M000078287

A Royal Priesthood?

The Scripture and Hermeneutics Series

Vol. 1 *Renewing Biblical Interpretation*
Vol. 2 *After Pentecost: Language and Biblical Interpretation*
Vol. 3 *A Royal Priesthood? The Use of the Bible Ethically and Politically. A Dialogue with Oliver O'Donovan*
Vol. 4 *'Behind' the Text? History and Biblical Interpretation* (forthcoming 2003)

A Royal Priesthood?

The Use of the Bible Ethically and Politically

A Dialogue with Oliver O'Donovan

Edited by

Craig Bartholomew

Jonathan Chaplin

Robert Song

Al Wolters

GRAND RAPIDS, MICHIGAN 49530 USA

First published 2002 jointly in the UK by Paternoster Press, an imprint of Authentic Media,
P.O. Box 300, Carlisle, Cumbria, CA3 OQS
Website: www.paternoster-publishing.com
and in the United States of America by Zondervan
5300 Patterson Ave SE, Grand Rapids, Michigan 49530

08 07 06 05 04 03 02 7 6 5 4 3 2 1

British Library Cataloguing in Publication Data
A catalogue record for this book is available from the British Library

ISBN 1-84227-067-2

Library of Congress Cataloging-in-Publication Data
A royal priesthood? : the use of the Bible ethically and politically /
edited by Craig Bartholomew … [et al.].
p. cm. — (Scripture and hermeneutics series; v. 3)
Includes bibliographical references and index.
ISBN 0-310-23413-1
1. Bible—Criticism, interpretation, etc.—Congresses. 2. Ethics in the Bible—Congresses. 3. Political theology—Congresses. 4. Christian ethics—Congresses. 5. O'Donovan, Oliver—Congresses. I. Bartholomew, Craig G., 1961– II. Chaplin, Jonathan III. Song, Robert
IV. Wolter, Albert M. V. Series.
BS680.E84 R69 2002
220.6'01—dc21
2002011428

Cover Design by Gert Swart and Zak Benjamin, South Africa
Typeset by WestKey Ltd, Falmouth, Cornwall
Printed in the United States of America
Printed on acid free paper

Blessed are you, Sovereign God of all,
to you be glory and praise for ever!
From the rising of the sun to its setting
your glory is proclaimed in all the world.
You gave the Christ as a light to the nations,
and through the anointing of his Spirit
you established us as a royal priesthood.
As you call us into his marvellous light,
may our lives bear witness to your truth
and our lips never cease to proclaim your praise,
Father, Son and Holy Spirit.

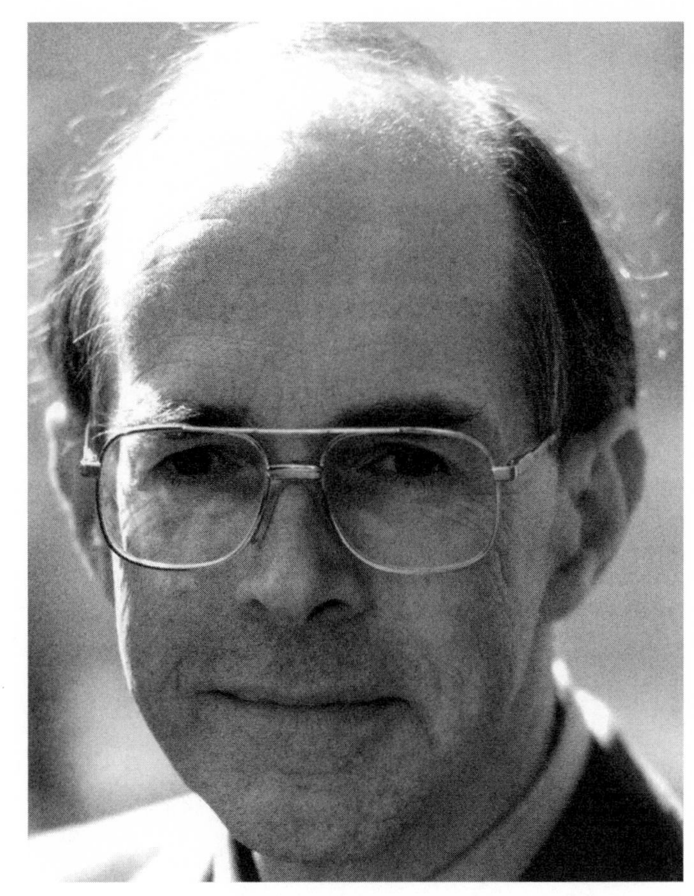

Oliver O'Donovan, respondent and dialogue partner

Contents

Contributors

Craig Bartholomew is Senior Research Fellow at the University of Gloucestershire. He is the author of *Reading Ecclesiastes: Old Testament Exegesis and Hermeneutical Theory*. He has also edited *In the Fields of the Lord: A Calvin Seerveld Reader* and co-edited *Christ and Consumerism: A Critical Analysis of the Spirit of the Age*. He is the series editor for the Scripture and Hermeneutics Series.

M. Daniel Carroll R. (Rodas) is Professor of Old Testament at Denver Seminary and adjunct Professor of Old Testament at El Seminario Teológico Centroamericano in Guatemala City. He is the author of *Contexts for Amos: Prophetic Poetics in Latin American Perspective*. He has edited *Rethinking Contexts, Rereading Texts: Contributions from the Social Sciences to Biblical Interpretation* and co-edited several other volumes. He is the chair of the Character Formation and Biblical Interpretation Group of the Society of Biblical Literature.

Jonathan Chaplin is Associate Professor of Political Theory at the Institute for Christian Studies in Toronto. He is co-editor of *Political Theory and Christian Vision*, has published a range of articles in the area of Christian political theory and is currently completing a book on the political thought of Herman Dooyeweerd. He is a member of a research project funded by Pew Trusts on *Politics and Human Nature*. He has worked with several Christian social and political organizations, including the Movement for Christian Democracy in the UK, the Center for Public Justice in the USA and, in Canada, Citizens for Public Justice, the Canadian Ecumenical Jubilee Initiative, and the Evangelical Fellowship of Canada.

Colin Greene is Head of Theology and Public Policy at the British and Foreign Bible Society, and Visiting Professor of Systematic Theology at Seattle Pacific University. He is the author of *Christology and Atonement in Historical Context* and *Marking Out the Horizons: Christology in Cultural Perspective* (forthcoming).

He is a contributor to *The Lectionary Commentary: Theological Exegesis for Sunday's Texts.* He is the consultant editor for the Scripture and Hermeneutics Series.

Gerrit de Kruijf is Professor of Christian Ethics at Leiden University. Prior to that, he was a minister of the Netherlands Reformed Church at Rijnsaterwoude and at Rotterdam. His works include *Watchful and Sober: On Christian Ethics in a Democratic Context* and *Christian Ethics: An Introduction with Key Texts.*

Andrew Lincoln is Portland Professor of New Testament at the University of Gloucestershire. He was previously Lord and Lady Coggan Professor at Wycliffe College, University of Toronto. His publications include *Paradise Now and Not Yet, Ephesians, Colossians* and *Truth on Trial.*

Joan Lockwood O'Donovan is a theologian living and working in Oxford. She has written many articles on political theology and philosophy and two books: *George Grant and the Twilight of Justice* and *Theology of Law and Authority in the English Reformation.* She is joint author of *From Irenaeus to Grotius: A Sourcebook in Christian Political Thought 100–1625.* She is a consultant editor and regular reviewer for the journal *Studies in Christian Ethics.*

Gordon McConville is Senior Lecturer in Old Testament and Hebrew at the University of Gloucestershire. His books include *Law and Theology in Deuteronomy, Grace in the End* and *Judgment and Promise.* He has co-authored *Time and Place in Deuteronomy* and co-edited *Reconsidering Israel and Judah: Recent Studies on the Deuteronomistic History.* He also writes on Old Testament theology and interpretation.

Gilbert Meilaender holds the Phyllis and Richard Duesenberg Chair in Christian Ethics at Valparaiso University. Among his books are *Friendship: A Study in Theological Ethics, Faith and Faithfulness: Basic Themes in Christian Ethics* and *Bioethics: A Primer for Christians.*

Walter Moberly is Lecturer in Theology at the University of Durham. His books include *The Bible, Theology, and Faith: A Study of Abraham and Jesus* and *The Old Testament of the Old Testament.*

Oliver O'Donovan is Regius Professor of Moral and Pastoral Theology and Canon of Christ Church at the University of Oxford. He is the author of *The Problem of Self-Love in Saint Augustine, Begotten or Made?, Resurrection and Moral Order, On the Thirty-Nine Articles, Peace and Certainty* and *The Desire of the Nations.* He is joint-author of *From Irenaeus to Grotius: A Sourcebook in Christian*

Political Thought 100–1625. He is a past president of the Society for the Study of Christian Ethics, and has been an active participant in Anglican-Roman Catholic dialogue. He is a Fellow of the British Academy.

Christopher Rowland is Dean Ireland's Professor of the Exegesis of Holy Scripture at the University of Oxford. He is completing a commentary on the Apocalypse that focuses on the history of its reception.

Peter Scott is Senior Lecturer in Theology at the University of Gloucestershire. He is the author of *Theology, Ideology and Liberation* and has written numerous articles on political theology and the theology of nature. He is currently completing *A Political Theology of Nature*.

James Skillen is President of the Center for Public Justice in Washington, DC. He is the author of *A Covenant to Keep: Meditations on the Biblical Theme of Justice* and *The Scattered Voice: Christians at Odds in the Public Square*.

Robert Song is Lecturer in Christian Ethics at the University of Durham. He is the author of *Christianity and Liberal Society* and *Human Genetics: Fabricating the Future*.

Bernd Wannenwetsch is an ordained minister of the Lutheran Church of Bavaria and is University Lecturer in Ethics at Oxford University. He is the author of many scholarly articles and books in German. His latest book on worship and ethics, *Oxford Studies in Theological Ethics*, is currently being translated into English.

Al Wolters is Professor of Religion and Theology/Classical Languages at Redeemer University College, Canada. His publications include *Plotinus 'On Eros': A Detailed Exegetical Commentary on Enneads III, 5*, *Creation Regained: Biblical Basics of a Reformational Worldview* and *The Song of the Valiant Woman: Studies in the Interpretation of Proverbs 31:10–31*.

Tom Wright is Canon Theologian of Westminster Abbey and is an SPCK Research Fellow. He has written over thirty books on early Christianity and its relevance for the present day. He has been Visiting Professor at many institutions including Harvard, Yale and the Hebrew University in Jerusalem, and he broadcasts regularly on radio and television.

Preface

The relationship between the Bible and ethics appears obvious. As Brevard Childs says, 'scripture functions towards sanctification'. However, in biblical studies and in theology this relationship has become anything but obvious. Oliver O'Donovan rightly asserts that we need to make the journey from what God said to Abraham to how to respond to Iraq today – indeed since 11 September 2001 this journey has become more important then ever – but in much biblical interpretation the very possibility of that journey is in doubt.

For these reasons, the Scripture and Hermeneutics Seminar has been committed from its inception to tackling the use of the Bible ethically as a major issue that any renewal of biblical interpretation needs to confront. We decided to do this by means of a dialogue with Oliver O'Donovan. Oliver's work in ethics and political theology is rightly acclaimed. Nick Wolterstorff describes *The Desire of the Nations* as 'the most important contribution to political theology in our century'. From our perspective, it is the surprising amount of biblical exegesis in Oliver's work that is so attractive – in this respect, his work represents just the sort of serious ethical engagement with Scripture that the Seminar wants to recover and promote.

Oxford is not far from Cheltenham, and I remember well the fine sunny day my colleague Gordon McConville and I drove to Oxford to discuss the possibility of a consultation on Scripture and ethics with Oliver. Much water has flowed under the bridge since then! The Scripture and Hermeneutics consultation on the use of the Bible ethically and politically was held at Glenfall House in Cheltenham from 25 to 27 June 2001. Oliver was both respondent and dialogue partner at the consultation. His commitment to patient, responsible listening was exemplary – it was only as the consultation progressed that I realized he had prepared a written response to each paper presented. We are most grateful to Oliver for his patient dialogue and hard work in revising his responses for publication.

The transformation of that rich dialogue into this book has been hard work. I am indebted to the editors – Al, Robert and Jonathan – who worked with us in a spirit of co-operation and rigour to ensure that we produced the best product we could in the time available. One of the great joys throughout has been ongoing contact with Oliver himself. He has introduced me to Bach's Cantatas and has without exception been hospitable at the personal and academic level.

Craig Bartholomew
University of Gloucestershire
Cheltenham, UK

Abbreviations

AB	Anchor Bible
AJJ	*The American Journal of Jurisprudence*
AnBib	Analecta biblica
APSR	*American Political Science Review*
BBB	Bonner biblische Beiträge
BETL	Bibliotheca ephemeridum theologicarum lovaniensium
BFT	Biblical Foundations in Theology
Bib	*Biblica*
BibInt	*Biblical Interpretation*
BJRL	*Bulletin of the John Rylands University Library of Manchester*
CD	*Church Dogmatics* (Barth)
Claud.	*Divus Claudius* (Suetonius)
CTJ	*Calvin Theological Journal*
DN	*The Desire of the Nations* (O. O'Donovan)
EuroJT	*European Journal of Theology*
ERT	*Evangelical Review of Theology*
EVV	English versions
ExAud	*Ex auditu*
HBT	*Horizons in Biblical Theology*
HSM	Harvard Semitic Monographs
HTR	*Harvard Theological Review*
HUCA	*Hebrew Union College Annual*
Int	*Interpretation*
ITQ	*Irish Theological Quarterly*
JAAR	*Journal of the American Academy of Religion*
JBL	*Journal of Biblical Literature*
JRE	*Journal of Religious Ethics*
JSNTSup	Journal for the Study of the New Testament: Supplement Series

JSOT	*Journal for the Study of the Old Testament*
JSOTSup	Journal for the Study of the Old Testament: Supplement Series
KD	*Die kirchliche Dogmatik* (Barth)
Mart. Pol.	*Martyrdom of Polycarp*
NIB	*The New Interpreter's Bible*
NICOT	New International Commentary on the Old Testament
NovTSup	Novum Testamentum Supplements
OBT	Overtures to Biblical Theology
OCD	*Oxford Classical Dictionary*
OTL	Old Testament Library
OTS	Old Testament Studies
PSB	*Princeton Seminary Bulletin*
R&T	*Religion and Theology*
RB	*Revue biblique*
RMO	*Resurrection and Moral Order* (O. O'Donovan)
Serm.	*Sermones* (Augustine)
SBLDS	Society of Biblical Literature Dissertation Series
SBTS	Sources for Biblical and Theological Study
SHS	Scripture and Hermeneutics Series
SJT	*Scottish Journal of Theology*
SNTSMS	Society for New Testament Studies Monograph Series
SCE	*Studies in Christian Ethics*
TS	*Theological Studies*
Them	*Themelios*
TSFB	*Theological Student Fellowship Bulletin*
ThSt	Theologische Studiën
TynBul	*Tyndale Bulletin*
USQR	*Union Seminary Quarterly Review*
VT	*Vetus Testamentum*
WBC	Word Biblical Commentary
WTJ	*Westminster Theological Journal*
WMANT	Wissenschaftliche Monographien zum Alten und Neuen Testament
WUNT	Wissenschaftliche Untersuchungen zum Neuen Testament
ZTK	*Zeitschrift für Theologie und Kirche*

The Artists

Zak Benjamin, Painter and Printmaker

Born Izak Benjamin de Villiers in 1951, Benjamin completed a BA Fine Arts degree, taught art and has worked full-time as an artist since 1991.

Benjamin grew up in Pretoria in a typical middle-class Afrikaner family. The discrepancies between the Christian values taught at church and the policies of the Nationalist government, and their expression in the status-seeking materialist Afrikaner middle class, caused him to rebel against his background. In the mid-1980s, Benjamin experienced a profound religious conversion that led to his friendship with sculptor Gert Swart in their mutual struggle to discover what it means to make contemporary art as Christians.

Benjamin's frustration with lingering apartheid in the Dutch Reformed Church and the challenges facing Christians in post-apartheid South Africa provide themes for some of his work. Calvin Seerveld has thus characterized his style: '… bright gaiety and humour combined with ethereal seriousness. Like the unusual world of *One Hundred Years of Solitude* (Gabriel Marquez), the paintings hold together, as natural, the most outlandish realities. Bold naïvete of forms and colours, stories of mysteries and conflict, trouble and healing – with a difference: friendly, zany, readable, provoking the viewer to look again … a wholesome pleasure in the grit of life.'

His work is represented in collections internationally. He is married and lives in Vereeniging, South Africa, and has two daughters.

< http://zakbenjaminartist.homestead.com/index.html >

Gert Swart

Gert Swart was born in Durban, South Africa, where he qualified and worked as a public health inspector before studying fine art for two years at the Natal Technikon. He now resides and works as a sculptor in Pietermaritzburg, South Africa. He is married to Istine Rodseth.

Gert Swart has lived and worked in Pietermaritzburg for the past ten years. His most important exhibition of this period was staged at the Tatham Art Gallery in 1997. This exhibition, titled 'Contemplation: A body of work by Gert Swart', expressed the redemption of an individual as a metamorphosis from the curse of death to the hope of resurrection and explored how this transition affects the individual's relationship to society, nature and God.

One of Swart's most significant commissions of the past decade was a monument erected on the battlefield at Isandlwana in 1999. Although the battle of Isandlwana is known for its stunning defeat of a colonial army by an unconventional army, only monuments to fallen British soldiers had been erected on the battlefield in the past. It was a privilege to be involved in redressing this injustice and a challenge to design a monument that honours the fallen Zulu warriors but does not glorify war.

Gert met Zak Benjamin at a Christian arts festival over a decade ago. He and Benjamin were among the founder members of the Christian Worldview Network initiated by Craig Bartholomew. They enjoy a rich friendship that is currently finding expression in the joint design of book covers for this series in collaboration with Craig. This design project is the fruit of Craig's concern for Christian artists and his friendship with Gert and Zak.

< http://gertswartsculptor.homestead.com/index.html >

Introduction[1]

Craig G. Bartholomew

In this introduction I do the following:

- introduce the theme of a royal priesthood and discuss the picture on the cover of this book;
- look at the obstacles to reading the Bible ethically and politically today;
- look at major ways in which the Bible has been and is being read ethically;
- describe and type O'Donovan's ethics and political theology;
- describe briefly the contents of the volume.

Sections of this introduction can be read independently or together, according to the reader's needs and desire. Some may want to proceed straight to the description of O'Donovan's ethics – it is an important background to the chapters that follow. Those familiar with O'Donovan's work may, however, wish to look only at the description of the contents.

Introduction: A Royal Priesthood

In a few compact verses, Exodus 19:3–6 sets out Israel's vocation. Yahweh instructs Moses to tell the Israelites:

> You have seen what I did to the Egyptians, and how I bore you on eagles' wings and brought you to myself. Now therefore, if you obey my voice and keep my covenant, you shall be my treasured possession out of all the peoples. Indeed, the whole earth is mine, but you shall be for me a priestly kingdom and a holy nation.

The whole earth belongs to Yahweh, but Israel has been brought to Yahweh at Mt Sinai, and she is to be a royal priesthood and a holy nation. 'Royal

---

[1] I am particularly grateful to Robert Song, Jonathan Chaplin and Gordon McConville for their helpful comments on this introduction.

priesthood' and 'holy nation' speak of Israel's particularity *and* her universal significance. Her particularity, because Yahweh has elected Israel from all the nations to be his people. She alone will be his 'treasured possession out of all the peoples'. Universal significance because, as a priestly royalty,[2] she is to mediate Yahweh's will to the nations. Just as priests mediate God to the nation, so Israel is to be committed to extend Yahweh's presence throughout the nations.[3] Israel is to be 'a display-people, a showcase to the world of how being in covenant with Yahweh changes a people'.[4] And, it should be noted, this includes the political dimension of Israel's life. As some have observed, 'treasured possession' has political implications; the Akkadian word is used to describe a vassal of a great king.[5] But stronger than this is the use of the word 'nation' (*gôy*) rather than the more common 'people' (*'am*) in 'holy nation'. This probably alludes to Genesis 12:2, where Israel as a political entity is in mind.[6] As Dumbrell says of Exodus 19:6, 'Probably then we are here, as we noted in connection with Gen. 12:2, thinking of Israel as offering in her constitution a societary model for the world.'[7] From this perspective Israel's political particularity, that is, as an ancient Near Eastern nation, is also of universal, political significance.

In 1 Peter 2:9 the image of a royal priesthood is applied to the church: 'But you are a chosen race, a royal priesthood, a holy nation, God's own people, in order that you may proclaim the mighty acts of him who called you out of darkness into his marvellous light.' 1 Peter draws here on Exodus 19 and other Old Testament passages to evoke the vocation of the church to 'proclaim the mighty acts of him who called you out of darkness into his marvellous light'. The question of the model(s) of the church and its relationship to society is no simple issue in the New Testament, let alone in 1 Peter.[8] Suffice it here to note that in a useful analysis of church and culture in 1 Peter, Miroslav Volf concludes that,

---

[2] This is a better translation of the Hebrew.

[3] On this point see also Brown, *Ethos*, 131.

[4] Durham, *Exodus*, 263.

[5] Sarna, *Exploring Exodus*, 131, Dumbrell, *Covenant*, 85.

[6] Dumbrell, *Covenant*, 66, says of Gen. 12:2, 'Certainly *gôy* in the Old Testament is normally reserved for the description of a political entity which can be delimited by appeal to geographical, ethnic, social or cultural factors, and the use of such a governmental term in this context could broadly have Israel's later political constitution in mind.'

[7] Dumbrell, *Covenant*, 87. See Durham, *Exodus*, 262, 263 for the different interpretations of this phrase.

[8] Niebuhr, in his justly celebrated *Christ and Culture*, finds the different Christ-culture relationships he discerns exemplified in different texts produced by the early Christian communities. Thus 1 John best expresses Christ against culture, the Pauline writings express Christ and cultures in paradox, and so on.

> The unusual child who looked like a sect, but did not act like a sect, was a Christian community – a church that can serve as a model even for us today as we reflect on the nature of Christian presence in modern, rapidly changing, pluralistic societies that resist being shaped by moral norms.[9]

Thus, in the Old Testament and the New, the image of a royal priesthood alerts us to God's intention for his people to mediate his presence and light in his good, but fallen, world. Christ is the 'author of life', and the life of his followers should shed light on all of that life of which he is author. This is not because of some inherent greatness about his people, but because of the presence of Christ and his word in their midst. Life as God has made it includes societies and politics, and we have called this volume *A Royal Priesthood?* to convey this sense that the Word which is at the heart of the church has important light to shed on society and politics today. This is no small hope on this side of 11 September 2001, and it should not be understood simplistically. Indeed, the cover of this book speaks of the immensity of the challenge of reading the Bible politically in a way that is truly liberating. Hence the question mark after 'Royal Priesthood?'

The Cover and Goya's *The Third of May*[10]

The cover image is a contemporary reworking of Goya's *The Third of May* by South African artists Gert Swart and Zak Benjamin. Goya's *The Third of May* depicts events in Spain at the start of the 1808–14 Peninsular War, when French troops invaded Spain in order brutally to suppress a popular uprising. Goya's painting depicts the public execution of insurgents by the French on 3 May 1808, in reprisal for the insurrection the previous day. It is a powerful comment on society, politics, violence and the church – themes that Goya returned to repeatedly.

In the history of art, Goya's *The Third of May* is a most significant painting, signalling a new way of seeing life at the threshold of the modern era.[11] 'With the creation of Giotto's frescoes in the Arena Chapel and Goya's *The Third of May* we come to works that sever the cord, that sound the signal of a fateful turn ... in the affairs of men.'[12] Goya's picture is brutal and frank, and to understand its significance we need to see it against the background of the genre of

---

[9] Volf, 'Soft Difference', 27.

[10] I am much indebted to Gert Swart and Istine Rodseth Swart for their help with this section.

[11] For much of the following comment on Goya's *The Third of May* I am dependent on Licht, *Goya*.

[12] Licht, *Goya*, 116.

The Third of May, Goya. Reproduced with the permission of the Museo Nacional Del Prado, Madrid.

paintings of martyrs, of which there was a long tradition. In this genre, martyrdom is frankly depicted – but in the context of eternal life and in a style such that one can enjoy the painting without being too shocked. In *The Third of May*, however, Goya 'insists on conveying the terror without the Aristotelian pity that in previous paintings of martyrdom led to catharsis'.[13]

In *The Third of May* two formations of men face each other across the narrowest of gaps. In contrast to the background darkness, the light in the picture is striking, especially as it illuminates the peasant about to be shot. However, the only source of light is a portable, stable lantern at the centre of the picture. The artistic technique that Goya uses here comes from early Baroque traditions that Caravaggio formulated. However, in Caravaggio's paintings the light is always an emanation of God. 'It is the gift of heaven which permits us to perceive the truth. It is also the visible evidence of God's blessing. This is especially true of martyrdom scenes in which light is manifest proof of the ultimate transfiguration of the tormented victim.'[14] By contrast, in *The Third of May* the light is not divine; it is man-made and merely focuses the targets for the executioners. Particularly telling, in this respect, is that the massive church buildings in the background participate in the darkness – no light emerges from these buildings, which seem so detached from the action, but they appear on the same side of the painting as the soldiers, providing a kind of hideous halo to the inhuman block of faceless executioners.

The church is not the only Christian motif in the painting. If you 'enter the painting' behind the soldiers, the light from the lantern irrevocably leads the viewer to the peasant in white and yellow, the canonical colours of the Catholic Church. The peasant is portrayed in the posture of Christ in Gethsemane, crying out in the context of the terrible darkness. His raised hands clearly bear the stigmata. This cry is what *The Third of May* is all about, and it is reflected in the figure of the monk with the tell-tale tonsure, to the right of the Christ-like peasant, pleading and praying. By contrast with earlier martyrdom paintings, there is no suggestion that this cry might be answered or that there will be any divine resolution of the horror. Instead, Goya's painting forces the viewer to take sides: either we line up with the soldiers or we join the victims. 'Whoever does not walk in the procession of the condemned stands among the executioners.'[15]

Swart and Benjamin, in their reworking of *The Third of May*, rightly recognize that the cry of the peasant is at the heart of the painting. In order to challenge us as strongly as possible with the task of reading and embodying the Bible politically as a royal priesthood, they have turned the peasant around to

---

13 Licht, *Goya*, 119.
14 Licht, *Goya*, 119.
15 Licht, *Goya*, 121.

face us directly – but in a mirror image of the original, so that we have no choice but to face the peasant.[16] Visually they do here what Levinas does with 'the face' philosophically.[17] 'The idea of infinity … is concretely produced in the form of a relation with the face … what is produced here is not a reasoning, but the epiphany that occurs as a face.'[18] By turning the peasant to face us, we are alerted unequivocally to the responsibility of reading the Bible politically.

> The face with which the Other turns to me is not reabsorbed in a representation of the face. To hear his destitution which cries out for justice is not to represent an image to oneself, but is to posit oneself as responsible, both as more and as less than the being that presents itself in the face. Less, for the face summons me to my obligations and judges me … The Other who dominates me in his transcendence is thus the stranger, the widow, and the orphan, to whom I am obliged.[19]

In their reworking of Goya, Swart and Benjamin thus remind us that there is much at stake in our reading of the Bible politically: the glory of God and the well being of creation. The terror on the peasant's face, his stigmata and the rubble that now forms the background to the peasant – perhaps reminiscent of Ground Zero in New York? – remind us that we need to be responsible in our quest to read the Bible politically. The rubble forms a dark halo around the peasant posing, as it were, the questions: 'How do we proceed into the twenty-first century and reverse man's self-destruction? What role does the church play in this process?' Too often the church has been complicit with oppression and a source of darkness, rather than a source of light. Hence our question mark after 'Royal Priesthood?'

This is not, however, to deny the potential light the Bible has to shed on politics. The reworked Goya needs to be juxtaposed, as it were, with the cover image from *Renewing Biblical Interpretation*, which evokes the potential in reading Scripture. It is through Scripture that God addresses us, and there is a long and rich Christian tradition of political theology, in which the church has taken the witness of Scripture for politics with the utmost seriousness. Oliver O'Donovan, who is our dialogue partner in this book, makes the point powerfully that this tradition of political theology is virtually unknown nowadays and needs to be recovered if we are to read the Bible for politics in a responsible way. However, there are considerable obstacles today to appropriating the Bible for ethics and politics.

---

[16] In the West we read from left to right. By reworking the peasant in mirror image and turning him towards us, they enhance the unavoidable confrontation with him.

[17] Levinas, *Totality*. For a Christian theological appropriation of this see Ford, *Self*, 17–29.

[18] Levinas, *Totality*, 196.

[19] Levinas, *Totality*, 215.

Obstacles to Reading the Bible Ethically and Politically

a) Modern biblical study and modern theological ethics

This may appear surprising because as canon, as the rule of faith, the Bible is all about lives lived in response to God, and one might therefore expect that biblical study would major on an issue like the use of the Bible ethically and politically. As Childs says, 'scripture functions toward sanctification'.[20] However, this is to ignore the legacy of historical criticism in biblical studies, which has bequeathed a separation of Bible and ethics. Indeed, in the academy there has been a strong resistance to moving from the Bible to normative ethics. Childs observes that,

> it comes as a great shock to discover how difficult it is to find good models for serious biblical interpretation involving both testaments, which approaches the material for guidance in the shaping of the Christian life.... even when biblical scholars seriously attempt to engage themselves in Biblical Theology ... there has been almost no attention directed to the nature of the faithful Christian life in the light of the two testaments.[21]

Similarly, Walter Wink asserts that historical criticism 'is bankrupt solely because it is incapable of achieving what most of its practitioners considered its purpose to be: so to interpret the Scriptures that the past becomes alive and illumines our present with new possibilities for personal and social transformation'.[22] Historical criticism has never been a simple entity, and those concerned to read the Bible as Scripture differ over its validity and usefulness in developing a Christian ethic.[23] Undoubtedly, though, it is disconcerting that the legacy of historical criticism is so limited in the area of biblical and theological ethics. A manifestation of the gulf between biblical studies and theology resulting from this sort of approach is that it is rare to find works on theological ethics that are deeply rooted exegetically, just as it is rare to find works on biblical ethics that have a sophisticated theological and philosophical perspective.

---

[20] Childs, *Biblical Theology*, 668.

[21] Childs, *Biblical Theology*, 706, 707.

[22] Wink, *The Bible*, 2.

[23] At a consultation on the use of the Bible in practical theology (Cardiff, University of Wales, June 2000), John Rogerson made the point that historical criticism is the great missed opportunity of the church. For a more critical view of historical criticism see Levenson's very stimulating *The Hebrew Bible, the Old Testament, and Historical Criticism*. History and hermeneutics is the topic for our 2002 consultation in Boston.

Siker analyses the use of Scripture in the works of eight major twentieth-century theological ethicists.[24] In his research, Siker observed the widespread woolly, selective use of Scripture. Thus, Reinhold Niebuhr rarely engages in exegetical discussion and tends not to let the biblical writers speak on their own behalf.[25] Bernard Häring rarely engages in the actual exegesis of texts, and when he does cite biblical texts he fails to take the larger contexts of the texts seriously.[26] Paul Ramsey's use of Scripture is personalistic and individualistic. According to Siker, he engages in special pleading and proof-texting.[27] Comparable comments could be made about the theological and philosophical sophistication of much biblical work on ethics.[28]

However, all is not as dismal as this suggests. An encouraging element in contemporary hermeneutics and the recovery of theological interpretation is a renewed interest in transformative reading of the Bible. Thiselton's massive *New Horizons* is subtitled 'The Theory and Practice of Transforming Biblical Reading', and in a different tradition the Yoder-Hauerwas-Hays narrative, ethical approach similarly aims at reading Scripture with transformation in mind. Hauerwas and Willimon assert at the outset of their stimulating book on the Ten Commandments, 'we hope to convince you that *knowing* the commandments requires a lifetime embodiment of a set of practices peculiar to the church – practises as basic as confessing belief in the Father, Son and Holy Spirit'.[29] In a different way, liberation theology returns to Scripture as it seeks 'a faith that transforms history'.[30]

Nevertheless, books like Hays' *The Moral Vision of the New Testament* and O'Donovan's *Resurrection and Moral Order* and *Desire of the Nations* remain the exception rather than the rule in their commitment to in-depth engagement with Scripture and biblical interpretation. Renewed interest in theological interpretation of the Bible and in theological ethics provides us with an opportunity to promote a fresh ethical engagement with the Bible as Scripture. Clearly such a direction is vital if we seek a renewal of biblical interpretation in line with the aims of the Scripture and Hermeneutics Seminar.

---

[24] Siker, *Scripture*.

[25] Siker, *Scripture*, 24.

[26] Siker, *Scripture*, 78.

[27] Siker, *Scripture*, 95.

[28] Thiselton, 'Communicative Action', 137, rightly notes that, 'Views and methods that students in philosophy of religion recognize as "positivist", "reductionist", or even "materialist" are often embraced quite uncritically in issues of judgement about, for example, acts of God in biblical narrative. In place of the more rigorous and judicious exploration of these issues in philosophical theology, biblical studies seems too readily to become polarized.'

[29] Hauerwas and Willimon, *The Truth About God*, 13.

[30] L. Boff and C. Boff, *Introducing Liberation Theology*, 12.

b) The particularity of the Bible and the enclosedness of the modern self-consciousness

We are familiar with this obstacle, relating as it does to Lessing's unbridgeable gap between the contingencies of history and reason.[31] Lessing's gap is part of that broader tendency of modernity to critique tradition on the basis of its belief in (modern) progress and the autonomy of (modern) reason. According to Gadamer, modernity's critique of tradition and prejudice is directly aimed at Christian Scripture:

> The historical critique of Scripture that emerges fully in the eighteenth century has its dogmatic base, as our brief look at Spinoza has shown, in the Enlightenment's faith in reason.[32]
>
> Enlightenment critique is primarily directed against the religious tradition of Christianity – i.e., the Bible. ... This is the real radicality of the modern Enlightenment compared to all other movements of enlightenment: it must assert itself against the Bible and dogmatic interpretations of it.[33]

For Scripture, rooted as it is in the life of Israel and Jesus of Nazareth, such an approach raises insuperable barriers, leading inevitably to reason judging Scripture to determine universal ethical norms, or some such approach. It is particularly when historical criticism has been embedded in such a world-view that it has impeded ethical reading of the Bible.[34] Elements of this obstacle resurface in the ideological barrier to the use of the Bible ethically, which we will discuss in more detail below.[35]

c) The diversity within Scripture

A third obstacle is the tension in the relationship between the OT and the NT. This remains a complex issue, and it extends to the diversity within each Testament. As we will see, O'Donovan acknowledges considerable diversity in the Bible and discontinuity between the OT and the NT. However, he holds this alongside a belief in the unity of Scripture. Many contemporary scholars stress the diversity at the expense of possible unity, to the point

---

[31] See Greene, 'Biblical Interpretation', 206ff.

[32] Gadamer, *Truth and Method*, 182.

[33] Gadamer, *Truth and Method*, 272.

[34] Any theological assessment of historical criticism must weigh the extent to which historical criticism is irretrievably rooted in an enclosed modern self-consciousness. See Harrisville and Sundberg, *The Bible*; Bartholomew, *Reading Ecclesiastes*, ch. 3; Möller, 'Renewing'.

[35] For a strong theological critique of this obstacle see Newbigin, *Foolishness*.

that reading the Bible ethically becomes problematic. Davies, for example, combining an argument about the ethical diversity of the OT with its ideological nature, says of the OT that,

> there are various ethical systems or models suggested or even expounded here, and ... most of them are not ethical at all, while those that are ethical are flawed.... Many biblical scholars – ultimately, most, I fear – not only fail to criticise such systems in their Bible, but even fail to identify them and analyse them. There is a tendency in some quarters to purvey them as values for our modern world. ... we might also, in the fashion of the postmodern era, consider the ethics of interpretation itself, and especially the manner in which its moral authority is invoked as a pretext for systems of belief and behaviour that deserve to be resisted. What is the ethical responsibility of a modern biblical exegete? ... My own anti-religious approach to ethics is, I hope, clear enough ...[36]

This kind of perspective is common among biblical scholars nowadays.

d) Postmodernism's suspicion of ideology

Postmodernism has fragmented biblical studies and raised questions about historical criticism and method in biblical studies. In the process, room has been created for the emergence of renewed attention to theological interpretation of Scripture, whereby the legacies of Barth and Childs are being strongly felt. Simultaneously, however, theological interpretation is easily relativized[37] and subject to radical, ideological critique. Hays, in his discussion of the hermeneutical issue of the relationship between Scripture and tradition, reason and experience, rightly notes that,

> Now, however, we have passed into an era in which the urgent question is the relative authority of Scripture and experience. Many feminist and liberation theologians are willing to assert explicitly that the authority of Scripture is in principle subordinate to the authority of the critical insight conferred by the experience of the oppressed or women. Here great caution is necessary to distinguish the appropriate – indeed,

---

[36] Davies, 'Ethics.' A less radical approach is that of Gustafson, *Theology and Christian Ethics*, 134, who asserts that, 'Scripture witnesses to a great variety of moral values, moral norms and principles through many different kinds of biblical literature ... The Christian community judges the actions of persons and groups to be morally wrong, or at least deficient, on the basis of reflective discourse about present events in the light of appeals to this variety of material as well as to other principles and experiences. Scripture is one of the informing sources for moral judgements, but it is not sufficient in itself to make any particular judgement authoritative.'

[37] Cf. Brett, *Biblical Criticism?*, and his suggestion that Childs's canonical approach is acceptable provided it is treated as one approach among many.

> inevitable – role of experience in shaping our interpretation of the text from the bolder claim that personal experience can be treated as a source of theological authority independent of Scripture.[38]

Hays is right. A strong strand of thought today argues that the Bible is a deeply ideological book with unhelpful nationalistic, patriarchal, ethnicist and sexist elements.[39] Recently Fretheim has addressed these issues. He maintains that,

> the [biblical] texts themselves fail us at times, perhaps even often. The patriarchal bias is pervasive, God is represented as an abuser and a killer of children, God is said to command the rape of women and the wholesale destruction of cities, including children and animals. To shrink from making such statements is dishonest. ... To continue to exalt such texts as the sacrifice of Isaac (Genesis 22), and not to recognize that, amongst other things, it can be read as a case of divine child abuse, is to contribute to an atmosphere that in subtle but insidious ways justifies the abuse of children.[40]

Fretheim has no desire to abandon the Bible as Scripture, but he seeks a hermeneutic that takes account of the ideological elements in the Bible. He proposes a dialogical model whereby the believer and the believing community dialogue with the Bible to determine what is of God and what is not. Fretheim suggests four criteria for assessing biblical statements about God.[41]

- First, we can get help from nonbiblical sources like academic disciplines and life experience generally. Psychology, for example, helps us to see how destructive Genesis 22 can be for children.
- Secondly, we can use other biblical material to assess biblical material we are concerned about. For example, Isaiah 49:14, 15, which portrays God as a loving mother, can be read against Genesis 22.
- Thirdly, the Christian community as part of the people of God has hermeneutic authority: 'From within this community, persons of faith have been given an authority to speak out against whatever in the Bible may be life-demeaning, oppressive, or promoting of inequality.'[42]
- Fourthly, Fretheim suggest six ways in which problematic texts may still be useful. For example, they may remind us that all language about God is inadequate, or they may negatively alert us to issues that are really important, and so on.

---

[38] Hays, *Moral Vision*, 211.

[39] So Clines, *Bible*. For a thorough introduction to socio-critical hermeneutics see Thiselton, *New Horizons*, 411–515.

[40] Fretheim, 'Part Two', 100.

[41] Cf. Clines's proposals for the use of the Bible in the church (*Bible*, 87–101).

[42] Fretheim, 'Part Two', 108.

It is not possible to deal here in any depth with the radical challenge that such socio-critical issues present to biblical authority.[43] Whereas previously theological interpretation of the Bible had to make an argument for some sense of its unity, now we face the considerable challenge of reading the Bible in its totality[44] *and* examining in detail how the Bible in its totality relates to feminism, power and issues of social location.[45]

How Has the Bible Been Used Ethically?

As we contemplate a renewal of the use of the Bible ethically and politically in dialogue with O'Donovan's work, it is helpful to bear in mind how the Bible has been and is being used ethically. It will also be helpful to focus in more detail on some of the creative renewals in the use of the Bible today.

1. The Bible as a *source of law* – the Bible has often been regarded as providing an absolute morality that can be applied in society like a law code. Treatises of this sort were particularly prominent in post-Reformation Protestantism.[46] A contemporary example of this type of use of the Bible is found in American Reconstructionism, a movement that has its origins in the work of Rousas Rushdoony, and particularly his book *The Institutes of Biblical Law* (1937). Reconstructionism is also known as 'theonomy' – theonomy is God's law, which identifies its commitment to applying biblical law to modern society. Such approaches fail to wrestle adequately with the cultural and historical (ancient Near Eastern/Graeco-Roman) contexts in which the Bible was written.
2. The Bible has also been appropriated for the description of ethics in *idealistic philosophical categories.* Such an appropriation is evident, for example, at the

[43] For a detailed discussion see Thiselton, *New Horizons*, chs. 11 and 12.

[44] An answer to these criticisms is the recovery of a strong notion of *tota scriptura*, or the sense that Scripture is God's word in its totality and needs to be read on all these issues as such.

[45] It is surely unhelpful and unnecessary to concede as much as Fretheim does in terms of the Bible being ideological. To conclude, for example, that Gen. 22 is in danger of affirming child abuse lacks sophistication in the light of the powerful, nuanced readings available of the story in its canonical context. See, e.g., Kierkegaard, 'Fear and Trembling', Childs, *Biblical Theology*, 325–36, and Moberly, *The Bible*. For O'Donovan's view of Gen. 22, see *RMO*, 43, 44. O'Donovan reads Gen. 22 as a conflict between the vocational and the ethical, between God's call to Abraham and the moral principle that forbids sacrificing Isaac. The conflict should be resolved like any other conflict of *prima facie* moral claims. What makes Gen. 22 distinctive is not this clash but that God's call to Abraham can only be privately discerned.

[46] Childs, *Biblical Theology*, 659.

birth of biblical theology in Gabler's inaugural. Gabler proposes a historical approach to the Bible, but the typical ideas of each author that result from this approach must then be examined to discern the universal ideas that are useful for dogmatic theology.[47] The relationship between Scripture and philosophy remains an important and controversial issue. The danger of imposing a framework on the Bible is that we mute its own voice.

3. *Scripture norms theology, which develops a theological ethic.* We refer here to the view that theological ethics is a subcategory of systematic theology, whose authoritative source is the Bible. The great example of this is Karl Barth, who understands ethics as a subcategory of the doctrine of God because it deals with the command of God to human beings. Thus Barth moves from the Bible through theology to ethical decisions. He does not derive moral decisions straight from the Bible. The extensive exegesis in the small print in *CD* is ample witness, however, to the continuing importance of exegesis in Barth's ethics, so that Scripture can also directly shape theology.

Barth anticipates the narrative turn in theology by reading the Bible as a history of God's covenantal relationship with humankind. It is important, however, to distinguish Barth's narrative approach from that of Hauerwas and Lindbeck. Kelsey, Lindbeck and Hauerwas privilege the imaginative construal that is brought by the community to the Bible. Biggar notes that

> whereas for Barth the biblical story is significant in its reference to the reality of the living God, for Hauerwas its importance lies immediately in its sociological function in forming the identity of the Christian community and thereby providing the rationale of its morality.[48]

Intriguingly Childs, at the conclusion to his monumental *Biblical Theology*, proposes that the way out of the present impasse in biblical ethics is a renewal and development of 'command ethics' as proposed by Brunner and Barth.[49] Childs refers to Richard Mouw's *The God Who Commands* as pointing in the right direction. In this way Childs connects with neo-Calvinism but distinguishes Bavinck's type of biblical neo-Calvinism[50] from what he sees as the current scholastic varieties.[51]

---

[47] See the translation of Gabler's inaugural, 'An Oration', in the appendix of Ollenburger, et al., eds., *The Flowering*, 492–502. Childs, *Biblical Theology*, 709, refers to the debilitating effect of idealistic categories in Ewald's four-volume *Biblical Theology*.

[48] Biggar, *Hastening*, 118. See Hays, *Moral Vision*, 253–66, for a useful analysis of Hauerwas's hermeneutics. See Vanhoozer, 'Voice', 85ff. for a creative defence of *sola scriptura*.

[49] Childs, *Biblical Theology*, 712ff.

[50] This is the Dutch Calvinism that developed out of Abraham Kuyper's work.

[51] Childs, *Biblical Theology*, 714, 715.

Childs interacts carefully and critically with Kelsey and Hauerwas, noting *inter alia* that 'Hauerwas has entered a veritable hornet's nest of biblical studies by his wholehearted embracing of a concept of the Bible as story or narrative', and he asserts that 'his actual use of the story increasingly turns out to be an abstraction without specific biblical content'.[52] Childs argues that, 'It is this hermeneutical function of canon which remains decisive for scripture's role in ordering the continuing life of the community of faith.' In OT ethics Childs acknowledges the significance of Barton's and McKeating's sociological work on the OT,[53] but he draws a very different conclusion:

> I would argue that the task of Old Testament ethics is to acknowledge this canonical corpus as a theological construct which is only indirectly related to an historical and empirical Israel, and to pursue rigorously the theological witness of this biblical witness as the privileged sacred writings of Israel, the people of God.[54]

For Childs, the canon has preserved its diversity as a theological witness to life under God's rule. Thus, the immorality of the patriarchs must be read also in terms of how these stories are received in the rest of the OT, such as in Psalms 105 and 106. 'Moreover, when a typological relation is established between the patriarchs and Israel, it is not in terms of accumulated virtue, but by means of paralleling events which adumbrated God's one purpose of salvation (e.g. Hos. 12.2ff.).'[55] Childs sees, especially in Paul's letters, the apostolic attempt to shape the everyday life of the diverse Hellenistic congregations in terms of the 'obedience of faith'. Ultimately, the final test for both biblical exegesis and preaching is the compatibility of human expression to the living will of God made known in Jesus Christ.[56]

4. In the context of Barth's huge legacy, it is important also to take note of *natural law ethics* in the Catholic tradition, stemming from Aquinas. Barth, of course, distances himself strongly from this tradition, but that does not mean it is not a fertile ethical tradition. In the natural law tradition, the Bible is understood to deal in the main with humankind's supernatural end, while natural law attends to moral questions. Principles such as the Ten Commandments can be equally well discovered through the use of 'untutored reason'. Spohn refers to this approach as 'Scripture as moral reminder'.[57] Scriptural support for it is found in the OT Wisdom literature and especially in Romans 1 and 2. Scripture, in this tradition, provides the

[52] Childs, *Biblical Theology*, 665.
[53] Barton, 'Understanding'; McKeating, 'Sanctions'.
[54] Childs, *Biblical Theology*, 676.
[55] Childs, *Biblical Theology*, 680.
[56] Childs, *Biblical Theology*, 672.
[57] Spohn, *Saying?*, 38ff.

motivation for ethics but not the content of ethics – the ought of ethics arises from [reflection on] what is.[58]

5. The recent groundswell of interest in *narrative ethics* is rooted in Barth's work, but has been considerably buoyed by the philosophical work of Alasdair MacIntyre, Charles Taylor and Paul Ricœur. Within theology, H.R. Niebuhr also made an important contribution with his use of story in explicating revelation.[59]

   Narrative has gained popularity in a variety of theological traditions, and fertile readings of the Bible such as those by Lesslie Newbigin and Tom Wright[60] also manifest a strong sense of the Bible as narrative, without necessarily holding, for example, to Hauerwas's views of community and pacifism. Vanhoozer has also recently advocated a dramatic hermeneutic which fits with a narrative approach.[61] Indeed there are a whole variety of positions that fit under the description 'narrative'. These different positions raise questions such as:

   - Is narrative an ontological notion – is story somehow basic to the human condition? Or
   - Is narrative related primarily to Christian/theological self-description? Or
   - Is narrative about the shape of the Bible or parts of the Bible as Scripture?

In this section we will outline some of the major narrative approaches to the Bible, in order to get a sense of what they yield ethically.

The *postliberalism* of Lindbeck and Frei is a major narrative approach to the Bible as Scripture. Lindbeck argues for a 'cultural-linguistic' understanding of theology. This distances itself from an understanding of Christian theology as a sub-group of the genus theology, and thinks rather of theology as religion-specific, an aspect of the self-description of Christianity. Theology, from this perspective, is a second-order discipline dependent on the first-order language of Christianity. Hans Frei, in his *The Eclipse of Biblical Narrative*, argues for a recovery of realistic reading of biblical narrative. Frei thinks that Barth's exegesis exemplifies the kind of narrative reading that can still be done, for Barth 'distinguishes historical from realistic reading of the theologically most significant biblical narratives without falling into the trap of instantly making history the test of the *meaning* of the realistic form of the stories'.[62] Frei's *The Identity of Jesus*

---

58 See Pavlischek, 'Questioning', for some of the current issues among Christian natural law theorists.

59 Nelson, *Narrative*, 64.

60 See Wright's chapter in this volume for an example of his creative use of narrative.

61 Vanhoozer, 'Voice'.

62 Frei, *Eclipse*, 6.

Christ indicates what this yields with the Gospels – narrative that renders the identity of Jesus Christ. For Lindbeck and Frei, the identity of God and Christ yielded by such an approach to Scripture must absorb our view of the world, rather than the other way around. In the Barthian tradition, such an approach to Scripture yields a theological reality, which integrally shapes a theological ethic.

Hauerwas and Hays place more importance on the Christian community as the context for reading the Bible as Scripture and less on dogmatics and *sola scriptura*. Hauerwas says that 'to claim the Bible as authority is the testimony of the church that this book provides the resources necessary for the church to be a community sufficiently truthful so that our conversation with one another and God can continue across generations'.[63] Narrative ethics develops from a sense of the fundamental role of story in human life, and the recognition of the storied shape of Scripture. For example, Hauerwas and Willimon say of the Ten Commandments:

> The commandments are stories in the sense that, to understand them properly, we must know the great overarching story – Creation, Exodus, kingship, prophets, exile, Jesus, death, Resurrection, Ascension, church. The commandments also *story* us, that is, they help subsume us into the story we call redemption. It is also true to say that the commandments make such a story possible.[64]

In his emphasis on the Christian community, Hauerwas leans on Blenkinsopp's point that the canon does not contain its own self-justification but directs our attention to the tradition which it mediates. We have problems, according to Hauerwas, with the moral authority of Scripture because we have forgotten that it is a political claim characteristic of a particular polity. Here Hauerwas is referring to the church. Central to a theological ethic is 'remembering' – the Scriptural narrative requires a community capable of remembering and for whom active reinterpreting remains the key to a distinctive way of life. Scripture creates more than a world – it shapes a community which is the bearer of that world: 'claims about the authority of scripture make sense only in that the world and the community it creates are in fact true to the character of God'.[65] Thus 'morality' and 'Scripture' must be thought in relation to community; real trouble develops with these concepts if they are thought apart from community. Ethicists need to know the text as Scripture for the Christian community. They often know much about current critical views of the development of the text, but

> It is my hunch that part of the reason for the misuse of the scripture in matters dealing with morality is that the text was isolated from a liturgical context ... reading

[63] Hauerwas, *Community*, 64.

[64] Hauerwas and Willimon, *The Truth About God*, 30.

[65] Hauerwas, *Community*, 55.

> must be guided by the use of scripture through the liturgies of the church. For the shape of the liturgy over a whole year prevents any one part of scripture being given undue emphasis in relation to the narrative line of scripture.[66]

In terms of morality, Scripture's function is to induct us into the stories of God for the guidance of our community and individual lives. Hauerwas is convinced that the most appropriate *discrimen*/image[67] for characterizing Scripture is story. Scripture must be seen as one long, loosely structured non-fiction novel that has sub-plots that at some points appear minor but later turn out to be central.

A characteristic of this approach is the 'turn to the community',[68] with its stress on the Christian community as the context in which the word is read and interpreted. For example, Hauerwas and Willimon say of the Ten Commandments,

> So to 'know the commandments', by which Luther claimed one can know the whole Scripture, means that these commands are not self-interpreting. They depend on the practices of a community (church) formed by the worship, in Spirit and in truth, of a Trinitarian God.[69]

This narrative and Anabaptist tradition is pacifist, and one of its characteristics is its insistence on the centrality of a non-violent ethic. Hays's *The Moral Vision* is a good example of this characteristic, with the use of force included under the rubric of 'violence'. The resulting radical critique of contemporary society and culture is refreshing, but it remains a moot point whether or not such an approach can deliver a transformative ethic. Recovery of the church as the Christian community is vital, but the sort of new monasticism being proposed in this tradition[70] seems to me to be in danger of withdrawing Christian influence from culture where it is most needed.[71]

6. We have already made some comments about *liberationist readings* of Scripture in the introductory section. Fretheim's hermeneutic could certainly be classified as *a* liberationist approach, although even to categorize it in this

---

[66] Hauerwas, *Community*, 240.

[67] *Discrimen* refers to the imaginative construal the reader brings to the Bible so that it functions theologically as Scripture.

[68] Cahill, 'New Testament', 386.

[69] Hauerwas and Willimon, *The Truth About God*, 21.

[70] See Wilson, *Living Faithfully*, esp. ch. 5.

[71] The Hauerwas-Hays position seems *to me* to be unable to deliver a constructive political ethic. For Hauerwas on politics see his chapter, 'The Politics of Justice: Why Justice is a Bad Idea for Christians!' in *After Christendom*. I recognize that Hauerwas and Hays would disagree with me on this.

way alerts us to the considerable diversity among liberation readers,[72] with their very different views of the role of Scripture in shaping a contemporary Christian ethic. Liberation theology has generated massive reengagement with the Bible, with an ethical focus. As O'Donovan notes:

> The excitement which accompanied the recovery of political theology in our time arose very evidently from the reading of the Bible. In Israel's political experience of YHWH's rule there was, it seemed, a word which shed light and understanding on the practical situations of the present day. The question of how adequately the theologians articulated their indebtedness to Scripture is important, but secondary.... The adventure into political questioning was driven by the energy of biblical discovery.[73]

Gutiérrez's definition of the task of theology as 'critical reflection on Christian praxis in light of the word of God'[74] expresses this ethical focus in the light of Scripture. Not all liberationist hermeneutics hold as high a view of Scripture as does Gutiérrez.

Feminist hermeneutics is strongly liberative. The progenitor of a feminist hermeneutic is Elisabeth Schüssler Fiorenza. Characteristic of her hermeneutic is the recovery of women's experience in the history underlying the NT in the early Christian society of equals. For Fiorenza, the Bible is inherently patriarchal so that, 'Biblical revelation and truth are given only in those texts and interpretative models that transcend critically their patriarchal frameworks and allow for a vision of Christian woman as historical and theological subjects and actors',[75] and,

> the revelatory canon for theological evaluation of biblical androcentric traditions and their subsequent interpretations cannot be derived from the Bible itself but can only be formulated in and through women's struggle for liberation from all patriarchal oppression ... The personally and politically reflected experience of oppression and liberation must become the criterion of appropriateness for biblical interpretation and evaluation of biblical authority claims.[76]

The real locus of authority is not the canon but the present-day struggle of women for liberation.[77]

Fiorenza's hermeneutic is characterized by sophisticated exegesis. She adopts a resolutely modern theological anthropology – human beings are

[72] See Thiselton, *New Horizons*, ch. 12, and also chs, 10 and 11.

[73] *DN*, 21.

[74] Guitiérrez, *Liberation*, 13.

[75] Schüssler Fiorenza, *In Memory*, 30.

[76] Schüssler Fiorenza, *In Memory*, 32.

[77] Cf. here Mosala, 'Biblical Hermeneutics', 55ff.

autonomous persons whose greatest fulfilment is to freely choose and decide their destinies. Her canon outside the canon can be contrasted with Ruether's canon within the canon. Ruether identifies two religions within the Bible, an oppressive religion of the 'sacred canopy' and a religion of prophetic critique that fights against the former. A Christian approach should stand with the prophetic against the oppressive trajectory. However, this contrast is relative since, for Ruether, Scripture is only authoritative when its descriptions are authenticated in contemporary experience.[78]

The hermeneutic of Fiorenza is, of course, controversial among theologians and biblical scholars. Childs comments in this regard with particular reference to McFague's work that, 'If Jesus Christ is not the norm, but various cultural criteria are, the result for Biblical Theology is an unmitigated disaster.'[79]

Looking at the obstacles to reading the Bible ethically and the ways in which the Bible has been/is being read ethically alerts one to the variety of issues that have to be attended to in any such reading. Issues like:

- Is it still possible to read Scripture as a unity?
- If so, how does one construe this unity?
- In particular, how does one construe the relationship between the OT and the NT?
- What role does historical criticism play in reading the Bible ethically and how does this relate to canonical and narrative readings?
- How does an ethical reading of the Bible respond to the challenge of the Bible as irretrievably ideological?
- What role do theology and/or philosophy play in reading the Bible ethically? How does one move from Scripture to contemporary ethical and political issues?
- What types of hermeneutic should be employed in theological, ethical interpretation of Scripture?

We now turn to O'Donovan's work and the way in which he responds to the challenge of reading the Bible ethically and politically today.

O'Donovan's Biblical, Theological Ethics

O'Donovan's work is, in my opinion, like a drink of cold water on a hot day.[80] An effect of historical criticism in biblical studies, as we noted above, has been

---

[78] See Siker, *Scripture*, 190ff.

[79] Childs, *Biblical Theology*, 721.

[80] Clearly I am very positive about O'Donovan's approach. In what follows I aim to describe his ethics and biblical hermeneutic. For more critical interaction with O'Donovan, see the chapters that follow and *Studies in Christian Ethics* 11.2.

such endless fragmentation that the obstacles to a unified use of Scripture seem insuperable.[81] O'Donovan respects historical criticism and draws on it in many different ways, but his work is driven by the possibility of a unified, biblical ethic. O'Donovan exemplifies the dictum of his 'mentor', St Augustine: 'The man who fears God seeks with diligence his will in the Holy Scriptures.' A profound commitment to the Bible as Scripture and diligence in reading, marking and inwardly digesting it are central to O'Donovan's scholarship.

In 1973, O'Donovan published an article about *the possibility* of a biblical ethic. In the light of the obstacles to a biblical, theological ethic that we looked at above, it is clear what a relevant issue this remains. Biblical interpretation – as well as O'Donovan's work – has moved on in many ways since then, but his argument remains valid and continues to motivate O'Donovan's work at its foundations. O'Donovan insists that the idea of a *biblical* ethic is neither absurd nor incoherent. Typically, O'Donovan never fears to confront the hardest problems that challenge his view of the Bible as Scripture. He confronts, for example, the relationship between the OT and the NT with respect to holy war and argues that for the Christian ethicist,

> No more than in the previous example does his method consist in ramming through a programme of New Testament interpretation of the Old, disregarding the features which do not easily conform to his pattern. His claim is more modest: in the midst of the ambiguities he claims to see a line of continuity relating Jesus and the Christian faith to the history of the Jewish people, and it is that continuity which he sets out to trace.[82]

In his ethics O'Donovan thus continues to affirm *sola* and *tota scriptura*: 'our decisions must arise out of long reflection on the biblical ethic understood in the light of biblical theology'.[83]

Scripture undergirds and informs all of O'Donovan's work. However, his ethic is not only biblical but also *theological*; it recognizes the need for concepts and models to mediate between Scripture and ethical issues:

> If we are to form and justify opinions on specific questions in ethics, we must do so theologically; which means bringing the formal questions of ethics to theological interpretation and criticism. This by no means implies, of course, that we shall accept the current understanding of the questions unhesitatingly from the lips of philosophers, for theology has something to say about how the questions are formulated as well as about how they are answered.[84]

---

[81] See obstacle 3, above.

[82] O'Donovan, 'Possibility', 20, 21.

[83] O'Donovan, 'Possibility', 22.

[84] *RMO*, 182.

DN, which O'Donovan describes as a work in political theology, is precisely an exploration of that which comes between Scripture and political ethics. We do have to make the journey from what God said to Abraham to how to respond to Afghanistan after 11 September 2001, but O'Donovan insists that while faith at an intuitive level may make that journey instantly, or the preacher in half an hour, it may take a lifetime of scholarship.[85]

What is fascinating about O'Donovan's work though, and unusual nowadays, is the way Scripture is never left behind as the theological concepts take hold.[86] Not only do the concepts come from Scripture, but they are set in motion in tandem with a willingness to return to scriptural exegesis at myriad points. The result is the blossoming of a thousand exegetical flowers amidst the emerging structure of a theological ethic which is nothing if not conceptually robust. *RMO* and *DN* contain nuggets of refined exegesis throughout, often in O'Donovan's distinctive small print. It is gloriously assumed that the development of theological concepts and the exegesis of Scripture will complement each other in a rich, overflowing ecology. And they do. It should also be noted that O'Donovan's exegesis is theologically and philosophically informed; it is thick exegesis. Genesis 22, to take just one example, is interpreted, as we noted above, through the philosophical distinction between kinds and ends.[87]

O'Donovan's commitment to a theological ethic is apparent from the start of *RMO*. A Christian ethic must be evangelical; it must arise from the gospel itself. And for O'Donovan this means not just that it must be biblical, but that its concepts must express the inner logic of the gospel.

> We are not attempting to deny the richness of the New Testament's ethical appeal; but it is the task of theology to uncover the hidden relation of things that give the appeal force. We are driven to concentrate on the resurrection as our starting-point because it tells us of God's vindication of his creation, and so of our created life.[88]

Just how fruitful the resulting conceptual scaffolding is to the edifice of O'Donovan's ethics is evident in *RMO*.

Similarly, in his quest for a political theology O'Donovan insists on the need for political concepts that will do the work of theory construction: 'Our search, then, is for true political concepts. But if the notion of "political theology" is not to be a chimera, they must be authorised, as any datum of theology must be, from Holy Scripture.'[89] The early chapters of *DN* argue

[85] *DN*, ix.
[86] The obvious parallel that comes to mind is Karl Barth's *Church Dogmatics*.
[87] See note 45, above.
[88] *RMO*, 13.
[89] *DN*, 15.

that the kingdom of God embodied in Israel and fulfilled in Jesus is the appropriate theme from which to develop political concepts for a political theology.

All of this alerts us unequivocally to the fact that the recipe for O'Donovan's ethic contains many ingredients, notably biblical exegesis, theology, philosophy and history – a profound awareness of the tradition in all these areas. *RMO* sets out the Christian moral concepts that arise from pursuing the inner logic of the resurrection.[90] Such an ethic will be *realist*. The logic of the resurrection resists the dichotomy that some discern between creation and kingdom ethics – the resurrection *is* the reaffirmation of creation.[91] The voluntarism that has dominated Western moral thought since the Enlightenment, and is central to postmodernism,[92] must therefore be resisted; humans do not impose order upon the world, rather morality is something to which one is called, it is 'man's participation in the created order'.[93] A robust doctrine of creation and history (eschatology) is fundamental to a Christian ethic, and Chapters 2 and 3 of *RMO* are devoted to this foundation. O'Donovan expounds the order of creation conceptually in terms of teleological and generic order, that is, order as 'end' and order as 'kind', carefully distinguishing a Christian realism from idealism and empiricism.[94]

The reaffirmation of creation which resurrection signifies does not mean that redemption leads creation back to the garden of Eden, but that it leads it forward to what God always intended creation's destiny to be. Redemption is thus not only restoration, but also transformation. The constancy this nevertheless affords to the structures of creation runs counter to the pervasive, contemporary historicism.[95]

Realism means that this order is truly present in the creation. This is O'Donovan's common ground with natural law ethics. But the fall, and this is where O'Donovan distinguishes his approach from natural law ethics, means that not only do humans resist the order, but they are confused about it. We must distinguish ontology from epistemology – the creation order is real and holds for all, but in a fallen world it cannot be grasped outside of Christ. O'Donovan discerns four characteristics of the moral epistemology we

---

[90] The paragraphs that follow explain the shape of O'Donovan's theological ethic and indicate how he avoids the enclosedness of modern consciousness and the creative anti-realism of postmodernism. See obstacles 2 and 4, above.

[91] *RMO*, 15.

[92] See *DN*, 271ff.

[93] *RMO*, 76.

[94] *RMO*, 35, 36.

[95] See *RMO*, 58–75, for O'Donovan's important and decisive critique of historicism. Theological attempts to provide a christological foundation for historicism amounts to replacing Christ with Barabbas.

require:[96] first, it must entail knowledge of things in their relations to the totality of things. Secondly, it must facilitate creaturely knowledge, or knowledge from within the creation, if it is to be truly human. Thirdly, it must be knowledge from a human's position in the universe. Fourthly, it must be ignorant of the end of history – knowledge of the shape history takes belongs to God alone. O'Donovan sums this up as follows:

> What, then, must such knowledge of created order be, if it is really to be available to us? It must be an apprehensive knowledge of the whole of things, yet which does not pretend to a transcendence over the whole universe, but reaches out to understand the whole from a central point within it. It must be a human knowledge that is co-ordinated with the true performance of the human task in worship of God and obedience to the moral law. It must be a knowledge that is vindicated by God's revelatory word that the created good and man's knowledge of it is not to be overthrown in history. Such knowledge, according to the Christian gospel, is given to us as we participate in the life of Jesus Christ. ... True knowledge of the moral order is knowledge 'in Christ'.[97]

In this way it could be said that O'Donovan articulates an ethic which forges a unity between Brunner's doctrine of creation and Barth's theological epistemology.[98] Like Barth, O'Donovan is quite clear on the epistemological priority and exclusivity of Christ: 'That small segment of reality, elect and chosen of God, shapes all the reality that we encounter, so that to be in touch with reality in any form we have to be in touch with that reality.'[99] And this is how O'Donovan responds to the arrogance of the self-enclosed modern consciousness. But, with Brunner, O'Donovan insists that there are objective orders in creation.

'Resurrection' points not only to the objective reality of creation order but, through its connection with ascension and thus Pentecost, it also points to the work of the Spirit in us. The Spirit makes the reality of God's redemption in Christ, a past event, present and authoritative to us, and it also evokes our free response to this redemption.[100] Through the Spirit, the authority of Christ exercises its claim upon us. The incarnation reminds us that Christ's authority is entirely in touch with the creation, it is a 'worldly moral authority'[101] so that we should not falsely conceive of the divine command as 'extraplanetary material'.[102] As O'Donovan notes, 'The meaning of Jesus' life and teaching

---

96 See *RMO*, ch. 4.
97 *RMO*, 85.
98 See *RMO*, 85–87.
99 *RMO*, 121.
100 See *RMO*, ch. 5.
101 *RMO*, 143.
102 Thielicke's phrase, quoted in *RMO*, 143.

must be a worldly meaning, a reality of human existence which can command our lives in the world and reorder them in the restored creation.'[103] Christ's authority is that of the 'concrete universal' – it is irreplaceable. With its goal of world-redemption, Christ's work is truly good news. O'Donovan again addresses here the historicist challenge – how can one small segment of reality be authoritative today and for all time? He rightly notes that the roots of this scepticism are in the belief in time as history so that events have no significance other than as contributions to subsequent developments.[104] O'Donovan also explains the historical authority of Christ in terms of his conferring on events their story shape as history, and in this context he discusses the relationship between Christ and the Old Testament.

According to O'Donovan, historical authority can hold contradictory elements together in one narrative. 'Historical authority can reconcile, where moral authority can only judge.'[105] Thus we should expect to find, within the narrative Christ forms around himself, moral contradictions that he reconciles historically.

> When we read, for example, of the conquest of Canaan and the terms of the ban, we will understand the Christological significance of these events only if we suspend the moral question which we immediately wish to put to them. The Christian reading of the Old Testament has been constantly baffled by a failure to understand this. ... Like the elder brother of the prodigal son, Christians reading the book of Joshua need to learn how to ask other questions before the moral ones: the history of divine revelation, like the waiting father in the parable, is not concerned only with justifying the good and condemning the bad. This Old Testament reality is concerned only to reveal the impact of the divine reality upon the human in election and judgement. We may wonder, of course, as we read the book of Joshua, what attitude this God of jealousy and wrath will take to the worldly order of things; and that question will be answered for us only as we follow the story of his self-revelation forward to its climax in Jesus Christ. The demand which this part of the story makes upon our faith is not that we should struggle to reconcile in moral terms the form of creaturely order which is shown us by Christ in Gethsemane with those unbridled acts of war, but that we should accept what is, perhaps, the greater scandal: a reconciliation in the history of divine revelation which can embrace even such a contradiction to the moral order.[106]

O'Donovan further suggests that in God's revelation it was necessary that the sort of material we find in Joshua – 'the transcendent fire of election and judgement' – had to precede his revelation in Christ and its vindication of creation,

[103] *RMO*, 143.
[104] *RMO*, 161.
[105] *RMO*, 157.
[106] *RMO*, 157, 158.

lest we take the incarnation for granted. Nevertheless, it is true that in the NT the creation order is vindicated in a way that is not anticipated in Joshua. The story that Christ shapes around himself is one of the election of humankind, and not just of Israel, as Joshua understands it. 'The moral questions, then, are only suspended, to allow the theological questions priority; they are not forgotten.'[107] Acceptance of the authority of Christ

> means belief that Christ turns these fragmentary utterances of God's voice, in warrior triumphs and legislative order, into a history which culminates in the divine manifestation and vindication of created order. Thus all the time, in one sense, the story of the Old Testament was the story of that order; and in reading the Old Testament as Christians we may expect to see this story, too, emerge from its pages.[108]

O'Donovan claims an ancient pedigree for this approach to the Old Testament, claiming *inter alia* Justin Martyr and Aquinas as practitioners.[109]

The form of the moral life is love,[110] but that requires unpacking. The form will relate to human acts and to moral character. In terms of the former, the great challenge morally is novelty. Ethicists try and cope with the challenge of change by drawing on tradition or anticipating the future. However, it is only if we have some idea of the order for change[111] that we can really face change, and this is precisely what the ancients called wisdom. Wisdom is 'the perception that every novelty, in its own way, manifests the permanence and stability of the created order, so that, however astonishing and undreamt of it may be, it is not utterly incommensurable with what has gone before'.[112] In the Old Testament O'Donovan locates this perspective in the 're-presentation of wisdom as law'.[113] 'In torah the moral authority of created order and the transcendent authority of the electing God were made one.'[114] Thus, the moral agent comes to new situations equipped with wisdom or the moral law.[115] Wisdom illuminates the situation but 'at the same time this illumination reflects back upon its

---

107 *RMO*, 158.

108 *RMO*, 159.

109 *RMO*, 159, 160.

110 *RMO*, ch. 11, is a wonderful analysis of the relationship between love of God and neighbour. O'Donovan's nuanced analysis is particularly important in the light of the recovery of ethics in the postmodernism of Levinas and Derrida, in which there is a tendency to collapse the neighbour into God (especially with Derrida, see *Gift*).

111 O'Donovan, *RMO*, 188, calls this 'what it is in the world which measures change and so stands beyond it'.

112 *RMO*, 189.

113 *RMO*, 189.

114 *RMO*, 190.

115 See *RMO*, 191, for useful definitions of created order, moral field, wisdom, etc.

source, so that he comes to understand not only the particular situation but the generic moral law itself with greater clarity'.[116] O'Donovan resists the notion that there can be formal rules, such as the Principle of Double Effect,[117] which apply equally to all acts. Particular judgements that are capable of different interpretations are thus occasions for moral learning. And this bears on how we ought to read Scripture ethically. Codes, such as the Ten Commandments, have their place – they express in a list our 'basic commitments'. However, to make moral judgements we need to access the principles of moral order that undergird these judgements:

> The items in a code stand to the moral law as bricks to a building.[118] Wisdom must involve some comprehension of how the bricks are meant to be put together.
>
> This has an immediate bearing on how we read the Bible. Not only is it insufficient to quote and requote the great commands of the Decalogue and the Sermon on the Mount. We will read the Bible seriously only when we use it to guide our thought towards a comprehensive moral viewpoint, and not merely to articulate disconnected moral claims. We must look within it not only for moral bricks, but for indications of order in which the bricks belong together. There may be some resistance to this, not only from those who suspect that it may lead to evasions of the 'plain' sense of the Bible's teaching, but from those who have forebodings of a totalitarian construction which will legislate over questions where it would be better to respect the Bible's silence. But in truth there is no alternative policy if we intend that our moral thinking should be shaped in any significant way by the Scriptures.[119]

In terms of the moral subject, O'Donovan argues that the unity of the moral law ensures the unity of the moral subject who respects it. Jesus' (and Proverbs') emphasis upon the heart tells us that God considers the moral subject as a totality.

O'Donovan's Reading of the Bible for Politics

The subtitle of *DN* is 'Rediscovering the roots of political theology'. A major element in *DN* is to alert us to the rich and relevant *tradition of political theology* and our lamentable ignorance of it. Recovery of this tradition would itself alert us to the fundamental ingredient in any political *theology*, namely Scripture. Indeed theology is political simply as a result of being true to the gospel:

[116] *RMO*, 190.

[117] See *RMO*, 192–94.

[118] O'Donovan, *RMO*, 203, describes a code as 'no more than a cultural form through which we communicate knowledge of the created order which is itself a whole'.

[119] *RMO*, 200.

'Theology must be political if it is to be evangelical.'[120] Political theology is concerned with opening up politics to the activity of God, and political theology should therefore be rooted in Scripture. O'Donovan insists that theology requires a full political conceptuality – indwelling of the narrative of Scripture, for example, would be inadequate on its own if it does not deliver concepts for political analysis. Such concepts must, however, be authorized by Scripture:

> For in any branch of theology concepts mediate between the reading of the scriptural text (the lector's task) and the construction of theology (the theologian's). Theory has to respond to the concepts found in Scripture, and its adequacy as theology will be measured by how well it has responded to them.[121]

The result of this perspective on O'Donovan's part is an exercise in political theology that is quite exceptional in its exegetical rigour and comprehensiveness. The biblical route into a contemporary political theology is, according to O'Donovan, *the kingdom of God*. O'Donovan notes that much of the language of Christian faith is politically charged; however, 'political theology ... does not suppose a literal synonymity between the political vocabulary of salvation and the secular use of the same political terms. It postulates an analogy ... grounded in reality[122] – between the acts of God and human acts, both of them taking place within the one public history which is the theatre of God's saving purposes and mankind's social undertakings.'[123] According to O'Donovan, it is in the analogy between God's rule and human rule as embodied in the kingdom of God that we find fertile soil for the development of a biblical, political conceptuality.

Taking seriously the reign of God will help us, according to O'Donovan, to recover the ground that has been lost to the notion of authority and the related notion of political activity as kingly.[124] A kingdom approach follows modern thought in positioning politics firmly within history, but it safeguards politics from historicism by first understanding it as an activity within creation and thus not arbitrary; it 'works within the covenant that is established through creation.'[125] Secondly, taking divine rule as a starting point clarifies the idea of

---

120 *DN*, 3.

121 *DN*, 15. This is one of O'Donovan's criticisms of liberation theology, which he refers to as the Southern School. See *DN*, 16.

122 On metaphor and Yahweh as king see *DN*, 35.

123 *DN*, 2.

124 *DN*, 19. See also *DN*, 30–32.

125 *DN*, 19. It is here that O'Donovan links *DN* back into *RMO*. See *DN*, 19, 20. The resurrection is the climax of a history of divine rule. An issue of controversy at our consultation was O'Donovan's view of history in relation to creation order. In *DN*, 19, he asserts that we must speak of a *history* of creation order and of a history of *creation order*.

authority by focusing on authority as firstly a human act rather than inhering in particular institutions. 'The political act is the divinely authorised act.'[126] The association of political authority with specific institutions is a mistake of the Western tradition; political theology will be interested in the authorized act and not attempt to discern the authorized institution(s).

Thirdly, taking the reign of God as our route into political theology will focus our attention on *the revealed history of Israel.* O'Donovan welcomes the fresh emphasis on Scripture that liberation theology has brought, but he rightly insists that a random appropriation of motifs out of their meta-context is inadequate. Motifs like that of exodus and *shālôm* are pregnant with political theology, but they have to be explicated within a unifying conceptuality if the resulting theology is to lay claim to Christian faith: 'What was needed was an architectonic hermeneutic which would locate political reflection on the Exodus within an undertaking that has its centre of gravity in the Gospels.'[127] And, of course, the major contender for such an undertaking is the kingdom of God/heaven, the major theme of Jesus' teaching in the Synoptics.[128] O'Donovan examines the different ways Hebrews and the Synoptics appropriate a kingdom vision – Hebrews' is heavenly, whereas the Synoptics' is earthly. This tension is not a contradiction; it serves to mediate the tension inherent in a theology of fulfilment and promise. Paul's discussion of the continuing role of Israel in Romans alerts us to the fact that:

> The public tradition of Israel carries an unrealised promise for the full socialisation of God's believing people, the appearing, as another prophet puts it, of the New Jerusalem from heaven. This means that any question about social forms and structures must be referred to a normative critical standard: do they fulfil that will of God for human society to which Israel's forms authoritatively point us?[129]

Thus, Israel herself is the hermeneutic principle that shapes a Christian political reading of Scripture: 'the governing principle is the kingly rule of God, expressed in Israel's corporate existence and brought to final effect in the life, death and resurrection of Jesus'.[130] This means that Israel's life must be taken seriously *as history* which unfolds through different periods and circumstances:

> To dip into Israel's experience at one point – let it be the Exodus, the promise of *shālôm*, the jubilee laws, or, with Thomas Cranmer at the coronation of Edward VI, the reign of Josiah of Judah – and to take out a single disconnected image or theme

126 *DN*, 20.
127 *DN*, 22.
128 John's equivalent is 'eternal life'.
129 *DN*, 25.
130 *DN*, 27.

> from it is to treat the history of God's reign like a commonplace book or a dictionary of quotations.[131]

O'Donovan opposes constructing a counter-history from the official account of Israel's history which would simply become at best a story of a group of the Israelites – we must cease from perpetual unmasking. Nor, in historicist fashion, should we tell Israel's history as one of progressive development. Israel's story must be read as a history of redemption, 'as the story of how certain principles of social and political life were vindicated by the action of God in the judgement and restoration of the people'.[132] As we take the narrative shape of the Old Testament seriously, we expose ourselves to the different forms of Israel's experience (tribe, monarchy, etc.), and the concepts employed by the narrators enable us to interpret this story. 'And from those concepts we may derive an orientation of political principle through which the legacy of Israel regulates our own political analysis and deliberation. YHWH's victory lays hold on our intelligence and claims us still.'[133]

O'Donovan develops his analysis of the kingdom of God by identifying four leading political terms associated with it – salvation, judgement, possession and praise (Israel's response). This conceptuality is central to O'Donovan's political theology. He acknowledges that it is not directly authorized by Scripture, but it does comprehend and illuminate the text of Scripture. O'Donovan notes that:

> The threefold analysis of divine rule as salvation, judgement and possession will provide a framework for exploring the major questions about authority posed by the Western tradition. The unique covenant of YHWH and Israel can be seen as a point of disclosure from which the nature of all political authority comes into view. Out of the self-possession of this people in their relation to God springs the possibility of other peoples' possessing themselves in God. In this hermeneutic assumption lay the actual continuity between Israel's experience and the Western tradition.[134]

From this conceptuality O'Donovan develops the following six theorems.[135] We cannot here describe the process by which he reaches each of these. Suffice it to note that they emerge through detailed exegesis and interpretation in dialogue with the tradition of political theology.

- Political authority arises where power, the execution of right and the perpetuation of tradition are assured together in one co-ordinated agency.

---

131 *DN*, 27.
132 *DN*, 29.
133 *DN*, 29.
134 *DN*, 45–46.
135 The first three in *DN*, 46–47, and the remainder on 65, 72, 80.

- That any regime should actually come to hold authority, and should continue to hold it, is a work of divine providence in history, not a mere accomplishment of the human task of political service.
- In acknowledging political authority, society proves its political identity.

This latter point O'Donovan develops in relation to Israel being a community of praise, and he suggests that in every political society there is some worship of divine rule.[136]

- The authority of a human regime mediates divine authority in a unitary structure, but is subject to the authority of law within the community, which bears independent witness to the divine command.

O'Donovan arrives at this theorem through a lengthy discussion of the role of mediators (judges, kings and prophets) in Israel. He argues that Israel rejected absolutism not by a distribution of powers, but by allowing a unitary government subject to Yahweh's law which has an independent authority made audible in Israel by the prophets.

- The appropriate unifying element in international order is law rather than government.
- The conscience of the individual members of a community is a repository of the moral understanding which shaped it, and may serve to perpetuate it in a crisis of collapsing morale or institution.

The story of Israel reaches its fulfilment in Jesus. But how do the political and the spiritual relate in Jesus' proclamation of the kingdom? Especially through Israel's experience of exile, an understanding of the people of God in the context of *two kingdoms* had arisen, and in the early church this was canonized by Augustine. Jeremiah, Esther and Daniel witness to the possibility of Israel living in two cities (Israel and Babylon) under two rules (Babylon and Yahweh), and exercising considerable influence in the process. Other OT texts, such as Second Isaiah, however, hold out the possibility of a return to Israel and recovery of one kingdom under one rule – that of Yahweh.

O'Donovan rightly notes that Jesus' ministry discloses the rule of God and thus challenges any concept of two kingdoms.

> Jesus ... unsettled the Two Kingdoms conception, which had, in one way or another, shaped Israel's understanding of its political position since the exile. He announced the coming of God's Kingdom to sweep away existing orders of government. Those orders were of a passing age.[137]

---

[136] *DN*, 49.
[137] *DN*, 137.

Jesus' preferred self-designation, 'Son of Man', with its background in Daniel 7, makes his political significance clear.[138] O'Donovan uses the same categories of salvation (Jesus' works of power), judgement (Jesus' proclamation of the judgement of Israel), possession (Jesus and the law), and praise (reception of Jesus) to explicate Jesus' teaching about the kingdom. O'Donovan finds Jesus' radical attitude to the authorities of the day exemplified in Matthew's story of the temple tax (17:24–27). Now that the king *is* present, citizens of the kingdom are free from the constraints of the empire, but purely as a concession Jesus and his disciples will pay taxes lest they are seen as rebels who repudiate God's mediated rule.[139]

Methodologically, O'Donovan insists that he is not using political concepts to explain the spiritual realities of the kingdom. The analogical movement is the reverse, and the 'first assumption of political theology must be that these analogies are valid, and that through them the Gospel of the kingdom offers liberation to an imprisoned culture'.[140]

Unlike Jesus, the early church did not proclaim the kingdom of God. It narrated the fact of the kingdom having come in Jesus. O'Donovan resists the practice of situating political theology more in the Gospels than in the rest of the NT. He argues that the movement from Jesus' proclamation of the kingdom to the Easter message elevates our sense of community: 'Political theology has an ecclesiological mode, which takes the church seriously as a society and shows how the rule of God is realised there.'[141] Christology opens up the connections between the Easter message and the kingdom of God. Christ is the mediator of God's rule and he is the representative individual. He is the *decisive* presence of God and the *decisive* presence of God's people.[142] Thus,

> To speak of God's rule from this point on must mean more than to assert divine sovereignty, or even divine intervention, in general terms. It means recounting this narrative and drawing the conclusions implied in it. ... We cannot discuss the question of 'secular' government, the question from which Western political theology has too often been content to start, unless we approach it historically, from a Christology that has been displayed in narrative form as Gospel.[143]

---

[138] See Ridderbos, *Coming*. The most significant recent work on Jesus and the kingdom is Tom Wright's *Jesus and the Victory of God*.

[139] *DN*, 92, 93. The radicality of this view is strengthened by O'Donovan's reading of Mt. 12:17ff. O'Donovan favours the view that Jesus' answer was neat-footed because, while he appeared to acknowledge Caesar's authority, in reality he brushed it aside. For different approaches to the politics of Mt. 12:17ff. see Cromartie, *Caesar's Coin*.

[140] *DN*, 119.

[141] *DN*, 123.

[142] *DN*, 124.

[143] *DN*, 133.

O'Donovan elaborates on this Christology through four moments of Christ's representative act: advent,[144] passion, restoration and exaltation. This is an exegetical rather than conceptual division.[145] O'Donovan finds the unfolding of the resurrection in two stages theologically significant. Christ's triumphant rising from the grave signifies the restoration of creation, but the invisibility of the ascension reminds us of what is still to come. With its coronation imagery, the ascension is politically charged: it is the conclusion of the story of Christ and the foundation which determines all future time.

From this flows the NT doctrine of the 'subjection of the nations'. According to O'Donovan, in the light of the ascension the primary thing to be said about the authorities, both political and demonic, is that they have been disarmed by Christ (Col. 2:15). Simultaneously, this disarming awaits the final return of Christ. 'Within the framework of these two assertions there opens up an account of secular authority which presumes neither that the Christ-event never occurred nor that the sovereignty of Christ is now transparent and uncontested.'[146] O'Donovan examines key NT texts to discern to what extent the secular authorities are compatible with the church's mission.[147] He argues that these texts indicate that secular authorities are authorized to provide the social space that the church's mission requires.[148] Romans 13 must be read with fresh eyes, namely in the context of Christ having vanquished the authorities. The authorities are reduced to the role once held by Israel's judges:

> St. Paul's new assertion is that the performance of judgement alone justifies government; and this reflects his new Christian understanding of the political situation. … Membership in Christ replaced all other political identities by which communities knew themselves. No respect can be paid to the role of government, then, as a focus of collective identity, either in Israel or in any other community.[149]

Such judgement restrains evil in society and facilitates the spread of the gospel.[150]

---

[144] O'Donovan makes the delightful point that when, at his baptism, Jesus prayed, he articulated faithful Israel's prayer for the kingdom to come. *DN*, 134.

[145] *DN*, 133.

[146] *DN*, 146.

[147] These are 1 Tim. 2:1ff.; Rom. 13; 1 Pet. 2:13–17; 1 Cor. 6:1; Mt. 18; 2 Thes. 3:2–9; Rev. 15.

[148] See also *DN*, 217, 218.

[149] *DN*, 148.

[150] With his strong ecclesial emphasis, one discerns similarities between O'Donovan and Hauerwas. But see *DN*, 151, 152 for O'Donovan's differences with Hauerwas concerning the role of the authorities.

The dual authority of two kingdoms is now changed in the light of the coming of the kingdom in Christ. 'A theological account of how this world is ruled, then, must proceed from and through an account of the church. … Decisions made about the nature of church authority have shaped and still shape what is said about secular government.'[151] The church is a political society in that it is brought into existence and held in existence by a government that demands absolute obedience. 'It is ruled and authorised by the ascended Christ alone and supremely; it therefore has its own authority; and it is not answerable to any other authority that may attempt to subsume it.'[152] It is Pentecost that speaks of the church's independent authority. Pentecost is not another moment in the Christ-event, but a uniting of the church with the authorizing of Christ. There is, according to O'Donovan, only one society that is incorporated into the kingdom of God – and that is the church.[153] However, the church's nature as a political society is hidden and to be discerned by faith. 'The shape of the pre-structured church, then, is the shape of the Christ-event become the dynamics of a social identity.'[154] In relation to the four moments of the Christ-event, O'Donovan identifies four characteristics of the church. In response to the advent, the church is a gathering or missional community. In response to the passion, the church is a suffering community. In response to the resurrection, the church is a glad community, as it perceives the recovery of God's order for creation in the resurrection. 'If the church's gladness is the gladness of creation, that means it is the gladness of Jesus himself; for this renewed order of creation is present in him.'[155] O'Donovan positions the moral life of the church in this context because it is evangelical; it springs from the reaffirmation of creation in Christ. In response to Christ's ascension the church prophesies; it speaks the words of God. Like Christ, the church establishes God's kingdom by God's word.

The remainder of *DN* focuses on how this theology of the kingdom worked itself out in the life of the church historically in terms of the doctrine of the Two.

> The passing age of the principalities and powers has overlapped with the coming age of God's Kingdom. … Secular institutions have a role confined to this passing age (*saeculum*). … Applied to political authorities, the term 'secular' should tell us that they are not agents of Christ, but are marked for displacement when the rule of God in Christ is finally disclosed. They are Christ's conquered enemies; yet they have an indirect testimony to give, bearing the marks of his sovereignty imposed upon them,

151 *DN*, 159.
152 *DN*, 159.
153 *DN*, 251.
154 *DN*, 171.
155 *DN*, 181.

> negating their pretensions and evoking their acknowledgement. Like the surface of a planet pocked with craters by the bombardment it receives from space, the governments of the passing age show the impact of Christ's dawning glory. This witness of the secular is the central core of Christendom.[156]

As our concerns are primarily with biblical interpretation, we will not describe O'Donovan's controversial defence of Christendom as an expression of Christian mission or his affirmation of early modern liberalism in any detail here.[157] O'Donovan discerns four ways in which early modern liberalism carries forward the positive legacy of Christendom: its discovery of freedom, its mercy in judgement, its tempered justice and its openness to speech. By contrast to this positive assessment, it is in the voluntarism of late-modernity that O'Donovan senses real danger:

> This helps us understand at once how modernity is the child of Christianity, and at the same time how it has left its father's house and followed the way of the prodigal. Or, to paint the picture in more sombre terms, how modernity can be conceived as Antichrist, a parodic and corrupt development of Christian social order.[158]

O'Donovan's Biblical Hermeneutic

O'Donovan's colossal attempt to rehabilitate the use of the Bible ethically and politically is comparable in its scale to Childs' work to recover the Bible as Christian Scripture. How successful is it, and does it really point the way towards a renewal in the use of the Bible ethically and politically? That is, of course, the debate to be had. In this section I will characterize O'Donovan's biblical hermeneutic and give some indication of how his approach relates to those we discussed above. Characterization is always an abstraction from the actual practice, and it inevitably diminishes some of its richness and complexity. This is especially the case with O'Donovan's work, which is not easily typified; nevertheless the attempt is, I trust, valuable.

O'Donovan reads the Bible as Christian Scripture, and that goes for the Old Testament as much as for the New. Scripture has the highest theological authority as God's word, and as such it exhibits a unity.

> To treat the books of the Old and New Testaments ... as *Scripture*, is to suppose that these historically diverse corpora, Hebrew, Jewish-Christian and Hellenistic-Jewish, cohere as a narrative; and that their narrative coherence, however it may be elaborated, constitutes a decisive testimony for faith.[159]

---

[156] *DN*, 211–12.

[157] See Colin Greene's chapter, 'Revisiting Christendom: A Crisis of Legitimization'.

[158] *DN*, 275.

[159] O'Donovan, 'Deliberation', 140.

Christ establishes the narrative unity within which the whole is to be read. The unity of Scripture is not, however, to be construed simplistically; O'Donovan's view of holy war indicates this clearly enough. However, O'Donovan does insist on the

> search for unity-in-relation. ... Are the biblical 'guilds', under cover of a proper insistence on source-differentiation, actually mounting an assault on any theology that proposes to read the Hebrew and Christian Scriptures? The term 'biblical theology' ... seems to have come back into circulation as a general term of abuse, as though we must all understand it as the duty of theology to be non-biblical and the duty of biblical studies to be untheological.[160]

Narrative is, according to O'Donovan, able to hold contradictory elements in the context of a whole, and 'despite' elements like holy war, a fundamental continuity and unity can be discerned in Scripture. The overarching inner logic of the whole that O'Donovan discerns is that of the resurrection of Christ as reaffirming and establishing creation order. This is complemented in *DN* by a salvation historical approach leading from God's action in Israel to God's action in Jesus, expressed in shorthand as the kingdom of God. O'Donovan invokes the kingdom as the appropriate point from which to develop a biblical, political theology, but I take it that he would be happy to describe the overarching theme of the Bible as the kingdom of God.

If this asserts the continuity in Scripture, O'Donovan also asserts discontinuity between the Old Testament and the New. This is apparent, for example, in his articulation of the change that the coming of the kingdom in Christ makes politically – politics is part of that which has been overcome, and its continuance is as a residual hangover. O'Donovan insists that this makes a real difference to the role of government in the period between the coming of the kingdom and its final consummation. Pentecost, with its connecting of the church with the exalted Christ, thus marks a real difference between the OT and NT eras. At the same time, Israel continues to exist as a challenge to the church to take society seriously.[161]

Much of O'Donovan's early work is in classics, and an important component of his hermeneutic, not least in relation to the Old Testament, is the 'once-valued discipline of historical reading'.[162] O'Donovan rightly critiques

---

160 O'Donovan, 'Response', 96.

161 I find this continued testimony of Israel to public life a most helpful insight. It connects with O'Donovan's twofold reading of Joshua in relation to the land. On the one hand, one can read Joshua along the line of Hebrews, whereby the land is fulfilled in Christ (O'Donovan, 'Loss', 49). At the same time, 'we can try to learn about place from the Old Testament theology of the land without flying in the face of all that the New Testament has done with it' (ibid., 50).

162 O'Donovan, 'Deliberation', 144.

our 'cheaply-won postmodern moralism', which quickly critiques ancient texts from a politically correct stance, and is endemic in biblical studies nowadays. His example in this respect is Lectionary 3 of the Church of England, which 'gingerly picks its way through the Old Testament like a scavenger on a garbage-tip, searching for morsels from the debris, topping and tailing its readings like a cook preparing rotten vegetables for the pan'.[163]

Old Testament society is a heroic warrior society, and we need, via patient, historical reading, to learn how to listen to a voice witnessing to Yahweh out of such a culture. Such an approach

> requires distance and suspension of moral judgement to allow an ancient society constructed on different terms from any we know to express its own moral priorities without our wanting to reprove it. We may not pretend to sink ourselves in that ancient past and lose ourselves there, forgetting what we are and how we have been led away from it since. But neither may we chide its heroic ambitions like a school prefect calling younger students to order.... to sustain it [such a distance] while avowing one God, one created human nature, one human vocation, and one supreme good that draws all generations, races and cultural varieties of mankind to itself, requires a serious historical sensibility.[164]

O'Donovan has little discussion of the discipline of biblical theology, but clearly his analysis of the unity of Scripture is along these lines. In OT circles, a salvation history approach is particularly associated with von Rad's approach to Old Testament theology, and the debates this generated, although it also exhibits similarities to the genetic-progressive method.[165] O'Donovan's discernment of the kingdom of God as the unifying theme in the Old Testament, at least for the purposes of developing a political theology, is less common, although *inter alia* Schultz, Klein, Helberg and Bright have argued along these lines.[166] The argument that the kingdom of God is the main theme of Jesus' teaching and of the New Testament is more common.[167]

Von Rad discerned two separate histories of Israel – that narrated in the Old Testament and that reconstructed by modern, critical historians. O'Donovan,

---

[163] O'Donovan, 'Deliberation', 143–44.

[164] O'Donovan, 'Deliberation', 143. O'Donovan makes the case for this sort of historical reading in a dialogue with Kenneth Cragg's discussion of Samson in his *Palestine*.

[165] See Hasel, *Theology*, and Hayes and Prussner, *Old Testament Theology*, for useful discussions of these views.

[166] See Hasel, *Theology*, 120, 138, 139; Helberg, *Die Here Regeer*; Bright, *Kingdom*. Dumbrell, *Covenant*, and others, have argued for covenant as a unifying concept in the Old Testament. O'Donovan speaks of the covenant of creation, but he makes little use of covenant in his theological ethics.

[167] See, e.g., Wright, *Jesus*; Ladd, *The Presence of the Future*, Ridderbos, *When the Time Had Fully Come*.

like Pannenberg, Rendtorff and others,[168] prefers to keep historical criticism and what he calls the 'revealed history' of Israel close together. The result is that O'Donovan combines a salvation historical, narrative approach with historical reconstruction, in a way that is reminiscent of Bright's approach in his *The Kingdom of God*. As O'Donovan reiterates in 'Response to Respondents: Behold the Lamb', he makes full use of biblical criticism but nevertheless remains committed to thinking 'out of' Scripture.[169] In Old Testament studies nowadays narrative, literary readings tend to diverge sharply from historical reconstructions – especially as such radical views of the latter have gained ground. Consequently, the way in which O'Donovan holds together a narrative approach with historical criticism was raised several times at our consultation.[170]

O'Donovan's use of a biblical theological approach is important as a way of bringing the authority of Scripture in its entirety to bear on the construction of an ethic. It undergirds his assertion of the need for an *architectonic hermeneutic*, or one that does justice to the shape of the edifice of Scripture as a whole. Motifs such as that of exodus or *shalom* must not be arbitrarily abstracted from the building of Scripture, but must be read in the context of the narrative structure of Scripture as a whole.

The role of the reading community in relation to this unity of Scripture is an issue nowadays – does the *discrimen*[171] inevitably come from the community or reader, or does Scripture norm the *discrimen*? How should we think of Scripture as connecting with ethical issues? A key issue is whether such a connection depends on the *discrimen* the reader/community brings to Scripture, or whether Scripture yields a key(s). O'Donovan opposes Kelsey's idea that the unified shape of Scripture for theology results from the *discrimen* the reader brings to Scripture. Rather, Scripture has a determinate shape that is authoritative for theology. However, O'Donovan helpfully alerts us to the mediating role of concepts between Scripture and theology. Theology requires a conceptual apparatus that we have to develop from Scripture.[172] In O'Donovan's ethics, these are the inner logic discerned in resurrection and the fourfold conceptual apparatus that he develops for political theology. As with Barth, O'Donovan continues to allow exegesis a major role even as the conceptual apparatus takes hold.

O'Donovan's understanding of how Scripture yields concepts which take hold in the development of a theology is, in my opinion, an important insight.

---

168 See Hasel, *Theology*, 106–15.

169 See O'Donovan, 'Response', 93–96.

170 See, in particular, the chapter by Moberly.

171 See Kelsey, *Uses*, 158ff. On *discrimen* see above, n. 67.

172 See 'Response', 93ff., for O'Donovan's defence of this position.

He insists that 'thought cannot live *sola narratione*. Narrative can authorise, but cannot supply, a deliberative discourse.'[173] As Schweiker thus observes of *DN*, 'O'Donovan's position is far more subtle than most narrative theologies that assume we can get along without concept formation and yet more hermeneutically sensitive than much political philosophy unmindful of the symbolic density of concepts.'[174] For reasons listed above, neither biblical scholars nor theologians generally focus attention on this aspect of interpretation. It is also one that probably requires rigorous scrutiny in terms of the whole process of theory construction.[175] It certainly raises the issue of the relationship between theology and philosophy and biblical interpretation. This cannot be pursued in detail here, apart from flagging it as an important issue for theological interpretation of the Bible.

O'Donovan's practice of biblical interpretation does, however, have important lessons for the contemporary, minority renewal of theological interpretation. Clearly O'Donovan's reading of Scripture is unashamedly theological, or 'thick', as opposed to thin, interpretation – it is exemplary in this respect. At the same time it resists the tension between theological interpretation and general hermeneutics, typified in the Yale-Chicago debate.[176] In his chapter on Romans 13, Gerrit de Kruijf suggests that O'Donovan's hermeneutic is a good example of what I type as 'Christ the clue to philosophy and theology' in *Renewing Biblical Interpretation*.[177] That typology is rudimentary, but it is a way of trying to discern the importantly different ways in which the ingredients of a biblical hermeneutic can be put together. As thick as O'Donovan's hermeneutic is theologically, it is powerfully and consciously undergirded philosophically. I am not sure how O'Donovan himself would construe the philosophy-theology relationship, but clearly, even when it comes to philosophy, his major commitment is to thinking out of Scripture, and he is clear that he does not assume the autonomy of philosophy. Although O'Donovan strongly affirms creation order which holds for all humans, he is clear that epistemologically we only read that order aright in Christ – this severs at its root any kind of natural theology which would support an autonomous philosophy.

In my opinion, it is just the kind of mix of (theologically informed) philosophy and theology that we find in O'Donovan's work that theological interpretation urgently requires. The complex interaction of these elements should not be underestimated. So, for example, O'Donovan's (critical) realism resulting from his view of resurrection and creation order, means that he is optimistic

[173] O'Donovan, 'Response', 94.
[174] Schweiker, 'Freedom', 117, 118.
[175] Analogy, for example.
[176] See Bartholomew, 'Uncharted Waters', 24–34.
[177] See Bartholomew, 'Uncharted Waters', 24–34.

that we can read an ancient text like the Old Testament and discern its meaning – after all, we inhabit ultimately the same world as ancient Israel, and this makes understanding a hope-full possibility. O'Donovan regards Gadamer's *Horizontverschmelzung* as a vain attempt to recover understanding, having already conceded a historicist framework, and he rejects it *inter alia* because of the realism embodied in the gospel.[178] In myriad such ways, theology and philosophy are interwoven in O'Donovan's hermeneutic.

Anyone in biblical studies will know how contested are the above features of O'Donovan's hermeneutic. In this regard, two comments are in order. First, important aspects of O'Donovan's hermeneutic are not even on the agenda of biblical studies as taught and practised in our universities and seminaries. If we are serious about a renewal in biblical interpretation, then O'Donovan is very helpful in identifying the issues we need to address, however much we may disagree with him. Secondly, O'Donovan's emerging corpus is an invitation to biblical scholars to read the Bible ethically and politically. It is an invitation that needs to be accepted, and in this volume the Scripture and Hermeneutics Seminar makes a start in that direction.

This Volume

As we have noted above, there are diverse elements that constitute the ecology of O'Donovan's ethic. O'Donovan's work ranges widely and penetrates deeply. The chapters in this volume consequently engage with O'Donovan from several angles. Chapters 1 to 10 attend particularly to O'Donovan's use of Scripture, 1–4 to the Old Testament and 5–9 to the New Testament. Some focus mainly on *DN*, while others (Carroll, Bartholomew) range across *RMO* and *DN*. In a reflection written after the consultation (ch. 10), Gilbert Meilaender ponders over the important question of how much difference exegesis actually makes to political theology. Chapters 11–15 are primarily concerned with O'Donovan's political theology rather than his use of Scripture, although they still keep their eye firmly on the biblical hermeneutical issues involved.

Walter Moberly examines O'Donovan's use of Scripture in *DN*. He questions whether O'Donovan has sufficiently faced the tricky questions of the relationship between the OT story of Israel and historically reconstructed histories of Israel, and the issue of ideology and the Old Testament story. Moberly also wonders whether the way O'Donovan construes the relationship between the OT and NT is adequate. O'Donovan is right, according to Moberly, to see the reign of God as central, but he suggests that a *canonical* hermeneutic would be more helpful – *inter alia* it would foreground covenant and Torah.

---

[178] *RMO*, 162.

Gordon McConville agrees with Moberly's question about how we read the OT and argues for a more canonical approach, and one that therefore prioritizes Deuteronomy in a political theology. McConville examines the difference such a focus would make to O'Donovan's political theology.

Craig Bartholomew suggests that Old Testament Wisdom literature is a relatively unexplored ally for O'Donovan's theological ethic, particularly as regards the centrality of creation order. In terms of *DN*, however, Bartholomew suggests that Old Testament wisdom indicates a stronger link between creation and politics than O'Donovan allows for.

Danny Carroll welcomes the emphasis on eschatology in O'Donovan's theological ethic but argues that it needs a more sustained exposition of the 'not yet'. Carroll contextualizes his discussion in terms of Latin American liberation theology and earths his discussion biblically in Isaiah and Amos.

Andrew Lincoln focuses on the Gospel of John as a whole. He shows that this Gospel, which is often regarded as apolitical, has a real contribution to make to political theology. Tom Wright alerts us to a recovery of the political dimensions of Paul's writings presently underway, and he initiates us into a fresh, political, narrative reading of Romans. Romans fares well in this volume, and two further chapters specifically address Romans 12 and 13. Bernd Wannenwetsch takes O'Donovan's view seriously that a theological account of politics must proceed via ecclesiology, and he examines Romans 12 with its teaching on the church as a test case to see how this ecclesial text might be read for politics. Gerrit de Kruijf focuses critically on O'Donovan's unusual reading of Romans 13 in *DN* by positioning it within the tradition of reading Romans 13 and arguing for an alternative view.

Chris Rowland shares O'Donovan's sense of the importance of the book of Revelation for political theology. Rowland's essay revisits the reception history of Revelation and argues for the relevance of appropriations of it such as that by William Stringfellow. He argues for a more imaginative hermeneutic in line with the spirit of the early Anabaptists, if we are to hear Revelations' powerful message for politics today.

Jonathan Chaplin expounds O'Donovan's political theology as 'Christian liberalism'. Chaplin subjects O'Donovan's political eschatology to searching critique and focuses in this respect particularly on O'Donovan's notions of the political act as judgement and his advocacy of unitary government. Chaplin is cautious of O'Donovan's discernment of a radically new dispensation in politics that is ushered in by the Christ-event, and he suggests that a Calvinist or Thomist affirmation of politics as part of creation order may have more going for it than O'Donovan allows.

Colin Greene and Peter Scott's chapters focus on O'Donovan's attempted recovery of political authority. Greene explains O'Donovan's quest to recover a robust notion of political authority by attending to the theme of the reign of

God, and he then interacts with O'Donovan's controversial defence of Christendom as an expression of the mission of the church. Greene suggests an alternative way of reading the narrative of Christendom. Peter Scott analyses O'Donovan's theology of authority in the context of his critique of liberation theology. In careful engagement with O'Donovan, Scott defends the authority of the poor against the charge of a return to 'the vomit of legitimation', and he goes on to ask how those of us who are not poor should read the Bible in the light of a liberation hermeneutic.

Joan Lockwood O'Donovan and Jim Skillen's papers alert us unequivocally to the relevance of political theology to contemporary political issues, in which the glory of God and the well-being of humans are at stake. Lockwood O'Donovan examines the idea of the nation-state which has become so central to our conception of political order. Lockwood O'Donovan argues that Christians armed with Scripture and the Christian tradition are well-placed to contribute in a major way to this vital debate. With a masterly knowledge of the tradition of Christian political theology, Lockwood O'Donovan explicates key elements in concepts of the nation in the last century or so, and then articulates the biblical framework for a theological concept of the nation and its outworking in the formation of Western Christian nations.

Jim Skillen anchors his chapter in the work of the Center for Public Justice (CPJ) in Washington, DC and its concern to bring Christianity to bear on American politics. CPJ made a significant contribution to the introduction of 'Charitable Choice', a lesser-known but innovative provision of the controversial 1996 Welfare Reform Act in the USA. As a result of this provision, it is no longer possible to discriminate against 'faith-based organizations' in the allocation of government funding for welfare purposes. In the context of this kind of practical engagement with politics, Skillen examines O'Donovan's ethics to see if it can adequately support such initiatives. There is much in *RMO* and *DN* that Skillen finds very helpful, but he argues that O'Donovan's church-centred political theology and his view of politics as a result of the fall are problematic and in tension with the best elements of O'Donovan's theology.

Bibliography

Bartholomew, C.G., 'Uncharted Waters: Philosophy, Theology and the Crisis in Biblical Interpretation', in *Renewing Biblical Interpretation* (ed. C. Bartholomew, C. Greene, K. Möller; SHS 1; Grand Rapids: Zondervan; Carlisle: Paternoster, 2000), 1–39

——, *Reading Ecclesiastes: Old Testament Exegesis and Hermeneutical Theory* (Rome: Pontifical Biblical Institute, 1998)

Barton, J., 'Understanding Old Testament Ethics', *JSOT* 9 (1979) 44–64

Biggar, N., *The Hastening That Waits: Karl Barth's Ethics* (Oxford: Clarendon Press, 1993)

Boff, L., and C. Boff, *Introducing Liberation Theology* (London: Burns and Oates, 1987)

Brett, M., *Biblical Criticism in Crisis? The Impact of the Canonical Approach on Old Testament Studies* (Cambridge: CUP, 1991)

Bright, J., *The Kingdom of God* (Nashville: Abingdon Press, 1953)

Brown, W.P., *The Ethos of the Cosmos: The Genesis of Moral Imagination in the Bible* (Grand Rapids: Eerdmans, 1999)

Cahill, L., 'The New Testament and Ethics: Communities of Social Change', *Int* 44 (1990), 383–95

Childs, B.S., *Biblical Theology of the Old and New Testaments: Theological Reflection on the Christian Bible* (Minneapolis: Fortress Press, 1992)

Clines, D.J.A., *The Bible and the Modern World* (Sheffield: Sheffield Academic Press, 1997)

Cragg, K., *Palestine: The Prize and Price of Zion* (London and Washington: Cassell, 1997)

Cromartie, M. (ed.), *Caesar's Coin Revisited: Christians and the Limits of Government* (Grand Rapids: Eerdmans, 1996)

Davies, P.R., 'Ethics and the Old Testament', in J.W. Rogerson, et al. (eds.), *The Bible in Ethics. The Second Sheffield Colloquium* (JSOTSup 207; Sheffield: Sheffield Academic Press, 1995), 164–73

Derrida, J., *The Gift of Death* (Chicago and London: University of Chicago Press, 1995)

Dumbrell, W.J., *Covenant and Creation: A Theology of the Old Testament Covenants* (Grand Rapids: Baker; Carlisle: Paternoster, 1984)

Durham, J.I., *Exodus* (Waco, TX: Word Books, 1987)

Ford, D.F., *Self and Salvation: Being Transformed* (Cambridge: CUP, 1999)

Frei, H.W., *The Eclipse of Biblical Narrative: A Study in Eighteenth and Nineteenth Century Hermeneutics* (New Haven and London: Yale University Press, 1974)

——, *The Identity of Jesus Christ: The Historical Bases of Dogmatic Theology* (Philadelphia: Fortress Press, 1975)

Fretheim, T.E., 'Part Two', in T.E. Fretheim and K. Froehlich, *The Bible as Word of God in a Postmodern Age* (Minneapolis: Fortress Press, 1998), 79–126

Gabler, J.P., 'An Oration on the Proper Distinction Between Biblical and Dogmatic Theology and the Specific Objectives of Each', in *The Flowering of Old Testament Theology* (ed. B.C. Ollenburger, et al.; Winona Lake, IN: Eisenbrauns, 1992), 489–502

Gadamer, H.-G., *Truth and Method* (London: Sheed and Ward, 2nd edn, 1989)

Gottwald, N.K., and R.A. Horsley (eds.), *The Bible and Liberation: Political and Social Hermeneutics* (Maryknoll, NY: Orbis Books; London: SPCK, 1993)

Greene, C., '"In the Arms of the Angels": Biblical Interpretation and the Philosophy of History', in *Renewing Biblical Interpretation* (ed. C. Bartholomew, C. Greene, K. Möller; SHS 1; Grand Rapids: Zondervan; Carlisle: Paternoster, 2000), 198–239

Gustafson, J.M., 'The Place of Scripture in Christian Ethics', *Int* 24 (1970), 430–55

——, *Theology and Ethics* (Oxford: Basil Blackwell, 1981)

Gutiérrez, G., *A Theology of Liberation* (London: SCM Press, 1973)

Harrisville, R.A., and W. Sundberg, *The Bible in Modern Culture: Theology and Historical-Critical Method from Spinoza to Käsemann* (Grand Rapids: Eerdmans, 1995)

Hasel, G., *Old Testament Theology: Basic Issues in the Current Debate* (Grand Rapids: Eerdmans, 3rd edn, 1982)

Hauerwas, S., *A Community of Character: Toward a Constructive Christian Social Ethic* (Notre Dame and London: University of Notre Dame Press, 1981)

——, *After Christendom* (Nashville: Abingdon Press, 1999)

——, *Unleashing the Scripture: Freeing the Bible from Captivity to America* (Nashville: Abingdon Press, 1993)

——, and J. Fodor, 'Remaining in Babylon: Oliver O'Donovan's Defense of Christendom', *SCE* 11.2 (1998), 30–55

——, and W.H. Willimon, *The Truth about God: The Ten Commandments in Christian Life* (Nashville: Abingdon Press, 1999)

Hayes, J.H., and F.C. Prussner, *Old Testament Theology: Its History and Development* (London: SCM Press, 1985)

Hays, R.B., *The Moral Vision of the New Testament: A Contemporary Introduction to New Testament Ethics* (New York: HarperCollins, 1996)

Helberg, J.L., *Die Here Regeer* (Pretoria: NGKB, 1983)

Hittinger, R., *A Critique of the New Natural Law Theory* (Notre Dame: University of Notre Dame Press, 1987)

——, 'Varieties of Minimalist Natural Law Theory', *AJJ* 34 (1989), 133–70

Kelsey, D.H., *The Uses of Scripture in Recent Theology* (London: SCM Press, 1975)

Kierkegaard, S., *Fear and Trembling: Repetition. Kierkegaard's Writings*, VI (Princeton: Princeton University Press, 1983)

Ladd, G.E., *The Presence of the Future* (Grand Rapids: Eerdmans, 1974)

Levenson, J.D., *The Hebrew Bible, the Old Testament, and Historical Criticism: Jews and Christians in Biblical Studies* (Louisville, KY: Westminster/John Knox Press, 1993)

Levinas, E., *Totality and Infinity: An Essay on Exteriority* (Pittsburgh: Duquesne University Press, 1969)

Licht, F., *Goya: The Origins of the Modern Temper in Art* (London: John Murray, 1980)

McKeating, H., 'Sanctions against Adultery in Ancient Israelite Society, with Some Reflections on Methodology in the Study of Old Testament Ethics', *JSOT* 11 (1979) 57–72

Moberly, R.W.L., *The Bible, Theology and Faith: A Study of Abraham and Jesus* (Cambridge: CUP, 2000)

Möller, K., 'Renewing Historical Criticism', in *Renewing Biblical Interpretation* (ed. C. Bartholomew, C. Greene, K. Möller; SHS 1; Grand Rapids: Zondervan; Carlisle: Paternoster, 2000), 145–71

Mosala, I.J., 'Biblical Hermeneutics and Black Theology in South Africa: The Use of the Bible', in N.K. Gottwald and R.A. Horsley (eds.), *The Bible and Liberation: Political and Social Hermeneutics* (Maryknoll, NY: Orbis; London: SPCK, 1993), 51–73

Nelson, P., *Narrative and Morality: A Theological Study* (University Park and London: The Pennsylvania State University Press, 1987)

Newbigin, L., *Foolishness to the Greeks: The Gospel and Western Culture* (London: SPCK, 1986)

Niebuhr, H.R., *Christ and Culture* (London: Harper Colophon, 1975)

O'Donovan, O., 'The Possibility of a Biblical Ethic', *TSFB* 67 (1973), 15–23

——, 'The Political Thought of the Book of Revelation', *TynBul* 37 (1986), 61–94

——, *Resurrection and Moral Order: An Outline for Evangelical Ethics* (Leicester: IVP; Grand Rapids: Eerdmans, 2nd edn, 1994)

——, 'The Loss of a Sense of Place', *ITQ* 55 (1989), 39–58

——, *The Desire of the Nations: Rediscovering the Roots of Political Theology* (Cambridge: CUP, 1996)

——, 'Response to Respondents: Behold the Lamb', *SCE* 11.2 (1998), 91–110

——, 'Government as Judgment', *First Things* 92 (1999), 36–44

——, 'Deliberation, History and Reading: A Response to Schweiker and Wolterstorff', *SJT* 54.1 (2001), 127–44

Pavlischek, K.J., 'Questioning the New Natural Law Theory: The Case of Religious Liberty as Defended by Robert P. George in *Making Men Moral*', *SCE* 12.2 (1999), 17–30

Pilgrim, W.E., *Uneasy Neighbours: Church and State in the New Testament* (OBT; Minneapolis: Fortress Press, 1999)

Ridderbos, H.N., *The Coming of the Kingdom* (Philadelphia: Presbyterian and Reformed, 1962)

——, *When the Time had Fully Come: Studies in New Testament Theology* (Jordan Station, Canada: Paideia, 1982)

Rogerson, J.W., et al. (eds.), *The Bible in Ethics: The Second Sheffield Colloquium* (JSOTSup 207; Sheffield: Sheffield Academic Press, 1995)

Rowland, C., and M. Corner, *Liberating Exegesis: The Challenge of Liberation Theology to Biblical Studies* (BFT; London: SPCK, 1990)

Sarna, N.M., *Exploring Exodus: The Heritage of Biblical Israel* (NY: Schocken Books, 1986)

Schüssler Fiorenza, E., *In Memory of Her: A Feminist Theological Reconstruction of Christian Origins* (New York: Crossroad, 1983)

Schweiker, W., 'Freedom and Authority in Political Theology: A Response to Oliver O'Donovan's *The Desire of the Nations*', *SJT* 54.1 (2001), 111–26

Siker, J.S., *Scripture and Ethics: Twentieth-Century Portraits* (New York: OUP, 1997)

Spohn, W.C., *What are They Saying about Scripture and Ethics?* (New York and Mahwah, NJ: Paulist Press, 1995)

Thiselton, A.C., 'Communicative Action and Promise in Hermeneutics', in R. Lundin, C. Walhout and A.C. Thiselton, *The Promise of Hermeneutics* (Grand Rapids: Eerdmans; Carlisle: Paternoster, 1999), 133–239

——, *New Horizons in Hermeneutics* (Grand Rapids: Zondervan, 1992)

Vanhoozer, K.J., 'The Voice and the Actor: A Dramatic Proposal about the Ministry and Minstrelsy of Theology', in *Evangelical Futures* (ed. J.G. Stackhouse, Jr.; Leicester: Apollos; Grand Rapids: Baker, 2000), 61–106

Volf, M., 'Soft Difference: Theological Reflections on the Relation Between Church and Culture in 1 Peter', *ExAud* 10 (1994), 15–30

Wenham, G.J., *Story as Torah: Reading the Old Testament Ethically* (Edinburgh: T. & T. Clark, 2000)

Wolterstorff, N., 'A Discussion of Oliver O'Donovan's *The Desire of the Nations*', *SJT* 54.1 (2001), 87–109

Wilson, J.R., *Living Faithfully in a Fragmented World: Lessons for the Church from MacIntyre's* After Virtue (Harrisburg, PA: Trinity Press International, 1997)

Wink, W., *The Bible in Human Transformation* (Philadelphia: Fortress Press, 1973)

Wright, C.J.H., *God's People in God's Land* (Grand Rapids: Eerdmans; Exeter: Paternoster, 1990)

Wright, N.T., *Jesus and the Victory of God* (London: SPCK, 1996)

1

The Use of Scripture in *The Desire of the Nations*

R. W.L. Moberly

It was an enlarging experience for me to read *The Desire of the Nations*. Professor O'Donovan is a profound and incisive thinker, from whom I have learned much. In particular, he has clearly thought long and hard about the meaning of Scripture, and the whole book is an exposition and application of Scripture – in conjunction with a robust sense of tradition, to be sure, but it is nonetheless Scripture that is fundamental. Although the primary explicit engagement with Scripture is in Chapters 2 to 4, the searching critique of modern political and social arrangements in the last two chapters, where it is argued that 'modernity can be conceived as the Antichrist, a parodic and corrupt development of Christian social order',[1] is in substance no less scriptural than the earlier chapters, even if the mode of argument differs. For to think and argue biblically involves understanding and applying the content of Scripture, regardless of overt reference to the biblical text. In an obvious sense, therefore, a study of the use of Scripture in the book could involve an engagement with the argument as a whole.

The specific context within which this paper is being written is a project seeking a renewal of the understanding and use of Scripture within contemporary church and culture. Any such renewal of Scripture requires that one considers some of the varying forms in which Christian use of Scripture can engage with the substantive political and ethical issues of our time. *DN* has been chosen as representative of such engagement. We are thus not only O'Donovan's primary audience of people engaged in political theology and political ethics, but also people coming at his book as possibly exemplary of a Christian use of Scripture. Given the range of contributions to the discussion, it is probably appropriate for this paper to take 'use of Scripture' in a rather conventional and restricted sense, and to focus more on questions of method than of content. This means that probably some of the discussion falls under the

---

[1] *DN*, 275.

heading of issues on which, in relation to O'Donovan's substantive thesis, 'nothing need be staked'.[2] He can probably concede many of my suggestions without loss (though of course he may not wish to do so!). However, the concern needs to be not only retrospective but also prospective. We need to consider not only what O'Donovan has as a matter of fact done with Scripture but also how future use of Scripture in this area might learn from his work, a learning that may not solely take the form of emulation.[3]

Let me at the outset, however, set out one axiom which underlies the following discussion: *how* one uses Scripture relates to *why* one is using it. Since there is more than one valid concern and context of use, so there is likely to be more than one valid method of use. To recognize this should not lead to any lazy pluralism, since for particular concerns some methods may be clearly better or worse than others. What matters is to identify the nature of particular contexts of use, and to discern the methods of interpretation appropriate to them.

O'Donovan's Scriptural Hermeneutic

In terms of approach, it will be appropriate initially to summarize the programmatic hermeneutic principles that O'Donovan himself sets out in Chapter 1. In the first place, O'Donovan sets out certain axioms that should be uncontroversial for a Christian. On the one hand there is the primacy of Scripture for the whole enterprise of political theology: 'true political concepts ... must be authorised, as any datum of theology must be, from Holy Scripture'.[4] On the other hand, Scripture as a whole must be engaged with, not least 'so that the moment of resurrection [the concern of his earlier *Resurrection and Moral Order*] does not appear like an isolated meteor from the sky but as the climax of a history of the divine rule'.[5]

Yet many hermeneutic problems instantly arise. Although 'the excitement which accompanied the recovery of political theology in our time arose very evidently from the reading of the Bible',[6] it is overwhelmingly the Old Testament rather than the New to which appeal has been made. This is clear both from the fact that O'Donovan follows the above reference to 'the Bible' with

[2] *DN*, 36.

[3] My evaluation of O'Donovan's use of Scripture has only limited common ground with that of Furnish, 'How Firm?', where a prime concern is O'Donovan's (apparently) insufficient attention to scriptural diversity. A far more searching evaluation is that of Hauerwas and Fodor, 'Remaining'. My concerns are wider in scope than those of Furnish but narrower in scope than those of Hauerwas and Fodor.

[4] *DN*, 15.

[5] *DN*, 20.

[6] *DN*, 21.

'Israel's political experience of YHWH's rule', and from the fact that the best-known categories of recent political theology – *shālôm*, the jubilee and especially the exodus[7] – are all Old Testament categories. The problem is thus presented as one of finding and utilizing a principled and unifying hermeneutic – 'a unifying conceptual structure ... that will connect political themes with the history of salvation as a whole', 'an architectonic hermeneutic which would locate political reflection on the Exodus within an undertaking that had its centre of gravity in the Gospels'.[8]

How should this be done? O'Donovan first sketches an obvious problem in the history of Christian thought,[9] to do with continuity and change between the Old and New Testaments (though O'Donovan generally prefers not to refer to discrete Testaments at all) in terms of the 'substance of religious hope in Israel and the early church'.[10] How far does the fulfilment of 'Israel's political hopes' lie 'beyond all experience of the public realm' and how far does it point to 'an earthly rule of Christ' with the church playing some key role? Although tensions here run through Christian history, O'Donovan sees this ultimately as a failure of scriptural understanding: 'Failure to attend to Israel is what left Christian political thought oscillating between idealist and realist poles.'[11] Indeed,

> ... the hermeneutic principle that governs a Christian appeal to political categories within the Hebrew Scriptures is, simply, Israel itself. Through this unique political entity God made known his purposes in the world. In relation to the crisis facing this unique entity, the church proclaimed those purposes fulfilled. Or, to express the same point differently: the governing principle is the kingly rule of God, expressed in Israel's corporate existence and brought to final effect in the life, death and resurrection of Jesus.[12]

This leads to four concluding comments about right and wrong use of the Old Testament in political theology. First, the OT must be treated '*as history*', by which is meant 'a disclosure which took form in a succession of political developments, each one of which has to be weighed and interpreted in the light of what preceded and followed it'. This is to rule out unprincipled or decontextualized use of a 'disconnected image or theme'.[13] Secondly, one must resist 'constructing a subversive counter-history, a history beneath the surface which defies and challenges the official history of Israel'. This relates to the

---

[7] *DN*, 22.
[8] *DN*, 22.
[9] *DN*, 22–27.
[10] *DN*, 23.
[11] *DN*, 27.
[12] *DN*, 27.
[13] *DN*, 27.

main theme of the first chapter, the need to move 'beyond suspicion'. Thus, 'a decision to take *Israel* with special seriousness implies a willingness to have done with perpetual unmasking'.[14] Thirdly, one must not 'rewrite Israel's history as a "Whig" history of progressive undeception', for by such means 'the past is recalled solely to justify the present against it, and has no standing as a point of disclosure. This is so that the history should remain normative in its own right.[15] Fourthly, Israel's history must be seen as the context where 'certain principles of social and political life were vindicated by the action of God in the judgement and restoration of the people'. The construal of God's rule must be that of Israel itself. Thus it is not just the history but also the meaning of that history which must be found within the biblical text.[16]

This is an admirable programme, as far as it goes (though it is perhaps curious that there is no comment upon appropriate use of the New Testament). I would like in what follows to contribute to its advancement. First and foremost, I will raise three general issues of principle with regard to O'Donovan's hermeneutic. But I will also select specific examples of textual interpretation that raise a variety of issues.[17]

General Issues of Scriptural Hermeneutics

Where is the history of Israel to be found?[18]

First, the prime challenge that O'Donovan apparently envisages to the history of Israel within the OT is the voice of suspicion, an ideologically subversive

---

[14] *DN*, 28.

[15] *DN*, 28.

[16] *DN*, 29.

[17] Unfortunately it is not possible here to do justice to the sheer freshness that regularly characterizes O'Donovan's exegesis of the text. One prime instance for me is O'Donovan's rendering of the perplexing narratives, Ex. 32:26–9; Num. 25:1–13, as 'making a case for the independence of Levitical jurisdiction ... removed from local loyalties, as against the court of landed squire or tribal elder' (*DN*, 59). O'Donovan's key moves are: i) ordination (32:29, 25:13) is to a judicial role, for it is this for which impartiality is the necessary qualification; ii) 'killing the brother, friend and neighbour is merely a colourful phrase for impartial vengeance'; and iii) the stories gain in point if directed against others with a judicial role who are not impartial. Whether or not this rendering is found to be persuasive (and it raises numerous questions), it displays a penetrative engagement with the text which is both instructive and memorable.

[18] I originally headed this section and conducted the following discussion in terms of 'the official history of Israel', a phrase used by O'Donovan (*DN*, 28), but he made clear in his response that the phrase does not represent his own position. The substance of the discussion nonetheless remains unchanged.

counter-history. This is indeed a major contemporary issue. Yet he says nothing about what for many students of Scripture is the more obvious problem – that is, the relationship between the history of Israel as presented by the OT itself and that constructed by modern 'historical-critical'[19] scholarship. The name of Julius Wellhausen remains the convenient shorthand for the insight, shared by all mainstream biblical scholars (however much they continue to dispute details), that the history of Israel and its religious development as perceived through the lens of modern critical historiography look very different from the picture presented by the OT itself. Does, for example, the mass of laws in Exodus to Deuteronomy derive from Moses and the origins of Israel's history? Or is it, as most post-Wellhausen scholars suppose, a composite of different law codes from different periods, the majority of which are exilic or postexilic in date? For much of the nineteenth and twentieth centuries, the OT's own presentation was seen by scholars as interesting chiefly as a springboard to recover something else – the 'true', 'original', 'authentic' course of history and religious development – and was hardly considered as significant in its own right.[20]

Among other significant recent developments, so-called 'canonical'[21] approaches, for which perhaps the name of Brevard Childs may serve as convenient shorthand, have argued for reconceptualizing the way the scriptural text is handled. Here there is a concern to find positive significance in Israel's own picture of its history without feeling any need to justify it as 'really more or less historical after all' (the standard 'conservative' approach). Rather, one may take for granted the kinds of traditio-historical and compositional developments that are commonly hypothesized but see the text in their light as representing

[19] I use the quotes because 'historical-critical' is a simplifying epithet which risks obscuring the diversity of methods and assumptions which have characterized modern biblical scholarship, and is of no help for distinguishing between enduring philological-cum-historical insights and the speculations and hypotheses that have usually accompanied them.

[20] In his response O'Donovan speaks of his dislike of a 'smug cunning' on the part of historical critics who seek to 'outwit' texts – a tendency he finds present in my account of the historical-critical approach. This, however, tends to misrepresent the historical-critical project, however accurately it captures some of its many crude popularizations. What makes the approach 'historical-critical', rather than merely 'historical', is precisely its ability to construct out of the biblical text a history significantly different from that which the Bible itself presents. The important questions for our purposes concern how this 'historical-critical' account is used, not least in relation to evaluations of the significance of the canonical presentation.

[21] I use the quotes again here because 'canonical' is also a simplifying epithet which risks obscuring the diversity of concerns and arguments which characterize such approaches.

Israel's mature reflection on the meaning and significance of its history. So, for example, even if (for the sake of argument) it is granted that 'covenant' did not develop as a way of depicting the relationship between YHWH and Israel before the Deuteronomists in the seventh century,[22] the fact that 'covenant' has been used to structure the formative moments in Israel's faith (especially in both Genesis and Exodus)[23] should be taken with total seriousness. Whatever the historical development of Israel's religion, 'covenant' has become the normative pattern within which Israel's faith should be understood and appropriated by those who subsequently seek to stand in continuity with it.[24] The mature perspective of the developed and received texts of the Pentateuch is that perspective in the light of which subsequent generations who seek to enter into Israel's heritage should engage with its enduring significance, even if Israel for some or much of its history existed without this perspective.

The motto of this approach could well be 'That which the ancient writers have joined together, let not modern scholars put asunder'.[25] It is not that one cannot, or should not, for certain analytical purposes in relation to certain contexts, abstract and recontextualize the text in relation to its possible origins and development. Rather, one should not rest content, at least if one is a believer concerned to engage with the text as Scripture, until one has returned to a renewed appreciation (and appropriation) of the whole. It is, perhaps, the difference between 'murder to dissect' and 'analyze to understand'. The real and contentious issue then becomes how to understand and evaluate the

---

[22] This is a thesis of Wellhausen, which was eclipsed by Eichrodt's major *Theology*, which put covenant at its centre, but has been forcefully renewed by Perlitt (*Bundestheologie*) in a way persuasive to many, though the evidence remains patient of more than one interpretation. Childs himself is doubtful about Wellhausen's thesis both in itself and in its renewed form (*Theology*, 134–37).

[23] Rendtorff suggestively observes that 'the word *bᵉrît* is never used in the plural. There is only one covenant, even if in different contexts and different shapes' ('Covenant', 133) – though this might lead one to expect more regular usage of covenant with the definite article, *habbᵉrît*, i.e., *the* covenant. Paul uses his Greek term for *bᵉrît*, i.e., *diathēkē*, in the plural (Rom. 9:4).

[24] O'Donovan recognizes the importance of covenant – 'the unique covenant of YHWH and Israel can be seen as a point of disclosure from which the nature of all political authority comes into view' (*DN*, 45) – although he does not discuss covenantal texts as such.

[25] One of the striking harbingers of current 'canonical' emphases is Franz Rosenzweig's 1927 letter 'Unity'. Rosenzweig accepts the kind of redactional developments within the biblical text generally surmised by modern scholarship, but comments that 'we, however, take this R [the common scholarly abbreviation for redactor] to stand not for redactor but for *rabbenu* [the common Jewish designation for Moses]' (23).

'constructed' nature of reality within Scripture that becomes apparent from such a process – something I take to be one of the major tasks of this Scripture and Hermeneutics Seminar.[26]

In the light of this, one problem I have with O'Donovan is to know what he understands as 'the history of Israel', especially given his concern that the construal of God's rule must be that of Israel itself. The 'history of Israel' for Jews and Christians is surely that history which the OT itself presents in the primary sequence from Genesis to 2 Kings (which can coexist with different tellings of the story, most notably in Chronicles). It is not that of the modern paraphrases with varying amounts of subtraction and reinterpretation of biblical texts (together with appeal to non-biblical material) according to varying *wissenschaftliche* premises – paraphrases that constitute a certain kind of analytical historiography under the heading of 'history of Israel'. O'Donovan is clearly happy to accept and utilize well-established scholarly constructs (the Yahwist and Elohist, the Deuteronomi[sti]c Historian[27]), which may suggest that his working model of Israel's history is that of the modern scholar, rather than of the OT itself, even though these constructs play little significant role. His first hermeneutic principle, that the OT must be treated '*as history*', by which is meant 'a disclosure which took form in a succession of political developments, each one of which has to be weighed and interpreted in the light of what preceded and followed it', seems to point in a similar direction. Likewise, his periodic discussion of texts as 'authentic' (e.g., that Jer. 51:59–64 is authentic to Jeremiah;[28] though most comments about authenticity relate to gospel texts)[29] suggests the presence of that modern scholarly frame of reference in which the Bible's own account of matters is to be judged by its conformity to a 'historical-critical' account. My concern here is not O'Donovan's specific judgements

---

[26] In his response at the consultation O'Donovan did not, I think, fully appreciate the nature of this argument. This canonical approach by its very nature could not set itself against a historical-critical approach as 'exclusive alternatives', for this canonical approach depends on recognizing the validity of a historical-critical account on its own terms but reconceiving its significance when it comes to reading the biblical text as Christian Scripture. His fear that a canonical approach will lead to a flattened or thinned reading of Scripture because of a loss of the historical depth and richness that historical-critical work could at its best produce is a fair one. I do not see it as a necessary consequence of a canonical approach (which needs at present to remain pragmatic rather than doctrinaire), but the test will need to be the long-term fruitfulness (or lack of it) of a canonical approach.

[27] *DN*, 67, 40.

[28] *DN*, 69.

[29] Comments concerning the 'authenticity' of OT texts are in *DN* on pp. 65 (Huldah's prophecy), 70 (Jeremiah's Book of Consolation), 79 (Jeremiah's hope for a future community), 124 (Jer. 23:5f.). For the 'authenticity' of dominical texts, see 99, 101, 103, 115f., 139.

about authenticity, which are consistently well-taken, but the frame of reference which his judgements presuppose, and whether such a frame of reference is appropriate or necessary for a political and ethical engagement with Scripture.

We may come at this from another angle. Elsewhere O'Donovan refers not unappreciatively to the work of narrative theology (which establishes a common 'story' as essential to social identity[30]), and he makes positive use of the 'narrative-structure of the Christ-event', a structure which is recapitulated in the life of the church ('the four moments [which] can claim to represent the essential structure of the story'[31]). If the Christ-event has a narrative structure, does not the history of Israel have some such structure, some shared story, also? And should not that story, for Jew and Christian, be the OT's own story, rather than the 'historical-critical' alternative?

In structural terms, therefore, there is surely a massive lacuna in O'Donovan's use of the OT. The use of the Psalms for the kingship of YHWH is significant and suggestive in many ways; though it is notable that although, in time-honoured Oxford manner, the dating of the Psalms as preexilic, exilic and postexilic is discussed, the shape of the Psalter itself, and how the Psalter as a whole may present the kingship of YHWH, is nowhere discussed.[32] The Psalter is easily the most cited book of the OT in O'Donovan's exposition, and herein certainly lies some of his freshness of approach. But where is the massive block of material, which the canon places in a foundational position, of the covenant between YHWH and Israel at Sinai? The relative invisibility of Exodus, Leviticus, Numbers and Deuteronomy is highlighted by the fact that a quick look at the index of scriptural references shows that, quite apart from the frequent citation of the Psalter, both Isaiah and Jeremiah respectively are cited more often than all the books of the Pentateuch together.

Why this neglect of Israel's primary Torah? To be sure, the Sinai texts do not as such depict YHWH explicitly as 'king' (*melek*). Yet it is abundantly clear throughout Exodus to Deuteronomy – quite apart from the much-vaunted extrabiblical treaties between suzerains and vassals, which have regularly been cited as parallels to parts of the Pentateuch – that Israel is in the position of a vassal (lit. slave, *'ebed*, esp. Lev. 25:55) to an overlord or master (*'ādôn*). Whatever the terminology, the sovereign authority of YHWH over Israel, given practical embodiment in law and commandments, is not in doubt. Indeed O'Donovan is aware of this, as in his passing reference to 'the covenant by which sovereign and subject are bound together'.[33]

---

[30] *DN*, 222f.

[31] *DN*, 250, 133.

[32] Among many recent studies of the shape of the Psalter as a whole, see esp. Seitz, 'Royal Promises'.

[33] *DN*, 48.

Two illustrations may suggest something of the disproportion of treatment. On the one hand, the Psalms indeed show that God's rule is somehow incomplete without Israel's response of praise, which does not constitute God's rule but demonstrates it.[34] But is this not also the point of the keynote of Deuteronomy, which Jewish tradition saw as the keynote of its faith as a whole – the Shema (Deut. 6:4–9)? Here the incomparability of YHWH as 'one', that is, the one and only lord and master of Israel, requires the response of total and undivided allegiance from Israel; and it would be difficult for the one to be meaningful without the other.

On the other hand, despite all that O'Donovan says about the importance of law as embodying the authority of God, both within Israel and for the nations, and all that he says about the structures by which law is mediated, little attention is given to the actual content of Israel's law, or how its emphases and priorities demonstrate the nature of the divine rule. Yet without focus upon the content, there lurks a danger that 'law' may become something of a cipher whose content can be filled in ways that owe less to scriptural priorities than might otherwise be the case.[35]

Alternatively, O'Donovan's account of the role of the individual raises related issues:

> In the Hebrew Scriptures the holy community is the prior and original fact; the individual member finds his or her significance within it. Yet that significance develops in the course of the First Temple period. The individual becomes, as it were, load-bearing, so that at the exile the future of the nation has come to depend on individual faithfulness. The logic of the development is perfectly expressed in the question of Psalm 11:6, 'When the foundations are destroyed, what shall the righteous one do?' ... It is a clear illustration of the principle that, to treat Israel's political tradition as normative, we have to wrestle with its history.[36]

The basic point about community and individual is well put.[37] But how precisely does it illustrate the need to 'wrestle with [Israel's] history'? If the basic concern is to avoid reading the OT flatly, with no sense of development and difference within it, that is fine. But, in terms of the question regarding what constitutes Israel's history ('canonical' story? 'historical-critical' story?), we should at least note that the OT does not present the load-bearing individual as

[34] *DN*, 48; cf. 113–19 for the comparable significance of faith in Jesus' proclamation of God's rule.

[35] Interestingly, O'Donovan does provide for the teaching of Jesus the kind of discussion he does not provide for Old Testament law.

[36] *DN*, 73f.

[37] Cf. *DN*, 80, 'the conscientious individual speaks with society's own forgotten voice'.

a phenomenon of the exile. For does not Noah fulfil this role in relation to the world in its infancy, *in illo tempore*? Does not Abraham in some way fulfil such a role in relation to Sodom and Gomorrah? Does not Moses fulfil this role during Israel's apostasy at Sinai, in Israel's infancy?[38] A case can, of course, be made for the late monarchic or exilic composition of all of these texts. Yet to think of them in the context of their possible composition (while fully valid for certain purposes) tends to undercut taking with full imaginative seriousness their position within the Hebrew story, in which Noah and Moses are paradigmatic for God's dealings with the world as a whole and Israel in particular.

My first concern, therefore, is that I have difficulties with knowing what constitutes 'the history of Israel' in O'Donovan's account.[39] The OT's own narrative structure, its own story, hardly features. The near-invisibility of Moses and the Sinai covenant is a prime illustration of this.[40]

Suspicion and the status of Israel's history

O'Donovan's desire to preserve 'the history of Israel' against possible suspicious subversion prompts one further observation. His primary, and laudable, concern is to resist the kind of scepticism from the outset which would 'set our face against the thought that in this people's history God has effectively made his rule known'.[41] His basis is the recognition that 'the documents we possess are, as they stand, critical of the exercise of government to a remarkable extent', together with the fact that they also contain positive 'affirmations'.[42] O'Donovan's depiction of an alternative 'subversive counter-history' is

---

[38] For the parallel roles of Noah and Moses as faithful individuals who in some way not only channel, but also enable, God's mercy to a sinful collective, see Moberly, *Mountain*, 91–93.

[39] Some not dissimilar observations could be made with regard to the nature of the Gospels in O'Donovan's interpretation. To argue about Q and the authenticity of dominical sayings is fully appropriate in certain contexts. But does O'Donovan need to engage such issues for the kind of use of Scripture that he proposes?

[40] O'Donovan in his response considers 'near-invisibility' to be an overstatement. His defence, 'that the longest passage of OT exposition by far is devoted to Exodus 33–34' [*DN*, 50–52] does not, however, alter my assessment. Such a small print discussion does not change the weight and tenor of the general discussion. Moreover, I am puzzled by O'Donovan's handling of the problematics of divine presence in Ex. 33–34, for he makes no reference whatever to the golden calf in Ex. 32 and the way in which Israel's sin in relation to God's commandments has problematized the divine presence.

[41] *DN*, 28.

[42] *DN*, 28.

> a history beneath the surface which defies and challenges the official history of Israel. That will not be the history of the people, but (at best) of a class within the people or (at worst) of a purely suppositious class that they [sceptical theologians] are inclined to think ought to have existed.[43]

Although this issue does not as such feature prominently in O'Donovan's discussion, his first chapter makes clear that an ability not to be limited or derailed by a certain kind of suspicious mentality is a prerequisite for his argument; and therefore some comment may not be inappropriate.

O'Donovan here, in common with many others, seems unconsciously to retroject a kind of democratic principle into the biblical period, whereby the official history must be of 'the people' rather than of 'a class within the people' (actual or suppositious). This, I suspect, may rest on a confusion between the reception of the biblical texts as authoritative within Judaism and among the Jewish people at large (where the identity of the Jewish people as a whole stands in a real, if indirect and varying, relation to the depiction of Israel within the biblical texts; so also subsequently, with further variations, within Christianity) and the reception of the texts as constructions of Israel's history in their own right. What became normative for the Jewish people may not always have been so. Or, to put it in other terms, there is some confusion between the theology of the Old Testament/Tanak (those particular interpretative construals of Israel's history and religion which now constitute an enduring literary and canonical deposit) and the course of Israel's history and religion as experienced by its participants at the time.

O'Donovan recognizes the formative role within the OT of 'the Deuteronomic literary culture', but he does not address the question of the status of the Deuteronomic movement within Israel. To take the sharp terms of Morton Smith's thesis, may not the 'Yahweh alone' party which shaped the OT have been an elite and unrepresentative minority within Israel and Judah?[44] Suppose, for the sake of argument, that one grants the substance of Smith's thesis, at least in terms of the minority nature of the movement (though the thesis of course remains contested and cannot readily be either confirmed or disproved). On one level, it should hardly come as a surprise, for the simple reason that the biblical writers themselves portray Israel, from the wilderness outside Egypt until the fall of Jerusalem to the Babylonians, as much more inclined to grumbling, disobedience and faithlessness than to loyal adherence to YHWH. That is, the writers' understanding of faithfulness to YHWH was not shared by many, probably a majority, of those whose history they depict. So if epigraphic discoveries mention Israel's deity as having a consort ('Asherah'),

---

[43] *DN*, 28.

[44] Smith, *Palestinian Parties*.

this should hardly be more surprising than Jeremiah's account of Judah's propensity for the queen of heaven (Jer. 44). The depth and truth (if such it be) of the Deuteronomic understanding of God and his covenant with Israel do not depend on its somehow representing a majority view or practice within Israel or Judah at the time of its composition. If it was the work of a 'class within the people', it need be none the worse for that.

In a not dissimilar way, it is quite possible that Paul, in his disagreements with the Corinthians, was untypical of early Christianity generally, and may have constituted a minority of one; and we do not know how many in the Corinthian church, if any, heeded him and embraced his vision of the Christian life. Again, the factor that makes the difference to us is reception – that process of discernment within the early church that recognized Paul as more truly articulating the inner logic and nature of the faith than those with whom he disagreed. A similar account can be given, *mutatis mutandis*, for the reception of Deuteronomy and the Deuteronomic literary culture within Israel's Scriptures. So those who come after are no longer in the same position as the initial recipients of the texts, but are in a privileged position to recognize their value, courtesy of the discernment and reception process of the community over time.

What is at stake here, I think, is that in an age which is suspicious of authoritative and canonical texts, we need to be clear about the grounds upon which Scripture's enduring authority should be based. My argument is not meant to imply some distaste or disdain for the vulgar religion of the masses (past or present) in favour of some quasi-gnostic superiority of a chosen few. Rather, I want to make clear that certain kinds of historical argument and historical construction do not get beyond ground-clearing to the heart of the matter – a heart which must consist of a discernment and demonstration by Christians (as by Jews also) of those realities of life before God (with both its affirmations and critiques) of which Scripture speaks. This discernment must be made (as O'Donovan recognizes) in critical continuity with classic discernments of the past. In short, what matters for Christian faith is not arguments that Israel and Judah (or the early church) were really (after all) more observant and faithful in relation to the criteria of the biblical text than doubtful critics have often suggested, any more than arguments that particular sayings are 'authentic' to Jeremiah or Jesus or whomever. What matters is the critical construal of the true nature of God and of life before God as discerned and received as holy Scripture within the continuing life of the people of God.

'An architectonic hermeneutic with its centre of gravity in the Gospels'

Thirdly, to move beyond the OT, how far is an 'architectonic hermeneutic' of Scripture as a whole 'with its centre of gravity in the Gospels', which

O'Donovan sees as necessary,[45] genuinely present? At the very least, any architectonic scriptural hermeneutic should surely present a dialectic between the two Testaments. On the one hand one must see how Israel prepared the way for the coming of the Christ, and so read the New in the light of the Old, as a fulfilment of the Old. On the other hand, one must see how Christ not only transforms those categories into which he was fitted by his contemporaries, but how, in the light of Christ, one can, and indeed should, reread and rethink that history which preceded him. New light may make existing truth look different. The concern here is not to impose a flat christomonism upon the whole of Scripture, but rather to seek a truly mutual and dialectical relationship between the Testaments. Yet it seems to me that for O'Donovan the traffic is largely one-way, a historical trajectory from Israel to Jesus.

The reading of texts in a composite collection such as Scripture can only in certain contexts and for certain purposes be in any way a straightforward matter. That is, one can look at certain texts in their own right. One can also look at their contextualization (which is often a recontextualization) within the narrative, the train of thought, or the book as a whole within which they stand. One can also consider their intertextual linkages and significance within the OT as a whole or NT as a whole. One can also consider the way in which the total canon, the OT and NT together, contextualizes them and creates multiple resonances. And all of this is quite apart from the possible influence of postbiblical developments for a reading of the biblical text.

In this regard, O'Donovan to some extent treats the NT differently from the OT. For he offers two readings of Jesus. The first is of Jesus in his ministry (Ch. 3), and then Jesus in his death, resurrection and exaltation (Ch. 4). This second reading to some extent reconfigures elements of the first.[46] Should one not, therefore, expect to have, in addition to a reading of the OT in its own right (whatever that involves), a rereading of the OT in the light of the NT? O'Donovan refers, for example, to Jesus' concern for a 'hermeneutic key which will order its [the law's] demand comprehensibly'.[47] One would expect, with regard to law, not only a reading of the OT law in terms of its own apparent priorities, but also a dialectical rereading of that same law in conjunction with Jesus' hermeneutic programme (and that of other NT writers, esp. Paul and John).

For example, O'Donovan makes clear at the outset that his dominant concern is *authority*. The words of the risen Jesus at the conclusion of Matthew's Gospel, 28:18–20, come readily to mind. Here Jesus makes the comprehensive claim that 'all authority in heaven and on earth has been given to me'. Such is the scope of Jesus' words that nothing/nowhere is exempted, and the

---

[45] *DN*, 22.
[46] Esp. *DN*, 133f.
[47] *DN*, 102.

passive form ('has been given') indicates that the gift is the work of God his Father. Divine authority has been definitively bestowed upon Jesus. Yet this is not allowed to remain at any abstract or theoretical level, for this claim has immediate implications for Jesus' disciples – 'Go therefore and make disciples of all nations ... and I am with you always ...' – that is a mandate for the church without limit of person or place or time. This passage is not only fundamental for understanding the whole of Matthew's Gospel, one prime purpose of which is the definitional depiction of what this authority means for Jesus and his disciples.[48] This passage also serves as an obvious point of reference whereby interaction between the Testaments as to the nature of divine authority might fruitfully be explored. How do Israel's depictions of divine authority prepare for Jesus? How do Israel's depictions of divine authority look in the light of Jesus? How does the contentious OT issue of the nations' submission to Israel as part of their submission to YHWH look in the light of Jesus' death and resurrection? Yet, remarkably, this passage is entirely absent from O'Donovan's discussions,[49] even in contexts where it would be an obvious text to discuss.[50] And there is minimal attempt to reconsider the OT's depictions of divine authority in the light of this or any comparable passage.[51] The overall hermeneutic, therefore, seems to me rather less architectonic than it might be.[52]

To be sure, O'Donovan can very interestingly reread the OT in the light of Christ:

---

[48] I have expounded Matthew's Christology and soteriology in this light in *The Bible*, 184–224.

[49] Other formative sayings of the risen Jesus, which could be significant for O'Donovan's argument, are also absent. Thus we are reminded that 'the relation of the church to Christ, to which the Pentecostal Spirit admits it ... is a *recapitulation* of the Christ-event, by which the community participates in the acts and experiences which the Representative first undertook on its behalf alone' (*DN*, 171), with no reference to Jn. 20:21, 'As the Father has sent me, so also I send you.'

[50] In a discussion of Luke 22 O'Donovan says, 'Those who have rejected the pursuit of authority in favour of service, as Jesus has, will, nevertheless, inherit authority, as Jesus will' (*DN*, 139). He discusses the resurrection as containing both 'restoration and empowerment' (*DN*, 142), but in relation to Luke and John among the evangelists, with only an insignificant passing reference to Matthew's knowledge of a special encounter of the risen Lord with his disciples in Galilee. He discusses the gathering of peoples in Matthew solely in relation to Jesus' pre-Easter ministry (*DN*, 175). He speaks of baptism as 'the sign that marks the gathering community' (*DN*, 177). In each context, Mt. 28:18–20 would have been germane. I hope that it was not discounted on the grounds of '(in)authenticity'.

[51] Such as Phil. 2:5–11, discussed in *DN*, 135.

[52] O'Donovan's response to my concerns in this paragraph was at the consultation couched in delightful and disarming Johnsonian mode: 'Ignorance, madam, ignorance.'

> Jesus' departure from the zealot programme showed his more theological understanding of power, not his disinterest in it. The empowerment of Israel was more important than the disempowerment of Rome; for Rome disempowered would in itself by no means guarantee Israel empowered. The paradigm of the Exodus was, we might say, being read with an emphasis not on the conquest of the Egyptians but on the conquest of the sea. The power which God gave to Israel did not have to be taken from Egypt, or from Rome, first. The gift of power was not a zero–sum operation.[53]

One may ask, however, what difference this makes to one's evaluation and appropriation of the *prima facie* sense of the OT narrative, where the deliverance of Israel is precisely at the expense of Egypt; and how, therefore, within the full context of Scripture, the exodus deliverance should best be understood and utilized.[54]

Cui Bono? What is at Stake in this Discussion?

One of the sharpest questions asked in the discussion of this paper at the Scripture and Hermeneutics Consultation was that of Gilbert Meilaender (which is helpfully contained in his short paper in this collection).[55] He picked up my opening remark about there being much which O'Donovan might 'concede without loss', a remark which I gaily repeated in my brief oral presentation, and he asked, 'Do you really mean that? If so, what does that imply for our project?' Meilaender's point is well taken. If this is really a discussion which makes no substantive difference to the political and ethical use of Scripture, then it would appear to be an 'academic' matter in the popular and pejorative sense of the term, a kind of wrangling over ideology and/or detail which rightly need be of no concern to the person who wants to get something done.

The force of my remark, apart from its being a diplomatic pleasantry, was primarily to indicate the restricted focus of my paper. I decided to look at the use of Scripture in a narrower sense than might be (as specified at the beginning), concerned more with method than content, on the assumption that

---

[53] *DN*, 95.

[54] O'Donovan responded most interestingly: 'How does my reading really find its centre of gravity in the Gospels? By finding its centre of gravity in the fall of Judah and the promise of return, the point at which Israel lives as a nation through the judgment of death and resurrection, becoming itself an anticipation of Christ, supremely focussed in the figure of Jeremiah'. Moreover this 'reading of the OT in the light of the cross … does not have to be obtrusively paraded – should not be, indeed, because we must attend to Israel in the light of the cross, not only to the cross as foreshadowed in Israel'. This is finely said. Yet I think that a fuller interaction and dialectic between the Testaments could not but strengthen the use of Scripture for political and ethical purposes.

[55] See pp. 259–64.

others, better qualified than I, would engage the substantive political issues (or, like Hauerwas and Fodor, engage both method and content). One way of putting this is that my paper probably more obviously addresses biblical scholars, who may wonder how far O'Donovan offers a model use of Scripture in terms of method, than it addresses political theologians and ethicists, whose interest in O'Donovan's use of Scripture is likely to focus more upon its content (and whose methodological debates will primarily be located elsewhere). In retrospect, I think this may have been a mistake, because the kinds of papers that I had thought might be forthcoming were on the whole not forthcoming, since the ethicists (unsurprisingly) tended to pursue different interests. That is, my pragmatic division of labour easily becomes a division of outlook or principle, a perpetuation of a divide between exegesis and ethics. If those who specialize in biblical interpretation do not relate their methodological concerns to substantive ethical and political questions, then it is likely that the task will simply not be done. In this final section, therefore, some brief comments about such issues are perhaps appropriate.

It is difficult, of course, to know how best to comment on a project such as O'Donovan's without appearing merely to nit-pick. For in any project of such size and scope it is always possible to make numerous small changes which may be not without significance in themselves and yet which leave the overall shape and tenor of the project unchanged. Extensive modification does, of course, at some point lead to a different overall shape, yet even so the force of the original vision and some of its details may endure (as, in biblical studies, Wellhausen's work continues to influence much OT study – even though there are few matters either of conception or of detail which have not been queried, and there is much which has been more or less abandoned). No such project becomes significant in the first place, however, unless its conception involves a constant correlation between a big picture and painstaking attention to detail. At the very least, any continuing engagement with a political vision as deeply rooted in Scripture as O'Donovan's is obligated to ask how well O'Donovan handles both the broad sweep and the detail of Scripture.

My reticence with regard to the difference my discussion might make to O'Donovan's project is also rooted in an agreement with the general direction of his handling of Scripture. When someone has thought so long and hard and in such an informed and sophisticated way about Scripture as a whole in relation to politics and ethics, then it is easy to disagree with any number of matters and yet still say that both the tenor and the detail of Scripture have been well captured. For example, although both Hauerwas and Fodor and also Meilaender express some reservations about the centrality which O'Donovan gives to the reign of God,[56] O'Donovan is surely right to have done so. Of

[56] Hauerwas and Foder, 'Remaining', 47f.; Meilaender, p. 263 in this volume.

course there are other important scriptural images, such as shepherd and sheep (one of those instanced by Hauerwas and Fodor), or husband and wife (instanced by Meilaender), but their usage and significance hardly approach that of kingship, for the pentateuchal books of Exodus to Deuteronomy and the Gospels each in their own way put the royal rule of YHWH and/or of Jesus at the centre. If, as I suggested, O'Donovan had, in addition to using the Psalms, given greater weight to Mosaic Torah, this would indeed have rooted his exposition more deeply within foundational OT texts, but it would not have suggested a shift of focus away from the reign of God.

Yet, within this general agreement, there remain problems. For example, O'Donovan argues that YHWH's rule over the nations lacks the mediatorial king characteristic of Israel, and is characterized rather by 'the imageless ideal of rule by law and providential action alone'.[57] Yet is this really so, even on the level of OT exegesis?[58] He allows that some voices within the OT envisage YHWH's rule over the nations as consisting in Israel's superiority over them, but he sees these as essentially isolated voices, moved to speak thus by times of affliction, and 'at no time' constituting 'the whole of the matter'.[59] Yet the canonical shape of the OT suggests that these voices are less isolated than O'Donovan allows. The Psalter as a collection is introduced by Psalms 1 and 2, and Psalm 2 clearly envisages the dominion of YHWH's king over 'nations', 'peoples', and 'the ends of the earth'.[60] Within the book of Isaiah as a whole, the reign of YHWH is a central image, as it is in Isaiah's commissioning vision (Isa. 6), and the consistent imagery in the later chapters is of other nations serving Israel and of Israel enjoying the resources of those nations (e.g., 45:14–17; 60:1–16). Likewise, the highly influential vision of enduring dominion over the nations as the role of the saints of Elyon (Dan. 7) hardly suggests a world order that is plurally constituted.[61] In other words, the OT provides much

[57] *DN*, 66–73; 72.

[58] One significant issue: Is 'law' the right term for that which is common among the nations? May not the OT's term be 'fear of God'? 'Fear of God' has a high moral content, shown especially in regard for the weak (one of the central concerns of Israel's laws), and is expected of other nations as well as of Israel (e.g. Gen. 20:11; 42:18; Lev. 19:14; Deut. 25:17–19). However, the OT consistently portrays nations other than Israel as needing to fear 'God' (i.e. the generic category of deity) rather than fear 'YHWH' (which is how Israel knows God), thereby preserving a distinction between the nations and Israel. Is not the common element thus something more like 'conscience' than 'law'?

[59] *DN*, 66.

[60] O'Donovan's response at the Consultation, that 'the Psalms ... speak of no more than Israel's victory over the nations in battle, not imperial rule', seems to me to evade the force of the text.

[61] O'Donovan gives considerable attention to Dan. 7: a recognition of Jewish expectations in terms of Dan. 7 (*DN*, 90), Jesus' appropriation of Dan. 7 for his disciples (*DN*, 116), and Paul's exposition of Dan. 7 in Rom. 13:1–7 (*DN*, 147).

more material for a Christian apologia for empire than O'Donovan allows, a fact which may be to some extent obscured by his own clear evaluative stance ('the theological impulse behind the conception of international law is altogether superior to the theology of empire'[62]).

Yet the use of Daniel 7 brings us back to the issue of reading the OT in the light of the NT. How should the OT pictures of the enduring dominion of Israel over subservient nations be read in the light of the clear NT construal of royal dominion in terms of self-giving service and witness to the truth? Might this material be reread in the kind of way in which O'Donovan rereads the exodus and the crossing of the sea? On the one hand, one could appeal to the OT's own vision of the enduring primacy of the Torah (e.g., Isa. 2:2–4) and so reconstrue Israel's dominion in moral and spiritual terms, as the nations' acceptance of Israel's understanding of God and life with corresponding ways of living (with modifications, as in Christianity). On the other hand, Israel's dominion could be construed as no longer at the expense of others but rather for their service (a move also found in Jewish theology). Whichever move one makes, the point is that a range of dialectical hermeneutical moves come into focus, which profoundly impact upon the way the OT is heard and utilized. Here I find O'Donovan's use of the OT to be fascinating in detail, but less nuanced and variegated than it might be in terms of overall hermeneutic.

To conclude, O'Donovan's use of Scripture is searching and distinctive, but others might find it difficult to replicate even if they wanted to. The purpose of this paper is to suggest how those who wish to follow in O'Donovan's footsteps might do well to adopt a more canonical perspective than O'Donovan himself does. For such a canonical perspective would, I suggest, best enable them to stand in genuine continuity with O'Donovan in taking Scripture with total seriousness for Christian engagement with contemporary political and ethical thought and practice.

Bibliography

Childs, B., *Biblical Theology of the Old and New Testaments* (London: SCM Press, 1992)

Eichrodt, W., *Theology of the Old Testament* (trans. J.A. Baker; 2 vols.; London: SCM Press, 1961)

Furnish, V.P., 'How Firm a Foundation? Some Questions About Scripture in *The Desire of the Nations*', *SCE* 11.2 (1998), 18–23

Hauerwas, S., and J. Fodor, 'Remaining in Babylon: Oliver O'Donovan's Defense of Christendom', *SCE* 11.2 (1998), 30–55

---

[62] *DN*, 267.

Moberly, R.W.L., *At the Mountain of God: Story and Theology in Exodus 32–34* (JSOTSup 22; Sheffield: JSOT Press, 1983)

——, *The Bible, Theology and Faith: A Study of Abraham and Jesus* (Cambridge: CUP, 2000)

Perlitt, L., *Bundestheologie im Alten Testament* (WMANT 36; Neukirchen-Vluyn: Neukirchener Verlag, 1969)

Rendtorff, R., 'Covenant as a Structuring Concept in Genesis and Exodus', in *Canon and Theology: Overtures to an Old Testament Theology* (OBT; Minneapolis: Fortress Press, 1993), 125–34

Rosenzweig, F., 'The Unity of the Bible: A Position Paper vis-à-vis Orthodoxy and Liberalism', in M. Buber and F. Rosenzweig, *Scripture and Translation* (trans. L. Rosenwald with E. Fox; Bloomington, IN: Indiana University Press, 1994), 22–26

Seitz, C., 'Royal Promises in the Canonical Books of Isaiah and the Psalms', in Seitz, *Word without End: The Old Testament as Abiding Theological Witness* (Grand Rapids: Eerdmans, 1998), 150–67

Smith, M., *Palestinian Parties and Politics which Shaped the Old Testament* (London: SCM Press, 2nd edn, 1987)

2

Response to Walter Moberly

Oliver O'Donovan

'Where is the history of Israel to be found?' A penetrating question such as that demands an exceedingly simple answer: it is found in the Old Testament.

On page 28 of *Desire* I spoke of an 'official history' in pointing to a position, which I reject, that the historiography of Israel can be of two contrasted kinds, an 'official' history and a 'subversive' history. Walter Moberly was not the only one to mistake my intention as being an endorsement of the distinction and support for the official alternative, though I meant to reject the alternative altogether. There is no 'official history' of Israel; there is only Israel's history. But this does not take the force out of Moberly's question. Is that history the *attested* history (as Childs thinks) or the *uncovered* history (as Wellhausen thinks)? In Moberly's words, is it 'the OT's own story' or 'the "historical-critical" alternative'? I shall be very unhappy indeed if I am forced to make a choice.

There was a certain smug cunning in the insistence of the historical-critics that 'it a'nt necessarily so, the things that you're li'ble to read in the Bible!' The very way Moberly puts it – 'the history of Israel and its religious development as perceived through the lens of modern critical historiography look very different from the picture presented by the OT itself'; or again, 'its ability to construct out of the biblical text a history significantly different from that which the Bible itself presents' – still shows the abiding influence of the 'cunning' project, of outwitting the text. Against this, the canonical project of finding 'positive significance in Israel's own picture' deserves endorsement for its piety – not only piety towards God, but piety towards texts, too. It believes in reading texts, not merely outwitting them. We shall not understand Deuteronomy without understanding why it is all put in Moses's mouth.

Yet the canonical project seems to consecrate the point of view from the closure of the canon, shutting us off, as it were, from the heat of the moment when Deuteronomy was being composed. I would like to reply to Moberly's question with one of my own: Where is the history 'which the Bible itself presents' to be found? In the canonical index of biblical books?

Out of the vast quantity of intellectual detritus left behind by the historical-critical project, a few (remarkably few) penetrating insights survive the test of time and impose themselves – simply by virtue of shedding such light on the text that when one reads the text one feels it would be doing it violence to read it apart from that light. Some of those have become part of my reading – far downstream from source, of course, because I am only a moral theologian who gets a biblical education at fifth hand. I receive them not because of the intellectual authority of the historical-critics, but in spite of the collapse of their intellectual authority. They are what is left behind when the project has been swept away.

These insights carry authority because the text reads itself so much more clearly with them than without them. They are now no more part of a 'cunning' reading but of a 'pious' reading. There is no 'Bible itself', one might say, apart from Deuteronomy itself, St Mark itself, the Psalms themselves. In their literary and traditional context, certainly, not in artificial isolation. But the 'Bible itself' is the *texts* of the Bible, not something else. The Old Testament's 'own' attestation of Israel's history is not restricted to the canonical order of the books and such literary features as the presentation of Deuteronomy in the mouth of Moses. It occurs at many levels. It includes such elements as the attestation in Deuteronomy 15 of the meeting between a rural pledge economy and an international trading economy based on money: 'You shall lend to many nations and shall not borrow.'

Can we read Deuteronomy so as to respect the *many* ways in which it attests history? I believe so. Can such a reading be established beyond the possibility of contest? Certainly not. It will be the result of an infinity of small judgements, any one of which may be wrong, and some of which are, in the case of any given judge, bound to be wrong. We should not expect to do our theology on the basis of incontestable findings. Protestants adopted the Catholic concept of philosophy as the foundational science of theology and put biblical studies in its place. The foundational model led us to look for 'sure' results on which to build. But it was a mistake.

I spoke of interpretation as having 'an architectonic centre of gravity in the Gospels'. Anyone who has encountered Moberly's own study of the figure of Abraham, *The Bible, Theology and Faith*, with its enchanting introduction from the story of the Emmaus Road, will doubt that this is a rule with which he has much sympathy. It remains interesting, however, that he and I seek our centre of gravity in the Gospels by a rather different route. Moberly calls on a sensitive and sophisticated version of something like a typological pattern: the moral matrix of the 'fear of God' provided by reflection on the narrative of Abraham provides a pattern out of which Christology must grow – an approach which, I have dared to suggest to him, would have resonated well with my predecessor of a century ago, R.C. Moberly. I, on the other hand, find my way to the

Gospels by finding a centre of gravity for Old Testament history *itself* first. (This, I suspect, is what I meant by the adjective 'architectonic', i.e., Israel's history as a whole, not only its several episodes, hold the key to Jesus as its fulfilment.) The fall of Judah and the promise of return is the point at which Israel lives as a nation through the judgement of death and resurrection, becoming *as a historical whole* a matrix for the figure of Christ, supremely reflecting the figure of Jeremiah.

This, perhaps, is why I disappoint Moberly by a comparative lack of interest in the Pentateuch. I think he overstates the position when he speaks of the 'near-invisibility of Moses and the Sinai covenant', since the longest passage of exposition of a single OT text by far is devoted to Exodus 33–34; but I accept the suggestion that I lay more weight, as a whole, on the crisis of Judah. That emphasis is born of an attempt to read the OT as a whole in the light of the cross as its historic culmination. Such a reading does not have to be obtrusively paraded – should not be, indeed, because we must attend to *Israel* in the light of the cross, not only to the foreshadowing of the cross in Israel.

I would understand better, perhaps, the dissatisfaction which Moberly expresses with my procedure, and the difference of perspective which, despite our agreements, lurks in the background, if I understood the meaning of his complaint: 'for O'Donovan the traffic is largely one-way, a historical trajectory from Israel to Jesus'. Doesn't history normally go one way? The virtue of my narrative approach would seem to be that it treats history as history. Yet Moberly is clearly of the opinion that in some sense the interpreter can dialectically defy history in this respect, going 'back' to 're'-read. Here is my puzzle: what kind of defiance am I being summoned to? In the most obvious sense every reading of history is a 're'-reading, simply because the reader is not in the midst of the history but beyond it; but there is something extra that Moberly wants to incorporate into the term, a kind of 're-re'-reading which I am failing to pull off.

The broadest hint he gives of what this may imply comes in an allusion to a passing comment I make on Jesus and the Exodus narrative, that 'the emphasis was not on the conquest of the Egyptians but on the conquest of the sea'. Moberly proposes: 'One may ask, however, what difference this makes to one's evaluation and appropriation of the *prima facie* sense of the OT narrative, where the deliverance of Israel is precisely at the expense of Egypt; and how, therefore, within the full context of Scripture, the exodus deliverance should best be understood and utilized.' What is this question trying to achieve: *understanding* of the *prima facie* sense, or *evaluation* of it? And what kind of 'appropriation' and 'utilization' is proposed here? To 'understand' a *prima facie* sense seems to require no work at all. The *prima facie* sense is by definition that which one understands immediately, guilelessly and without second thoughts. We have a *prima facie* sense in which Egypt is to blame, and that is that; we have a further reflection from Jesus in which the sea is to blame (never mind whether there is any sense in this); and now Moberly wants some further step, some going back *from* the reflection *to* the *prima facie* sense.

To do what? It may be that once our eyes are opened, our *prima facie* reading of the exodus story will change, and we shall never be able to read it as mainly about the Egyptians again. But that is not something we could arrange for; either it will simply happen, or it will not. Anything more than this, it would seem to me, could only take the form of a kind of contest in which we champion the reflection against the *prima facie* sense, aiming to suppress it, neutralize it or overcome it in some way. To 'evaluate' it clearly implies some form of acceptance or rejection of a moral claim it makes. But what authority has the *reader* to do this? Perhaps a moralist may, but he has to do it on his own authority, not pretending merely to interpret. But if we are frankly engaged in moralizing, must we be compelled to moralize on *this* sense of *this* unit of text, just because a literary critic, who has no moral authority, chooses to pick it out? Why should we not insist that the essential prerequisite to moralizing is some serious theological organization of what we propose to moralize *about*. All of this, I have to confess, makes me nervous, renewing suspicions of the hermeneutical project, which was often suspected of ambitions to justify and insure the reader's present against the text's past. Promiscuous moralizing is a great cause of alarm to the professional moralist. Is interpretation, he worries, simply going to be used as a cover for an undisciplined excitement about the moral *differences* of the past?

3

Law and Monarchy in the Old Testament

J. Gordon McConville

The following paper comes out of a great appreciation for Oliver O'Donovan's *The Desire of the Nations*, especially because he roots his thesis about political authority in the idea of the revelation of God's rule in the history of Israel, and because he gives close attention to Old Testament texts and their interpretation. In offering a contribution to the discussion of the thesis, I focus on that foundational part of the discussion. While I am in agreement and sympathy with large parts of the analysis, especially the victory-judgement-tradition triad as well as the belief that Israel's political categories can serve as a paradigm for all others, I shall suggest that the picture that emerges would look somewhat different if the OT material were handled in a different way. The argument also has a bearing on O'Donovan's postulate of the priority of the political act.

In particular, I want to argue that Israel's political categories, and the OT's presentation of them, are best understood if Deuteronomy – the OT's supreme political text – is allowed to have priority, rather than being seen as a late minority critical voice. Other pentateuchal texts, such as the book of the covenant (Ex. 20:22 – 23:19), might also be brought into the argument. The focus here is on Deuteronomy, however, because it is the most extensive development of the theme of law in the Old Testament. This treatment of law is also set in the context of a theory about the organization of the covenant people that has been called a 'constitution'. It is the only OT book to have an extended discourse on the topic (with the possible exception of Ezekiel, to which I return below). Recognizing this puts the question of suspicion in our reading of the texts in a different light from that taken by O'Donovan. And it shows that the OT has a more sophisticated concept of the constituents of a political theory than O'Donovan has allowed.

My proposal pursues two lines of argument. First, the thesis that Deuteronomy should have some priority in an OT political theology poses a methodological question about how we read OT texts in relation to each other. Specifically, how do we decide what the OT articulates about a history of

Israel, and thus about political categories that can be regarded as normative? Second, the proposal requires an elucidation of Israel's political categories derived from Deuteronomy in critical dialogue with the Davidic-Zion theology.

Locating Israel's History

I begin with some remarks about methodology, which are largely in line with Walter Moberly's paper 'The Use of Scripture in *The Desire of the Nations*'. I echo Moberly's question concerning O'Donovan's understanding of the history of Israel as an 'official history' reconstructed by historical-critical means, and his suggestion that such a history ought not to be abstracted from the canonical shape of the Old Testament. He rightly observes that the Pentateuch generally is under-represented in *DN*, at the expense of the Psalms and the Prophets. This profiling of the Old Testament, surprising in view of the prominence of law in the argument, corresponds to the focus on kingship as the unifying centre of the political categories that O'Donovan finds relevant to a biblical political theology. He is well aware that the monarchy in Israel was born amid controversy, with fears that the unifying of God's own kingly functions in a human monarch ran the risk of making an image of deity.[1] Yet he concludes an opening discussion of this by saying: '... in the end nobody opposed the monarchy'.[2] And he goes on to show how the monarchy won through because of felt inadequacies in Israel's premonarchical political institutions.[3]

In arguing for the need to treat Israel's political tradition as history, O'Donovan makes four qualifications which theologians should respect: i) they should consider the full range and diversity of Israel's history; ii) they should treat its 'official history', not 'a subversive counter-history'; iii) they should not think in terms of a progressive 'Whig' history; yet, iv) they should understand it as a history of redemption.[4]

My initial concern is with the second of these qualifications (on 'official history', again with Moberly), although the argument as a whole also relates to the first and third qualifications. According to the second qualification, Israel's 'official history' is opposed to a subversive history, which is then linked with the prophetic and Deuteronomic critique of government. This poses a

---

[1] O'Donovan, *DN*, 52–53. Cf. his reconstruction of Israel's politics before the monarchy, 56–57.

[2] *DN*, 53.

[3] *DN*, 56–57.

[4] *DN*, 27–29.

problem in O'Donovan's analysis that in my view is not resolved. He admits, 'Actually, the documents we possess are, as they stand, critical of the exercise of government to a remarkable extent, a fact owing to the influence of the prophetic movement in the Deuteronomic literary culture.'[5] But how should these 'critical' elements in the biblical account of Israel's history be assimilated? In particular, to make an association between Deuteronomy (here cast in the role of an oppositional 'culture') and a sceptical attitude towards the proposition that in Israel God has made his rule known, is to beg a fundamental question about the way we read the texts of the Old Testament. To set the issue up in this way supposes at the outset that Deuteronomy has only a limited and secondary role in the Old Testament's articulation of what Israel, as revealer of God's rule in the world, actually is. O'Donovan says we must affirm the biblical picture as well as criticize. My questions are: What do we affirm? And what must be criticized? And how are we guided in these things by the biblical texts themselves?

O'Donovan's view of Deuteronomy is based on established tenets of historical criticism. This raises crucial methodological issues, especially the late modern conflict in OT studies between historical criticism and approaches based on readings of the texts as such.[6] Some of these approaches are anti-historical in principle. Historical criticism, in my view, provides no bulwark against these, because those who hold to these approaches can claim not only that there is profound disagreement among practitioners of historical criticism, but also that the OT is precisely history written by the winners, a postexilic, *post hoc* falsification of history. Historical criticism paradoxically leaves us without a history – or at least with an inconclusive debate about whether King David even existed. Israel thus becomes an Israel of the imagination only, with no 'political categories' that ever entered the real world. And it opens the door to kinds of study that are 'merely' literary or ideological, the 'suspicious' readings that O'Donovan rightly wants to avoid. The dependence on historical criticism to secure the relevance of the texts for a view of history, therefore, is unsafe.

To these reservations about the capacity of historical criticism as such to yield answers for theological interpretation, I add a concern about how it has affected Deuteronomy studies in particular. Because of the place given to 2 Kings 22:8 in reading Deuteronomy, my concern is that it has been read according to an interpretation of a text outside it, and indeed that the force of that interpretation derives from a hypothesis about that text's relation to

---

[5] *DN*, 28.

[6] In using the term historical criticism, I accept Moberly's distinction between 'enduring philological-cum-historical insights and the speculations and hypotheses that have usually accompanied them' (p. 50, n. 19).

historical events. It is as if Josiah's reform itself, as a historical event, has been canonized. But the effect of this is to absolve us from the obligation to read Kings critically. The reform is narrated by Kings, and consequently stands under the questioning of the narrative. It is not self-evident that the reform as such should pass unexamined into Scripture. Josiah's intention in carrying out the reform may or may not have been congruent with the intention of the narrator in telling us about it. As to Josiah's intent, we may speculate whether it was piety or nationalistic opportunism. As to the author's intent, the narration of the reform is inseparable from that of the curious, untimely death of the king while embarked on a misadventure (2 Kgs. 23:29–30), and from the fall of the kingdom that (in both narrative and history) came so soon after. These outcomes inevitably cast a shadow over the passing triumph of the reform and suggest a reservation on the author's part.

If Kings itself cannot be read as an apologia for the reform, how much less Deuteronomy. Here, too, the neatness of the critical axiom that 'the book of the law' (2 Kgs. 22:8) equals (a form of) Deuteronomy has led beguilingly to the conclusion that Deuteronomy was written to support the reform. But now we bypass the need not only to listen carefully to Kings in its own terms, but also Deuteronomy.

Of course, we might read Deuteronomy as if Moses were a cipher for a king in the mould of Josiah. I have tried to argue below, on the contrary, that Moses is a figure without strict parallel. And though in some respects he behaves like a king, he does so only in the act of establishing certain principles and structures which are incompatible with the kind of kingship that emerged in Israel's history.

As part of my proposal to raise the profile of Deuteronomy in the discussion, I argue that the 'political categories' of historical Israel are best identified by an approach that gives due weight to the canonical shaping of the Old Testament. To give primacy to such an approach does not, of course, by itself deliver solutions to all the problems of reading texts in relation to each other, since the reading of texts entails a range of reading skills, such as the recognition of genre, sensitivity to theme and structure, as well as to rhetorical characteristics, including irony. But it registers a readiness to understand texts both in their entirety and in relation to each other.

Nor does this prioritizing of canonical interpretation answer historical questions. In a sense, historical questions are postponed by adopting such an approach. That is, they are postponed until it can be judged that these texts, together, actually tell about a history, specifically (in the context of our discussion) a history of God's rule in Israel. Decisions about the relevance of individual books or events to history are as complicated for canonical interpretation as for historical criticism. However, when the OT is read according to its own order and relative priorities it is clear that, for the canonizers at least, the concept of God's rule in history, and Israel's part in relation to it, play an important role. The story that emerges is predicated on the assumption that God chose this people, made a covenant with them, accompanied them in a variegated history, blessed them, judged them and restored them (as the NT story makes no sense apart from the life, death and resurrection of Jesus).

The OT canon, then, witnesses to the history of Israel. The shape and significance of that history is perceived by faith on the basis of a reading of the canonical Scriptures. Exactly how one conceives this is a question that can be shelved for the present purpose.[7] The point is that the history of God's dealings with Israel, culminating with Christ, is constructed on the basis of a reading of the canonical texts in terms of each other and of the canon as a whole. But this history cannot be identified with the 'official history' of historical-critical reconstruction. The immediate point is that the place of the critical strain in the OT must be embraced more wholeheartedly than O'Donovan embraces it. Further, this is not only because it is part of the story (and not a disposition of the suspicious reader), but also because – canonically – the critique comes first, rather then coming along after as a reactive movement ('the prophetic movement in the Deuteronomic literary culture'). Programme and critique are one and the same – because the programme critically confronts the ancient Near East generally, and not just the Davidic development within Israel.

Deuteronomy and David/Zion in the Old Testament Story

O'Donovan begins his analysis of Israel's recognition of God's authority in the liturgical refrain 'Yahweh reigns' (as in, e.g., Pss. 93, 96–99). This is taken to be an expression of the faith of 'the Jews of the First Temple period', and cautiously understood in the context of the theory of an 'enthronement ceremony'. The privileged place given to the First Temple period is apparent in the rider that follows, that even if the hypothesis of preexilic enthronement Psalms should fail, 'we would still have no cause to doubt that the ideas expressed in them are continuous with conceptions prevalent in the monarchy and before'.[8]

The effect of this derivation of Israel's political categories from conceptions current in Israel in the First Temple period is to graft them into a particular set of OT political concepts, namely those which may be characterized as the

[7] One model is provided by von Rad, *Theology*, whose faith-history (distinguished categorically from 'scientific history') is structured by the notions of promise-fulfilment and salvation-history (esp. 106–27). Von Rad's specific thesis has been criticized by, for example, Watson, *Text*, 205–7. Watson argues for a structure of canonical reading that begins firmly in the New Testament.

[8] *DN*, 32–34.

'Zion-Davidic theology'. Form-critically, the essential elements of the 'Zion-tradition' (classically contained in the so-called 'Songs of Zion', esp. Pss. 46, 48, 76) are God's triumphs in Zion over natural forces and over kings and nations.[9] Other closely related Psalms draw in his election of the Davidic king, whom he installs on Mt Zion as the seat of his (God's) rule on earth, from where he demonstrates his victory over the nations (Ps. 2), and the king's place in the establishment of justice and the defence of the weak (Ps. 72). (The 'Songs of Zion' and the Davidic-messianic Psalms are treated here as a unity, and referred to as the Zion-Davidic theology).[10] O'Donovan draws on this set of concepts when he finds in the symbolism of kingship the threefold guarantee of the stability of the natural order, the security of Israel among the nations, and the ordering of Israel's social existence by means of justice and law.[11]

I have already said that the problem with this choice of focus is that it does not pay attention to all the canonical voices. To that methodological point may be added another, namely the time-honoured dilemma about how the task of synthetic OT interpretation should be addressed. This dilemma resolves itself into attempts that characterize themselves as 'Old Testament theology' and those that set out to do 'history of Israelite religion'. That these are not simply distinct disciplines, but rival bids to make the integrative link between exegesis and theology, is clear from recent work. (The point is elaborated by James Barr in his sympathetic treatment of R. Albertz's *A History of Israelite Religion in the Old Testament Period*.)[12] The issue may be roughly expressed as whether to give priority to the religious ideas of Israel in their development through time and in their wider religious environment, or to the theology of the texts considered systematically in relation to each other. O'Donovan's preference for the concepts of Zion-Davidic theology, though he makes no theoretical distinction between these methods, involves an attachment to certain religious-historical ideas, since the Zion-Davidic theology has close kinship with ideas found widely in the ancient Near East. The attendant problem of such a method is that it may not examine with sufficient rigour the filter through which the Old Testament writers put those ideas.

---

9 Ollenburger, *Zion*, 15.

10 It is a debatable point whether the Psalms that celebrate David's kingship belong properly to the 'Songs of Zion'. Clements sees a 'general similarity' between Ps. 2 and these songs; (*Isaiah*, 79). But Ollenburger contests this, thinking that the Songs of Zion may even have been 'theological attempts to modulate the claims of monarchy, especially since the kingship of Yahweh is stressed, while that of the earthly kings goes unmentioned' (*Zion*, 194, n. 71). The distinction is not directly relevant to the immediate point. It does illustrate the difficulty, however, of making historical criteria indispensable for interpretation.

11 *DN*, 32–33.

12 Barr, *Concept*, esp. 118–39.

In this connection, too, the secondary role assigned to Deuteronomy in *DN* is problematic. It is not just that Deuteronomy may have additional points or insights, but that the force of its critique of the Zion-synthesis is missed. Indeed Deuteronomy is even assimilated to the Zion viewpoint in one important respect, in that its law of the place of worship is regarded as supporting the unique place given to Jerusalem in a range of other OT texts.[13] While this is in line with a major strain in OT scholarship, I have argued in a number of places that Deuteronomy, in its formulation and context of the altar law, aims to prevent the claims of any particular place becoming absolute.[14]

My suggestion in what follows is that, within the story that constitutes the 'primary history' of the OT (Genesis–Kings), there is a progression from Deuteronomy to the narrative of the establishment of the royal temple cult in Jerusalem that allows critical questions to be asked of those political institutions. In reading Deuteronomy as an overture to the history of David, Solomon and the kings, factors can be brought to bear that are specifically narratological and hermeneutical. In particular, a distinction should be made between the logic of the surface narrative and the symbolic universes disclosed by it.[15] Deuteronomy and Samuel–Kings, though part of the same surface-narrative, exhibit quite different concepts of political authority. For this reason, the concept of 'suspicion' appears to be embodied in the narrative, and cannot be entirely elided. If Deuteronomy sets out the standards and limits of political life in Israel, the story of Israel that follows tells how an actual history unfolded – one of a number of possible histories – which falls under the judgement of the Deuteronomic standard. Finally, if the actual history, which involved elements of accommodation of Yahweh to the recalcitrance of Israel, gave rise to concepts that were then absorbed into its literature of worship and prophecy, this does not neutralize such adverse judgements as are invited by the narrative.

It remains to show how Deuteronomy's concept of political authority differs from that of the Zion–Davidic synthesis, and to ask what difference a recognition of this might make to O'Donovan's thesis.

Deuteronomy as Critique of the Zion–Davidic Synthesis

Deuteronomy contrasts with the Zion–Davidic synthesis in specific ways. While the narrative of 2 Samuel, echoed by the Psalms and Isaiah, proclaims that David (more exactly Solomon in 2 Sam. 7:14) is God's 'son' (cf. Ps. 2:7; Isa. 9:5 [9:6 EVV]), and the traditional covenantal terminology is applied to the

---

13 *DN*, 41–43.

14 See, e.g., McConville, *Time*, 89–139. Cf. Olson, *Deuteronomy*.

15 I developed this point in 'Metaphor'.

king rather than to the people (in the same text), Deuteronomy attaches both covenant and sonship to the people (Deut. 5:2; 14:1). The same is true of election (1 Sam. 13:14; Deut. 7:6). That this direct relationship between Yahweh and people is an important part of the book's thought is borne out by its structure, with its well-known similarities to both treaties and law codes. It is also enunciated by the regular insistence that Israelites are 'brothers'.

The contrast between the two views of political authority is most pointed when Deuteronomy deals with kingship, in the only OT law to address the theme (Deut. 17:14–20). Here, while a king is permitted, he has no essential role. The three most striking things about the law of the king are, first, its counter-portrait of Solomon (no horses, no wives, no gold and silver); second, the king's status as a 'brother' in Israel; and third, his subjection to the Torah. (It is true that the king-law is often taken to be supportive of kingship, but this interpretation is forced by the belief that Deuteronomy is a programme for King Josiah's reform. The law in its own terms can hardly be taken in this way, however, but is directed exactly against the style of kingship adopted by every king after David.[16])

The king-law corresponds to the book's wider view of political authority. In particular, Moses, though he behaves in certain respects like a king, is never called a king, nor does he ultimately receive royal privileges. The kingly functions in Deuteronomy are reserved strictly for Yahweh: he wins the war of occupation, and he gives the land. Moses mediates the covenant, and teaches the law, but he is succeeded by one who is not his son, and who in turn has no single successor.

The subject of succession leads into the most significant feature of Deuteronomy's concept of political authority, namely, what may be called its 'separation of powers'.[17] The text for this theme is Deuteronomy 16:18–18:22. This passage, unique in the OT, incorporates the king-law, but only in the marginalizing way that we have observed. The real thrust of the passage is to elaborate the several responsibilities of various offices in Israel in a distributed political authority. Here we find provision for judges and officers throughout the cities of Israel (16:18–19), for priests (18:1–8), for a high court comprising these two offices (17:8–13), and for the prophet, who has, incidentally, the best

---

[16] The point is accepted by Levinson, *Deuteronomy*, 138–43, even though he advocates the general view that Deuteronomy supports Josiah's reform.

[17] In the consultation for which these papers were prepared, O'Donovan pointed out that I was using a seventeenth-century concept here (which he himself does not favour, *DN*, 65), in a seventeenth-century reading of Deuteronomy. I respond to this below. But the presence of this idea in Deuteronomy has modern support too, in Halpern, *Constitution*, 226–33; and Lohfink, 'Sicherung'. Jonathan Chaplin directly addresses O'Donovan's reservations about this principle in the present volume.

claim to be Moses' successor (18:15–22). All of these offices are enjoined upon Israel; only the king is merely permitted, on the initiative of the people (though in that case he must be one whom Yahweh chooses). The dispersed exercise of authority outlined in Deuteronomy 16:18–18:22 is echoed in a prominent position in the book, in 1:9–18, where Moses delegates the authority of judging to representatives of the people.

In these provisions it is the people itself to whom responsibility for the administration of Torah is assigned. It is the people who appoint their judges (in 1:13–14 and 16:18),[18] though the appointment of priest and prophet is reserved to Yahweh. It is the assembly of Israel (the *qahal*) that stands before Yahweh at Horeb in the archetypal covenantal event, the place of the fundamental political decision by which they accept their status as Yahweh's covenant partners and the responsibility to keep the Torah (4:9–14). It is the assembly of Israel that stands before him again at Moab in the renewed covenant that they enter into on the verge of the land (28:69 [29:1 EVV]). And it is the assembly of Israel that will stand before him at the covenant renewal in the land (Deut 27:9–26), and regularly thereafter in worship events at the sanctuary (Deut 31:9–13).

This system of authority is entirely predicated upon the rule of Israel by Yahweh's Torah. The supremacy of the Torah is symbolized by the deposit of the 'book of the law' beside the ark of the covenant in perpetuity (31:25). (A second copy of this is kept by the king for his own use and symbolizes the fact that he too, like his brother-Israelites, is subject to it; 17:18–20). By this means, the substance of the Torah preached by Moses on the border of the promised land is conveyed to subsequent generations. It is, indeed, Israel's submission to the Torah, in the context of the Mosaic covenant, that is its identifying mark.

Furthermore, this identity of Israel is secured for all its future. Deuteronomy's unique concept of a solidarity of Israel across all its generations into an open future is based on its perpetual recommitment to covenant with Yahweh, whose substance is Torah. This contention of the book is secured in two ways. First, the teaching of Moses is put on a par with the Ten Commandments. This is the point of the dual focus in 4:13–14: Yahweh gave the Ten Commandments to *the people*, but charged *Moses* with the task of teaching 'statutes and ordinances' in the promised land. That teaching, furthermore, is conceived as a paradigm for all future teaching of the Torah in Israel, primarily by families (6:6–9), but also by judges and priests as they interpret the Torah (16:18–17:13). Second, the continuity of Israel throughout its generations is secured by the transition from Horeb to Moab, a paradigm of perpetual covenant-renewal, the key text being 28:69 [29:1 EVV] – 30:20.

---

[18] The singular address in this context, as typically in Deut., is directed to the people as a whole; see my 'Singular Address'.

Finally, the concept of Torah has aspects of both stability and novelty. The stability is signalled by the command neither to add to nor subtract from the word that Moses speaks (4:2). The possibility, even necessity, of novelty is conceded, however, by the relationship of Deuteronomy to other law codes in the Pentateuch. The nature of the relationship of the Deuteronomic law code to its closest cousin, the 'book of the covenant' (Exod. 20:22–23:22), is much debated (does it reinterpret it, for example, or entirely replace it?). The most satisfactory answer is one that accounts for the preservation of both codes in the Pentateuch, and this suggests that Deuteronomy canonizes an ongoing activity of reinterpretation.

The concept of an open future for Israel involves a vision that goes far beyond the merely foreseeable. Israel in Deuteronomy has its origins in creation: both the exodus and the attachment of Israel to Yahweh are put in the context of the creation of the world (Deut. 4:32–34; 32:8–9). And it has its horizon in the eschaton: images of the land are markedly paradisal (Deut. 8:7–10), and visions of the people at worship portray everything that a people might be and might enjoy in terms of the divine blessing (Deut. 16:13–17). In this rapprochement of a concept of creational order with a politics based on a people's covenantal relationship with God in willing obedience to the Torah, Deuteronomy challenges profoundly the ancient Near Eastern concept of a political order with fixed hierarchical forms based on analogous hierarchies in the divine realm.

Deuteronomy as a 'Constitution'?

The comprehensive political vision of Deuteronomy has led some commentators to claim that it contains a 'constitution', based especially on Deuteronomy 16:18–18:22.[19] The argument in favour of this is that the book provides for a whole political life, in a concept that is carefully worked out in dialogue with prevalent theories of political authority. The quality of *ṣedeq* ('righteousness', 'justice') is embodied in the laws and commands that constitute the *torah* (= Torah; 4:8) – an unusual attribution of the term *ṣaddiq* ('righteous'), which is otherwise attached to individuals – and responsibility for it is entrusted to officials appointed by the assembly of Israel (16:18–20 – note the exhortation to the judges that in their decisions they should be guided by *ṣedeq*, v. 20). The responsibility of the people for implementing *torah*, vested in the assembly and delegated to appointed officials, is perhaps the single most radical feature of the book. Their constitution as a religious assembly symbolizes the source of the authority of *torah* in God. Finally, the argument that Deuteronomy is a 'constitution' rests not only on the laws of 16:18–18:22, but on the structure of the

19 Halpern, *Constitution*, 226–33; Rüterswörden, *Gemeinschaft*, 89–90.

whole book, which aims to provide a way of governing the people after the death of Moses.[20]

That Deuteronomy's laws of officials amount to a constitution, or a concept of statehood, has been strongly challenged, both on the grounds that these laws are insufficiently comprehensive, and that they are merely 'Utopian', since no king could possibly have allowed such a law to be promulgated.[21] The former point is perhaps met by the consideration that Deuteronomy provides a framework for ongoing interpretation of the law. The latter rests on the assumption that any thinkable doctrine of statehood would have to be in monarchical terms, which precludes the possibility that Deuteronomy conceives statehood in deliberate opposition to monarchy as such. In the canonical story, in contrast, Deuteronomy stands over the history of the kings. In its insistence that kingship, with all its mythological overtones, could not have an unchallenged place in Israel's political arrangements, it had the final word.

Deuteronomy, Government and Creation

I propose to go one step further in attempting to characterize the political reach of Deuteronomy. I have suggested already that the Zion-Davidic set of concepts has echoes in the wider religious environment of Israel. Among Israel's neighbours, kingship was conceived in a mythological framework, embracing a certain approach to deity, creation and providence. The challenge that Deuteronomy presents to the political thought of the ancient world is at heart a religious one.

I argued above that Deuteronomy places Israel's origins in creation, and that its telling of Israel's history puts it finally in an eschatological context. In this comprehensive vision, the covenant with Israel is a realization of possibilities entailed in creation. Deuteronomy's view aims precisely to challenge other (mythological) views that are equally comprehensive in their embrace of creation and politics. This is the full extent, and the genius, of the Deuteronomic covenantal theology. It is also the context of Deuteronomy's understanding of *ṣedaqah* and its related terms. We have observed that *ṣedeq/ṣedaqah* is to be the quality that governs the political, social and legal life of Israel (1:16; 4:8; 16:18, 20). But *ṣedaqah* goes deeper than this. God himself is *ṣaddiq* (just, righteous), in an ascription of perfection to both his character and his 'work' (32:4). People may be *ṣaddiq* (sometimes in the sense of 'innocent', 16:19; 25:1). *Ṣedaqah* can refer to the innocence or righteousness of Israel (9:4–6). Finally, and importantly, it also connotes a condition that exists when the covenant is kept, and

[20] Olson's stimulating interpretation of Deuteronomy (*Deuteronomy*) recognizes how much its whole argument is predicated on the death of Moses.

[21] Perlitt, 'Staatsgedanke'.

that is best understood by its parallels in 'good' and 'life' (6:24–25).

The concept therefore embraces the character of God, his commands, and the conditions that he seeks to realize in and for his covenant people. It is clear from the concentration of the *ṣedaqah* vocabulary in 16:18–20, that is, in the prelude to the laws about officials and their roles, that it is to this end that the structures are put in place for the governance of the people. I have tried to argue that Deuteronomy's provision for the political organization of the people (including its 'separation of powers') arises out of a belief in a fundamental moral order, which is rooted in the character of God, expressed in his creation, and applied in his making of a covenant with Israel.[22]

This point finds echoes, I think, in the papers of Jonathan Chaplin and James Skillen in the present volume. My suggestion is that the restrictions placed on the power of an individual in Deuteronomy's polity indicate the perception of something important and abiding about the nature of human government. So I respond sympathetically to Chaplin's questioning of O'Donovan's prioritizing of the political act over (in Chaplin's terms) 'a universally valid normative principle of social order'. Chaplin, referring to the biblical laws of Jubilee (Lev. 25), asks whether biblical justice can be 'adequately grasped as corrective (remedial) action without a prior intuition of the normative principle which has been violated'. This is a question about justice and creation. *Ṣedaqah* is about established orders of relationship. More than this, it is an attribute of God, which is reflected in his creation.[23]

Implications for O'Donovan's Thesis

How much difference would it make to O'Donovan's thesis if one were to look for Israel's political categories first in Deuteronomy rather then in 'Zion' texts? In certain respects his thesis will be unaffected. The basic ingredients of political authority, identified by O'Donovan, will be the same – namely God's victory or salvation, his judgement, and the community's tradition (land/possession and law).[24] He has also, in practice, brought the Deuteronomic critique of kings to bear in such a way as to take account of the OT's deprecation of the concentration of power.

---

[22] Chaplin has argued that O'Donovan, in his notion of the lawfulness of political order, comes closer to sanctioning the 'separation of powers' in actuality than he does in theory.

[23] This point reflects a discussion at the consultation. Against O'Donovan's concept of justice (or as he prefers, judgement) as act (*DN*, 39), it was urged that *ṣedaqah*, in characterizing a creation order, differed from *iustitia*.

[24] *DN*, 36–48. Cf. *RMO*, 128–29.

However, there are places where I think a higher profile for Deuteronomy would have nuanced the argument somewhat differently. For example, in relation to the acceptance of political authority by members of a community,[25] the best models are in the covenantal texts – in Exod. 19–24 as well as Deuteronomy – in which Israelites together agree to be bound by the terms of the covenant (Deut. 26:17–19). Covenant, indeed, plays a surprisingly small part in the argument in *DN*, in view of its prominence in the OT, and its usefulness as a concept for the commitment of individuals to each other, in a community under the authority of law and committed to justice. It furnishes a paradigm for consent to be governed that is more far-reaching than that which is entailed in Israel's confession '*yhwh mālak*' as understood by O'Donovan. In that connection he speaks of 'an initial moment of political faith', with the assumption that Israel's religion was at that time relatively undeveloped. The point at which this assumption emerges is in connection with Israel's place among the nations, and the confession is taken to mean that Israel looks to Yahweh as king for protection from enemies, in line with the Zion-Davidic theology that informed the worship of the First Temple. Only later did Israel understand its relation to the nations differently.[26] The 'initial moment of political faith' might have been differently conceived, according to a more integrative (canonical) approach to Old Testament theology, as the moment of consent in covenant. In that connection, Israel's whole body politic is portrayed as offering a witness to the nations (Deut. 4:6–8).

The place of the individual, incidentally, is carefully addressed in Deuteronomy – not only by means of its rhetoric, with its pointed oscillations between singular and plural address, but also by explicit reflection. The main text for this is Deut. 29, in which groups and individuals are enumerated as participants in the covenant (vv. 9–10 [vv. 10–11 EVV]), and where the effect of an individual's rejection of the covenant is considered (vv. 17–20 [18–21 EVV]). The responsibility of the individual for covenant obedience is thus part of the Deuteronomic political vision.[27]

---

[25] *DN*, 30–1.

[26] *DN*, 33.

[27] O'Donovan's idea that the individual is not in a position to make private judgements in relation to the law, *RMO*, 152–53, may need to be qualified in the light of this. I think individual judgements are implied by the exhortation in Deuteronomy, and in instances such as the case of making loans (Deut. 15:9), where the capacity of the law to compel behaviour reaches its limit. A recognition that the responsibility of the individual for covenant obedience lies deep in the canonical record, rather than supposing that it emerges at a late stage, with Jeremiah for example, may help avoid the danger O'Donovan sees of superimposing a 'Whig' notion of progressive history on the OT story – an ever-present danger with certain historical-critical reconstructions.

The other elements in the *yhwh mālak* confession (stability of the natural order, ordering of social existence by justice and law) also have primary expositions in Deuteronomy, as we have observed.

But it is in the main exposition of the elements of political authority (salvation, judgement, tradition/possession)[28] that I think Deuteronomy might be brought to bear in a rather different way from that which we find. O'Donovan's exposition of the progress of salvation-judgement-possession in Israel has its centre of gravity in the Zion-Davidic synthesis and the period of the monarchy, while other parts of the OT are drawn in at points for confirmation and criticism. Deuteronomy finds a place in this section, but I think that in one respect it is misconstrued, and that in another it could add a significant depth-dimension to the discussion.

First, the misconstrual of Deuteronomy lies in the supposition that in its demand for one Yahweh-sanctuary it is simply echoing the tenets of the Zion-Davidic theology.[29] I have tried to show above that the book fundamentally challenges the royal-mythological concepts that fed into Israel's religious history from the ancient world. Deuteronomy's approach to 'possession' is quite different, being based rigorously on diversification. O'Donovan recognizes this theme: 'At the opposite pole from this unitary focus on the possession in the city, there is the tradition of tribal and family landholdings, which still deeply engaged the interest of the Deuteronomic historian'; and '... tribal and family landholding established, in principle, the membership of Israel'.[30] He illustrates the point by referring to the extremely telling incident of Naboth's vineyard, which symbolizes the cultural clash between the autocratic monarchical way and the distinctively Israelite culture of possession.[31]

However, there is no sustained explanation of where the oppositional ideas come from, or of what status they have. They are attributed simply to groups that oppose the concentration of power, and eventually to the Deuteronomists and prophets. The former are credited with a retrospective view of Israel's history, in which certain fundamentals are safeguarded, especially that Israel's possession was the gift of Yahweh himself and the king could only ever have a guardian's role in connection with it. In the same connection, the king-law is mentioned as illustrating a Deuteronomic concern for the limitations of his power.[32]

The result of this kind of appropriation of Deuteronomy, however (that is, as secondary and posterior), is that the full import of its thinking is muted. This

---

28 *DN*, 36–81.

29 *DN*, 41–43.

30 *DN*, 43–44.

31 *DN*, 44.

32 *DN*, 62.

emerges in certain places. The idea of a 'separation of powers', for example, is mentioned only as an option that the OT did not take up in its resistance to absolutism.[33] The authority of law, too, is exhibited more clearly in a framework that does not have to reckon with the complicating claims of human royal authority. It is Deuteronomy that guarantees more carefully the concepts of the contingency of political arrangements (in its resistance to prevailing autocratic political systems, and in its own refusal to name a 'place', as if one place, or set of political arrangements, should be thought to have final and unchallengeable authority). And by the same token it is open to the pluralism that O'Donovan considers to be a *bonum* at the level of international politics.[34]

Second, Deuteronomy could add a depth-dimension to the account of political authority in Israel by allowing the story of the kings to be read more systematically in the light of it. The tensions that O'Donovan sees between the claims of kings and the criticism of them by opposition groups has been cast in a story by the OT authors. Opposition to kingship is not just a historical factor (though it is also historical; modern versions of this include Halpern's important analysis[35]), but the struggle over it is embodied in the canonical record. Deuteronomy sets out a programme for Israel's 'history', and the historical books that follow (Joshua–Kings) narrate one among many possible 'histories'. An element of measure and critique is built into the structure. The evidence for this is well known, and O'Donovan notices it. It includes the passages which dispute in principle the compatibility of human dynastic kingship with the postulate of divine kingship (Judg. 8:22–23; 1 Sam. 8:4–20) and Yahweh's initial repudiation of a royal-temple synthesis (2 Sam. 7:5–7). It also includes those passages which portray kings as coming into conflict with law (2 Sam. 11–20, a narrative which follows hard on a brief glimpse of David the righteous ruler; 1 Sam. 8:15, but in which a series of destructive events is triggered by David's adultery and murder; 1 Kings 1–11, in which Solomon's God-given wisdom is always in counterpoint with his self-aggrandizing tendencies; and 1 Kings 21, in which the clash of political cultures is exposed, and leads to the murder of a fellow-Israelite by the king).

It follows that the record of events that lead to Zion may indeed be subjected to a suspicious reading, with a suspicion that is sown by the canonical record itself. Must Israel have been governed by kings at all? Would it still have been Israel had it not been? Is Zion a necessary or inevitable symbol reconciling, as O'Donovan has it, the themes of possession and victory?[36]

The canonical record also embraces the notion of kings upholding law (1 Sam. 8:15; 1 Kings 2:2–4; Ps. 72). There is, therefore, a kind of

[33] *DN*, 65.
[34] *DN*, 71–72.
[35] Halpern, 'Jerusalem'.
[36] *DN*, 45.

accommodation built into the story. The idea of king as lawgiver is built into the interaction between the law tradition and history. And it is out of the Davidic idea that messianic hopes are born and its images arise ('a righteous branch for David', Jer. 23:5–6; the 'shoot of Jesse', Isa. 11:1). But kings are finally judged by the tradition, so that the messianic idea derives as much from failure of kings as from success.

It may be that the story of failure and success comes close to O'Donovan's idea of 'compromise'.[37] Compromise is the best that can be done within the limits of possibility imposed by a society's tradition. Do David-Solomon-Josiah simply represent the 'tradition' of Israel? The truth is more complicated, for in a sense they subvert it. Yet in some measure, and varyingly, they also uphold it. In this sense I agree with O'Donovan's insistence that 'after Ahab Elisha must anoint some Jehu, some Hazael'[38]. The idea of compromise is also close to that of the contingency of political arrangements – there is no single or final ideal political structure.[39]

The Zion–Davidic Theology Beyond Deuteronomy

Finally, I want to put my reading of Deuteronomy in a broader Old Testament context. The idea of David as king under Yahweh is almost everywhere problematized in the Old Testament. But the re-evaluation of the Davidic tradition in the Old Testament takes a variety of forms, rather than a simple opposition of the Deuteronomic to the Davidic. The Chronicler, for example, portrays David positively, in a vision which some see as eschatological.[40] But some of the solutions offered relativize or diminish, or even erase, the idea of monarchy. This may be briefly illustrated by some examples. The canonical shaping of the Psalms is a case in point, with its reaffirmation of the royal rule of Yahweh after the great lament for the failure of the Davidic covenant (Ps. 89, followed by Pss. 93, 96–99).[41] These are precisely the *yhwh mālak* Psalms, of course, which are an important ground of O'Donovan's argument about kingship.[42] The book of Isaiah is a further instance, with its retreat from the Davidic-messianic themes of chapters 1–12, and the notable absence of these, especially in chapters 40–66. That this is not an accident is clear from the famous 'democratization' of the Davidic covenant in Isaiah 55:3.[43]

---

[37] *RMO*, 93–97.

[38] *DN*, 11–12.

[39] I have pursued this in *Time*.

[40] Williamson, 'Eschatology'.

[41] See Wilson, *Editing*.

[42] *DN*, 32–34.

[43] See Williamson, *Variations*, 113–66.

Ezekiel 40–48 is the other section of the Old Testament (besides Deut. 16:18–18:22) which has some claim to be a 'polity' for Israel. For Jon Levenson, 'Ezek. 40–48 tells not of the fall, but of the birth of the ideal political state.'[44] The vision is like Deuteronomy in certain respects.[45] It is comprehensive, in that it provides for the building and administration of the temple and for the roles of priests and 'prince', it legislates for ritual and other matters, and it allocates land. Leadership functions are a major focus, with an important role falling to the priests (Ezek. 44:9–45:5, cf. Deut. 17:8–13). Ezekiel's own prophetic role is like that of Moses, since it is by his word that the institutions are given to Israel (Ezek. 40:4).

The place of the monarch has been refashioned here, too, though in a distinctive way. The 'king' has become a 'prince' (Hebrew *naśi'*), which makes him like a tribal chief from Mosaic times (cf. Num. 2, throughout). Like the king in Deuteronomy, he does not seem to have a clear authority-bearing function, being accommodated in a somewhat conventional way into the temple-palace geography of Zion in this radical revision of it. The real power lies elsewhere. The point is apparently to warn against a too-powerful monarchy, and to insist that the political chief is subject to the Sinai covenant and law of Moses.[46] K.R. Stevenson goes further, arguing that the spatial geography of Ezekiel aims 'to restructure society from pre-exilic monarchy to a post-exilic temple society without a human king'.[47] It will be fairly pointed out in response that Ezekiel also has room, in his vision of the future Israel, for the idea of 'David' ruling under God (Ezek. 34:23–24; 37:22–24), in this latter case with the title *melek* ('king'). Even so, it is in Ezekiel 40–48 that the *role* of the king is articulated alongside those of other agencies in Israel, and therefore the book, at the least, does not merely reiterate traditional ideas of the monarch's supremacy.

A quite different development regarding kingship is found in the book of Daniel. Daniel, too, rethinks law and kingship for another age. His obedience to the law of God, contrasted with the intransigent injustice of the 'laws of the Medes and Persians' (Dan. 6:5, cf. v. 15) is the conflict point in this story of Jewish faithfulness under pagan rule. Here the false claims to kingship by Nebuchadnezzar and successors are met, not by a Davidic messianism (here in direct contrast to the Chronicler), but by the piety of certain faithful Israelites (Daniel and his friends), and by 'one like a son of man', at once a

---

[44] Levenson, *Theology*, 57.

[45] Steven Shawn Tuell sees Ezek. 40–48 as a 'polity', 'like Deuteronomy and the Book of the Covenant', *Law*, 175.

[46] Levenson, *Theology*, 57–69; 111–25.

[47] Stevenson, *Vision*, 160.

heavenly figure and identified with the (earthly)[48] 'saints of the Most High' (Dan. 7:13–14, 18). On this figure Lacocque has well said:

> ... [the author of Daniel] relinquished the king title or the Messiah title for his hero. In fact, he refrained from using any title at all, for 'son of man' is no title. He preferred to call him simply 'Man', exhibiting thus the root of all kingly or messianic '*ṣemaḥ*' (shoot) in Israel.[49]

I think this brief review shows that the attempt to implement the law of God in Israel repeatedly found the idea of human kingship to be a problem. That being so, it may not be surprising after all that the one text in the Pentateuch to speak directly about the relationship of king and divine law should express hesitations, rather than promote unequivocally the idea of the monarch's supreme responsibility under God. The moral and intellectual struggle over how to accommodate kingship in a people bound to the law of God runs right through the Old Testament witness.

Have I pushed Deuteronomy too hard in the direction of an anti-monarchical reading as such? It is only fair to concede that its king-law was applied theologically to Christian monarchy for centuries of church history.[50] And, indeed, concepts of monarchy are not all the same. Kingship as conceived in Christendom need not be tarred with the same brush as the mythologized politics of the ancient Near East. Perhaps I have been (inadvertently) too much influenced by the seventeenth century.[51] I would respond by suggesting that if some seventeenth-century people were exercised by the difficulty of reconciling human claims to kingship with divine claims, they were not the first! If that difficulty is not always felt acutely, it may be because other factors make the fact of kingship more or less unquestionable. (Incidentally, I think this is why Josiah may have thought he was doing a good reading of Deuteronomy.) It is when the possibility occurs to the public consciousness that kingship may not after all belong to the eternal pattern of things that the logic of a contrary view takes on a powerful clarity.

---

[48] As I think, though 'heavenly' interpretations may be found alongside 'earthly' ones. An influential advocate of the former is Collins, *Daniel*.

[49] Lacocque, *Daniel*, 133.

[50] This was pointed out to me by Joan Lockwood O'Donovan at the consultation. Documentary evidence for it may be found in O'Donovan and O'Donovan, *From Irenaeus*. At the time of writing I am able only to note the point as made to me verbally.

[51] As Oliver O'Donovan gently suggested at the consultation.

Bibliography

Albertz, R., *A History of Israelite Religion in the Old Testament Period* (2 vols.; London: SCM Press; Minneapolis: Fortress Press, 1994)

Barr, J., *The Concept of Biblical Theology: An Old Testament Perspective* (London: SCM Press, 1999)

Clements, R.E., *Isaiah and the Deliverance of Jerusalem* (JSOTSup 13; Sheffield: JSOT Press, 1980)

Collins, J.J., *Daniel, with an Introduction to Apocalyptic Literature* (Grand Rapids: Eerdmans, 1984)

Halpern, B., *The Constitution of the Monarchy in Ancient Israel* (HSM 25; Chico, CA: Scholars Press, 1981)

——, 'Jerusalem and the Lineages in the Seventh Century BCE: Kinship and the Rise of Individual Moral Liability', in *Law and Ideology in Monarchic Israel* (ed. B. Halpern and D. Hobson; JSOTSup 124; Sheffield: Sheffield Academic Press, 1991), 11–107

Lacocque, A., *The Book of Daniel* (London: SPCK, 1979)

Levenson, J.D., *Theology of the Program of Restoration of Ezekiel 40–48* (HSM 10; Missoula, MT: Scholars Press, 1976)

Levinson, B., *Deuteronomy and the Hermeneutics of Legal Innovation* (New York/Oxford: OUP, 1997)

Lohfink, N., 'Die Sicherung der Wirksamkeit des Gotteswortes durch das Prinzip der Schriftlichkeit der Tora und durch das Prinzip der Gewaltenteilung nach den Ämtergesetzen des Buches Deuteronomium (Dt 16,18–18,22)', in *Testimonium Veritati* (Festschrift W. Kempf; ed. H. Wolter; Frankfurt: Knecht, 1971), 143–55; ET: 'Distribution of the Functions of Power: The Laws Concerning Public Offices in Deuteronomy 16:18–18:22', in *A Song of Power and the Power of Song* (ed. D.L. Christensen; SBTS 3; Winona Lake, IN: Eisenbrauns, 1993), 336–52

McConville, J.G., with J.G. Millar, *Time and Place in Deuteronomy* (JSOTSup 179; Sheffield: JSOT Press, 1994)

——, 'Metaphor, Symbol and the Interpretation of Deuteronomy', in *After Pentecost: Language and Biblical Interpretation* (ed. C. Bartholomew, C. Greene and K. Möller; Carlisle: Paternoster; Grand Rapids: Zondervan, 2001), 329–51

——, 'Singular Address in the Deuteronomic Law and the Politics of Legal Administration', *JSOT* 97 (2002), 19–36

O'Donovan, O., *Resurrection and Moral Order: An Outline for Evangelical Ethics* (Leicester: IVP; Grand Rapids: Eerdmans, 2nd edn, 1994)

——, *The Desire of the Nations: Rediscovering the Roots of Political Theology* (Cambridge: CUP, 1996)

——, and J. O'Donovan (eds.), *From Irenaeus to Grotius: A Sourcebook in Christian Political Thought 100–1625* (Grand Rapids: Eerdmans, 1999)

Ollenburger, B.C., *Zion, the City of the Great King: A Theological Symbol of the Jerusalem Cult* (JSOTSup 41; Sheffield: JSOT Press, 1987)

Olson, D., *Deuteronomy and the Death of Moses* (Minneapolis: Fortress Press, 1994)

Perlitt, L., 'Der Staatsgedanke im Deuteronomium', in *Language, Theology and the Bible: Essays in Honour of James Barr* (ed. S.E. Balentine and J. Barton; Oxford: OUP, 1994), 182–98

Rad, G. von, *Old TestamentTheology* I (Edinburgh: Oliver & Boyd, 1962)

Rüterswörden, U., *Von der politischen Gemeinschaft zur Gemeinde: Studien zu Dt 16,18–18,22* (BBB 65; Frankfurt am Main: Athenäum, 1987)

Stevenson, K.R., *The Vision of Transformation: The Territorial Rhetoric of Ezekiel 40–48* (SBLDS 154; Atlanta: Scholars Press, 1996)

Tuell, S.S., *The Law of the Temple in Ezekiel 40–48* (HSM 49; Atlanta: Scholars Press, 1992)

Watson, F.B., *Text and Truth: Redefining Biblical Theology* (Edinburgh: T. & T. Clark, 1997)

Williamson, H.G.M., 'Eschatology in Chronicles', *TynBul* 28 (1977), 115–54

——, *Variations on a Theme: King, Messiah and Servant in the Book of Isaiah* (Carlisle: Paternoster, 1998)

Wilson, G.H., *The Editing of the Hebrew Psalter* (SBLDS 76; Chico, CA: Scholars Press, 1985)

4

Response to Gordon McConville

Oliver O'Donovan

There are two paradoxes about Gordon McConville's paper: 1) He chides me gently for not adopting an intra-textual reading of the Old Testament, but attaching myself exclusively to the Zion tradition, yet he assumes a much sharper opposition between the Zion-strand and the Deuteronomic strand of OT thinking than I think tolerable. 2) He chides me gently for succumbing – despite my methodological protestations – to a progressivist 'Whig history' by adopting a seventh-century date for Deuteronomy, yet he pulls out of Deuteronomy a much more markedly 'Whig politics' than I think possible. Which of us has succumbed more to the temptations of mainstream biblical criticism? I, with my choice of the seventh-century date? Or he, with his Hegelian antithesis of royal-mythological strands over against covenantal-legal strands, brought to a synthesis in the histories?

I make it plain, I think, that I do not see the *yhwh mālak* theme of the Psalms as yielding a theology of monarchy. David and the Davidides are only a small part of what is implied there, only one of the mediations of YHWH's kingship. The law is a much larger part. Inadequate as my remarks on law may be, they are also fairly copious, though more in connection with the New than with the Old Testament. Here I must demur at the imputation that I think 'that the individual is not in a position to make private judgements in relation to the law'. This is supported with a reference to *Resurrection and Moral Order*, which is devoted to the Pauline antithesis of 'law' and 'Gospel'; but I do not find this suggestion in what I wrote there. I plead guilty, on the other hand, to saying too little about 'covenant', thinking, on the one hand, that it was accounted for within the category of law, and on the other that it was a temptation to the modern mind, for which the slide from 'covenant' to 'contract' was a fatally easy one.

I confess to not having read Deuteronomy closely enough when I wrote *Desire*, but I have done something to correct that since. Let me justify (as far as I can) the Josianic date. Its attraction is that it places Deuteronomy at the very centre of the sacred history, in the drama of Judah's fall and restoration. The centrality I assign to this period (rather than to David), and to the figure of Jeremiah in particular, has been noticed by some readers of *Desire*. The hypothesis of a Josianic date for Deuteronomy sheds wonderful light upon that period, its failed project of reform, and the way it viewed the tradition it received. It reads Deuteronomy extremely well, explaining many of its puzzling literary features. As a serious working-tool of citizens and judges, Deuteronomy displays features common to all law books: adaptation of old provisions to new circumstances, combinations of complementary statutes, commentary and application, etc. The often irritating fondness of critics for distinguishing layers of composition really does have a place in Deuteronomy, because all law texts are layered like that. Unlike a sixth-century date, a seventh-century date takes the practical pretensions of the book seriously. The parallel with the closing chapters of Ezekiel, which McConville explores, strikes me as very implausible. These are my main reasons – not conclusive, I admit, but strong. I support them with ancillary considerations: a seventh-century date makes this great law-project of Israel contemporary with the awakening to law that transpires elsewhere in the Mediterranean at the end of the seventh century, notably in Greece. Lykourgos, Drakon and Solon are all contemporaries of Jeremiah. Furthermore, since we know that Josiah carried out a law reform just before the exile (unless we have torn up preexilic history altogether), is it not reasonable to expect to find some literary traces of it in the Pentateuch?

It is a gloriously seventeenth-century reading of Deuteronomy that McConville offers us, a 'constitution', complete with limited monarchy, separation of powers and individualism; and I thank him for it warmly, but I can't quite believe it.

My chief point of scepticism is that I don't believe it is an anti-monarchical book. The little 'law of the king', modest as it may be, puts forward a profoundly important view of the relation between monarchy and law. I cannot believe it backed into it by mistake while trying to cut monarchy down to size. It is a positive view, though, of course, it corrects some other views. But the role assigned to monarchy is large, especially if, as I and McConville both think, the figure of Moses is quasi-monarchical. The fact that he isn't called king matters less than what he does. First, he takes responsibility for delegating authority to tribal leaders – note that! The tribal leadership holds its authority at the monarch's behest (1:9–18). Secondly, he promulgates the law code. In a passage which McConville draws attention to but fails, I think, to see the whole force of (4:13f.), Moses says that the Decalogue was given to the people directly, but 'the Lord commanded me … to teach you statutes and ordinances'. The Decalogue is, so to speak, *Grundgesetz*; but the monarch determines the form in which its principles are to be elaborated as law. Josiah has, I think, fully protected his own role in the legal reform here.

5

A Time for War, and a Time for Peace: Old Testament Wisdom, Creation and O'Donovan's Theological Ethics

Craig G. Bartholomew[1]

Introduction

Oliver O'Donovan's theological ethics is remarkable for its interdisciplinary range and depth. The exegetical detail in *RMO* and *DN* is surprising and refreshing, and for biblical scholars it holds great hope for breaking down the divide between biblical studies and theology, and thereby renewing both disciplines. For all the exegesis in *RMO* and *DN*, not surprisingly some parts of the Bible are attended to more than others. In *DN*, for example, Psalms is a major OT source. In other chapters in this volume authors suggest ways in which closer or different attention to other parts of Scripture would affect O'Donovan's project. In this chapter my main aim is to point out the ethical contribution of Wisdom literature and to suggest that in all sorts of ways O'Donovan has a relatively unexplored ally in Old Testament wisdom.

Creation Order

O'Donovan discerns the inner logic of Scripture in the resurrection as reaffirmation of creation. Thus creation order is central to O'Donovan's (critically) realist ethic; morality is 'that to which one is summoned',[2] it is humankind's 'participation in the created order'.[3] In the Old Testament Wisdom literature we find a similarly strong articulation of creation order. Indeed, an important

---

[1] I am grateful to Al Wolters, Gordon Wenham, Gordon McConville and Karl Möller for their helpful comments on an earlier version of this chapter.

[2] *RMO*, 43.

[3] *RMO*, 76.

factor in helping wisdom to come in from the cold, theologically, was Zimmerli's 1964 essay in which he argues that OT wisdom is theological in its doctrine of creation. 'If we now try to characterise the theological attitude of Wisdom, we must say: Wisdom thinks resolutely within the framework of a theology of creation.'[4] Wisdom knows nothing of salvation history, according to Zimmerli, but it is rooted in Genesis 1. This view of wisdom as based on a theology of creation is now widely accepted.[5]

The extent of wisdom influence in the Old Testament is much debated.[6] Within the books of the Old Testament normally classified as Wisdom literature, it is in Proverbs and Job that we find extensive considerations of creation and its order. In Proverbs 1–9, the hermeneutical key to the book as a whole,[7] there are two key passages on creation: Proverbs 3:19, 20 and Proverbs 8:22–31. Proverbs 3 stresses that it is *by wisdom* that Yahweh created the world.[8] Because Lady Wisdom is not actually said to create in 8:22–31, some commentators suggest that there is a different view of wisdom here from that in 3:19, 20. However, an instrumental understanding of wisdom is common to both texts. Not only does the counter-argument depend on a diachronic separation of Proverbs 8 from its context, but clearly wisdom in Proverbs 8 is with Yahweh in his creative activity and continues to be deeply relevant to humans (v. 31). If the translation of *'āmôn* as 'craftsman' or 'artisan' is correct,[9] then wisdom is here 'personified as the king's architect-adviser, through whom the king puts all things in their proper order and whose decrees of cosmic justice are the standard for human kings and rulers (v. 15)'.[10]

In Proverbs, these passages about wisdom and creation occur in the context of exhortations to seek wisdom. Proverbs 3:19, 20 and 8:22–31 contain the theological rationale for wisdom being so valuable and so worthy a goal. Wisdom is so desirable because it is by *wisdom* that Yahweh founded the earth and by *understanding* that he established the heavens. The very things that are the goal of the quest for wisdom in Proverbs (cf. 3:13 – the same two words are used as in 3:19) are the means by which Yahweh created the world in which

---

[4] Zimmerli, 'Place', 148.

[5] See, e.g., Day, Gordon and Williamson, 'Introduction', in *Wisdom*, 1; Murphy, *Tree*, 118–21; Perdue, *Wisdom*.

[6] See Murphy, *Tree*, ch. 7.

[7] I am assuming the possibility of reading Proverbs as a whole. See Bartholomew, *Proverbs*.

[8] The meaning is instrumental (Murphy, *Proverbs*). Von Rad, *Wisdom*, 155, suggests that Yahweh creates the world 'into wisdom'. I agree with Murphy that the b^e here is instrumental, but von Rad rightly discerns that the *effect* of this means of creation is creation order.

[9] I agree in this respect with Murphy and Van Leeuwen.

[10] Van Leeuwen, 'Proverbs', 94.

humans live. And the reference to 'the earth', 'the heavens', and 'the deeps' in 3:19, 20 speaks of the entire creation.[11] The entire, complex fabric of the world, as it were, has been woven by Yahweh, so that to attain wisdom is truly to find the tree of life,[12] because it positions one to live according to the warp and woof of the world. As Clifford says, 'Whoever lives in accord with wisdom will not go against but with the grain of the world. Such a person will receive all the goods a wisely constructed world can offer.'[13]

Creation order, it can be argued, is the root or organizing metaphor in Proverbs 1–9, which consists of instruction for a young, adolescent man. Thus there is much about avoiding sexual temptation. However, the specific applications are less obvious than the hortatory nature of the speeches, encouraging the reader to choose wisdom and life in the conflict between wisdom and evil, righteousness and wickedness. Proverbs depicts humans as drawn by either wisdom or folly, and it piles exhortation upon exhortation to encourage allegiance to wisdom.

The rhetorical effect of Proverbs 1–9 sets the context for the book as a whole by opening up a symbolic world in which the rest of Proverbs is to be interpreted.[14] Proverbs 1–9 does this through the recurrence of powerful metaphors: the two types of eros, the two paths or ways,[15] the two women, Lady Folly and Lady Wisdom, and the culmination of chapters 1–9 in the two houses (Prov. 9), with the two invitations and the two meals. Such world construction generally operates with a root metaphor that is the organizing centre for the surface metaphors. There is disagreement among wisdom scholars as to what the root metaphor(s) are for Proverbs. Camp[16] suggests that Woman Wisdom is the root metaphor in 1–9, whereas for Habel it is the two ways.[17] Van Leeuwen is right, I think, that

> underlying the bipolar metaphorical system of positive and negative youths, invitations/calls, 'ways', 'women', and 'houses' in Proverbs 1–9, is a yet more fundamental reality which these images together portray. These chapters depict the world as the arena of human existence. This world possesses two fundamental characteristics. First is its structure of boundaries or limits. Second is the bipolar human eros for the beauty of Wisdom, who prescribes life within limits, or for the seeming beauty of Folly, who offers bogus delights in defiance of created limits. Love of Wisdom means staying within her prescribed cosmic-social boundaries ... Thus, recognition of cosmic structure or limits is inseparable from proper eros or direction. ... The

[11] Van Leeuwen, 'Proverbs', 53.

[12] Prov. 3:18. The only other place this occurs in the OT is Gen. 2.

[13] Clifford, *Proverbs*, 54.

[14] In this section I am using material from my *Reading Proverbs*.

[15] Cf. also Ps. 1, which is a wisdom psalm.

[16] Camp, 'Woman Wisdom'.

[17] Habel, 'Symbolism'.

> socio-ethical order of Proverbs 1–9 is grounded in the creation order revealed by Wisdom who accompanied God as he set the cosmic boundaries.[18]

Clearly, therefore, the shape that God has given to creation and human response to that shape is fundamental to Old Testament wisdom, as it is to O'Donovan's theological ethic. O'Donovan rightly opposes any disjunction between creation and kingdom ethics, and Proverbs 1–9 is an important biblical source for a creation ethic.[19] Proverbs' articulation of the wise life also provides a biblical endorsement of O'Donovan's notion that 'Authority is the objective correlate of freedom. It is what we encounter in the world that makes it meaningful for us to act.'[20] Proverbs, like O'Donovan, envisages humans as free agents with real choices to make. For Proverbs, the possibility of folly is ever present. Such freedom implies limits or boundaries: 'For if possibilities are to be meaningful for free choice, they must be well-defined by structures of limit.'[21] O'Donovan rightly notes that 'Freedom can alienate itself and produce unfreedom.'[22] Nowhere is this more powerfully pictured than in Proverbs 9, which starts with Lady Wisdom's house and her call to 'Come and eat', and ends with Lady Folly also calling passers-by to enter her house. 'But they do not know that the dead are there, that her guests are in the depths of Sheol'(Prov. 9:18)!

Central to Proverbs is the doctrine of the two ways. O'Donovan comes to the two ways, or what he calls the 'simplicity of decision', at the end of *RMO*:[23]

> We can speak of the simple choice for or against God's new creation, the simple alternative of a broad way and a narrow way, the straightforward either-or opposition of sin and virtue. We can speak of the life of the believer as one in which there is love and no sin, and of the life of the unbeliever as one in which there is sin and no love. This is the second way in which love qualified by faith takes on a distinctively eschatological form. Such absolute oppositions cannot be avoided in Christian thought, for without it morality loses its eschatological relation to the new creation and becomes no more than a reflection of the ambiguities and complications of this world.[24]

---

18 Van Leeuwen, 'Liminality', 116–17.

19 It might be thought that Job and Ecclesiastes subvert Proverbs' view of creation order. But, as Gladson shows, retributive paradox is already present in Proverbs. Furthermore, much depends on how one reads Job and Ecclesiastes. See Knierim, *Task*, 201–202, for some helpful comments on Job and creation order. As we will argue below, Ecclesiastes is about *knowing* that order, and particularly about *wrong* ways to try and get to know it.

20 *RMO*, 122.

21 *RMO*, 107.

22 *RMO*, 108.

23 See *RMO*, 259–64.

24 *RMO*, 260.

O'Donovan refers to 1 John 3:1–12 as the most famous passage of perfectionist language in the Bible. John connects the two possibilities of love and hate with Cain and Abel. O'Donovan rightly notes that there is an important eschatological dimension in this doctrine; it stresses that *ultimately* it will become clear that these two ways are distinct. Failure to note the eschatological dimension leads either to the danger of legalism or to that of antinomianism: 'when moral thought has not made or has lost contact with the eschatological ground, the emphasis on simplicity of choice will be immanentized, and so will obscure the complexities and ambiguities which concrete moral decisions actually present'.[25]

Now, of course, there is no developed eschatology in Old Testament Wisdom literature. There is an openness to the mystery of God in wisdom and there is also the fact that, like Yahwism, wisdom insists on pursuing righteousness even while aware of the injustices in the world.[26] But certainly there is no developed eschatology. Does Proverbs, therefore, fall into the trap of legalism or antinomianism? Proverbs *is* concerned to inculcate into its readers the ultimate simplicity of life-direction, comparable to the way Jesus ends the Sermon on the Mount, but it is well aware of the complexity of ethics in a good, but fallen, world. Proverbs has often been represented as articulating a simplistic act-consequence ethic. However, there is growing evidence that, read as a whole, Proverbs evinces a far more nuanced ethic that is well aware of the complexities of life. Thus, for example, its view of wealth and poverty is not the simplistic one of virtue leading to prosperity.[27] Especially in chapters 1–9, Proverbs does articulate the character-consequence principle, but this is carefully nuanced in later chapters in which the complexities of individual cases are observed.

We have already noted how human wisdom is the human correlate of the divine wisdom that made the world. Another fascinating aspect of the human imaging of the divine wisdom can be discerned in O'Donovan's discussion of the marks of the church in *DN*. One of his characteristics of the church is that it is *a glad community*. O'Donovan relates this to the resurrection as the recovery of creation order. 'If the church's gladness is the gladness of creation, that means it is the gladness of Jesus himself; for this renewed order of creation is present in him. ... Our very joy places us within that order, and by our gladness the ordered creation of God is made complete.'[28] In this way the church images Lady Wisdom, for she too rejoices in the inhabited world and delights in the human race (8:31). Creation is concluded with delight and celebration. As Job

[25] *RMO*, 261–62.

[26] See von Rad, *Wisdom*, ch. 6.

[27] See Van Leeuwen, 'Wealth'.

[28] *DN*, 181–82.

38:7 puts it, 'the morning stars sang together and all the heavenly beings shouted for joy'.[29]

In many ways, therefore, O'Donovan's resurrection ethic finds strong support in Old Testament wisdom. Morality for him is a summons to participate in creation order, and even this element of call is present in Proverbs. Lady Wisdom is present to creation in an ongoing fashion; she is portrayed as calling out to Israel's inhabitants to embrace wisdom. In Proverbs 1:20, 21, and in 8:1–3, her voice is heard in all the great public sectors of life: the squares, the busiest corner and the city gates. Strong biblical support for O'Donovan's ethic of resurrection and moral order can therefore be found in wisdom. Two major objections could nevertheless be raised in response to his project. First, there is the issue of creation order and the overall shape of Scripture. And, secondly, there is the theological/philosophical issue of the contemporary viability of creation order. We will discuss them in this order.

O'Donovan's theological ethics assumes a certain unity to the Bible, as I note in the introduction. A moot point in this regard is the extent to which creation order is an important element of a (unified) biblical theology. Covenant and election have often been understood to be quite distinct from wisdom's theology of creation order. Thus, Clements says that,

> ideas of an ordered creation, and of the universal applicability of the teachings of wisdom, contrast with the emphasis upon God's unique actions towards Israel in Old Testament prophecy and historical writings. In the very formative application of the concept of *torah* by the Deuteronomists to describe God's revelation, this is specifically presented as truth uniquely vouchsafed to Israel (cf. Deut. 4:32–40). Contrastingly wisdom is proudly offered to the inquiring spirit of every nation.[30]

This sense that salvation history and wisdom sit uneasily together goes back in recent scholarship to an influential essay by Gerhard von Rad published in 1936.[31] Von Rad argued that, for Israel, creation was secondary to redemption: 'in genuinely Yahwistic belief the doctrine of creation never attained to the stature of a relevant, independent doctrine'.[32] However, more recently a series of studies have argued that creation is a fundamental part of biblical theology. H.H. Schmid pointed out that a belief in creation order is common to the religions of the ancient Near East, and that this order included nature, law and politics. In Hebrew, Schmid connects this order with *ṣedeq* (= righteousness). He

[29] Cf. Ps. 104 for similar emphases. Commenting on Gen. 1, Westermann, *Creation*, 62, says that 'The joy of Creation is thereby opened up to man. That is the meaning of the sentence that in God's eyes all was very good.'

[30] Clements, *Wisdom*, 20.

[31] Von Rad, 'The Theological Problem of the Old Testament Doctrine of Creation'.

[32] Von Rad, 'Theological Problem', 62.

notes that the ancient Near Eastern law codes enact 'the establishment of the order of creation seen in its juristic aspect'.[33] Schmid examines the Old Testament texts on creation and concludes that, 'Israel participated fully in the thought world of the ancient Near East and understood – and indeed could only understand – her particular experiences of history and experiences of God in this horizon.'[34] Thus, for Schmid, creation *is* the broad horizon of biblical theology.

Similarly, Knierim argues for the centrality of creation in Israel's faith. He rightly points out that however Israel arrived chronologically at a belief in creation, the important question is

> whether the purpose of the creation of the world is the history and existence of Israel, or whether the purpose of Israel's history and existence is to point to and actualise the meaning of creation. In the former, creation would have its meaning by standing in the service of Israel. In the latter, the meaning of the history and existence of Israel would be to stand in the service of God's creation of the world.[35]

Knierim strongly supports the latter view. He finds the idea of creation as structured space in much of the OT.[36] The view of the world as creation means it is structured or ordered in a particular way. By his oneness, Yahweh is the guarantee of the unity and wholeness of the world. In this respect Knierim makes much of the bipolar cosmological description 'heaven and earth'. The earth – home for humans – is understood as ordered in relation to heaven – the 'home' of God – as a structured place. This distinction provides for the tension between God's kingdom and human history: 'It expresses in nuclear form the foundational concern of the Old Testament and ... of biblical theology: the concern for the meaning of God's creation as universal cosmic order, especially in view of the acute threat to this order arising from humans on earth.'[37]

Knierim and others note that already in the eschatology of the Old Testament, redemption is viewed as a recovery of the order of creation. Knierim refers to Second Isaiah, in which the new exodus involves the reintegration of human history into creation order.[38] Similarly, Goldingay notes that '[t]he object of redemption is the restoration of creation'.[39]

---

[33] Schmid, 'Creation', 105.

[34] Schmid, 'Creation', 111.

[35] Knierim, *Task*, 181.

[36] See Knierim, *Task*, 199ff., for a discussion of some of the Hebrew vocabulary for creation order.

[37] Knierim, *Task*, 191.

[38] Knierim, *Task*, 200.

[39] Goldingay, *Diversity*, 229. See the whole of his ch. 7. See also Scobie, 'Structure', for the view that God's order should be a major theme in any biblical theology.

An issue that arises from a reading of Knierim's suggestive work is the precise nature of the relationship between creation order and history. Indeed, there is a tension in Knierim's work between creation order and history, and he appears to find it difficult to integrate the two. On the one hand he makes the startling statement that, 'For the Old Testament itself, however, "order" is a basically "historical," i.e. an always changeable, reality.'[40] However, he simultaneously affirms that creation is an event which remains an ever-present reality, it is not just the beginning of history but 'the place and moment which contains the criterion for the meaningful correlation of cosmic reality and human history, and at the same time for the critical evaluation of human history'.[41] If this is so, it is difficult to see how the order can be always changeable. A similar tension exists in his distinction between cyclical and historical time.[42]

The recovery of creation for biblical theology has not, of course, gone uncontested. In my view, the work of Schmid and Knierim moves in the right direction, but apart from this it serves at the very least to validate O'Donovan's understanding of creation as *a* legitimate reading of Scripture.

Secondly, there is a possible philosophical objection to the centrality of creation order in O'Donovan's ethics. This comes from Paul Ricœur's recent discussion of the theology and philosophy of creation.[43] In a variety of ways Ricœur's discussion concurs with O'Donovan, and so I will outline Ricœur's discussion before focusing on the important difference between them.

Ricœur rightly notes that there are several metaphors or models for creation in the Bible. He finds Jon Levenson's treatment of the combat motif particularly attractive, with its focus upon the confrontation between the goodness of the creator with the persistence of evil.[44] Ricœur discusses creation under the two aspects of separation and foundation. The similarities to O'Donovan's perspective in his discussion of creation as separation are striking. By separation he refers to the Creator-creature distinction. This distinction is originary in the sense that the world exists as 'a manifold reality, hierarchically organized and closed-in on itself'.[45] Creation means that the world exists 'in itself' without being 'for itself'. 'Prior to' any transgression, 'the commandment is a structure of the created order for man',[46] so that originarily there is a limit, and the primordial limit 'is constitutive of a distance that, far from excluding proximity, constitutes it'.[47] In this way Ricœur makes the same point as O'Donovan when

[40] Knierim, *Task*, 183.
[41] Knierim, *Task*, 193.
[42] Knierim, *Task*, 185ff. See further discussion of this issue below.
[43] Ricœur, 'Thinking Creation'.
[44] Levenson, *Creation and the Persistence of Evil.*
[45] Ricœur, 'Thinking Creation', 40.
[46] Ricœur, 'Thinking Creation', 41.
[47] Ricœur, 'Thinking Creation', 41.

the latter points out that to describe the world as created is 'already to speak of an order'.[48]

In his discussion of 'thinking creation', Ricœur refers to H.H. Schmid's view of creation order as the horizon of biblical theology, and he proposes some correctives to this view. Firstly, according to Ricœur, we need to speak of the *contingency* of creation order and to think of creation as an event rather than as an idea: 'a doing, an act is at the origin of what is'.[49] For Ricœur, if we join the ideas of necessity and contingency, our concept of order becomes more dynamic, especially as we move from the cosmic to the human level of justice. This objection to creation order is not compelling. Creation as event and creation as idea are not mutually contradictory – creation is depicted as event in Genesis 1, but that does not disqualify the validity of creation as concept, as evident in Proverbs 3 and 8, for example. We surely need both. As regards the protection of the contingency of creation, this is a proper concern but one ably present in a nuanced doctrine of creation order such as that in *RMO*. It is in the Platonic tradition that universals tended to be thought of as divine, thus placing God under necessity to create this world:

> there is no reason why this proper theological concern should not be fully accommodated within a teleological and generic understanding of created order. In speaking of kinds as independent of time-place particularity there is certainly no need to attribute to them an eternal transcendence such as belongs to God himself. … Our contention that the relation of the creation to the Creator is teleological, but not in any way generic, has properly safeguarded the absolute contingency of the creature and the freedom of the Creator.[50]

Secondly, Ricœur suggests that Schmid, by including justice within the creation order, opens up a fragility at the heart of his view of creation. By setting creation order against historical evil, Ricœur thinks that Schmid calls into question the efficacy of order.

Thirdly, the relationship between creation order and contemporary justice is deeply problematic for Ricœur:

> The critical point is as follows. We no longer know how to think the 'justice of God' both as a structure of the Creation of the world and as a demand organizing the practical field, that is, the field of human action. Of all the concepts to which Schmid refers, and with which he ends his essay, it is assuredly the 'justice of God' that has become the most enigmatic to us. If the justice of God belongs to the same kind of thinking as does Creation and Salvation, then we must say that we have left the field where that connection is still conceivable. … The irreducibility of the lesson of

---

[48] *RMO*, 31.

[49] Ricœur, 'Thinking Creation', 57.

[50] *RMO*, 39, 40. See *RMO*, 42, for a defense of God's 'arbitrariness'.

> Genesis 2 to the totalising ambitions of Genesis 1 already bear witness to this. . . . The injustice of the world constitutes such a massive fact that the presumed tie between the idea of justice and that of creation loses almost all its pertinence. Creation may remain the surrounding horizon, but it ceases to be the encompassing idea that would constitute its identification with the idea of order.[51]

These are, of course, big issues that Ricœur raises – questions of creation order, theodicy and contemporary justice. In his earlier work, Brueggemann raised similar questions about creation order as conservative and oppressive.[52] More recently, Brueggemann has acknowledged that creation theology is not inherently conservative: 'Thus creation theology is neither inherently nor inevitably conservative, but functions most often in a conservative fashion.'[53] Trigo, writing from a liberationist perspective, is more positive about the implications of creation order for justice:

> To profess that our God is the creator of heaven and earth, then, means denying a sacred foundation to that which enslaves and subjects the world today; and it means proclaiming as real what has all the appearances of the contemptible, the nameless, or the impossible. To call God our creator is to proclaim that the poor shall behold their liberation, that the dispossessed shall inherit the earth, and that a world where justice dwells is destined to become reality.[54]

One suspects that Ricœur's real problem is not with creation order itself, but with certain distorted perceptions of creation order, of which there have been notable examples in the twentieth century. This surfaces in his unusual reading of Genesis 2 in relation to Genesis 1. The juxtaposing of these accounts is surely not about Genesis 2 resisting the totalizing ambitions of Genesis 1, as Ricœur suggests, but about a false, autonomistic way of knowing the whole. It is a view of order with humankind at the centre that Genesis 2 and 3 firmly resist, not an understanding of the whole rooted in reverence for Yahweh Elohim. Of course, how we relate (contemporary) justice to creation is no simple issue. According to O'Donovan, we do have to make the journey from what God said to Abraham to how to respond to Iraq today, but he rightly insists that while faith at an intuitive level may make that journey instantly, or the preacher in half an hour, it may take a lifetime of scholarship.[55] *DN* is itself an exercise in the theological moves required, and clearly the task is complex and much contested. However, as O'Donovan stresses, if politics is to resist the idol of contemporary historicism, then the journey must be undertaken.

---

[51] Ricœur, 'Thinking Creation', 60–61.
[52] Brueggemann, 'Trajectories'. However, see Middleton, 'Creation Theology'.
[53] Brueggemann, 'Response', 283.
[54] Trigo, *Creation*, xvii.
[55] *DN*, ix.

Epistemology

Clearly there are similarities between O'Donovan's theological ethic and OT wisdom in terms of creation order. But one might suspect that any such similarities would vanish when it comes to the issue of *how we know* that order – the issue of epistemology. Is not Old Testament Wisdom literature empirical in its epistemology, depending on reason and observation in a way that runs counter to O'Donovan's theological epistemology? Would not OT wisdom fit better with a kind of natural theology,[56] rather than O'Donovan's Barthian epistemology?

There are some, perhaps many, who would argue along these lines. But, at the very least, the situation is not that simple. In recent years the epistemology of OT wisdom, and especially that of Ecclesiastes, has received close attention, and with some surprising results. This interest has arisen regarding the relationship between Qoheleth's epistemology and that of Proverbs. Michael Fox, rightly in my opinion, distinguishes Qoheleth's empirical epistemology from that of wisdom, and of Proverbs in particular.[57] Many of the sages' teachings undoubtedly derive from the observations of generations of wise men, but they are always shaped in accordance with prior ethical-religious principles. Whatever the actual source of their teaching, the sages do not, according to Fox, offer their experience as the source of new knowledge, and they rarely invoke experiential arguments. The rare appeal to what is seen is a rhetorical strategy and not a fundamental methodological procedure, as with Qoheleth.[58]

A positive description of the epistemology of wisdom as represented in Proverbs will depend on whether one reads the book as a whole, and on how one relates the overarching motif of the fear of the Lord as the beginning of wisdom to the quest for wisdom. It is well known that historical critics discern various layers of wisdom in Proverbs, and McKane, for example, thinks that the earliest layers are secular and that the introduction of Yahwism is late. The effect of such diachronic analysis is that one ends up debating the extent to which the Yahweh-sayings radiate beyond their immediate context in the book.[59]

---

[56] See Barr, *Biblical Faith*, esp. ch. 5, and Collins, 'Precedent'.

[57] Fox, *Contradictions*, 90. See Crenshaw, 'Understanding', and *Education*, esp. ch. 9, for a different perspective. Crenshaw, 'Understanding', 224, argues that, 'With respect to subjectivity, or the amount of involvement of the ego in the learning process, Qoheleth differs from other biblical sages only in degree ... As for the empirical base of his insights, Qoheleth resembles earlier sages at the time of initial discovery. ... In his understanding of the intellectual enterprise, he was quite at home with sages who preceded him and who came after him ... Perhaps Qoheleth was epistemologically less revolutionary than some critics have imagined.'

[58] Fox refers to Prov. 24:30–34; 7:6–20 and 6:6–8 as examples.

[59] So Whybray, 'Yahweh-Sayings.'

However, if one takes the book in its final form seriously, then the *inclusio* in 1:7 and 31:30[60] provides important clues to the overarching epistemology of wisdom.[61] It asserts that the foundation and starting point of wisdom is a reverence for *Yahweh*. There is much debate about the relationship between wisdom and the narrative tradition of the OT.[62] In my opinion it *is* significant, especially in Proverbs' final form, that the fear of *Yahweh* is the beginning of wisdom.[63] Yahweh is quintessentially the name of the covenant God of Israel, who rescued the Israelites out of Egypt and brought them to himself.[64] Whatever the history of wisdom in Israel, and I do not deny that reconstruction of its history is important, in its final form Proverbs asserts that the only way to read the creation order aright is to start with Yahweh, and, by implication, the redemption he has secured. In this way, it seems to me, Proverbs 1:7 performs the same function as the unusual name for God in Genesis 2 and 3, namely, Yahweh Elohim.[65] The juxtaposition of Yahweh with Elohim alerts the reader unequivocally to the fact that Israel's God is Elohim, the creator God. As L'Hour notes, 'Its meaning in each case stands out clearly: it is about showing and proclaiming that Yahweh, the God of the Hebrews, is also the God of all the earth over which his lordship shines forth through the hail and thunder.'[66]

From this perspective, then, in a pre-theoretic way the epistemology of wisdom is closer to O'Donovan's than we might have suspected. For O'Donovan, we require an epistemology which provides for the following: knowledge of things in their relations to the totality; creaturely knowledge from within the creation and which is appropriate for humans but makes no pretence of ultimate transcendence; and knowledge which is ignorant of the shape and end of history as this belongs to God alone. The parallels with wisdom are remarkable: wisdom is all about knowing how things fit in the whole and, in the light of this, what is fitting in a particular situation.

There is a strong sense of the creatureliness of humans in OT wisdom and of their need for wisdom from above if they are to discern wise ways in God's world. In a short discussion of Ecclesiastes, O'Donovan notes that it

---

[60] And 9:10.

[61] Newbigin, *Gospel*, 75, uses this point against Barr and asserts that, 'It is in the light of this knowledge which is Yahweh's gift to Israel that Israel can learn from and appropriate the wisdom which has been developed among the nations on the basis of that which God gives freely to all.'

[62] See Murphy, *Proverbs*, on Prov. 8:30. He discerns in the double use of אהיה an intertextual reference to Ex. 3:14.

[63] But cf. here Murphy's 'Excursus on Fear of the Lord', in *Proverbs*, 254–58.

[64] See esp. Ex. 3 and 6.

[65] See L'Hour, 'Yahweh Elohim'.

[66] L'Hour, 'Yahweh Elohim', 530.

> is in fact simply anxious to place human wisdom firmly in its existential context and rebuke its pretensions to transcendence. ... Wisdom, like any other goal that man may set himself, does not take one outside the world of flux and change. It, too, is a temporal activity, and like all such activities will yield in due time to its contrary. ... man's wisdom does not afford him a total purchase on the cosmos and its history; he can reach out towards apprehension only from within.[67]

O'Donovan is quite right to relate Ecclesiastes to the issue of epistemology. Michael Fox, who has written by far the most creative material on Ecclesiastes in recent years, asserts that '[t]he problem of epistemology is one of the main concerns of his book – in a sense, it is the central one'.[68] However, there is considerable debate about how Qoheleth's doctrine of the 'autonomy of individual reason'[69] plays out in the book as a whole. The majority opinion is that Ecclesiastes articulates a sort of empiricism, which leads him to his despairing conclusion. O'Donovan, however, rightly in my view, suggests that Ecclesiastes humbles human arrogance in its attempt to grasp the totality of life.

In my opinion, as I have argued elsewhere in some detail,[70] Ecclesiastes does indeed humble arrogant human pretensions by its ironic exposure of an empiricistic epistemology, which seeks wisdom through personal experience and analysis alone, without the 'glasses' of the fear of God. Qoheleth's empiricistic epistemology keeps coming up against the enigma (*hebel*) of life when pursued from this direction. This is the negative pole of Qoheleth's thought, which keeps running down to its *hăbēl hăbālîm* conclusion. However, there is another pole or strand in Ecclesiastes, namely a shalomic, creation-affirming pole embodied in the joy passages. Ecclesiastes dramatically illustrates the difficulty of relating these juxtaposed strands as long as one works with an empiricistic epistemology. The resolution of this paradox is found in the fear of God (rejoicing and remembrance), which enables one to rejoice and apply oneself positively to life in the midst of all that one does not understand – including, and especially, death. Ecclesiastes, in my opinion, thus exhorts Israelites struggling with the nature of life's meaning and God's purposes, presumably in an exilic context, to pursue genuine wisdom by allowing their

---

67 *RMO*, 79–80.

68 Fox, *Time*, 71.

69 Fox's words, *Time*, 81.

70 I cannot here rehearse the complex debate about Ecclesiastes and the details of my own arguments. See my *Reading Ecclesiastes*, and for an accessible outline of my approach see 'Qoheleth in the Canon'. My approach is akin to the dialogical approach of Perry, and I am delighted to see that Ian Provan and I agree about the message of Ecclesiastes. See Provan, *Ecclesiastes*. Other readings of Ecclesiastes, such as that by Longman, *The Book of Ecclesiastes*, would fit equally well with O'Donovan's description of Ecclesiastes.

thinking to be shaped integrally by a recognition of God as Creator so that they can enjoy God's good gifts and obey his laws amidst the enigma of his purposes. In this way it is an exhortation to be truly wise in difficult and perplexing situations.

A moot question is how Job relates to this issue. Mainline historical criticism has tended to see Proverbs, Job and Ecclesiastes as being at odds with each other. Thus Job 28 can be read as asserting the mystery of wisdom while Proverbs asserts its availability. In my opinion, the commonality among these three wisdom books is considerably greater than is often assumed. Job 28 must be read in the broader context of wisdom and theodicy, and it shares with Proverbs and Ecclesiastes a strong sense of Yahweh as the source of wisdom and the necessity of existential relationship with him in the quest for wisdom. Knierim's comments on Job are perceptive. He points out that in Israel it was because of Yahweh's presence that the world order was regarded as intact, and 'in this intactness, Yahweh was experienced as cosmically present in everyday reality'.[71] The authors of the biblical texts knew about the dark side of reality, and in their discussion of it they 'fall back on one kind of reality which is also true and present, and which is ultimate and unshakeable: the order of creation in which God is present and in which they are at home'.[72] Psalm 104 and Job do not contradict each other. Creation order cannot be verified either by Job's friends or by himself: '[t]hrough Yahweh's own theophanic appearance as the creator and sustainer of the world, the order of the world itself theophanically appears in its intactness. This is the book's answer to the crisis of wisdom.'[73]

Naturally, neither Proverbs, Ecclesiastes or Job manifest a strong eschatology as we find it in the NT. Nevertheless, they do assert a confidence in righteousness and justice while maintaining an awareness of injustice and unrighteousness. They are also conscious of the mystery of God. Thus, in all these ways, it is apparent how the inner shape of wisdom's epistemology is similar to that of O'Donovan's theological ethic.

Wisdom and Politics

Thus far our concern has mainly been with wisdom and O'Donovan's theological ethic as articulated in *RMO*. However, there is a surprising amount of material in Proverbs about kingship and rule, none of which is referred to in *DN*.[74] Because wisdom is the means by which Yahweh creates the world, there

71 Knierim, *Task*, 200.
72 Knierim, *Task*, 201.
73 Knierim, *Task*, 203.
74 *DN* contains no references to Proverbs.

is no area of life in which wisdom is not required. Consequently all areas of life, and not least politics, come up for discussion in OT Wisdom literature. The difficulty that interpreters have had in coming to grips with wisdom's view of all of life as the terrain for exercising wisdom and understanding is exemplified in the history of interpretation of the Proverbs 31 woman.[75] O'Donovan rightly says that 'Theology must be political if it is to be evangelical.'[76] We might say in the light of Proverbs that theology must be political if it is to be wise.

Proverbs deals with rule and kingship primarily in 16:10–15, 28, 29; 31:1–9. However, the verses which establish unequivocally the connection between creation, wisdom and politics are 8:15, 16:

By me kings reign,
And rulers decree what is just;
by me rulers rule,
And nobles, all who govern rightly.

In these verses the closest connection is made between wisdom and government, and this not just in Israel but universally.[77] And the practice of government is made possible by and is a response to Yahweh's creation order. The play on *ḥqq* alerts us to the close connection between the ruler and God: 'Just as the Lord "marked out" חקק (*ḥāqaq*) "the horizon on the face of the deep" and "gave to the sea its boundary" (*ḥāqaq*), and as God "marked out" (*ḥāqaq*) "the foundations of the earth" (vv. 27, 29), so also do human rulers "decree" (*ḥāqaq*) "what is just" (v. 15).'[78]

Several matters are worth noting at this point. Government is here viewed as a human activity within history in diverse nations, but it derives its authority from being an ordained activity within creation. Throughout Proverbs, as in the ancient Near East generally, God's kingship is paralleled closely by that of the human ruler. The emphasis in these verses, furthermore, is at least partly on the political *act* as decisive: 'rulers decree what is just', whether exercised by king, rulers or nobles. This may provide biblical support for O'Donovan's view that a political theology should focus first on authority as act rather than as institution: 'The political act is the divinely authorised act.'[79] The triple terminology of office – of kings, rulers and nobles – may suggest flexibility about institution, but not about the exercise of judgement.

[75] See Wolters, *Song*, and Bartholomew, *Reading Proverbs*.

[76] *DN*, 3.

[77] The meaning of *rôzᵉnîm* is unsure, but always refers to foreign officials (Fox, *Proverbs 1–9*, 273).

[78] Van Leeuwen, 'Proverbs', 92.

[79] *DN*, 20.

O'Donovan notes that we need to recover the ground lost to the idea of authority and of political activity as kingly.[80] O'Donovan leans heavily on the notion of the kingdom of God as it unfolds around Israel to achieve this recovery. It is worth noting that Proverbs indicates a parallel route to such recovery through the doctrine of creation. This is not to suggest that O'Donovan does not take creation seriously in his political theology. Indeed, his kingdom approach resists historicism in that it 'works within the covenant that is established through creation'.[81] Nevertheless, *covenant* plays a marginal role in *DN*, and O'Donovan's pregnant phrase 'the covenant of creation' is never unpacked and explored for its political implications. O'Donovan develops his political theology not from Genesis 1, 12, 15 and 17, and Exodus 19, but primarily from the story of Israel. His theology of politics develops through an analogy between the kingdom of God in Israel and political rule.

If I am right about Proverbs 1:7, and if there is a closer link between wisdom and narrative in the OT than is generally assumed, then there may be more of kingdom theology in Proverbs and its view of government than most expect. However, even if this is true, it does seem to me that Proverbs makes the link between God and government through the doctrine of creation rather than through the kingdom of God. Political rule, we might say, is according to Proverbs a specific way in which the wisdom of God is imaged in his creation. Wisdom in Proverbs implies a myriad of ways of such imaging, but politics is specifically mentioned here in Proverbs 8 as a major example.

And here, it seems to me, is where covenant and Genesis 1 may be significant. I think O'Donovan is right to refer to the 'covenant of creation'. No one, in my opinion, has better defended this view exegetically than Dumbrell in his *Covenant and Creation*. Dumbrell argues that Genesis 1 is *the* covenantal text, and that the other biblical covenants are subsets of the creation covenant. Two points flow from this.[82]

The first is that in the doctrine of the *imago dei* in Genesis 1, we already have a political analogy between God as king and humankind. Covenant is a highly political concept with its background in kingship and treaties, and Genesis 1 is full of royal imagery presenting God as the great king.[83] The term *ṣelem* (= image) is a potent metaphor which is brought into relation with Elohim and

---

[80] *DN*, 19.

[81] *DN*, 19.

[82] John Stek, in '"Covenant" Overload', argues that it would be better to think of the kingdom of God as the overarching theme of the OT. I have argued against this. See Bartholomew, 'Covenant'. In fact, Stek's view makes clearer my point about O'Donovan here, namely that a discussion of the kingdom of God should begin in Gen. 1 and not with Israel's confession of Yahweh as king.

[83] On this see Stek's fine chapter, 'What Says the Scriptures?'

humankind in Genesis 1 as a way of 'explaining' humankind. It is a mistake to tie such a metaphor down to one precise meaning. Its very metaphorical richness means that different readings, such as humankind as a speech creature, humankind as relational, and humankind as called to exercise royal stewardship or dominion, may be complementary aspects of 'image' rather than alternative, contradictory definitions. However, in the context of Genesis 1:26–28, 'image' clearly refers to human reign over the creation that images Elohim's reign. This means that the analogy between Yahweh's reign and human activity relates to the whole gamut of human 'being', and not just to politics. And the challenge this presents to O'Donovan's political theology, I think, is to articulate how the political analogy of Yahweh's kingship for politics relates to the significance of this analogy for other areas of life such as economics, family life, and so on. O'Donovan finds the image of kingdom a fertile *political* analogy; Genesis appears to find *rule* an appropriate image for all of human life. How do these relate to each other?

Secondly, there is the question of *wisdom and history*. A big issue in wisdom studies is the relationship between wisdom and historical literature in the Old Testament.[84] How does wisdom relate to story and Torah? For the ancients, O'Donovan notes, wisdom was the view that every novelty manifested in some way the permanent creation order so that however new it was, it was not totally incommensurable with what preceded and could therefore be understood.[85] Some have suggested that Israel did not have the same sense as Greek thinking of stability set against change and history, but O'Donovan disagrees:

> The re-presentation of wisdom as law declares, in fact, the central point of Israel's faith, which is the meeting of life-in-the-world with life-before-God. ... On the one hand, the understanding of the world-order, so necessary for the life in the world, was known to be the personal and gracious gift of the God who had chosen Israel for himself. On the other, the burning fire of election, that transcendent storm which swept through history as the Lord revealed himself, intended nothing other than the blessing of life upon the earth. Wisdom, with its cool observational detachment and its inherent restriction to the educated, was made available to all in the form of law, and was co-ordinated in the covenant with the summons to worship and rejoice.... In *torah* the moral authority of created order and the transcendent authority of the electing God were made one. That was the source of Israel's security, the watch-tower from which her prophets could comprehend the events of the ancient Near East, always threatening dissolution and meaninglessness, and make of them a song of praise and thanksgiving.[86]

[84] See Goldingay, *Diversity*, ch. 7, for a useful discussion.

[85] *RMO*, 189.

[86] *RMO*, 189–90.

O'Donovan's overall position is exactly right, in my opinion. Canonically, wisdom and story/law complement each other. In OT studies, the relationship between wisdom and law is much debated.[87] In Proverbs 28 and 29, there is a close association of wisdom, government and Torah. Torah here is both the law of Moses and the teaching of the wise.[88] In these chapters, wisdom and law fit comfortably and easily together. It may be that covenant, with its foundation in creation *and* its strong sense of historical development, provides a biblical link between order and history.

An intriguing question is whether a stronger rooting of government in creation/covenant affects political theology in any major way. It does not affect the possibility of critique of rulers – Proverbs combines an affirmation of kingly rule with some devastating critiques of misdirected authority.[89] What it *may* do is contribute to the Aquinas versus Reformed debate about whether politics is a result of the fall or part of God's original intention with creation. OT wisdom links government strongly to creation. Clements, for example, says that for wisdom, 'the holding of political office and the wielding of political power were understood as part of the grand design of the universe'.[90] Clements relates this to the needs of Israel in the exilic and postexilic era, in which more of an international perspective was required. Proverbs' rooting of government in creation may provide support for a Thomist perspective, but clearly this is only a small part of the biblical data of which political theology needs to take account.

Underlying this question of the relationship between wisdom and story/law is the question of *time and history*. Wisdom is sometimes considered static and universal, whereas story is considered to be particular and dynamic. Theologically, this raises the question of how creation order relates to history. At our consultation, the view of history underlying O'Donovan's political theology caused some debate, with the suggestion made that O'Donovan may have succumbed to a partial historicism by failing to root his theology of history in creation order.[91] This issue surfaces more strongly in O'Donovan's recent response to Wolterstorff when he says that,

> politics belongs within the category of history, not of nature. Families and schools arise from natural structures of relating, created, fallen and redeemed. But political

[87] On this issue, see, e.g., Blenkinsopp, *Wisdom*.

[88] Van Leeuwen, 'Proverbs', 246.

[89] See 16:12; 28:3, 15, 16; 29:2, 7, 12, 16; 31:1–9, etc. Note, too, Prov. 8:16b – 'all who govern rightly'. If the NRSV translation is right, which I think it is, then this verse already distinguishes appropriate government from misdirected government, and associates wisdom only with the former!

[90] Clements, *Wisdom*, 96.

[91] A similar criticism could be made of Knierim. See above.

> order is a *providential* ordering, not a created one, and so it has become diaphanous to the redeeming work of God, taking on new forms in the light of the Christ-event.[92]

We do need to be cautious in suggesting that Old Testament wisdom might illuminate this issue. The OT wisdom books say little about Israel's history, and the extent to which they complement the historical books of the OT remains controversial. However, we have already suggested in this chapter that wisdom is more complementary to story than is generally admitted. A key chapter of the Old Testament in terms of creation order and history is Genesis 1. The genre of this chapter is much debated, but its content clearly connects with wisdom's interests. Importantly for our discussion, Genesis 1 understands history to be part of creation order. Jenson overstates this I think, but his articulation of the doctrine of creation nevertheless gets at the importance of including history firmly within creation:

> the world God creates is not a thing, a 'cosmos', but it is rather a history. God does not create a world that thereupon has a history; he creates a history that is a world, in that it is purposive and so makes a whole. The great turnings in God's history with his creation, at the call of Abraham, the Exodus, the Crucifixion and Resurrection and the final Judgement, are not events within a creation that is as such ahistorical; they are events of the history that is created. Even the biblical account of the absolute beginning is itself a narrative; the six days of Genesis do not recount first an absolute beginning on the first day and then what happens to the creation on subsequent days; the whole story of one week tells the one absolute beginning. ... The loss of this insight is the great historical calamity of the doctrine of creation. ... Perhaps the key diagnostic question is whether redemption is understood to fulfil creation or merely to restore it; theology has too much tended to the latter.[93]

Jenson's reference to the great events of salvation history alerts us again to the extent to which Old Testament wisdom really does complement Old Testament story. We cannot engage that debate again here. Suffice it to note, however, that in the ancient Near East and in Israel, as Schmid points out, creation order *always* includes culture and politics. This in itself gives a certain dynamic to creation order and certainly resists seeing politics as not part of created order.

A place in Old Testament Wisdom literature where there is a sustained reflection on time is, of course, Ecclesiastes 3. This poem has provoked much discussion, and how one interprets it is closely related to how one reads the book of Ecclesiastes as a whole. Clements rightly notes the concern in the poem with how humans relate to and experience time.[94] In a lengthy excursus on time in

---

[92] O'Donovan, 'Deliberation', 137.

[93] Jenson, *Systematic Theology*, II, 14, 15.

[94] Clements, *Wisdom*, 50–51.

Ecclesiastes, Fox rightly argues that in Ecclesiastes 3, 'the fact that there is a "time for war" does not mean that God predestined the Congressional declaration of war against Japan on December 8, 1941. Rather, there are conditions right for war, situations when war is called for and can be effectively prosecuted.'[95] Of course, in Ecclesiastes 3 the *hebel* from this is that on the basis of experience and reason alone humans cannot know this time.[96] But if I am right in thinking that this is not Ecclesiastes' last word on the subject, but that starting with 'remembering one's creator' Ecclesiastes suggests that one can make considerable progress towards discerning the time for war and the time for peace, then we arrive once again at a place similar to that occupied by O'Donovan.

Conclusion

In his work O'Donovan invites us to a sumptuous feast at which theology and biblical exegesis are fully present in their own right. In this chapter we have suggested that O'Donovan might do well to serve up more dishes of Wisdom literature in the smorgasbord of delights at his feast. In Old Testament Wisdom literature O'Donovan has an ally, but it is one of which he has taken little note thus far. We have also suggested that wisdom's doctrine of creation order may raise some critical questions about O'Donovan's theology of history. Long may this feast continue!

Bibliography

Anderson, B.W. (ed.), *Creation in the Old Testament* (London: SPCK; Philadelphia: Fortress Press, 1984)

Barr, J., *Biblical Faith and Natural Theology* (Oxford: Clarendon Press, 1993)

Bartholomew, C.G., 'Covenant and Creation: Covenant Overload or Covenantal Deconstruction', *CTJ* 30.1 (1995), 11–33

——, *Reading Ecclesiastes: Old Testament Exegesis and Hermeneutical Theory* (AnBib 139; Rome: Pontifical Biblical Institute, 1998)

——, 'Qoheleth in the Canon?! Current Trends in the Interpretation of Ecclesiastes', *Them* 24.3 (May 1999), 4–20

——, *Reading Proverbs with Integrity* (Cambridge: Grove, 2001)

Blenkinsopp, J., *Wisdom and Law in the Old Testament: The Ordering of Life in Israel and Early Judaism* (Oxford: OUP, 1995)

Brown, W.P., *Character in Crisis: A Fresh Approach to the Wisdom Literature of the Old Testament* (Grand Rapids: Eerdmans, 1996)

[95] Fox, *Time*, 198.

[96] See my comments above about epistemology and Ecclesiastes.

——, *The Ethos of the Cosmos: The Genesis of Moral Imagination in the Bible* (Grand Rapids: Eerdmans, 1999)

Brueggemann, W., 'Trajectories in Old Testament Literature and the Sociology of Ancient Israel', *JBL* 98 (1979), 161–85

——, 'Response to J. Richard Middleton', *HTR* 87.3 (1994), 279–89

Camp, C.V., 'Woman Wisdom as Root Metaphor: A Theological Consideration', in *The Listening Heart* (ed. K.G. Hoglund, et al.; JSOTSup 58; Sheffield: JSOT Press, 1987)

Clements, R.E., *Wisdom in Theology* (Carlisle: Paternoster; Grand Rapids: Eerdmans, 1992)

Clifford, R.J., *Proverbs* (Louisville, KY: Westminster/John Knox Press, 1999)

Collins, J.J., 'The Biblical Precedent for Natural Theology', *JAAR* 45.1, Supplement (Mar. 1977), B: 35–67

Crenshaw, J.L., *Education in Ancient Israel: Across the Deadening Silence* (New York: Doubleday, 1998)

——, 'Qoheleth's Understanding of Intellectual Inquiry', in Schoors (ed.), *Qohelet in the Context of Wisdom*, 205–24

Day, J., R.P. Gordon and H.G.M. Williamson (eds.), *Wisdom in Ancient Israel: Essays in Honour of J.A. Emerton* (Cambridge: CUP, 1995)

Fox, M.V., 'Qoheleth's Epistemology', *HUCA* 58 (1987), 137–55

——, *Qoheleth and His Contradictions* (JSOTSup 71; Sheffield: Almond Press, 1989)

——, *A Time to Tear Down and a Time to Build: A Rereading of Ecclesiastes* (Grand Rapids: Eerdmans, 1999)

——, *Proverbs 1–9* (AB; New York: Doubleday, 2000)

Gladson, J.A., *Retributive Paradoxes in Proverbs 10–29* (Ann Arbor, MI: University Microfilms International, 1979)

Goldingay, J., *Theological Diversity and the Authority of the Old Testament* (Grand Rapids: Eerdmans, 1987)

Habel, N.C., 'The Symbolism of Wisdom in Proverbs 19', *Int* 26 (1972), 131–57

Jenson, R.W., *Systematic Theology*, II: *The Works of God* (Oxford: OUP, 1999)

Knierim, R.P., *The Task of Old Testament Theology: Method and Cases* (Grand Rapids: Eerdmans, 1995)

LaCoque, A., and P. Ricœur, *Thinking Biblically: Exegetical and Hermeneutical Studies* (Chicago and London: University of Chicago Press, 1998)

Levenson, J., *Creation and the Persistence of Evil: The Jewish Drama of Divine Omnipotence* (San Francisco: Harper & Row, 1988)

L'Hour, J., 'Yahweh Elohim', *RB* 81 (1974), 524–56

Longman, T., *The Book of Ecclesiastes* (NICOT; Grand Rapids: Eerdmans, 1998)

McKane, W., *Proverbs* (London: SCM Press, 1970)

Middleton, J.R., 'Is Creation Theology Inherently Conservative? A Dialogue with Walter Brueggemann', *HTR* 87.3 (1994), 257–77

Murphy, R.E., *The Tree of Life: An Exploration of Biblical Wisdom Literature* (Grand Rapids: Eerdmans, 2nd edn, 1996)

——, *Proverbs* (WBC 22; Nashville: Thomas Nelson, 1998)

Newbigin, L., *The Gospel in a Pluralist Society* (Grand Rapids: Eerdmans, 1989)

O'Donovan, O., *Resurrection and Moral Order: An Outline for Evangelical Ethics* (Leicester: IVP; Grand Rapids: Eerdmans, 2nd edn, 1994)

——, *The Desire of the Nations: Rediscovering the Roots of Political Theology* (Cambridge: CUP, 1996)

——, 'Deliberation, History and Reading: A Response to Schweiker and Wolterstorff', *SJT* 54.1 (2001), 127–44

Perdue, L.G., *Wisdom and Creation: The Theology of Wisdom Literature* (Nashville: Abingdon Press, 1994)

Provan, I., *Ecclesiastes* (Grand Rapids: Zondervan, 2001)

Rad, G. von, 'The Theological Problem of the Old Testament Doctrine of Creation', in B.W. Anderson (ed.), *Creation in the Old Testament*, 53–64

——, *Wisdom in Israel* (London: SCM Press, 1972)

Schmid, H.H., 'Creation, Righteousness, and Salvation: "Creation Theology" as the Broad Horizon of Biblical Theology', in B.W. Anderson (ed.), *Creation in the Old Testament*, 102–17

Schoors, A. (ed.), *Qohelet in the Context of Wisdom* (Leuven: Leuven University Press, 1998)

Scobie, S., 'The Structure of Biblical Authority', *TynBul* 42.2 (1991), 163–94

Stek, J., 'What Says the Scriptures?', in *Portraits of Creation: Biblical and Scientific Perspectives on the World's Formation* (ed. H.J. van Til; Grand Rapids: Eerdmans, 1990), 203–65

——, '"Covenant" Overload in Reformed Theology', *CTJ* 29 (1994), 12–41

Trigo, P., *Creation and History* (Kent, UK: Burns & Oates, 1991)

Van Leeuwen, R., 'Wealth and Poverty: System and Contradiction in Proverbs', *Hebrew Studies* 33 (1992), 25–36

——, 'Proverbs', in *The New Interpreters Bible*, V (Nashville: Abingdon Press, 1997), 19–264

——, 'Liminality and Worldview in Proverbs 1–9', *Semeia* 50 (1990), 111–44

Weeks, S., *Early Israelite Wisdom* (Oxford: OUP, 1994)

Westermann, C., *Creation* (Philadelphia: Fortress Press, 1974)

Whybray, R.N., 'Yahweh-Sayings and Their Context in Proverbs 10:1–22:16', in *La Sagesse de l'Ancien Testament* (ed. M. Gilbert; BETL 51; Leuven: Leuven University Press, 1979), 153–65

Wolters, A., *The Song of the Valiant Woman: Studies in the Interpretation of Proverbs 31:10–31* (Carlisle: Paternoster, 2001)

Zimmerli, W., 'The Place and Limit of Wisdom in the Framework of Old Testament Theology', *SJT* 17 (1964), 146–58

6

Response to Craig Bartholomew

Oliver O'Donovan

'Three things are too wonderful for me, four I do not understand: the way of an eagle in the sky, the way of a serpent on a rock, the way of a ship on the high seas, and the way of a man with a maiden' (Prov. 30:18f.). Wonder and incomprehension are not the first aspect of Wisdom that is usually spoken of; yet they are, it seems to me, fundamental to the wisdom project. The estimate of wisdom-epistemology as 'empirical' seems to me, as to Craig Bartholomew, to leave a great deal too much unsaid. And where Bartholomew points us to wisdom as a quest of fear of the Lord, we can reply that fear of the Lord begins in uncomprehending wonder.

The particular cause for wonder in this case, the common factor that is shared among the different phenomena that catch the proverbialist's eye, is *tracklessness*. Without map, road-mark or concrete guidance, the bird finds its way to the nest, the serpent to the hole, the helmsman to harbour, and the man to his sweetheart. They display an ordered sense of direction, but precisely how that sense of direction is given them does not meet the eye. And it is with what does *not* meet the eye that wisdom has its business.

Wisdom, then, is not merely about creation order, in the abstract. It is about the *disclosure* of creation order to the enquiring, believing and patient observer. It is about a painful process of making plain, which has, in its own terms, the character of a journey and a discovery. We cannot quite speak of a 'history', since the journey remains for the most part at the level of the individual enquirer, symbolically represented as the young man venturing upon life, the object of solicitous parental counsel. But the dialectical structure of ordered reality and temporal discovery is present in wisdom conceived as an existential task. This is what allows in wisdom the same dialectic between ultimate decision and detailed discernment which I attributed in *Resurrection and Moral Order* to eschatology, although, as Bartholomew shrewdly points out, eschatology is absent from wisdom. What there is, however, is a kind of personal eschatology represented by the twin possibilities of disaster for the foolish and success for the wise.

There is also in wisdom the phenomenon of objective disorder, the surd in the appearance of the ordered universe. 'Under three things the earth trembles; under four it cannot bear up: a slave when he becomes king, and a fool when he is filled with food; an unloved woman when she gets a husband, and a maid when she succeeds her mistress' (30:21–23). How such earth-shaking nonsense can ever be resolved is left unclear in such a text as Proverbs, which remains poised at the point of wonder. But as the legacy of wisdom is turned towards theodicy in texts such as Psalm 73, the patience of the wise enquirer corresponds to a willingness of events to disclose a longer meaning, a disclosure of God's goodness in the immanent shape of history.

Creation cannot be thought as existing apart from history; it exists *with* history and *under* history, in a dialectic that allows neither order nor event to disappear into the other. I cannot follow Craig Bartholomew in his endorsement of Robert Jenson's saying that 'the world God creates is not a thing ... but ... a history. God does not create a world that thereupon *has* a history; he creates a history that is a world, in that it is purposive.' I do not see how that can be excused from conflating moral and historical teleology, 'the good' and 'the future', precisely as in *Resurrection* I complained that the (younger) Pannenberg did. (The older Pannenberg of *Grundlagen der Ethik* makes full amends.)

We do not need Jenson's historicist move at this point to be delivered from the *impasse* in which Paul Ricœur finds himself, of not knowing how to relate justice and creation order. The problematic of Ricœur, that justice is not simply *given* in creation order, seems to me to be an entirely biblical one. But the discovery of justice in history is, in an important way, a *re*-discovery of creation order, too. The decisive text for me at this point is the diptych of visions in Revelation 4 and 5, in which the intelligibility of creation is impugned by the sealed scroll of history, but vindicated by the disclosure of history through the Lamb that was slain.

How, then, do we accommodate political order to this dialectic of creation and history? This question may be put in a more *alttestamentliche* form as: 'What are we to make of cosmic kingship?' Learning again from the proverbialist's sharp eye: 'Three things are stately in their tread; four are stately in their stride: the lion which is mightiest among the beasts and does not turn back before any; the strutting cock, the he-goat, and a king striding before his people' (30:29–31). That appears to situate political leadership pretty decisively in the created order, but the observation is not, in the end, quite unambiguous. For he has also commented: 'Four things on earth are small, but they are exceedingly wise: the ants are a people not strong, yet they provide their food in the summer; the badgers are a people not mighty, yet they make their homes in the rocks; the locusts have no king, yet all of them march in rank; the lizard you can take in your hands, yet it is in kings' palaces' (30:24–28). There is a paradigm in nature, too, for the spontaneous sociality of creatures, an ability to organize and fend for themselves without the pretentiousness of rule; and set beside such models, are we not invited to think that the strutting cock and the king striding before his people have a touch of the ridiculous about them? In the lizard who creeps into kings' palaces we have an ironic metaphor for the role of wisdom itself, unpretentious but infinitely versatile. The reptilian wise man who finds his way across the trackless rock will insinuate himself into the pretentiousness of power and make it possible to do something to the point. '*By me* kings reign.' Standing at the king's right hand is the advisor, the one who knows the world outside the palace, the link between the king and the cosmos.

My formal answer to the question is this: Political authority or kingly rule, including God's own, belongs to the category of *act*. It is something that is done, not something that simply is. The question about the political act, as about every act, is whether it is well, or wisely, done. A universe of pure regularity without the risks of history and freedom would be a universe without space for human action and so without space for kingly rule. That is why the mechanistic Natural Theology of the seventeenth century led inexorably to Deism, which is belief in God without belief in the kingdom of God.

This leaves me with a version of the *felix culpa* motif. Some variants of this say that the fall was happy because it made Mary queen: 'Blessed be the day that apple taken was ...' My own, more daringly, says that it made God King. But the appearance of blasphemy is merely a trick of perspective. There never was a time when God was not king, because there never was a time when God did not foredestine a universe of freedom and action. When we are presented in Scripture with visions of creation surmounted by the throne of God (and I gladly take the point that this is implicitly the case in Genesis 1, too, with its culmination in man as the royal 'image' of God), we see creation order *from the context* of history. In viewing creation we see what underlies the history through which we move; in viewing God as seated in creation's throne, we see the implications for creation of what has been shown us of God's rule in history.

7

The Power of the Future in the Present: Eschatology and Ethics in O'Donovan and Beyond

M. Daniel Carroll R.

Introduction

One of Oliver O'Donovan's many contributions to the enterprise of elaborating an evangelical ethics is the inclusion of the eschatological dimension in his presentation of what should define a Christian perspective on the moral life. Any discussion of the 'eschatological', of course, can incorporate a variety of components, even as it does in O'Donovan's construal. It is my hope that the synopsis of O'Donovan's position and the subsequent comments on how this perspective might be further enriched will do justice to the intricate and multilayered nature of his argument.

This essay is divided into four parts. My own interest has been in Old Testament social ethics, and it might be helpful to first observe how several scholars in the field of Old Testament social ethics have incorporated eschatological matters into their own ethical constructs before turning to O'Donovan's views.[1] This brief survey will be instrumental in bringing to the surface some of the issues that will be pertinent to our own concerns. The second section will provide the summary of O'Donovan's position. The third part will then shift attention to theological reflections from Latin America, where the topic of eschatology has assumed important ethical relevance. Some of the burdens from that context underscore some of the questions we would put to O'Donovan's presentation; in other words, eschatology matters in very real

[1] An example of a recent volume on New Testament ethics is Hays, *The Moral Vision of the New Testament*. One of the three major elements of his study is eschatology – the new creation. Not only does Hays dedicate a separate section to an exposition of Revelation (169–85), he also incorporates that perspective into the examination of each of his five 'test cases' (Part IV, 313–461).

ways. The fourth and final major section of this essay offers a synchronic reading of two Old Testament prophetic books (Isaiah and Amos) in order to provide biblical examples of the role of eschatology in the ethics of the people of God.

Old Testament Ethics and Eschatology

On the one hand, the focus on the eschatological can serve as a welcome complement to those presentations of Old Testament ethics that grant but a minor role to the future. For example, Walter Kaiser's *Toward Old Testament Ethics* mentions eschatology only in passing, in a brief reference to eternal rewards (or punishment) for an individual's actions.[2] The primary concern of his volume is to highlight the theme of holiness, which he considers the fundamental virtue of Old Testament ethics, and to elaborate lasting principles for today from an exegesis of the Pentateuch. John Barton also speaks of the future, although more extensively than does Kaiser, as a motivation for moral behavior. In contradistinction to Kaiser's treatment, Barton's discussion goes beyond the individual to encompass the community and considers passages dealing with material prosperity (or natural disasters) within this life rather than in the one to come.[3] Neither Kaiser nor Barton deals with the 'eschatological' within the Old Testament in the sense of the irruption into human history of the reign of God in the more distant future.

Several other recent, substantial monographs on Old Testament ethics also give the eschatological dimension little attention. Eckart Otto's detailed work concentrates on the legal codes and tries to reconstruct the historical development of Israel's ethical thought. His discussion of the prophets is brief and deals primarily with the announcement of judgment.[4] For his part, Gordon Wenham concentrates on the narrative material of the Old Testament and, through careful readings of many texts, probes how these 'tales' communicate

---

[2] Kaiser, *Toward*, 10–11. As an aside, it is interesting to note that Kaiser cites two early articles by O'Donovan to establish the theoretical basis of his ethics. He appeals extensively to O'Donovan ('The Possibility') in a section entitled 'The Possibility of Old Testament Ethics' (*Toward*, 24–48) and in his discussion of the threefold use of the Law (ibid., 44–50; O'Donovan, 'Towards an Interpretation').

[3] Barton, *Ethics*, 82–90. Kaiser will allude to this aspect as well, but under 'eudaemonism' within an apologetic section entitled 'The Morally Offensive Precepts and Sanctions in the Law of God' (*Toward*, 301–4).

[4] Otto, *Theologische Ethik*, 104–11. In light of our commitment to the relevance of Old Testament ethics, it should be mentioned that Otto is reticent to move from the descriptive task of presenting the ethical thought of ancient Israel to suggestions for modern prescription and application.

moral ideals through literary structure, characters, scenes and language. He does offer a brief consideration of the vision of an age of peace, but this is imbedded within a broader discussion of the relationship between the ethics of the Old and New Testaments. He says in passing that this 'golden age' has been inaugurated with the coming of Jesus.[5] Cyril Rodd expounds a more negative agenda, which is encapsulated very well in the title of his work: *Glimpses of a Strange Land*. In his opinion, the modern reader must recognize the impressive – and unbridgeable – gap that exists between modern views of ethics (both in method and content) and the perspectives of ancient Israel transmitted through the Hebrew Bible. Through that text we are given simply bits and pieces of a way of life and thinking very different from our own. Today the notion of an eschatological age brought through the sovereign hand of God would be dismissed as anachronistic.[6]

On the other hand, some scholars do give the more global aspects of eschatology – such as the renewal of creation, the predicted exaltation of Israel and the conversion of the nations – a more prominent place within their Old Testament ethics. Janzen mentions the hope of a future beyond the exile within the prophetic literature and explains how the prophets communicated the contours of an 'interim' ethic for the intervening time before the restoration.[7] In his exposition of Jeremiah 29, Ezekiel 18 and sections of Isaiah 40–66, Janzen argues that the prophets pointed back to the 'familial' paradigm (of life, land and hospitality) that was evident from the beginning of Israel's existence. When Janzen coordinates this proposal with his understanding of the contribution of the New Testament, the hoped-for eschatological fulfillment of the Old Testament appears to be reinterpreted (even reduced) as fulfilled in the assurance of salvation and heaven for the individual believer.[8]

Birch also relates the prophetic descriptions of a more glorious time beyond the impending judgment to the moral life of Israel.[9] In his view, the words foretelling its restoration would have served as an indictment of the nation's actual socio-political context, while at the same time they would have

---

[5] Wenham, *Story*, 146–49.

[6] Note this closing comment in a section on the ethics of the prophets: 'They hold that Yahweh will intervene personally with direct action, and this we no longer believe' (Rodd, *Glimpses*, 296). He does on occasion allude to the hope of a future different from what ancient Israel experienced (e.g., in regards to war, animals and nature, *Glimpses*, 185–249). But he mentions this fact only in passing – not to explore its ethical relevance (then and now), but rather to underscore in detail how the modern reader would not agree with the text's point of view.

[7] Janzen, *Old Testament*, 166–73.

[8] Ibid., 200–9. Janzen is not unaware that this is the impression his view can suggest.

[9] Birch, *Justice*, 269–74, 300–2, 311–13.

empowered the faithful to both embody and work for the realization of the ideals pictured there. Birch believes that these prophetic oracles of salvation are relevant for the Christian church today, as they form part of the moral vision that the people of God now should claim as their own.

Christopher Wright incorporates the far future within his scheme of a God-Israel-the Land triangle.[10] He develops this relationship throughout the Bible in (to use his terminology) 'paradigmatic' (God-Humanity-the Earth), 'typlogical' (God-the Church-*koinonia*) and 'eschatological' (God-Redeemed Humanity-the New Creation) fashion. He illustrates this triple pattern in an examination of the Jubilee legislation of Leviticus 25. For Wright, the Old Testament hope can serve as a guide for evaluating modern social structures, for suggesting concrete ethical action and legislative initiatives, and for imagining an alternative world of human existence.

This cursory overview demonstrates that, within studies on Old Testament ethics, there is a spectrum of opinions as to what 'eschatology' might refer and as to how (or if) it might be useful to Christians.[11] This is evidence of the importance of O'Donovan's concentration on eschatology for theological and biblical ethics. Although any number of issues of definition and application are readily apparent, we will deal with only two related areas. These will be the focus of the dialogue with O'Donovan in this essay. First, if, as Christians, we believe that the kingdom of God has come already in the person and work of Jesus Christ at his first advent (the 'already'), then what is the essence of the 'not yet' aspect of our eschatological hope? In other words, what is *the nature of the hope*: Is it an expectation of the final judgment and triumph of the righteous, or does it also entail a transformation of human existence as we now know it? If the latter, what would that look like? Will there be a degree of continuity between that final disclosure of the eschaton and today? If so, is it possible to speak of mediations of that future within the present? A second

[10] Wright, *Walking*, 13–45. This chapter ('The Use of the Bible in Social Ethics') originally appeared as an article in *Transformation* 1.1 (1984), 11–20.

[11] Differences regarding what the term 'eschatology' refers to have also characterized Old Testament studies in general. Debate tends to revolve around three issues: 1) What does 'eschatology' mean? Does it describe a this-worldly hope at the end of history (i.e., in continuity with present reality) or a developed doctrine of events beyond history, more within the realm of apocalyptic than the prophetic (i.e., with an emphasis on discontinuity)? 2) Where did Old Testament eschatology originate? Was it borrowed from other cultures, or was it a natural feature or outgrowth of Israel's own faith? 3) When did eschatology, however understood, make its appearance within the faith of Israel? Does it find its roots early in Israel's history, or was it a late development? If late, are the 'hope' passages then to be classified as exilic or even postexilic redactional additions? For a collection of essays on these sorts of topics by a wide variety of scholars, see Preuss, *Eschatologie*.

issue follows on this set of questions: What might be *the possible impact* of this eschatological vision on the moral life of the church?[12] We now turn to the work of O'Donovan and will attempt to understand his appreciation of the eschatological within Christian ethics.

Eschatology in the Ethics of O'Donovan

We begin this section by offering a general outline of O'Donovan's utilization of eschatology by looking in turn at *Resurrection and Moral Order* and *The Desire of the Nations*. This summary will function as a backdrop for a narrower focus on the two issues mentioned at the close of the previous section, which in our view deserve greater attention: the nature of the eschatological hope, and the possible impact of that hope on the people of God.

In *RMO*, O'Donovan proposes that a proper appreciation of the creation is foundational for Christian ethics. It provides the objective grounding for human moral order and the appropriate *telos*, or natural purpose designed by God, for every created thing.[13] With the resurrection of Jesus Christ from the dead this created order, although fallen, is vindicated.[14] The resurrection marks the dawning of the eschaton, the kingdom of God, and signals several profound realities. Creation is redeemed from sin, life is affirmed, and humanity sees its true significance revealed – as rulers through the victorious and exalted Christ. Nevertheless, the kingdom is not present in all of its fullness. Thus, the resurrection both heralds a new beginning and points toward a more glorious future. It is a definitive moment that establishes a notion of history that is moving forward under the sure sovereignty of God to a final and complete manifestation of the renewed created order, when its transformation will be universalized.[15]

---

[12] This is the same sort of question Gowan asks at the end of his own reflections on the nature of the Old Testament hope: 'Two aspects of the ethical implications of eschatology may be identified and designated as the *object* and the *impetus*. By *object* is meant *what* eschatology says human beings can and should be doing in the world, and by *impetus* is meant *why* eschatology impels us to want to do something about the present world' (*Eschatology*, 125).

[13] *RMO*, 31–52, 58–67.

[14] The term 'vindication' is perhaps O'Donovan's favorite to describe what is accomplished by the eschaton. In some ways this choice is interesting, because it gives a certain 'legal' flavor to his understanding of eschatology that corresponds to his perspective on the nature and role of human government. (See below, n. 23.)

[15] *RMO*, 53–58. At this juncture, O'Donovan distinguishes this divinely oriented *telos* from what he labels a historicist perspective, which says that movement in history is based on a dynamic immanent within history itself.

Through the redemption realized in the resurrection, individual believers and the community which is the church are now authorized as moral agents and are empowered by the Spirit; they are free to act in obedience and according to their true *telos*.[16] Here, too, there is an anticipatory and provisional character to life today in light of the future. Knowledge can only be partial, and compromise – properly understood – is unavoidable;[17] the church witnesses as well to the fullness of the kingdom and to the final judgment in its inner order and in its ecclesiastical rulings.[18] Lastly, that end of history, guaranteed even now by the resurrection, is the assurance of eventual comprehensive justice on behalf of the innocent and of a final resolution to the problem of evil.[19] The eschaton is partially realized in this present time (which he describes as the overlapping of the two eons) but will culminate in the future with the total vindication of the created order.

O'Donovan expands on some of these same points in *DN*, but his purpose there is to articulate a political theology. Accordingly, he links his view of history with a theological exploration of the nature of politics based on the rule of God.[20] This goal leads O'Donovan to see how the divine purposes were worked out in the laws, institutions and worship of Old Testament Israel. This part of his study is designed to instruct us concerning some basic elements of God's authority and its relationship to human government.[21] O'Donovan goes on to explain that God's rule, demonstrated in the history of Israel and the nations, was present and disclosed in new and powerful ways in the ministry, passion, resurrection and ascension of Jesus.[22]

The bulk of the rest of this volume examines how the initial triumph of the eschaton, the rule of God confirmed in such a unique way at the resurrection and exaltation, is to be realized within the church and through its mission in societies and under rulers that are subject to Christ and now serve him for a time with a circumscribed authority.[23] This theoretical foundation leads to further reflection on the nature of the church as a political community with a singular identity and to an investigation of Christendom as a fruitful (theological and historical) model

---

16 *RMO*, 101–20, 163–78.

17 *RMO*, 76–97.

18 *RMO*, 169–76.

19 *RMO*, 74–75, 82–85.

20 *DN*, 19–20.

21 *DN*, 30–81.

22 *DN*, 88–119, 133–46

23 O'Donovan dedicates much of his discussion to the judicial basis and responsibility of human government vis-à-vis the law of God. It is not surprising that he devotes so much space to Augustine and to the Christendom model. Cf. O'Donovan's 'Augustine's *City*' and 'Government'.

that might inform Christian thinking about politics in the modern (post-Christendom) world.

The victory of Christ over all principalities reconfigures the role of secular authorities. They are to serve the church's mission by guarding a social context for its existence through proper governance, and they are also to be the instrument of God's wrath in this period before the end (Rom. 13:1–7; 1 Pet. 2:13–17). The church is to respect this appointed function, while at the same time recognizing that the judgments within the community of Christ are to be resolved by a different set of criteria in light of the cross and the future judgment of God upon all humanity (1 Cor. 6ff.; Rom. 8:33–34). Secular legal pronouncements, therefore, are only 'provisional and penultimate judgments' within the present divine economy. This eschatological perspective yields a new view of the rights of Christians within the world's system: they are not to be defended, as no government can offer a conclusive word of vindication.[24]

The other side, so to speak, of the new view of secular powers emerging out of the eschatological triumph of Christ comes from the descriptions of demonic human empires found in biblical apocalypticism in general and in the book of Revelation in particular.[25] In Revelation, John presents a vivid unmasking of the idolatrous nature of dominating states and a vision of the vindication of the church. This cosmic justification of the saints is anchored in the victory already achieved by the Lamb, but before the final judgment the life of the church is marked by persecution and even martyrdom. The antichrist and this diabolical type of government mimic in perverse ways the kingdom of God and his Christ, but in the end the evil city that is Babylon is claimed and utterly transformed by God. O'Donovan treats suffering in at least two other places. The topic reappears within his discussion of the sacraments, specifically the Eucharist.[26] There he posits that the suffering of Christians, like that of Jesus, is vicarious and can serve as a living testimony of the mission of the church to suffer for the sins of others. The celebration of the Eucharist remembers the suffering of Jesus and marks the church's identity as inexorably linked to that suffering. The problem of suffering also surfaces in O'Donovan's critique of liberal society.[27] This societal system has displaced the divine order for life with the championing of the individual and conceives of human society as a formal arrangement grounded in the voluntary consent and will of said individuals. Within this conceptual framework the notion of sacrificial or 'sympathetic' suffering loses its significance as something that coheres with the nature of existence, the pursuit of the common

---

[24] *DN*, 146–52; cf. 112f.

[25] *DN*, 153–57, 214–17; cf. 'Political Thought'.

[26] *DN*, 178–81.

[27] *DN*, 276–78.

good and the person of God himself. Instead, God – if even granted existence – is maligned as unfeeling and unfair.

In sum, O'Donovan presents a (partially) realized eschatology, which understands the kingdom of God as having come with the resurrection and exaltation of Christ. This sequence of events signals the vindication of the created order and anticipates its complete restoration, establishes the bases for the identity and mission of the church, and provides a fresh understanding of the nature and role of secular authorities and societies. This eschatological reality of the inauguration of the kingdom determines the provisional nature of human government and its limited judicial obligations and exposes the rebellious nature and cruelty of the nations as part of a cosmic struggle. This orientation is complemented throughout by the awareness that the future will bring yet a more comprehensive manifestation of the eschaton.

O'Donovan's utilization of eschatology for ethics is impressive, and one hopes that this has been a fair, albeit short, representation of his richly textured argument. Nevertheless, from our perspective from within Old Testament studies and our experience in Latin America,[28] we would suggest that O'Donovan's understanding of the eschaton could be deepened by more extensive consideration of the two aspects of eschatology that we highlighted in the first part of the essay. The first point is that *his eschatology offers no sustained exposition of the 'not yet' of eschatology*, and this lack has several implications for ethical reflection and practice. His primary (and very commendable) concern is to delineate the various facets and many implications of the 'already' – that is, of the resurrection and ascension of Christ. On occasion O'Donovan does allude to the coming eschatological consummation, but it is never described with concrete details. In *RMO* he mentions several times the transformation of the created order, but one is left wondering what that future will actually be like. On at least two occasions he talks of the 'new heavens and the new earth'[29] and the 'Holy City' of Revelation 21–22,[30] but the language of these few portrayals is limited to theological terminology – to the jargon of the text, as it were. This is where discussion surely must begin. The biblical text, through its very vivid and realistic metaphors and descriptions, does offer abundant and relevant material for reflection and ethical application. O'Donovan, however, does not mine this richness. Once again, the reader finds it hard to grasp any true tangibleness in his view of the eschaton.

This omission, quite obviously, is a contrast to what one finds in more systematic treatments of eschatology, which go to great lengths to sketch the outlines of the future state. Among other matters, these debates deal with

---

[28] The contribution of Latin America appears in the next section.

[29] *RMO*, 56.

[30] *DN*, 155–56.

whether the eschaton will involve a millennium as a prelude to the new heavens and new earth, or whether the judgment of God is to be followed immediately by the New Jerusalem.[31] Our purpose here is not to enter into what have sometimes been heated debates (especially within North American evangelicalism) over the precise nature of the eschaton. Rather, what is pertinent to our discussion is to recognize that theologians do venture some sort of description of that future state, and for many this picture has great ethical import. One can mention Jürgen Moltmann, who since his now classic work, *Theology of Hope*, has strived to establish the relevance of the future for the present. More recently, in *The Coming of God*, he champions what he calls 'eschatological millenarianism' as the only position that can give hope in a troubled world.[32] Others argue against a millennial age, but at the same time they do present a vision of the new heaven and new earth as a literal fulfillment of the Old Testament prophetic passages.[33] In both cases, in other words, there is a purposeful attention to detail for ethics in the present.

Some sort of notion of the shape of the future naturally leads to attempts to determine the degree of continuity between that future and the world today.[34] Discussions on the nature of the continuity (or its lack) revolve in large measure around its import for motivating ethical behavior. Recognition of some continuity can also bring the contemplation of mediations of the eschatological kingdom within the present order, both within and beyond the bounds of the Christian church. Continuity and mediation are related, but theoretically distinct, concepts. The former envisions the present extending forward into the future; the latter seeks the presence of the future reaching back, so to speak, into the present. O'Donovan is clear that the church manifests the rule of God in many ways and that secular authorities in an indirect manner are subject to the exalted Christ in their governance. Concerning the presence of the kingdom of God outside the church and this limited role of human authorities, however, one catches but brief glimpses. Examples of these rare statements include, 'Earthly events of liberation, rule and community-foundation provide

---

[31] In 'Political Thought' O'Donovan does state that he disagrees with the idea of 'a this-wordly millennium' (70).

[32] Moltmann, *Coming*, 192–202. For Moltmann's comments on the new heaven and new earth, see *Coming*, 308–19. Of course, there would be many evangelicals who would argue for the millennial position. For a thoughtful discussion of the relevance of the millennium, note, e.g., Berkhof, *Christ*, 122–93.

[33] E.g., Berkouwer, *Return*, 211–34, 291–322; Hoekema, *Bible*, 274–87; Bauckham, 'Christian Eschatology'.

[34] Each of the theologians mentioned in the previous paragraph does speak to this very issue. In addition to these theologians, note the discussion in Williams, 'Evangelicals'. Williams himself does not believe that continuity is that important an issue. He offers his own critique of O'Donovan's eschatology on pp. 301–4.

us with partial indications of what God is doing in human history',[35] and, 'It will include discerning the signs of promise which alert us to the appearance of Christ's future coming.'[36] But what exactly are these 'signs of the times', which Christians are to discern?[37] Of what do they consist?

These comments seek a more viable hope and move in a direction different than O'Donovan's eschatological emphasis. If, from our point of view, in *RMO* a prime issue of concern is the need for more substantial *content* for the eschatological hope, an additional shortcoming (that is, along with the 'content' problem) in *DN* is the absence of a more 'positive' *tone* in regards to the Christian hope. There, O'Donovan consistently underscores judgment as the focus of the future, especially in relation to human societies and governments. Judgment surely is a crucial component of biblical eschatology, and our observation in no way intends to dismiss or minimize the demonic character of secular authorities (an analysis of earthly powers with which we are in hearty agreement) or the necessity of the confrontation of human authorities with the true Lord. This is important and indispensable. There should be no movement into discussions of a new world, especially for those who are oppressed and marginalized, without an assurance of a final vindication of their humanity and a comprehensive righting of wrongs by a just God. Indeed, a suffering world groans for this – and any ethical construct must demand it. Yet, having said that, this can be considered as an initial phase of both those movements. That is, beyond vindication and justice is the offer of true life.

Our desire is to pursue a wider conceptualization, one that sees more clearly and consistently the glories after that judgment. Why limit the source of the 'gladness' of the church to the 'recovery of the created order' and the 'vindication of God's rule' gained through the resurrection, and to remembering acts of redemption accomplished in the past?[38] Should not this joy and its Sabbath rest also celebrate the coming triumphs of the end? The joy in this case, of course, would be of a different substance than what is motivated in remembering. It is the kind of joy found in the psalms of lament, for example, that looks forward to the deliverance of God in the future, even in the midst of trials. It is a joy that is nurtured in perseverance and in the settled convictions of faith in a supremely sovereign and gracious God, who will see history to its rightful end.

The topic of suffering, too, acquires a distinct nuance in light of this first issue of a more concrete view of the awaited eschaton. O'Donovan does well

---

[35] *DN*, 2.

[36] *DN*, 273.

[37] E.g., *DN*, 224, 267, 273.

[38] *DN*, 181–86. The discussion of gladness appears in a section O'Donovan labels 'moments of recapitulation'.

to incorporate the reality of the suffering of the saints within his paradigm. Yet, one hears almost nothing of general human suffering due to racism, ethnic cleansing, socio-political and economic oppression, hunger, war and disease. What does Christian eschatology have to say to the hundreds of thousands, perhaps millions, of wounded, widows and orphans of the wars in Bosnia, Guatemala, Rwanda, the Sudan and Afghanistan? Is there a future for the victims of the HIV/AIDS epidemic in Africa? Examples could be multiplied. O'Donovan appears to circumscribe his treatment of suffering essentially to that of believers, to those who remain true to their testimony and calling as Christians in the face of persecution and opposition. This concern is fundamental, of course. But suffering humanity is part of the created order that longs for the transformation of its existence into a different world not characterized by violence and want. Once again, one seeks to expand the horizon of his theological-ethical reflections. Could not, for example, the support of Jesus for the poor and love for the neighbor of which O'Donovan speaks so eloquently have eschatological dimensions as good news that moves beyond Jesus' earthly ministry and the present commitments of his church?[39]

Our first criticism, then, has been to single out the importance of a more extensive and explicit view of the eschaton. The second point, *the impact of the eschatological vision*, builds on the first. Here we will be brief. Mention has already been made of continuity and mediation. Continuity can function as a motivation for living a life commensurate with that hope and assures the Christian and the church that certain human accomplishments, those which would reflect the character and will of God, have lasting value. On the other hand, the discernment of a sign, or mediation, of the future eschatological kingdom of peace, justice and plenty should force believers and the church to consider very seriously if it is not indeed incumbent upon them to participate in its further realization in response and commitment to God's rule. In other words, a clearer comprehension of the 'goods' of the eschaton might very well dispose them to and inspire them to certain kinds of ethical projects.

There is one further dimension of the relevance of the eschatological vision that merits consideration: the power of the text to shape the imagination of the people of God. In his treatment of Revelation O'Donovan describes how the text presents a different perspective on the realities of life. At one level this is an issue of ethical discrimination and perspicacity; at the same time, using insights from the field of philosophical hermeneutics can enhance this awareness of a different appreciation of reality communicated through the biblical text. With the appeal to literary theory to inform their work and the commitment to more literary readings of the text, some Old Testament scholars have become sensitized to the role of texts in molding

---

[39] Cf. *DN*, 97ff.

perceptions of life and orienting behavior.[40] For instance, Barton has utilized the work of Martha Nussbaum to explore how the Old Testament helps inform and fashion the moral vision of the people of God; we also have drawn from Nussbaum and others in the analysis and appropriation of the last lines of Amos for engendering hope beyond the horrific realities of recent Latin American history.[41] In *Let Justice Roll Down*, Birch relates the function of the text to a particular concept of biblical authority.

Perhaps the scholar most associated with this sort of multidisciplinary approach to the Old Testament is Walter Brueggemann. In his seminal *The Prophetic Imagination*, Brueggemann delineates two tasks of this 'prophetic imagination'. The first is to offer appropriate metaphors and language sufficiently powerful to empathize with the reigning disillusionment and to call into question the hegemonic socio-political and economic powers and their imposed self-serving, destructive 'reality'. The second responsibility is to 'energize' people, to encourage them 'to engage the promise of newness that is at work in our history with God' and to embrace a counter-vision of the world.[42] In *Texts under Negotiation* he speaks of means to 'fund' the imagination, and in his *Theology of the Old Testament* Brueggemann discusses in detail the impact of biblical rhetoric on the imagination. In a later section of the latter volume he traces the trajectory of the narrative of God's dealings with Israel, humanity, the nations and creation. The biblical 'drama' of the trajectory of each of these entities moves from 'brokenness' to 'restoration', from judgment to ultimate blessing.[43] O'Donovan's presentation of the prophetic message emphasizes denunciation: the unmasking of the demonic powers and the announcement of judgment.[44] The possibility of allowing the text's more 'positive' visions to shape moral vision is truncated.

The first section of this essay presented a survey that showed that eschatology does not always occupy the place it should in some recent studies in Old Testament ethics. In that discussion two specific aspects of eschatology were

---

[40] A key influence has been Paul Ricœur, who has explored the power of metaphor and the role of the text in shaping the existential and moral imagination (cf., e.g., his 'Language', *Essays*, and 'Imagination'). From an evangelical perspective, note especially Thiselton, *New Horizons* (31–35, 294–307) and 'Communicative Action'. Of special interest is his consideration of the importance of 'promise' for hermeneutics.

[41] Barton, 'Reading' (cf. idem, *Ethics*, 15–18, passim); Carroll R., 'Reflecting', 'Prophetic Text', and 'Living'.

[42] Brueggemann, *Prophetic Imagination*, 44–79. The cited phrase comes from p. 63.

[43] For extended theoretical discussions on the imagination, see *Texts* and *Theology*, 64–71; for the trajectories and their significance for today, see *Theology*, 407–564, 707–50. In addition to *Prophetic Imagination*, for the prophets also see, e.g., *Creative Word*, 40–66; *Theology*, 622–49.

[44] *DN*, 62–65, 76–79, 186–88; cf. 153–57.

singled out that have served in this second section as the guiding questions for the dialogue with O'Donovan's explanation of the role of eschatology within his own construct: the nature of the future hope and its possible impact on contemporary moral reflection. We now turn to the treatment of eschatology from a different part of the globe, Latin America. The reflections done in that particular social and political cauldron will serve to illuminate our two points in other ways.

The Demands on Eschatology in Latin America

For Latin American Liberation Theology, the term 'utopia' has proven to be a most helpful term to communicate the substance and implications of their eschatological convictions.[45] Their use of the word clearly draws some inspiration from Marxist thought, but this does not entail a naïve or wholesale acceptance of that philosophy's understanding of its meaning. This is even more evident after the demise of socialism, both worldwide and in Latin America in the late 1980s and early 1990s.

The interest in utopia is driven by a very important *inquietud* ('disquiet') from within the Latin context. Míguez Bonino's comments summarize the concern nicely:

> The real question, however, is whether the kingdom of God is irrelevant to policy and therefore 'existing social processes' are closed in themselves, or whether the kingdom is a horizon which commits us to an effort at transforming the 'existing conditions' in its direction.[46]

Liberation Theology decisively opts for the second alternative. 'Utopia' stresses the concrete nature and partial realizations of hope; that is, the promise of a new world unfolds within history. Christology is foundational. This hope is guaranteed by the resurrection of Jesus: the kingdom has come, although not in its fullness. This progressive unfolding, however, does not mean that history blindly moves forward, as humanity passively awaits its outcome. Instead, it

---

[45] For helpful discussions of Liberation Theology's concept of utopia, see Gutiérrez, *Theology*, 160–68, 213–50; Míguez Bonino, *Doing Theology*, 132–53; *Toward*, 87–94; Ellacuría, 'Utopía'; and Batista Libânio, 'Esperanza'. It is important to be cognizant of the dates of the publications in order to appreciate shifts in thinking (such as the different evaluations of socialism). Also note the recent issue of *RIBLA* (*Revista de Interpretación Bíblica Latinoamericana*) that is dedicated to the topic (24 [1997]). It is entitled 'Por una tierra sin lágrimas: Redimensionando nuestra utopía' ('For an earth without tears: reconceptualizing our utopia').

[46] Míguez Bonino, *Toward*, 90.

requires participation and cooperation in positive social change from the side of the poor (*praxis*), in what are deemed to be possible mediations of that future eschaton on behalf of all humanity. Nevertheless, because the Christian conception of utopia is grounded in the 'already'/'not yet' tension of the biblical teaching regarding the kingdom of God, utopia can never be totally identified with or limited to any particular social context or stage in time.

To be truly efficacious, involvement in significant change needs diligent and scientific analysis (hence, the appeal to the social sciences in Liberation Theology). Prophetic action, thus critically informed, will involve both radical critique of unjust situations and the annunciation of an alternative world toward which society and oppressed groups can strive. Old Testament passages about a new world, as well as the book of Revelation (through its matchless symbolic language that portrays the cruelty and defeat of the beast), can be a source for encouragement in the struggle.[47] In general terms,[48] the ultimate manifestation of the utopia of the kingdom of God will entail complete peace, solidarity and equitable social relations, abundant provision of the necessities of life, and the absence of violence: in other words, this is a socio-economic, political and material hope, and not only a spiritual or religious one.

This eschatology is intimately intertwined with new evaluations of, for instance, what it means to be the church of Jesus Christ, the nature of liturgy and the significance of martyrdom.[49] Liberation Theology has questioned the classical hierarchical structure and institutional politics of the Roman Catholic Church and proposed a reformation to a more democratic ecclesial body (embodied in the *communidades eclesiales de base*). Any talk of a Christendom model would be met with deep suspicion, because the Latin American experience of 'Christendom' came in the form of the Spanish Conquest of the sixteenth century and the socio-religious structures it left in place (some of which continue in some fashion even today) and in the crass foreign policy interventions by the United States, whose civil religion has often sanctified that country's policy of 'manifest destiny'. Liturgies have been reformulated to embody and proclaim liberationist ideals: some of the sacraments have been given new meaning, and other elements have been added to traditional ceremonies. Liberation Theology also has mourned a large number of martyrs, the most

---

[47] Note especially Richard, *Apocalypse*; cf. Rowland and Corner, *Liberating*, 131–55; Ramírez Fernández, 'Judgment'.

[48] One who has provided very detailed description of the 'new heaven and new earth' is Ellacuría, 'Utopía', 424–42. This is presented in very this-worldly terms. The question that naturally arises is whether there is any element (or, if so, to what degree) of transcendence in the Liberation Theology conception. Answers would vary from theologian to theologian.

[49] Note, e.g., Boff, *Church*; Jiménez Limón, 'Sufrimiento'.

celebrated of which is Archbishop Oscar Romero of El Salvador. Death has come not from the persecution of the Christian faith *per se*, but rather because some believers paid a heavy price for trying to live out that faith authentically, sacrificially and with integrity.

This emphatic commitment to concreteness for the Christian hope helps explain why, years ago, Liberation Theology appreciated, yet strongly criticized, Moltmann's *Theology of Hope*.[50] Their argument was that Christians should comprehend that it was not so much that the future draws us forward, as much as that the misery of the present is the birthplace and arena for that yearning to be nurtured, and for the mediations of the future to be worked out. It is also important to recognize that this desire for a realistic eschatology cannot be limited to liberationist circles. Latin American evangelical theologians and missiologists, such as Padilla, Escobar and Costas, have also called for a more solid and contextual orientation to eschatology (especially in contradistinction to the sensationalistic variety propagated by certain fundamentalist groups).[51] In his exposition of the book of Revelation at CLADE III (a continent-wide gathering of evangelicals in Quito, Ecuador, in September 1992), Juan Stam links eschatology to *la misión integral* (holistic mission).[52] And in CLADE IV, celebrated in September 2000, one of the statements of the final declaration of the commitments signed by the delegates reads:

> Vivir la esperanza escatológica del Reino de Dios en la sufriente América Latina de hoy, participando activamente en los procesos de la sociedad civil que promuevan y defiendan la vida y la dignidad humana. [To live the eschatological hope of the kingdom of God in today's suffering Latin America, actively participating in the processes of civil society that promote and defend life and human dignity.]

Eschatology within many circles in Latin America can exemplify a comprehensiveness that is also evident in O'Donovan. It is clear, however, that this eschatology has a different *content* and thus conceives of a distinct ethical *impact* for eschatology. Clearly, the complex socio-political and economic situation and tragic history of Latin America have yielded a different construct. Latin America's demand for a concrete, hopeful eschatology, one that must be

[50] Gutiérrez, *Theology*, 217–18; Míguez Bonino, *Doing Theology*, 144–50.

[51] Padilla, 'El reino'; Escobar, *Evangelio*, 113–77; Costas, *Christ*, 174–94. What these authors demonstrate is the importance of eschatology for Christian mission. For a more global perspective, see Bosch, *Transforming*, 313–27, 500–10. Liberationists have been very suspicious of the socio-political implications and commitments of more popular, sensationalistic and fundamentalist eschatology. See Pixley, 'El final'; Schäfer, 'Algunas consideraciones'.

[52] Stam, 'El evangelio'. Note more recently his commentary on the book of Revelation (*Apocalipsis*).

accompanied by a peculiar lifestyle and orientation toward the context, reinforces the value of a more substantial view of the eschaton than what is found in O'Donovan's work. It embraces the suffering of the masses and gives the eschaton a more human face. There is hope beyond our misery.[53]

Contributions from the Books of Isaiah and Amos

From the more theoretical discussions of the first two sections and our brief survey of a contemporary situation in which eschatology is of great importance, we now turn to the prophetic books of Isaiah and Amos to illustrate our two points regarding the *content* and *impact* of eschatological hope from the Bible itself. Our approach to the biblical text will be based on a literary reading of the final form.[54] This sort of reading can track a dynamic movement from the opening chapters to the end, from the tumultuous context of eighth-century Judah and Israel to a future of restoration and blessing. The purpose of this part of the essay is to demonstrate that within the biblical text itself there is a hope for a gracious work of Yahweh beyond the announced devastating judgments, and that this hope is presented as a motivation for ethical life in the present. Even those scholars who would assign this progression to the work of creative redactors of different periods that actualized the prophetic word to meet the demands of new contexts recognize an eschatological thrust within the present shape of these books. The limitations of this essay require that our readings be quite concise, rather than detailed.[55]

---

[53] Perhaps O'Donovan can learn more from the 'southern school' than he allows (*DN* 12–17; 'Political Theology').

[54] For Isaiah, sources that we have found that offer particularly suggestive readings include Dumbrell, 'Purpose'; Webb, 'Zion'; Conrad, *Reading*; Seitz, 'Isaiah 1–66' and *Zion's Final Destiny*; Williamson, *Variations*. Seitz (in the works just cited, but also in *Word*) and Williamson are distinct in their interest in explaining the redactional activity in some detail. Two more substantial sources, which deal with the final form of Isaiah but from very different vantage points, strategies and goals are Brueggemann, *Isaiah 1–39* and *Isaiah 40–66*; Childs, *Isaiah*. A distinctively evangelical reading, which reflects some literary sensitivities, is Motyer, *Prophecy*. A number of literary approaches to the book of Amos have appeared in the last two decades. For the concerns of this essay, see esp. Carroll R., *Contexts*, 'Reflecting', 'Prophetic', 'God', and 'Living'; Noble, 'Remnant' and 'Amos'. Also note Möller, 'Rehabilitation' and '"Hear"'.

[55] The reading we will present attempts to reflect the flow and tenor of the texts. The question of whether the ancient community of Israel would have read these prophetic books in the fashion presented here is a good one, but it is perhaps finally beyond our knowing with a high degree of certainty. Barton has discussed the several ways in which prophetic texts were interpreted and used by Jewish and early Christian

Isaiah

From the various constituent parts of the hope in Isaiah, we will only consider the destiny of Jerusalem/Zion in our investigation of the *content* and *impact* of eschatology.[56] Of course, this theme is inseparable from reflections on the royal hope for Israel in the first part of the book and from the Servant theology of chapters 40–66.[57] Strictures of space will confine our comments, however, to the Zion theme. To begin with, many have observed that the city of Jerusalem frames the entire book: chapters 1–2 describe the sin, judgment and subsequent glorification of the 'Faithful City' (1:26); chapters 65–66 picture Jerusalem within the context of a new heavens and new earth (65:17–18; 66:2, 22). Our task is to briefly trace the significance of this movement.

The initial chapter paints a grim picture of life on Zion: the people (especially the rulers) demonstrate their rebelliousness through hypocritical

---

communities (*Oracles*). Several studies have tracked the theological reception and ethical appropriation of the books of Isaiah (e.g., Brueggemann, 'Five'; Sawyer, *Fifth Gospel*) and Amos (e.g., Martin-Achard, *Amos*, 161–271) in different contexts.

[56] For Zion as the central theme of the book, note the works of Dumbrell, Webb and Seitz, which are cited above in n. 54. Mention should also be made of Gowan's *Eschatology* and Ollenburger's *Zion*, which organize their discussions of Old Testament eschatology around the Zion theme.

[57] Those who discuss the Zion theology of the book of Isaiah tend to develop the two together (also note Gowan, *Eschatology*, 32–41). It is possible to see development of this theme with a literary approach, too. For example, the prediction of the Immanuel child in 7:13–17 appears to be fulfilled initially in ch. 8 with the birth of the prophet's son (note the repetition of vocabulary and concepts in 8:3–10, 18). However, 9:1–7 reveals that this one, who is to deliver Jerusalem from the Assyrians, is to be a royal child (cf. 11:1ff.; 16:5; 32:1–9), so the reader must set aside Maher-Shalal-Hash-Baz as an option. This person remains nameless apparently until chs. 36–39, as Hezekiah seems to fulfill this hope (again through a series of echoes of ch. 7; note, e.g., the place, 36:1–2; a sign, 37:30; 38:7, 22; the need to trust in Yahweh's help, 37:1–20). Yet, his failure in ch. 39 disqualifies him as well. Isaiah 40–66 presents the Servant, one of whose tasks is to establish justice in Israel and among the nations. This and other characteristics (e.g., the Spirit, light) link him to the royal hope of chs. 1–39. The person that the people of God must wait for, then, is a composite figure, whose ultimate identity keeps pushing the reader forward through a series of historical eras yet without final closure. In addition, the many lexical and thematic connections between the Servant and the people in chs. 40ff. yield an even more complex picture, which is full of theological and ethical implications. Of course, a Christian reader would identify Jesus as the final fulfillment of this literary movement. Nevertheless, our concern at this juncture is to demonstrate the flow and power of the eschatological hopes within the Old Testament itself.

worship divorced from the law's demand for the care of the needy. Zion is sick and weak, and Yahweh's chosen city has become much like Sodom and Gomorrah. From this chapter on, 'righteousness', 'justice', and 'faithful(ness)' become the watchwords throughout the various sections of the book for the kind of society which Yahweh requires and that he has ordained for Israel and all of humanity. Here in chapter 1, sin brings divine chastisement, but this is designed to purge Zion of its transgressions and transgressors so that it might again be called the 'City of Righteousness' (1:24–28). With 2:2–4, the reader sees that judgment brings reversal: Jerusalem will become a place of obedience to the law by those made holy (cf. 4:2–6), and peace will replace violence; worship on Yahweh's mountain is restored to its central place, but it is also universalized to include all the nations of the world.

As one continues through the first five chapters of Isaiah, one finds no specific historical allusions.[58] Instead, the reader encounters characterizations of groups of people and of the nation as a whole within what might be considered a typological understanding of history. In this manner the pattern of sin resulting in judgment, which then in God's grace leads to the exaltation of Zion, is set in place (and in motion). As the book progresses, these broad themes are enacted in actual life settings in a series of narratives that give the text a greater historical grounding and realistic impression. Interspersed among these passages are predictions of an ultimate, more distant vindication in 'that day'.

The first extensive concrete scenario appears in chapter 7.[59] The city is under threat of attack by Aram and Israel, and king Ahaz is challenged by the prophet to respond in faith to Yahweh, who is able to deliver (7:1–11). Yahweh's gesture is rebuffed, and judgment is announced: Assyria, whom those two nations had wanted to thwart (and to whom Ahaz actually appealed for help), ironically will arrive as the divine instrument of punishment (7:12–8:10; 10:5–11). The empire also will suffer the rod of his anger (10:12–34), but Assyria will continue to loom as the preeminent enemy through chapter 39. The first major section of the book closes with chapter 12, with a celebration of song on Zion for a future restoration.[60]

---

[58] This is not to suggest that these chapters had no historical setting as their impetus. Scholars, for instance, debate whether allusions to the events of 701 or 587 lie behind these oracles. The literary fact, however, is that historical specifics are obscured and hidden by the language of the text, in contrast to the rather clear historical markers that begin to appear at 6:1.

[59] The heavenly court and holy king of ch. 6, with the angels and obedient prophet, serve as a stark contrast to the faithless Ahaz in ch. 7.

[60] Note the juxtaposition with ch. 11, which describes a reign of justice, harmony, the cessation of hostilities and the return of God's people to the land under a glorious ruler who is full of the Spirit.

The oracles against the nations (chs. 13–23) include another general denunciation of Jerusalem, but some particularity is achieved with the mention of Shebna and Eliakim (ch. 22). Chapters 24–27 contrast the sinful state of Zion in the present with its more glorious future:[61] the mountain of God is now secure, and the righteous enjoy the kindness of Yahweh with a banquet and victory over death. As in chapters 1–12, this sequence of chapters also includes a song for the victory of Yahweh and the reversal of the conditions of sin and loss (ch. 26). Chapters 28–35 again represent Jerusalem as sinful, lacking in faith and deserving of punishment, but there is impending redemption and blessing for the righteous; Zion, now made holy, will echo with the praises of Yahweh's holy ones (35:10). Chapters 13–35 are somewhat vague in terms of explicit historical references, but the menace of Assyria continues to cast a long shadow (e.g., 14:24–26; 30:1–5; 31:1–3); nevertheless, it (along with Egypt) will some day come to Yahweh in a fulfillment of that surprising earlier oracle (19:23–25; cf. 2:2–4).

A new political crisis and then a miraculous victory are depicted in some detail in chapters 36–39. Readers might be tempted to read the wondrous pictures of 'that day' in previous chapters as exaggerated descriptions anticipating this triumph, or at least to see this salvation of Jerusalem as a type of Yahweh's future, more grand liberation. A careful reading of chapters 36–38 would yield theological and lexical connections (especially with ch. 7), which do point to continuity of some sort.[62] Hezekiah will later speak of singing God's praises in the temple for his healing from sickness (38:15–20). These lines would seem to offer a fitting close to this section, parallel to the pattern thus far of singing following deliverance, but 39:5–7 shockingly predicts the sacking of the palace and signals the rise of another foe, Babylon. What now of Zion after that coming defeat?

Time and the literary flow march on under the sovereignty of God, in other words.[63] The dramatic intervention of the angel of death cannot be the climax of Yahweh's plan for Zion (37:36f.). The new oppressor, Babylon, must be defeated before a subsequent exaltation is possible. Chapters 40–66, however, are less specific in terms of historical details than the first part of the book; there will be no narrative like that of chapters 36–39. However,

---

[61] Scholars debate whether the evil city of ch. 24 is Babylon or Jerusalem. We have chosen the second option.

[62] Note, e.g., the observations in n. 57, above.

[63] The interconnectedness of the second half of the book with chs. 1–39 is communicated through phrases such as 'the former things' and 'new things' in chs. 40–48. One of the theological points of this section is that Yahweh is unique among the gods of the earth, because he has known the end from the beginning (cf. 42:9; 43:18; 46:9f.; 48:3–8).

Babylon's defeat (already anticipated in chs. 13–14 and 21:1–10) is announced in chapter 47, and Yahweh reveals that the coming 'anointed' deliverer will have the name 'Cyrus' (44:24–45:13). Beginning in chapter 40, quite a number of passages encourage the people of God and Zion itself with stirring pictures of Yahweh's incomparable power and irresistible word and of the return to and restoration of Jerusalem (note especially chs. 51–52). Worship of Yahweh on Zion is again the response (51:11; 55:12–13).[64] Chapters 56–66 provide no explicit historical particulars whatsoever. The reader now is encouraged to look for still another deliverance of Zion beyond the fall of Babylon. This ultimate view of eschatological restoration and victory (chs. 61–62) is connected to a new heavens and earth. Worship in the temple by the consecrated ones from Israel and the nations will characterize that last age of blessing (66:19–21; cf. 56:1–8; 2:2–4). The book in a sense has come full circle – beginning and ending at Zion – even as it has pushed forward through time to a final exaltation of Yahweh's city.

A full and exhaustive reading also would be able to explore related dimensions that are important for O'Donovan's concerns, such as the ideals for human government, the role of the law envisioned for Israel and the other nations, the arrogance of those in power, and the kingship of Yahweh. Our purpose has been to illustrate how the text portrays a progression toward a final eschaton, foretastes of which are available to the people of God in their history. No one event or setting ever fulfills that last eschatological hope in all of its details, but the successive victories of God are steps in that direction: there is continuity in the reversals of the present in the eschaton(s) and mediations of the miraculous presence and activity of God at each stage. All along the way Israel is to rejoice and praise the God of future restoration and vindication, even as they are to embody his demands in the here and now. The pictures of the future vary in the amount of detail. Nevertheless, even if they are vague in chronological and geographical reference, they are still palpable imaginative construals, because they reflect the actual activities and settings of Israel's life. Generality does not mean irrelevance.

The text also reveals the impact this pattern should have upon the people of God. Time and space do not allow us to trace the ethical themes for each stage of this unfolding, but they are there and are part and parcel of the trajectory toward final glory. This topic could be investigated at several different levels. One can begin with the textual descriptions and divine evaluations of the various named and type characters within the eschatological story line of the text. Ahaz and others (like the 'rulers' and 'women of Zion') are negative object lessons of sinful behavior and its consequences, whereas Hezekiah is an ambiguous model in his vacillations. On the other hand, the royal figure of

[64] Chs. 49–55 in general have Zion as their main focus.

the hope in chapters 1–39, the persevering remnant[65] and the Suffering Servant (whatever his identity might be) are moral exemplars of a life pleasing to Yahweh, profound in its integrity in the expectation of his future judgments and blessing. The relevance of the eschaton for God's moral demands also is communicated through the portrayals of contrasting scenes, especially in relationship to acceptable worship in the temple on Zion. In addition, the book directs multiple ethical imperatives to its real and implied readers in light of that coming punishment and vindication (note, e.g., 2:5 and 56:1–3). Here again, a more exact reading would distinguish between the different kinds of exhortations commensurate with each of these messages. Finally, philosophical hermeneutics would encourage us to probe how the visions of eschatological glory in Isaiah might shape the moral imagination and ethical initiatives today at personal, communal, social, national and international levels.[66]

Amos

The eschatological framework in the book of Amos is not as complex as that of Isaiah, but still a general pattern holds: the necessary, comprehensive divine judgment upon Israel and the other nations for their oppression, cruelty and arrogance is followed by a word of promise of national restoration (9:11–15). In Amos, the judgment is imminent and inescapable; the hope of a different world lies beyond that horror and will entail rebuilding from out of the rubble. In other words, there are two phases within Israel's eschatological future; the second builds off the first and makes no sense without it.

The soon-coming judgment is described as an invasion sent by Yahweh. Israel in its sin has become one of the nations that stand condemned before God. In its literary form, the declaration of the punishment of God's chosen people (2:6–16) unmistakably now is part and parcel of the oracles against the nations (chs. 1–2). In fact, Israel has become worse than the others: Ashdod (part of the Philistine group of city states, which is condemned in 1:6–8) and Egypt (that paradigm of evil and Israel's oppressive past; cf. 2:10; 3:2) are invited to come as witnesses to the violence within Israel and the chastisement Yahweh will bring (3:9)! Yahweh himself has ordered and will execute Israel's downfall and ruin (3:6,14–15; 5:6, 9, 17, 27; 6:8–11; 7:7–9; 8:9–11; 9:1–4, 9f.). The text enumerates seven kinds of soldiers who will die 'on that

[65] Of the studies cited in n. 54 above, the work by Webb ('Zion') most fully develops the topic of the remnant. Williamson's *Variations* does as well, but in a different direction. He argues for an increasing 'democratization' of the royal hope within the book.

[66] Note, e.g., the reflections in Brueggemann, *Isaiah 1–39* and *Isaiah 40–66*; Childs, *Isaiah*.

day' (2:14–16) before an unnamed enemy (3:11; 6:14; 9:4); death and mourning will be everywhere (5:1–3,16f.; 6:9; 8:3). The sanctuaries will fall (3:14; 7:9; 8:3; 9:1); the walls of Israel's cities will be breached (4:3; 6:8); and homes and possessions destroyed (3:15; 5:11; 6:11). The anonymity of the invader makes it clear that it is with Yahweh Ṣ^{e}bā'ôt that Israel (and the other nations) ultimately must contend (cf. 4:12f.; 5:8–9; 9:5f.). All of Israel's religiosity, both official and popular, stands rejected and cannot save the nation (2:8; 4:4f.; 5:4–6, 21–24; 7:9–17). Yahweh will not be manipulated and domesticated as a god of national victory and blessing.

In light of these sweeping statements of judgment, how can the passages that seem to offer small glimpses of hope (5:4–6,14–15; 9:8) – let alone 9:11–15 – be interpreted as part of a coherent message? Just how absolute is the 'no' of Amos? Scholars have proposed a variety of solutions, such as that some of the more optimistic lines come from an earlier time in the prophet's ministry before Israel's definitive rejection of Yahweh's overtures, or that the language of total judgment is hyperbolic and designed to bring the nation to repentance, or that the condemnation rests upon the sinful within the nation and will not affect the oppressed and the innocent, or simply that these passages (and especially 9:11–15) are later additions. From a literary point of view, none of these explanations seems warranted. If one remembers that the judgment of Yahweh is coming as an invasion, then the totalizing language is very understandable. War is indiscriminate in its destruction and brutality. Rich and poor, righteous and unrighteous alike will suffer, die or go into exile. This stark reality heightens the guilt of Israel's religious, political, military and economic leaders – those who seem secure in Samaria (6:1; 9:10), enjoy their lifestyles at the expense of others (4:1; 6:4–6), glory in their victories (6:3,13) and promote the worship of a benevolent deity (7:13). The blood of the innocent is on their hands, both now in that oppressive society and in the future when the invader comes.

The few words of hope before the war (5:4–6, 14–15; 9:8) do not guarantee avoiding the terror of the imminent conflict. What kind of meaning, then, can these offers of life have in this litany of death? On the one hand, in their literary contexts, they stand as part of an uncompromising call: to seek Yahweh and life requires that they establish justice in the gates. On the other hand, they might simply suggest to the audience the possibility that in God's mercy some might survive the attack and be part of the 'remnant of Joseph'. Yet those who endure also will experience the mourning, the burial of the dead and the destruction of their society – no temple, no king, no walls and no homes. If in the past the nation had suffered want and adversity (4:6–11), how much more now. Yahweh will have decisively enacted his justice and responded to the cry of the poor in a fashion that would bring those most responsible under even greater condemnation.

Against this backdrop, the closing lines of the book make powerful sense (9:1–15). Chastisement is not God's final word. The ruins are to be rebuilt; there will be plenty of food and drink for all, and not just for the privileged; Israel at last will be a peaceful land and will face neither defeat nor further exile, as Israel will be 'planted' and the nations will be called by Yahweh's name. Instead of the disastrous policies of the house of Jeroboam, the 'fallen tent of David' will be lifted up: a new socio-political construct (with its religious center on Zion, 1:2?) will replace the pretensions of the dynasty of Jehu and the perversions of the 'sacred canopy' (to use the sociological term) legitimated at Bethel.[67] A careful reading of these verses demonstrates that their vocabulary consciously reverses the negative experiences of the past.[68]

The *content* of 9:11–15 allows those who face the coming conflict in faith to see beyond it to another time; its *impact* is that it gives a reason for making the most of the opportunity to choose life in Yahweh and to not follow the example of those who have brought Israel to this point.[69] Justice does demand that there be an accounting for the sins of Israel and the nations. Amos has announced that justice will be achieved through the invasion – but what is there after the war? Is there hope on the other side of the horror? 'Yes,' says Yahweh, 'your God' (9:15), who no longer presents himself as Yahweh Ṣᵉbā'ôt.

In sum, both prophetic books devote much attention to eschatological issues. Both also attempt to provide some sort of concrete picture of hope through images related to the situations and experiences of their context. Hope then becomes imaginable and now can serve as an invitation to live in a way that reflects the ethics that Yahweh wills in the here and now. The prophets can function similarly today, as the reader moves into the world of the text, begins to see life today through its lens, and decides to follow Yahweh in light

---

[67] The political implications of the phrase in 9:11 and the rest of the message of Amos are evident perhaps in Amaziah calling the Judean prophet's activity a 'conspiracy' (7:10–13).

[68] In light of these literary connections, it is surprising for Gowan to say, 'The book concludes with two short oracles of promise. They are not thematically related, and neither of them shows any close relationship with the rest of the book' ('Amos', 426). Apparently, although he desires to present a rhetorical approach to the text, he has not been able to extricate himself completely from some of his critical historical reconstructions.

[69] As in the book of Isaiah, one could also trace the ethical impact of the characters and settings within the world of the text. Few names are given (just Amos, Jeroboam and Amaziah), but there are certain types of people described with participles ('those who…') or as groups (the Nazarites, the prophets, the needy), as well as type scenes (such as the sanctuaries, the city gates and the market place), that can function as lessons, both good and bad, for the reader.

of the hope set before the people of God. The Christian reader can assert that the 'desire of the nations' has come in Jesus, but the New Testament – as did the Old – looks forward in expectation to another day and another world.

Conclusion

O'Donovan has done well to emphasize the eschatological in his theological ethics. Our criticism is that, in his emphasis on the realized aspect of the Christian hope in the resurrection of Christ, he has neglected important aspects of the 'not yet'. What is lacking is a fuller view of the *nature of that hope*. What is it that we are to hope for? How is it related to the present (the issues of continuity and mediations)? Second, once we have established a better picture of that future, *how should it impact* the church and the world today? We have attempted to demonstrate the importance of these questions by looking at some reflections on eschatology in Latin America and by offering a reading of two Old Testament texts that suggests that these concerns are inherent within the canon itself.[70] Our hope is that our observations might prove constructive for O'Donovan's continued work in Christian ethics

Bibliography

Barton, J., *Oracles of God: Perceptions of Ancient Prophecy in Israel after the Exile* (London: Darton, Longman & Todd, 1986)

——, 'Reading for Life: The Use of the Bible in Ethics and the Work of Martha C. Nussbaum', in *The Bible in Ethics: The Second Sheffield Colloquium* (ed. J.W. Rogerson, M. Davies and M.D. Carroll R.; JSOTSup 207; Sheffield: Sheffield Academic Press, 1995), 66–76

——, *Ethics and the Old Testament* (Harrisburg, PA: Trinity International, 1998)

Batista Libânio, J., 'Esperanza, utopía, resurrección', in Ellacuría and Sobrino (eds.), *Mysterium Liberationis* II, 495–510

Bauckham, R., 'Must Christian Eschatology Be Millenarian? A Response to Jürgen Moltmann', in K.E. Brower and M.W. Elliott (eds.), *'The Reader Must Understand': Eschatology in Bible and Theology* (Leicester: Apollos, 1997), 263–77

Berkhof, H., *Christ: The Meaning of History* (trans. L. Burman; Grand Rapids: Baker, 1979)

[70] Of course, we leave to O'Donovan the articulation of a clear hermeneutic for appropriating the Old Testament today within his theological ethic. He has done this to quite some degree already, but perhaps our work might suggest some reconsideration of his formulations.

Berkouwer, G.C., *The Return of Christ* (Studies in Dogmatics; Grand Rapids: Eerdmans, 1972)

Birch, B.C., *Let Justice Roll Down: The Old Testament, Ethics, and Christian Life* (Louisville, KY: Westminster/John Knox Press, 1991)

Boff, L., *Church, Charism and Power: Liberation Theology and the Institutional Church* (trans. J.W. Diercksmeier; London: SCM Press, 1985)

Bosch, D.J., *Transforming Mission: Paradigm Shifts in Theology of Mission* (Maryknoll, NY: Orbis Books, 1991)

Brueggemann, W., *The Prophetic Imagination* (Philadelphia: Fortress Press, 1978)

——, *The Creative Word: Canon as a Model for Biblical Education* (Philadelphia: Fortress Press, 1982)

——, *Texts under Negotiation: The Bible and the Postmodern Imagination* (Minneapolis: Fortress Press, 1993)

——, 'Five Strong Rereadings of the Book of Isaiah', in M.D. Carroll R., D.J.A. Clines and P.R. Davies (eds.), *The Bible in Human Society: Essays in Honour of John Rogerson* (JSOTSup 200; Sheffield: Sheffield Academic Press, 1995), 87–104

——, *Theology of the Old Testament: Testimony, Dispute, Advocacy* (Minneapolis: Fortress Press, 1997)

——, *Isaiah 1–39* (WBC; Louisville, KY: Westminster/John Knox Press, 1998)

——, *Isaiah 40–66* (WBC; Louisville, KY: Westminster/John Knox Press, 1998)

Carroll R., M. Daniel, *Contexts for Amos: Prophetic Poetics in Latin American Perspective* (JSOTSup 132; Sheffield: Sheffield Academic Press, 1992)

——, 'Reflecting on War and Utopia in the Book of Amos: The Relevance of a Literary Reading of the Prophetic Text for Latin America', in M.D. Carroll R., D.J.A. Clines and P.R. Davies (eds.), *The Bible in Human Society: Essays in Honour of John Rogerson* (JSOTSup 200; Sheffield: Sheffield Academic Press, 1995), 105–21

——, 'The Prophetic Text and the Literature of Dissent in Latin America: Amos, García Márquez, and Cabrera Infante Dismantle Militarism', *BibInt* 4.1 (1996), 76–100

——, 'God and His People in the Nations' History: A Contextualized Reading of Amos 1 and 2', *TynBul* 47.1 (1996), 49–70

——, 'Living between the Lines: Reading Amos 9:11–15 in Post-War Guatemala', *R&T* 6.1 (1999), 50–64

Childs, B.S., *Isaiah* (OTL; Louisville, KY: Westminster/John Knox Press, 2001)

Conrad, E.W., *Reading Isaiah* (OBT; Minneapolis: Fortress Press, 1991)

Costas, O.E., *Christ outside the Gate: Mission beyond Christendom* (Maryknoll, NY: Orbis Books, 1982)

Dumbrell, W.J., 'The Purpose of the Book of Isaiah', *TynBul* 36 (1985), 111–28

Ellacuría, I., 'Utopía y profetismo', in Ellacuría and Sobrino (eds.), *Mysterium Liberationis* I, 393–442

—— and J. Sobrino (eds.), *Mysterium Liberationis: Conceptos fundamentales de la teología de la liberación* (Colección Teología Latinoamericana 16; 2 vols.; San Salvador, El Salvador: UCA Editores; Madrid: Trotta, 1993).[71]

Escobar, S., *Evangelio y realidad social: Ensayos desde una perspectiva evangélica* (Lima: Ediciones Presencia, 1985)

Gowan, D.E., *Eschatology in the Old Testament* (Philadelphia: Fortress Press, 1986)

——, 'Amos', in *New Interpreter's Bible* VII (ed. L.E. Keck, et al.; Nashville: Abingdon Press, 1996), 339–431

Gutiérrez, G., *A Theology of Liberation: History, Politics and Salvation* (trans. Sister C. Inda and J. Eagleson; Maryknoll, NY: Orbis Books, 1973)

Hays, R.B., *The Moral Vision of the New Testament: A Contemporary Introduction to New Testament Ethics* (San Francisco: HarperCollins, 1996)

Hoekema, A.A., *The Bible and the Future* (Grand Rapids: Eerdmans, 1979)

Janzen, W., *Old Testament Ethics: A Paradigmatic Approach* (Louisville, KY: Westminster/John Knox Press, 1994)

Jiménez Limón, J., 'Sufrimiento, muerte, cruz y martirio', in Ellacuría and Sobrino (eds.), *Mysterium Liberationis* II, 477–94

Kaiser, W.C., Jr., *Toward Old Testament Ethics* (Grand Rapids: Zondervan, 1983)

Martin-Achard, R., *Amos: l'homme, le message, l'influence* (Geneva: Labor et Fides, 1984)

Míguez Bonino, J., *Doing Theology in a Revolutionary Situation* (Philadelphia: Fortress Press, 1975)

——, *Toward a Christian Political Ethics* (Philadelphia: Fortress Press, 1983)

Möller, K., 'Rehabilitation eines Propheten: Die Botschaft des Amos aus rhetorischer Perspektive unter besonderer Berücksichtung von Amos 9,7–15', *EuroJT* 6.1 (1997), 41–55

——, ' "Hear this word against you": A Fresh Look at the Arrangement and the Rhetorical Strategy of the Book of Amos', *VT* 50.4 (2000), 499–518

Moltmann, J., *Theology of Hope: On the Ground and the Implications of a Christian Eschatology* (trans. J.W. Leitch; New York: Harper & Row, 1967)

——, *The Coming of God: Christian Eschatology* (trans. M. Kohl; Minneapolis: Fortress Press, 1996)

Motyer, J.A., *The Prophecy of Isaiah: An Introduction and Commentary* (Downers Grove, IL: IVP, 1993)

Noble, P.R., 'The Remnant in Amos 3–6: A Prophetic Paradox', *HBT* 19.2 (1997), 122–47

——, 'Amos' Absolute "No"', *VT* 47.3 (1997), 329–40

[71] The two volumes of *Mysterium Liberationis* have been translated into English and condensed into one: *Mysterium Liberationis: Fundamental Concepts of Liberation Theology* (Maryknoll, NY: Orbis Books; North Blackburn, Australia: CollinsDove, 1993). My references are to the Spanish edition.

O'Donovan, O., 'The Possibility of a Biblical Ethic', *TSFB* 67 (1973), 15–23
——, 'Towards an Interpretation of Biblical Ethics', *TynBul* 27 (1976), 54–78
——, 'The Political Thought of the Book of Revelation', *TynBul* 37 (1986), 61–94
——, *Resurrection and Moral Order: An Outline for Evangelical Ethics* (Leicester: IVP; Grand Rapids: Eerdmans, 2nd edn, 1994)
——, 'Augustine's *City of God* XIX and Western Political Thought', *Dionysius* 11 (1987), 89–110
——, *The Desire of the Nations: Rediscovering the Roots of Political Theology* (Cambridge: CUP, 1996)
——, 'Political Theology, Tradition and Modernity', in *The Cambridge Companion to Liberation Theology* (ed. C. Rowland; Cambridge: CUP, 1999), 235–47
——, 'Government as Judgment', *First Things* 92 (1999), 36–44
Ollenburger, B.C., *Zion the City of the Great King: A Theological Symbol of the Jerusalem Cult* (JSOTSup 41; Sheffield: Sheffield Academic Press, 1987)
Otto, E., *Theologische Ethik des Alten Testaments* (Kohlammer Theologische Wissenschaft 3/2; Stuttgart: Kohlhammer Verlag, 1994)
Padilla, C.R., 'El reino de Dios y la iglesia', in *El reino de Dios y América Latina* (ed. C. René Padilla; El Paso, TX: Casa Bautista de Publicaciones, 1975), 43–68
Pixley, J., 'El final de la historia y la fe popular: el reino milenario de Cristo (Ireneo y el fundamentalismo)', *Pasos* 41 (1992), 11–16
Preuss, H.D. (ed.), *Eschatologie im Alten Testament* (Wege der Forschung 480; Darmstadt: Wissenschaftliche Buchgesellschaft, 1978)
Ramírez Fernández, D., 'The Judgment of God on the Multinationals: Revelation 18', in *Subversive Scriptures: Revolutionary Readings of the Christian Bible in Latin America* (ed. and trans. L.E. Vaage; Valley Forge, PA: Trinity Press International, 1997), 75–100
Richard, P., *Apocalypse: A People's Commentary on the Book of Revelation* (trans. P. Berryman; Maryknoll, NY: Orbis Books, 1995)
Ricœur, P., 'The Language of Faith', *USQR* 28.3 (1978), 213–24
——, *Essays on Biblical Interpretation* (ed. L.S. Mudge; Philadelphia: Fortress Press, 1980)
——, 'Imagination in Discourse and in Action', in *Essays in Hermeneutics* II: *From Text to Action* (trans. K. Blamey and J.B. Thompson; Evanston, IL: Northwestern University Press, 1991), 168–87
Rodd, C.S., *Glimpses of a Strange Land: Studies in Old Testament Ethics* (OTS; Edinburgh: T. & T. Clark, 2001)
Rowland, C., and M. Corner, *Liberating Exegesis: The Challenge of Liberation Theology to Biblical Studies* (BFT; London: SPCK, 1990)
Sawyer, J.F.A., *The Fifth Gospel: Isaiah in the History of Christianity* (Cambridge: CUP, 1996)

Schäfer, H., 'Algunas consideraciones acerca de la función de la escatología milenarista en los conflictos sociales de Centroamérica', *Pasos* 31 (1990), 11–14

Seitz, C.R., 'Isaiah 1–66: Making Sense of the Whole', in *Reading and Preaching the Book of Isaiah* (ed. C. Seitz; Philadelphia: Fortress Press, 1988), 105–26

——, *Zion's Final Destiny: The Development of the Book of Isaiah. A Reassessment of Isaiah 36–39* (Minneapolis: Fortress Press, 1991)

——, *Word without End: The Old Testament as Abiding Theological Witness* (Grand Rapids: Eerdmans, 1998)

Stam, J., 'El evangelio de la nueva creación', in *CLADE III: Tercer Congreso Latinoamericano de Evangelización, Quito 1992* (ed. C.R. Padilla; Buenos Aires, Argentina: Fraternidad Teológica Latinoamericana, 1993), 228–45

——, *Apocalipsis*, I (Comentario Bíblico Iberoamericano; Buenos Aires: Kairós, 1999)

Thiselton, A.C., *New Horizons in Hermeneutics: The Theory and Practice of Transforming Biblical Reading* (London: HarperCollins; Carlisle: Paternoster; Grand Rapids: Zondervan, 1992)

——, 'Communicative Action and Promise in Interdisciplinary, Biblical and Theological Hermeneutics', in *The Promise of Hermeneutics* (ed. R. Lundin, C. Walhout, A.C. Thiselton; Grand Rapids: Eerdmans; Carlisle: Paternoster, 1999), 133–239

Webb, B.G., 'Zion in Transformation: A Literary Approach to Isaiah', in *The Bible in Three Dimensions: Essays in Celebration of Forty Years of Biblical Studies in the University of Sheffield* (ed. D.J.A. Clines, S.E. Fowl and S.E. Porter; JSOTSup 87; Sheffield: Sheffield Academic Press, 1990), 65–84

Wenham, G.J., *Story as Torah: Reading the Old Testament Ethically* (OTS; Edinburgh: T. & T. Clark, 2000)

Williams, S., 'Evangelicals and Eschatology: A Contentious Case', in *Interpreting the Bible: Essays in Honour of David F. Wright* (ed. A.N.S. Lane; Leicester: Apollos, 1997), 291–308

Williamson, H.G.M., *Variations on a Theme: King, Messiah and Servant in the Book of Isaiah* (Carlisle: Paternoster, 1998)

Wright, C.J.H., *Walking in the Ways of the Lord: The Ethical Authority of the Old Testament* (Downers Grove, IL: IVP, 1995)

8

Response to Daniel Carroll R.

Oliver O'Donovan

Daniel Carroll would like me to have offered an account of eschatological realization which differed from the one I actually offered in three respects: 1) It would have been less apophatic and reserved, fuller of content about the shape of things to come. 2) It would have been more joyful and affirmative, less exclusively oriented to judgement, more to fulfilment. 3) It would have had more of an unfolding form, allowing each phase of fulfilment to satisfy the previous, without providing the ultimate satisfaction. These are three rather different requests, though they circle around a single issue: how may we delineate a positive political hope that is beyond our direct political experience? Let me make an observation about each in turn.

1. Carroll complains of a 'lack of true tangibleness', of 'concrete detail' in my depictions of the future state, and of being confined to 'the jargon of the text'. This raises the question of an epistemology for eschatology. The authority for any 'utopian' depiction of the shape of things to come must, in the first place, be scriptural depiction, which has simply to be read and believed. On the one hand, theology would be pretentious and in bad taste if it were to elaborate Scripture's eschatological images and claim that they were truths of reflection that it had reached on its own – suggesting, for example, that the final state of human community would have no socialized medical care, since medicines would be immediately available from natural vegetational resources. On the other hand, theology would be idolatrous if it were to project random aspirations of the political present and proclaim them as God's will for the end of history. For Scripture treats the relation of the political present to the final purposes of God not simply as one of striving to plenitude, the satisfaction of felt needs, but as a moment of immediate confrontation. Theology, then, cannot declare that the future is one of socialized medical care simply because that is what we presently want. The scriptural depictions must be correlated with some interpretation of our

present political condition, either affirmatively or critically. We may hold that scriptural eschatology supports socialized medicine, or that it denies it support. But in either case it is the political witness *of the present* to the future that we are talking about, not about the political future *as such*. Our depiction of the political future as such, then, must be indirect, mediated through the possibilities of witness in the present on the one hand and through the 'jargon of the text' on the other. To this extent an apophatic element in what we say is, in my view, inescapable.

2. My account of joy, according to Carroll, is exclusively related to creation and history, not to the future. The reasons for this lie with the subjective conditions for the experience of joy. Gladness is a subjective condition, objectively caused. The subjective condition must lie in a correspondence between the object and the subject, and where the object is future, in a correspondence between future and present. Without that, the future could not be a joyful one *for us*, however joyful it might be for God and the angels. Gladness lies in the vindication and confirmation of what is already given and loved. 'Pure' future is always terror. That we may find joy in what is still unrealized is true, but it is a truth not about joy as such, but about faith and hope, which become the basis of joy. So scriptural language about joy in the future is in self-conscious dialectic with the language of faith and hope, and understands it as a negation of present suffering.

   The expectation of judgement, on the other hand, is not merely a negative cancellation of desire. I have, I believe, consistently refused an understanding of the gospel in terms of 'first the bad news, then the good news'. When speaking of future judgement, theologians may not think in terms merely of a bad 'penultimate' which leads to a good 'ultimate'. True judgement itself is what human community longs for. So I wrote of Christ as 'the *desire* of the nations', borrowing the phrase from the *kethib* text of Haggai. Though Amos warns us not to look for the Day of the Lord because it will be a day of darkness and not light, the fulfilment of human community is not something simply *other* than judgement. Judgement is the negative form in which we grasp the positive hope. There is a truth about the world that depends on judgement for its disclosure; and that truth can be, and insuppressibly is, hoped for.

3. Carroll's model of an unfolding eschatology is suggestively illustrated from a canonical reading of the book of Isaiah, and for this use of the prophetic corpus I must express my gratitude. Yet without opening up once again the questions that must be raised about such a reading (What point of view within Israel's history is actually privileged by it? When do the readers of these prophecies finally find themselves in a position to grasp the unfolding eschatology that has guided them?), we may note that it is a reading of Isaiah in which the Zion theme is curiously independent of the messianic one.

> Would Isaiah's eschatology come to more of a point, if Carroll were to conclude his account of it with St Matthew's affirmation that it was fulfilled in the ministry and work of Jesus of Nazareth? I am not sure of the status of the disclaimer at note 39, which sets such a consideration gracefully to one side: 'our concern at this juncture is to demonstrate the flow and power of the eschatological hopes within the Old Testament itself'. Is *that* canonical criticism?

The issue between us is about the perspicacity of history in the light of the Christ-event. In the *aevum Christi* the shape of history cannot appear to us as it did to Isaiah (or to any of his anonymous followers), but can only appear to us as it appeared to Matthew. The desire of the nations has come. The continued strivings of the nations for other forms of satisfaction are, to those who have believed in Jesus risen from the dead, no longer a guide to the shape of history.

9

Power, Judgement and Possession: John's Gospel in Political Perspective

Andrew T. Lincoln

When the resources of the New Testament gospels are employed in political theology, it is either the Jesus of the synoptic tradition or the 'historical Jesus' reconstructed from that tradition who features most prominently. John's Gospel, thought to have little value in the quest for the historical Jesus because of its christological concerns and perceived 'spiritual' nature, does not immediately spring to mind as a source conducive to political reflection. After all, in contrast to the Synoptics, the Fourth Gospel has no parables about the kingdom reflecting the economic conditions of first-century Palestine and no explicit teaching about possessions or paying taxes. Whereas in Luke the poor are blessed because theirs is the kingdom of God (6:20), in John the poor are simply 'always with you' (12:8). Indeed, one scholar, J.T. Sanders, has likened the ethics of the Fourth Gospel to that of a fundamentalist Christianity unconcerned 'with war, poverty, racial inequities, and the rights of women'. In contrast to the neighbourly love and concrete aid shown to the man who was robbed, beaten and left for dead in the Lukan parable of the Good Samaritan, says Sanders, 'Johannine Christianity is interested only in whether he believes. "Are you saved, brother?" the Johannine Christian asks the man bleeding to death on the side of the road. "Are you concerned about your soul?" ... "If you believe you will have eternal life," promises the Johannine Christian, while the dying man's blood stains the ground.'[1]

How, then, does the Fourth Gospel fare in Oliver O'Donovan's wide-ranging and stimulating political treatment of the New Testament in *The Desire of the Nations*? O'Donovan deals with NT material over three chapters. Chapter 3 focuses on the mission and proclamation of the earthly Jesus, Chapter 4 treats the proclamation of the early church about Jesus, and Chapter

[1] Sanders, *Ethics*, 99–100. Rensberger, *Johannine Faith*, in particular, has made a significant contribution to redressing such an individualistic and dualistic interpretation of John.

5 incorporates New Testament material on the church. This division would be unlikely to produce raised eyebrows from most professional NT scholars. O'Donovan differs from many of them, however, in not adopting the rigorously critical perspective that requires a sifting of the synoptic material in order to filter out traces of the evangelists' and previous early Christians' colouring or inventing of material before anything about authentic Jesus material can be said. It is not that he is unaware of such issues and, indeed, he sometimes pauses to justify briefly the use of a particular passage.[2] On the whole, however, he is content to assume that most of the synoptic material corresponds closely to what happened in the life of Jesus. In this sense it could be said that he uses his sources to depict an earthly Jesus rather than to reconstruct from them a 'historical Jesus'. Even so, the Gospel of John features only minimally in Chapter 3. This is not because O'Donovan is radically sceptical about its historical value,[3] and it is certainly not because he has pigeon-holed it as 'spiritual' rather than 'political'.[4] Equally clearly, it is not because he believes that Jesus material rather than Christology is of primarily political interest.[5] It appears to be more a result of the decision about organization and presentation (including presumably, to some extent, considerations of space).

The fourth chapter of *DN* – on the proclamation of the early church – is presented in terms of Jesus Christ as representative in the four 'moments' of advent, passion, restoration and exaltation. Here under passion is found the most extensive, though still relatively brief, treatment of Johannine material, in the helpful exposition of the trial before Pilate.[6] This also underscores that the previous chapter on the earthly Jesus does not include his arrest, trial and crucifixion, which might not unreasonably be thought to belong to Jesus' earthly career. It is not clear, to take one example, why what Jesus says to Pilate about the kingdom in the Johannine trial narrative should not be treated as part of the earthly Jesus' proclamation about the kingdom, unless a prior judgement has been made (and there is no indication of this) about how much of this discussion is likely to be authentic, about how much is Johannine theologizing in the form of narrative, and about how far it is possible to make such distinctions. The point is made not in order to adopt a particular stance on this matter but in order to illustrate that, whatever arguments might be made for its usefulness, O'Donovan's division of the gospel material is not without some inconsistencies and methodological problems. He himself recognizes that his organization

[2] Cf., e.g., *DN*, 99, 101 with its discussion of the healing miracles involving Gentiles or of Jesus' anti-Pharisaic polemic.

[3] Cf., e.g., *DN*, 97.

[4] From the outset he has asked his readers to question such a distinction, see *DN*, 82.

[5] See the treatment of this matter in *DN*, 121–23.

[6] Cf. *DN*, 140–41.

of the material does not correspond to the literary form of the NT.[7] He talks also of the unity of each gospel's presentation,[8] and yet his own presentation only allows him to hint at the distinctive way each evangelist presents his narrative proclamation of the life, death and resurrection of Jesus.

When what is on offer in *DN* is such excellent fare, it might well seem ungenerous and nit-picking to look for gaps in its treatment of the NT. Yet since we do not find the political theology of each of the gospels in any substantial form,[9] what we have touched on may be more than merely a trivial issue of method or presentation. A strong case can be made that, in using the gospels as Scripture to inform and shape the attitude of the church, it is precisely their four stories of Jesus Christ, in the form we have them, that should primarily occupy our attention. For various purposes it may be necessary to decipher gospel sources, such as Q, or to attempt to discern behind the gospels' witness what can be established about the ministry of Jesus, using the tools of present-day historiography. The results of such investigations, interesting and valuable as they may be, are not, however, what count as authoritative for the church's theology.[10] It can hardly be objected against this point of view that, since the four stories are written from a post-resurrection perspective, to treat each as a whole might detract from any proper insistence that the narratives are more than fiction and that 'the politics of Jesus' were played out in a real and particular first-century historical context. After all, O'Donovan has employed parts of these four canonical stories in a composite fashion to portray the earthly Jesus' proclamation and deeds.

What will be attempted here, though far less elegantly, eruditely and incisively than O'Donovan himself might present it, is a sketch of what taking a gospel as a whole might look like in the case of John's Gospel. This exercise is one that both complements and is parasitic on O'Donovan's discussion. Indeed, the motifs of power (the mighty deeds of salvation), judgement and possession (with its conferral of community identity), which O'Donovan has employed so illuminatingly for his treatment of the political dimensions of the Old Testament and of the earthly Jesus' ministry, will be borrowed from him.[11] They will be shown to be appropriate and effective analytical categories for this gospel's message, which enables a reading rather different from one that finds

---

[7] *DN*, 120.

[8] *DN*, 121.

[9] O'Donovan has, of course, provided this type of treatment for the book of Revelation. See 'Political Thought', and the greatly abbreviated version of this in *DN*, 153–57.

[10] A similar point is made by Moberly in his essay in the present volume, 'The Use of Scripture in *The Desire of the Nations*.'

[11] See esp. *DN*, 36–46, 93–113. These categories are likely to be equally fruitful in the similar probes that would need to be carried out on the distinctive messages of Matthew, Mark and Luke.

only a notion of the individual's possession of an otherworldly salvation. O'Donovan indicates his awareness of this potential when he begins his discussion of the passion of Christ by highlighting the Johannine theme of judgement.[12]

Variations on Old Testament Judgement Themes

An evangelical political theology, according to O'Donovan, proclaims 'God's rule demonstrated and vindicated, the salvation that he has wrought in Israel and the nations',[13] and this is indeed the burden of John's evangel. God's sovereign rule, depicted primarily in terms of Jesus' inauguration of the kingdom of God in the Synoptics and of Christ's lordship in Paul, is expressed in John as God's judgement of the world carried out in Jesus. And, as is commonly recognized, the positive verdict of that judgement – eternal life – functions as John's equivalent to the synoptic motif of the kingdom of God. In John's narrative, the motifs of judgement, testimony and truth coalesce and take the shape of a cosmic trial in which Jesus acts as both witness and judge.[14] John takes up and reworks major themes and specific language from the Septuagint version of the controversies between God and the nations and God and Israel in Isaiah 40–55. So the account of the trial of Jesus before Pilate in John, the most extensive of all four Gospels and singled out by O'Donovan as particularly significant, functions as a climactic expression of the broader trial motif.

Within the OT, judgement and kingship are frequently closely associated, whether with reference to humans (e.g., 1 Kgs. 3:28; 10:9; 2 Chr. 9:8; Prov. 20:8; 29:4; Jer. 23:5) or to God (e.g., Pss. 89:14; 97:1, 2; 99:4; Isa. 33:22; Dan. 4:37).[15] The trial before Pilate in John also links the two concepts, because Jesus is interrogated about whether he is 'the king of the Jews', and the irony throughout this account plays on who is the true judge in this situation – the alleged king of the Jews or his Roman interrogator. At one point this irony appears to become blatant as the accused, dressed in mock royal insignia, is seated on the judge's bench (19:13).[16]

In the OT, judgement is related not only to kingship, but also to salvation. Judgement does not, of course, primarily have negative connotations of punishment for wrongdoing. In Isaiah, in particular, God's righteousness or righteous judgement and God's salvation are often paralleled (cf. Isa. 33:22;

---

[12] Cf. *DN*, 136.

[13] *DN*, 81.

[14] See my *Truth on Trial*, 12–262, for a fuller discussion.

[15] Cf. also *DN*, 35–36, 38.

[16] For discussion of the interpretative options, see Lincoln, *Truth on Trial*, 133–35.

46:13; 51:5, 6, 8; 56:1; 59:11). For God to save is for God to act justly. For God to establish justice is for God to right wrongs and to restore conditions of well-being. As is widely recognized, John's characteristic terminology that serves as an equivalent for salvation is life, or eternal life. This, too, is intimately associated with the trial motif, since the judgement of God has two possible outcomes. It is meant to produce the positive verdict of life, and only when this verdict is refused does condemnation come into play. The purpose of God's sovereign judgement in putting the world on trial is stated explicitly in John 3:17 – 'God did not send the Son into the world to condemn the world, but in order that the world might be saved through him.' The motivation for bringing judgement or justice is God's love for the world, and the salvation the divine judgement effects is the gift of eternal life, with its reversal of the condition of perishing (cf. 3:16). When the focus is on Jesus' initiative, a similar point is made – 'I came not to judge the world, but to save the world' (12:47), where 'judge' in the first clause has the negative connotation of 'condemn'. So, as John's narrative replays these political themes already encountered in the OT, it tells of a fresh initiative on the part of Israel's God, a new judgement on behalf of Israel and the world that entails an act of rescue from humanity's present plight of death and a provision of life and well-being. Jesus' expression of his role in this act is 'I came that they may have life, and have it abundantly' (10:10), and the person who receives his witness 'does not come under judgement [as condemnation], but has passed from death to life' (5:24).

Truth is another concept that is frequently paired with righteous judgement or justice in the OT (cf., e.g., Pss. 45:4; 96:13; 119:142, 160; Isa. 42:3; 45:19; 48:1; 59:14). For Yahweh, to judge justly is to determine, declare and demonstrate the truth. In the context of a lawsuit, truth will stand for the whole process of judging, culminating in the verdict, and its specific content will be dependent on the particular issue at stake. In the case of the Fourth Gospel, that issue has at its heart whether the crucified Jesus is the Messiah, the Son of God, and is therefore one with God, and whether through this Jesus God has effected a judgement that means life for the world (cf. 20:31). Jesus, in his witness, claims to be the embodiment of this truth that is life-giving (14:6).

Power and Judgement in Jesus' Mission

The presupposition of judgement and trial is clearly that, as its Creator, God has sovereign rights over this world, and that all humanity and especially Israel, with whom God has entered into a special covenantal relationship, owe God acknowledgement and allegiance. The dispute recounted in John's Gospel is about whether this trial is now taking place with Jesus as its unique divine agent. The language of the prologue makes the assumptions of the lawsuit explicit. God's Logos, who was God (1:1c), is the one through whom all things came into being (1:3, 10). So in taking up the mission to pursue the divine lawsuit, the Logos 'came to what was his own' and to 'his own people' (1:11). The prologue both establishes the rightful divine claim and makes clear that the subsequent narrative's focus on the incarnate Logos' mission is to be seen as the pursuit of God's claim. Not only does its first verse both distinguish the Logos from God and identify the Logos with God but it also, in what is probably the best attested reading of its last verse (1:18), asserts that it is one who is 'only God' who makes God known. In John's account of a cosmic trial, it is through the incarnate Logos that God comes to expression as witness and judge. God and Jesus are at one in the task of bringing the world to judgement.

John's Gospel, unlike the Synoptics, has no trial of Jesus before the Jewish Sanhedrin. This is because Jesus' public ministry has already been depicted as a trial before Israel, in which the controversy with 'the Jews' takes the form both of a number of acts of judgement and a series of interrogations, or mini-trials. After John the Baptist has been introduced as the first witness (cf. 1:6–8, 15, 19–34), it soon becomes clear that Jesus is to be the chief witness in the lawsuit (cf. 3:11–21, 31–36; 8:14). Not only so, but just as in Isaiah 40–55, in the controversies with the nations and with Israel, Yahweh could be accuser, accused and judge, so Jesus, as God's uniquely authorized agent, will combine these functions. As a witness, he is sometimes the accuser and sometimes the accused, yet at the same time he is the judge (cf. 5:22, 30; 9:39; 12:47, 48). Particularly in the disputation of John 5 and the interrogation of John 8, Jesus, as the accused, gives witness, which then becomes prosecution as he mounts his own counter-accusations. The prosecuting role shades over already into a judging one. Witness becomes a form of judgement when it is witness against evil: 'The world ... hates me because I testify against it that its works are evil' (7:7). Indeed, the very content of Jesus' witness as truth and its nature as ultimately self-authenticating (8:14) entail that Jesus' witness is the criterion of judgement, and he is at the same time the judge. The goal of both the testifying and the judging remains the positive verdict of life. Only where there is wilful refusal to receive this life and its light is there the secondary outcome of a judgement of death and blindness. Because some of the Pharisees refuse to admit any blindness and are so adamant that they do see, they receive the negative judgement – 'your sin remains' (9:41). This perspective on the purpose of Jesus' role as judge is reinforced at the end of the public ministry to Israel in 12:47b, 48, where he can say, on the one hand, 'I came not to judge the world, but to save the world.' On the other hand, he can then add, 'the one who rejects me and does not receive my word has a judge; on the last day the word that I have spoken will serve as judge'.

Whereas others judge by appearances (cf. 7:24) or judge according to the flesh (cf. 8:15), Jesus does not. Instead, his judgement is in line with that of the messianic king of Isaiah 11:2–5, who 'shall not judge by what his eyes see, or decide by what his ears hear; but with righteousness he shall judge the poor'. This judge was to be one on whom the Spirit of the Lord rests and, of course, John the Baptist had testified to seeing the Spirit remain on Jesus (1:32, 33). That Jesus' judging is not ordinary human judging is clear from 2:23–25, where we are told that Jesus did not entrust himself to those who believed on the basis of his signs. This was 'because he knew all people and needed no one to testify about anyone; for he himself knew what was in everyone'. Jesus' omniscience about humans means that he can dispense with the need for witnesses in making his own judgements. He judges from the divine standpoint. Again, in the work of judgement Jesus and God are at one (cf. 5:30; 8:16; 12:48, 49).

The works, or signs, that Jesus performs can be seen both as witness to his being sent by the Father (5:36; 10:25) and as powerful acts of positive judgement, overturning dearth, disease and death and producing plenty, wholeness and life. They are anticipations of *eternal* life, which does not simply signify duration but also takes up the notion of the life of the age to come and denotes the quality of life appropriate to that age. The present experience of this life is not to be viewed as simply on some separate 'spiritual' level. Its centre lies in a believing relationship to the God made known through Jesus and the Spirit, yet this affects all of human living. All of Jesus' signs bear witness to this life, whether it is through supplying the wine and joy of the new order, restoring people to health and sight, providing bread, mastering the chaos waters through walking on the sea, or raising Lazarus from the dead. This last sign in particular makes clear that the judgement's positive verdict includes resurrection and thus that created bodily life is embraced by eternal life. Not only the witness of Jesus' works, but also that of his words, conveys life (cf. 6:63, 68). Many of the symbols in his discourses, such as bread, water and light, have life as a primary referent. With reference to light, Jesus can declare, 'Whoever follows me will never walk in darkness but will have the light of life' (8:12). Light can in fact serve as a symbol for the whole judging function of Jesus' mission (cf. 3:19–21) but, because for those who come to the light it means receiving sight (9:39a) and no longer remaining in darkness (12:35, 36, 45), it is also particularly appropriate as a reference to the positive outcome of this judgement.

The incident in the temple, which in this gospel is placed close to the outset of Jesus' mission, can also be seen as an act of judgement on the old order within Israel.[17] Since Jerusalem and the temple were regarded as God's own possession in a special way, Jesus' activity there is a graphic illustration of the prologue's formulation about the Logos coming to 'what was his own' (1:11a). To focus solely on the account's main point – that Jesus himself is now the fulfilment or

---

[17] Cf. also *DN*, 97.

replacement of the temple and all that it stood for – can lead to ignoring some of the more immediate political ramifications in John's account. Buildings can be powerful and substantial symbols, as we have been reminded forcefully by the attacks on the World Trade Center and the Pentagon, and the temple had massive religious, economic and political significance for Israel. Jesus' action in this building represents a shaking of its foundations. The presence in the temple precincts of animals and birds to be bought for sacrifice was a necessity if the Torah's requirements for sacrifice were to be obeyed. The moneychangers had to be there, too, if the money in the possession of pilgrims was to be changed into the coinage acceptable to the temple. Driving all these out at one of the most significant feasts of the year is a symbolic action that temporarily brings to a halt the sacrificial system understood to be ordained by God in the law. The saying that interprets this action – 'do not make my Father's house an emporium or house of trade' contains an allusion to Zechariah 14:20, 21. This passage looks forward to God's presence in a renewed Jerusalem on the day of the Lord. At that time all nations will keep the Feast of Tabernacles, and the final words of the prophecy are 'there shall no longer be traders in the house of the Lord of hosts on that day'. The trading previously associated with the sacrificial system will not be necessary, because, in the end-time worship of Yahweh as king, all aspects of life will have become sacred. Jesus' saying underlines that his action constitutes a prophetic gesture pointing to the end of the present temple order and its sacrifices in the expectation of their replacement by the new arrangements appropriate for God's eschatological presence. It is not so much that the traders Jesus drives out were doing anything wrong as that, in the new order Jesus has come to bring, their presence will not be needed at all. The evangelist makes clear that Jesus' further words – 'Destroy this temple and in three days I will raise it up' – refer to his body. The response of 'the Jews', however, which remains on the literal and merely earthly plane, as they think in terms of the impossibility of rebuilding the temple in three days when it had taken forty-six years to construct, ensures that the saying's play on what has in fact happened to the temple building is not missed. The evangelist is writing at a time when he and his readers knew that the temple had been destroyed. A major shift in the locus of presence and power has manifestly taken place, and John's Gospel claims that this was precipitated by God's presence now being located in the crucified and risen body of Jesus. The temple incident displays the fact that this new locus of the divine presence means that there can no longer be 'business as usual'. Instead, an eschatological era of holiness and justice for all has been inaugurated. The vision of the time of the new temple in Zechariah 14:20, 21, where traditional distinctions between sacred and secular are transcended, is held to have become a reality in Christ.

The issue of truth is most to the fore in Jesus' mission to Israel in the heated contest of claims in 8:12–59. In response to accusations about the invalidity of his single witness, Jesus declares that both his witness and his judgement are nevertheless true because of his divine origin and destiny (8:14, 16). Later, he asserts that continuing belief in his word enables people to know the truth of the issue at stake in the trial and to experience the salvific effect of its true judgement in liberation from sin (8:31, 32). As becomes clear from the parallel statement in 8:36 – 'If the Son makes you free, you will be free indeed' – the truth that emancipates is God's revelation embodied in Jesus. Those who are said to have believed immediately cast doubt on the nature of their belief by the incomprehension they reveal in their response. They show more concern about being descendants of Abraham than about being followers of Jesus, and they deny the need for liberation with the claim that they have never been slaves to anyone. There is obvious irony on the political level about such a claim being made by those under Roman occupation, though presumably they intend it more as an expression of their freedom from idolatry and sin on the basis of their relation to God through the covenant with Abraham. Jesus does not allow them to get away with their claim even on this level, pointing out that all who sin thereby show themselves to be slaves to sin. How far, we might be prompted to ask in our present context, are those groups or nations which most defiantly proclaim either their political or religious freedom really free? Here in John it is not that the emancipation Jesus proclaims has nothing to say to the situation of Israel's subjection to Rome but that, because it deals with sin as the root cause of all subjection, this freedom will give a profoundly different perspective on the values held by those on both sides of this political divide. The issue becomes clearer in the trial of Jesus before the representative of Roman power, Pilate.

Power and Judgement in the Trial before Pilate

The climactic trial before Pilate sets divine judgement squarely on the world stage and in the context of the nations. God, through Jesus as the divinely authorized representative, is to be seen as judging the nations, represented by this official of the Roman Empire, behind whom Caesar himself hovers as an influence. The account revolves around what is true judgement and who speaks truly and has sovereign power. Jesus' mission statement about bearing witness to the truth (18:37) comes in the context of this trial when, as he knows, Jesus is about to be sentenced to death. Its setting involves a struggle for power between Pilate and the Jewish religious leaders, and it also comes in the midst of a dialogue about power. The Jewish leaders have used their power to arrest Jesus and to hand him over to Pilate (18:35). They are impotent to carry out by themselves the death sentence that they believe Jesus merits under the law (cf. 18:31; 19:7), but they expect to use their influence to persuade Pilate to carry out the sentence on a different charge – that of being a politically subversive claimant to messianic power. Pilate is not anxious to be manipulated, but Jesus' first words in reply to Pilate's question – 'Are you the King of the Jews?' – are also a question that reminds him of the power struggle in which he has become involved – 'Do you ask this on your own, or did others tell you about me?' (18:34). Later Pilate will warn Jesus that he, Pilate, has the power in this situation, and Jesus will respond that any authority Pilate possesses has in fact been delegated to him from above (19:10, 11). In the power struggle between Pilate and the Jewish religious leaders, the latter get their way by using intimidation, suggesting to Pilate that by releasing Jesus he could well be seen as disloyal to the emperor (19:12). But Pilate gets his way by not handing Jesus over to be crucified until he has extracted from the religious leaders a confession of complete allegiance to the emperor and his powers that amounts to a betrayal of their supposed allegiance to God as their one King (19:15). This is such a major concession, however, that at the level of the play for power the narrative portrays Pilate as having kept the upper hand. There is, of course, another element in the contemporary political power struggle that is brought to our attention in this episode. In contrast to the Jewish religious leaders' willingness to accommodate to Roman imperial power, there is the response to that power represented by Barabbas, the brigand and insurrectionist. The narrative presents a choice between Jesus and Barabbas, just as it will present one between Jesus and Caesar.

Jesus' delayed reply to the question of whether he is the king of the Jews, and therefore, from Pilate's perspective, whether he is staking out some claim to political power, is that his royal power, his kingdom, is not of this world. This does not mean that it is totally otherworldly. It is exercised and displayed in this world, but it has its source elsewhere – with God (cf. 8:23). It cannot, therefore, be neatly categorized from within Pilate's this-worldly value system, where power means political dominance, diplomatic manoeuvring and strategic treaties. It is a power that will not be co-opted by the destructive forces of this world's cycle of violence. If it were, Jesus' followers would be fighting for him (18:36). Both the programmatic use of force against an oppressive system by an insurrectionist like Barabbas (18:40) and the attempt to wield the sword in self-defence by a follower like Peter (cf. 18:10, 11) are called into question in the light of Jesus' kingdom programme. Jesus in fact subordinates the whole question of royal power to that of truth – 'You say that I am a king. For this I was born, and for this I came into the world, to testify to the truth' (18:37a). His witness in apparent weakness becomes the arbiter of the nature, purpose and use of power. The truth of his cause is one that subverts normal human assumptions about power, and, as we shall explore later, thereby also subverts human assumptions about truth that see it as simply a form of power. Jesus adds, 'Everyone who belongs to the truth listens to my voice' (18:37b). Again, the power of his cause is not that of physical force or of manipulation. It draws in adherents as they accept his witness. For 'truth creates a socially centripetal force; it gathers its following of those who "belong to" the truth. Thus Jesus commands a social authority – the root of all social authority, in fact.'[18]

Though his kingdom will not be achieved by political means, it will have political implications, as this trial itself reveals. Religious and political dimensions of the kingdom are inextricably interwoven, since, for both 'the Jews' and Pilate, acknowledgement of Jesus' kingship is shown to clash with loyalty to Caesar's rule. This emerges in the last scene of the trial – 19:12–16a. 'The Jews' are depicted as playing on Pilate's political relationship with a suspicious Tiberius, who was known to act swiftly and brutally in response to any hint of treason. They present Jesus' kingship as a rival to Caesar's power – 'Everyone who claims to be king sets himself against the emperor' (19:12b). The dilemma of Pilate's own situation of trial now becomes even clearer. He is faced not simply with a decision between Jesus and 'the Jews', but also with a decision between Jesus and Caesar. The narrative, however, presents the Jewish religious leaders as victims of the very dilemma they have posed for Pilate. When Pilate does not give up on his sarcastic jest and provokes and enrages them with his question – 'Shall I crucify your King?'[19] – this produces the final and shockingly ironic words of the chief priests – 'we have no king but the emperor' (19:15c). Not only is Jesus cast aside as messianic King but so also, apparently, are all expectations of a royal Messiah who would deliver Israel from foreign oppression. Instead, 'the Jews' proclaim their loyalty to the oppressor. But what is more, by proclaiming their loyalty to Caesar as a way of securing Jesus' death, they end up renouncing their God. Through their own words, the chief priests are portrayed as judging and condemning themselves. They have accused Jesus of blasphemy, but now they are shown to be guilty of apostasy by pledging exclusive allegiance to Caesar rather than to God as King. In this episode, then, 'Rome is seen as hostile to the hope of oppressed Israel, but Rome's authority is undermined and relativized by the assertion of God's sovereignty in the kingship of Jesus. Israel's true allegiance must be to God, not Caesar, and for John this allegiance is now fittingly expressed in adherence to Jesus the King.'[20]

---

[18] *DN*, 140.

[19] *DN*, 141, suggestively sees this as part of 'the irony whereby Caesar's representative is denied, by the logic of Caesar's rule, the final privilege of impotence ... His position forces him to confront God's Kingdom and to concede its claim. The title "King of the Jews" on Pilate's lips begins as a joke against the Jewish leadership (18:39) and ends as a capitulation.'

[20] Rensberger, *Johannine Faith*, 116. For his treatment of the trial before Pilate, see 87–106.

Power and Judgement in the Death and Resurrection of Jesus

As signalled by his final words on the cross – 'it is completed' (19:30), Jesus' witness to the truth is established in and through his death. This is also the death of the judge. The profound ironies of the mocking of the royal judge at the Roman trial and the superscription on the cross – 'Jesus of Nazareth, the king of the Jews' – reinforce the notion that, in the cosmic perspective, the power of the judge is exhibited in the weakness of suffering and death. The superscription proclaims in the major languages of the first-century world that Israel does have a sovereign over the world and its powers, but it also makes clear that this sovereign is enthroned on and rules from a cross. Jesus remains judge while transforming the criteria normally associated with judgement. The one to whom has been delegated all judgement at this point submits himself to the world's judgement in the conviction that he is also submitting himself to the Father's judgement in the cosmic trial. If his dying on the cross is the completion of Jesus' witness, then it is to be expected that this will also be the time at which the Father's judgement is rendered. By absorbing the violence of the negative verdict of death, Jesus as the judge who is judged becomes the source of the positive verdict of life, as blood and water flow from his side (19:34). The symbols of the blood and the water have been explained earlier in the narrative in 6:53, 54 and 7:38, 39. They point unmistakably to the saving judgement in which life for humanity is effected through the death of the victim.

The accounts of the empty tomb and of the appearances complete the vindication of the judgement concerning Jesus.[21] They confirm Jesus' earlier witness to his resurrection (cf., e.g., 2:19; 10:17, 18) and are also integral to his role as judge, in which 'just as the Father has life in himself, so he has granted the Son also to have life in himself' (5:26). At the heart of the account of Jesus' final sign in the witness of works before Israel, the temporary restoration of Lazarus to human bodily life, is the saying of 11:25 – 'I am the resurrection and the life.' Jesus claims to be the embodiment of both eschatological expectations of the resurrection of the dead and of the verdict of life. That claim is substantiated in Jesus' own resurrection, in which, unlike Lazarus, he needs no one to unbind him as he leaves his grave clothes behind (cf. 11:44, with 20:7).

Jesus' death is seen as the hour of glory, but that evaluation does not obviate the need for his own restoration to life. It is significant that the message the risen Jesus tells Mary to pass on is not that he is risen, but that he is ascending (20:17). This links the resurrection accounts with the earlier discourse about Jesus' ascent (cf. 3:13; 6:62) and his return to the Father who sent him (cf., e.g., 7:33; 14:28; 16:28). Now both the death and the resurrection can be seen as

---

[21] Cf. also *DN*, 136.

vital stages of the ascent in glory. The climax of Jesus' story is not the death itself, nor the resurrection itself, but the return of the crucified Jesus to the Father in a resurrected body. So the weakness of the truth does at the same time involve power – the power of life over death. Yet the narrative does not allow us to forget that these remain in a dialectical relationship, whereby the power of life is only possible in and through the powerlessness of death. It makes clear that the resurrection does not triumphalistically supersede the crucifixion, because the marks of the victim's woundedness remain in the hands and side of the risen Jesus (20:20).

Possession and Community Identity

In discussing Israel as Yahweh's possession, O'Donovan can see this notion in political terms because it shows 'how the judgements of God could give order and structure to a community and sustain it in being'.[22] John's prologue introduces the theme of possession in relation to Israel and the world. The Logos was in the world that came into being though him, and yet the world did not know him (1:10). The focus then becomes narrower in the parallel statement of 1:11. The Logos came to his own property, to his own home within the world, and in that setting his own people did not accept him. But in contrast to those who oppose him, there are those who do take up the role that Israel was meant to have as God's possession. The Logos authorizes a new group of children of God from all – both Jews and Gentiles – who receive him (1:12). His believing followers will later be designated as 'his own' (13:1). Jesus possesses them as he abides in them and will preserve them by raising them up at the last day (6:54–56). As the good shepherd, Jesus knows his own sheep, laying down his life for them, while they know and listen to his voice (10:3, 4, 14–16). Such followers are to be seen as the shared possession of the Father and the Son (17:6, 9, 10).

Acknowledgement of Jesus' authority in this new community is through believing, which is synonymous with receiving or accepting his witness (cf., e.g., 3:11, 12). Jesus' word now fulfils the role the law had previously played in ordering Israel's existence and providing life. In 12:48–50, where Jesus' summary of his mission recalls what is said of the prophet like Moses, his word, which is the Father's commandment of eternal life, will serve as the ultimate criterion of judgement. The teachings Jesus gives to his disciples can therefore be called commandments that they are to keep (cf. 13:34; 14:15, 21; 15:10, 12).

Those who have accepted Jesus' testimony have aligned themselves with God's verdict and are now in a position to play their own part as a community

---

[22] *DN*, 41.

of witnesses in God's continuing judgement of the world. The announcement of the continuation of the trial into their own time forms a significant part of the preparation Jesus gives his followers in John 13–17. Particularly in 15:18–16:15, Jesus tells them that, after he has returned to the Father, they will face the hatred of the world, expulsion from the synagogue and even death, but his cause must still be argued. The disciples themselves are now to be witnesses – 'You also are to testify because you have been with me from the beginning' (15:27). Just as Jesus' witness had entailed humiliation and a martyr's death, so social ostracism and martyrdom may well characterize the witness of his followers, including Peter in a later Roman context (cf. 21:18, 19).[23] Martyrdom is a political act – the result of non-violent resistance for the sake of the truth in the face of an oppressive power.[24]

But the disciples are not alone as they play their role in the lawsuit of history. 'When the Paraclete or Advocate comes, whom I will send to you from the Father, the Spirit of truth who comes from the Father, he will testify on my behalf' (15:26). Just as Jesus was accompanied by the divine witness of the Father, so now his followers are accompanied by the divine witness of the Spirit. An advocate was a person of influence who could be called into court to speak in favour of defendants or their cause. This Advocate will be with the disciples (14:16, 17). He will aid them in their witness to the truth, because, as the Spirit of truth, he will guide them into all truth (16:13, 14; cf. also 14:26). As was the case with Jesus, the Spirit in his advocacy moves from witnessing to accusing and judging. He becomes the Prosecutor as he presses home the divine verdict of the lawsuit, confronting the world with the negative judgement that has been passed on it and convicting it of its guilt in the issues that are contested in the trial (16:8–11). As the Spirit promotes the divine verdict, that verdict is seen as overturning the world's values and the criteria for judgement that it has used. As O'Donovan has put it, 'The Holy Spirit brings God's act in Christ into critical opposition to the falsely structured reality in which we live.'[25] This takes place with respect to three interrelated topics. It is sin that causes the plight of death from which the trial is intended to rescue the world. The prosecuting work of the Spirit entails showing the world that it is culpable in its sin and that the chief manifestation of that sin and its culpability is its very refusal to believe in the one who has brought the salvific judgement it needs. In convicting the world of its sin, the Spirit convicts it also of the rightness or justice of Jesus' cause, since without such a conviction there would be no

---

[23] For observations on this tradition, see Lincoln, *Truth on Trial*, 305–6.

[24] It differs radically, therefore, from any notion of martyrdom in the context of terrorism, where for the sake of some higher cause one voluntarily takes one's own life in order to take the lives of others.

[25] *RMO*, 104.

awareness that it had been guilty in its refusal to believe. The other corollary of the truth or right judgement of Jesus' cause is that the same verdict that vindicated Jesus was the one that condemned the world. The Spirit convicts the world that it is the recipient of this negative verdict, just as the world's ruler has been.[26] Through the Spirit, then, the believing community continues to point to the true state of affairs in the world, that political reality brought about by God's judgement in Christ. The Spirit is more characteristically associated with the positive verdict in the lawsuit, that of life (cf. 6:63; 7:37–39). Because Jesus has himself experienced this verdict in the resurrection, he can pass on the life-giving Spirit to the disciples when he commissions them (20:21, 22). Easter and Pentecost come together in John's narrative, as the risen Jesus breathes on his disciples and says to them, 'receive the Holy Spirit' (20:22).

The believing community as Christ's possession carries out its witness in a world which may well at present be hostile, but which is also rightfully Christ's possession. To the question 'Whose world is it?', the answer of John's Gospel is unequivocal. It is not that of the Jewish religious authorities who are depicted as impotent to carry out their own law and as dependent on and confessing their allegiance to Rome (cf. 18:31; 19:15). It is not that of Rome, whether represented by Pilate or the emperor, since the former is reminded that whatever power he has is from above (19:11). It is not that of the powers of evil and their ruler. In the trial's verdict, 'the ruler of this world' is driven out (12:31), has no power over Jesus (14:30), and has been condemned (16:11). Instead, the world rightly belongs to the one who has come into it from above to bring salvific judgement.

But, of course, the evangelist also uses the term 'world' in a negative sense, where it stands for the world of humanity that rejects the claims of the judgement that is taking place. Jesus' followers do not belong to the world in this sense, but they have been chosen out of it or have been given to him out of it (cf. 15:19; 17:6, 9, 14, 16). But it is also made clear that they are not taken out of the world in its neutral sense (17:15), since this is the territory in which they have a mission to make clear the nature of the verdict in the true judgement that has been given. The point of their presence in the world is that the rest of humanity might come to its senses, recognize God as the rightful instigator of the lawsuit and Jesus as the divine agent, and, through the unity of the believing community, perceive the love that has been the motivation for the process of salvific judgement (17:21, 23). That this vocation of Jesus' followers in the world is expected to have positive results is indicated by the fact that Jesus prays not only for them, but also for those who will believe in him through their witness (17:20). As he goes to his death, Jesus himself can see his mission as

---

[26] For a fuller discussion of 16:8–11, compare *RMO*, 105–6, with Lincoln, *Truth on Trial*, 117–20.

already accomplished – 'In the world you face persecution. But take courage; I have conquered the world!' (16:33). This is a ringing announcement that he has emerged triumphant in the lawsuit with the world, having reclaimed what was rightfully his, and that this makes all the difference for his followers who are to carry out their mission in that world, willing to accept persecution and pain because they are confident in their knowledge of whose world it is.

O'Donovan speaks of life in the church as providing a bridgehead for God's rule over society.[27] The political character of the believing community in John's gospel lies in its embodied witness to that rule of justice through its love, unity and hospitality. It is noticeable that, when Jesus is speaking to the disciples in the farewell discourse, the language of love rather than that of eternal life predominates. Love, it seems, is the primary manifestation of the present experience of the positive verdict of eternal life. A community that enacts the pattern of loving service seen in Jesus' witness is essential for the credibility of the continuing witness in the world – 'By this everyone will know that you are my disciples, if you have love for one another' (13:35). Jesus' prayer for his disciples and for those who will believe through their witness makes clear that this community is to be a united one and that the issues at stake in the overall judgement hinge on this – 'that they may become completely one, so that the world may know that you have sent me ...' (17:23). Since the truth established in John's version of the lawsuit is the oneness between Jesus and God, it is not surprising that the testimony to that truth is displayed by the oneness of the witnesses.

As a number of recent writers, including O'Donovan,[28] have highlighted, one of the forms which justice takes is hospitality, the welcome of the other. In the Fourth Gospel, God's saving judgement on behalf of humanity can be seen as an act of hospitality that takes place in the face of human inhospitality toward God. God's welcoming love is such that, in the gift of the Son, God suffers humanity's violence in order to make space within God's self for this hostile other by sharing the divine life (cf. 3:16). The divine persons who in their self-giving make space for one another without abandoning their own identities also open up their divine life to provide the space that is the ultimate home for humanity. Jesus can pray, 'As you, Father, are in me and I am in you, may they also be in us' (17:21). Jesus himself memorably breaks with all conventions about the act of hospitality when he washes his disciples' feet himself. The one into whose hands all things have been given exercises his sovereign authority

---

[27] Cf. *DN*, 266.

[28] Cf. *DN*, 73, 268. 'There are always "others", those not of our fold whom we must respect and encounter.' 'The act of recognition and welcome, which leaps across the divide between communities and finds on the other side another community which offers the distinctive friendship of hospitality, is a fundamental form of human relating.'

by taking on the role of servant (13:3, 4). Accepting this gesture of hospitality is said to be necessary for having a share in him (13:8b). His act then becomes the paradigm for the outworking of justice among humans, as his followers are told that they are to take the same vulnerable stance in relation to others by washing their feet (13:14–17). Jesus knows that among those whose feet he washes is a betrayer, an enemy, and he later continues to extend his hospitality to Judas in the special gesture of offering him the dipped piece of food (13:26). The extension of loving justice to the hostile other by God and Jesus, especially in the verdict rendered at the cross, suggests that there is no reason to interpret the injunctions to wash one another's feet and to love one another as exclusively restricting believers' responsibility to others to those in their community.[29] These injunctions also by no means assume that the others encountered in such actions will be congenial. Instead, they require a self-giving regard for those who may well be radically different in many ways. Both the divine grounds and the community practice of hospitality mean that difference need not be interpreted as inevitably leading to violence. Christian community is to be both a witness to the prior ground of unity in our world and an anticipation of the full revelation of the just and merciful judgement in which all differences will be embraced.

The welcome of the other is not, however, a relativism that simply accepts all differences as equally valid. John 8 notoriously contains strong judgement against those who are seen as manipulating the truth for violent ends. There is deceit and there are enemies. Such differentiating judgements have to be made without them becoming exclusionary ones. When they are made by human witnesses rather than the divine judge, there always has to be the recognition that such necessary judgements are provisional and fallible. But beyond that, there has to be the willingness, which has now been made possible, to show hospitality, with all its attendant risks, to those whom one also feels compelled to acknowledge as enemies of the truth. The fallibility and imperfection of Christians' understanding and practice in their witness to God's saving justice in Jesus means that these are always in need of correction and enrichment, and, particularly in the public sphere, recognition of this should ensure an ability to negotiate and to come to terms with the inevitability of compromise. As O'Donovan observes,

> Even at its best, public right action can bear only an indirect relation to the demands of truth and goodness considered absolutely ... The exercise of political authority is

---

[29] As O'Donovan, *RMO*, 242, rightly observes, 'Far from denying universal love of man for man, the love of the believer for Christ and for his fellow-believer is the form in which it is restored and re-enters the world. For the church anticipates restored humanity, and all humanity lies implicitly within the church.' For his fuller discussion of the love-command and respect for persons, see *RMO*, 237–44.

> the search for a compromise, which, while bearing the fullest witness to the truth that can in the circumstances be borne, will, nevertheless, lie within the scope of possible public action in the particular community of fallen men which it has to serve.[30]

Justice, Truth and Life

To read the Fourth Gospel in the light of power, judgement, possession and associated themes allows one to place its treatment of the individual believer's experience of communion with God through Christ, which has frequently been emphasized in an interpretation of John as 'the spiritual Gospel', in a broader context where its political dimensions emerge. In the OT, just judgement was seen as the condition for life. In many instances the setting for appeal to divine judgement was that Israel was experiencing concrete injustices and crying out for Yahweh to intervene in order to deal with oppression and restore what was necessary for Israel's well-being. In Jewish eschatological hopes also, there would be a last judgement in which wrongs would be righted and at which the resurrection of the righteous would be followed by their enjoyment of the life of the age to come. Against this background, John's Gospel can be seen as depicting how in Jesus the God of Israel, the one true God, is bringing to the world the justice for which it longs and the fullness of life that accompanies such justice. As God's unique agent, Jesus functions both as the witness to the goal of justice and life for all and as the judge who has authority to achieve it. The truth of the divine verdict in the judgement process has to do, therefore, not only with claims about Jesus' identity, but also with the relation of human existence to the divine purpose.

A good case can be made that one of the catalysts for the evangelist's employment of the judgement motif was the experience of the community from which the Gospel emerged.[31] Its themes addressed the concrete issues of what Johannine Christians considered the injustice of Jesus' treatment at the hands of Jewish and Roman authorities, and of their own treatment at the hands of the Jewish authorities in their area – in which their expulsion from the synagogue was considered a substitute for a sentence of death and accompanied by social deprivation and shaming. The Gospel's narrative proclaims that such events did not mean the absence of God but were to be viewed in the light of God's sovereign judgement achieved in a just verdict for both Jesus and believers in him, a verdict that entailed life rather than death. This verdict would not only have been taken to mean that they had been placed in a right relationship to the world's Creator and Judge, but it would also have been seen to entail religio-political and social consequences as concrete as those the verdict of the

[30] *RMO*, 130.

[31] Cf. Lincoln, *Truth on Trial*, 263–307, for a fuller discussion.

earthly authorities had produced. The positive verdict in the cosmic trial was an assurance that, in Jesus, God was at work in this world against all that threatened life – including injustice, oppression and suffering – and was restoring the conditions that make for human well-being, even though these would be experienced at present in the midst of continuing hostility and physical death.

To engage adequately the political theology O'Donovan draws from his reading of Scripture would take us far beyond an interpretation of this one Gospel and severely stretch this writer's levels of competence. In what follows I simply suggest, therefore, some basic implications for Christian political attitudes that appear to follow from the preceding presentation of the Fourth Gospel's message. If their emphasis is seen to differ slightly from O'Donovan's, it may be due to the conviction that the believing community's appropriation of the message is itself always caught up in relations of power and domination, and therefore it needs to be conscious of the role its social location plays in its interpretation of Scripture.[32] In the course of these concluding reflections, I will attempt to draw attention to elements of this Gospel's political message which have the potential to address such concerns. And the notion that right judgement about its message is inextricably bound up with just action is, of course, not foreign to John's Gospel. It holds that those who do what is true come to the light (3:21), and John's Jesus asserts that anyone who resolves to do the will of God will know whether his teaching is from God (7:17).

Present-day readers, like the evangelists' community, belong to a world that desires to see true judgement. It is a world of suffering and death for millions of victims of oppression and genocide, and for the many casualties of the ambiguities of international power politics, a world in which there remains the cry of humanity for justice. It is a cry to which even the setting up of international tribunals to punish war crimes can never be an adequate response. Where is there a comprehensive judgement that will demonstrate the difference between justice and injustice as it remembers the forgotten victims of starvation, rape, torture and barbaric savagery? On a very different, personal level, much of the appeal of therapy in Western culture springs from a deep desire for someone from outside one's situation, yet sympathetic with it, to understand, evaluate and reveal the truth about the messiness of one's particular story. There is a longing for a safe place to be judged in the context of mercy and forgiveness. On both levels, judgement is essential to hope. There can be no enduring hope if we have only the ambivalences of our present, the continuing interplay between power and victimization without resolution. Indeed, our very ability to recognize ambiguity in the present and to be torn apart by injustice is parasitic on a sense of ultimate justice. John's Gospel holds that there will be an

---

[32] This, of course, points us to some of the issues raised by Peter Scott's contribution to this volume in 'Return to the Vomit of "Legitimation"'?

ultimate reckoning, a final hour at the end of history when the dead will be raised for a judgement of either life or condemnation (cf., e.g., 5:28, 29). Justice will be seen to have been done – hence, the notion of a resurrection even for condemnation. The particular contribution of John's story of Jesus, however, is its stress that in him this judgement has been decisively anticipated and inaugurated. The verdict of the Creator and Judge that reveals the purpose of the cosmic story no longer only awaits the end. It has been rendered in the life and death of Jesus and therefore already supplies the decisive clue to the whole of history from within its midst. The 'realized' aspect of the trial does not render the rest of history meaningless. Rather, it is what enables there to be the basic trust about a justice that has in view human well-being, a trust without which human activity is in danger of being undermined by despair or cynicism. But, more than this, the decisive verdict given in the death of Jesus reveals the nature of the divine judgement. Judgement at the last day will be in the hands of the judge who has been judged, the crucified one, and so the justice that will be displayed remains his merciful and life-giving judgement.

One of the features that distinguishes John's Gospel is that it so explicitly makes the death of the witness and judge as victim of the world's violence the criterion for true judgement. Through Jesus' death, the power of true judgement is revealed through the weakness of self-giving love. Power and truth converge in Jesus as victim to provide a radically different view of the relation between truth and power than that which prevails in late modern thought, where claims to truth become simply a disguise of the will to power. Following Nietzsche, truth claims are seen as ways of asserting one's place in the world and as inevitably leading to manipulation and violence. Interestingly, Nietzsche himself referred to John's Gospel in expounding his views:

> Do I still have to add that in the entire New Testament there is only *one* solitary figure one is obliged to respect? Pilate, the Roman governor. To take a Jewish affair *seriously* – he cannot persuade himself to do that. One Jew more or less – what does it matter? The noble scorn of a Roman before whom an impudent misuse of the word 'truth' was carried on has enriched the New Testament with the only expression *which possesses value* – which is its criticism, its *annihilation* even: 'What is truth?'[33]

After Nietzsche, Foucault has stated the case for truth as power as clearly as anyone:

> Truth is a thing of this world: it is produced only by virtue of multiple forms of constraints. And it induces regular effects of power. Each society has its regime of truth, its 'general politics' of truth: that is, the types of discourse which it accepts and makes function as true ...[34]

---

[33] Nietzsche, *The Anti-Christ*, 162.

[34] Foucault, *Power/Knowledge*, 131.

If the explanation of truth is that what passes for it is produced by power and such truth becomes the means by which the powerful wield more power, then not only are any supposed criteria for judging between truth claims undermined, because they too are socially produced, but we are simply left to the competing claims of rival groups that inevitably produce violence. The earlier quotation from Nietzsche shows the cost of such an explanation of truth, a cost to its victims. The person who treats the question about truth with contempt has no compelling reason not to treat human life with contempt, as Nietzsche's horrendous throwaway line, 'One Jew more or less – what does it matter?' illustrates. We need to be alert not only to the dangers, but also to the potential for human well-being bound up with claims to truth, including that of the Fourth Gospel that sees truth embodied in Jesus.[35] Jesus embodies the truth of divine judgement while subverting the notion that truth is simply power. The power of the ultimate arbiter of truth is exhibited in the weakness of suffering and death. In contrast to the pattern of the dominant myth of redemptive violence in our time,[36] as Jesus absorbs the violent judgement of humans in this world, instead of passing on its destructive consequences, he opens up the possibilities of new life.

Again, the goal of the divine judgement is life, and John's Gospel claims that in the verdict given in Jesus the power to experience it has been released. A new quality of life is now available within history through the death and resurrection of Jesus and the presence of the Spirit. As we have seen, witness to this transforming judgement has been entrusted to the community of believers for the sake of all humanity, and its justice and life are at present displayed in this community's unity, loving service and hospitality. The life of the witnessing community foreshadows the divine judgement intended for creation as a whole. After all, the goal of the cosmic trial was the establishment of God's just claim on the world in enabling the experience of life as God intended it to be. Eternal life in this Gospel begins with the creative life of God in the Logos. It moves through both the verdict that took place in Jesus' life-giving death, whereby the alienation and death of humanity is overcome, and through the confirmation of that verdict in the resurrection of Jesus that empowers his believing followers, and that will end with the latter's own bodily resurrection. Eternal life is not the abandonment of the created world but the establishment of God's judgement through its renewal. Because God's promise of eternal life includes the body, it also embraces both society, since the body provides a person's connectedness with others, and the cosmos, since the body is intimately

---

[35] I am indebted for this point about truth and power to Söding, 'Macht', and its excellent development in Volf, *Exclusion*, esp. 264–71.

[36] On the way this myth undergirds Western popular culture, notions of national security and foreign policy, see, e.g., Wink, *Engaging*, 13–31.

linked to the rest of the creation. The believing community's physical and tactile practice of washing one another's feet is a prime indication of the way in which the body already plays an essential part in the new relationships that characterize the present experience of eternal life. If what can be said of believers' present experience and eschatological expectation of the divine judgement is to shape their views and practice of justice in the public arena, in line with John's account of the goal of the cosmic trial, they will see public justice as entailing not only the righting of injury and wrong but also the provision of conditions in which life and well-being can flourish, including the encouragement of a culture in which conflicts are managed without violence.

Because the Gospel of John is itself a written testimony to the divine judgement that is intended to provoke or consolidate a decision (cf. 21:24; 20:31), its readers are caught up in the continuing cosmic trial. At the very least, being faced with having to make a judgement on the Gospel's witness ought to make readers aware that, if this witness is not accepted, some other verdict about justice and life is being preferred and endorsed. For readers in the West the pervasive rival modern verdict, reinforced by the advertising business, involves the claim that individual persons, seen as autonomous units, have the right to whatever well-being and happiness they choose, and that these can be found through gaining and consuming a variety of material goods. Where this is the vision of life, the accompanying notion of justice holds that having a disproportionate amount of whatever it takes to gain happiness and security is justified and that exploiting others by various means, including the use of force and violence, in order to gain or maintain this disproportion, may also be justified. Even those readers who accept the Gospel's witness do not, of course, live solely out of its narrative but also out of their own culture's story. They discover that the power of the weakness of the crucified Christ, witnessed to and vindicated in John's narrative, inserts itself into the network of other kinds of power in their world and does so particularly through the community of believers. The witness of this community and its members is always given from some point within that complex of interacting powers. The nature of the divine judgement displayed in the victim of this world's violence, to which they witness, should keep them asking whether that point is more closely aligned with the victims or with the oppressors in their world. The Gospel's own history provides ample proof of the difference this can make. The evangelist who produced this Gospel represented Jewish Christians who had at one stage been excluded, oppressed and marginalized by the Jewish majority. But, when its content was later appropriated by a powerful Gentile Christian majority, its perceived anti-Judaism became a weapon in the oppression of a Jewish minority. Yet to commandeer the Fourth Gospel's truth claims to pursue intimidation and hatred of those with whom one disagrees would be to succumb to the notion of truth as self-serving power. Any appeal on the part of the powerful to John's Gospel to justify the waging of holy war for the sake of truth would be a travesty of all that its Christ stands for as the crucified one, the truly innocent victim of this world's injustice. The whole thrust of this Gospel's message renounces such attitudes and calls for the suffering and death of Jesus as *the* witness to be the paradigm for bearing one's own witness to the truth. Readers of the Gospel who find themselves among the persecuted and the victimized, whatever their temptation to reciprocate the hostility of oppressors, are also continually reminded by its witness that the death of Jesus is the radical openness of God toward the hostile other. In accepting that witness, they acknowledge that they themselves were part of the antagonistic world for which God gave God's self in the Son, and so they are not free to view themselves as a completely innocent 'us' against an evil 'them', but rather as those who also need the Judge's positive verdict. In the Gospel of John that positive verdict of life resulting from the divine judgement is offered not to one group that can lay exclusive claim to it but to a world to which all, both Jew and Gentile, both victim and oppressor, belong.

Bibliography

Foucault, M., *Power/Knowledge: Selected Interviews and Other Writings 1972–1977* (New York: Pantheon, 1980)

Lincoln, A.T., *Truth on Trial: The Lawsuit Motif in the Fourth Gospel* (Peabody, MA: Hendrickson, 2000)

Nietzsche, F., *Twilight of the Idols: The Anti-Christ* (ET Harmondsworth: Penguin Books, 1968)

O'Donovan, O., 'The Political Thought of the Book of Revelation', *TynBul* 37 (1986), 61–94

——, *The Desire of the Nations: Rediscovering the Roots of Political Theology* (Cambridge: CUP, 1996)

——, *Resurrection and Moral Order: An Outline for Evangelical Ethics* (Leicester: IVP; Grand Rapids: Eerdmans, 2nd edn, 1994)

Rensberger, D., *Johannine Faith and Liberating Community* (Philadelphia: Westminster Press, 1988)

Sanders, J.T., *Ethics in the New Testament* (London: SCM Press, 1975)

Söding, T., 'Die Macht der Wahrheit und das Reich der Freiheit. Zur johanneischen Deutung des Pilatus-Prozesses (Joh 18,28–19,16)', *ZTK* 93 (1996), 35–58

Volf, M., *Exclusion and Embrace* (Nashville: Abingdon Press, 1996)

Wink, W., *Engaging the Powers* (Minneapolis: Fortress Press, 1992)

10

Response to Andrew Lincoln

Oliver O'Donovan

The thematic theologian thinks through ideas, the exegetical theologian through texts; yet neither is capable of doing his own work without the other, for where are the ideas to come from if not from the texts, and how are the texts to speak to us, if not through ideas? So the two learn from each other – but how well? Andrew Lincoln has given us a model, for which I can only express gratitude, of how an exegete may use categories drawn from my thematic study to shape a penetrating and illuminating exegetical survey of the Gospel of John. At the same time he properly raises the question how well I have learned from exegetes in my rather limited handling of St John, and he hints that I may have absorbed more than I admit from the now rather elderly exegetical tradition that treats John solely as a *post hoc* reflection on the Christ event rather than a living witness to it. What follows is not a full defence against this charge, which I think has an element of justice in it. I do not, as he observes, believe the older sceptical account of St John. Nevertheless, having received my exegetical education a generation ago, I can see that I did not know *how* to carry through an alternative view consistently, and that this has resulted in St John's being significantly less well represented in my index than the Synoptic Gospels.

I am educable on this matter, and more than grateful for the education that Lincoln is offering me. But to sharpen the focus a little, let me at least offer a plea in mitigation. The distinction between my third and my fourth chapter Lincoln takes to be that the former 'focuses on the mission and proclamation of the earthly Jesus' while the latter 'treats the proclamation of the early church about Jesus'. Up to a point. The way I put it was, 'Jesus proclaimed the coming of the Kingdom of God, but the apostolic church … told the story of what happened when the Kingdom came.'[1] In that formulation the distinction is not *epistemological*, but *thematic*. The third chapter makes no pretence at getting behind the Gospels' witness to Jesus, to 'the real thing', which has then to be contrasted with what the evangelists made of it; it is concerned precisely with

[1] *DN*, 120.

the *display of the kingdom at the fulfilment of the times*, the climax of Israel's hope and expectations. The third chapter contains some of the most crucial Old Testament discussion, too. The *unfolding* of the fulfilment, which departs so far from expectations in the way it fulfils them, is then the subject of the fourth chapter, which, again, makes no pretence at leaving 'the real thing' behind for the constructions of the evangelists. Lincoln's puzzles about why the trial-narrative belongs in the fourth rather than the third chapter solve themselves from this point of view. The willingness which he predicts of 'professional NT scholars' to keep their eyebrows steady at my procedure, may possibly come from a sense of familiarity that turns out to be misleading. My way of sorting out the issues may appear to resemble what they are used to more than it really does.

But that provides no explanation of why we meet St John primarily in the fourth chapter of *Desire*, not in the third. And for this, as I say, there may be no sufficient explanation to be had. Yet Andrew Lincoln's own exploration of the judgement theme suggests at least one, though it may be insufficient. St John's treatment of Jesus as the judge and witness in God's 'lawsuit', as he puts it, always has the final confrontation in view: the disclosure is never uncontested. The drama of refusal, division and vindication dominates the Johannine narrative from the first moment. He never entirely recreates Israel's moment of innocent wonder, from which the 'Who is this?' question is put within the Synoptics. (Though it is not wholly absent, either: we think of the 'Israelite without guile' wondering under his fig tree how Nazareth can be the source of him whom the law and prophets wrote.) Yet the division of belief and unbelief shapes the disclosure: from the prologue in which we learn that he 'came unto his own', we know that 'his own received him not'. As Lincoln observes from this same passage, the theme of community identity is worked out in relation not to an 'undivided' Israel, but to 'a new group of children of God ... who receive him'.

The principles on which I have separated out thematically the elements of fulfilment of the times and narrative of the kingdom's coming, then, are arguably more open to easy demonstration from the Synoptics than from John – not because all the themes are not present in John, but because they are woven together so tightly there. Yet there is plenty of material in St John that could have fed a discussion in Chapter 3, as Lincoln demonstrates. And to build on his remarks about the importance of the disclosure of truth for John, I would like to point to the great tabernacles episode (chs. 7, 8). It has long been an unfulfilled ambition of mine to explore this most pregnant and difficult section at the heart of St John's Gospel simply for my own sake, not in relation to any writing project. An ideal *Desire*, one that wholly answered the conceptions that dictated its composition, would surely have devoted some space to it. It begins with the question of the 'hour' of Jesus' self-disclosure, and then probes through a long series of dialogic exchanges how his authority proves itself in relation to the tradition of Moses, David and Abraham, and the common expectations of the coming of the Christ. It is at the summit of these exchanges that we reach the great assertion of the liberating power of truth. Here is John's exploration of the thematic of *fulfilment*: of what it means to see that Jesus was the true climax, not the prisoner, of a tradition of expectation and hope.

11

Paul and Caesar: A New Reading of Romans

N. T. Wright

Introduction

We have moved away quite rapidly in recent years from the old split, which was assumed by and built into the fabric of Western biblical studies, between 'religion' and 'politics'. We have come to see that trying to separate the two in the ancient world, not least in the Middle East, is as futile as trying to do so in certain parts of the modern world. There is a quantum leap now being made from the old way of reading the Bible, in which certain political 'implications' could be drawn here and there from texts which were (of course) about something else, and the occasional concentration on rather isolated texts – one thinks of the 'Tribute question' in the synoptic tradition, and of the notorious first paragraph of Romans 13 – as being the only places in the New Testament at least where real 'political' issues came to the fore. (Until recently, Revelation remained outside the implicit canon of many New Testament scholars, and even when it was considered its striking political significance was often limited to reflections on its thirteenth chapter.)

Now, however, we have all been alerted to the fact that the kingdom of God was itself, and remained, a thoroughly political concept; that Jesus' death was a thoroughly political event; that the existence and growth of the early church was a matter of community-building, in conflict, often enough, with other communities. There is of course a danger, not always avoided in recent studies, of seeing the New Testament now simply the other way up but still within the Enlightenment paradigm: in other words, of declaring that it's all 'politics' and that to read it as 'religion' or 'theology' is to domesticate or privatize it. The fact that for some that might still be so doesn't excuse us from doing our best to reintegrate what the Enlightenment had pulled apart, both in the name of serious ancient historical study and in the name of responsible biblical study for today's world.

I want in this paper to introduce, by means of a sharply focused piece of exegesis, the question of how to rethink and remap Paul within this new world.[1] I have a proposal to make which I have been developing for the last few years in dialogue with a group of scholars, mostly American, who are working in this area, whose most obvious leader is Richard A. Horsley of the University of Massachusetts, the editor of two volumes of collected essays entitled *Paul and Empire* and *Paul and Politics*.[2] To understand where this proposal is coming from and going to, we need to back up for a moment and consider what's been happening in Pauline studies over the last generation.

Nearly a quarter of a century ago, Pauline studies received a shot in the arm which still continues to invigorate – or, depending on your point of view, a deep wound from which it is still trying to recover. In his *Paul and Palestinian Judaism*, E.P. Sanders offered what one writer called a 'new perspective on Paul'.[3] Sanders' main thesis, which I regard as securely established in outline if not in all its details, is that the picture of Judaism assumed in most Protestant readings of Paul is historically inaccurate and theologically misleading: first-century Jews were not proto-Pelagians, and Paul did not attack them as such. Sanders' thesis was explicitly advanced as a case about the religion of Judaism and of Paul; this was always a partial proposal, screening out or downplaying large areas of Pauline theology, so that the responses to Sanders from aggrieved Protestant theologians have sometimes missed the target.[4] Sanders' proposal had its own agenda at the level of the study of religions; it was not the same sort of thing as the Lutheran perspective it controverted, and indeed it was in some ways a plea to see Christianity from a modernist comparative-religion perspective rather than a classic theological one. These questions invite further reflection for which this is not the place.

The subsequent debates as to the validity of the 'new perspective' as a whole and in its parts (with such related matters as the interplay between covenant and apocalyptic, and the phrase 'the faith of/in Jesus Christ') have continued to engage scholars and to inform different readings of the text.[5] I do not wish to

---

[1] What follows is a lightly revised version of my 2000 Manson Memorial Lecture, to be published in *BJRL*.

[2] A more general and wide-ranging treatment which shows the way these winds are blowing is Horsley and Silberman, *Message*. See also Elliott, *Liberating*.

[3] See Dunn, 'New Perspective'.

[4] Gundry, 'Grace'; Schreiner, 'Paul'; Seifrid, *Justification*, 'The "New Perspective"', and *Christ*. A major new project is under way to refute Sanders, of which the first volume has appeared at the time of going to press: Carson, et al. (eds.), *Justification*.

[5] On the convergence of covenant and apocalyptic in Paul's thought, see especially Martyn, *Galatians*. On the basic arguments surrounding the 'faith of Jesus Christ' versus 'faith *in* Jesus Christ' debate, see the interchange between Richard B. Hays and James D.G. Dunn in Johnson and Hay (eds.), *Pauline Theology*.

suggest that this phase of work could or should now come to an end. I wish rather to complicate matters by suggesting that there is a whole further dimension to Paul which both old and new perspectives have ignored, and which must be factored in to subsequent discussion.

A Fresh Perspective?

I begin with a fact that I confess I had not appreciated until very recently, which is itself revealing about the directions in which New Testament scholarship has been looking and not looking. In the Mediterranean world where Paul exercised his vocation as the apostle to the Gentiles, the pagans, the fastest growing religion was the Imperial cult, the worship of Caesar.[6]

In Rome itself, as is well known, the Julio-Claudian emperors did not receive explicit divine honours until after their deaths, although being hailed as the son of the newly deified Julius was an important part of Augustus' profile, and that of his successors, at home as well as abroad. But in the East – and the East here starts, effectively, in Greece, not just in Egypt – the provinces saw no need for restraint. With a long tradition of ruler-cults going back at least to Alexander the Great, local cities and provinces were in many cases only too happy to demonstrate their loyalty to the emperor by establishing a cult in his honour, and indeed by vying for the privilege of looking after his shrine.[7]

This feature of the Roman empire has been extensively studied, and the continuing debates – on, for instance, the precise relationship between this cult and that of earlier Eastern rulers – do not affect the basic point I am making. The religious world of the day was of course thoroughly pluralistic, and there was no expectation that this new cult would displace, or itself be threatened by, the traditional Graeco-Roman religions in all their variety. Indeed, frequently the two were combined, as demonstrated by statues of the emperor in the guise of Jupiter or another well-known god.[8] But, whereas traditional books and lecture courses that cover the religious world of late antiquity tend to add the emperor-cult simply as one element within a treatment of the multiple religions, philosophies and theologies of the ancient world, giving students the impression that it was a relatively insignificant addition to more important aspects of pagan thought and life, it is increasingly apparent that to many ordinary people in Greece, Asia Minor, the Middle East and Egypt – with the exception of the last, the focal points of Paul's

[6] Price, *Rituals*, 1–22; Zanker, *Power*, 1–4; Wright, 'Paul's Gospel'.

[7] For the direct impact of this on Corinth around the time of Paul's establishment of the church there, cf. Winter, *After Paul*, ch. 12.

[8] See Zanker, *Power*, 318.

missionary work – the Caesar-cult was fast-growing, highly visible, and powerful precisely in its interweaving of political and religious allegiance. As various writers have recently urged, you don't need such a strong military presence to police an empire if the citizens are worshipping the emperor. Conversely, where Rome had brought peace to the world, giving salvation from chaos, creating a new sense of unity out of previously warring pluralities, there was a certain inevitability about Rome itself, and the emperor as its ruler, being seen as divine. Rome had done – Augustus had done – the sort of thing that only gods can do. Rome had power: the power to sweep aside all opposition; the power, in consequence, to create an extraordinary new world order. Rome claimed to have brought justice to the world; indeed, the goddess *Iustitia* was an Augustan innovation, closely associated with the principate.[9] The accession of the emperor, and also his birthday, could therefore be hailed as *euaggelion*, good news (we should remember of course that most of the empire, and certainly the parts of it where Paul worked, were Greek-speaking). The emperor was the *kyrios*, the lord of the world, the one who claimed the allegiance and loyalty of subjects throughout his wide empire. When he came in person to pay a state visit to a colony or province, the word for his royal presence was *parousia*.

With all this in mind, we open the first page of Paul's letters as they stand in the New Testament, and what do we find?[10] We find Paul, writing a letter to the church in Rome itself, introducing himself as the accredited messenger of the one true God. He brings the gospel, the *euaggelion*, of the son of God, the Davidic Messiah, whose messiahship and divine sonship are validated by his resurrection, and who, as the Psalms insist, is the Lord, the *kyrios*, of the whole world. Paul's task is to bring the world, all the nations, into loyal allegiance – *hypakoē pisteos*, the obedience of faith – to this universal Lord. He is eager to announce this *euaggelion* in Rome, without shame, because this message is the power of God which creates salvation for all who are loyal to it, Jew and Greek alike. Why is this? Because in this message (this 'gospel of the son of God'), the justice of God, the *dikaiosynē theou*, is unveiled. Those of us who have read Romans, written essays on Romans, lectured on Romans, preached on Romans, written books about Romans over many years, may be excused if we rub our eyes in disbelief. Most commentators on Romans 1:1–17 insist that it forms the thematic introduction to the whole letter. None that I know of (myself included) have suggested that it must have been heard in Rome, and that Paul must have intended it, as a parody of the imperial cult.

---

[9] See, e.g., Ovid, *Epistuale ex Ponto* 3.6.25; *Acts of Augustus*, ch. 34, and *OCD*, s.v., Iustitia (791).

[10] More details on all of the following may be found in my forthcoming commentary on Romans, *NIB* 10.

If we go for a moment to the other end of Romans, the impression is the same. The thematic exposition concludes with 15:7–13, where the mutual welcome of Jewish Christian and Gentile Christian in the one family of God in Christ, producing united worldwide worship in fulfilment of scriptural prophecy, is the goal of the whole gospel. Paul builds up a careful sequence of scriptural passages to make the point, emphasizing on the way the universality of the rule of Jesus Christ, the *kyrios* (Ps. 117:1, quoted in v. 11, repeats 'all': all the nations, all the peoples). The final quotation is from Isaiah 11:10, one of Isaiah's great messianic passages, and Paul has chosen a passage which, in its Septuagintal form, looks right back to Romans 1:3f.: 'The root of Jesse shall appear, the one who rises up (*ho anistamenos*) to rule the nations; in him shall the nations hope.' Jesus' Davidic messiahship, once more, is confirmed by his resurrection, and means that he is the true ruler of the nations. This cannot, I suggest, be other than a direct challenge to the present ruler of the nations, Caesar himself.

Austin Farrer, when lecturing on Romans in Oxford in the early 1950s, used to read Romans 1:8–15 aloud, and run straight on to 15:14 and the following passage. He would then ask his hearers: why did Paul break off and include all that other material? In similar fashion I want to pose the question: if Paul has framed this great letter with an introduction and a theological conclusion which seem so clearly to echo, and thus to challenge, the rule of Caesar with the rule of Jesus Christ, is the rest of the letter in some sense about this as well, and if so, how? And what does this do to all our traditional readings of Paul, in both old and new perspectives?

Before I can address this, some initial comments are in order on where we have come so far.

Initial Comments

First, a note about scholarly treatment of Romans 1:3–4. When I was first working on Romans in the mid-1970s, I was conscious of what I can only call a powerful undertow in scholarship that resisted any attempt to allow Paul to be interested in, let alone to affirm or make central, the Davidic messiahship of Jesus. Romans 1:3–4 was regularly seen as a pre-Pauline formula – not so much, I suggest, for reasons of its structure and phraseology, but because messiahship, especially with an explicit reference to David, was deemed to be extraneous to Paul's theology.[11] Commentators then regularly hurried on to 1:16–17, which was seen as the real statement of the theme of the letter, and

[11] See, e.g., Käsemann, *Commentary*, 5, who states that messianism is a category Paul 'does not emphasize'. Similarly Jewett, 'Redaction', 101.

indeed of 'the gospel'. I thought then, and think still, that this represents part of a de-Judaizing of Paul, an insistence that he cannot have thought in categories like messiahship; and I have argued extensively for the opposite point of view elsewhere.[12] I now realize that this tendency also represents part of a depoliticizing of Paul, a desire to move his theology away from confrontation with the powers of the world and into the safer sphere of a faith, a religion, a theology in which the only thing one needs to say about the rulers of the world is that God has ordained them and that they must in principle be obeyed. (I shall return to Rom. 13 in due course.) The roots of this de-Judaizing and depoliticizing of Paul are outside the scope of this paper, but I suspect they would not be hard to find.

My second comment is to note that Romans is by no means unique in having this apparent covert reference to, and subversion of, Caesar.[13] I have written elsewhere of how Philippians 2:5–11 and 3:19–21 can be seen to have explicit reference to the imperial cult and theme, with, once more, the main thrust that Jesus Christ is the true *kyrios* of the world, so that of course Caesar is not. Indeed, I have argued that the whole of Philippians 3 can and should be read as a covert anti-imperial exhortation: as Paul had abandoned his Jewish privileges to find Christ, so the Philippians should be prepared, at least, not to take advantage of their belonging to a Roman colony, with the same end in view (finding Christ). Philippi was, of course, a Roman colony (not all of the Philippian Christians were Roman citizens, but all will have gained, or might have expected to gain, as a result of being part of the colonial city).[14] It can be shown that some hints in 1 Thessalonians run the same way: when people say 'peace and security', then sudden destruction will come upon them unawares (1 Thes. 5:3). And 'peace and security', it has been argued, was part of the Roman propaganda of the first-century empire.[15]

Third, while highlighting the imperial context of Paul's writings, and proposing that at least at some points Paul is consciously parodying and subverting imperial ideology, I do not at all suggest that Paul derived his theology, either in outline or in detail, from the world of Graeco-Roman paganism in general or the imperial cult in particular. We must not confuse derivation with

[12] Wright, *Climax*, 18–55.

[13] I gratefully acknowledge the work of Dr Peter Oakes of Manchester University, whose studies of Philippians first alerted me to this whole theme, though he should not be held responsible for the larger picture I am trying to draw, with all its dangers and loose ends. See Oakes, *Philippians*.

[14] See Wright, 'Paul's Gospel and Caesar's Empire'. I do not see Paul's occasional exploitation of his own Roman citizenship in Acts as in fundamental conflict with this position.

[15] Georgi, *Theocracy*, 28; Hendrix, 'Archaeology', 109; Koester, 'Imperial Ideology', 161–62.

confrontation. Some who have made these connections seem to be using them as a way of rolling back fifty years of work, from W.D. Davies to E.P. Sanders and beyond, of locating Paul within the world of Second Temple Judaism, and returning history instead to an earlier history-of-religions project in which Paul derived his central themes from the non-Jewish world of late antiquity.[16] As I hope I have already indicated, but here wish to emphasize, my reading depends precisely on Paul being and remaining a Jewish thinker, addressing the pagan world with the news that the God of Abraham, Isaac and Jacob is the true God, and that this God has now proved the point by raising from the dead Jesus, who is thereby the Jewish Messiah *and therefore* the Lord of the whole world. This, indeed, is the logic underneath the whole Gentile mission: not that Paul was abandoning Judaism, but claiming to fulfil it. Here, not for the last time, we find fascinating parallels between Paul and the roughly contemporary Wisdom of Solomon, which addresses the rulers of the world with the news that Israel's God is the true God who not only gives wisdom to rulers, but who will vindicate his people against pagan oppression.[17]

Fourth, if there is indeed a reference to Caesar and his cult in Romans, Philippians and elsewhere, it would be a mistake to universalize this, and suppose that Paul is covertly opposing Caesar in all sorts of other places as well. The theme is not so obvious in the Corinthian correspondence, though a case has recently been made for seeing it there too.[18] It is even harder to see this theme in Galatians – though there, too, a recent writer has attempted to do so.[19] Rather, I suggest that Paul's anti-imperial stance is part of a wider strain in his thinking which has also been marginalized in many systematic treatments of his thought, but which should be acknowledged and rehabilitated: the confrontation between the gospel and the powers of the world, between the gospel and paganism in general. Paul's gospel remained thoroughly Jewish: his critique of idolatry and immorality, again paralleled in the wisdom tradition, is the standard wide-ranging Jewish critique, sharpened up but not significantly modified through the gospel of Jesus. The fresh perspective I am proposing, that we take seriously Paul's subversive references to Caesar, is part of the larger point I have made in various places: that we take Paul seriously as the Jewish apostle to the pagan world, and think through his theology and religion not just as the

---

16 See, e.g., Georgi, *Theocracy*; Koester, 'Imperial Ideology'.

17 See Wisdom 6:1–11; 15–19.

18 See Winter, *After Paul*. On the imperial cult in Corinth see Chow, *Patronage*. See also Horsley, 'Rhetoric'. It may be that we should explore further in this respect the conflict between the gospel and the powers in 1 Cor. 2, the reign and victory of Christ in 1 Cor. 15, and other themes as well (a point made to me in conversation by Dr Andrew Goddard).

19 Cf. Winter, 'Imperial Cult'. See Winter's forthcoming monograph, *The Imperial Gods and the First Christians: Conflict over the Beginning of All Things*.

outworking of a Jewish history-of-religion in the abstract, but as confrontation with paganism in its many varieties – the Caesar-cult being one of the most powerful, high-profile, fast-growing and usually ignored in scholarship.[20]

Fifth, and perhaps most important, I am not proposing that we give up looking at Paul as a theologian and read him simply as a covert politician. There is a danger, which Horsley and his colleagues have not always avoided, of ignoring the major theological themes in Paul and simply plundering parts of his writings to find help in addressing the political concerns of the contemporary Western world. To be sure, Paul has not been much used in Christian political thinking, and much work remains to be done in this area. But we would be foolish to suppose that we could substitute a one-dimensional political reading for a one-dimensional theological one. On the contrary: my proposal is that we recognize in Paul, in full integration, what post-Enlightenment Western culture has pulled apart. Our struggles over the integration of faith and history, of church and society, of natural and supernatural, simply did not look like that in the first century. The question is, rather, how we can appropriately describe *what appear to us as* 'different dimensions of Paul's thought' in ways that will do justice to the exegesis of the text, and that will also, perhaps, give to the early twenty-first century a lesson in joined-up thinking. It is perhaps ironic that theologians and exegetes should find themselves discovering the importance of serious political thought just when politicians themselves seem finally to have abandoned it.

Towards a Multi-Dimensional Fresh Reading of Paul

Once all these issues are raised, it should be clear that we shall not do justice to Paul simply by arranging bits and pieces of his letters according to the doctrinal schemes of regular dogmatic theology – God, humankind, sin, salvation, and so forth – or according to the patterns of religion (getting in, staying in, and the like). Doctrinal belief matters; religious theory and practice matter; but they matter as part of a larger whole, and I am suggesting that this larger whole must include Paul's sense of the conflict of the gospel with the principalities and powers in general and with Rome, and Caesar, in particular. How can we describe all of this coherently without allowing one element to gain a false prominence over the others?

---

[20] As Horsley ('Introduction', in *Paul and Empire*, 3) puts it: 'Since so little attention has been devoted to the Roman imperial context of Paul's mission and his relations to it, we are only at the point of attempting to formulate appropriate questions and provisional research strategies.' On my own wider proposals see *Climax* and also *What St Paul Really Said*.

I have elsewhere proposed a method of worldview analysis, which I have employed on a large scale in my historical treatment of Jesus.[21] Worldviews, I have suggested, can be understood as a combination of praxis, story, symbol and theory, which give rise to, and are expressed within, a set of aims and motives on the one hand and of specific beliefs, at various levels, on the other. Without entering into a full exploration of this, I will offer a bird's-eye view of some of these elements, attempting to show how the fresh perspective I am proposing not only finds a place alongside other elements, but changes the shape and balance of the whole. This will lead me back, in my final main section, to some further reflections on the parts of Romans between 1:1–17 and 15:7–13.

The passages I have just mentioned, and the rest of Romans 15, offer quite a full statement of Paul's aims and motivations, which are backed up by what we know of his actual habitual praxis (in other words, we have good reason to think that what he says to the Romans about his overall goals is not just a rhetorical smokescreen, but really does represent the way he thought). He believed himself to have a unique vocation from the God of Israel, the creator and covenant God, which put him in debt to the whole world, since it was his task to bring to the world the announcement that Jesus was Lord and that God had raised him from the dead. His developed strategy for obedience to this vocation involved the sustained work of proclamation and church development in Greece and Asia Minor, with Jerusalem and Antioch as his back markers; now it was time to move to Italy, Spain, and presumably (though he does not mention it) Gaul. His aim was to extend the rule of Jesus, the world's true Lord, planting cells of people loyal to Jesus, whose loyalty would be evidenced not least by their unity across traditional ethnic and cultural lines. To that end, he had taken a collection from Gentile churches and was on his way to Jerusalem to give it to the Jewish Christians there; it was a powerful symbol that Jesus is Lord and that the principalities and powers, who kept the world divided up into separate categories and allegiances, were not.

Paul's symbolic praxis as outlined in Romans 15 thus points to the controlling narrative out of which he was living, which can of course be checked against the various stories he tells, explicitly and implicitly, throughout his writings. We may trace six interlocking stories, working from the largest scale to the smallest. In each case, the story is about the one true God, revealed in climactic and decisive action in Jesus and the Spirit, challenging and defeating rival gods. It is, in other words, a Christian variation on regular Second-Temple Jewish stories, confronting, as did many such stories, the world of paganism.

---

[21] See *New Testament*, Part II, chs. 3–5; and *Jesus*.

The outer story that Paul tells frequently, not least in Romans, is the story of creation and new creation. This is the Jewish story of a good creator God bringing to birth a good creation, and then, when creation has been spoiled by the rebellion of humankind, accomplishing its rescue not by abandoning the old and starting afresh, but as an act of new creation out of the old. The resurrection of Jesus is, for Paul, the prototype of the new creation; the Spirit is the agent, already at work. Paul applies to the creation itself the motif of the exodus, of redemption from slavery.

The second story is the covenantal narrative from Abraham, through Moses and the prophets, to the Messiah, and on to the mission of the covenant God to the wider non-Jewish world. Again, this is seen classically in Romans, particularly in 9:6–10:21, but is everywhere presupposed and frequently alluded to. As with the story of creation, the covenant story is of God's original design spoiled by sin, this time by the rebellion of the covenant people, highlighted and exacerbated by the law. But, once more, God's solution is not to destroy and start from scratch, but to redeem through the new exodus, which has been accomplished in the death and resurrection of Jesus and the gift of the Spirit.

The third story is that of Jesus himself. Paul notoriously has little to say about the life of Jesus prior to the crucifixion, but there should be no doubt that he regarded Jesus' public career as messianic; the resurrection alone would not have been sufficient to convince him that someone was the Messiah unless it vindicated what had gone before. Every time Paul tells the story of Jesus' death and resurrection it comes out differently, but the constant note is, as he says in the summary tradition in 1 Corinthians 15, that it took place 'according to the scriptures'. What he means by this is not just that these events fulfilled a few specific prophecies, but that they brought the long story of Israel to its God-ordained climax and goal, in both its positive aspects (focused especially on the fulfilment of the promise to Abraham) and its negative aspects (focused especially on the ambiguous role of the law). The narrative of Jesus is, for Paul, the supreme revelation of the one true God. In the gospel, God's justice and love are revealed definitively and decisively. This is again, of course, central to Romans (3:21–26; 5:6–10).

In the complex relation of this third narrative to the first two we find the heart of what can loosely be called Paul's atonement-theology; but we also find, in one of the most powerful moves within the fresh perspective I am proposing, Paul's treatment of the cross as the means of the defeat of the powers. As everyone in the Roman world knew well, the cross already had a clear symbolic meaning; it meant that Caesar ruled the world, with cruel death as his ultimate, and regular, weapon.[22] For Paul, throughout his writings, the cross is far more than simply the means whereby individual sins are forgiven, though of

---

[22] See, e.g., Hengel, *Crucifixion*.

course it is that as well. It is the means whereby the powers are defeated and overthrown (1 Cor. 2:6–8; Col. 2:13–15). The resurrection demonstrates that the true God has a power utterly superior to that of Caesar. The cross is thus to be seen, with deep and rich paradox, as the secret power of this true God, the power of self-giving love which (as Jesus said it would) subverts the power of the tyrant (Mk. 10:35–45).

The fourth story Paul tells is the story of the church, the renewed people of God in Christ. In one sense, of course, this is an aspect of the second story: the church is not something other than the multi-ethnic family God promised to Abraham. But Paul also, I think, tells this story as complete in itself, because in the present age of inaugurated eschatology, living between Jesus' resurrection and his final reappearing, the church goes through its own complete cycle of call, mission, suffering, struggle and vindication. The very existence of the church is an affront to the principalities and powers in general (Eph. 3:10) and to Caesar in particular, because here within his empire is a growing group of people giving allegiance to a different lord – as Luke says, to 'another king' (Acts 17:7). The church, through its exodus-shaped life (1 Cor. 10:1–13), is also a revelation of the true God. Paul's strong pneumatology, which he does not retract in the face of muddle, sin and rebellion in the Corinthian church, ensures that he sees the very existence, let alone the obedient life, of the church as a vital sign to the world of who its rightful God and Lord now are.

The fifth story is that of the individual Christian. (We may note in passing how narrow has been the focus of much study of Paul, limited to stories 3 and 5, with only occasional glances at 1, 2 and 4.) The call of each person to hear the gospel, and to respond in believing obedience, is vital to Paul, even though what he means by 'justification' is hardly what the majority of Christian theologians have meant by that term since at least Augustine. The story Paul tells about how people become Christians is clear at several points. The gospel is preached – that is, Jesus is announced as the risen Lord of the world – and God's power is thereby unleashed, through the Spirit, who causes some hearers, no doubt to their surprise, to believe it (see, e.g., 1 Cor. 12:3; 1 Thes. 1:4–5; 2:13). Their submission to Jesus as Lord is expressed in the new-exodus symbolism of baptism, which by its link to Jesus' death and resurrection is understood as bringing them 'into Christ', that is, into the Messiah's people (Rom. 6:1–11; 1 Cor. 10:1–2; Gal. 3:26–29). They are thereby not only given secure promises of future salvation (Rom. 8:29–30; Phil. 1:6), but also charged with responsibilities and obligations in the present, including that of undergoing the suffering which will result from thus standing with the true God against the powers (Rom. 8:31–39; Phil. 1:29–30; 1 Thes. 3:3). And at every moment in this story they are turning away from the idols of their pagan past to serve a living and true God (1 Thes. 1:9–10); which must have meant, for many of Paul's hearers as for his successors in the following centuries, turning away from the Caesar-cult and worshipping Jesus instead. Finally, all must appear before the *bēma tou theou* or *tou Christou*, the 'judgement seat', at which the true Lord, as opposed to Caesar and his delegated officers, would preside, justice would be seen to be done, and those who had already been declared to be God's people on the basis of faith alone would have that declaration ratified in the final act of their being raised from the dead, and so 'saved' from the ultimate powers and 'justified', found to be in the right, before the final court.[23]

Controversially but crucially, when Paul uses the language of 'justification' he is not referring to this whole process, this *ordo salutis*. Rather, he is referring to God's declaration about those who believe the gospel (confessing Jesus as Lord and believing that God raised him from the dead, as in Rom. 10:9; cf. 4:24–25). This faith is the solitary badge which marks out who belongs to God's renewed, eschatological people; any attempt to propose other badges leaves the 'powers' still in charge. This divine declaration in the present only makes sense because it is based on the death and resurrection of Jesus in the past, and because it looks forward to the future judgement at which there will be 'no condemnation' for these same people because of what the Holy Spirit has done in their lives.[24] Those whom God justified, God has also glorified (Rom. 8:30). This is the basic meaning of justification by faith; this is how, in Romans, Galatians and elsewhere, it can be integrated with the fresh perspective I am proposing. The 'faith' because of which God justifies (in this sense) is a believing loyalty which upstages that demanded by Caesar; the 'judgement' which will be issued at the last day, and which is anticipated in present 'justification', is by the one God, through the one Lord, as opposed to that meted out within Caesar's system. The 'gospel' through which the Spirit works powerfully to bring people to this believing obedience, this loyalty, and so to justification, is the true gospel as opposed to that of Caesar. The true gospel focuses on the crucifixion of the Messiah as opposed to being backed up by the crucifixion of Caesar's opponents.

The sixth story I have already told, but I recapitulate to make it clear. It is the story of Paul himself: Paul as, at one level, an agent of new creation; at another, the minister of the new covenant; at another, a member of Christ's body; at another, the founder of the Gentile church; at another, a classic example of both a converted Jew and a converted human being, the unique apostle to the Gentiles. Paul sees his own story of mission and suffering, and his expectation of vindication, as revelations in action of the true God, and as embodiments of the exodus, through both of which the false gods – including now the idolatry of Israel's own ethnic status and pride – are confronted and rebuked.

---

23 Rom. 2:1–16; 14:10–12; 2 Cor. 5:9–10.

24 See again Rom. 2:7, 10, 26–29; 8:1–17.

Paul's narrative world thus integrates what theologians and historians of religion have regularly held apart, including indeed aspects which both have marginalized or ignored completely. The hardest question for the fresh perspective to face is: how can this be integrated with the traditional topics of Pauline theology (justification, the law, Christology, and so forth)? I believe that through this means, of worldview analysis and particularly narrative analysis, a way may be found towards a fuller answer, to which I shall presently return. Paul's stories are all God-stories, confronting and subverting the stories of other gods; they all focus on Jesus and the Spirit, and on the new exodus, itself the unveiling of God's sovereign power over the gods.

The symbols of Paul's worldview are the outward and visible points at which the characteristic stories and praxis find expression. Preaching the gospel, baptism, the Eucharist, the collection, the coming together of Jew and Gentile in one body – all of these and more must count as symbols, signs within the world that a different God is at work, warnings to the powers that their time is up. That is why each of these arouses fierce opposition. To explore this would take us too far afield, but we must note that just as the Lord's Supper was seen by Paul in 1 Corinthians 10–11 as the reality of which the pagan temple meals were the parody, so the summons to Jew and Gentile alike to worship Jesus as the ruler of all nations must be seen, from Paul's point of view, as the reality of which Caesar's grandiose claims were also the parody. And since that summons was absolutely central to all that Paul was and did, we must also declare that at the symbolic level, as well as at the level of praxis and narrative, his challenge to Caesar was central and decisive. When Polycarp of Smyrna refused the oath a hundred years later, he was being a true follower of Paul.[25]

How would Paul answer the five key world-view questions that comprise the level of theory?

1. Who are we? We are the people of God in Christ, indwelt by the Spirit. We are the renewed Israel, the people of the new covenant. We are those who acknowledge Jesus as Lord and believe that God raised him from the dead. And this defines us over against those who worship other gods, and other lords.
2. Where are we? We are in God's good creation – citizens now not of a particular country so much as of the world that God is going to make, where we shall share the rule of the Lord Jesus. We are living, as it were, in a house that is being rebuilt around us, though there is yet to come a final moment of rebuilding on a scale hitherto unimaginable. We are part of the Jewish movement designed by God to spread to the ends of the earth. Our location is defined not by Caesar's empire but by God's creation and covenant.

[25] See *Mart. Pol.*, 8–12.

3. What's wrong? Though Jesus' resurrection has ushered in the new creation, we live between that event and the redemption still awaited by ourselves and the rest of the world; and, since most of the world still does not acknowledge Jesus as Lord, we are persecuted. We ourselves, too, are not yet perfect, but live in the tension between what we are already, in Christ and by the Spirit, and what we shall be when Jesus appears again and when his work in us is complete. Caesar still rules the world, despite Jesus' enthronement as its rightful Lord.
4. What's the solution? The work of the Spirit, in the present and the future, will put into practice, for us and for the whole cosmos, what has been accomplished in Christ. God will put the world to rights, achieving at last what Caesar claimed to have done.
5. What time is it? We live in the overlap of the ages: the age to come has already broken in in Jesus, but the present age still continues. A great crisis is looming shortly, involving fierce suffering and worldwide convulsion, from which the church will emerge stronger; and one day, though nobody knows when, Jesus will reappear, when God finally remakes the cosmos. The Roman world is tottering; only God's kingdom will last.

Out of praxis, story, symbol and theory there emerge not only aims and motivations, at which we have already glanced, but also explicit beliefs, or theology. Paul's theology can best be understood as the radical revision, in the light of Jesus and the Spirit, of the triple Jewish beliefs of monotheism, election and eschatology. Just as each element of the Jewish theology Paul is modifying already stood over against the principalities and powers, so too, in his revision, each element continues to confront the powers of the world.

The Jewish belief in one God was always a polemical doctrine over against pagan idolatry. In some of its greatest expressions this opposition is explicit: the exodus was God's victory over the gods and pharaoh of Egypt, and the revelation of God's saving righteousness in Isaiah 40–55 meant the overthrow of Babylon, its rulers and its gods. Jews of the first century, especially hard-line Pharisees, would have had no difficulty in rereading these texts and others like them in relation to the victory of the true God over first-century paganism in general and the Caesar-cult in particular. The Wisdom of Solomon offers an instructive parallel. Paul, drawing upon these sources and rereading them around Jesus Christ and the Spirit, has given them new focus and application, and has thereby launched a movement in which the heirs of Israel's Scriptures would confront paganism with a new weapon, looking for a new kind of victory. Paul's high Christology and pneumatology, controversially forming the basis of the later doctrine of the Trinity, were designed as a way of giving Jewish monotheism a new focus and polemical power against the pagan gods, especially Caesar. Recognizing this raises interesting questions about what is really going on in the regular attempts to deny Paul's high Christology.[26]

The Jewish belief in the election of Israel to be the people of the one true God was always, likewise, a polemical doctrine over against pagan idolatry. The Torah, Israel's covenant charter, is from one point of view a lengthy elaboration of what it means to have no gods but YHWH alone. Paul's radical revision of the doctrine of election, focusing on justification by faith apart from works of Torah and on the creation in Christ and by the Spirit of the one body, the worldwide church, is simultaneously a challenge to all the powers, from Babylon to Rome, that tried to create new empires which gave unity, peace and justice to the wider world. For him, the intention of Torah is fulfilled in Christ and by the Spirit; those who are defined as God's people in this renewed way are thereby defined over against the peoples who give allegiance to false gods, emperors included. The reflex of Paul's revision – the continuing debate and sometimes bitter controversy with unbelieving Judaism, and with right-wing Jewish Christians – must be seen as just that, the reflex of his mission to the world, not as the centre in its own right of his theological understanding and endeavour.

Finally, the Jewish belief in the coming age when God's righteousness would be unveiled in action, vindicating Israel, defeating pagan wickedness, and putting the whole world to rights, was always likewise a polemical doctrine over against paganism. One only has to think of Daniel to see how this played out. For Paul, the decisive revelation had already taken place in Jesus Christ, and his death and resurrection, through whom the age to come had been inaugurated; and the Spirit was now at work to complete what had been begun (through the resurrection) in the world, and (through the preaching of the gospel) in human beings. The Day of the Lord had split into two: the day which happened at Easter, and the day which was yet to come when Jesus reappeared and the cosmos was finally liberated.[27] This radical revision of the Jewish doctrine was, like the rest, designed to enable Paul and his hearers to stand boldly and cheerfully as Christians despite the rage of the powers, including Caesar's henchmen.

The fresh perspective I am proposing is not, then, an odd extraneous feature which might have crept in by accident, or might be read in by mistake, in Paul's thinking. Polemic against the powers, and against the blaspheming emperor-cult in particular, is to be expected precisely because of those Jewish traditions to which Paul was heir and which he reshaped around the gospel.[28] How, finally, might this work out in a reading of Romans, with which we began?

---

[26] Cf. again Wright, 'Paul's Gospel', 181f.

[27] Cf. 1 Cor. 15:20–28.

[28] On continuing subversive themes within Jewish mystical literature see Alexander, 'Family'.

New Creation, New Covenant: The Heart of Romans

In conclusion, I want to draw attention to key features of Romans which show, I believe, that the initially surprising fresh reading of its opening and closing are not accidental, but inform the whole – without detracting in any way from all the other things that Romans is about.

The centre of Romans, arguably, is the double climax of chapters 8 and 11. I cannot here go into the complex relation between the different sections of the letter; I simply comment that chapters 5–8 are a kind of formal centre, the tightly compressed driving motor for the rest, which energizes the discussions of major issues facing the Roman church in 9–11 and 12–15. Chapters 1–4 prepare the way for 5–8 in one way, and for 9–11 and 12–15 in other ways.

There should be no doubt that Romans 8 forms one of the climactic moments of all Paul's writing. It stands to the letter, and perhaps to his thought as a whole, like the climax of the Jupiter symphony to the preceding movements and, in a measure, to Mozart's oeuvre as a whole. And the main thrust of Romans 8 – marginalized, ironically, in much Protestant exegesis! – is the renewal of all creation by God's great act of new exodus. The cosmos itself will be redeemed, set free from slavery, liberated to share the freedom of the glory of God's children. God's children in turn have their inheritance, the new covenant equivalent of the promised land, in this entire new world. They will therefore, as Romans 5 stresses, share the *reign* of Jesus over the whole new world.[29] This, I suggest, cannot be other than subversive when set as the climax of a letter to the small struggling church in Rome, whose emperor claimed to rule the world, whose poets had sung of the new age of peace, freedom and prosperity that had come to birth through Augustus' defeat of all enemies. Though of course the vision of new creation is far more than a mere political polemic, in its context it must be seen as offering a vision which was bound to make other visions of world empire pale into insignificance as the cheap imitations they really were. God will put the world to rights; the *dikaiosynē theou* is that covenant faithfulness by which God will accomplish the new creation in which justice will triumph.

All is achieved, in Romans 5–8, by the love of God. David Aune has recently suggested, in his commentary on Revelation, that some Roman thinkers saw their city as having a secret name, the name of Rome spelled backwards, forming the word AMOR, love.[30] If this is so, Romans 5 and 8 could be more subversive again, claiming that true love is found in God's self-giving in

---

[29] We should not overlook, in this context, the remarkable promises that God's people in Christ will 'reign' (*basileuein*) (5:17). To be sure, the main contrast here is with the reign of death; but any hint at a *basileus* other than Caesar is fighting talk in the Roman Empire, as Luke knew well (Acts 17:7).

[30] Aune, *Revelation*, 926–27.

Christ, not in any aspect of Rome's civic pride or imperial achievements. But even if this is irrelevant, or at best an unproveable possibility, the theme of God's victory over the powers through his love revealed in Jesus, which forms the substance of the final paragraph of Romans 8, remains not only pastorally powerful but, in a world where crucifixions proclaimed that the power of death was the way to rule the world, politically of enormous importance. Anyone taking Romans 8:31–39 as their motto would be able to stand up to Caesar, knowing that he could only do that which tyrants normally do, while the true God had already revealed a weapon more powerful still, in the love seen on the cross and in the power seen in the resurrection.

Romans 1:18–4:25 is, of course, the classic statement of the revelation of God's covenant faithfulness, his saving justice, in and through the death of Jesus, against the background of a world in rebellion and of the failures of God's covenant people. By itself this does not appear to be explicitly subversive, except in the general sense that if this is how the creator God has accomplished his purpose, he has clearly upstaged the ambitions of Caesar. (We might note that in 4:13 Paul speaks almost casually about Abraham's family 'inheriting the world', anticipating the conclusion of 8:18–27.)[31] But since this is one of the passages in which 1:1–17 is spelled out more fully, and a key move on the way to Romans 8, we may say that the saving death of Jesus, for Paul, unveils not just the plan of salvation for individual sinners, but God's overthrow of all the powers of the world. That, indeed, is why already in 3:21–31 and 4:1–25 a major emphasis is the unity of Jew and Gentile in the covenant family on the basis of the same faith, the same loyalty to God's action in Jesus.

Romans 9–11 deals, of course, with a very specific issue, to which questions of Caesar and Rome seem at first sight irrelevant. We must not become so keen on coded meanings that we miss the main thrust of the text.[32] However, the long argument that God has in fact done, in Christ and through the Gentile mission, that which he promised all along in the Scriptures is in itself, as we saw, a version of that Jewish election-theology which was designed to show that Israel is the true people of the one creator God. And the story of Abraham's two sons, and then of Isaac's two sons, and of tracing the true lineage through the right ones in each case, could not but strike a Roman hearer as remarkably similar to the great founding stories of Rome itself, going back to Romulus and Remus.[33] Paul is telling a much older story; like Josephus, he is suggesting that Rome's stories are upstaged by the far more antique Jewish story of origins.

---

[31] Wright, 'New Exodus', 30–31.

[32] On coded political polemic within first-century theological writing see esp. Goodenough, *Politics*.

[33] On the connection between Esau and Rome see, e.g., Hengel, *Die Zeloten*, 309; Feldman, *Jew and Gentile*, 493.

Thus, though his main purpose is to explain to Gentile Christians in Rome that they must not look down on Jewish non-Christians, part of that very argument, weaning them away from any latent pride in being Roman rather than Jewish, is so to tell the Jewish story, albeit then with its radical Christian modification, that the great story of Rome itself is subverted.

A final word is necessary about Romans 13 in particular. Romans 13:1–7 has of course long been regarded as the one point at which Paul nods in the direction of Caesar, and the nod appears quite respectful. This, obviously, I consider radically misleading. There are six points to be made.[34]

First, the fact that Paul needs to stress the need for civil obedience itself tells fairly strongly, if paradoxically, in favour of my overall case. It implies that, without some such restraining counsel, some might have heard his teaching to imply that the church was to become a Christian version of the Jewish 'fourth philosophy', owing allegiance to no one except God and therefore under obligation to rebel violently against human rulers, and to refuse to pay taxes. The paragraph can therefore be seen, not as evidence that Paul would not have been saying anything subversive, but that he had been, and now needed to make clear what this did, and particularly what it did not, imply.[35]

Second, to say that the ruler is answerable to God is itself a Jewish point over against pagan ruler-cult. Caesar did not, normally, owe allegiance to anyone except himself, and perhaps, though at a surface level, the traditional Roman gods. Paul declares, with massive Jewish tradition behind him, that Caesar is in fact responsible to the true God, whether or not he knows it. This is an undermining of pagan totalitarianism, not a reinforcement of it.

Third, the power and duty of the ruler *qua* ruler is emphasized in the context of the prohibition against personal vengeance at the end of the previous chapter (12:19–21). What Paul says at this point belongs on the map of one of the regular theories as to why magistracy matters: without it, everyone will take the law into their own hands. This fits closely with the following points.

Fourth, Paul's underlying point is that the victory of the true God is not won by the normal means of revolution. Rome could cope with revolutions; she could not cope, as history demonstrated, with a community owing imitative allegiance to the crucified and risen Jesus. God did not intend that the church should be the means of causing anarchy, of refusing normal civic responsibilities; anarchy simply replaces the tyranny of the officially powerful with the tyranny of the unofficially powerful, the bullies and the rich. The real overthrow of pagan power comes by other means.

---

[34] It is sadly impossible to enter here into debate with the many scholars, including some in this book, who have written importantly on this passage. A fuller statement of my present position is found in the *NIB* commentary.

[35] I owe this point to Dr David Wenham, in conversation.

Fifth, if in Romans 9–11 Paul is concerned with Christian attitudes to non-Christian Jews, in 12–15 he is concerned with mutual relationships within the church itself. He almost certainly knew of the riots in the late 40s, *impulsore Chresto*;[36] this kind of behaviour, he says, is to be avoided. Though the church does indeed give allegiance to another king, this allegiance must not be seen by the watching powers to result in civic disturbance, in strife between different sections of a community. God is the God of order, not chaos; the Christian response to tyranny is not anarchy but the creation of a community worshipping Jesus as Lord.

Sixth, as the succeeding passage makes clear, Paul wants the Roman Christians to live appropriately in the tension between present and future. This does not mean, as Paul's own example bears out, that one must be politically quiescent or repressed until the final reappearing of Jesus. Preaching and living the gospel must always mean announcing and following Jesus, rather than Caesar, as the true Lord. But the eschatological balance must be kept. The church must live as a sign of the coming complete kingdom of Jesus Christ; but since that kingdom is characterized by peace, love and joy it cannot be inaugurated in the present by chaos, hatred and anger. This, I think, is what motivates Paul in Romans 13:1–7.

Conclusion

When we set Paul's gospel, not least the letter to the Romans, against the context of the widespread and increasing Caesar-cult of his day, with all that it implied, we discover a fresh perspective, a new angle on familiar passages, which informs and to an extent modifies traditional readings.

This is not to suggest in any way – to anticipate the most obvious criticism! – that the major theological or religious subject matter of Romans has been set aside or relativized. On the contrary. The critique of the powers which Paul has in mind depends precisely on a thoroughgoing and well worked out theology, not least a very high Christology and a strong doctrine of justification, and is fortified by the explicitly Christian religion from which and to which Paul writes. To show how this works out – to integrate Paul's explicit and implicit polemic against paganism in general, the powers in particular, and the Caesar-cult especially, within his wider theology and exegesis – is a long and complicated task. I hope I have shown that it is both necessary and fruitful.

---

[36] The phrase is from Suetonius, *Claud.* 25.4. Cf. my *New Testament*, 354.

Bibliography

Alexander, P.S., 'The Family of Caesar and the Family of God', in *Images of Empire* (ed. L. Alexander; JSOTSup 122; Sheffield: Sheffield Academic Press, 1991), 276–97

Aune, D.E., *Revelation* (WBC 52c; 3 vols.; Dallas, TX: Word Books, 1997)

Carson, D.A., P.T. O'Brien and M.A. Seifrid (eds.), *Justification and Variegated Nomism*, I: *The Complexities of Second Temple Judaism* (WUNT 2/140; Tübingen: Mohr Siebeck; Grand Rapids: Baker, 2001)

Chow, J.K., *Patronage and Power: A Study of Social Networks in Corinth* (JSNTSup 75; Sheffield: JSOT Press, 1992)

Dunn, J.D.G., 'The New Perspective on Paul', *BJRL* 65 (1983), 95–122; reprinted in *Jesus, Paul and the Law: Studies in Mark and Galatians* (London: SPCK, 1990), 183–206

Elliott, N., *Liberating Paul: The Justice of God and the Politics of the Apostle* (Biblical Seminar 27; Sheffield: Sheffield Academic Press, 1995)

Feldman, L.H., *Jew and Gentile in the Ancient World* (Princeton: Princeton University Press, 1993)

Georgi, D., *Theocracy in Paul's Praxis and Theology* (Minneapolis: Fortress Press, 1991)

Goodenough, E.R., *The Politics of Philo Judaeus* (Hildesheim: Georg Olms Verlagsbuchhandlung, 1967 [1938]).

Gundry, R.H., 'Grace, Works and Staying Saved in Paul', *Bib* 66 (1985), 1–38

Hendrix, H.L., 'Archaeology and Eschatology at Thessalonica', in *The Future of Early Christianity: Essays in Honor of Helmut Koester* (ed. B.A. Pearson; Minneapolis: Fortress Press, 1991), 107–18

Hengel, M., *Die Zeloten* (Leiden: E.J. Brill, 1961)

——, *Crucifixion in the Ancient World and the Folly of the Message of the Cross* (London: SCM Press, 1977)

Horsley, R.A. (ed.), *Paul and Empire: Religion and Power in Roman Imperial Society* (Harrisburg, PA: Trinity Press International, 1997)

—— (ed.), *Paul and Politics: Ekklesia, Israel, Imperium, Interpretation: Essays in Honor of Krister Stendahl* (Harrisburg, PA: Trinity Press International, 2000)

——, 'Rhetoric and Empire – and 1 Corinthians', in Horsley, *Paul and Politics*, 72–102

—— and N.A. Silberman, *The Message and the Kingdom: How Jesus and Paul Ignited a Revolution and Transformed the Ancient World* (New York: Grossett/Putnam, 1997)

Jewett, R., 'The Redaction and Use of an Early Christian Confession in Romans 1:3–4', in *The Living Text: Essays in Honor of Ernest W. Saunders* (ed. D.E. Groh and R. Jewett; Lanham, MD: University Press of America, 1985)

Johnson, E.E., and D.M. Hay (eds.), *Pauline Theology*, IV: *Looking Back, Pressing On* (Symposium Series 4; Atlanta: Scholars Press, 1997)

Käsemann, E., *Commentary on Romans* (Grand Rapids: Eerdmans, 1980)

Koester, H., 'Imperial Ideology and Paul's Eschatology in 1 Thessalonians', in Horsley (ed.), *Paul and Empire*, 161–62

Martyn, J.L., *Galatians* (AB 33A; New York: Doubleday, 1998)

Oakes, P., *Philippians: From People to Letter* (SNTSMS 110; Cambridge: CUP, 2001)

Price, S.R.F., *Rituals and Power: The Roman Imperial Cult in Asia Minor* (Cambridge: CUP, 1984)

Sanders, E.P., *Paul and Palestinian Judaism: A Comparison of Patterns of Religion* (London: SCM Press, 1977)

Schreiner, T.R., 'Paul and Perfect Obedience to the Law: An Evaluation of the View of E.P. Sanders', *WTJ* 47 (1985), 245–78

Seifrid, M.A., *Justification by Faith: The Origin and Development of a Central Pauline Theme* (NovTSup 68; Leiden/New York: E.J. Brill, 1992)

——, 'The "New Perspective on Paul" and its Problems', *Them* 25 (2000), 4–18

——, *Christ, Our Righteousness: Paul's Theology of Justification* (Leicester: Apollos, 2000)

Winter, B.W., 'The Imperial Cult and the Early Christians in Pisidian Antioch (Acts 13 and Galatians 6)', in *First International Conference on Antioch in Pisidia* (ed. T. Drew-Bear, M. Tashalan, and C.M. Thomas; Ismit: Kocaeli Press, 2000), 60–68

——, *After Paul Left Corinth: The Influence of Secular Ethics and Social Change* (Grand Rapids: Eerdmans, 2001)

——, *The Imperial Gods and the First Christians: Conflict over the Beginning of All Things* (forthcoming)

Wright, N.T., *Climax of the Covenant: Christ and the Law in Pauline Theology* (Edinburgh: T. & T. Clark, 1991)

——, *What St Paul Really Said: Was Paul of Tarsus the Real Founder of Christianity?* (Oxford: Lion; Grand Rapids: Eerdmans, 1997)

——, *Christian Origins and the Question of God*, I: *The New Testament and the People of God* (London: SPCK, 1992)

——, *Christian Origins and the Question of God*, II: *Jesus and the Victory of God* (London: SPCK, 1996)

——, 'Paul's Gospel and Caesar's Empire', in Horsley (ed.), *Paul and Politics*, 160–83

——, 'New Exodus, New Inheritance: The Narrative Structure of Romans 3–8', in *Romans and the People of God: Essays in Honor of Gordon D. Fee on the Occasion of His 65th Birthday* (ed. Sven K. Soderlund and N.T. Wright; Grand Rapids/Cambridge: Eerdmans, 1999), 26–35

——, *Romans* (*NIB* 10; Nashville: Abingdon Press, 2002)

Zanker, P., *The Power of Images in the Age of Augustus* (Jerome Lectures, 16th Series; Ann Arbor, MI: University of Michigan Press, 1988)

12

Response to N.T. Wright

Oliver O'Donovan

During the earlier stages of my work on *DN*, while Tom Wright was still in Oxford, I learned a great deal from our discussions, and especially from the ways in which he hoped to carry Ed Sanders' interpretative proposal forward, that Jesus' preaching had to be understood in terms of aspirations for the national renewal of Israel. So I am not surprised to find myself in sympathy with his approach. The political overtones of the theological vocabulary of Paul, not least *dikaiosunē*, I underline myself. That this should imply that Paul has a critical front towards the imperial establishment is a natural corollary; the remarks on Romans 13 I take to be largely in parallel with my own, and since that has been a contested area I am grateful for the support. Though Paul in Romans and John the Seer in Revelation come at the question of Rome from different angles and with different emphases, there is a fundamental compatibility between their outlook which, after all, one might reasonably expect from a tightly self-conscious minority movement at the beginning of its existence.

After this central and entirely resonant 'Yes', I trust a friendship of one third of a century to allow me the prerogative of a sharp, if more circumferential, 'No'. Wright does not appreciate the extent to which his own interpretation belongs in the mainstream tradition. His remark about 'what the majority of Christian theologians have meant' by justification 'since at least Augustine' will cause some distress to those who know *City of God* 19, where Augustine consciously and resolutely exploits the continuities of meaning from *ius* to *iustitia* and *iustificatio*. As for 'Lutheran', a term which regularly signals the displeasure of this aforetime enthusiast for the Reformation, who else, after all, has a better claim to have reawakened the Western church to the enactive, performative sense of the noun *dikaiosunē* and its relation to the Hebrew verb *ṣaddîq* than Brother Martin? To which I would add that the post-Hildebrandine popes and their advisors were quite well aware that the successors of Charlemagne with whom they had to deal were, by the same token, successors of Divus Augustus, and that when it came to religion, the imperial tradition was dangerous. What

Tom Wright reacts against is a kind of Kantian pietism, which has, however, little claim to speak as the majority voice of the tradition. (And perhaps not for Kant either, but that is for another day!)

Now, let me try a 'Perhaps'. Wright would like us to be aware that some of Paul's theological vocabulary carries overtones (though secondary ones) from the imperial cult, and therefore suggests a confrontation (though as an implication, rather than as a goal of his argument). The test must be: would Paul have thought such overtones audible to his likely audience? These were Greek-speaking Jews and Jewish sympathizers, living in the city of Rome as a marginalized oriental subculture in the modern Trastevere. Their word for 'love' would have been *agapē*, not *amor*, and they would have called the city they lived in *Rhōmē*, not *Roma*. A play on words in Latin would surely have been beyond them. In Ephesus Paul is possibly surrounded by evidence of the imperial cult; but are the Romans themselves? The Julio-Claudians promoted the cult slowly, and initially only in the Orient, though Claudius judged Britain sufficiently exotic and barbarous for its introduction. In Rome itself the political priority was to establish quasi-republican constitutional legitimacy: *Res Gestae Divi Augusti*, 34, tells not of the cult of a goddess Iustitia, but of Augustus' so-called 'transfer of power to the SPQR'. In the 50s AD the imperial cult would surely have been a muted affair in Rome; though perhaps Paul was unaware of that, or counted on recent immigrants to have a lively sense of what was going on from their previous homes.

On a rather different front, I would welcome some clarification of the work done in Tom Wright's construction by the concept of 'narrative'. Of the six 'stories' he identifies, three look like 'narratives' in a recognizable sense: the 'covenantal narrative' from Abraham to the Messiah, the story of Jesus, and the story of Paul himself. But 'creation and new creation' is only marginally narratival in structure, and the 'story of the church' hardly more so (unless we mean what Wright does not mean, i.e., the history of the church up to the Second Vatican Council). The 'story of the individual Christian' does not look like a narrative at all. *Which* individual Christian, one would have to ask, is it supposed to be the story of? A regular and repeated pattern of events is not, as such, a narrative; a narrative has to be particular. Would it make any difference, I wonder, if Tom Wright were to abandon his attempt to make every theme look like a story?

13

'Members of One Another': *Charis*, Ministry and Representation: A Politico-Ecclesial Reading of Romans 12

Bernd Wannenwetsch

Ecclesiology and Politics

> A theological account of how this world is ruled, then, must proceed from and through an account of the church. ... Decisions made about the nature of church authority have shaped and still shape what is said about secular government.[1]

Thus reads a central claim of Oliver O'Donovan's political theology as expounded in his *The Desire of the Nations*. His account of political authority has sought its conceptual basis in an analysis of Israel and the church as political societies par excellence. This hermeneutic rests on the basic assumption that 'We assert first the true character of the church as a political society.'[2] While in the case of Israel as God's chosen people who actually did form their own civil community the political nature has always been obvious enough, in the case of the church it has been widely overlooked. Two related aspects appear to ground O'Donovan's understanding of the church as political society. First, the fact that the church is not just a social entity, following the pattern of an undirected 'process', but is a *governed* society, 'brought into being and held in being, not by a special function it has to fulfil, but by a government that it obeys in everything'. A second foundation is the eschatological vision of the 'eternal city'.[3] 'If the Christian community has as its *eternal* goal, the goal of its pilgrimage, the disclosure of the church as city, it has as its *intermediate* goal, the goal of its mission, the discovery of the city's secret destiny through the prism of the church.'[4]

---

1 *DN*, 159.
2 *DN*, 159.
3 *DN*, 159.
4 *DN*, 286.

The way in which O'Donovan understands the church to inform the worldly city and its political culture is not so much envisioned in terms of analogies, as in Karl Barth's famous proposal 'The Christian Community and Civil Community',[5] but explored in terms of the free sharing of conceptual discoveries. As the church learns to understand and describe its own life politically, it offers the world an opportunity to rethink its dominant conceptualizations of the political life, in the hope that it may readjust its practices in a way which is less caught up in narrow frameworks and unfruitful alternatives.

If the church witnesses to the rule of Christ in its own life as a society ordered according to the 'law of the Spirit of life in Christ' (Rom. 8:2), keeping the 'bond of peace' (Eph. 4:3), it cannot expect the civil communities to simply adopt this law, nor will the peace for which the church prays and gives thanks directly inform secular policies. Yet, if the secular *polis* becomes attentive to this witness, it cannot but question a whole range of prejudices on which much of its political life is based: the assumption, for example, that peace is 'manageable' if only the right strategies are employed, or that it is just another word for proportioned reciprocity, and so on. The deconstructive potential of the politics of God as enacted in the life of the church begets, however, constructive hope. Though renewal of secular rule will hardly start from the peace that Christ has wrought, it may begin as important recognitions penetrate into the political consciousness. For instance, the recognition that peace, as a concept, is not exhaustively or not even primarily conceivable in terms of political *poiesis*, but must be anticipated in its reality ('the bond of peace', Eph. 4:3) in order to become actual, may considerably reset the stage for, say, the terms and conditions of impending negotiations in a particular conflict.[6]

We must not forget that worldly rule makes an impact on the disciples, too, as the Lukan narrative makes especially clear in the recurrent theme of striving for greatness (Lk. 22:24ff.; 9:46ff.). Jesus' followers are not exempt from the *schemata* of this *aion*. In order to be able to witness to the worldly city with *transforming* power, the church must acknowledge the *formative* power of the dominant patterns of reaction within the worldly city. Though Christ has deprived this power of rule, the *schemata* are nevertheless still powerful. Therefore, the new understanding and practice of political authority within the church must be formulated over against the dominant conceptualizations, such as those of power as force, peace as balance of fear, and so on.

---

[5] Barth, *Against the Stream*, 15–50.

[6] In order to be able to enter into negotiations in the course of a violent conflict, we must simply assume the reality of peace in a sense; we must take for granted that it is not a utopian idea, that both parties know what it is about and that an envisioned peace treaty would therefore not necessarily suffer from mutually incompatible interpretations, etc.

The glory of the political existence of the church does not lie in the possession of a superior political ontology that has only to be applied to praxis in church and world.[7] Rather, the church's concepts are to be understood in a verbal sense: they must be 'grasped' (*concipere*) in their meaning and significance. The church does not make but is given its core practices. Nor does the church 'have' better political concepts apart from its *actual* process of grasping the meaning of its own practices – an act which is best seen as a discovery bound up with the imperative to be renewed in its perception, as it refuses to conform to the *schemata* of the worldly city.

In describing the task of ecclesio-political hermeneutic in this vein, I am drawing on Paul's *paraklesis* in Romans 12. What I would like to undertake here is an exegesis of these verses, which are often said to mark the beginning of the 'ethical part' of Paul's letter to the Romans. They have, however, as far as I can see, rarely been read with a keen sensitivity to the possibility of their having an implicit political theory. If political authority is to be informed by the way in which the *polis* of the co-citizens of the saints (Eph. 2:19) is governed, we should expect Paul's account of the 'body politics' of the Christian church also to be of interest in the political context.

My considerations operate on the basis of the positive suspicion that there is a political ethic in Paul's account of the church. I wish to explore what we can gain from examining Romans 12 in this light, and whether the conceptual gain can inform our understanding of the exercise of political authority elsewhere. In particular, I will pay special attention to the idea of representation. The fact that this motif, which is central to any account of political authority, is also heavily featured in Paul's *paraklesis*, may be seen as justifying my hunch concerning the political fecundity of this chapter. And its exegesis will help us to understand and assess Oliver O'Donovan's claim that, 'The responsible state is ... minimally coercive and minimally representative.'[8]

Furthermore, as a kind of inner-exegetical test case, we may ask whether echoes of the ecclesio-political concept as analyzed in chapter 12 can be found in Paul's own account of worldly authority in the subsequent chapter. Is there a way from Romans 12 to Romans 13? And if we grant that there is, can there be a proper understanding of the latter without considering the hermeneutical impact of the former?

A note of caution is appropriate. From what I can see, Romans 12 does not seem to feature much in the history of Christian political thought. An indication of this is the index of the superb source book in Christian political thought, *From Irenaeus to Grotius*, which Joan Lockwood O'Donovan and Oliver O'Donovan have recently published. In this comprehensive collection we find

---

[7] See my criticism of John Milbank's anti-political metaphysic in 'Political Worship'.

[8] *DN*, 233.

only one single reference to Romans 12, pointing to an anonymous text from the eleventh century.

It should therefore be obvious that my attempt has an experimental flavour, and I am aware of the danger of over-interpretation. At any rate, such attempts need much help and refinement from others who have more expertise in Paul and political thought. Still, the possible gain seems worth the risk. I shall confine my analysis to those eight verses, which I quote from the RSV:

> I appeal to you therefore, brethren, by the mercies of God, to present your bodies as a living sacrifice, holy and acceptable to God, which is your spiritual worship. [2]Do not be conformed to this world but be transformed by the renewal of your mind, that you may prove what is the will of God, what is good and acceptable and perfect. [3]For by the grace given to me I bid every one among you not to think of himself more highly than he ought to think, but to think with sober judgment, each according to the measure of faith which God has assigned him. [4]For as in one body we have many members, and all the members do not have the same function, [5]so we, though many, are one body in Christ, and individually members one of another. [6]Having gifts that differ according to the grace given to us, let us use them: if prophecy, in proportion to our faith; [7]if service, in our serving; he who teaches, in his teaching; [8]he who exhorts, in his exhortation; he who contributes, in liberality; he who gives aid, with zeal; he who does acts of mercy, with cheerfulness.

If we allow that Paul's account of the body and its members in verses 3 and following may have a political overtone – after all, the 'body' was not an unusual metaphor in contemporary political rhetoric – we may also find it legitimate to engage in a political reading of these well-known opening verses.

Such a presupposition should alert us to Paul's use of plural pronouns, which should not just be interpreted as an artefact of the literary setting of a letter which is written to a number of people. We should rather understand this fact as conceptually demanded by the subject: Paul is addressing a corporate 'we', not just a multitude of individuals. This assumption inaugurates a different way of understanding the following imperatives: what it means to sacrifice the bodies *as a body*, what it means to renew the sense of perception *in a communal way*, what it means to become a *community* of discernment, and so on.

If we allow the first two verses to be read in the light of the subsequent account of Christian body politic, we may in turn also read Paul's considerations on the charismatic body in the light of the opening imperatives and understand these imperatives to be outlined in the subsequent exhortations. Is the way in which the different members of the body are to receive one another in Christ (vv. 3ff.) perhaps identical with the holy and living sacrifice, the reasonable worship of which Paul has spoken (v. 1)? And what light does it shed on the politically conceived differentiation of the body according to the distribution of *charismata* (vv. 3ff.) when understood as the practical expression of the call to renewal, non-conformism and discernment (v. 2)?

Let us first look at the particular speech act, which is Paul's address to the church at Rome. This will provide us with an initial sense of the kind of authority which marks the political nature of the church.

Paraklesis: The Genuine Political Speech Act of the Church

'I appeal to you …' The Greek verb is *parakalein*. Its tone is one of authority, as Paul speaks as an apostle, and the formulation recalls the famous passage in 2 Corinthians 5:20, where he says: 'We stand before you as Christ's ambassador, as though God were exhorting you through us (*parakalountos di' hēmōn*)'. However, the content of the *paraklesis* is specified immediately by what follows in that passage: 'We implore you: be reconciled with God.' The authority of *paraklesis* does not employ the language of command. In his letter to Philemon, Paul makes the juxtaposition explicit: 'Though I had complete freedom in Christ to *command* you (*epitassein*) what is decent, for love's sake, I rather *appeal* (*parakalō*) to you' (v. 8f.).

The difference between appeal and command reflects not a downgraded authority but a different *kind* of authority, which does not rely on the power to compel but on the freedom of the addressees to assent. For this reason, it does not invoke the particular status of the one who exercises *paraklesis* ('as apostle'), but rather invokes the status of the addressees ('brothers'). Or, more precisely, it invokes the status which both, addressees and addresser, share.

The kind of exhortation that *parakalein* denotes mirrors the particular address ('brothers'), which is in itself an appeal to a reality (the brotherhood of the children of God) that embodies an inherent moral imperative. And it seems that the detailed exhortation that follows is merely specifying the imperative that is already inherent in the invoked reality. Thus, the appeal is not directed to 'moral subjects' as a summons to them to *realize* what is not yet real or not yet fully there; rather the appeal is to a *given reality*. Therefore, we must deem the translation 'exhortation' insufficient insofar as it reduces Paul's *paraklesis* to a moral appeal, an expression of an 'ought' to become rather than an 'is' which is given.

The actual etymology of *parakalein* confirms this suspicion. While the profane Greek meaning was focused on the moral motif, ranging from 'admonishing', 'summoning' to 'beseeching', in the Septuagint the term is used for the translation of the Hebrew *nachat* (niphal or piel) which means 'consoling' or 'comforting'.[9] In the New Testament, we find both individual

[9] Schlier, 'Vom Wesen', 75f.

meanings respectively, but the characteristic novelty is that the concepts seem to merge. So in some contexts, such as the one with which we are concerned here, *paraklesis* is only fully intelligible if we allow for the double sense of 'consoling exhortation', or 'exhorting consolation'. In the German language, *Trost* (comfort) has the same root as the English 'trust', and it may be apt to say that because *paraklesis* is an appeal to a *trustworthy reality*, the imperative to trust in it can in itself be comforting. As we have seen, in the case of Romans 12, this reality is the brotherhood of the church as implied and invoked in Paul's address to the 'brethren'.[10]

What I wish to highlight here is this: within the speech act of *paraklesis*, the address 'brothers' should be understood in political terms. Certainly, its normal usage belongs to the language of the household, which according to the perspective of classical philosophy marks exactly the pre-political sphere – a sphere where there is only command and obedience, but no freedom and (therefore no need of) moral exhortation. Yet, as it seems to me, in Paul we have to reckon with a specific theologically-subverted language of the 'household-*polis*' of God, where the representatives of *polis* and *oikos* have been reconciled into one body, overcoming the separation of public and private and the antagonism between the hitherto mutually exclusive spheres of life.

Again, the letter to Philemon is an illuminating example. If Paul sends Onesimus back to his master 'no longer as a slave ... but as a beloved brother', what is employed here is not really family language; instead, for Paul, 'brother' must now be a political notion. As if confirming this point, Paul adds, '... both in the flesh and in the Lord'. 'Beloved brother' is not a mere spiritual status, but a bodily one also. As a member of God's household, the former slave in Onesimus' household is at the same time a co-*citizen* of the saints with the same *politeuma*, with the same civic right as his master (cf. Eph. 2:19).[11] At stake is a political reality in which they are now all brothers and sisters – master, slave, and also the apostle.

It is true, as Heinrich Schlier[12] has reminded us, that *paraklesis* is a warm form of exhortation, which mirrors the emotional bonds of a familial relationship such as father and children share with each other. But even within this familial emphasis, the difference from the patriarchal household pattern is prominent.

[10] It should be noted here, that while mere exhortation would obscure the political character of the church, *paraklesis* could not be sufficiently translated with 'consolation' either. The reality, which is invoked, must be 'appealed' to, since it is still hidden and not obvious to all observers. Therefore the moral imperative, though inherent, must be formulated and addressed.

[11] As to the programmatic 'conflation' of household and *polis* language, see my *Gottesdienst*, 153ff.

[12] Schlier, 'Vom Wesen', 77. See also 1 Thes. 2:10ff.

So, for example, Paul introduces his *paraklesis* with the claim to imitate him by appealing to the contrast between his own 'fatherly' relationship with the Corinthian community and the kind of authority which a *paidagōgos* exercises: 'I am not writing this to make you ashamed, but to admonish you as my beloved children. For though you might have ten thousand guardians (*paidagōgous*), you do not have many fathers. Indeed, in Christ Jesus I became your father through the gospel. I appeal (*parakalō*) to you, then …' (1 Cor. 4:14ff.).

Though Paul sees this warm *paraklesis* motivated in his special fatherly 'familiarity' with the Corinthian community that he has founded, the general logic, which allows him to address the still unknown Roman body in the same way, is the politico-familial status of 'brotherhood' that he shares with them.

What can we infer for the concept of authority from our analysis of the genuinely Christian form of moral exhortation? On the one hand, *paraklesis* is a speech act that brings the apostle in a sense 'down' to the same level as his addressees. In this vein, Paul can introduce his *paraklesis* through the explicit reminder that 'we speak to you as your fellow-workers (*synergountes*), adding our exhortation (*paraklesis*)' (2 Cor. 6:1), and thus we may affirm that Oliver O'Donovan is certainly right to describe the authority in the church as a common standing under the authority of the gospel.[13] However, the picture is complicated by the observation that the apostle in exercising *paraklesis* does also in a way represent God's voice and authority, as the preceding verse (5:20) suggests: 'Representing Christ we appeal to you as though God was exhorting you through us.' And to make things even more puzzling, we observe that at the end of his letter to Philemon, Paul expects Philemon to 'obey' as a result of his *paraklesis* (v. 21). What are we to make of this puzzling finding that comes down to the notion of *obedience without command*?

Let us at this point just note a perplexing duality: the language of *paraklesis* seems to be characteristic of the kind of authority in the church as political body; although juxtaposed with the patriarchal[14] language of command, it

---

[13] *RMO*, 172. This is related to (while not identical with) the distinction between counsel and command which O'Donovan has identified as an essential mark of the church:

> Counsel, indeed, is the Church's most characteristic address to the individual, because it respects his status of one whom God also addresses directly and whose particular decisions are partially hidden from public gaze. … The Church commends its case by argument, persuasion and the exposition of Scripture, and regards itself as having in some measure failed if the matter is ultimately brought to the level of command. Its counsel, therefore, is authoritative without being coercive. (*RMO*, 171f.)

[14] O'Donovan labels the command/force pattern 'pure political authority', drawing on the ruler's monopoly of violence that can mistakenly be thought to be a sufficient rationale for the exercise of authority. In classical terms, however, the idea of unlimited power to force and command belongs to the sphere of the household rather than to the

nevertheless aims at obedience.[15] It is rooted in the shared status of 'brotherhood' and citizenship in the household-*polis* of God. In this sense, the authority by which *paraklesis* is exercised can be said to be an authority which belongs to the nature of the political body itself. On the other hand, this can only be the authority of Christ in whom the body has its life. Yet, everything depends on how the authority of Christ is understood to be represented within the 'natural' authority of the church. The straightforward answer will certainly be 'as his body'. But this is exactly what requires spelling out: *how* the obedience to Christ is embodied in a community in which *paraklesis*, not command, is the dominant political language.

At least to some degree, I think, our chapter provides an answer. I take the key to be Paul's strange-sounding idea of the Christians being 'members of one another' – an idea that invites an essential reconceptualization of the idea of political representation.

But before we address this issue, we must see how our understanding of *paraklesis* is deepened when we look at the way Paul frames it: *dia tōn oiktirmōn tou theou*, 'by the mercies of God', as the NRSV translates the phrase. It is certainly right to say that this echoes what Paul has outlined in the previous chapters in terms of the great deeds of the merciful God. However, we would underrate the theological quality of *dia*, were we to understand it as a mere rhetorical emphasis, adding the weight of divine authority to what Paul has to say. 'For the sake of God's mercies' would, in a sense, still leave the great deeds of God 'behind', by turning them into motivating considerations that add to the plausibility of the exhortation by appealing to the inner sense of gratitude on the side of the addressees.

Yet the 'acts of mercy' are not Paul's individual motivation, nor are they meant to provide a motivation for the morality of the community. Rather, Paul addresses the congregation 'through' them, by putting what he has to say into the light of God's merciful deeds that are already known to the Romans. Those 'mercies' are in fact authorizing his speech, but in a potentially critical way. He is not saying, 'Look what God has done for you, now consider it fair to listen to my exhortation as a kind of moral duty for the sake of all those

---

polis, so it might be more advisable to speak of a depoliticization taking place when the patriarchal pattern of the household with its *potentia absoluta* of the *pater familias* is transposed into the political sphere. In spite of this terminological difference, O'Donovan makes it clear enough that 'pure political authority' is not 'true political authority', which must encompass both compelling 'natural' authority (including force in the name of status and tradition) and 'moral' authority (of truth). See *RMO*, 124ff.

[15] In the light of this observation or qualification, I would prefer to describe (the insufficient) 'pure political authority' in O'Donovan's terms as concerned with command, rather than, as O'Donovan does, as 'concerned … with obedience' (*RMO*, 174).

goodies.' Rather, his words carry this tone: 'Judge my claim as to whether it is in accord with the *oiktirmōn tou theou* – judge my exhortation as to whether it can be seen as outlining the moral claim which is inherent in those mercies.'

It would perhaps not be exaggerating to say that for Paul, those divine mercies are the genuine *subject* of the *paraklesis*.[16] Having said this, we must remind ourselves again that this authority is not claimed in a direct sense but mediated in the particular way in which the genuine political language of the church addresses its addressees. I say deliberately 'of the church', not only 'in the church', since the clue lies in the particular freedom of the addressees to respond to a non-commanding authority with obedience. The nature of this political language is intelligible only in a community for which 'authority' is never a monolithic concept – a community that is less concerned with divine legitimation of human authority than with human *mediation* of divine authority.

As Oliver O'Donovan has pointed out, any direct claim for divine authorization would deny the public and historical character of God's work and of the church, respectively. Any claim to obedience must be made in the light of the public history of Jesus' life, death and resurrection. Divine authority is not a private matter of inner prompting and compulsion deprived of speech.[17] The voluntarist tradition which roots the authority of command in the sheer and naked *potentia absoluta Dei* was therefore, we must say, an anti-political regression, incapable of distinguishing the particular sense of Christian obedience from the sheer function of commanding power.

The Transformation of the Body

Having analysed the concept of *paraklesis* as characteristically political, we now turn to the individual expressions in Romans 12. Here we must keep in mind that they are all governed by the *pluralis politicus* in which Paul addresses the believers as a body.

'Present your bodies as a living sacrifice, holy and acceptable to God which is your spiritual worship.' Commentators often remark that the verb *paristanō*, especially when combined with *thysia*, is a technical term belonging to the

---

[16] This claim finds support from various similar constructions in Paul's theological rhetoric. See, for example, 1 Cor. 1:10: *Parakalō de hymas, adelphoi, dia tou onomatos tou kyriou hēmōn Iēsou Christou*. As Heinrich Schlier has remarked, it would be odd to understand Paul here as only referring to the name 'Christ' and not appealing to the efficacious name *of* Christ ('Vom Wesen', 79). See also Rom. 15:30: *Parakalō de hymas, adelphoi, dia tou kyriou hēmōn Iēsou Christou*.

[17] *RMO*, 141.

language of cultic sacrifice. So the translation 'presenting' or 'giving away' seems perfectly in order. However, the profane Greek offers another possibility, in which it translates into 'standing together' as in military action – forming a military unit as a densely woven web of mutual support in order to ward off a hostile attack.[18]

So the meaning: 'stand together with your bodies as (or even, in order to become) a *thysia*', can be considered as a plausible translation.[19] In this case, the imagery would not be individual martyrdom and its symbolic representation in the moral life of the individual Christians. If this were the case, would Paul not have used the plural for the sacrifices, too? *Thysia*, however is a singular, suggesting that the presentation of the individual bodies is not meant to comprise sacrifices in the immediate sense, everyone offering his or her own sacrifice. Rather, we have another characteristic immediacy here: the offerings of the individuals become a living, holy and God-pleasing sacrifice only by their 'standing together', by contributing to the *thysia* in the singular. Anticipating our further analysis, we may say that the true worship that Paul invokes is the offering of *the* body (the church) through the communal offering of the individual bodies to become one body in mutual service. From this perspective, a 'living' sacrifice does not merely mean, as most commentators point out, that the bodies are not consummated (as in a holocaust) but stay alive. Instead, Paul speaks of a *living* sacrifice because the *thysia* is a matter of the *corporate life* of the body of Christ.

In a sense, we can see foreshadowed here what was to be elaborated in the eucharistic theology of the Patristic period, especially in its conceptualization of the offertory rite. Here, the subject of 'sacrifice' is explicitly said to be the church, however cast in the idea of a double identification: 1) of the individual believers with the material elements (oblations, 'fruit of the earth and human labour') which are offered by the church on the altar (according to Augustine, 'there you are on the table … there you are in the chalice'[20]), and 2) of the

[18] Bauer, *Wörterbuch*, 1243. Interestingly, John Chrysostom has taken up the military imagery in his account of *parastēsai*, though giving it another slant. He interprets Paul along the following lines: Do not make your bodies into a sacrifice, but surrender them to God, hand them over … like a military horse; likewise your bodies, handed over to God and his fight against the devil … are not any longer to be harnessed to private usage (*Twentieth Homily*, my translation).

[19] Luther's original German translation *begebet eure Leiber* is perhaps a perfect representation of the theological oscillation between the (usual) transitive use of *parastēsai* and the (politically pregnant) intransitive meaning towards which my suggestion points. So the German *begeben* is normally used intransitively, but in this case it is ruled by the transitive thrust of sacrificial language without losing its pointer to the 'line up', which those will form who 'move their bodies to become living sacrifices'.

[20] Augustine, *Serm.*, 229.

essential identification of Christ with the elements by taking up those sacrifices into his own sacrifice on Golgotha.[21]

Hence, on a political reading of Romans 12, the literal sense is all important: the singular of *thysia* should not be overlooked or deprived of its theological meaning by explaining it as just another grammatical possibility; nor, on the other hand, should the plural of *sōmata* be overlooked or explained away as a *pars pro toto*, meaning just 'self'. Paul's emphasis on the bodies is essential to understand the polemic irony in the perplexing formulation of *logikē latreia*. 'Spiritual worship' (RSV) is actually a very good translation, but only if we have in mind that this is phrased against the background of the Hellenistic–Jewish juxtaposition of 'cultic' sacrifice (of beasts) and 'ethical or spiritual' (self-) sacrifice. This had found a special expression in the tradition of the *Corpus Hermeticum*, where *logikē latreia* was meant to be the wordless prayer of the mystic. However, over against such a background, the polemic thrust of Paul's redefinition of 'spiritual worship' as precisely a *bodily* enterprise jumps out.[22]

The difference, however, is only fully understood if we take into account the meaning that the body (in generic terms) has for the communal aspect. While the *logikē latreia* of the mystic was by virtue of its spiritualist, body-denying nature ideally a solitary undertaking, the 'spiritual worship' which Paul has in mind must be, by virtue of its bodily nature, a communal affair.[23]

Our bodies are the media through which we communicate; it is our bodies that turn us to others. Yet, for Paul, it is not the natural social capacity of the physical bodies that lends itself to the metaphorical imagination of 'one social body'. In order to envision the socio-political reality of the body of Christ, there must be a sacrifice of our bodies into the body – *of* our bodies *into* the body, and of our *bodies* into the *body*. This sacrifice is to include the 'natural'

---

[21] Dom Gregory Dix, in his seminal work *The Shape of the Liturgy*, offers an excellent summary:

> Each communicant from the bishop to the newly confirmed gave *himself* under the forms of bread and wine to God, as God gives Himself to them under the same forms. In the united oblations of all her members the Body of Christ, the church, gave herself to *become* the Body of Christ, the sacrament, in order that receiving again the symbol of herself now transformed and hallowed, she might be truly that which by nature she is, the Body of Christ, and each of her members members of Christ. In this self-giving the order of laity no less than that of the deacons or the high-priestly celebrant had its own indispensable function in the vital act of the Body. The layman brought the sacrifice of himself, of which he is the priest. The deacon, the 'servant' of the whole body, 'presented' all together in the Person of Christ, as Ignatius reminds us. The high-priest, the bishop, 'offered' all together, for he alone can speak for the whole Body. In Christ, as His Body, the church is 'accepted' by God, 'in the Beloved'. Its sacrifice of itself is taken up into His sacrifice of Himself (117).

[22] See Schlier, 'Vom Wesen', 86.

[23] See my discussion of Hannah Arendt's claim that Christianity has notoriously overemphasized the *vita contemplativa* at the cost of *vita activa*, in *Gottesdienst*, 197ff.

concepts of political society and political authority, which come to our minds as they are shaped by our experience of secular politics.

In this light, the special character of the required sacrifice as expounded in verses 2 and 3 becomes visible. Here, Paul summons the community to a transformation, which entails the abdication of the *schemata* of this world. As the church is called to be a community of the discernment of God's will,[24] the renewal of the *nous* is required.

Nous refers to the mind in a specific sense, addressing its faculty to comprehend reality as it is especially associated with the ability to conceptualize, to grasp reality in its generic sense.[25] The renewal of the mind is necessary, given the schematizing power of the *aion*. *Mē syschēmatizesthe*: 'do not be conformed to this world'. Here, the passive voice is no less in place than it is in the subsequent call to be transformed. The latter case is certainly a matter of *passivum Divinum* – the transformation cannot be a simple 'rethinking' of things as an increased effort of the human mind itself; transformation requires[26] nothing less then a *renewal* of the mind. And a new mind can only be a gift, part and parcel of the *kainē ktisis*, God's creation of a new humanity, so that the imperative can only mean to watch out for God's activity of renewing the mind.

Yet, the initial call *mē syschēmatizesthe* has a passive voice, too, which indicates 'recognition of a power or force which moulds character and conduct and which "this age" exercises'.[27] And while this exhortation is certainly of general validity for Christians of all ages in every aspect of their lives, we may again be well advised to take it at face value, as we take Paul's further appeals. As his subsequent call to 'appropriate self-esteem' in verse 3 suggests, he is concerned in

---

[24] In the biblical usage, *dokimazein* is construed in a significantly comprehensive sense, integrating the transitive and intransitive meanings of 'probing' and 'testing'. The probing of God's will is not separable from the probing of our hearts (1 Thes. 2:4) and deeds (1 Cor. 3:13) through God. Therefore, the translation 'discerning' aims at more than mere intellectual practice and must assume a specifically moral meaning, wherein the discernment of God's will is identical with the discovery of the 'good and acceptable and perfect'.

[25] In Aristotle's philosophy of mind, the *nous* occupies the central position between *sophia* (immediate vision of the ends) and *phronesis* (means-to-end rationality) as the conceptualizing faculty of the mind.

[26] John Chrysostom has emphasized the qualitative difference between the *schema* of the world and the *morphe* of the new life. While the *schema* is mere appearance and pretence of reality, *morphe*, or 'form', has a natural beauty that does not deceive. While the virtual character of the *schemata* does not foreclose (perhaps rather explain) their spell, the 'form' can only emerge in its own right as a matter of transformation. 'Away with the *schema*, and there you have the form!' (*Twentieth Homily*, v. 12.2 [my translation])

[27] Dunn, *Romans*, 712. Dunn opts for the passive rather than the middle voice.

the first place with the ecclesio-political aspect of the schematizing power of the age.

What the transformation is meant to overcome is precisely 'disordered' thinking about the way in which the individual members relate to the whole body by way of relating themselves to the other members. At the base of the *hyperphronein* that Paul wants to foreclose may lie a version of the classical idea of the political sphere as an arena for striving for excellence at the cost of others. In this perspective, place and status in the political society are seen as a 'natural claim' by virtue of heritage or personal achievement. And Paul's call to renewal of (this pattern of) thought recalls Jesus' response to the competition over greatness between his disciples (Lk. 22:24ff., Mk. 10:35–45).

Here, the *schema* of rule in the secular world ('the rulers of the nations lord over them, and those in authority are called benefactors'), in which 'natural authority', the authority of means, dictates status, is confronted ('but not so with you') with a new way of understanding and exercising authority. 'The greatest among you must become like the youngest and the leader like one who serves.'

Jesus' claim, 'not so with you', is not in an egalitarian fashion doing away with the notion of authority and greatness altogether. Rather, it aims at a reconceptualization of what it means to be great – from striving to excel over others, which means to let them appear smaller in one's own presence, towards a notion of service or ministry which marks out a greatness that makes others grow rather than diminish in the presence of this greatness.

Paul seems to follow Jesus' lead by presenting a sophisticated though thoroughly practical account of the church as a community of authority where ordered thinking about one's own role is cast into the measure of *charis*. I cannot resist a reference to Luther's German translation here, as he has brought out this coincidence so nicely in rendering verse 3 in this way: Everybody should think of him or herself '*maßvoll*' (*sōphronein*), according to the '*Maß*' (the measure) of faith. As the new order of social status in the church is essentially an order of baptism where the waters of the sacrament have washed away every 'naturalist' claim to authority and lordship ('as many of you as were baptized into Christ ... there is no longer Jew or Greek, slave or free, male or female, for all of you are one in Christ' (Gal. 3:27ff.), it is not that surprising to find the word which Paul uses for the renewal of the mind, *anankainosis*, bearing a certain baptismal overtone.[28]

In the light of baptismal equality and inclusiveness, the address *panti* is qualified: the focus on the inclusiveness of 'everyone' must be understood emphatically, ringing as it were throughout the whole of Paul's subsequent expounding. This emphasis is warranted not only because of the universality of

---

[28] Schlier, 'Vom Wesen', 88. Cf. Tit. 3:5; 2 Cor. 4:16; Col. 3:10.

the 'Zebedeian temptation' to strive for lordship, but it is also called forth by the political nature of the sacrifice and the sound worship of the church, and ultimately by the church's own nature. In order to be a truly political society, it is not enough to have in good order the basic functions that are necessary to sustain communal life. Instead of *functioneers*, there must be *citizens* if there is to be a political society. And in accord with the classical definition of a citizen as someone 'holding an office' in the *polis* (Aristotle[29]), Paul is keen on characterizing the church as a community in which 'everybody has something to contribute' (1 Cor. 14:26).

Now, the most interesting question with regard to political hermeneutics is exactly how this universal citizenship in the church is related to the ordering of the communal life, how it relates to the question of authority and representation.

Approaching this question, we note at first that Paul's appeal to *sōphrosynē* is not simply a call to moderation and modesty. He does not say, 'Do not think higher of yourself than you are', but '… than you ought to think', immediately qualified by, 'according to the *metron pisteōs*, the measure of faith'. A *metron* can, of course, be both the result of measuring as well as the criterion by which something is measured, quantity and quality. Yet the whole thrust of Paul's argument seems to discourage the quantitative understanding of the 'measure of faith' in terms of the *genitivus obiectivus*. This would in effect come down to a strange ranking of the charismata according to the *quantum* of faith, suggesting that in political terms, the one with the greatest faith would have to rule, not unlike Plato's philosopher king. As this is clearly ruled out for Paul, we take the *metron pisteōs* to be a *genitivus subiectivus*, introducing the diversity of *charismata*, not their weighting or ranking.[30] The individual believers should think of themselves and their role according to the divergence of gifts that God has distributed through faith. This is to be read in close conjunction with '*kata tēn charin tēn dotheisan hēmin diaphora*'. In a typical move, Luther in his commentary on Romans has made the point that, since faith is the 'main' gift or good that brings all the others with it, the 'measure of faith' rules out the lurking danger of understanding our own role according to our own will or the measure of our own merit.[31]

---

[29] *Politics*, 1275b, 18f.

[30] John Chrysostom has made this point especially clear, stating, 'the *charisma* which is given to us, is one and the same. … Therefore it is spoken of the *charismata* not in terms of a more or a less which has been attributed to the one or the other, but that they are different; you have *charismata* not greater or smaller but different' (*Twentieth Homily*, my translation).

[31] Luther, *Der Römerbrief*, 210.

Members of One Another: The Representation of *Charis* and Ministry

Now we have to come to terms with the most striking of Paul's claims: that the members of the body are to consider themselves as 'individually members of one another' (*kath' heis allēlōn melē*). What James Dunn calls a 'slightly odd variation of the body metaphor'[32] is actually not a variation but a transgression of its natural logic. While we can imagine what it is to be members of the same body, to be a member *of someone else*, as Paul phrases, can hardly be understood within the logic of the body metaphor. And it is exactly in this 'unnatural' imagery that Paul makes clear that the acceptance of the body of Christ is a political task.

The thrust of the chapter is not grasped if we overhear Paul merely summoning the Christians to actively play their part, to accept their assigned role and fulfil their ministry. Though this is certainly included, the thrust of Paul's words goes in a perhaps annoyingly different direction, as it aims at the recognition of the ministry of the *others*. Yet Paul aims not just at our allowing others to be part of the community, to have a task, role and place in their own right. He goes much further in ascribing to them the dignity of becoming *part of ourselves*: 'members of one another'. This is a description of the political existence of the body of Christ that is as intriguing as it is radical.

Of course, it is more difficult to accept the *charisma* of the other than it is to accept his or her weakness. Their weakness is an opportunity to express my strength, but their charisma is a possible threat to my charisma, letting comparison and competition become the regular order of relationships.

Accepting the other as 'a member of my own (body)' goes beyond accepting his or her charisma as such. It is precisely accepting the ministry of the other *towards* myself. In this vein, Luther paraphrased Paul's claim by the phrase '*sich das Werk gefallen lassen*'[33] in the (active and passive) double sense of to *delight* in someone else's work and to *receive* or *accept* it for oneself.

We should be aware that Paul's claim does not merely challenge our *natural* human instinct to protect ourselves from each other. It is even *more* difficult when it comes to the *Christian* community of baptismal equality. Let me explain this with an example. It is relatively easy to accept the ministry of another person within the framework of an 'expert' model. I have no idea how to repair my television, therefore I am more than happy to accept the service of the technician. This willingness to recognize his 'ministry' is helped by the fact that I do have my own areas of expertise where I appreciate the acceptance of my ministry by others with less knowledge in this field. Perhaps the repairman needs a bit of theological advice some time? So far, so easy. The model of

---

[32] Dunn, *Romans*, 724.

[33] Luther, *Der Römerbrief*, 209.

recognition of expertise draws its plausibility and practicality from the process of differentiation and specialization of modern societies, with its ongoing tendency to compartmentalization and fragmentation of knowledge.

The reverse side of the expert model is, however, an increasing inability to accept the authority of another if it touches on my own expertise. Of course, I am happy to receive a collegial suggestion from another theologian from time to time, but it would be harder for me if my college were to decide that, from now on, there would be an appointed college theologian in charge of responding to all theological questions. Am I not a theologian myself, perhaps more knowledgeable than this colleague, at least in some areas?

When it comes to political order, the challenge faced by the communities that Paul addresses is no less threatening. Some should be teachers in a way in which others are not, some are to be prophets in a way in which others are not, some are called to exercise moral discernment in a way in which others are not, and so on. We must be aware that the claim that there should be such special ministries (offices) and representation is not self-evident in a community where *the* ministry belongs to the body as a whole.

When Paul says in 1 Corinthians 14:29, 'let some prophesy, let the others judge', the ministry of prophecy is obviously thought to be a matter of the whole body, where the 'weighing' of what is said is no less important than what is said. Given this inclusive nature of the ministry (which is even more strongly confirmed in verse 31: *dynasthe gar kath' hena pantes prophēteuein*), it is not an easy lesson to learn that there should be still 'some' to represent it, some who are given a specific authority over the others in a particular sphere. For the charismatic communities that the charismatic Paul addresses, it is a lesson that must be learned – the political life of the church is not solely built on charisma or 'natural authority'. In addition to charisma, there is also a sense in which 'pure' political authority called forth the acceptance of the special ministry or office of others. Taking up O'Donovan's distinction again, we must hasten to add that this acceptance is bound up with the authority of *truth*, since the addressees of the ministers actually *share* in the ministry. Therefore, in all his apostolic exhortations, Paul can ultimately claim to be 'not master of your faith but collaborators *(synergoi)* of your joy' (2 Cor. 1:24).

It is exactly this acceptance of mutual representation that allows the church to become the community of discernment that probes and explores God's will (Rom. 12:2). For to know God's will is to do it, and it is only in doing God's will that it will be known. The political existence of the church is itself the practice of exploring God's will.

The way in which the body is at stake in Paul's account of 'everybody a member of one another' is not focused on the membership of *the other* in the body – and our own like or dislike of it – but on something more radical, as John Chrysostom has put it: 'Why do you amputate *yourself* from this body through your pride?'[34] It is our own possession of the body, our own share in it, which is threatened by a denial of this principle of mutual representation and equality: 'As he is a member of you, so you are a member of him, and the equality is in this respect, too, a complete one.'[35]

In order to understand the nature of representation within the body of Christ, we should begin by becoming aware of the reflexive form of the noun 'representation', which denotes a presentation of something which is already there. We can say, first of all, that this presence is true of the body as such. It is not that the congregation should *become* the body of Christ by the application of Paul's principles. Rather, the mystical body of Christ is already present, and the congregation shall be ever more transformed into it. Ministry does not create order but presupposes it. Derived from the already present body is another 'given', the membership of the believers in the body. As Luther has commented on our passage: the members have their own praxis within the body since they are members of the body; they are not members of the body by virtue of their praxis. They have become members by birth (baptism) before any work.[36]

What is it now that is represented in the political existence of the church? We shall see that the answer will be given in terms of an account of differentiated representation that includes *charis*, *charismata*, ministry and special ministries (offices). How can we describe the different modes of representation in the Christian body?

a) Charis *and the one ministry*

At the most basic level, we have to speak of the representation of the one *charis* and the one corresponding ministry: to receive it and live up to its reality. As all baptized Christians are charismatics and ministers in this sense, representation at this level is a basic notion as it is provided through every member and for every member: 'everyone a member of one another'.

b) Charismata *and ministries/office*

Differentiation is inaugurated through the *charismata diaphora*: they are represented by the ministers who exercise them. Yet the emphasis is on representation, not exclusive ownership. The individual minister is but a personal reference to the presence of the charisma in the whole body. Were she the only one to have a particular charisma she could not *re*-present it. There

---

[34] Chrysostom, 21st Homily, emphasis mine.

[35] Chrysostom, 21st Homily.

[36] See Luther, *Der Römerbrief*, 206.

would be no 're-', no presence to refer to apart from her own personal gift. So the minister is by her exercise of a *charisma* to others exactly witnessing to the commonality of the *charisma*. The discernment of what is prophesied is part of the ministry of prophecy as much as learning is part of the teaching ministry.

It is of singular importance to understand that the specific unfolding of the ministry into several offices is *not* a function of the specific *charismata* of the individuals. The office of a teacher is not established because one member or a few members of the congregation happen to be just so pedagogically gifted. Rather, God has established 'teaching', the particular praxis of making the rationality of the Christian faith intelligible to one another because grace is, among other things, 'instructive grace';[37] thus, the ministry of teaching is *charis*, a gift of God to the whole body and which awakens different *charismata* in different members, often but not always by ordaining natural talents to serve the *oikodomē* of the whole body.

In this light, the odd participial construction that Paul employs when introducing the particular *charismata* and ministries takes on a critical implication: 'As one who serves, in *diakonia*; as one who teaches, in *didachē*; as one who exhorts, in *paraklesis*.' The RSV is obviously unaware of an important difference when it reads 'he who teaches, in his teaching, he who exhorts, in his exhortation'. Yet, what the one who teaches is to represent is not 'his' own teaching, but the ministry of teaching. What is at stake in teaching is the *sacra doctrina*, which is already there in a transpersonal, political sense (as the possession of the body), just as the *paraklesis*, which we have analysed as a political language game par excellence, is a given *morphe* (form) which is the object of the attention of those who are called to this ministry. These *charismata* are not a property of the ministers as officeholders but the possession of the church, a possession which makes it into a *society*.[38] The business of individual ministers and officeholders is precisely to represent this communal charisma or ministry to the body, an act which has the effect of maintaining the church as a *political* society, insofar as the recognition and acceptance of this representation is the political form which obedience to Christ's rule takes on.

---

[37] I am happy to adopt this notion from O'Donovan's response to this paper.

[38] I borrow the way in which the distinction between possession and property informs the theory of society from Oliver O'Donovan. It is noteworthy that 'having' gifts (v. 6, '*echontes de charismata*') may also be translated 'holding' (*echo* can be both) of *charismata*, echoing the political language of 'holding' an office. As its exercise is from the outset directed towards the *oikodomē* of the *ekklesia*, a *charisma* is therefore a common possession of the church, not a property of individual charismatics.

Representation and Political Society

If we claim that the acceptance of the representation of ministry (the ministry of regular office-holders as well as of its spontaneous actualizations) is what makes the church a truly political entity, this calls forth a qualification: neither the offices nor the charismata are able do this in their own right. (Herein lies the limitation of the debates on 'charisma and/or institution'.)

The account of the distribution of charisma and ministry in the Christian body should be distinguished from accounts that draw on the functional distribution of labour according to a view of the nature of society as a 'system of needs' (Hegel). The political will in the Christian body is not immediately directed to the preservation of the community or its 'unity', but towards Christ's rule in his body.[39] Therefore, in this chapter, we see Paul not rushing into the political rhetoric of 'keeping the unity' and employing the suggestive 'body' metaphor to this end; instead, as we have seen, he starts by exhorting the believers to offer themselves communally into the consumption of God's rule. What he has to say further – on the diversity of praxis, the acceptance of ministry and the honouring of office – is not meant to establish ecclesiastical authority but invokes the political *morphe*, which the authority of Christ takes on through the authorization of the Spirit's gifts.

However, if we are saying that the political form of the body is to embody Christ's rule, we must not forget the inclusion that Christ's rule is *hidden* in a pattern of practices, which, when observed from outside, may look pre-political or even 'purely political' (in O'Donovan's pejorative use of the term).[40]

---

[39] It is this theological priority of *charis* over *charisma*, of ministry over ministries or office, that Karl Barth addressed in his own way when he spoke out against what he took to be a 'Romantic Catholic ecclesiology' of the body as an organic being, understood within the logical framework of 'whole and parts'. Over against this tradition, Barth maintains that the community is '*neither* aggregate *nor* organism' (*Der Römerbrief*, 428).

In one sense the individual believer is not 'part' of the whole, but 'is' the whole inasmuch as the *charis* dwells in him as a whole, making the individual 'one body' in Christ (429). Therefore, the just way of referring and relating to the individual is not *suum cuique*, but rather '*jedem das Eine*': the One for everyone (430). On the other hand, Barth talks about the divine disturbance of the individuality of the individual, where every individual can only want and do 'one thing': the recognition of *charis*. Only if this is clear, if everybody has recognized his or her bestowal of the one-same grace, then the '*suum*' may come to bear on the community and must be honoured and appreciated (431). Yet if this is to happen – and Barth's provision is a repeated 'perhaps' – we do not think of it in terms of job sharing, disciplines or resorts. Rather, everybody, in doing his or her own thing, does the 'one' thing, which is the whole.

[40] 'The political character of the church, its essential nature as a governed society, is hidden, to be discerned by faith … Looked at from outside, it presents the appearance

Let us take preaching as an example. The very fact that there are many who listen to what one individual has to say could well be understood as a natural function of what Friedrich Schleiermacher has called 'religious consciousness' and its inner drive to sharing; or it could be understood as evidencing the structural heteronomy and patriarchal command-structure in the church. It is virtually impossible for an observer to discern whether listening to the words of a preacher is an *active* engagement with the word of God. For disengaged observation cannot discern whether or not this particular social phenomenon is an incidence of 'accepting the other as one's own member', meaning that the preacher proves herself to be a listener, while the listening community is actively sharing in the proclamation. With only the limited conceptualization of authority as either 'natural' (charisma) or 'purely political' (institutional) at hand, we are incapable of understanding what is going on in the church as a political entity in its own right.

Though as a baptized member of the church I myself have been bestowed with the word, I have still to listen to it as a *verbum alienum*, authoritatively passed on to me through the voice of another person. The inextricable externality of the gospel is embodied in the practice of bodily representation where 'we are members of one another'.

So we can sum up our account of differentiated representation:

- Every charisma represents the one *charis* just as every special ministry (e.g., teaching) represents the one ministry (of witnessing God's *charis*) of the church by representing one charisma (e.g., understanding doctrine) in particular.
- Every office (e.g., teacher) represents the ministry (of teaching) in a (publicly ordered) way which differs from the way in which the ministry is represented by every other member.

These different and gradual modes of representation imply a critical function over against all possible claims to immediacy such as claiming the authority of the one ministry for one's own execution of an office. This is why there has to be a *paraklesis* such as Paul's which summons the body to a sound form of recognition of its peculiar political nature as highlighted in his account of differentiated representation. In this light, that of the free yet obedient response to the apostolic *paraklesis*, we can describe a differentiated sequence of recognition that mirrors the differentiated account of representation:

- The recognition of office is a way of recognizing ministry, which is a way of recognizing charismata, which is a way of recognizing *charis.*

---

of a functional religious organism rather than a political one, having no visible source of government' (*DN*, 166). Cf. also Luther's famous saying: 'abscondita est ecclesia, latent sancti'.

Charis as the fundamental level of representation is, of course, a highly critical principle which does allow every single charisma and its exercise in office and spontaneous service to be tested against its very own nature. Does the concrete way in which the office/service is exercised account for the gift character of grace? Or does it instead subvert grace in making its exercise look like an achievement, expecting praise, gratitude, and so on? Does it live up to the communal character (*panti*), or does it reclaim the charisma for the office-holder, denying the participation of others in it?

As we have seen, this account does not employ a *theologia politica naturalis*, as it does not feed on the 'organic evidence' of the body metaphor. Instead, it goes beyond and even against the grain of the body metaphor. This 'unnaturality' is emphasized again by the significant order in which Paul lists charismata and ministries. As Luther has pointed out, this order exactly mirrors the thrust of Paul's account of the nature of Christian ministry in which prophecy is first and leadership (*proistamenos, proistamai*) comes last. This biblical order, as Luther states, is itself the work of the Spirit, as though it was anticipating the future pall that the devil would cast over Christianity: namely, the tyranny wrought in the church in which ruling is seen as the highest and most desirable good and everything else must be bent to this tyranny of rule.

In contrast to this, Paul, as Luther understands him, has assured us 'that there is no higher thing than the word of God, the ministry over every ministry, the office over offices'. The ministry of government is the word's slave who might have to occasionally stimulate it at times, just as a slave may have to wake up his master or remind him of his office.

Luther concludes with an account of the dialectical relationship between the 'high' and 'low' ministries which seems but a reaffirmation of the concept of differentiated representation: 'Therefore, the ministry of ruling is the lowest, and yet the others are subject to it, and – conversely – it is of service to the others of care and oversight. In turn, prophesying is the highest, and yet, it is subject to the one who governs.'[41]

What could our theological analysis of Romans 12 mean for a theory of political representation in the secular sphere? Whom or what do the carriers of temporal authority represent? The obvious answer, the people or the country, makes sense in regards to international relationships, but looked at from the inside of a political society, it is not that straightforward. At least, politicians should not (want to) represent the citizens in the *direct* sense of having an imperative mandate that would render them mere agents of their voters' wills. Over against such an administrative model of politics, a political representative can be understood to be something more, if we say, for example, that she should be free to follow her conscience rather than party discipline.

---

[41] Luther, *Der Römerbrief*, 214.

Hence it seems more suggestive to say that what political representation is meant to represent is the 'common good'. And it is true: without the assumption of a common good there could be no political ministry, there could be no officeholders, only lobbyists. The sense of objectivity that surrounds the idea of an office cannot be upheld without the claim of an existing common good. However, the representation of the common good is a matter of the existence of political authority as such and cannot be claimed in a straightforward way by any holder of a political office. Though she must certainly strive to act on behalf of the common good and in accord with her assuming it in any given case, her actual understanding of that good and proposed course of action must at the same time be held accountable to the common good in terms of the perception that others have of it. This dialectics seems to be an obvious feature of democratic societies where the common good is a matter of public dispute.

Rather than representing the people in an abstract sense, elected politicians as members of parliament represent the people in their common *deliberation*. Even this, however, must be understood not exclusively but inclusively, as parliamentary debates must not replace but focus and stimulate public debates.

Therefore, we notice a peculiarly dialectical relation of political representation and the common good: political office as such is authorized by its being ordained to serve and represent the common good, yet must be tested against it by calling into question the representative quality of political action. This dialectics often tempts us to a hasty resolution on one side or the other: either to equip political authority with the claim of representing the common good by virtue of its sheer existence and staying power or by virtue of a special insight (Plato's philosopher king) or legitimacy (through divine investiture or the surrender of the collective will); or the dialectic can be dissolved into the idea that the common good has no claim to existence prior to political negotiation within society, leaving for the political officeholder the role of representing exactly this ongoing negotiation with its inherent imperative to moderation.

If our collective political memory leaves us with this dialectic and yet this dialectic leaves us puzzled, is there anything we can learn from Paul's political ecclesiology? The first thing to note is that in the light of an ecclesiological account, representation cannot be conceived in exclusivist terms. Following Paul's hermeneutic, we may say: 'She who represents: in representation!' Representation is a matter of the whole political body, differentiated and gradually defined. Even though it is necessarily bound to single persons and bodies, it cannot be translated into a personal quality, but will always refer to specific *acts* and to a particular *ministry*. So rulers do not simply represent the people, nor do they represent God (a pagan idea), but rather they represent quite simply 'rule', as the creator has instituted it.

In the secular sphere, political ministries cannot be said to be *charismata* as they are not expressions of the *charis* as a gift of the Spirit. Yet they must be regarded in theological terms as expressions of a divinely instituted *ordo*: the *ministerium politicum* (*politikē leiturgia,* cf. Rom. 13). Though a theologically understood secular authority is still different from leadership in the church, as it cannot rule out the use of force ('the sword'), it shares with ecclesial authority the particular concept of inclusive representation: the ruler is not capable of representing the *ministerium politicum* on her own. This is why certain acts of recognition from the side of the citizens are essential for (though not constitutive of) political authority. On the other hand, as a theological account of representation calls forth, acts of recognition of the people's sharing in the rule are equally essential for the way in which rulers exercise their special ministry. Though this will hardly become as radical as Paul's account of mutual representation and 'members of one another', it will be decisive for the political culture that the concept of 'rule' is not absorbed into claims of the sufficiency of personal authority ('charisma') or purely political authority (command).

Therefore, if we turn again to Oliver O'Donovan's claim which we quoted at the beginning, the claim that the 'responsible state' is to exercise a *minimum* of representation, we are now in a position to understand its critical thrust, but we also feel the need to relocate the accent. If the political life of the church is to bear on our concepts of political authority and political act, the first thing that needs to be emphasized is that representation *per se* must not be regarded as a problem. The responsible state is, in fact, representative. Representation is not ruled out as it has been suggested in the tradition of political Romanticism, where the idea of absolute individual self-possession leads to the ideal of a plebiscite democracy. As we have seen in our exegesis of Paul, the way in which the Christian community exercises 'obedience without command' is shaped by a particular praxis of political representation (grace, charisma, ministry, office). If we are to speak of a 'minimalism' in this account of representation, it lies in the differentiation, which carefully avoids any claim of immediacy to the divine power.

Therefore the critical thrust of Pauline ecclesiology takes a twofold direction. It challenges both 'realist' accounts in the vein of Hobbes' *Leviathan* or Machiavelli's *The Prince*, which would emphasize a 'thick' notion of political representation without any social mediation, and also 'idealist' accounts such as Rousseau's, which rule out political representation altogether.

In concluding, let us with the help of an example test whether those conceptual considerations find echoes in the more explicit account of political authority and participation that primitive Christian practices and Paul's famous passage in Romans 13 offer. The example I have in mind is the Christian practice of interceding for those in authority (1 Tim. 2:2).

On the one hand, the intercession for temporal authority is an indication of the acceptance of political authority in and through the church, including the authority of hostile rulers such as Nero. But there is more to it than simple acceptance. On the other hand, the intercessions entail or rest upon a theological qualification of worldly authority, which goes beyond the knowledge and self-understanding of those who are the actual bearers of it. Whatever they may think of themselves, they are, as Paul claims in Romans 13:4, *leiturgoi* of God, ordained to serve 'towards the common good': *eis to agathon*.

This ascription provokes another important consequence: As the very term '*leiturgos*' indicates, being the personal form of '*leiturgia*', it is an office/work (*orgia*) of/for the people (*laos*): as *leiturgoi*, the bearers of worldly authority are seen to represent the *ministry* of the people in inclusive terms.

This is why the practice of interceding for the temporal rulers finally indicates that Christians share in their ministry. Even in those times when Christians were deprived of the possibilities of civil engagement, as in places which are remote to modern democracy today, Christians have always participated in the *ministerium politicum* through their intercessions. Those prayers have been understood as a political action for the sake of the *salus publica*, and theologically as representation in the strong sense: to stand before God, presenting the people, the rulers and the whole political society to God by commending them to his grace. This peculiar representation did not go unnoticed in the world and could be acknowledged even by Gentile rulers.[42] And it seems fair to say that this mutual recognition of political representation and sharing in the ministry of rule has certainly prepared the way for a wider participation of Christians in the political culture and for the general development of this culture towards enhanced participatory chances.

But even in times and places of little or no official possibilities for political participation, the Christian view on temporal authority could not help but be shaped by the specific idea and experience of a society where its members are 'members of one another'. In this light, members of the body of Christ have never been and can never be mere subjects, but must always be citizens, no matter what their status in worldly terms might suggest. And if the political character of the church is as hidden as the rule of Christ in the world is hidden, we should not be surprised to learn about sublime ways in which certain aspects of ecclesiology spill over to inform our political imagination.

---

[42] In the Edict of Tolerance by Galerius in 311 there was a passage according to which the Christians, in return for the emperor's favour, were obliged to pray for the authorities: 'Unde iuxta hanc indulgentiam nostram debebunt Deum suum orare pro salute nostra et rei publicae ...'

Bibliography

Barth, K., *Against the Stream: Shorter Post-War Writings 1946–52* (London: SCM Press, 1954)

——, *Der Römerbrief* (Munich: Kaiser, 11th edn, 1924)

Bauer, W., *Wörterbuch zum Neuen Testament* (Berlin: Alfred Töpelmann, 5th edn, 1963)

Chrysostom, J., *20th Homily on Romans* (A Library of Fathers of the Holy Catholic Church; Oxford: Parker, 1841)

Dix, D.G. *The Shape of the Liturgy* (London: A. & C. Black, 1945)

Dunn, J.D.G., *Romans* (WBC 38B; Dallas: Word Books, 1988)

Luther, M., *Luthers Epistelauslegung*, I: *Der Römerbrief* (ed. E. Ellwein; Göttingen: Vandenhoeck & Ruprecht, 1963)

O'Donovan, O., *Resurrection and Moral Order: An Outline for Evangelical Ethics* (Leicester: IVP; Grand Rapids: Eerdmans, 2nd edn, 1994)

——, *The Desire of the Nations: Rediscovering the Roots of Political Theology* (Cambridge: CUP, 1996)

——, and J.L. O'Donovan (eds.), *From Irenaeus to Grotius: A Sourcebook in Christian Political Thought 100–1625* (Grand Rapids: Eerdmans, 1999)

Schlier, H., 'Vom Wesen apostolischer Ermahnung', in *Die Zeit der Kirche. Exegetische Aufsätze und Vorträge* (Freiburg, Basel, Wien: Herder, 5th edn, 1972)

Wannenwetsch, B., *Gottesdienst als Lebensform: Ethik für Christenbürger* (Stuttgart, Berlin, Köln: W. Kohlhammer, 1997)

——, 'The Political Worship of the Church: A Critical and Empowering Practice', *Modern Theology* 12 (1996), 269–99

14

Response to Bernd Wannenwetsch

Oliver O'Donovan

I warmly welcome a contribution that explicitly connects ecclesiology and politics, and does so exegetically; but I welcome it especially because it does so in such an original way. We are familiar with the line of thought which begins with the 'conciliar' representation of the local in the universal, and concludes to the 'federal' constitution of secular government. We are familiar with the line of thought which begins with the Pentecostal equality of the member of the church and ends with a civil society marked by equal rights. Bernd Wannenwetsch's line of thought is in a way like these, but in another way unlike them: the church is a body in which each relates to the other by representing (or re-presenting) a prior grace with its own pre-structured possibilities of special ministry; in the same way the different offices of civil society must represent something higher than the people; they must represent the pre-structured form of 'rule' itself.

The complex weave of relationships is summed up in three important statements near the end: 'Every charisma represents the one *charis* as every special ministry ... represents the one ministry ... by representing one charisma ... in particular.' 'Every office ... represents the ministry ... in a publicly ordered way, which differs from the way in which the ministry is represented by every other member.' 'The recognition of office is a way of recognizing ministry, which is a way of recognizing charismata, which is a way of recognizing *charis*.' Taking these sentences as our key, we may perhaps chart Wannenwetsch's view of the relations diagrammatically in two columns as follows:

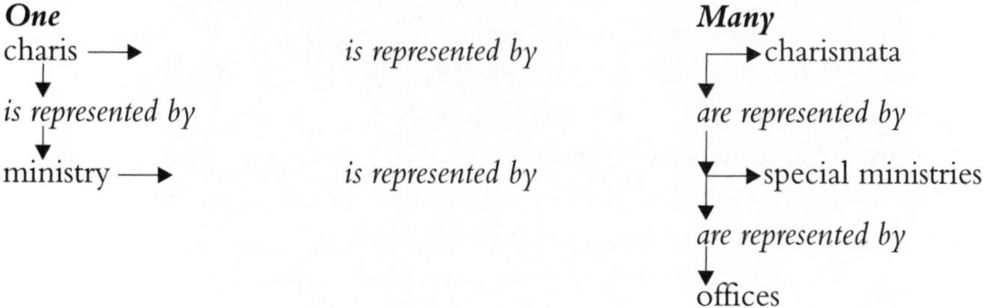

This diagram makes it clear that there are in fact two kinds of representation: the representation of the one by the many, and the representation of the pre-structured by the structured. It is from the one pre-structured *charis* of God that all of the authority within the community to perform any differentiated task derives. The authority of the community is the mercy we show one another; and to the extent that we communicate God's mercy, we command the authority of that mercy. But our communication of God's mercy becomes defined in two ways: as a *witness* to it, which is the key content of the term 'ministry' for Wannenwetsch, and as a *differentiated expression* of it, in the plurality of forms. Special ministries arise as a combination of these two forms of definition: we *witness to the differentiated expression* of the grace of God. And out of these special ministries there arises a further level of witness, that which is provided by the formalized offices of the church.

The principal implication Wannenwetsch draws from this is that charismata, as differentiated forms of the divine mercy that we present to one another, are not merely native endowments taken up, as it were, into the ecclesial project of God, but are shaped by a logic of *self*-differentiation within the mercy of God. There are two complementary routes from *charis* to special ministries: one passes through the different charismata of individuals, the other through the common witness of the church. These two routes explain and limit each other. So that any person's exercise of a charisma is not an agonistic exercise of display, where personal endowments are shown to good effect in the service of others, it is an exercise of 'alignment' (as he provocatively renders Paul's verb *paristano*) in a corporate sacrifice which is the living body of the church. This same principle shapes the way we understand the special ministries and offices, too. As he tellingly insists: 'what the one who teaches is to represent is not "his" own teaching, but the ministry of teaching. What is at stake in teaching is the *sacra doctrina*, which is already there in a transpersonal political sense.' The special ministry of teaching is not defined by the fact that the church has people who can teach, but by the fact that the grace God gives us demands teaching because it is, among other things, instructive grace.

I do not think that Wannenwetsch intends to identify charismata with special ministries, though sometimes his emphasis on the corporate ministerial destination of the charismata is such as to make the difference not very clear. In the examples he gives, however, he identifies 'understanding doctrine' as a charisma, and 'teaching' as the corresponding special ministry. Here the charisma clearly corresponds to the individual's power and the ministry to the use he is called to make of it. What we are being told, however, is that the power itself, the 'makings' of a teacher which an individual may have to fit him for the ministry, is not an independently grounded contribution out of his personal endowment, but is called forth by the pouring out of God's instructive grace.

The individuality of the endowment is, as it were, fully accounted for in the logic of the whole, and needs no further accounting for. How would I ever have a gift of 'understanding doctrine' unless grace were given *as* doctrine? How would I encounter doctrine as an object of understanding without encountering it as a destiny to ministry? The individual endowment is a distinct moment, but no more than a moment, in the distributive administration of God's grace.

There is, however, an interpretation of this very ecclesial understanding of gifts and ministries that Wannenwetsch wants to caution against. He tells us that his account should be distinguished from accounts which draw on the functional distribution of labour according to a Hegelian 'system of needs'. I would have been grateful for more explanation of this warning. The brief explanation that he gives us is that the logic of the church's ministry is not one of self-maintenance, but one of witness. This seems to suggest that precisely the *ecclesial* emphasis may mislead, if we do not understand what kind of a body the *ecclesia* really is. If the distribution of gifts and ministries is not simply a matter of the native endowments of individuals, neither is it simply a matter of the current needs of the church. The church needs more ordained ministers to maintain its parish churches, so we look to see who there is that God has made half-suitable for the task. The need-driven conception can, alternatively, assume an anti-clerical guise. Sometimes we hear it lamented that the lists of *charismata* in 1 Corinthians turn into a list of offices in Ephesians: should the early church not have understood the *charismata* as infinitely open to new possibilities, so that the list could go on, 'she that makes sandwiches, in sandwich-making; he that makes critical comments on the sermon, in critical commentary', etc. But these indefinite extensions of the list still spring from a kind of immanent logic of community self-perpetuation; they are a matter of what the church finds *useful* (sandwich-making) or *interesting* (critical comments), rather than of the forms of the grace of God. I suspect that Wannenwetsch has a rather clear idea in his mind of the forms that divine grace has taken and will take, and thinks in terms of an essentially determinate range of possible *charismata*, ministries and offices, shaped by the once-for-all gift of Christ present through the Holy Spirit.

As the charis is represented by every member to every member, so is the common good in political society. The offices represent that common good which is, as it were, already present and already represented mutually; and the office-holders represent the office which is already present as a mediation of the common good. It seems that we can ask two kinds of question about political structure: 1) does this office-holder discharge the office rightly? and 2) are the terms of this office well conceived as a mediation of the common good which we all, as citizens, serve? Concrete political questions and constitutional questions both appear on the horizon in Wannenwetsch's scheme.

He then denies that any ruling office represents either God ('a pagan idea') or the people. Rulers represent 'rule', which I presume is the active aspect of the common good, as authority is the active aspect of God's mercy. To this I would like to wonder whether if, besides the pneumatological basis of representation, Wannenwetsch had explored a christological basis, he would be forced to qualify his negatives here. Of Christ's authoritative representation we say that he represents both God and the people, *alēthōs theos, alēthōs anthropos*. The negative point is, of course, clear: on the one hand, the ordered social reality of the people stands between God and ruler; on the other, God as the source of ordered rule stands between people and ruler; so the ruler does not stand between the people and God. Vitoria would have said as much. To that extent Christ in his two natures is unique, not replicated in any ruler; there is *one* mediator between God and humankind. Yet must we not insist that Christ is also paradigmatic? As it is *God's* rule over the people that the ruler represents, and for that very reason the *people's* rule under God, we cannot avoid a sense in which the ruler speaks both with God's authority and the people's.

15

The Function of Romans 13 in Christian Ethics

Gerrit de Kruijf

Introduction

Parallel to the developments in philosophical ethics in which analytic and procedural ethics have lost ground to ethics based upon consideration of virtue or the good,[1] in Christian ethics we are also again beginning to locate discussions of moral dilemmas in broader moral fields and to relate to the moral subject, and even to see the discussions in the light of salvation history. This means that the coherence of dogmatics and ethics has become more visible, and that we do not limit the use of the Bible in ethics to the search for pointers in admonitions and commandments. We can now extend it to seeking the will of God (Rom. 12:2) in the light of the whole biblical narrative. This is the direction we must certainly go in our thinking, because the question in Christian ethics is not about the action of humankind abstracted from the acts of God, but about the actions of humankind in light of God's acts.[2]

Although it was very clear in *Resurrection and Moral Order* that O'Donovan wanted to define and discuss the concept of moral order from the history of the mighty acts of God, his work has nevertheless sometimes been classified under the heading of 'natural ethics'.[3] The seriousness with which he takes the primacy of the history of God's acts can be seen in *The Desire of the Nations*, and he narrates that history in such a way that the centuries after the Christ-event actually are a part of that history as well.[4] These centuries are not merely

---

[1] Cf. the work of Alasdair MacIntyre and Charles Taylor.

[2] In his introduction to this volume (*A Royal Priesthood?*), Bartholomew has categorized this position as ethics as an extension of dogmatics (type 3). One may ask what dogmatics is about when Christian ethics is about something else than dogmatics.

[3] *DN*, 19.

[4] O'Donovan's concept can be subsumed under Bartholomew's 'type 4'conception, 'Christ the clue to theology and philosophy', outlined in 'Uncharted Waters', 33.

labelled as the epoch of the Holy Spirit, but rather are discussed in the light of the Holy Spirit. In this description it is, then, perceptible that the aim of accenting creation within history is to accent that the gospel is not gnostic but involved in mundane, human, and even political reality. Once again, the resurrection also plays a central role in this history. In fact, *DN* deals with the question of how, in discussions of political reality, we can legitimately bring to bear the fact that Christ is risen and has defeated the powers. Precisely because of the desire to do so, the use of the Bible acquires a surprising dynamism: can the words of the Bible be heard in such a way that they actually affect political reality rather than merely skimming along its surface?

Many Christian ethicists do indeed confess that Christ has in principle defeated the powers, and therefore they expect the coming of the kingdom of God, but they see no way to actually charge their vision of political reality with that belief. It usually goes no further than a very general indication – 'patience', for instance – after which follows a discussion that seems to presume (to cite O'Donovan) 'that the Christ-event never occurred'.[5] The reason that O'Donovan precedes his political ethics with a political theology lies precisely in his desire to promulgate an ethic 'which presumes neither that the Christ-event never occurred nor that the sovereignty of Christ is now transparent and uncontested'.[6] That second possible, triumphal premise (which holds that the reign of Christ is visible in the power of the church) in theological discussions of politics has been characteristic of the tradition of Christendom, while the general critique of it has as a rule produced an ethic with the (albeit concealed) first premise (Christ's resurrection seems of no real significance). O'Donovan wishes, in a non-triumphal manner, still to take seriously that Christ has made a public display of the powers.

I was trained up in the school of Barth. I was left with questions regarding the connection between commandment and creation in Barth's work. I consider *RMO* to be a convincing answer to these questions: God's commandments and deeds articulate and transform the created moral order until the eschaton. Barth also left me with questions about the connection between confessing Jesus as Lord and political deliberation. According to Barth, political choices should reflect the confession of Christ as Lord, they should even be seen as confessions themselves, but Barth does not make clear how the church can debate about what is the right political confession. One may even wonder whether the use of the term 'political confession' allows for political discussion. Only O'Donovan's next book can be interrogated on that point, because in

---

[5] *DN*, 146. By 'exponent' Barth means that the state as such (not just the Christian or the church-promoting state) functions within the circle of authority (*Herrschaftskreis*) of Christ (cf. Barth, 'Bürgergemeinde', 55).

[6] *DN*, 146.

DN we receive no answer to the question of the use of the Bible regarding the deliberative question of 'whether or not we should bomb Iraq'.[7] For he only treats the reflective question – important enough – of whether such a question is theologically relevant. But O'Donovan does speak just as passionately as Barth does about political reality *zwischen den Zeiten* – albeit somewhat differently than Barth did. O'Donovan candidly advocates striving for a Christian state, while Barth sees the state as such as an exponent of the kingdom of God.[8] However, I do not suspect that O'Donovan even for a moment desires the restoration of ecclesiastical political power; on the contrary, I sense that he shares the critique of such power. With him I feel the urgency of the question of whether we, in a post-Christendom situation, and without losing the critical distance, can and must speak again about the church as a political reality.

It is with this background that I wish to discuss O'Donovan's reading of Romans 13.[9] Our task is to test whether O'Donovan helps us to experience the ethical relevance of the Bible anew. It is a reading that O'Donovan himself already characterizes as the result of looking 'with fresh eyes'.[10] The suggestion is thus that we will arrive at surprising new insights if we throw off the weight of our preconceptions. From the perspective of hermeneutics this is, of course, a suspect manoeuvre, but it is correct that new insights are offered, and I thus understand the remark as intended to stimulate openness for his reading. What follows is an attempt to summarize that reading, to place it in the *Wirkungsgeschichte* of Romans 13, and to evaluate it. This discussion in fact involves two points: a) the state has the task of providing space for the mission of the church; and b) the paradigmatic political act is judgement. The first sounds familiar, the second totally unfamiliar.

At first sight, Romans 13 is about submission to authorities, but according to O'Donovan it is primarily about the subjection of the nations. His reading is clearly from the standpoint of salvation history.[11] The authorities to which we must be obedient are precisely those forces which, according to Colossians 2:15, are defeated by Christ. The victor's power is present and visible in the church's life and mission. The quiet and peaceful life which, according to 1 Timothy 2, it is the responsibility of the government to provide, does not appear there in the context of quietism, but rather in the context of God's will for everyone to be saved and to come to recognize the truth. According to O'Donovan, the idea expressed in these two texts also underlies Romans 13.

---

[7] O'Donovan, 'Response', 93.

[8] Cf. *DN*, 213.

[9] *DN*, 146ff.

[10] *DN*, 147.

[11] Cf. A. Wolters, 'Confessional Criticism', 102.

O'Donovan uses the word 'underlies' with respect to the context. For in making this argument he does not limit himself to Romans 12–15, as is usually the case, but on the contrary fixes his attention on Romans 9–11! Just as Israel still remains important, so too do the authorities: both entities are affected by Christ's victory but are also taken up into God's plan for final redemption.

We can see this idea further expressed in the use of the term 'prevailing authorities' for governments, rather than 'rulers', 'kings', and so on. O'Donovan adopts the 'angelic powers' interpretation of this term, and moreover accepts the conclusion that the choice of this term places government in the context of the victory of Christ. Paul, he asserts, is undertaking to show that it is by God's purpose that the structures of the old age 'continue to exercise their sway', serving the church's mission.

The task of the government in this supportive ('servant') function consists of the exercise of judicial responsibility. For this description, O'Donovan refers to Romans 13:3–4: the government must praise those who do good and visit wrath on the wrongdoer. And he uses these verses as support for the statement that this is the *sole legitimating* task of the government. He further supports this idea that judgement is the biblical concept of authority by appealing to the Old Testament, particularly looking to the concept of *mishpat*. He does distinguish other tasks for the authorities in ancient Israel: the preservation of the integrity and identity of Israel itself, and, in service of this task, military leadership. But it is precisely at this point that the Christ-event makes a difference: something has 'changed'. There is no place any more for the experience of identity in, for instance, ethnicity. The only identity which is valid now is 'membership in Christ'. The fact that God is gathering a community which is called from all nations decisively relativizes the position of the nations. This view lies behind O'Donovan's bold assertion that, 'No government has a right to exist, no nation has a right to defend itself.'[12]

But judgement must be respected, for it is the form in which God expresses his wrath, and this secular expression of God's wrath is necessary as a restraint in society, preserving the social order and furthering the spread of the gospel. Note that O'Donovan by no means limits the task of government to the work of the courts. For him, judgement is the paradigm for all political acts. Christian ethics should therefore examine what the privileging of judgement implies for the other functions of government, such as lawmaking and warfare.[13]

Within this framework, Paul's admonition is that Christians, too, are, and should be, subject to that 'regime' of God administered through secular government. They should have no problem with it, because they should behave well. They should be the first to be happy with the judicial function of

---

[12] *DN*, 151.

[13] O'Donovan, 'Government'.

the government, because it serves the mission of the church. Therefore they should also pay taxes, and joyfully. O'Donovan notes that where Jesus, according to Matthew, was ironic on this point, Paul speaks more positively. O'Donovan interprets this difference historically: Paul speaks after the kingdom's challenge to (and triumph over) all established authorities.

Two Visions of the Relation Between Government and God in Romans 13

Having summarized O'Donovan's interpretation and positioning of Romans 13, I will now attempt to place this in the exegetical tradition – devoting the most attention to the first element. That involves the relation in which the government stands to God, and the consequences this relationship has for the position of the Christian community vis-à-vis the government. There are two lines of interpretation we can distinguish here. The first line says that Romans 13 bases the necessity of being subject to the state within a view of the government as a gift of God's creative or providential activity. The emphasis lies on the role of the state in the protection of humanity. The second, soteriological (*heilsgeschichtliche*) line focuses on the relationship of church and state: the state is the servant of God, by advancing the mission of the church. This second line provides for much more space for the prophetic witness to the state than the first. I will briefly provide historical illustrations for both these traditions.[14]

The first interpretation stands, of course, in the wider context of the philosophical/theological concept of natural law, which encompasses views of the state as belonging to a natural, or creational, structure of reality and as a gift of divine providence. Already in the early church, the accent in Christian theology lies more on providence than on creation. The difference between the view of the state as an institution of creation or of providence is important, for these views underlie completely different attitudes to the state – such as those of Locke and Hobbes, respectively. But both are (modern) natural law views. For according to both models, the state does not have a function in salvation – it is an instrument of God for humanity as long as history endures.[15] Irenaeus emphasizes that governments are not demonic but human powers, given by God after the fratricide of Genesis 4 in order to rein in the passions of human beings. Chrysostom offers the interpretation that the phenomenon of government, and not any particular government, is what is intended in Romans 13. Government mediates God's providence, and the structure of government and subjects reflects the natural order. This line was thus being sketched out very

[14] Cf. Wilckens, *Römer*, 43–66, and O'Donovan and O'Donovan (eds.), *Irenaeus*.

[15] I use the term 'natural law' in a very general sense here.

early, and for many centuries thereafter it was hardly disputed. For that matter, in the ensuing centuries of Christendom, those who placed the accent on the other, creation-based, interpretation generally did not contrast it with this line. That is true not only for the Catholic Middle Ages, but also for the Reformation theologians.

In the dominant political theories after Althusius and Grotius, the appeal to the idea of the *ordinatio dei* disappears into the background in favour of more generally acceptable terminology. That is roughly in agreement with O'Donovan's observation that, after Grotius, political reflection was stripped of any determinative theological dimension. But it was precisely the natural law interpretation that remained, and, after Grotius, made itself felt in social contract theories. In religious thought within the church, however, the concept survived all the innovations that occurred in philosophy, and even Barth does not challenge it. The most recent Protestant ethics (Rendtorff and Pannenberg, for instance)[16] still maintain the idea of politics as regulation, without appealing to Romans 13 as playing an important role in this. Because of the mutual interdependence of human beings, life itself calls for political order, and that insight is an inheritance from antiquity which has been taken over by Christian theology. We would expect that O'Donovan would choose this classical use of Romans 13 at least as the point of departure for his argument. But he leaves it entirely out of consideration. We must assume that it is precisely by doing this that he seeks to create room for a fresh reading – indeed, along the second line.

We find this second soteriological line, majestic and compelling, in Augustine – who viewed government from the perspective of the history of the City of God. To be sure, Augustine gives considerable attention to the view of the state along the first line, which had become the norm by that time. This even forms the basis for his political theory, and to it he attaches considerations about the educational value of governmental power, in relation to salvation: subjugation serves to combat the pride that hinders people from acquiring heavenly treasures. But what is striking about his vision – although to my mind it is not the dominant aspect – still lies in the idea that the sword must serve the advancement of the gospel. The 'evildoers' of Romans 13:3 are the heretics who must be brought to repentance by the sword. In other words, the government is in service to the church.[17]

---

[16] Cf. Rendtorff, *Ethik*, II, 23, 48, and Pannenberg, *Grundlagen*, 133.

[17] That this has not only a severe but also a merciful side, becomes clear in Augustine's Letter 153.19, to which O'Donovan devotes a penetrating and enlightening discussion (cf. *Irenaeus*, 107). Augustine writes that the government needs to be severe in its actions against criminals, but that the church has the task of praying for mercy for them, and that the government must be moved to 'love' by this: 'Let nothing be done through desire of hurting, but all through love of helping, and nothing will be done cruelly, inhumanely.'

This interpretation only raised the curtain for a struggle for primacy in God's order which would go on for centuries. Some resolved the issue by granting the government a limited terrain in which to exercise power (John Damascene), others by arguing that the monarch given by God, responsible for both the church and state, must also obey God (Sedulius Scottus), while still others stipulated that obedience to God ran through the church (Honorius Augustodunensis), and others disputed that (John of Paris). But do all of these interpretations really convey a salvation-historical reading? Are they about the advancement of the mission of the church? They rather seem to be about trying to settle the power struggle within the natural law framework of the first interpretation. This struggle was, after all, about the state challenging the church's theocratic use of the natural law idea.[18] The distinction between natural (state) and supernatural (church) still is a distinction within the natural law framework – it is not about the progress of salvation history. True religion must be encouraged, but for a long time, it appears, the task of the government was hardly seen in a historical-eschatological perspective.

That was not so with Thomas Müntzer. He exegeted Romans 13 in such a way as to show that Christians owe their kings obedience only so long as the kings employ their power to protect the devout and so help to bring the eschatological kingdom closer. Luther and Calvin had their hands full combating Anabaptism (although the Anabaptists rejected resistance against governments, they were often seen as rebels), while they themselves were also in conflict with governments. But, appealing to Romans 13, Luther and Calvin permitted little or no disobedience on the part of citizens.[19] In Calvin's view, the task of the state is always *humanitas* plus support of the true faith – without accentuating the salvation-historical idea with any special force. The salvation-historical approach only returned in Barth. In the most mature of his many considerations of Romans 13, *The Christian Community and the Civil Community*, we find the state as one of the constants in God's providence and,

[18] It is interesting to note how Troeltsch uses the terms 'natural law' and 'theocracy' in his *Social Teaching*. For instance, in his chapter on early Catholicism he says, 'The Church, therefore, had at her disposal two entirely different theories to guide her in her attitude towards social and political problems: the theory of relative Natural Law and the theory of theocratic absolutism. With the aid of the theory of relative Natural Law she learned, on the one hand, how to tolerate the actual social situation – which in itself was opposed to her fundamental principles, but which the very fact of her sense of sin and her orientation towards the future life led her to depreciate – and, on the other hand, how to regulate it according to her theories of Natural Law. The theocratic absolutist theory enabled the Church to adopt the position that the Emperor and the State might act freely in earthly matters, but that in everything which concerned religion and the Church, the Church must have the upper hand' (*Social Teaching*, 158).

[19] Calvin, *Institutes*, IV.20, 2, 4, 19.

as included in God's plan of salvation, it is an exponent of the kingdom of Jesus Christ. By 'exponent', Barth means that the state belongs to the powers that are created in Christ and which cannot separate us from the love of God because, as has been revealed in the resurrection of Jesus Christ, they have been given over to him. Barth works here with the controversial definition of *exousiai* as angelic powers – a definition he says had not been used by exegetes since Irenaeus.[20]

O'Donovan's own position is not all that different from this, except that Barth (as noted earlier) thinks directly from God acting with the world while O'Donovan, with Augustine, concentrates on God acting with the world through the church. For Barth, the church is essentially not more (nor less either, of course!) than the witness to what God has done and is doing. For O'Donovan (as for Augustine), on the other hand, the mission of the church has an essential place in God's work.[21] We might even conclude that O'Donovan, in *DN*, has presented us with a contemporary version of *The City of God*! But we can also conclude that this sort of historical thinking was not characteristic of what O'Donovan calls 'the Great Tradition'. On the contrary, it was rare. To a great extent, the Great Tradition thought scholastically, and unhistorically.

Most modern exegetes resolutely reject the deeper christological interpretation of *exousiai*.[22] After long hesitation, Cranfield also sides with them.[23] Drawing upon the study by C.D. Morrison, *The Powers that Be: Earthly Rulers and Demonic Powers in Romans 13:1–7* (1960), Cranfield weighs the pros and cons. Among the counter-arguments there are two which appear to me to be of special importance for our discussion:

1. The New Testament affords no evidence in support of the contention that hostile spiritual powers were recommissioned to a positive service to Christ, after being subdued.
2. Nowhere else does Paul give any indication that the subjection of the powers to Christ involves their being placed over believers; on the contrary, it is affirmed that in Christ believers are no longer subject to the spiritual powers of the world.

---

[20] Barth, 'Rechtfertigung', Ch. 2. Cf. also note 5, above.

[21] Barth, *KD* IV.3, par. 72, 'The Holy Spirit and the Mission of the Christian Community'.

[22] Cf. Wilckens, *Römer*, 32, Käsemann, *Römer*, 340–41, Moo, *Romans*, 795–96. Ziesler, *Romans*, 310–11 speaks of a consensus.

[23] See for the following passage Cranfield, *Romans*, II, 653–59.

I must admit that the christological, salvation-historical explanation is not convincing to me either. Quite the reverse: for me, it is the minimalistic interpretation that results from reading 'with fresh eyes'! By 'minimalistic' I mean that, for Paul, participation in social life appears to be entirely on the edge of his mind, receiving minimal concentration. The contextual point is really the admonition to the community to join in the *Pax Romana* and not to invite persecution.

N.T. Wright criticizes this view. According to Wright, Paul is very much addressing politics because he is opposing the imperial cult. For that reason, Romans 13 is not one of the few but one of the many Pauline passages on politics. In Wright's contribution to this volume, however, it appears that he uses the term 'politics' in two different ways. I will consider the fourth of the six points he makes in this regard.

> Paul's underlying point is that the victory of the true God is not won by the normal means of revolution. Rome could cope with revolutions; she could not cope, as history demonstrated, with a community owing imitative allegiance to the crucified and risen Jesus. God did not intend that the church should be the means of causing anarchy, of refusing normal civic responsibilities; anarchy simply replaces the tyranny of the officially powerful with the tyranny of the unofficially powerful, the bullies and the rich. The real overthrow of pagan power comes by other means.[24]

I think Wright correctly makes clear that the battle with Caesar is not of a 'political' nature in the normal sense: the kingdom of God comes 'by other means'. But Romans 13 evidently speaks about 'the political' in the normal sense of subordination to governmental authority! So, when we read Paul with political interest in the normal sense, we may rightly conclude that this interest is on the edge of his mind.

The New Testament contains political directives, but no doctrine as to how the state should be shaped. It merely suggests an *attitude* toward the state, based on the distinction between church and world, and on eschatological expectation. O'Donovan's argument is exciting, taking our contemporary life up into the biblical drama, and therefore the Bible seems to speak more directly to the present than we are accustomed to. But I am of the opinion that the minimalistic reading of Romans 13 does not make the Bible politically irrelevant – far from it. On the contrary, I consider that relativizing the significance of the state in the light of God's history, and limiting its task, to be extremely important directives for political ethics. They give every reason for critical participation in political life and constant vigilance against totalitarian tendencies such as Caesar's.

---

[24] Wright, 'Paul and Caesar', 190.

> The effect of declaring before Roman ears that government is a mere 'servant' is first to repudiate Roman claims to the deity of the Emperor, and secondly, by bringing government under the limits of divine law, to undermine the Roman concept of absolute political sovereignty.[25]

Like O'Donovan, I willingly seek support in Augustine, but I would accentuate more than O'Donovan does the importance of the value-neutral politics described in *The City of God* 19, over against the theocratic line deployed in defence of the coercion of Donatist heretics.[26] My use of the term 'value-neutral' is not meant in any idealistic sense, but more in the sense of an armistice (truce): in a pluralistic society, we simply need a certain neutral space in order to survive.

Judgement and the Paradigmatic Political Act

O'Donovan's discussion of the *task* of the state – the second element in his exposition of Romans 13 – is at least as interesting and compelling as his christological interpretation of the status of the state. Proceeding from its changed status, he concludes that there is also an altered – or, better, a limited and more focused – task for the state:

> The role of civil authority according to Saint Paul is to reward the just and punish the evil. No other role that a political authority might have played could have any interest for a world in which God has conferred the supreme Kingdom on his Christ. Israel's identity is complete in him; the identities of the other nations are of no account except in so far as they acknowledge him; the winning of earthly victories over earthly enemies has been superseded by the great victory over sin and death won once for all on the cross. But this usefulness the rulers of the earth still have: pending the final judgment at which the secrets of all hearts shall be revealed, they can maintain a distinction between the just and the unjust.[27]

To a great extent I find the concept of judgement that O'Donovan develops convincing, as I do his handling of biblical, chiefly Old Testament, concepts that contribute to this understanding. But if we focus strictly on the use of Romans 13, then we must say that it is overcharged here. The christological interpretation is extended into verse 4 and, as far as I know, no one has ever supported that exegesis. Nothing more is said than that subjection to the government can not be a bad thing if one behaves decently. It is impossible for this

---

[25] Chaplin, 'Government', 416.

[26] Cf. O'Donovan and O'Donovan (eds.), *Irenaeus*, 105–11, where the interpretation of 'value-neutral' in a modern liberal sense (e.g., R.A. Markus) is contested.

[27] O'Donovan, 'Gerechtigkeit und Urteil', 1, 2.

text to carry the weight necessary for it to function as a definition of the political act in the exclusive way O'Donovan claims.[28]

This is not to say that I am not curious about precisely how this concept may help us in deliberations in political ethics, and about the way in which Scripture can then function in this deliberation, because here we are dealing with nothing less than the distinction between good and evil, and indeed with this distinction as it is made by governments and in service of the mission of the church.

Here I will confine myself to one further reflection on the use O'Donovan makes of Romans 13 in his political theology. Romans 13 tells him that the church has to challenge governments, announcing the Lordship of Christ over secular gods and their final disappearance. It does not tell me that; and most exegetes support my view.[29] It would be nice if I could claim that this support has been decisive in the process of my own theological deliberation, because that would create the impression of really wanting to listen to the Bible. But that is not the case. For if I were eventually to find O'Donovan's theopolitical concept of history convincing, then I would join him in using the Barthian escape hatch of the *exousiai* interpretation. I do indeed find his accent on the historical character of God's acts convincing, but I think that he exaggerates the role of 'the two' (church and state): they are certainly very important historically, but that does not mean that they are important in terms of salvation history. The gospel challenges people, publicly, and in public cultural debate, too. But I cannot but read Western history other than as rightly leading to the conviction that political government is about the ordering of society amid various challenges in order to avoid violent confrontation. The minimalistic interpretation of Romans 13 fits admirably with that. I also cannot read church history other than that the church's mission is universal. Although it does not leave cultures undisturbed, nevertheless political support or acceptance is not the first thing that the church seeks or needs. The church does not ask for more room than is allowed to other movements. I find that amply documented in the New Testament, too. But I must concede that in ethics we indeed make *use* of the Bible, and we do that in good conscience, hopefully, and our insights and concepts are often inspired by the Bible – but we rarely let ourselves be convinced by a concept purely on the basis of exegesis.

---

[28] Cf. Skillen, 'Acting Politically', 410: 'Quite in contrast to this interpretation [of O'Donovan], it seems to me that Paul is telling the Roman Christians, who at the time did not hold positions of high governmental authority, to recognize the authorities as servants of God for their good. For that reason, they were to pay taxes, give honor, and not rebel. These authorities are first of all God's servant *for good*, and they are supposed to punish people only when they do wrong.'

[29] Cf. note 17.

It is, of course, attractive to try to demonstrate how the understanding of biblical passages is normative for one's ethical deliberation. But when confronted with two or more exegetical options, as we are in the case of Romans 13, it seems to me that a wider view of what is at stake makes us choose the option that fits within that view. I consider it to be a matter of intellectual honesty to admit this. And I think this is also a way of describing the hermeneutic circle: there is a reciprocity between the understanding of the whole of a text and of its parts.

More important, perhaps, than this deconstructive remark, is the observation that I made at the start – namely, that O'Donovan's moral theology is a sign of the return of the Bible in ethics. Moral reflection and deliberation among Christians should take place in the shadow of the story of God's history with Israel and the Gentiles. On that we agree. Otherwise it will in fact be (and indeed often is and has been) merely philosophical ethics that we are doing.

Bibliography

Barth, K., *Die kirchliche Dogmatik* IV.3 (Zurich: Evangelischer Verlag, 1959)

——, *Rechtfertigung und Recht, Christengemeinde und Bürgergemeinde* (ThSt 104; Zurich: Theologischer Verlag, 1989)

Bartholomew, C.G., 'Uncharted Waters: Philosophy, Theology and the Crisis in Biblical Interpretation', in *Renewing Biblical Interpretation* (ed. C. Bartholomew, C. Greene and K. Möller; SHS 1; Carlisle: Paternoster; Grand Rapids: Zondervan, 2000), 1–39

——, 'A Royal Priesthood? Reading the Bible Ethically and Politically in Dialogue with Oliver O'Donovan: An Introduction' (in this volume)

Chaplin, J., 'Government', in *New Dictionary of Christian Ethics and Pastoral Theology* (ed. D.J. Atkinson, D.H. Field, A.F. Holmes and O. O'Donovan; Leicester: IVP, 1995), 415–16

Cranfield, C., *The Epistle to the Romans*, II (Edinburgh: T. & T. Clark, 1979)

Dunn, J.D.G., *The Theology of Paul the Apostle* (Edinburgh: T. & T. Clark, 1998)

Käsemann, E., *An die Römer* (Tübingen: J.C.B. Mohr, 1974)

Moo, D.J., *The Epistle to the Romans* (Grand Rapids: Eerdmans, 1996)

Morrison, C.D., *The Powers that Be: Earthly Rulers and Demonic Powers in Romans 13.1–7* (London: 1960)

O'Donovan, O., 'Gerechtigkeit und Urteil', in *Neue Zeitschrift für Systematische Theologie* 40 (1998), 1–16

——, 'Response to Respondents: Behold the Lamb', *SCE* 11.2 (1998), 91–110

——, *Resurrection and Moral Order: An Outline for Evangelical Ethics* (Leicester: IVP; Grand Rapids: Eerdmans, 2nd edn, 1994)

——, *The Desire of the Nations: Rediscovering the Roots of Political Theology* (Cambridge: CUP, 1996)

——, and J.L. O'Donovan (eds.), *From Irenaeus to Grotius: A Sourcebook in Christian Political Thought 100–1625* (Grand Rapids: Eerdmans, 1999)

Pannenberg, W., *Grundlagen der Ethik: Philosophisch-theologische Perspektiven* (Göttingen: Vandenhoeck & Ruprecht, 1996)

Rendtorff, T., *Ethik: Grundelemente, Methodologie und Konkretionen einer ethischen Theologie*, I, II (Stuttgart: W. Kohlhammer, 1990)

Skillen, J.W., 'Acting Politically in Biblical Obedience?' (in this volume)

Troeltsch, E., *The Social Teaching of the Christian Churches*, I (trans. Olive Wyon; Chicago: University of Chicago Press, 1960)

Wilckens, U., *Der Brief an die Römer*, III: *Teilband (Römer 12–16)* (Zurich: Benzinger Verlag; Neukirchen-Vluyn: Neukirchener Verlag, 1982)

Wolters, A., 'Confessional Criticism and the Night Visions of Zechariah', in *Renewing Biblical Interpretation* (ed. C. Bartholomew, C. Greene and K. Möller; SHS 1; Carlisle: Paternoster; Grand Rapids: Zondervan, 2000), 90–117

Wright, N.T., 'Paul and Caesar: A New Reading of Romans' (in this volume)

Ziesler, J., *Paul's Letter to the Romans* (Philadelphia: Trinity Press International, 1989)

16

Response to Gerrit de Kruijf

Oliver O'Donovan

One of the interesting side-questions of the consultation, in which the influence of Dutch neo-Calvinism of the Kuyper school, mediated through its North American versions, was discernible in a number of contributions, was how much difference would appear between this and the Calvinism of the established church represented by Gerrit de Kruijf. In his paper I was struck at first by the similarities of his concerns with those of the neo-Calvinists, notwithstanding the Barthian elements in his culture. Where they talk about creation structures, he talks about natural law; yet it is the same move on my part that troubles him: my refusal to locate politics within created nature. That said, his concern has a different shape. He sees the alternatives not in Old Testament terms (creation vs. history), but in New Testament terms (nature vs. salvation). Where James Skillen thinks me in danger of refusing to say that government does us good, Gerrit de Kruijf sees my danger as that of Christonomic politics – a danger that he also sees in Barth. I seem to be including government too readily in the good news.

This places me, in his view, in a peculiar relation to the tradition. It is very welcome that he brings the Great Tradition in at this point, quite apart from the satisfaction Joan and I take in his use of *From Irenaeus to Grotius*! The natural-law orientation to Romans 13 prevails, he thinks; while I stand alone with Barth, Cullmann and Thomas Müntzer. He does not shrink from quoting Barth in support of the view that the whole tradition was 'scholastic' – to which I must reply that of all the things on which I am ready and eager to accept instruction from Barth, the character of the mediaeval tradition is not one. I would like to suggest that de Kruijf's account underestimates the tendency of Augustinianism to subordinate civil rule to the church. Augustine himself he sees as belonging to both camps, persuasively – although his conception of Augustine as defender of a 'value-neutral' state follows Robert Markus down a path which Markus himself is no longer quite ready to walk. Augustine's mediaeval successors are much more marked in their state-church subordinationism, and Gregory VII was tempted even to assign a diabolic origin to the state.

I would like to suggest further exploration of another thing de Kruijf says about the early tradition: that it did not contrast the one possibility with the other. Why not? Because it also made a distinction between creation and history (or providence), and assigned political authority to the latter, not to the former. That is where the earlier tradition drew the dividing line. And this creates the possibility of an intersection – between 'history' and 'saving history' – which the sharp alternative he poses does not, I think, take seriously enough.

There is, of course, an evangelicalization of political order that I would repudiate. The doctrine of 'the two' must not be collapsed into a doctrine of the one. The triumph of Christ is manifest in the vis-à-vis of church and government, the challenge to the principalities and powers – not in the simple absorption of the one by the other. Certain things could be understood by my term 'reauthorization' of the state by Christ (which disturbs de Kruijf, as it did Nicholas Wolterstorff), which I would not endorse. I think that Cullmann drifted into some of them, and gave the state a more directly christological status than I could. The state, in my view, remains under the direction of the First Person of the Trinity; it is not filled with the Holy Spirit at Pentecost; but it attests, negatively and by the yielding up of its powers, the fulfilment of the Father's purpose in the Son. My 'reauthorization', you might say, is a 'merely partial deauthorization' of the political power, rendering it 'secular' in the sense of merely secular. The 'secularity' of the state can correctly be expressed as 'desacralization', although that negative must be supplemented by a positive. The secular can only exist in the light of Christ's triumph; but it cannot exist apart from the light of Christ's triumph and must be put to positive service.

De Kruijf concludes that I 'advocate a Christian state'. In what sense is this true? I advocate the virtues of various Christian states of the past which have received an unfairly bad press. I am keen to leap to the defence of the project of Savonarola, a much better example than Thomas Müntzer, but I am even more keen to say a word for some less dramatic projects. That means I am prepared to advocate the theological *possibility* of the Christian state, but not its *necessity*. I believe I made clear that the Christian state is not, in my view, on the agenda at the present, and that I have no restorationist aims. I am not a de Bonald.[1] The point, rather, is to free the Christian witness of our day from a range of inhibitions which paralyse it when it is too nervous of the very appearance of a 'Christian politics'.

---

[1] Though no one, I think, could refuse de Bonald respect after reading Robert Spaemann's fascinating study, *Der Ursprung der Soziologie aus dem Geist der Restauration* (Stuttgart: Klett-Cotta, 2nd edn, 1998).

I am aware that these issues look different from the Netherlands. This is not a point that Gerrit de Kruijf has allowed to enter an exegetical argument; yet it is easier to have doubts about confessionalism in the Netherlands, where a tradition of pluralistic confessionalism was still strong in the early twentieth century, than it is in Britain, where the confessional state collapsed in 1828–32. The subsequent career of Gladstone, who would certainly have been a confessional politician had he found a way to be, sealed in British minds for ever the secular principle that politics was susceptible of Christian motivation, but not of Christian content. An engagement between those experiences can only be instructive – though each side will have to remember that a particular interpretation of a given alternative may not be the only possible one, and that adverse circumstances may defeat even the best possible interpretation in practice.

The 'fresh eyes' with which I hoped to read Romans 13 were refreshed, essentially, by a contextualization of the chapter within the preaching of the kingdom of heaven within the Gospels themselves, an orientation from outside. In that sense, I think Gerrit de Kruijf looks for refreshment to other sources than I do. Does he have doubts, perhaps, about intertextuality?

17

The Apocalypse and Political Theology

Christopher Rowland

The language of apocalypse has featured in contemporary discourse since the events of 11 September 2001. The banner headline over a picture of the burning twin towers on the front of the British tabloids on 12 September said, simply, 'Apocalypse'. The use of such language is understandable. The death and destruction on 11 September conjure images of the book of Revelation from the chapters of the Apocalypse in which the Lamb's opening of the seals, the trumpet blasts and the pouring of the bowls disclose the violence in the world. An apocalypse is also a revelation or disclosure, however. This means that it is not so much the Christian equivalent of Nostradamus' enigmatic predictions, outlining what will happen in the days leading up to the last judgement (though there have always been some who have read the Apocalypse in this way), as it is a creative way of shedding light on the complexities of the present and pointing in new directions. There has been an ancient interpretative tradition, in which apocalyptic images have offered readers a way of understanding the struggle going on in persons, between contrasting obligations, between the Lamb and the Beast, Jerusalem and Babylon, which include economic and political affairs, and the need to resist in the light of a different kind of political vision epitomized by the new Jerusalem.

The essay that follows is in three, loosely related, parts. In it I want to consider different ways of interpreting the Apocalypse and its contribution to political theology. I shall do this first by a reference to Oliver O'Donovan's discussion of the book. Then I shall consider two contrasting North American interpretations, which in turn form the basis of the hermeneutical reflection in the third and final section on the contribution which the Apocalypse makes to the method of political theology.

Oliver O'Donovan on the Apocalypse

In Oliver O'Donovan's writing on the Apocalypse I found much with which I agree, and I welcome his grasp of the significance of this book for Christian theology.[1] Of importance is his challenge (echoed now in recent study of Second Temple Judaism) to views which question the role of apocalypticism for political theology,[2] and the recognition that the Apocalypse has a significant role in expounding the role of prophetic witness to the earthly powers, a view which has been canvassed in various recent studies.[3] There are certain key differences between us with regard to the interpretation of the Apocalypse, not least the differing attitudes to the earthly reign of Christ, the important role of which within early Christian thought and practice (as exemplified by Justin basing a this-worldly kingdom on Rev. 20) I would want to affirm. Indeed, the hope for a this-worldly reign of God seems to me to be an important ingredient in the eschatology of the theology of liberation.[4] Also, while recognizing the central role that the Apocalypse played in Augustine's understanding of history, I think the evidence is clear that the answer to O'Donovan's question, 'Are we to believe in a counter-cultural tradition of political thought within Christendom, historicist in character, taking its root from John of Patmos?' is in the affirmative. It is a tradition whose roots are in second-century chiliasm, nurtured in different ways in the mediaeval church. It flowered in Joachite interpretation and has been an important counterpoint to the more familiar themes of political theology.[5]

For Oliver O'Donovan, the Apocalypse is a work of 'disciplined theology and poetic imagination',[6] in which Christ's crucifixion is regarded as the decisive achievement of God's purposes, and the manifestation of the idolatrous empire is provoked by Satan's downfall on Calvary. In other words, we have an apocalyptic presentation of the essence of the gospel, whose political and cosmic frame is best served by apocalyptic imagery. There is political significance given to the role of prophetic witness in the period before the eschaton. Followers of the Lamb can learn from the Apocalypse's images something of

---

[1] O'Donovan, *DN*, and 'Political Thought'. I have also had access to an unpublished essay, 'History and Politics in the Book of Revelation', which sets the arguments of the latter in the context of recent writing on the Apocalypse.

[2] Cook, *Prophecy*, against Hanson, *Dawn*.

[3] Bauckham, *Theology*; Hays, *Moral Vision*; Collins, *Cosmology*.

[4] O'Donovan, 'Political Thought', 63; and further Rowland and Corner, *Liberation Exegesis*, 114–30.

[5] O'Donovan, 'Political Thought', 66 and see Emmerson and McGinn, *Apocalypse*; Cohn, *Pursuit*; Rowland, *Radical Christianity*; and Bradstock and Rowland, *Radical Christian Writings*.

[6] *DN*, 153.

their call to be witnesses to the peaceable kingdom of the Lamb. The outcome of the church's martyr-witness is to call forth the first hesitant and abashed confession of the rule of God, out of which beginning the Holy City will come to be.[7]

O'Donovan's grasp of the challenge that the Apocalypse offers to an inward-looking preoccupation with ecclesial matters, or the comfortable assumption that to be part of the church is to be part of, or on the way to, the kingdom of God, are some of the most cogent sentences in his long account of a biblical political theology in *The Desire of the Nations*.[8] In the Apocalypse there is, unsurprisingly, a sense of exile, for the church as community seems to have become 'attenuated', in the sense that the corporate identity of the church as the body of Christ is subverted by the positive response of some of its members to the culture of Babylon. This is unmasked in the Apocalypse by the relentless probing of that which shows its lack of conformity to the way of the Lamb and which requires the prophetic and costly witness of individuals to the new Jerusalem, over against 'lukewarm Laodiceans' who desire to be at ease – as if the Zion of Christian hope is virtually coterminous with Babylon.[9] This witness is carried out in the shadow of the cross, which is itself the catalyst which provokes the last desperate assertion of a 'defiant and expansive empire' over against which the kingdom of Christ stands. Commitment to the kingdom of God and the Messiah leads to a situation where 'the faithful will be scattered, isolated witnesses before the massive solidity of the idolatrous empire'. This is true prophecy when the outsiders, 'the strangers and aliens in a strange land', angular in their personalities and who make uncomfortable social companions, relentlessly 'call for the endurance of the saints, those who keep the commandments of God and the faith of Jesus' (Rev. 14:12).

The horizon of the messianic reign when Satan is bound and God's throne dwells, no longer in heaven but in the new Jerusalem, provides an impetus to social criticism and hope. John's vision equips him with the resources such that he 'needs no modern Marxist to tell him that economic domination is a more effective key to world-empire than military might'.[10] Revelation 17–18 offer a critique of the way in which a nation becomes rich and invite us to consider the business of what passes for international order (18:13). Oliver O'Donovan summarizes the point of the vision: 'trade as much as conquest violates the integrity of communities which become dominated by the influence of the stronger trading partner'.[11] Babylon commits fornication with the kings and

[7] *DN*, 155–56.

[8] *DN*, 155.

[9] *DN*, 155.

[10] *DN*, 154.

[11] O'Donovan, 'Political Thought', 85.

mighty, suggesting the lengths to which nations and culture can go in order to achieve wealth, status and power. O'Donovan points out that 'trade is fornication. It is a cultural promiscuity by which one power exploits and drains the resources from many others.'[12] In the extravagance and luxury of life and wealth of the few there lies a hidden cost to human lives and societies (Rev. 18:13). Acts of trade and commerce and political processes are shown to be shot through with conflicts of interest. The Apocalypse does not allow a view of society which accepts that it can be understood without reference to God in its various constituent parts. The story of Christ casts its shadow over every human transaction. Readers (and hearers) of the Apocalypse are offered the resources, in their own circumstances, to work out what faithfulness to the testimony of Jesus might mean. In a few pages of *DN*, there is encapsulated the heart of Oliver O'Donovan's political theology – around which, if he allowed it, the rest of the New Testament and the ongoing tradition can be fitted. It is a reading of the Apocalypse with which, in general terms, I find myself in agreement. Although I think, unlike him, I would see this as a fundamental component of political theology in much the same way as we find in Yoder's theology.[13]

The United States of America, the Beast and Babylon

Exegesis of the Apocalypse may appear to be kaleidoscopic. In fact, there is a fairly limited set of hermeneutical options. Among these, O'Donovan and I on the whole follow a well-worn path which can be traced back to the early church, at least to Tyconius and probably long before.[14] In this section, I will outline the interpretative contrast between two North American interpretations of the beast and Babylon. I will also locate O'Donovan's hermeneutic within the Tyconian tradition. In outlining this tradition, the importance of the history of interpretation (which I know O'Donovan regards as central to Christian moral reasoning) is given its place in the discussion of the contribution of the Apocalypse to political theology.

From very different parts of the Christian spectrum, the beast and Babylon in Revelation 13 and 17 are linked with the culture and society of the United States of America. First, since the very foundation of the Seventh Day Adventist Church after the Millerite disappointment at the failure of their eschatological hope in the mid-nineteenth century, a key doctrine has been the

[12] O'Donovan, 'Political Thought', 85.

[13] Yoder, 'To Serve'.

[14] Rowland, *Revelation*, and my forthcoming commentary on the reception-history of the Apocalypse for the Blackwell Bible Commentary series.

identification of the second beast of Revelation 13 with the United States of America, its culture and religion. This is worked out on the basis of minute exegetical discussion.[15] It is an exegetical exercise of considerable sophistication and ingenuity (similar to what we find in the Scofield Reference Bible), which one may admire even if one disagrees with the approach to the text on which it is based. From very early in Christian interpretation of the Apocalypse, the beast in Revelation 13 was linked in one way or another with Rome. This kind of interpretation, though with a distinctly Protestant hue, as the Roman Catholic Church was linked with the whore of Babylon, was widespread in mid-nineteenth century North American interpretation – not least in the Millerite tradition, which was the forerunner of Seventh Day Adventism. What emerged in Adventism, however, was a very distinctive interpretation of the second beast of Revelation 13, in which the beast was identified with the United States of America.[16] This contrasted with the very different sense of being an elect nation, with a peculiar destiny in the divine economy, which was deeply rooted in American public theology from the very early years of the colonization.[17] In the Adventist interpretation, the USA was to be an ally of the antichrist in the last days because support for enforced Sunday worship is the mark of the beast. The USA, according to this interpretation of Revelation 13, which appears to be concerned with civil and religious liberty and with equal rights, masks a very different reality: in fact what appears to be like a Lamb speaks as the dragon. In this eschatological scenario, the USA will join with the Roman Catholic Church in a final attempt to stamp out the faithful remnant. Such a view of the USA and its government may have prompted the Branch Davidians at Waco, Texas to regard the FBI siege as being of apocalyptic moment because the federal agents' persecution of the followers of the Lamb seemed to prove that they were the followers of the beast.[18]

A rather different approach to the image of the Apocalypse is to be found in a book written in the middle of the Vietnam War. Although William Stringfellow was hailed by Karl Barth as the theologian to whom America should listen, he was an obscure figure on the North American theological scene.[19] He was an early civil rights activist and protester against the war in Vietnam. He turned his back on a distinguished legal career and worked in East Harlem. He was an early advocate of the theology of the 'principalities and powers' and their contemporary social reality. Stringfellow's *An Ethic for Christians and Other Aliens in a Strange Land* is a book geared to enabling his audience

15 Newport, *Apocalypse*, and Numbers and Butler, *The Disappointed*.
16 Boyer, *Time*, 225–53.
17 Smolinski, 'Apocalypticism'.
18 Newport, *Apocalypse*, 224–25.
19 Wylie-Kellermann, *Keeper*.

to read America biblically, 'rather than allow the United States of America, its culture and values to determine the way the Bible is read'.[20] 'America', he writes, 'is a demonic principality, in which death is the reigning idol', and resistance to the power of death is the only way to live humanly. At the heart of his method is this conviction that the Bible, and particularly the Apocalypse, can assist one to understand a particular moment of time because it enables an enhanced vision of reality.[21] The Apocalypse does not offer a timetable about the end of the world, but a template by which one can assess the theological character of the world in which one lives. As a result there can then be opened up, in reading the Apocalypse in humility before God, something of the reality of death at work in the world, that which is demonic and dehumanizing and also the power of the resurrection. Stringfellow follows in a long and distinguished tradition which sees Babylon and Jerusalem as types of two different kinds of religious communities.[22]

Stringfellow does not expect to go to the Scriptures as if to a self-help manual that will offer off-the-shelf solutions. Nor is he interested in abstract principles or grand theories to apply to human situations. For him, the ethics of biblical people concern events, and not moral propositions: 'Precedent and parable, not propositions or principle.'[23] There is no norm, no ideal, no grandiose principle from which hypothetical, preconceived or carefully worked out answers can be derived – because there are no disincarnate issues. The Apocalypse's stark contrasts offer an interpretative key to understanding the cosmos under God and the situation in the USA in the 1970s and 1980s.[24] The images of Babylon and Jerusalem are not only eschatologically future images, but they are also important for how one relates to reality here and now. Babylon is a description of every city, an allegory of the condition of death, the principality in bondage to death, and ultimately the focus of apocalyptic judgement. Jerusalem is about the emancipation of human life in society from the rule of death. It is a parable, he says, of the church of prophecy – an anticipation of the end of time.[25]

Stringfellow applies the antichrist imagery to the situation which confronted him in the 1970s as the USA was torn apart by conflicting views about the Vietnam War. Stringfellow offers an apocalyptic hermeneutic which is not just talking about some future eschatological figures, but about real, contemporary people of flesh and blood. Picking up ideas from the book of Revelation

---

[20] Stringfellow, *Ethic.*

[21] Stringfellow, *Ethic*, 152.

[22] See the influential view of John Bale, outlined in Bauckham, *Tudor*, 68–90.

[23] Stringfellow, *Conscience*, 24.

[24] Stringfellow, *Ethic*, 114.

[25] Stringfellow, *Ethic*, 21.

and 1 John (2:17–22), he sees the antichrist as mimicking and displacing Christ. The church is in particular danger of being taken in by such 'antichrists' in culture, for ecclesiastical institutions may find themselves converted into functionaries of the state, or banished if they fail to conform. For Stringfellow, there are always signs of that happening. In that situation, however, under God's grace, the marks and beginnings of Jerusalem are always going to be found. Stringfellow describes the ideal 'confessing' church. It is 'spontaneous; episodic; radically ecumenical; irregular in polity; zealous in living; extemporaneous in action; conscientious; meek and poor'.[26] Its role is to expose the reign of death while affirming the aspiration to a new life.[27]

Contrasting Interpretations of the Apocalypse

From the earliest period of the interpretation of the Apocalypse (probably responding to different signals in the text of the Apocalypse itself), there have been two major contrasting approaches to interpretation. In one approach, corresponding to that of the Adventists, interpretation involves detailed textual analysis, incorporating passages from other parts of the Bible, to produce a detailed eschatological synthesis. The Apocalypse occasionally prompts the quest to 'decode' the meaning of the apocalyptic mysteries (e.g. 17:9; cf. 1:20; 4:3). Such allusions have prompted the quest for a precise equivalence between every image in the book and figures and events in history. This has resulted in a long tradition of interpretation based on the 'decoding' principle, in which we find the translation of the imagery of the Apocalypse into a more accessible mode of discourse. As a result, the book has been treated as an account of the end of the world, and therefore none of its details relate to present ecclesiastical and political realities. Such interpretation usually links the Apocalypse with other prophetic and eschatological texts like Daniel, Ezekiel and 1 Thessalonians 4:16ff. to produce a coherent eschatological chronology. Alternatively, the visions have been decoded and related to their ancient, first-century context. The complex symbolism is decoded in its relationship to (ancient) contemporary historical realities. In both interpretations the images are left behind and the peculiar ethos of the apocalyptic symbolism and its hold on the reader and hearer is lost. The 'translation' of those images becomes all-important, as the key to the meaning of the Apocalypse.

The other approach is more orientated towards the present role of the church in the world. In this approach, the apocalyptic images helped Christians to understand the struggle in which they were engaged, personally and

[26] Stringfellow, *Ethic*, 122.

[27] Stringfellow, *Ethic*, 87.

politically. Tyconius' reading of the Apocalypse (c. 400) reflects the ongoing task of being the church in the world as being of eschatological significance.[28] He used the book to interpret his own times, particularly the struggles between his persecuted, minority church (the Donatists) and a 'great church'. Although Tyconius' commentary on the Apocalypse no longer exists, its influence was pervasive – as is evidenced by the ongoing citations from it in authors such as Bede (eighth century) and Beatus of Liébana (eighth century). His hermeneutics of the Apocalypse and his general biblical hermeneutics were closely intertwined. His approach offered a basis for an ethical/ecclesial reading of the Apocalypse, in which the book's images were used to inform the present life of the church, with Jerusalem and Babylon symbolizing an ongoing struggle between the demonic and the divine, in the individual and also in society. The biblical text becomes for Tyconius a tool that facilitates discernment of the moral and spiritual. Present and future are always mingled, therefore. Tyconius sees the world as divided into two societies in opposition, which are represented by the imagery of the whore of Babylon (Rev. 17) and the new Jerusalem (Rev. 21). Throughout Scripture he finds references to these societies in opposition, reflecting what the Donatists were experiencing in Africa in Tyconius' days – an experience which he may have regarded as an anticipation of the end. The mature Augustine was indebted to, and continued, the Tyconian tradition of interpretation. Augustine's approach to empire in *The City of God*, where he contrasts the 'city of God' with the 'city of the world', is in certain key respects at one with the dualistic and suspicious attitude evident in earlier Christian apocalyptic interpretation.

It is this 'Tyconian' model that is, in general terms, followed by both William Stringfellow and, in a less homiletic vein, by Oliver O'Donovan. They juxtapose the imagery of the Apocalypse with their own circumstances, whether personal or social, so as to allow the images to inform understanding of contemporary persons and events and to serve as a guide for action. In contrast, the 'decoding' of the Apocalypse, in which the images are translated into another discourse, whether historical or eschatological, preserves the integrity of the textual pole and does not allow the images from the Apocalypse to be identified solely with one particular historical or eschatological personage or circumstance. This method does not prevent the text from being actualized in different ways over and over again, while it implicitly allows the eschatological significance of the ongoing witness to Jesus Christ. In the imaginative and ethically orientated readings in the 'Tyconian' method, the biblical text is a springboard, a creative frame of reference for the world which confronts the interpreter. It is a form of typological exegesis, in which the apocalyptic images are in a dialectical relationship with the persons and events connected to the

[28] Fredriksen, 'Tyconius'.

reader. The Apocalypse allows this in a way that the book of Daniel does not, as interpretations of the visions reduce the illuminative potential of the visions.

Such typological interpretations, of course, are not without dangers (as is evident from the cavalier way the Apocalypse was applied at the Reformation to serve the needs of various Protestant polemicists).[29] Nevertheless, our modern queasiness should not inhibit our embarking on such typological interpretation. This kind of interpretation is carried out within the constraints of human fallenness, and those who point to others as incarnating the beast and supping at the table of Babylon always need to ask themselves searching questions about the extent to which the humble Christ summons them to repent, just as he did the assertive and confident Laodicean angel (Rev. 3:14–22). In embarking on this interpretative journey we may glimpse the contribution of the Apocalypse to political theology (and for that matter to theology in general), and why its absence from theological and ethical discussion leads to the impoverishment and distortion of Christian theology. As our ancestors in the faith from Irenaeus to Joachim of Fiore realized, the Apocalypse offers the paradigm for a Christian understanding of history.[30] It reveals the meaning of history in the formation of a new human race, international in character, around the Lamb that was slain, and was no longer determined by Caesar's violent rule.[31]

Practical Engagement in Political Theology in the Light of the Apocalypse

There is one further issue to consider. The Apocalypse suggests a rather different approach to the practical engagement of political theology. It is such a different approach, in fact, that there is a question whether theology (at least as it is understood in 'Northern' academies) is the most appropriate way of describing the quality of the engagement. It will be more meandering (though it will not be without direction), embracing different kinds of routes. The poetry of image and oxymoron will lead as often to lateral thinking, in which anecdote and analogy, rudely juxtaposed, all contribute to the pursuit of truth. An interpretative method that is in some ways similar is William Blake's expansion of moral sensibilities by interweaving his text with complementary illuminations. The precise function of the visual impact on the reader often results in a destabilizing effect, when text and picture seem to have little relationship one with another. As a result, the possibility is opened up of a critical re-examination of the premises of one's own (and one's society's) life.[32]

---

29 There is a summary with a bibliography in Rowland, *Revelation*.

30 Yoder, *Politics*, 237; Yoder, 'To Serve'; McClendon, *Systematic*, 97–102.

31 Wengst, *Pax Romana*.

32 Dörrbecker (ed.), *Continental Prophecies*, 153.

However much we may relate the Apocalypse to its original historical context, the peculiarities of its form drive us to new ways of engagement with its discourse and to the quest for a hermeneutical strategy that is appropriate to it. The quest for ancient, related and apocalyptic texts has seemed to give us our interpretative bearings, thereby allowing us to read this text in a way that differs little from the approach to a Pauline letter. But does this really do justice to its character? Occasionally in the comments of interpreters there is an unconscious sense of aesthetic or theological superiority with regard to the apocalyptic mind and its lack of system and glory in enigma. Luther's comments in the Preface to his 1523 German Bible ('Christ is not taught or known in it') and Bultmann's 'weakly Christianized Judaism' are typical. Perhaps there is an indirect reference to this kind of attitude in the dismissive words the 'phantom of the overheated brain' in Blake's *Jerusalem* 1.23. Blake and John do not fit: it is the lot of visionaries and mystics throughout history.[33]

The Apocalypse summons us to be confronted by, and infused with, its images. We are called, like John, to 'come up here, and I will show you what must take place' – not primarily as interpreters or calculators of a precise eschatological programme, or even as providers of careful explanation. Rather, we become participants in a spiritual and moral agony, which wrenches us from our prejudices concerning the nature of our obedience to God, shot through as it is with the *easy* compromises we make with the beast and Babylon. The reader (or hearer) of the Apocalypse is summoned to participate in another way of speaking about God and the world which refuses to be tied down to the niceties of carefully defined formularies. Like the parables of Jesus, which have consistently refused to be tied down to one particular meaning, the Apocalypse offers a mode of moral reasoning which prompts and tantalizes in ways which are unpredictable in their effects and may offer those who persevere a means of understanding reality which leads to a changed life. The Apocalypse exemplifies Adorno's demands expressed in *Minima Moralia*: 'Perspectives must be fashioned that displace and estrange the world, reveal it to be, with its rifts and crevices, as indigent and distorted as it will appear one day in the messianic light.'[34] Reading the Apocalypse engages us and can transform us so that 'apocalypse' takes place with every reading, every 'digesting' of the text (to use the image derived from Ezekiel's prophecy and used by John of his prophetic vocation in Rev. 10). We may be curious about the meaning of symbols or preoccupied by the possibility of historical reference, but the fundamental task is reading, hearing and appropriating the contents of this book and thereby having our perspective transformed. What we are offered in the Apocalypse is

---

[33] Ozment, *Mysticism*; Dronke, *Women*; Jantzen, *Power*.
[34] Adorno, *Minima Moralia*, 247.

not a manual of eschatology, ethics or theology, though it enables all of these by its disturbing and destabilizing effects.

Oliver O'Donovan writes of John's apocalypse as 'disciplined theology'. I would not dissent from this. Nevertheless, 'disciplined theology' in the context of a discussion of this apocalyptic text means that John obediently writes down what he has seen, given to him by Jesus Christ. He is a theologian in this sense, in that he writes of the things given to him by God. It is a discipline, a teaching, whose form as well as whose content demands engagement. There is the temptation to 'translate' this particular discipline, to make it more 'user friendly', for its imagery sits uneasily with what we understand theology to be about. It is *this* particular blend of visionary imagery, however, with its different images oscillating between one another, that demands our engagement and our theological response.[35] If this beckons us to a different kind of theological engagement, that is what we need to learn from the Apocalypse of Jesus Christ, rather than render it in more prosaic discourse. John has bequeathed to us an apocalypse, a prophecy – not a narrative or an epistle. It is a text requiring different interpretative skills from its readers – imagination and emotion, for example. Like a metaphor, it disorientates us before we can be pointed to a fresh view of reality. The theological function of apocalypse depends on the ability of the reader to allow its images to inform by means of a subtle interplay of text, context (biblical and social) and imagination. We are summoned to see things from another, unusual, point of view, and to be open to the possibility that difference of perspective will lead to difference of insight and practice. The Apocalypse does not provide the currency of our normal theological exchange, and it summons us to engage in political theology in a rather different way. It will demand that the less ordered, imaginative part of ourselves is more active. The Apocalypse typifies the kind of writing offered by 'the wisest of the ancients' who 'consider'd what is not too explicit as the fittest for instruction, because it rouzes the faculties to act'.[36] Responses to it defy the neat and the systematic and beckon those who engage with it to do exegesis less analytically and more imaginatively. In such a situation, the theologians may find themselves less expositors than those who facilitate the active faculties and assist with the outcome of the spiritual stimulus which apocalypse offers.

I hope it will be apparent that the difference between O'Donovan and myself is not so much on the content of our interpretation. Indeed, there is a surprising degree of similarity in what we would want to say about the text. Where we do differ is on the question of hermeneutical approach. I have suggested an imaginative approach to this visionary text, in which the actual practice of bearing witness to Jesus is a more appropriate context for understanding than a detached study of the text in an academic context. The sort of

---

[35] Bengel, *Gnomon*.

[36] Letter to Trusler in Keynes (ed.), *Complete Writings*, 793–94.

engagement with the text in which imagination is allied to practical discipleship suggests a different kind of Christian pedagogy. At the risk of oversimplification, I would characterize the pedagogical preference in the third part of this essay as in the spirit of the early Anabaptists, whereas O'Donovan's is more indebted to the magisterial Reformers.[37] So, it is not that I opt for a liberationist reading where O'Donovan does not (indeed, there is much in the content of O'Donovan's interpretation which liberationist exegetes would echo). Rather I want to ensure that we put at the centre of reading the Apocalypse (and indeed any part of the Bible) a politically committed, engaged discipleship of Jesus as a necessary component of understanding the divine will. This is the hermeneutic which is typical of the pedagogy of the Basic Ecclesial Communities from which all liberationist exegetes have learned so much.[38]

Let me end on a personal note. I have suggested that the Apocalypse prompts an engagement with political issues which does not sit easily with much modern theology. I have pointed to the study of William Stringfellow as an example of this. Stringfellow is at the academic end of an engagement with the Bible which has a long history. This tradition has also been given prominence by the engagement with Scripture in the grassroots communities of Latin America, linked with the emergence of liberation theology (though the antecedents are much older).[39] Theologians in these contexts have struggled to discover another way of exercising their responsibility as theologians.[40] It is less about explanation and more about facilitating, less about making judgements on the interpretations and more about enabling the judgements to be made, as people seek to draw wisdom, new and old, from the theological treasure trove. It is episodic, aphoristic and oral, and it fits with difficulty into the carefully measured discussions of academic debate. Nevertheless, this tradition offers insights and a grasp of the political claim of the gospel that bears out Jesus' words that God reveals wisdom to the 'little ones'. If I have any role in discussions of political theology, it is to try to broker a mutual recognition between the kinds of things I have witnessed in Latin America and in urban theology groups in the British Isles, and the 'Great Tradition' of political theology and its most articulate and influential modern exponent, Oliver O'Donovan. Such an exchange will not be easy, for the character of the intellectual currencies will not be immediately compatible. Nevertheless, it is not only the health of the subject but a fully informed Christian political theology which requires such a quest for complementarity.

---

37 See the outline of early Anabaptist scriptural study in Bradstock and Rowland, *Radical Christian Writings*, 89.

38 See the marginal notes on the Apocalypse in *Bíblia Sagrada* and Richard, *Apocalypse*.

39 Some examples are collected in Bradstock and Rowland, *Radical Christian Writings*.

40 See the helpful sketch by Ken Leech in *Through our Long Exile*, 111–229.

Bibliography

Adorno, T.W., *Minima Moralia: Reflections from Damaged Life* (trans. E.F.N. Jephcott; London: New Left Books, 1974)

Bauckham, R., *The Theology of the Book of Revelation* (Cambridge: CUP, 1993)

——, (ed.), *Tudor Apocalypse* (Oxford: Sutton Courtenay Press, 1978)

Bengel, J.A., *Gnomon of the New Testament* (Edinburgh: T. & T. Clark, 1857)

Bíblia Sagrada Edição Pastoral (São Paulo, 1991)

Blake, W., *The Continental Prophecies* (ed. D.W. Dörrbecker; Blake's Illuminated Books IV; London: William Blake Trust; Princeton, NJ: Princeton University Press, 1995)

——, *Blake: The Complete Writings* (ed. G. Keynes; Oxford: OUP, 1972)

Boyer, P., *When Time Shall Be No More: Prophecy Belief in Modern American Culture* (Cambridge, MA: Belknap Press, 1992)

Bradstock, A., and C. Rowland, *Radical Christian Writings: A Reader* (Oxford: Basil Blackwell, 2002)

Cohn, N., *The Pursuit of the Millennium* (London: Paladin, 1957)

Collins, A.Y., *Cosmology and Eschatology in Jewish and Christian Apocalypses* (Leiden: E.J. Brill, 1996)

Cook, S.L., *Prophecy and Apocalypticism: the Post-Exilic Social Setting* (Minneapolis: Fortress Press, 1995)

Dronke, P., *Women Writers of the Middle Ages* (Cambridge: CUP, 1982)

Emmerson, R.K., and B. McGinn (eds.), *The Apocalypse in the Middle Ages* (Ithaca, NY: Cornell University Press, 1992)

Fredriksen, P., 'Tyconius and Augustine on the Apocalypse', in R.K. Emmerson and B. McGinn (eds.), *The Apocalypse in the Middle Ages* (Ithaca, NY: Cornell University Press, 1992), 20–37

Hanson, P.D., *The Dawn of Apocalyptic* (Philadelphia: Fortress Press, 1975)

Hays, R., *The Moral Vision of the New Testament* (Edinburgh: T. & T. Clark, 1996)

Jantzen, G., *Power, Gender and Christian Mysticism* (Cambridge: CUP, 1995)

Leech, K., *Through our Long Exile: Contextual Theology and the Urban Experience* (London: Darton, Longman & Todd, 2001)

McClendon, J.W., *Systematic Theology Doctrine*, II (Nashville: Abingdon Press, 1994)

Newport, K., *Apocalypse and the Millennium* (Cambridge: CUP, 2000)

Numbers, R., and J. Butler, *The Disappointed: Millerism and Millenarianism in the Nineteenth Century* (Bloomington, IN: Indiana University Press, 1987)

O'Donovan, Oliver, 'The Political Thought of the Book of Revelation', *TynBul* 37 (1986), 61–94

——, *The Desire of the Nations: Rediscovering the Roots of Political Theology* (Cambridge: CUP, 1996)

Ozment, S., *Mysticism and Dissent: Religious Ideology and Social Protest in the Sixteenth Century* (New Haven: Yale University Press, 1973)

Richard, P., *Apocalypse* (Maryknoll, NY: Orbis Books, 1995)

Rowland, C., *Radical Christianity: A Reading of Recovery* (Oxford: Polity, 1988)

——, *The Book of Revelation* (*NIB* 12; Nashville: Abingdon Press, 1998)

——, and M. Corner, *Liberating Exegesis: The Challenge of Liberation Theology to Biblical Studies* (BFT; London: SPCK, 1990)

Smolinski, R., 'Apocalypticism in Colonial North America', in *The Encyclopedia of Apocalypticism*, III: *Apocalypticism in the Modern Period and the Contemporary Age* (ed. S.J. Stein; New York: Continuum, 2000), 36–71; 140–78.

Stringfellow, W., *An Ethic for Christians and Other Aliens in a Strange Land* (Waco, TX: Word Books, 1973)

——, *Conscience and Obedience* (Waco, TX: Word Books, 1977)

Wengst, K., *Pax Romana and the Peace of Jesus Christ* (London: SCM Press, 1988)

Wylie-Kellermann, B., *A Keeper of the Word: Selected Writings of William Stringfellow* (Grand Rapids: Eerdmans, 1994)

Yoder, J.H., *The Politics of Jesus* (Grand Rapids: Eerdmans, 1972)

——, 'To Serve our God and to Rule the World', in Yoder, *The Royal Priesthood* (Grand Rapids: Eerdmans, 1994), 127–42

18

Response to Christopher Rowland

Oliver O'Donovan

Christopher Rowland suggests two contrasts in types of Apocalypse interpretation: *a*) First there is the contrast between the Adventist use of the book and that of William Stringfellow. Both of these spring from important moments in dissident American self-criticism, but they proceed very differently: i) by constructing an inter-textual schedule of eschatological events, ii) by an intra-textual application of eschatological images to contemporary events. This second type constitutes the best tradition of Apocalypse interpretation, from Irenaeus to Tyconius, to Augustine to Joachim to Stringfellow and (thank goodness!) to O'Donovan. *b*) Secondly, there is the contrast between i) an interpretation which proceeds 'analytically' and by 'translation', and ii) one, again represented by Stringfellow, which functions by displacing perspectives, loosely, imaginatively, challenging and destabilizing the reader.

How do these two pairs of contrasting approaches relate to each other? It could appear that they are in effect the same contrast made in two ways. But that falls foul of O'Donovan, who is located in *a*) ii), but also in *b*) i). We could focus the question by asking whether the contrary combination of approaches is thinkable, *a*) i) with *b*) ii). We are left with an impression that it is not. Yet the Adventists could themselves be a case. There, if anywhere, the Apocalypse was read 'because it rouzes the faculties to act'; there, if anywhere, the contemporary context – US Sabbath legislation – was the precipitating factor that sent the interpreters back to the text to find imaginative stimulus for their dissidence. And if it seems that their reflections are altogether too systematized to fit the approach described in *b*) ii), we could point out that the system woven by their intertextuality serves as a cover for a fair degree of anarchy in their treatment of the single text.

This then prompts the question whether in setting up the first contrast, *a*), Rowland has been quite fair: he finds in i) 'a timetable about the end of the world' and in ii) 'a template by which one can assess ... the world in which one lives'. Yet attempts to provide a minute prediction of the progress of the eschaton do not arise out of sheer vacant curiosity. They trace their origin back to some precise moment of contemporary crisis which invoked a sense of the unfolding end. (Who does not remember the sudden quickening of eschatological speculation in some circles a couple of decades back, as the number of member-states of the European Community approached the Danielic ten?) I am unpersuaded by Rowland's attempt to draw the line between i), those who think of apocalypse as future, and ii), those who think of it as present. The real line, I think, separates those who think of it as *historically unique* (both present and future) and those who think of it as *repeated and generic* (past and present and future).

Girolamo Savonarola, a figure for whom Christopher Rowland and I share a common affection, explained that St Thomas's doctrine of the superiority of monarchy over other forms of government was *true*, but no longer *relevant*, because the fifth age of the church as predicted by the fifth horseman in the Apocalypse, the age of civil and ecclesiastical Reformation, had now (1494) begun with the invasion of Italy by Charles VIII of France. Henceforth the church must live in civil polity – democracy, or something like it. He stoutly denied that his theory of ages derived from Joachim of Fiore, whose work he boasted of having hardly read. How, then, can a Christian know about the significance of the events of his day in relation to the overall shape of history? Savonarola's answer was uncompromisingly biblical: by prophecy.

This is close to the spirit of John of Patmos, who, when he provides carefully coded references to particular Roman emperors, lays claim for the events of his own day to a unique and unrepeatable significance. But that means, if John of Patmos is right, Girolamo Savonarola and the Seventh Day Adventists must be wrong. If the fifth horseman of the Apocalypse appeared first in AD 69, he did not appear first in AD 1494. Claims for a particular and unique historical meaning for any one period are incompatible with similar claims for other periods. So there is something of a struggle ahead for interpretations of this type: they are likely to pin John down to an interest in future events – not because *they* are interested only in the future, but because they need to find room within his vision to accommodate *their* present.

The alternative favoured by Rowland and, on his account, by Stringfellow, is to assign a generic character to apocalyptic events. This turn was undoubtedly taken by Augustine, for whom the eschatological character of the time between ascension and Parousia could be stated only in terms of the church's pilgrimage through the world. The centuries AD form a unique era, but one that allows of no further particularization in terms of world events. Neither the persecutions, nor the conversion of Constantine, nor the spread of the Christian Roman empire can be assigned a 'once for all' character. They could all be reversed and done again a hundred times before the Lord came. So they assume a generic, repeatable character.

Problematic as particular historical claims are, it is not clear that they can be avoided entirely. Savonarola's bold claim that a new era of civilization was beginning at the turn of the sixteenth century turned out in fact to be so formative for historiography, morals and politics that even today the heirs of the Whig historians hardly pause to question it, though they might wince at the proposal that Savonarola knew it by prophetic inspiration. (Christopher Rowland does not wince at it, and I salute him for that!) No serious defence of the development of Western democracy fails to presuppose some such historical periodization as that which he propounded. One-directional historical development from barbarism to civilization, from antiquity to modernity, is an irresistible fact of world history; both in politics and theology it has to be conceived of somehow, whether guardedly or enthusiastically. John presents the canonical Christian reading of history that marks the decisive turning point in history not in the Renaissance or Reformation, but in the crucifixion and resurrection of Jesus of Nazareth. The question every Christian must ask and answer is on what terms that account of history can be sustained in the light of *subsequent* history – which means, I suppose, on what terms Christianity itself can be sustained in the light of subsequent history. For all the bizarre features of Adventist eschatological exegesis, it managed, at least, to keep that question in play. If the question whether nineteenth-century Sunday Observance legislation was the actual moment of the appearance of the beast as predicted by John of Patmos seems all too easy to answer, here is another question, which is more difficult: did we, or did we not, ask the same question about the Vietnam War, and should we have asked it?

In broaching the *second* contrast, *b*), Rowland displays an aspect of his intellectual disposition which his grateful colleagues cherish: a willingness to stand outside the bounds of the literary-historical criticism that prevails in New Testament studies, and to entertain alternative theological approaches to the biblical text. It is welcome indeed to have him remind us that the first stop in our enquiry into the meaning of the Bible must be the community's existential search for help and inspiration in its own context of action, and that no 'criticism' has the right simply to bypass that primary hermeneutical enterprise and its discoveries. Disapproval of the homiletic is an academic affectation that well deserves to be punctured.

Still, I wonder whether Rowland's warnings against the 'analytic', the 'disciplined' and the 'neat' are correctly focused. To say that the apocalypse is 'not a narrative or an epistle' is true enough; but the question remains what an apocalypse, or what John's apocalypse, *is*. A kaleidoscope of oscillating images, yes, but also, on my account, a carefully structured composition. This judgement is not reached a priori, but a posteriori. The book wears its structural features on its face, and there is nothing else in the New Testament quite like them. In one way, it is all a great embarrassment. Revelation claims to be a vision dictated red-hot, and we *want* a certain untidiness, as only proper to such a thing. (Commentaries of an earlier generation liked to remark approvingly upon its poor grammar.) Rowland is unwilling to let that self-presentation go, and very properly; but the interpreter cannot simply rest in it, but must think how to reconcile the book's visionary appearance with its complex and highly studied form. Of the two scholars, both of whom I count as friends, who have most recently enriched my understanding of Revelation, and to whom I feel great gratitude, I find something in each which I find lacking in the other: in Christopher Rowland, an acute sensibility to the political context of the book and the political questions it poses, and in Richard Bauckham a highly attuned sense of the complex way it is put together.

Let me turn back in conclusion to Rowland's strongly affirmative answer to my question about a counter-cultural tradition within Christendom taking its root from John of Patmos. Neither agreeing nor disagreeing, I should like to remark on the paradoxical combination of ideas we deploy when we think of a *counter-cultural tradition*. Culture and tradition are strongly bound up with each other, and counter-cultural moves are inevitably counter-traditional. Christians have resorted to the Apocalypse, especially at moments of cultural crisis, when their sense of where they are within their wider society has been badly shaken. Such moments of resort are determined by the collapse which prompts them. Whether wisely or unwisely, lines of connection are drawn between the experience of the first-century church and the events they now have to engage with, and their own disturbances appear as the harbinger of that ultimate disturbance which shall come upon the world. Sometimes, after providing strength for their day, these lines of connection disappear and strike successors as bizarre; surprisingly often they, or something that remains of them, prevail. So Friar Girolamo's view of the coming Reformation as the dawning of a democratic age became the stuff of Protestant historiography up to and beyond Hegel. John of Patmos' own experience and the Asian martyrdoms it attested became the ground on which the post-Constantinian church proudly took its stand. In the beautiful church of St John *ante Portam Latinam*, Rome assures its visitors that the city so scornfully depicted by the seer of Patmos did not fail to secure the blessing of his presence (and of his remarkable resistance to boiling oil).

Is there, then, an 'alternative' tradition that runs like a subterranean stream? Or is there just *one* tradition, which has come to bear within itself the witness of those to whom the tradition of their own day offered no peace?

19

Ethics and Exegesis: A Great Gulf?

Gilbert Meilaender

When, in that moment of great turmoil in his life, Augustine heard a voice saying 'take and read', he took it as a command to open the Scriptures and read the first passage upon which his eyes fell, a passage from Romans 13: 'Not in rioting and drunkenness, not in chambering and wantonness, not in strife and envying; but put ye on the Lord Jesus Christ, and make no provision for the flesh.' It seemed to provide the guidance and direction he needed, for he writes, 'it was as though my heart was filled with a light of confidence and all the shadows of my doubt were swept away'.

As it happened, some other themes from Romans 13 were important for the Scripture and Hermeneutics Seminar on the use of the Bible ethically and politically. As a participant in that consultation, I was struck once again by just how complicated a topic this is. Serious Christians turn to the Bible for guidance about the moral life, yet they seldom get it as directly and unequivocally as Augustine did in that garden in Milan. Only rarely are we able to go, as it were, directly from Scripture passage to judgment about what should be done. More often a process – sometimes a complicated process – of theological and moral reasoning marks the move from text(s) to judgment.

A great gulf seems fixed between exegetes and moral theologians. If it is not as great as that between the rich man in Hades and Lazarus in Abraham's bosom, it may sometimes seem to be. One of the great virtues of Oliver O'Donovan's *The Desire of the Nations* is that it seeks to bridge this gulf and seems to do just that. O'Donovan gives a reading of the Bible that turns out to provide a Christian understanding of politics. Craig Bartholomew, in his paper for the consultation, helpfully notes several reasons why it has seemed difficult to use the Bible for ethics. It is instructive to note how *DN* implicitly responds to these problems.

First, the Bible's story is a particular one – about Abraham, Isaac and Jacob; about God's elect people Israel; and about that one Israelite, Jesus of Nazareth, and the community of his followers. How can such a particular story provide general guidance for morality and politics? Yet, O'Donovan begins precisely with that story. He finds within the story of Israel an understanding of the political, which turns out to have been culture-forming in the West.

Second, the modern belief in human autonomy has made it difficult to bend the knee before an authoritative scriptural command. Indeed, to allow one's life to be decisively governed by any authority external to the self has been thought to be a betrayal of our humanity. Yet the story of Yahweh's rule, as O'Donovan reads it at any rate, reveals that it is Yahweh's authority, directing us toward our true fulfillment, that makes genuine freedom possible.

Third, one might think that diversity within the Bible, and particularly between Old and New Testaments, might make it impossible to formulate any single direction of guidance for the moral life. Yet although some readers will, I suspect, think that O'Donovan's reading of the two Testaments needs more discontinuity, it is instructive to watch him derive his understanding of politics from the story of Israel, retain that understanding throughout, but permit the triumph of Christ and the presence of the church to reshape the meaning of politics.

Fourth, contemporary fashions, gathered together under the term 'post-modern', reject and deconstruct any attempt at metanarrative, any 'totalizing' account that makes universal claims. Yet, here again O'Donovan's approach is instructive. He begins not with a metanarrative, but with a particular story (of Israel, Jesus and the church). He starts, that is, from within one single story – not from any purportedly uncommitted, universal account. But the particular story he narrates invites all who hear to acknowledge their Lord.

If these are some of the chief obstacles to using the Bible for ethics, then we may say that O'Donovan has, at least, not ignored them when attempting to develop a political theology grounded in the Bible. This does not mean that all problems are solved, of course. And at several points in the consultation it struck me that the gulf between exegesis and use of the Bible for ethics remained in place. I want to illustrate this from two directions, first from an angle that questions O'Donovan's critics, then from an angle that questions O'Donovan.

Two exegetical papers in particular – by R.W.L. Moberly and J.G. McConville – intrigued me. From each I learned a good bit about useful critical angles on O'Donovan's work. Moberly raises hard questions – especially about O'Donovan's characterization of the official history of Israel, about the relative lack of emphasis upon Israel's primary Torah, and about the relation between the two Testaments in *DN*. McConville shares Moberly's worries about how one locates and describes Israel's 'official' history, and he argues that greater attention to the Deuteronomic witness within the Old Testament would offer an internal critique of the David/Zion synthesis so central to O'Donovan's account of the meaning of the political.

At least to the outsider, to one whose specialty is not exegesis, these critiques carry weight. That does not make them unanswerable; indeed, O'Donovan found ways to respond forcefully to each. Here, though, I am less interested in their ultimate validity than in a larger issue they force upon us. Despite raising the serious questions noted above about O'Donovan's reading of the biblical texts, Moberly suggested that O'Donovan might 'without loss' be able to concede many of his claims. And despite raising serious questions about the degree to which O'Donovan's first four chapters (in particular) really make a place for central voices in the Old Testament narrative, McConville offered the disclaimer that, even were O'Donovan to look for Israel's political categories more in Deuteronomy than in the Zion texts, 'the differences will be marginal'.

Can this possibly be right? It seems to suggest that the exegesis – however learned, careful and detailed – is not doing as much work in moral and political reasoning as it seemed to be. We can come round to a similar question if we start from a different angle. In his analysis of O'Donovan's Christian politics, Jonathan Chaplin makes some acute observations about the relation between *Resurrection and Moral Order* and *DN*. In the first of these books O'Donovan gives an account of political authority whose formal similarity to the account given later in *DN* is striking. Noting this, Chaplin also notes that in *RMO* this analysis is presented entirely without the extensive exegetical work of the first four chapters of *DN*. Hence, from a quite different angle we may find ourselves wondering whether the exegesis – however learned, careful and detailed – is doing as much work in moral and political reasoning as it seemed to be.

When we find ourselves at such a point, however, we might wonder whether something has gone awry. I think it unlikely, in fact, that the views of serious Christians, pondering issues of moral and political significance, should really float free of their understanding of biblical narrative and teaching. Perhaps the lesson we should draw from the examples above is not that exegesis is idle in ethics or that the gulf between the two is so great as to be unbridgeable, but, rather, that only rarely can any single exegetical detail be decisive. Our reading of the Bible shapes moral and political insight not, usually, by proofs almost mathematical in character, but by something better described (in Mill's phrase from a quite different context) as considerations 'sufficient to determine the intellect'. The Bible is far too variegated a book for our use of it to be otherwise. It is altogether likely that our ethical reflection will draw on the Bible in a number of ways (many of which Craig Bartholomew noted in his paper). We will find in the Bible law and command (though that will force us to think theologically about the relation between the Testaments and about the meaning of freedom from 'works of law'). We will find in it a sense of created order that may seem to authorize rational analyses of natural law. We will find in it narratives that exemplify virtue and shape character – and, in particular, the narrative of a community within which we are trained to discern what is good and right, which community has first claim on our loyalty.

But whatever use for ethics we make of these, they must all be drawn into the overarching account the Bible gives of humankind as claimed and graced by God in creation, reconciliation and redemption. And there is movement in this account. The end is not simply the restoration of the beginning. That he sees this explains, I think, the power of O'Donovan's reading of the Bible. Jonathan Chaplin recognizes this when he writes of 'the full force of his [O'Donovan's] panoramic, Augustinian eschatological vision of political history'. Likewise, Gerrit de Kruijf describes *DN* as 'a contemporary version of the City of God', for which even 'government is part of the history of the City of God'. The history of redemption must make a difference to our understanding of every aspect of the moral life – politics certainly included.

The attempt to permit it to make such a difference is what really makes O'Donovan's political thought biblical. Once we see this, we may be more ready to say – with Moberly and McConville – that many (though, of course, presumably not all) of the exegetical details could shift, but the overall direction of thought remain the same. So, for example, in his illuminating discussion of 'The Function of Romans 13 in Christian Ethics', de Kruijf takes issue with O'Donovan's adoption of the view that interprets the 'governing authorities' of Romans 13:1 as not only civil rulers but also as 'angelic authorities'. This matter came in for a good bit of attention at the Consultation – and reasonably so, since this interpretation works beautifully for the general thrust of O'Donovan's argument. These 'authorities' have been disarmed by the triumph of Christ; hence, government has now been placed in service of the church and her mission.

Surely, however, O'Donovan's 'dispensationalist political eschatology' (as Chaplin puts it) could get along without the 'angelic authorities' interpretation of Romans 13. It would still be true that political authority had, in the providence of God, been ordered toward the coming of the Christ in whom all principalities and authorities had been created and in whom all things hold together (Col. 1:16–17). It would still be true that the rulers of this age had crucified the Lord of glory (1 Cor. 2:8) and that the kings who serve the beast had been conquered by the Lamb (Rev. 17:14), who is the ruler of kings on earth (Rev. 1:5) and, indeed, King of kings and Lord of lords (Rev. 19:16). Christian theology, reflecting on the phenomenon of political authority, will necessarily draw upon the dynamic movement of this story of Christ's triumph, even if different Christian thinkers may draw upon it in somewhat different ways and in service of somewhat different conclusions. Such differences do not mean that the Bible is really idle in their reflections; it means, rather, that the Bible's account of God's creating, reconciling and redeeming action is a complex one.

Thus, for example, I am inclined to think (as does Chaplin) that the 'humble state' which acknowledges the triumph of Christ might – contrary to O'Donovan's argument – adopt something precisely like the First Amendment of the US Constitution. To be sure, it would not be understood in quite the way that the First Amendment has come to be read in the last quarter of a century of US Supreme Court interpretation – a reading which may, in fact, have influenced O'Donovan. On that reading, one sets in tension a 'free exercise' clause and a 'no establishment' clause. It is, I suspect, just such a reading that led O'Donovan in our discussion at the consultation to reject (as idolatrous!) a 'no establishment' clause while affirming that 'free exercise' is almost required by the very meaning of religious faith. But if, as some scholars have argued, there is really only one religion clause (that Congress shall make no law respecting an establishment of religion or otherwise prohibiting the free exercise thereof), we might learn not to pit establishment against free exercise but, instead, to think more clearly about the sorts of 'establishment' that are injurious and the sorts that are not. Then kings might bring their homage and the humble state might acknowledge its limits by explicitly disavowing any godlike claims on the final loyalty of a citizen's conscience. One could, I think, say that – reading the implications of the biblical story in a different manner from O'Donovan – without departing from the general outlines of his project.

One might, of course, also give a quite different reading of the biblical story; I do not at all intend to deny this. O'Donovan is successful, I think, in his attempt to paint with a bigger brush than many political theologies do. His account does not depend on as narrow a strand of biblical witness as some political theologies (that depend largely on the story of the exodus, for example). One could also, however, find a radically different starting point. O'Donovan's is shaped by his belief that 'no destiny can possibly be conceived in the world, or even out of it, other than that of a city'.[1] But the Bible does, after all, teach us to think not only of a city in which Yahweh rules, but also of a marriage in which Yahweh takes to himself a bride. A story in which the dominant motif is not command but love might give quite a different interpretation of the point and purpose of politics. My aim is not to develop such a reading here, but simply to acknowledge its possibility.

Chiefly, though, I am led by the consultation to wonder whether we should worry less about the supposed gulf between ethics and exegesis, spin fewer methodological wheels looking for ways to bridge this chasm, and devote more energy actually to thinking about ethics and politics in light of the Bible's account of the history of redemption. The great virtue of *DN*, at least in my view, is that O'Donovan, so to speak, 'gets on with the work'. We cannot, of course, simply ignore questions of method. But the Scripture and

---

[1] *DN*, 285.

Hermeneutics project may serve us best if its attention to method grows out of work whose focus is not method but theology. That is what O'Donovan himself has done, and he might say to the rest of us something like Augustine said at the end of his mammoth *City of God*: 'It may be too much for some, too little for others. Of both these groups I ask forgiveness. But of those for whom it is enough I make this request: that they do not thank me, but join with me in rendering thanks to God.' And, of course, one way to render such thanks is by continuing the hard work of thinking biblically about our moral and political life.

20

Political Eschatology and Responsible Government: Oliver O'Donovan's 'Christian Liberalism'[1]

Jonathan Chaplin

Introduction

As someone engaged in the quest for a contemporary Christian political philosophy oriented to the pursuit of a just state, I have found Oliver O'Donovan's *The Desire of the Nations* to be the most arresting, challenging and rewarding work of political theology[2] to have appeared in a long time. While I part with some of

[1] An earlier version of this paper was presented at a roundtable on *The Desire of the Nations* at the Second National Conference of Christians in Political Science, Calvin College, 17–20 June, 1999. I profited from contributions by participants in that session, esp. from Eric Gregory's paper, 'Our Traditions? Christendom and Liberalism in Oliver O'Donovan'.

[2] I find it helpful to distinguish between *political theology*, defined as reflection on political material in (or the political implications of) *biblical and theological sources*, and *Christian political philosophy* (or theory), defined as reflection on *political reality* in the light of those sources. O'Donovan refers to the latter as 'an ordered exploration of the political concepts that are required for authentic Christian political discourse', but styles it 'political ethics' ('Response', 92). *DN*, while mainly consisting of political theology (though O'Donovan defines this somewhat differently, 2–3), also contains many forays into Christian political philosophy – which is why I find the book so valuable. Examples of works mainly consisting of what I term Christian political philosophy would be Maritain's *Man and the State* or Dooyeweerd's *Roots of Western Culture*. O'Donovan expresses hesitation about the 'evangelical' character of the first of these on account, it seems, of its supposed attempt to elaborate a publicly accessible political philosophy insufficiently responsive to the particularity of political theology. I am somewhat less inclined so to charge Maritain, but I certainly accept the legitimacy of O'Donovan's question. I suspect, however, that he might classify this genre of Christian political philosophy as 'a theological type of political theory' rather than 'an evangelical political theology' – a 'Law' rather than a 'Gospel' (*DN*, 81).

O'Donovan's most fundamental claims, I believe that *DN* performs an invaluable service to those seeking to ground their Christian political reflections as deeply as possible in biblical and theological foundations and to avoid capitulation to secular modernity. Inevitably the work has come in for a wide range of criticisms. Among those criticisms that pertain most directly to its substantive political theology, several seem to me to reach premature, indeed at times ideologically tilted, conclusions for want of sufficient attention to what the text actually says.[3] This is not entirely surprising, since what the text says, with its dense prose and multiple, interlocking themes, is not obvious even after repeated readings. This paper was initially stimulated by a disappointment that the illuminating commentaries in *Studies in Christian Ethics* responded only in part to the political theology of *DN*.[4] One of this paper's primary purposes, accordingly, is to attempt to remedy that situation by exhibiting in some detail its intended systematic coherence and by exploring some of its central difficulties. One way of approaching such difficulties is to query the role of 'concepts' in the hermeneutical task, as several critics do. O'Donovan announces his ambition of developing 'true political concepts' authorized by the scriptural narrative and capable of structuring a political theology and ethics.[5] I shall suggest that his

---

[3] This is how I read Gorringe's suspicion of a 'patrician defence of the hegemony of the ruling class' in *DN*, in 'Authority', 25. Such tilt seems even more evident in Shanks's counterposings of a politics of 'authority' with one of 'solidarity' (Shanks, 'Response'), as if we were faced with a straightforward choice between these two options. O'Donovan convincingly rebuts both these misconstruals in 'Response' (99–103). He names the alleged plague supposedly detected by such critics as 'conservatism', repudiating it as 'a quite precise heresy regarding the status of tradition' ('Response', 99). By contrast, Hauerwas and Fodor have O'Donovan exactly right on this point ('Remaining', 30–34).

[4] The contributions by Hauerwas and Fodor ('Remaining') and Rasmusson ('Not All Justifications') press questions of particular interest to political theorists. I find several of these to be searching and pertinent, although I accept O'Donovan's critique of a political theology proceeding *solely* on the basis of 'narrative' ('Response', 97–99). Regrettably, the issue of *Studies in Christian Ethics* in which these exchanges occur contains no response by any representative of one of the most significant contributors to the premodern Christian thought O'Donovan seeks to rediscover, namely Thomism. This may be partly explained by the unfortunate absence of any sustained interaction with Thomism in *DN*.

[5] *DN*, 12ff. In 'Response', O'Donovan notes that his proposal to develop such concepts created a 'flutter of alarm' among his critics. As someone professionally engaged in deploying such concepts, and often disappointed not to find them in other works of political theology, I experienced rather a rush of excitement. But I think O'Donovan's energetic and often cogent reply to this concern ('Response', 93–98) will not calm that flutter entirely, and, as noted above, I share some of his critics' reservations about his account of the content of and interrelationships between some of these concepts.

accounts of some of these concepts, notably 'society' and 'government', may not be as directly authorized as he implies, but may instead reveal the influence of larger theological commitments through which Scripture is read.[6]

O'Donovan's systematic political theology can, I propose, be disclosed with particular clarity through its confrontation with 'liberalism'. His critical reflections on modern social and political thought in *DN* display an affinity with those advanced by contemporary Christian modernity-critics such as Alasdair MacIntyre, Stanley Hauerwas and John Milbank, as well as those of an earlier generation such as Jacques Ellul and especially George Grant.[7] O'Donovan certainly poses a stark antithesis, informed by his reading of Augustine, between the unique and universal claims of the gospel and the hubristic pretensions of a secularized late-modernity premised on a denial of transcendence, an assertion of the primacy of subjective will and a salvific pursuit of the technological domination of nature. To these aspects of late-modernity, the primary word sounded by the gospel, for O'Donovan as for his fellow modernity-critics, is one of judgement.

O'Donovan also identifies contemporary liberalism – not primarily liberal political philosophy (John Rawls is nowhere mentioned – one of the many pleasures of the book) but rather liberal society – as the foremost expression of such late-modernity.[8] Most modernity-critics have little positive to say about the liberal tradition. Its historical association with and contribution to a discredited modernity is deemed to be sufficient to require its repudiation. As O'Donovan puts it, 'the critique of liberalism is now a standard element in the work of modernity-critics, who find in the meeting of liberal voluntarism and technological reasoning the nuclear fusion that energises the Leviathan of our age'.[9]

In *DN*, however, O'Donovan is interested not primarily in reinforcing or elaborating this negative critique of the deficient aspects of modern liberalism, but rather in going behind it to retrieve an authentic tradition of Christian political wisdom – especially its insights into the nature of authority[10] – from

---

[6] Although technical hermeneutical issues lie beyond my professional expertise, I have tried to pose this and other core hermeneutical issues in a way that assists debate among those possessing such expertise.

[7] Cf. J.L. O'Donovan, *George Grant.*

[8] O'Donovan notes two significant 'counter-theses' to liberalism, namely historicist idealism and modern sociology. He alludes to them as sources of that captivity to 'suspicion' which has foreclosed the capacity of contemporary political theology to articulate genuinely constructive alternatives (*DN*, 9–11).

[9] *DN*, 227.

[10] 'A central thesis in what follows is that theology, by developing its account of the reign of God, may recover the ground traditionally held by the notion of authority. That notion has wasted away into unintelligibility, and with it the idea of political activity as kingly' (*DN*, 19). Liberation theology – perhaps the clearest example of a

the mists of premodern obscurity and to reappropriate its positive contribution for Christian political thought and witness today.[11] The tradition he seeks to rediscover is the product of ideas and practices of over a thousand years of historical interactions between church and political authority, reaching its clearest expression in the early modern period. He opts to describe its culminating formulation simply as 'early-modern liberalism' in order to highlight its contrast with the 'late-modern liberalism' which he regards as its secularized antithesis.[12] He also terms it 'Christian liberalism',[13] and I think it is not misleading to employ in this paper what for him is an occasional usage.

His fullest account of the core political principles of Christian liberalism is found in Chapter 6 of *DN*.[14] The location of this discussion in the structure of the book is significant: over-simplifying a richly-textured and interweaving narrative, the flow of the argument moves from gospel (chs. 2–4),[15] to church

---

political theology regarding political activity not as 'kingly' but as 'prophetic' – is cited as a leading instance: 'Building itself on an acephalous idea of society, dissolving government in deconstructive scepticism, lacking a point of view which can transcend given matrices of engagement, the Southern school has lacked a concept of *authority*' (*DN*, 16). This large claim cannot be tested here. Another reading might be, not that liberationism has lacked *any* concept of (political) authority at all, but that – at least in its earlier manifestations which O'Donovan seems mainly to have in mind – it uncritically endorsed the notion of popular sovereignty. This may be an erroneous notion, but it is still a 'concept' of authority. (Cf. Peter Scott's chapter in this volume for a thoughtful, and rather more positive, account of a liberationist notion of authority.) Valuable insights on what a liberation theology prepared to take up its 'kingly' duties might look like can be found in, for example, Villa-Vicencio, *Reconstruction*, esp. chs. 2 and 3 on constitutionalism and the rule of law.

[11] This is also the purpose of O'Donovan and O'Donovan (eds.), *From Irenaeus to Grotius*, a magnificent scholarly achievement which will make ignorance of the wealth of premodern Christian political thought much less excusable than it has been.

[12] *DN*, 226.

[13] *DN*, 278.

[14] I do admit to a 'flutter of alarm' at O'Donovan's disclosure, in 'Response', that 'someone who reads *Desire* omitting chapter 6 would read that book that I first sat down to write' (103). Had I been obsessing about a mere afterthought, I wondered? Clearly not – the 'Doctrine of the Two' and its implications for a rereading of 'Christendom' in that chapter are, he states, integral to the final product. His explanation of how this notion intruded into a rainy Cotswold walk, however, still leaves me in a fog.

[15] Ch. 2 of *DN* is devoted to the 'revelation of God's kingship' in Israel, of which his redeeming work in Jesus Christ is presented as the climax. The Old Testament plays a crucial role in O'Donovan's political theology (21–29), not primarily as a source of discrete political principles (22, 27) but as the foundation of God's entire redeeming activity in church and world: 'the governing principle is the kingly rule of God, expressed in Israel's corporate existence and brought to final effect in the life, death and resurrection of Jesus' (27).

(ch. 5), to world (chs. 6 and 7). This structure discloses the fundamental shape of O'Donovan's political thought, which is essentially this: what God has done in Jesus Christ is focused in the life and mission of the church,[16] which is called to bear witness to the triumph of Christ before the world and its rulers, and to summon them to obedience to him. On a first reading of *DN*, someone interested in its usefulness for political philosophy might wonder why the author devotes so much space to details of the biblical narrative (in both Testaments), and to aspects of the internal constitution of the church, which seem to have little immediate political reference. But it is fundamental to the grand sweep of his theological vision that it is the victory of Christ which creates the church, and that ecclesiology is prior to political theology (or, rather, is an integral part of it).[17] In this respect, O'Donovan lines up with narrative theologians like Hauerwas in asserting that the foundation of the church's witness to the world must be the existence of a faithful witnessing community. Where he departs from them is in his denial that the mere existence of such a community *just is* the church's political witness to the world.

Christian Liberalism

Christian liberalism is 'the legacy of Christendom'. O'Donovan refers to this legacy not, as we are wont to do, simply as 'the influence of Christian faith on the Western political tradition' (or some such formulation), but audaciously, and with striking novelty, as 'the triumph of Christ in liberal institutions'.[18] What he offers is a radically christological reading of Western political thought.[19] His intention is precisely not to supply a theological legitimation of a (secular) political ideology or practice, but to demonstrate how the victory of Christ over 'the rulers of this age' has taken actual historical, institutional effect as political authorities in Christian Europe 'bowed before' the throne of the risen and ascended Christ. He summarizes his case in a characteristically compressed statement, which the remainder of this paper will hope to elucidate:

---

[16] O'Donovan uses the term 'church' to refer to two realities which I believe need to be distinguished, namely, church as organized worshipping community, and church as 'People of God' redemptively active in all dimensions of creaturely life (as were the Old Testament people of God). The latter includes, for example, Christian families, publishing houses, colleges, political organizations, etc., which are not part of the church in the first sense. James Skillen elaborates a similar point in his contribution to this volume.

[17] *DN*, 159.

[18] *DN*, 228.

[19] *DN*, 123, 133.

> To display the liberal achievement correctly, we have to show it as the victory won by Christ over the nations' rulers … Apart from this salvation-historical background, liberal expectations lose their meaning, which is to point to a *bene esse* of political society which presumes an *esse*. They represent a (provisional) perfection and fulfilment of *political* order which derives its political character from the rule of divine providence.[20]

There could hardly be a starker contrast between this approach to interpreting liberalism and that found in most other Christian commentaries, which typically (and often valuably) expound a series of interlocking liberal assumptions and principles and then bring them into critical confrontation with central tenets of Christian political thought as drawn from Scripture and theology.[21] O'Donovan's fundamental concern is not so much philosophical as *missiological*: his leading question is not how far liberal political principles survive such a confrontation (though that is searchingly addressed), but rather how the inauguration of the kingdom has impacted upon the political arrangements we have come to inherit as 'liberal'.[22] 'Christian liberalism', then, is an identifiable historical fruit of the proclamation of the gospel by the church. It offers a uniquely significant testimony to the success of the church's mission. The liberal tradition 'has right of possession. There is no other model available to us of a political order derived from a millennium of close engagement between state and church. It ought, therefore, to have the first word in any discussion of what Christians can approve, even if it ought not to have the last'. Liberalism, indeed, 'has the status of a church tradition.'[23]

Unfortunately, O'Donovan does not identify very clearly the leading individual representatives of such Christian liberalism. American Christians revering the supposed biblical wisdom of the founders will be chagrined to discover

---

[20] *DN*, 229.

[21] A good example of this genre is Mott, *Christian Perspective*, which presents a critical survey of the main modern political ideologies in the light of an evangelically inspired realist socialism. (For a critique of Mott's approach, and Ronald Sider's, see my 'Prospects'.) Sophisticated Catholic reflections are gathered in Grasso et al. (eds.), *Catholicism* (see esp. Grasso, 'Beyond Liberalism'), and in Douglass and Hollenbach (eds.), *Catholicism*. See also the outstanding analysis of liberalism, evaluating critiques propounded by Grant, Niebuhr and Maritain and itself indebted to O'Donovan's approach, in Song, *Christianity*.

[22] This is why he cannot be content with formulating the 'general conception of authority' which he elicits from the OT in ch. 2. Political theology, he holds, must go beyond such a general conception and engage in 'proclamatory history'. 'Unless it speak in that way it can only advance a theological type of political theory, not an evangelical political theology, a "Law", in the theological sense, rather than a "Gospel"' (*DN*, 81).

[23] *DN*, 228, 229.

that Locke, for example, is evidently not regarded as a champion of Christian liberalism.[24] Rather than specific authors, O'Donovan has in mind a broad complex of notions evolving over many centuries and reaching a more or less definitive formulation in the early modern period. The political legacy of Christendom, he writes, 'lies in a fruitful constellation of social and political ideas which came together in a decisively influential way in the sixteenth and seventeenth centuries'.[25] The seventeenth-century Spanish scholastics, such as Suárez and Vitoria, are noted as significant late contributors to this constellation, though they too are criticized for conceding too much autonomy to natural law and thus abandoning 'an evangelical basis for civil rule and justice'.[26] O'Donovan's account of the Calvinist contribution is less overtly critical,[27] yet the obvious figure of Johannes Althusius, who achieved an original synthesis of scholastic and Calvinist political and legal theory at the turn of the seventeenth century, is nowhere cited (though he appears in *Irenaeus*). So historians of political thought will be inclined to press O'Donovan for a more precise identification of the early modern bearers of the Christian liberalism which he seeks to retrieve. In any event, his concern is not firstly historical: an idea is constitutive of the Christian political tradition not merely by being advanced by a leading Christian author, but only insofar 'as it is shown to be organically derived from the guiding principles of Christian society'.[28]

---

[24] Locke is mentioned only once in the book, as evidence of a secularizing, contractarian trend which undermined a key principle of Christian political thought – its conception of 'natural right' (*DN*, 279). There is more trouble ahead for Americans harbouring feelings of piety towards the First Amendment. Those inclined to honour the genius of the Elizabethan Settlement emerge from the book rather less discomfited.

[25] *DN*, 226. O'Donovan refers to a 'High Tradition' spanning the period 1100–1650. This periodization, and indeed the content O'Donovan finds generated within it, are confirmed in Tierney, *Religion*. For a lucid interpretation of that tradition, see J.L. O'Donovan, 'Political Authority'. On *DN*'s method of engagement with Christendom, see Gregory, 'Traditions?'.

[26] *DN*, 210. They are contrasted unfavourably with John Wyclif, whose notion of 'dominion by grace' is cited as a salutary instance of an attempt at such an evangelical basis (*DN*, 26). O'Donovan does have some positive things to say about these Salamancan scholastics, on which more later. For a fine analysis of Wyclif and other Reformation political theologians, see J.L. O'Donovan, *Theology of Law*.

[27] *DN*, 210–11.

[28] *DN*, 229. Of course, that formulation, too, evokes the question of how such organic derivation occurs and how it may be reliably identified. Perhaps O'Donovan concedes too much in 'Response', when he tells us that he saw his task as 'historico-theological' – not the historian's one of merely 'presenting' the past, but the theologian's one of 'exploiting' it for our time, which means 'selecting quite precisely what commands *our* interest *from* it' (92).

Christianity and Liberal Society

At this point I interrupt O'Donovan's account of Christian liberalism in Chapter 6 of *DN* in order to examine his discussion of 'liberal society', which appears in Chapter 7, entitled 'The redemption of society'. O'Donovan has deliberate, if somewhat obscure, reasons for treating liberal political institutions prior to liberal society, but reversing his order of treatment may, I suggest, make his position clearer (to me, at least).[29] What his discussion of 'liberal society' attempts to achieve is an account of the way in which the gospel, and the church as its witness, have over the centuries framed the enduring character of European Christian society. That character, he claims, displays *analogically* the same narrative structure as is present in the gospel and the church – a structure that turns on 'four moments'. The four features of liberal society disclosing the impact of the gospel are *freedom*, *merciful judgement*, *natural right* and *openness to speech*. These witness to the four moments of the gospel itself: *advent*, *passion*, *restoration* and *exaltation*.[30] In turn, these four moments find their parallels in four features of the church, which exists as a *gathering* community, a *suffering* community, a *glad* community and a *prophetic* community.[31]

I am not qualified to assess the full hermeneutical plausibility of this analogical methodology, but I can at least underscore O'Donovan's own recognition that summarizing the core of the gospel in these four notions is not the only possibility.[32] And perhaps it is not the best. Why, for example, not opt for the arguably more comprehensive triad of motifs, 'creation-fall-redemption/salvation', as such a summary? But what would we then posit as corresponding features of liberal society? Has not the biblical faith in 'creation', for instance, found its outworking in modern liberalism's commitment to affirming, exploring and controlling 'nature' (*prior* to the idolatrous distortion of that vision in the modernist faith in technological mastery, which O'Donovan justly denounces)?[33] Or, as others have noted,[34] why does the theologically central notion of 'covenant' play such a minor role in a political theology so indebted to the Old Testament idea of kingship, whereas it proved absolutely

[29] For an explanation of these reasons, see *DN*, 193–94, 241–42, 246–52. His distinction between 'society' and 'political authority' plays a crucially important systematic role, and I return to it later.

[30] *DN*, 133–46.

[31] *DN*, 174–92.

[32] O'Donovan, 'Response', 98–99.

[33] E.g., Charles Taylor rightly identifies the 'affirmation of ordinary life' as one of the outcomes of Reformed Christianity which came to be constitutive of the best in modern liberalism. Cf. *Sources*, Pt. III.

[34] E.g., Furnish ('How Firm?', 21), Hauerwas and Fodor ('Remaining', 38), and, in this volume, Gordon McConville.

decisive for Calvinist and Puritan writers equally so indebted?[35] And, if covenant had played a more prominent role, might it have required a guarded recognition that some version of the idea of 'contract' at the root of modern liberal political theory might yet be salvaged as having some biblical warrant (which, to be sure, has been uprooted in later liberalism's grounding of contract in supposedly naturally free and equal individuals)? I confess to finding a certain artificiality in O'Donovan's analogical reading of modern liberal society. It fails to persuade me that the four features of liberal society he identifies display the necessary connections to the core of the gospel message that he suggests they bear, or that other features might not equally qualify as authentic manifestations of Christian faith.

Nonetheless, the four features he selects do indeed take in many of the commanding heights of modern Western society, and his account of their appearance and destiny in liberal society is penetrating. First, Christian *freedom* is ultimately what made possible the civil freedom we have come to associate with liberal society. The 'paradigm for … [a] free society', says O'Donovan, is 'the recognition of a superior authority which renders all authorities beneath it relative and provisional'.[36] And further,

> God has done something which makes it impossible for us any more to treat the authority of human society as final and opaque. He has sent the anointed one to rule; and wherever he has appeared … he has loosened the claims of existing authority, humbling them under the control of his own law of love.[37]

Freedom is not primarily 'an assertion of individuality' but rather 'a social reality'; Christian freedom always remains engaged in society. Yet it issues forth in a form of individual liberty guaranteed by the prior claims of Christ over any existing social structure.[38] Historically, such 'evangelical liberty' served as the basis on which a wide range of freedoms could be asserted, including, most importantly, freedom of conscience. The affirmation that the primary religious duty of the individual is to God, and not to any human authority, limits the competence which may be granted to governments to regulate that religious relation. Thus was demarcated 'a sphere of individual responsibility before God in which the public good is not immediately at stake'.[39]

---

[35] See, e.g., Franklin (ed.), *Constitutionalism*; Gardner, *Justice*; Burns (ed.), *Cambridge History*, ch. 7; Skinner, *Foundations*, II.3. Contributions from John Knox and the author of the highly influential Huguenot tract *Vindiciae, contra Tyrannos* are included in the O'Donovans' *Irenaeus*.

[36] *DN*, 252. On his view of the relation between freedom and authority, see *DN*, 30–32, 252–55; and *RMO* pt. II, 'The Subjective Reality'.

[37] *DN*, 253.

[38] *DN*, 254–55.

[39] *DN*, 255.

The second feature of liberal society is its acquisition, after the coming of Christ, of the capacity to temper the execution of the judicial function of the state with *merciful judgement.* Liberal society 'is forced to acknowledge the redemption that God has made in every act of judgment that it performs'.[40] The proclamation of God's mercy did not undermine, but rather strengthened, the church's confidence in the judicial paradigm for secular government. Under the spreading influence of the church, especially as modelled in its distinctive penitential order, society, 'respecting the judicial function as the core of political authority, must shape its conception of justice in the light of God's reconciling work'. 'The church asserted its own evangelical justice in society's midst, and society, to a degree, had to defer to it.'[41] What this practically implied is exemplified in the minimizing of the intensity of coercive penal sanctions, the application of the virtues of humility and mercy to the task of judging, and, in the sixteenth century, the development of a novel Christian concept of 'equity'.[42]

The third characteristic of liberal society manifesting its Christian provenance is its recognition of *natural right*, which laid the basis for four profoundly significant affirmations. 'Natural equality' led to the ultimate undermining of the institution of slavery; the 'structures of affinity' form the human home (family, local community, language, tradition, culture and law); 'universal humanity' is expressed most fully in international law; and, finally, there is our 'creaturely cohabitation' with the non-human world.[43]

Finally, liberal society displays the formative influence of the gospel (specifically its Pentecostal founding) through its *openness to speech.* The prophetic speech of the church confronted Western society with the possibility of

> ... an order in which power, judgment and tradition, the staple elements of political authority, have to confront and accommodate the free discourse of a society which has learned to recognise authority also in the word spoken from God by manservants and maidservants (as the prophecy of Joel had said). Any voice within the public realm which could address the community about the common good had to be heard, lest the voice of true prophecy should go unheard.[44]

O'Donovan recognizes this as one of the contributing factors in the emergence of modern Western democracy. While he is dismissive of any interpretation

---

[40] *DN*, 256.

[41] *DN*, 259, 260.

[42] *DN*, 260–61.

[43] *DN*, 262–68.

[44] *DN*, 269. This was prefigured in Israel, especially in the prophetic function (*DN*, 73–80). 'The mediators of YHWH's rule do not monopolise the knowledge of YHWH's *mishpāt*, but must concede the relevance of individual insight in discerning it' (*DN*, 75).

of democracy as direct self-rule and is unimpressed by any equation of popular consent with universal suffrage, he provides a considered appreciation of how modern democratic procedures can assist in requiring rulers to be 'responsive to a widely based context of public deliberation which is open to the community as a whole'.[45]

Christian Political Liberalism

These, then, are the principal characteristics of Western liberal society insofar as it has borne the permanent imprint of the gospel. In section 5, below, I return to O'Donovan's analysis of the radical perversion, in late-modern liberalism, of each of these four characteristics. Here I take up again his account of the distinctive contribution of Christianity to liberal *political* institutions and ideas. He has, of course, already ventured well into the terrain of politics in his account of liberal society; that account showed how the infusion of Christian norms into European society already created conditions for the emergence of a distinctive form of political order. Now our focus is on his assessment of the distinctive Christian elements in (early-modern) liberal conceptions of government and law. In this assessment, the full force of his panoramic, Augustinian eschatological vision of political history will appear more clearly.[46]

What was the substance – the 'normative political culture' – of Christian political liberalism?[47] Only a general sketch is possible, O'Donovan concedes, for 'There is no one political structure that can claim to have carried forward the traditions of Christendom in untainted lineage; there is only a family of political structures which may reflect them variously and with variable

[45] *DN*, 270. He resists the interpretation of popular elections as expressions of popular sovereignty or as exercises in self-government (cf. *DN*, 18), and he specifically laments the reduction of the role of (the British) parliament from a deliberative assembly oriented to the common good to an arena for the resolution of conflicts of sectional interests, a mere 'court of common pleas' (*DN*, 271). I think few Americans would disagree that the US Congress would be an even better example. I return to his view of representation below.

[46] On O'Donovan's interpretation of, and indebtedness to, Augustine, see his 'Augustine's *City of God* XIX'.

[47] *DN*, 230. O'Donovan suggests that such a normative political culture must satisfy three requirements: it must be 'genuinely political' and not merely Utopian fantasizing – it must 'yield policies of government that are practicable in at least some recognisable social conditions'; it must accommodate 'the proclamatory presence of the church in its midst', which means that an account of it must also engage in ecclesiology; and, to avoid abstract idealism, what it requires of government must correspond to what may be expected of society (*DN*, 230–31).

success.'[48] But uniting all members of that family is the central political doctrine that 'government is responsible'. From what has been said so far about O'Donovan's approach, we would hardly expect the previous 230 pages of closely argued political theology to culminate merely in a defence of the principle that executives should be accountable to legislatures.[49] What O'Donovan means by 'responsible government' is something far more momentous:

> Rulers, overcome by Christ's victory, exist provisionally and on sufferance for specific purposes. In the church they have to confront a society which witnesses to the Kingdom under which they stand and before which they must disappear.[50]

This terse summary presupposes lengthier expositions earlier in the book, especially one in Chapter 4 on 'The triumph of the Kingdom'. This kingdom is the foundation of all future history. Although in this age it remains, in one sense, hidden from public view, yet:

> … in no sense is it a private foundation, but one which determines all public existence. It determines the ultimate and most truly public existence of all, when the contradiction between private and common is to be resolved and disorder overcome. Prior to this it determines the public existence of the church, which participates in the coming of the Kingdom and witnesses to it; and through the church it determines the provisional public life of the world, in which the authorities are subdued, reformed and given a limited authorisation.[51]

Hence the primary eschatological assertion about the 'principalities and powers' must be that 'they have been made subject to God's sovereignty in the Exaltation of Christ', even though that will not become fully apparent until Christ is universally present.[52] Rulers are not simply responsible in some general way to God as origin of all authority, but specifically to the kingdom of Christ, the historical inauguration of which two millennia ago established an entirely new providential dispensation under which political authority is now required to acknowledge the authority of Christ. We might describe this position as a *dispensationalist political eschatology*.

To clarify O'Donovan's meaning here, it is essential to note that he subscribes to the patristic notion, most fully articulated by Augustine and continued by Luther, of government as a post-lapsarian, remedial institution providentially established by God to curb human sinfulness and enforce a

---

[48] *DN*, 230.

[49] I take up his view on this specific institutional question in section 6, below, under 'Unitary government'.

[50] *DN*, 231.

[51] *DN*, 146.

[52] *DN*, 146.

measure of 'earthly' justice until the return of Christ, who will usher in a new, heavenly order of peace and harmony in which political authority will be redundant and so pass away. O'Donovan supplements this patristic conception with the strategically important assertion that, after the exaltation of Christ, God *now* commands governments publicly to lay down their own pretensions to supreme authority and concede sovereignty to him upon whom all authority in heaven and earth has been conferred. (The church, we may add, is to proclaim this divine injunction, and, when and to the extent that governments actually heed it – as the early church believed had occurred at the conversion of Constantine, and in the Edict of Milan in 313 – they may gladly accept the fruits of such political humility. I consider what this might mean in institutional practice in section 5, below.)

The coming of Christ, then, functions as an eschatological turning point for political authorities. It precipitates an awesome moment of decision for all who bear political authority Anno Domini: will they acknowledge their responsibility to the exalted Christ, accept their limited, provisional authority as mere servants of earthly justice and peace, concede the legitimacy of the church as witness to a higher sovereignty, guarantee it the necessary social space, and listen attentively to its insights into what God has revealed about the requirements of justice and peace during this age? Or will they cling on, defiantly, to the glory and power of the old order which now stands under the judgement of Christ, repudiate the church's witness to the higher authority of the kingdom and presumptuously define for themselves what their political responsibilities are? As O'Donovan puts it: 'The Messianic age ... [propels political authorities] to a simple decision between two governments: the creative government of the Word of God and the predatory self-destructive government of human self-rule. In this age that decision must underlie all other decisions.'[53]

This eschatologically charged notion of 'responsible' government, then, is the core of the political legacy of Christendom that has come to be crystallized in the early-modern liberalism which O'Donovan presents as the distinctive political contribution of the gospel.[54] The confession that political authorities

---

[53] *DN*, 157.

[54] O'Donovan complicates, needlessly in my view, an already complex line of argument by claiming that the appearance of the very term 'state' is itself evidence of the unique impact of the gospel on Western political thought. Without exact parallel in classical culture, the term 'state' – which refers neither to 'the government' nor to 'the community as a whole' (which he seems to identify, problematically, with 'the political community'), but rather to 'a structure of relations within the community that can perfectly well coexist with other structures that serve other purposes' (*DN*, 231) – could only appear when it became possible to grasp that political authority need no longer be regarded as the ultimate source of people's identity (*DN*, 231–33). His substantive point about the challenge which the existence of the church, as a rival source of

are subordinate to a higher sovereign whose transient historical purposes they serve is the central consequence of 'the triumph of Christ' over the rulers of this age. What will such 'responsibility' consist in? O'Donovan's answer appears to be twofold: first, it will involve (or at least open up the possibility of) a public, constitutional confession of Christian faith – this claim is developed in the last chapter of *DN* and I return to it below; second, and more pertinently for our present purposes, it will require the faithful discharge of the state's definitive *judicial* function, the task of 'judgement'. Political authority has always involved this judicial task – 'the execution of right' – as one of its essential functions, the other two being the 'exercise of power' and the 'maintenance of tradition'. But Christ's triumph has not only radically relativized political authority under his supreme authority, but also *these other two functions in comparison to the judicial function*, which now alone legitimates the continuation of secular government in this age. For St Paul, O'Donovan writes (interpreting Rom. 13), 'the authorities are … chastened and reduced to the familiar functions that were once assigned to Israel's judges'.[55] In the light of this new reading of the political situation, the early church was thus able to view government as 'thrust back by Christ's victory to the margins, there to be reauthorised to perform a single function of which the church outside the world stood in need for the time being'.[56]

In the final section, below, I critically assess this fundamental assertion, but here I want to raise an immediate problem. The reference to this function as one needed by *the church* is by no means incidental. It turns out that O'Donovan conceives of the judicial function of secular government (in the gospel era) as being justified essentially – indeed *exclusively* – in terms of the enabling of the church's mission. Given that Christ's authority is revealed in that mission, the

---

authority to that of the political community, brought to classical political understanding, is certainly persuasive. Whether this point is wedded to a claim about the etymology of the term 'state' is less certain.

[55] *DN*, 147. The practice of judgement in Israel is discussed in *DN*, 56–61.

[56] *DN*, 156. For a searching analysis of O'Donovan's 'reauthorization thesis' and his account of the reordering of the three functions as a result of the victory of Christ, see Wolterstorff, 'Discussion', the argument of which parallels my own. In his reply to Wolterstorff, O'Donovan makes clear that his insistence on the state's need for reauthorization is an immediate consequence of his notion of the church as a 'political' community. The 'thrusting back' he refers to is not simply moral, but sociological: 'This use of "political" is not, for me, a metaphor, but an analogically proper application of the term to a law-governed social reality which structures social relations and consequently restricts the boundaries of secular political authority within hitherto unknown limits' ('Deliberation', 132). (He also makes clear, however, that this 'thrusting back' is not at all to be construed as a Thatcherite 'rolling back of the frontiers of the state', but is quite compatible with the state claiming a potentially wide brief.)

new question which confronted the New Testament writers is: 'to what extent is secular authority compatible with this mission, and, so to speak, reauthorized by it?' Their answer is that the purpose of secular government now becomes the creation of a social space for that mission, in order to 'serve the needs of international mobility and contact which the advancement of the Gospel requires'.[57] Secular government's task of judgement must be respected, 'for it is the form in which God expresses his wrath; and that wrath cannot cease yet for ... it is a restraining element in society which preserves the social order that furthers the spread of the Gospel'.[58] Here the consequences of O'Donovan reading political theology through the lens of ecclesiology appear in their clearest light.[59] Many would take exception to the suggestion that the role of secular government Anno Domini is limited merely to the facilitation of the mission of the Christian church. Of course, O'Donovan would immediately repudiate the term 'merely' here, declaring that the destiny of the whole creation is bound up with that of the church. It is for me, too (Eph.1:15–23), yet this exclusively ecclesiocentric legitimization of government seems to conflict with his view, noted earlier, that political authority has a universally valid *esse* which existed prior to, and *is not suspended by*, the triumph of Christ. If political authority is a universally valid calling which God wills (providentially) for all of humanity, both before and after Christ, then its current legitimacy is *not* grounded solely on the mission of the church.[60]

This seems to be confirmed as we delve deeper into O'Donovan's account of the role of political authority. As we saw, earlier in the book (Ch. 2) he sets forth a general account of the inherent nature of political authority, its abiding *esse*. Now he elaborates on how the three functions linked to this *esse* are reconceptualized in the gospel era:

> The responsible state is the *bene esse* which corresponds to the *esse* of political authority ... [namely] the union of power, the execution of right and the perpetuation of tradition in one centre of action ... But the *bene esse* cannot undo the *esse*. The

[57] *DN*, 146–47.

[58] *DN*, 148.

[59] In his contribution to this volume, James Skillen levels a justified criticism at O'Donovan's ecclesiology on this point.

[60] At one point, discussing the New Testament understanding of authority, O'Donovan says that Jesus refashions the notion 'on the model of how God exercises his own'. Thus, 'Within the people of God's rule authority is directed to providing for the weak' (*DN*, 106). This seems to lay the basis for a much wider notion of the judicial responsibilities of rulers – one embracing all human beings wherever they stand in need of just judgement, and not one directed essentially to making room for the church's mission. This, of course, is the Old Testament 'general conception' of that role (and O'Donovan expounds it brilliantly).

> subjection of all authorities to Christ's authority does not mean the dissolution of authority ... The accumulation of power and the maintenance of community identity cease to be self-evident goods; they have to be justified at every point by their contribution to the judicial function. The responsible state is therefore minimally coercive and minimally representative. Not everything that it could cause to happen should it cause to happen; and not every energy within society that it could maintain should it maintain, but only what is necessary to its task of judging causes. This is not a restraint imposed by the nature of political authority as such ... it is imposed by the limits conceded to secular authority by Christ's Kingdom ... [H]owever much political authority survives from the old aeon, it does so upon terms set by the new.[61]

The triumph of Christ thus brings about 'a reorientation of politics to the task of justice'.[62] However, if the *bene esse* does not undo the *esse*, then an exclusively ecclesiological legitimization is ruled out. I return to this point below, but now I want to trace further O'Donovan's account of the political consequences of the triumph of Christ.

The reorientation of politics to justice has come to more detailed expression in distinctive conceptions of law and constitutional legitimacy which emerged from the legacy of Christendom and formed the core of early-modern liberalism. In the *first* place, it has generated an acknowledgement by states of a higher law under which their judicial function is to be administered. 'The state exists in order to give judgment; but under the authority of Christ's rule it gives judgement *under law*, never as its own law ... within Christendom ... all political authority was the authority of [the law of the ascended Christ].'[63] Three specific convictions about law came to characterize Christian Europe: 'all law derives from the will of God; all law is one; all secular rulers are subject to law'. Legislation, accordingly, came to be seen not as a creative but as a responsive activity, 'an answer to the prior lawmaking of God in Christ'.[64] This implied the repudiation of the classical pagan conflation of the personal authority of ruler with the authority of law in the figure of the ruler as 'living law'. Christian thinkers, by contrast, came to conclude that the decree of a sovereign would be invalid if it conflicted with divine or natural law. From this development O'Donovan draws a key systematic conclusion which generates some controversial jurisprudential implications:

> In situating human legislation under the law of God in this fashion, the tradition stressed the juridical character of *all* governmental activity. Even making statutes

[61] *DN*, 233.

[62] *DN*, 233. This achievement is, O'Donovan suggests, illustrated in sixteenth-century efforts to contain the excessive assertions of the claims of power and tradition within the norms of a 'just war' theory.

[63] *DN*, 233.

[64] *DN*, 234.

> was giving effect to law that already existed, acting like a court that makes law in the course of administering it.[65]

Drawing on the implications of the Christian confession of Christ's authority for the question of the legitimacy of particular governments led to a *second* decisive advance on the part of Christian political thinkers. O'Donovan here traces the distinctively Christian roots of the constitutionalist conception of government that came to be established in the Christian liberalism of the early modern period. The question it faced was this: given that government derives its general legitimacy from its execution of a providentially authorized judicial function, how could any *particular* government claim to be the legitimate government of *this* or *that* people?

O'Donovan calls this the problem of 'representative legitimacy', and he discerns three distinct phases in the Christian attempt to answer it. The first was the assertion of the legitimacy of a universal secular government, required to correspond with Christ's universal rule of the world and the church. The 'people' is here understood simply as the whole human race. The earliest expression of this was the support for the notion of a world empire, but a more adequate version alluded to the existence of a regime of international law rooted in natural law.[66] The second phase of the answer focused on the notion of Christian kingship. Kingship, it was held, found its legitimacy not in any existing natural characteristic such as nationality, race or language, but rather was 'imposed upon an essentially unformed social material by divine appointment of kings'.[67] The legitimacy of kingship was deemed to be rooted in law – hence the maxim 'law makes the king'. O'Donovan suggests that in this phase we witness the birth of a distinct species of law regulating the holding of political office, namely constitutional law. In this phase it comes to be recognized that, 'What gives a regime its entitlement is a law-structure which defines rights of succession as well as rights and obligations of tenure, just like any other right and obligation. With this, political authority begins to be conceived as office.'[68]

In the third phase, this emergent constitutional law is clearly differentiated from other types of law and becomes 'constitutional principle'. For this to occur, the nature of the relationship between ruler and people had to be clarified, and this led to the notion that the people may play a distinct role in the

---

[65] *DN*, 234. This argument is developed further in his 'Government as Judgment'.

[66] *DN*, 235–36. In ch. 2 O'Donovan describes how Israel's conception of the model of YHWH's rule of the world produced a radical critique of world empire (*DN*, 72–73): '"humanity" ... is not a reality that we can command politically. We do not meet it in any community, however great, of which we could assume the leadership. We meet it only in the face of Christ ...' (*DN*, 73).

[67] *DN*, 236.

[68] *DN*, 236–37.

process of conferring legitimacy on a ruler. At this point, an element of voluntarism entered into the development of constitutionalism. O'Donovan is not suggesting that representation can only be conceived voluntaristically (a typically modernist misconception): the first two phases (universal rule and kingship) were also answers to the question of how a political authority may be representative of a people. But a voluntarist contribution to the understanding of representation marks a significant departure for Christian political thought (though not one without precedent in earlier mediaeval political theory).[69] In its earliest, Christian, phase, however, the voluntarist component remains firmly under the control of the constitutional principle:

> ... the act of will does not account for the nature of political authority as such. If later contractarians found the essence of political rule in the capacity of a community to will as one, the constitutionalists found only the occasion. The source of authority for them was the will of God. In appointing itself a head, society entered into a provision for political structure that God had decreed, and began to enjoy a power of political agency that it had not enjoyed while it was still acephalous.[70]

The political logic of such constitutionalism led some Christian thinkers to conclude that there might be lawful ways actually to remove rulers if they breached the divinely established terms of their office and became tyrannical. The 'Calvinist theory of resistance' was simply the culmination of an exploration of such ways beginning in the fourteenth century.[71] As early as that, the notion is entertained that

> Given that the highest office is received from God not immediately but through the hands of a collective body, there is within the structure of political order itself a principle that allows the correction of an abusive ruler ... [however] since the removal of a ruler is an act of law, not an act performed in a legal vacuum, it must be done lawfully.[72]

---

[69] For one account of the journey of voluntarist conceptions in the history of Christian political thought, see Black, 'Christianity and Republicanism'. I trace some of the implications of these lines of thought for contemporary Christian political theory in 'Christian Theories', though I suspect that neither Oliver nor Joan O'Donovan would endorse all my tracings (and even less so Black's, against which I too would enter some reservations). For a more detailed survey of the emergence of early-modern constitutionalism, see the contrasting analyses of Tierney, *Religion*; Burns (ed.), *Cambridge History*; Skinner, *Foundations*.

[70] *DN*, 237. O'Donovan remarks that the notion of 'sovereignty' was understood quite differently in Christian constitutionalism than in those later contractarian theories which came to attribute the source of all political authority not to divine ordination but to 'popular sovereignty' alone (240–41).

[71] *DN*, 238.

[72] *DN*, 239.

This crucial qualification is continued into the classic sixteenth-century formulations, in which 'the removal of a corrupt ruler is an expression of the operation of the rule of law. Only later, with the earliest contractarians, does the old opinion reassert itself that the deposition of a ruler is a reversion of society to a pre-political state of nature.'[73]

After Christian Liberalism

This 'legal-constitutional conception', declares O'Donovan, 'is the essence of Christendom's legacy'. It may be summed up as 'Christian constitutionalism'.[74] What happened to it? Let us first record what O'Donovan takes late-modern liberalism to have done to the four characteristic gospel-infused features of 'liberal society' considered above (again reversing his order of treatment). Having traced 'how modernity is the child of Christianity', he now charts the path by which 'it has left its father's house and followed the way of the prodigal'.[75] More portentously, he alerts us to the need to discern, in the late-modern degeneration of a society which once bore the imprint of the Christ, the marks of the antichrist. This is modernity-critique on the grandest scale, with the late-modern world being envisaged as a menacing totality whose spirit it is the task of the church to discern.[76] The fundamental shift away from the Christian liberalism of the early-modern period occurs with the appearance of

> the notion of the abstract will, exercising choice prior to all reason and order, from whose *fiat lux* spring society, morality and rationality itself … the paradigm for the

---

[73] *DN*, 240.

[74] *DN*, 240. This term is also used by John Courtenay Murray to describe the central principle of Christian political thought. See *Religious Liberty*, 67, 162. The term 'Christian constitutionalism' might, I suggest, have been a more apt designation of 'the legacy of Christendom' than either 'early-modern liberalism' or 'Christian liberalism'. The term 'liberalism' seems now to be irrevocably associated with a theory in which individual liberty functions as the primary political value. While Christian political thought, as noted above, certainly contains a powerful affirmation of liberty, its most fundamental principle is, as O'Donovan masterfully demonstrates, the subservience of political authority to divinely given norms of justice governing the nature and purpose of the state and law. Clearly this notion powerfully conditioned the minds of some of the earliest thinkers to whom the epithet 'liberal' may legitimately be applied, so that we might justifiably say that Christian constitutionalism has been a major contributor to the liberal tradition. But while we should acknowledge the premodern Christian roots of early-modern liberalism, we may pre-empt misunderstanding if we reserve the term 'liberal' for the distinctive school of political thought originating with Locke.

[75] *DN*, 275.

[76] *DN*, 271–75.

> human presence in the world is creation *ex nihilo*, the absolute summoning of reason, order and beauty out of chaos and emptiness.[77]

Such radical ontological voluntarism can only twist the fourfold societal legacy of the presence of the gospel out of all recognition. First, Christian *freedom* is reduced to an absolutization of individual free choice, manifested in the myth of the social contract in which 'society's demands are justified only in so far as they embody what any individual might be expected to will as his or her own good'.[78] Among the deleterious consequences of this are the devaluing of 'natural communities in favour of those created by acts of will', the reduction of justice to a mere procedure by which occasions for free choice can be multiplied, and the 'fissiparation … of a singular notion of "right" into a plurality of subjective "rights"'.[79]

Second, by making suffering unintelligible, the notion of *merciful judgement* is rendered incoherent, insofar as the transcendent basis for issuing and accepting judgement is occluded.[80]

> Christian liberalism taught judges to look over their shoulders when they pronounced on fellow-sinners' crimes. It taught them they were subject to the higher judgment of God, who would judge mercifully those that judged mercifully. Ex-Christian liberalism inherited all the hesitancy; but, no longer grounded in religious humility, it became moral insecurity.[81]

Third, *natural right* was 'Reconstructed from below … [and] given a new derivation in the interest of individuals in their own self-preservation. Political association was interpreted correspondingly as a conventional construct to protect individual rights.'[82] Damaging outcomes followed in the field of international law and in the understanding of equality. The basis of a regime of international law was undermined, since international relations fell outside the scope of civil order, but no grounds remained for the assertion of a prior order of natural law by which such relations could be moderated.[83] The belief in natural equality, once interpreted against the background of the differentiated claims of given communities of affinity, now 'has the role of pulling down whatever walls of differentiation the builders of social order have erected … it is a changed notion altogether, atomic in its vision of human individuals, suspicious of any form of non-reciprocal relation'.[84]

---

77 *DN*, 274.
78 *DN*, 275.
79 *DN*, 276.
80 *DN*, 276–77.
81 *DN*, 278.
82 *DN*, 278.
83 *DN*, 278–79.
84 *DN*, 280.

Finally, whereas Christian society made possible an *openness to speech*, late-modern liberalism strives at its 'totalising', rendering us incapable of distinguishing between wisdom and mere information or communication. So the press, for example, obstructs informed discourse 'by amplifying to a deafening level the dicta of an unreflective punditry'. Moreover, since 'the normal content of political communication ... has come to be the conflict of competing wills, speech has lost its orientation to deliberation on the common good and has come to serve the assertion of competing interests', a development consolidated by political parties posing merely as 'competing constellations of interests'.[85]

With the prophetic challenge posed by this analysis of late-modern liberalism, O'Donovan closes *DN*. But the question which is left outstanding is this: what form of public witness should the church *now* pursue, in the chastened context of a late-modern liberal social and political order? O'Donovan does not explore what the shape of that public witness might be in response to the four features of liberal society, and their corruption in late-modernity. Nor are his discussions of the appropriate political ambitions to which Christians should now aspire anything more than pointers (an in-depth treatment of which he has presumably reserved for his projected second volume on political ethics). However, he says enough to suggest the general direction. We can best clarify that direction by considering his analysis of the institutional consequences of 'the end of Christendom'. In doing so, we take up his claim, raised earlier, that one implication of the Christian conception of government as 'responsible' is the prospect that it might make a public confession of Christian faith.

O'Donovan takes it as beyond dispute that Christendom has now come to an end. If its symbolic origin was the Edict of Milan in 313, its symbolic abandonment was the passing of the First Amendment in 1791.[86] It is not entirely clear whether O'Donovan thinks that the end of Christendom also amounted to the effective end of the influence of Christian constitutionalism (he seems to imply that significant residues remain even today), but it is abundantly clear that he interprets the First Amendment as the paradigmatic negation of the central premise of Christian political thought.[87] Contrary to the intentions of at

---

85 *DN*, 282–83.

86 *DN*, 244, cf. 195.

87 In 'Not All Justifications', Rasmusson pointedly asks why the establishment of Henrician Erastianism (in 1532 when Henry VIII is acknowledged by the clergy as supreme head of the English church) is not chosen instead as the symbolic end of Christendom. O'Donovan might reply that this did not actually amount to the public declaration that political authorities were *incapable* of evangelical obedience. But did it not in effect mean that political authorities were virtually declaring *themselves* as the authoritative interpreters of what such obedience was concretely to amount to? The fact that this model later evolved into a kinder, gentler Erastianism (under Elizabeth) does not

least some of its framers, the First Amendment 'ended up promoting a concept of the state's role from which Christology was excluded, that of a state freed from all responsibility to recognise God's self-disclosure in history'.[88] Many contemporary commentators would agree with O'Donovan that 'a measure first conceived as a liberation for authentic Christianity has become, in this century, a tool of antireligious sentiment'.[89] Many might also agree with him that the formative theological impulse at work in the framing was not the orthodox, redemptive-historical Trinitarianism which produced 'Christian liberalism'. Rather, 'A Deist religion of divine fatherhood seemed sufficient to support the authority which government needed.'[90] But many will dissent from his concluding judgement[91] that, 'By denying any church established status in principle, the framers of the First Amendment gave away more than they knew. They effectively declared that political authorities were incapable of evangelical obedience. And with this the damage was done.'[92]

The First Amendment is, however, only the most specific constitutional expression of modernity's repudiation of Christendom. It is important to note precisely what the end of Christendom means for O'Donovan. If the beginning of Christendom occurred when secular authorities bowed before the rule of Christ, its end was heralded when they formally declined to pay such homage. Thus, 'Our contemporaries no longer think that the rulers of the earth owe service to the rule of Christ ... [they deny] that the state should offer

---

change this basic point. One might have expected O'Donovan to highlight this as a fundamental assault on the freedom of the church to be the church, especially as he specifically notes and repudiates a weaker example of ecclesiastical failure of nerve, when the church, earlier in Christendom, first looked to secular rulers to defend its mission coercively (*DN*, 218). O'Donovan alludes to but then sets aside the moment which many modern Christians have taken to be the most evocative repudiation of Christendom, namely the French Revolution (*DN*, 244), and I remain at a loss to know why that cataclysmic, overtly anti-Christian event could be evaluated as less antithetical to Christendom than the passing of the First Amendment. (Another equally plausible dating of the 'end of Christendom', as Colin Greene notes in his contribution to this book, is the conclusion of the religious wars of the seventeenth century.) I am also sympathetic to Hauerwas and Fodor's view that the loss of Christendom (whenever it is dated) should be regarded not only as the refusal of the state to render evangelical obedience, but also as 'God's disciplining of the church in order that we might better understand how our habitation in Babylonia should proceed' ('Remaining', 42). I imagine O'Donovan is, too.

[88] *DN*, 245.

[89] *DN*, 245.

[90] *DN*, 246.

[91] Other factors are also alluded to in his assessment of the context and significance of the First Amendment (see *DN*, 246–47).

[92] *DN*, 246.

deliberate assistance to the church's mission.'[93] And, given the need of society for government in order to express its shared moral and religious agency, excluding government from 'evangelical obedience' also undermines the capacity of society for such obedience. To be sure, without the infusion of gospel norms through the church into society itself – from the bottom up, so to speak – secular government would have failed in its attempt to discipline society under the law of God. But since only government is able to define the unifying moral vision which every society needs, a vital part of the task of the church now is to proclaim anew the legitimate function of political authority as mediating the authority of God.[94]

What might this involve? Is the achievement of Christendom recoverable today? O'Donovan poses the following question:

> Has [Christendom] fulfilled itself in the transition from the rule of the kings to the rule of Christ, or has it simply been eclipsed by the vicissitudes of mission, perhaps to return in another form or, if not to return, to provide a standing reminder of the political frontier which mission must always address?[95]

No very precise answer to that question is given, but the tendency of his thought seems to be as follows. In the first place, the church must protect itself against the temptations of civil religion. It need not always refuse the social or moral support which political authorities are inclined to seek from it, but it must vigilantly safeguard the integrity of its mission and message against the distortions which such co-operation may, in different circumstances and to differing degrees, render it vulnerable.[96] For O'Donovan, the heart of the problem of civil religion is that the church's witness is 'cut loose from its evangelical authority'.[97] I noted earlier that the sixteenth-century Spanish Thomists were chastised by O'Donovan for promoting such a severance in their theory of the

---

[93] *DN*, 244.

[94] *DN*, 246–50.

[95] *DN*, 243–44.

[96] '"Never mind how you vote, just make sure you go to the poll!" Messages like that delivered from the pulpit are the archetypal civil religion of modern democracy. They maintain the appearance of political neutrality, while actually suppressing important possibilities for Christian criticism: that the Gospel may raise serious difficulties for an order that conceives itself as democratic, that the Christian population may need to send a message of disapproval not to the governing party but to the political classes at large, and so on' (*DN*, 225). Here O'Donovan cannot resist another sideswipe at the US constitution: 'we need to be clear about what civil religion is. Not every gauche adventure into lay Christian leadership, such as US political leaders like to practise from time to time, will count. Could it not more often take the form of finding religious reasons to support the First Amendment?' (*DN*, 225).

[97] *DN*, 225.

natural law foundation of government. Jacques Maritain, their twentieth-century descendent, comes in for the same criticism. His 'democratic secular faith' was offered as a public creed endorsable by all, but which could be justified differently in private by Christians and non-Christians. For O'Donovan, this means that the democratic creed, rather than the gospel, becomes the core of the church's political message. 'Granted, the church may always make the best of any coincidence of political doctrine between Christians and non-Christians that it lights upon; but "making the best" means *making the evangelical content of the doctrine clear*, not veiling it in embarrassment.'[98] What that specifically implies for the practical conduct of Christian political speech and action, O'Donovan does not elucidate in this book.

Towards what *constitutional* implications might an authentic Christian political witness tend today? The coercive character of Christendom was never necessary to its aspirations and has now rightly been repudiated.[99] But this does not necessarily imply the incoherence of the very notion of 'the Christian state':

> Imagine a state that gave entrenched, constitutional encouragement to Christian mission not afforded to other religious beliefs, and expected of its office-holders deference to these arrangements as to constitutional law. Such a state would have no need to restrict the civil liberties of any non-Christian, even to the point of allowing the highest offices to be free of religious tests.[100]

O'Donovan pays gentle tribute to existing models of Establishment in Europe as limited reminders of the political truth realized in Christendom. Although they only amount to 'a qualification of the prevailing [post-Christendom] ethos', in them, nevertheless, 'states continue to acknowledge the church's mission'. The English model is not singled out for special appreciation. In fact, O'Donovan points to the Finnish triple establishment of Lutherans, Catholic and Orthodox as 'a model which could have been more widely imitated'.[101]

He realizes, however, that a Christian state which accorded such constitutional privileges to the church could not insure such arrangements against

[98] *DN*, 219 (emphasis mine).

[99] *DN*, 220–22.

[100] *DN*, 224. As noted above, this commitment to equal religious liberty is a fruit of the Christian impact on 'liberal society' – the outworking of 'evangelical liberty' in 'freedom of conscience'.

[101] *DN*, 244. Sympathy for similar arrangements is expressed by Lesslie Newbigin in *Faith and Power*. Where O'Donovan speaks of a 'Christian state', Newbigin refers to a 'Christian society' – both fully respecting individual and corporate religious liberty. Newbigin's notion of the 'the Gospel as public truth' lines up closely with O'Donovan's approach.

future constitutional reform, 'should that secure the necessary support'.[102] An awareness of the contingencies of history and mission requires of Christians that they sit loose to any particular arrangement of church-state relations. Thus,

> we should not expect of the Christian state the permanence of Byzantium. Like various aspects of the church's life, the Christian state may be disclosed from time to time as a sign of the Kingdom, disappearing at one moment to return at another. It cannot pretend (as Augustine understood) to be an irreversible datum of history.[103]

O'Donovan, then, is no dogmatic advocate of the principle of Establishment, though he holds out as theologically permissible its legitimacy in principle and its possibility in some circumstances.

But is any form of constitutional privilege for the church necessary for the state faithfully to execute its judicial role (even in a dominantly Christian society), or even helpful towards that end? An alternative, Christian pluralist reading of that role could argue that the inner logic of *the judicial task itself* renders such privilege unacceptable in principle even when attainable in practice.[104] To argue this is not necessarily to support the letter (or even the spirit) of the First Amendment, nor is it to lapse into the temptations of civil religion,[105] nor to exclude the state from 'evangelical obedience'. The debate between O'Donovan and the pluralist model is not over *whether* the state should be encouraged towards evangelical obedience – as distinct from a mere conformity to the imperatives of a rationally accessible, universal natural law, or, worse, the confining requirements of a Rawlsian 'public reason' – but over *what form* such evangelical obedience should take. For O'Donovan this form should, where possible, include a public confession of

---

[102] *Entrenching* such arrangements, however, would either block any such reform in the short- or medium-term (or, in the case of a 'rigid' constitution such as that in America, with its demanding amendment procedures, the rather longer-term), or make it virtually impossible (as in the case of certain provisions in the German Basic Law which are deemed to be unamendable).

[103] *DN*, 224.

[104] For Protestant examples of such Christian pluralism, see Lugo, 'Caesar's Coin'; Skillen, *Recharging*; Mouw and Griffioen, *Pluralisms*; Guinness, *American Hour*, ch. 6; Monsma and Soper (eds.), *Equal Treatment*. For classic Catholic statements, see Murray, *Religious Liberty*; Maritain, *Man and the State*; for contemporary discussions, see Grasso, 'Beyond Liberalism' and 'Special Kind of Liberty'.

[105] It seems that O'Donovan might indeed lay this specific charge against a pluralist approach, which conceived of the state's judicial task as requiring equitable treatment of different religions. At one point he implies that 'pluralism' exemplifies the current Babylonian captivity of the church, although it is not entirely clear whether he has *religious* pluralism, or its *political* and *legal* accommodation, in mind (225–26).

Christian faith by means of some model of Establishment. For the pluralists, the state demonstrates its willingness to bow before the reign of Christ to the degree that (among other things) it relates to plural religious communities (churches, Christian organizations, etc.) in an impartial way. I take such impartiality to rule out the according of any privileged political or constitutional status to particular churches, even those which have occupied a predominant role in shaping a nation's tradition (though not every slight deviation from that norm is worth actively campaigning over).[106] The deeper motivation for O'Donovan's preference can, however, best be disclosed through a discussion of his dispensationalist political eschatology, to which I now turn.

O'Donovan's 'Dispensationalist Political Eschatology': Critical Reflections

I now want to examine more fully what I take to be a central difficulty of the systematic political theology of *DN*, arising from what I earlier termed its 'dispensationalist political eschatology'. I will approach this first by assessing O'Donovan's problematic use of two specific political concepts – 'judgment' and 'unitary government' – since these point towards the wider problem, which emerges most fully in the distinction between the created structures of *society* and the remedial nature of *government*.

---

[106] This 'anti-establishment' stance does not, however, imply or depend on a liberal neutralism of the Rawlsian type (of which the best recent Christian critique is Wolterstorff's half of Audi and Wolterstorff, *Religion*). It is not a consequence of an aspiration to a religiously-neutral (or 'naked') public square – I take such an aspiration to be hopeless at best and pernicious at worst. But it follows, rather, from a conviction about the jurisdictional incompetence of the state in matters of faith. But the lack of legal competence over such matters – the absence of a right to public adjudication on them – does not imply that the state is not in fact substantially, inevitably and legitimately shaped by the cumulative impact of the faith commitments of its citizens and officers. Given the necessary dependence of law and policy upon principles of political morality (and, behind them, faith commitments), it cannot be otherwise. So where a large Christian majority (or indeed a substantial minority) actively takes up its political responsibilities through the representative process, the result will be a state bearing the impact of Christian political convictions. Thus while the state will, on this pluralist model, officially retain a posture of (what O'Donovan during the consultation termed) 'confessional silence', this should not be construed as confessional *nakedness*. The design and colour of the clothing will be plain for all to see, only it will not sport any *constitutional* designer label.

'Judgment'

In *DN*, O'Donovan always refers to the essential task of political authority in the form of the verbal noun 'judgment' (a notion he adopts from Paul Ramsey). For him, the question of the nature of political authority is not first one of the authority of *institutions*, but of the political *act*.[107] Thus 'judgment', not 'justice', is his preferred term:

> It is impossible to overestimate the importance of this concept for a study of biblical political ideas. It is often obscured by the influence of a quite different conception of justice, classical and Aristotelian in inspiration, built on the twin notions of appropriateness and proportionate equality – justice as receiving one's own and being in social equilibrium. *Mishpāt* is primarily a judicial *performance*. When 'judgment' is present, it is not a state of affairs that obtains but an activity that is duly carried out.[108]

I suggest that the *act of judgement* is so accentuated because O'Donovan wishes to present political authority as an expression of God's providential *will*, of which political institutions are merely the contingent, historically variable, channels. This prioritizing of judicial agency is influenced by his larger understanding of salvation as the history of divine *action*, and his specific grounding of political authority in soteriological, not creational, categories. The core point is not simply that political institutions exist providentially. We already know this from O'Donovan's first *theorem*: 'That any regime should actually come to hold authority, and should continue to hold it, is a work of divine providence in history, not a mere accomplishment of the human task of political service.'[109] The point is rather that the *providential* character of such authority is most pointedly revealed in the authority's *acting* judicially. Just as God's saving acts are decisive demonstrations of judgement, so the preservative acts of those authorized to exercise political authority in this present age are essentially, and analogically, *acts of judicial intervention*.

Now it may well be that the predominant biblical mode of discourse about justice refers to divine action. I suggest, however, that O'Donovan may be over-emphasizing this literary feature at the expense of the (arguably equally pervasive) affirmation of a perdurable order of social justice, of which OT covenantal law codes may be seen as uniquely authoritative historical instantiations. Take, for instance, the OT principle of inalienable family land tenure, which seems to lie at the basis of the Jubilee provisions in Leviticus 25. Does this not point towards a universal principle of justice requiring an equitable distribution of essential material resources (however that might be realized

---

107 *DN*, 20.

108 *DN*, 39.

109 *DN*, 46.

in very diverse historical contexts)? Thus a just king intervening to invoke the Jubilee laws, or other related provisions, would be acting to restore (or perhaps implement for the first time) a universally valid normative principle of social order. Can biblical justice be adequately grasped as corrective (remedial) action without a prior intuition of the normative principle which has been violated?[110] While the term *mishpāt* itself may not refer to a 'state of affairs', its meaning surely depends upon principles intended to order states of affairs.[111] Such 'principles' are, of course, instances of the implications of what the classical tradition has termed 'natural law' or 'creation order', and I comment on O'Donovan's relation to this aspect of the tradition below.[112]

'Unitary government'

The same prioritizing of the moment of political action emerges in O'Donovan's reservations about the modern constitutional principle of the 'separation of powers'.[113] I noted above that by 'responsible government' he

---

[110] In this case it would be an original equitable distribution of land – similar to what John Paul II, in *Centesimus Annus*, calls 'the universal destination of material goods'.

[111] O'Donovan is, of course, fully versed in such OT social and political principles. I remarked above (note 15) that his main interest in the OT is its narration of the saving activity of God through Israel (his new recognition of 'divine decisiveness' in contrast to 'legal and cosmic stability' is intimated in *DN*, 40). Yet the significance of Israel is not only soteriologically, but also in some sense sociologically, normative: 'any question about social forms and structures must be referred to a normative critical standard: do they fulfil that will of God for human society to which Israel's forms authoritatively point us?' (*DN*, 25). And 'Israel's history must be read as a *history of redemption*, which is to say, as the story of how certain principles of social and political life were vindicated by the action of God in the judgment and restoration of the people' (*DN*, 29). Perhaps it is his intention to elaborate the meaning of such principles in his work on political ethics.

[112] I would emphasize strongly my anchoring of what I have called 'universal principles of justice' in the concrete structures arising from created order. I do not have in mind *abstract* or *formal* principles of either the classical Aristotelian or the modern Kantian variety. A principle can be universal without being abstract or formal, by virtue of its being grounded in the order of creation which holds universally (though neither statically nor unhistorically) for all creatures. What I have in mind is close to what I believe Joan Lockwood O'Donovan is referring to in her characterization of the classical Christian view of the common good of society as composed of 'a multiplicity of communal structures of right and law ... *defined by universal principles of right or justice*' ('Political Authority', 14, emphasis mine).

[113] This may be further evidence of a bias against American, and towards English, constitutional history. On the other hand, O'Donovan's reading of the latter is far from uncritical, as is made clear in his enlightening analysis of the contemporary

does not have in mind simply the idea of the accountability of executives to legislatures. To clarify this point it will be helpful to note the way O'Donovan elaborates his judicial conception of government and law in 'Government as Judgment'. His approach stands in contrast to contemporary usage, in which 'judicial' typically refers to the activity of judging according to the law and declaring guilt or innocence under it – hence constitutional theory speaks of 'the judicial system' as that arrangement of institutions and practices which perform this function, contrasting this with the legislative function of lawmaking, and the executive function of law-implementation. In his view, by contrast, 'the court is the central paradigm of government – all government, in all its branches'.[114] O'Donovan's entirely laudable concern here is to resist any absolutization of one branch of government and to ensure the subordination of each to the definitive governmental task of judgement. For example, whereas advocates of the secularized doctrine of popular sovereignty might, under the idolatrous notion of *vox populi, vox Dei*, uncritically venerate popularly elected assemblies and resist external constraints on them, O'Donovan urges that it is necessary to curtail the creative hubris of legislatures and recall legislators to their duty of drafting laws which realize principles of justice (or 'right'). Legislators are not to suppose that they are entitled to generate public norms *de novo*. Rather, they are to discern the practical meaning, for this or that item of public policy, of the prior claims of justice rooted in divine and natural law (and, perhaps, already embodied in 'custom'). Equally, where there is evidence of 'judicial usurpation' of the legitimate representative process, other branches of government must act to rein in such judicial excess, such as, for example, by narrowing the meaning of constitutional provisions capable of ideologically-coloured jurisprudential interpretation.

Thus it is quite consistent with his idea of 'accountability' for him to support a horizontal *distribution* of legislative, executive and judicial functions across different organs of state.[115] What he firmly opposes, however, is the attempt – an inherently fruitless one, he believes – to *separate* powers with the intention of deliberately pitting them against each other and so risking governmental incoherence or paralysis.[116] Indeed, he takes such an arrangement to be indicative of

---

compromising of the independent representative function of the British parliament by an executive-dominated party system (cf. 'Government', 41–42).

[114] O'Donovan, 'Government', 39.

[115] O'Donovan, 'Government', 39–40, 42. I would add that, in my view, his notion of accountability also need not exclude a vertical distribution of functions within a federal system, though I am not clear whether he would agree with this.

[116] His particular concern is with safeguarding the necessary moment of 'legal closure', which every workable constitution needs: the requirement that at some point deliberation must end in authoritative decision. Now suppose that one acknowledged, as I do,

social decline: 'The constitutional separation of functions within government has risen in favour when confidence in the effective authority of a common social "possession" of moral principles has been weak.'[117] Israel's way of containing the danger of absolutism was not the distribution of powers but rather 'unitary government subject to the independent authority of YHWH's law, which had its independent voice in society through the prophetic movement'.[118] O'Donovan ventures, rather speculatively, that Jesus' remarks about 'a kingdom divided against itself' reveal a sympathy for the view that 'the establishment of multiple centres of competing power is a recipe for political weakness'.[119] It appears that he advocates unitary government because it allows for clarity in the expression of a society's shared moral conscience. The prophetic community – and in the gospel era the church – then serves, not as a countervailing constitutional power, but as an alternative source of communal authority, calling such a unified government back to its subordination to divine and natural law. This OT duality of king and prophet is now mirrored in the NT principle of 'dual authority', where the church stands over against political authority as the chastening voice of divine revelation.

But does this preference for a concentration rather than a dispersal of political power really follow from a biblical political theology?[120] Certainly a powerful tradition of constitutional thought with precedents in O'Donovan's 'High Tradition' eventually reached the conclusion that, since all power corrupts, it had better be spread thinly rather than concentrated. A crucial implication of

that every constitution makes provision for such formal closure. This, however, does not mean that such decisions are closed in perpetuity. All constitutions make provision for revisiting the 'sovereign' decisions of their own government, and indeed for amending themselves, and it must be right that they do, in order not to 'frame mischief by [unchangeable] statute' (Ps. 94:20, RSV). Even in the USA, Supreme Court decisions can in principle – if only infrequently in practice – be undone by constitutional amendments. In any event, conceding O'Donovan's insistence on the need for legal closure, we are still left with the question of the *degree* to which a legitimate distribution of functions allows for, or even encourages, the kind of jurisdictional competition which O'Donovan finds problematic. We also wonder whether such competition might, up to a point, be a *healthy*, or even *essential*, form of mutual restraint. Thus while I find myself in agreement with O'Donovan's systematic claim about the shared judicial character of all governmental activity, I am inclined to tug the principle of functional distribution in a competitive, rather than a unitive, direction.

[117] *DN*, 65.

[118] *DN*, 65.

[119] *DN*, 94.

[120] Gordon McConville's chapter in this volume provides substantial evidence, from Deuteronomy at least, that it does not.

this recognition was that the only truly effective way to hold executives accountable to the imperatives of divine and natural law was to constitutionalize that accountability by interpreting the principle of 'the rule of law' not merely as a moral duty upon executives to abide by a higher law, but as a legal duty to do so, enforceable if necessary by alternative organs of political authority, especially representative organs (and, later, courts). In other words, O'Donovan's *eschatological* notion of 'responsible government' does, after all, lend a measure of support to the *constitutional* principle of the 'separation of powers'.

In fact, he comes very close to recognizing this explicitly. As I noted above, he pays tribute, for example, to the Calvinist theory of resistance, and its corollary that 'there is within the structure of political order itself a principle that allows the correction of an abusive ruler', an act which, moreover, 'must be done lawfully'.[121] Yet he refrains from taking the next step and concluding that this corrective process might be constitutionally regularized in the requirement that executives be permanently accountable to representative bodies (or courts). O'Donovan is aware of the role played by the emerging representative assemblies of early modern Europe in the development of 'Christian liberalism'. And, as we have seen, his notion of 'openness to speech' offers an original reading of how the gospel assisted in the legitimation and expansion of that role.[122] I would want to press the point, however, that the representative function of a popular assembly must go together with an accountability function. That is, it is necessary not simply to suggest that such representative assemblies enable popular participation in deliberation about the activities of executives, but also to say that executives must answer for those activities at the bar of such assemblies (and, perhaps, at the bar of courts), on pain of censure – or worse – for failure. And I believe that this can all be said without in any way implying the myth of 'popular sovereignty' or entertaining the illusion of direct democratic 'self-government'.

---

[121] *DN*, 239.

[122] He might, perhaps, have stretched the implications of this point further. His endorsement of the notion that governments should be 'responsive to a widely based context of public deliberation which is open to the community as a whole' (*DN*, 270) – elsewhere encapsulated as his 'Pentecostal republican ideal' ('Response', 102) – seems to sit uneasily alongside his seemingly less enthusiastic suggestion that 'responsible government' is only 'minimally representative' (*DN*, 233, as cited above). Why 'minimally'? His concern, it seems, is not to allow the raucous clamour of interests to drown out the dulcet tones of justice – obviously a legitimate concern. So representation can never be merely the unmediated representation of whatever demands democratic activity happens to throw up. But might not a government, conceding its need for help from its citizens in remaining 'responsible' (acknowledging its citizens as *co-responsible*, if not equally responsible, in the pursuit of justice) actually seek to facilitate, even *maximize*, an appropriately mediated representation?

'Society' and 'government'

Governmental action must be decisive, unified action because it is analogous to the decisive, saving interventions of divine action in a fallen world. The emphasis on the active judicial character and unitary nature of government derives, I am suggesting, from this analogy. But this analogical approach itself needs to be interpreted against the even larger canvas of O'Donovan's view of the relation between the orders of creation, providence and salvation. Creation furnishes a given, stable, natural order, while providence both sustains created order and orders history according to divine purposes. A fundamental question is the way in which the divine activity of salvation relates to both created and providential orders. This question emerges at its sharpest in O'Donovan's crucial distinction between 'society' and 'government': his position seems to be that salvation *restores and vindicates* the created orders of *society*, but *restrains and disciplines* the providential order of *government*.

He tells us, on the one hand, that the natural structures of *society* (e.g., 'structures of affinity' such as family, local community, nation) are based in the order of creation.[123] Like the whole of creation, such structures are vindicated and restored in the resurrection, and, perhaps, will be carried over, transformed, into the age to come. At this point O'Donovan reaffirms a central thesis of *RMO*: the history of divine action, climaxing in the resurrection, 'is demonstrated precisely in its vindication of creation order as a basis for rational action'.[124] Now the 'natural structures' mentioned in *DN* are presumably those possessed of what in liberal society came to be known as 'natural right'. And they are evidently parallel to the varying manifestations of 'natural authority' discussed in *RMO*.[125] The language of the 'natural', O'Donovan reminds us, is simply another way of saying (as he does in *RMO*, Ch. 2) that, 'There is given in creation an order of kinds and ends, within which our actions, too, attain their intelligibility. Our task as moral agents is to participate in this order, understanding it and conforming to it.'[126]

---

[123] Cf. *DN*, 14.

[124] *DN*, 19.

[125] '[C]reated beings can evoke free action from us … [T]he "authorities" themselves, are few and recurrent. We may mention four: beauty, age, community and strength (a word which includes the whole range of natural virtue, from might to wisdom) have the capacity, as we encounter them in individuals, in human institutions and in the natural world, to inspire and order our actions in distinctive ways' (*RMO*, 124). Such authority, however, is not unconditional, but 'subject to the review of a higher authority which can presume to order and criticize it … the authority of truth', which may also be called 'moral authority' (*RMO*, 125–26).

[126] *RMO*, 127.

We are presented, then, with a strong affirmation of the inherent goodness of created, natural structures of authority as given conditions of human social life, and of their openness to redemptive restoration. He does not dwell on what such transformed structures might look like in the age to come, although he seems to envisage a renewed humanity fully unified under the immediate reign of Christ. Whether he believes that the *differentiation* of natural social structures, a feature which he seems to conceive as rooted in creation and as contributing to human well-being, will remain under that reign, or rather be dissolved into a single unmediated communal whole, remains unclear.[127]

What is emphatically clear, however, is his assertion throughout *DN* that society needs some kind of ruling authority.[128] This explains his animus against modern sociological theories which depict society as 'acephalous', capable of operating solely under its own internal, unconscious dynamics apart from a directing political agency.[129] Now, in the present age, that function is served by secular *government*. Without government, society lacks the capacity to order its affairs under a coherent moral and religious principle; it lacks moral agency: 'the societies we actually inhabit are *politically formed*. They depend upon the art of government'.[130]

Government, then, is needed in our present age, but it is not grounded in created order in the same way that natural social structures are. This is made even more explicit in O'Donovan's most recent statement,

> ... politics belongs within the category of history, not of nature. Families and schools arise from natural structures of relating, created, fallen and redeemed. But political order is a *providential* ordering, not a created one, and so it has become diaphanous to the redeeming work of God, taking on new forms in the light of the Christ-event.[131]

A providentialist view of government was, in fact, already present in *RMO* (though without its overt grounding in a full-fledged dispensationalist political eschatology). To the four instances of natural authority cited above, he there adds a fifth, 'the authority of injured right to command our resentment and

---

[127] In *DN*, however, he admits to agnosticism on the 'eternal destiny' of families, tribes and nations (*DN*, 219).

[128] *DN*, 16–17.

[129] *DN*, 10, 16.

[130] *DN*, 16.

[131] O'Donovan, 'Deliberation', 137. One implication here seems to be that, for O'Donovan, history is solely the outworking of *providence*, rather than (as I hold) simultaneously the human unfolding of creation's potentials in response to the 'cultural mandate' of Gen. 1:28. Another implication appears to be that created order is not 'diaphanous' to the redeeming work of God, which strikes me as, at least, puzzling.

vengeance, the authority which shapes our structures of justice and government' (which reappears in *DN* as 'the execution of right'). This, however, is one which 'would be classed as "natural", according to medieval thinkers, "in a relative sense", which is to say that it *belongs to the natural order as it is encountered under the conditions brought about by Adam's sin*'.[132] His account in *RMO* already introduced the other two aspects of the task of government, rendered in *DN* as the 'exercise of power' and the 'maintenance of tradition' – but *these*, *RMO* tells us, *are indeed 'natural' in the sense of being rooted in created order.*[133] So the picture emerging can be clarified even more sharply: the two functions of power and tradition are indeed rooted in created order, while the third, the execution of right, is a providential, remedial response to sin. Hence we are offered this fuller statement, which helps shed light on his later account in *DN*:

> The distinctive form of authority which we call 'political' is, then, at its simplest, a concurrence of the natural authorities of might and tradition with that other 'relatively natural' authority, the authority of injured right. When these three authorities are exercised together by one subject, then they are endorsed by a moral authority which requires that we defer to them. They are exercised together when the first two are put at the disposal of the third; that is, when one whose possession of *might* is in accord with the *established order* of a society takes responsibility for the *righting of wrongs* within that society … For justice, in the relative sense in which it is appropriate to speak of it in human communities, can be realized only by this triad of authorities in combination.[134]

O'Donovan can then define justice as 'public right action', each term referring to one of the three indispensable dimensions of political authority:

> Tradition safeguards the sphere of *public* life; for the substance of any community, that which its members hold in common, is determined by what they can 'pass on' from one to the other. Resentment of injured right is the form in which concern for *right* lays hold upon us at the instinctual level. Might, the power to coerce, is the guarantee that *action* can be effective.[135]

Note that he was able to propose this formulation in *RMO* without dependence upon the extensive exegetical work of justification he presented only in *DN*. Of course it is perfectly possible that a theologian can intuit correct biblical insights prior to laying out (or even discovering) their full biblical warrant. But the apparently 'free-standing' nature of the account of political authority in *RMO* does at least evoke the question of whether this account is *derived from*

[132] *RMO*, 124, emphasis mine.
[133] *RMO*, 127–30.
[134] *RMO*, 128–29.
[135] *RMO*, 129.

biblical exegesis or rather *brought to* it. That question can only be satisfactorily answered after detailed exegetical testing by specialists. But let me at least pose some questions. To do that I need to say still more about O'Donovan's account of the essential functions of political authority in *DN*.

This account is derived from the deep structure of his conception of God's redemptive activity in the world. The revelation of God's kingship in Israel (expounded in Ch. 2) is displayed in three fundamental moments: *salvation* (understood as 'victory'), *judgement* (in which the righteous are publicly vindicated), and *possession* (of the 'land' by the 'community').[136] By means of a complex process of reasoning – documented with wonderfully rich exegetical insights, but proceeding according to a logic which I have yet to find persuasive[137] – these three moments generate the following definition: 'Political authority arises where power [salvation], the execution of right [judgement] and the perpetuation of tradition [possession] are assured together in one coordinated agency.'[138] This, of course, is simply a reformulation of the

[136] *DN*, 36–46.

[137] O'Donovan suggests that possible confusions on this point may be dispelled by his sequel on political ethics. His explanation that the tripartite analysis of political authority is 'theory', while the four-moment analysis of the Christ-event is 'exegesis', is certainly helpful ('Response', 97–99). My question, however, essentially turns on the nature and status of the *method of 'analogy'* used by theory in deploying exegesis (cf. *DN*, 2–3). One way to approach it could be this: if the moments of power and tradition are revealed only as *soteriological* categories (salvation and possession), how can they also be conceived as *creational* (natural)? I would look for further clarification of this point in that sequel.

[138] *DN*, 46. In fact, in *DN*, this turns out to be only the first of six 'theorems' summarizing the nature of authority. The remaining five are usefully summarized by Hauerwas and Fodor ('Remaining', 39) thus:

> 2. That any regime should actually come to hold authority, and should continue to hold it, is a work of divine providence in history, not a mere accomplishment of the human task of political service (*DN*, 46).
>
> 3. In acknowledging political authority, society proves its political identity (*DN*, 47).
>
> 4. The authority of a human regime mediates divine authority in a unitary structure, but is subject to the authority of law within the community, which bears independent witness to the divine command (*DN*, 65).
>
> 5. The appropriate unifying element in international order is law rather than government (*DN*, 72).
>
> 6. The conscience of the individual members of a community is a repository of the moral understanding which shaped it, and may serve to perpetuate it in a crisis of collapsing morale or institution (*DN*, 80).

We have encountered most of these in our account so far. Insofar as they are presented as a summary of key themes in OT political theology, they are certainly insightful, though hardly complete. But while I can agree with some interpretation of each of these six theorems, their hermeneutical status and conceptual connection remain unclear to me. For a start, they derive entirely from the OT, and the possible

definition quoted above from *RMO*. And it derives, so far, entirely from reflection on the OT. Now, however, it is taken up – indeed *shaken* up – by O'Donovan's comprehensive vision of the triumph of Christ over secular political institutions (thus effecting a move beyond the OT's 'general conception of authority' to 'proclamatory history'[139]). As we have seen, this recasting amounts to an eschatologically driven reordering of the three core functions of political authority. In the new dispensation brought about by Christ's victory, political authority receives its legitimacy *exclusively from its judicial function* (the execution of right), which must henceforth govern and limit the discharge of its two other functions ('the exercise of power' and the 'maintenance of tradition').

But here a significant puzzle arises. Has not O'Donovan *already* indicated in *RMO* that the judicial function should control the other two? In the passage quoted above, he states that the three functions 'are exercised together when the first two are put at the disposal of the third; that is, when one whose possession of *might* is in accord with the *established order* of a society takes responsibility for the *righting of wrongs* within that society'. But isn't this 'putting of power and tradition at the disposal of justice' precisely what the triumph of Christ is supposed *uniquely* to have effected? Can this be reconciled with his claim that the priority of the judicial over the other two functions is 'not a restraint imposed by the nature of political authority as such'?[140] Perhaps O'Donovan has simply changed his mind in *DN*. If so, we might have expected such a significant shift to have been announced; after all, it is at the heart of his claim about the triumph of Christ over secular government.

In any event, he also suggests that under this triumph 'the authorities are … chastened and reduced to the familiar functions that were once assigned to Israel's judges'.[141] Now if this is the case, then it seems possible to reconstruct an account of the historical (dispensational) evolution of the role of political authority as follows: the political functions of power and tradition[142] arise naturally out

---

transformative impact of the NT on them is not made explicit. It is perhaps plausible to see how the threefold revelation of God's kingship is concentrated in the first, since this is the very definition of political authority – but then what is the precise relation between the first and the remaining five?

[139] *DN*, 81.

[140] *DN*, 233.

[141] *DN*, 147.

[142] For the purposes of this hypothetical reconstruction, I am supposing the possibility of a non-coercive form of power based in unfallen creation, though O'Donovan may not be open to this possibility. On 'tradition', I venture simply this: in Western political thought, this has not always been accorded the same status as an indispensable function of political authority as 'might' and 'right' (or power and law). O'Donovan might then say, so much the worse for Western thought. Perhaps so, though I am not yet

of the requirements of created social order, whereas the advent of sin generates the need for a third, remedial, judicial function. In early Israel, the judges performed this judicial function (at times) in a normative way, subordinating the imperatives of power and tradition to the requirements of the 'execution of right'. But then – at some unspecified point (the emergence of the monarchy perhaps?) – rulers lose such restraint, allowing power and tradition to trump justice (climaxing in Solomonic excess?). The implication is that a parallel deterioration also occurs *outside* Israel, if it has not already become the standard fare of Gentile political order (since Noah, Nimrod, Cain?).[143] But then comes the advent and victory of Christ, proclaiming the restoration of the proper subordination of power and tradition to justice. In other words, salvation restores the functional equipoise within government, such that the created functions of power and tradition are honoured and kept in their proper place under the remedial, judicial function.

I wonder whether O'Donovan would accept this as a faithful reconstruction of his position. Either way, the following problem may still be posed: is it scripturally necessary to characterize the judicial function of government *exclusively as remedial*? While Romans 13 can, and often has, been read in this way, I have yet to be persuaded that this is the only legitimate reading. This is because I read the corrective, remedial features mentioned there (and elsewhere) in the same way that I read, say, the corrective thrust of the Jubilee laws: as remedies dependent for their meaning upon an anterior (though still dynamically holding) universally valid normative order of justice expressive of the social requirements of our created being.

Accordingly, I am prepared to credit Thomism with greater evangelical integrity than does O'Donovan, and it is instructive to explain why. In conceiving of political order in this fashion, the Salamancan school, he suggests, still remained 'decisively Christian' and politically critical, yet produced a 'Christian secularism', lacking revolutionary potential because it 'had no

---

convinced that 'tradition' is the most accurate way to designate the political analogy of the OT idea of the possession of the land. Compare O'Donovan's threefold distinction with, for example, that of D'Entrèves, whose *The Notion of the State* distinguishes 'might', 'law' ('power') and 'legitimacy' ('authority'); or with that of Dooyeweerd, who reformulates the conventional pairing of 'might' and 'right' and seeks to explain their inner coherence in the creational structure of the state (e.g., 'Christian Idea').

[143] Wolterstorff notes a potentially highly subversive implication of O'Donovan's account at this point: that, during the Babylonian exile, not only was there no genuine human political authority in Israel (which few would contest), but that there was no legitimate political authority in Babylon, either. By aspiring idolatrously to world empire (a central political theme in *DN* I have said little about), Babylon had forfeited its legitimacy ('Discussion', 92–93).

place for the interventions of divine judgment'.[144] O'Donovan compares them unfavourably with Wyclif, for their 'admirable venture' 'lacks a comparable sense of divine immediacy. To have God present in judgement, it seems, makes political institutions unstable; to have stable institutions requires that God's purposes be kept at ground level, as the founding cause of political existence ... The tension between the two traditions needs the mediation of a political order which *itself* discloses and reveals the judging presence of God in society.'[145]

But why is this 'immediacy of divine judgment' incompatible with a grounding of the judicial function in the imperatives of created order? Is a public order of justice required only because of sin? Whatever the limitations of the specific Salamancan formulations, it is surely possible to assert *both* that such authority arises from created possibilities, *and* that the coercive, corrective character of its post-fall judicial interventions to restore a just public order are also instances of divine judgement. This is possible if we view the triumph of Christ in the political order not essentially or primarily as the disciplinary curtailment of a providential institution run amok, but as one among many equally dramatic demonstrations of God's restorative action across the whole of human culture and history. The political consequence of *Christus Victor* is then not primarily the *defeat and displacement* of political authority, but its *rehabilitation* as a created, fallen, judged, but now redeemable, social good. Political authorities are not then 'thrust back by Christ's victory to the margins', but, simply, *put in their proper, creational place.*[146] Now this place is not centre-stage and was never intended to be. To the extent that it has become so, Christ's victory, insofar as it becomes historically effective,

---

[144] *DN*, 26. The full quotations reads: the Salamancan school 'found a basis for political order in creation, especially in the sociality of human nature and its natural capacity for justice. This allowed them to look for universal categories of political experience, while still maintaining a relation to the Gospels, for grace, they held, restores and perfects nature. Political theory was to be constructed as the Natural Law of social existence. Here was a Christian secularism – still decisively Christian, though it is easy to see how a later generation would find in it the *point d'appui* for an autonomous political science – unrevolutionary, for it had no place for the intervention of divine judgment, but far from uncritical as its noble protest against colonial slavery and conquest makes clear'.

[145] *DN*, 26–27.

[146] *DN*, 156. As Wolterstorff puts it: 'The *telos* of the Christ-event is the redemption of humanity and cosmos from the onslaught of evil, and the enabling once again of *proper* functioning. So why would the Christ-event imply the *re-authorization* of governmental regimes? Why would it not instead imply the healing of their malformations?' ('Discussion', 102).

will indeed be met with resistance and experienced as a painful humbling as 'the mighty are brought down from their thrones'.[147]

Yet nor is it peripheral to the real drama, as if this were appropriately conceived ecclesiocentrically. Christ calls government to what it has always been called to – if indeed with renewed eschatological urgency ('Now is the day of salvation'): namely, the establishment of justice in the public realm of society,[148] with the church summoned to prophesy accordingly. I submit that this calling is not in itself occasioned by the presence of sin, but that it arises from the need for authoritative public determinations of the requirements of just interrelations, distributions or allocations inherent to any human community. The Creator's call to justice precedes our sinful violations of it – indeed it *defines* them: without that call ringing in the ears of our conscience, without some intuitive sense of justice implanted in our created nature (however obscured or twisted by sin), we would not be able to recognize something as an *in*justice at all. The implication I draw from this is that the institution we have found it necessary to erect in order to secure the administration of such justice in the public realm – government – must be seen as arising from created social needs. While the presence of sin necessitates the employment of coercive means (the 'sword') to enforce the public authority of government, that authority does not originate from beyond created order but rises up from within it. And, like all created goods, in so 'rising up' it reveals the sovereign and loving purposes of God: we can therefore still claim that political authority derives from divine authority.

If so, then it becomes unnecessary to suggest that Christ's triumph *reorders* the essential functions of government. Power and tradition were from the beginning *always* supposed to be subservient to justice, and that triumph

---

[147] In an evocative passage, O'Donovan writes that secular political authorities are 'not agents of Christ, but are marked for displacement when the rule of God in Christ is finally disclosed. They are Christ's conquered enemies; yet they have an indirect testimony to give, bearing the marks of his sovereignty imposed upon them, negating their pretensions and evoking their acknowledgment. Like the surface of a planet pocked with craters by the bombardment it receives from space, the governments of the passing age show the impact of Christ's dawning glory. This witness of the secular is the central core of Christendom' (211–12). This is a singularly clear expression of the view that redemption confronts the providential order of political authority as an *alien* force. I would put it this way: Christ only confronts *sin and rebellion*, and never anything given either in creation or in God's providential ordering of history, as an alien force. No doubt O'Donovan would agree on this with respect to *created* goods; the disagreement centres on the nature, status and destiny of *providentially* instituted orders.

[148] Or, in O'Donovan's phrase, the pursuit of 'public right action', which is as good a candidate as any.

amounts to the decisive reaffirmation of that original ranking. If so, then government does not stand in need of an eschatological re-authorization by Christ nor an ecclesiocentric re-legitimation, but rather a humble acceptance of its calling to 'public right action', not only for the church but for every person and community under its stewardship. If this is the case, then a political theology should not be 'dispensational', but simply 'restorative'.

O'Donovan, however, wishes to insist that secular government now bear the imprint of Christ's triumph in a *wholly unique* fashion, one not characteristic of other social institutions. He does not, for example, claim that institutions like families, schools, or voluntary associations bear this specific imprint. Why? Because, it seems, *they lack a specific analogy with the activity of divine salvation*. Or, rather, since divine salvation is manifested decisively, uniquely, in the exercise of *kingly* authority, the human analogy of such authority is its leading challenger, and so *the principal target* of divine judgement. Critics have observed that selecting the theme of 'the reign of God' as the unifying hermeneutical key to the biblical story is not the only legitimate option.[149] But even if we hold (as I do) that it is indeed close to the heart of the biblical narrative, we need not conclude that the assertion of the kingly rule of God is necessarily addressed uniquely or in any privileged way to human *political* authority. If such an assertion really is creation-wide, then while 'theology must be political if it is to be evangelical',[150] it must be many other things as well. It will not speak any *more* directly to political life than it does to any other dimension of human social life (economic, technological, familial, cultural, educational, and so on). Perhaps what we need, then, is not a dispensationalist political eschatology setting a creation-based 'society' at odds with a providence-based 'government', but rather a seamless creational eschatology laying all creatures – persons and institutions – equally open to the restorative impact of the gospel in this age and to the transformative hope of participation in the new earth under the just and gentle rule of Christ.[151]

---

[149] E.g., Hauerwas and Fodor, 'Remaining', 47.

[150] *DN*, 3.

[151] A point on which an apparently deep disagreement briefly surfaced during the Consultation was the theological legitimacy of the notion of a *felix culpa* (a 'happy fall'). The position we take on this will be intimately linked with our larger theology of creation, providence, salvation and history. If these linkages are indeed significant, this would seem to substantiate the important hermeneutical claim, made by Al Wolters in *Renewing Biblical Interpretation*, regarding the indispensable role, in any particular interpretative dispute (such as whether Rom. 13 teaches a 'remedial' concept of the state), of 'redemptive-historical analysis' as one of nine levels of interpretation he there distinguishes (Wolters, 'Confessional Criticism', 102). My critique of what I have called O'Donovan's dispensationalist political eschatology is closely linked to my rejection of the idea that the fall was in any way 'happy', in the sense that it was either always part of

Bibliography

Audi, R., and N. Wolterstorff, *Religion and the Public Square: The Place of Religious Convictions in Political Debate* (Lanham, MD: Rowman & Littlefield, 1997)

Black, A., 'Christianity and Republicanism: From St. Cyprian to Rousseau', *APSR* 91.3 (1997), 647–56

Burns, J.H. (ed.), *The Cambridge History of Political Thought 1450–1700* (Cambridge: CUP, 1991)

Chaplin, J.P., 'Christian Theories of Democracy', in *Contemporary Political Studies 1998*, II (ed. A. Dobson and J. Stanyer; Nottingham: Political Studies Association of the UK, 1998), 988–1003

——, 'Prospects for an Evangelical Political Philosophy', *ERT* 24.4 (2000), 354–73

D'Entrèves, A.P., *The Notion of the State* (Oxford: OUP, 1967)

God's plan of salvation, or necessary to the display of God's loving purposes for his good creation, or necessary to the revelation of God's kingship. Probing this further may take us close to the border of theological speculation (it certainly takes me beyond the territory of my own professional competence), but let me suggest – or rather *confess* – this: the creation of the universe was, as it were, a completely 'adequate' display of God's power and love, not in any way standing in need of further demonstrative assertion. The gradual, historical disclosure of its bountiful potentials by human discovery could only confirm that power and love. In the face of sin – that wholly unprecedented, inexplicable, culpable human deviation from God's good purposes – God determines to remain faithful to his creational intentions and so graciously, sovereignly, embarks upon an enterprise of cosmic redemption, climaxing in the Christ-event and culminating in the new heavens and new earth. This need not, and in my view should not, be seen as involving an 'improvement' on God's original creational design – how could the Creator's work be improved upon? Nor is it necessary to imply that creatures stood in need of redemption from the outset, nor that humans are in need of 'divinization', as if creatureliness were some form of temporary privation. It is true, of course, that, situated as we now are on the far side of the fall, we now know God not only as creator but also as redeemer: we have experienced things 'into which angels long to look' (1 Pet. 1:12) – we have been forgiven. I am open, therefore, to the proposal that we can now experience the love and power of God with a quality or intensity which would have been 'unavailable' to us in an unfallen world (not that this point thereby implies any kind of primordial incompleteness or deficiency). But this does not support the notion that the fall was, in anything other than a poetically suggestive sense, 'happy'. My approach to these questions has been partly shaped by the views of neo-Calvinist theologians such as Herman Bavinck (cf. Wolters, 'Nature and Grace') and is represented (theologically) in works such as Spykman, *Reformational Theology*; Mouw, *When the Kings*; and Wolters, *Creation Regained*; and (philosophically) in Dooyeweerd, *Roots*.

Dooyeweerd, H., *Roots of Western Culture: Pagan, Secular and Christian Options* (Toronto: Wedge, 1979)

——, 'The Christian Idea of the State', in H. Dooyeweerd, *Essays in Legal, Social and Political Philosophy* (Lampeter: Edwin Mellen Press, 1997), 121–55

Douglass, R.B., and D. Hollenbach (eds.), *Catholicism and Liberalism: Contributions to American Public Philosophy* (Cambridge: CUP, 1994)

Franklin, J.H. (ed.), *Constitutionalism and Resistance in the Sixteenth Century: Three Treatises by Hotman, Beza and Mornay* (New York: Pegasus, 1969)

Furnish, V.P., 'How Firm a Foundation? Some Questions About Scripture in *The Desire of the Nations*', *SCE* 11.2 (1998), 18–23

Gardner, E.C., *Justice and Christian Ethics* (Cambridge: CUP, 1995)

Gorringe, T., 'Authority, Plebs, Patricians', *SCE* 11.2 (1998), 24–29

Grasso, K.L., et al. (eds.), *Catholicism, Liberalism and Communitarianism* (Lanham, MD: Rowman & Littlefield, 1995)

——, 'Beyond Liberalism: Human Dignity, the Free Society and the Second Vatican Council', in *Catholicism, Liberalism and Communitarianism* (ed. K.L. Grasso, et al.; Lanham, MD: Rowman & Littlefield, 1995)

——, 'A Special Kind of Liberty: *Dignitatis Humanae*', in *Building the Free Society: Democracy, Capitalism and Catholic Social Teaching* (ed. G. Weigel and R. Royal; Washington, DC: EPPC; Grand Rapids: Eerdmans, 1993), 107–30

Gregory, E., 'Our Traditions? Christendom and Liberalism in Oliver O'Donovan', paper presented at the Second National Conference of Christians in Political Science, Calvin College, 17–20 June, 1999

Guinness, O., *The American Hour* (New York: Macmillan, 1993)

Hauerwas, S., and J. Fodor, 'Remaining in Babylon: Oliver O'Donovan's Defense of Christendom', *SCE* 11.2 (1998), 30–55

Lugo, L.E., 'Caesar's Coin and the Politics of the Kingdom: A Pluralist Perspective', in *Caesar's Coin Revisited: Christians and the Limits of Government* (ed. M. Cromartie; Washington, DC: EPPC; Grand Rapids: Eerdmans, 1996), 1–22

Maritain, J., *Man and the State* (Chicago: University of Chicago Press, 1951)

Monsma, S.V., and J.C. Soper (eds.), *Equal Treatment of Religion in a Pluralistic Society* (Grand Rapids: Eerdmans, 1998)

Mott, S.C., *A Christian Perspective on Political Thought* (New York: OUP, 1990)

Mouw, R.J., *When the Kings Come Marching In: Isaiah and the New Jerusalem* (Grand Rapids: Eerdmans, 1983)

——, and S. Griffioen, *Pluralisms and Horizons: An Essay in Christian Public Philosophy* (Grand Rapids: Eerdmans, 1993)

Murray, J.C., *Religious Liberty: Catholic Struggles with Pluralism* (ed. J.L. Hooper; Louisville, KY: Westminster/John Knox Press, 1993)

Newbigin, L., et al., *Faith and Power: Christianity and Islam in 'Secular' Britain* (London: SPCK, 1998)

O'Donovan, J.L., *George Grant and the Twilight of Justice* (Toronto: University of Toronto Press, 1984)

——, *Theology of Law and Authority in the English Reformation* (Atlanta: Scholars Press, 1991)

——, 'Political Authority and European Community: The Challenge of the Christian Political Tradition', *SJT* 47 (1994), 1–17

O'Donovan, O., 'Augustine's *City of God* XIX and Western Political Thought', *Dionysius* 11 (1987), 89–110

——, *Resurrection and Moral Order: An Outline for Evangelical Ethics* (Leicester: IVP; Grand Rapids: Eerdmans, 2nd edn, 1994)

——, *The Desire of the Nations: Rediscovering the Roots of Political Theology* (Cambridge: CUP, 1996)

——, 'Government as Judgment', *First Things* 92 (1999), 36–44

——, 'Response to Respondents: Behold the Lamb', *SCE* 11.2 (1998), 91–110

——, 'Deliberation, History and Reading: A Response to Schweiker and Wolterstorff', *SJT* 54.1 (2001), 127–44

——, and J.L. O'Donovan (eds.), *From Irenaeus to Grotius: A Sourcebook in Christian Political Thought 100–1625* (Grand Rapids: Eerdmans, 1999)

Rasmusson, A., 'Not All Justifications of Christendom Are Equal: A Response to Oliver O'Donovan', *SCE* 11.2 (1998), 69–76

Shanks, A., 'Response to *The Desire of the Nations*', *SCE* 11.2 (1998), 86–90

Sider, R., 'Towards an Evangelical Political Philosophy: An Agenda for Christians in the United States', *Transformation* 14.3 (1997), 1–10

Skillen, J.W., *Recharging the American Experiment: Principled Pluralism for Genuine Civic Community* (Grand Rapids: Baker Book House, 1994)

Skinner, Q., *The Foundations of Modern Political Thought* (2 vols.; Cambridge: CUP, 1978)

Song, R., *Christianity and Liberal Society* (Oxford: Clarendon Press, 1997)

Spykman, G., *Reformational Theology: A New Paradigm for Doing Dogmatics* (Grand Rapids: Eerdmans, 1992)

Taylor, C., *Sources of the Self: The Making of the Modern Identity* (Cambridge, MA: Harvard University Press, 1989)

Tierney, B., *Religion, Law and the Growth of Constitutional Thought 1150–1650* (Cambridge: CUP, 1982)

Villa-Vicencio, C., *A Theology of Reconstruction: Nation-building and Human Rights* (Cambridge: CUP, 1995)

Wolters, A., 'Nature and Grace in Bavinck', trans. of pp. 345–65 of J. Veenhof, *Revelatieen Inspiratie* (Amsterdam, 1968; Toronto: Institute for Christian Studies, n.d.)

——, *Creation Regained: Biblical Basics for a Reformational Worldview* (Grand Rapids: Eerdmans, 1985)

——, 'Confessional Criticism and the Night Visions of Zechariah', in *Renewing Biblical Interpretation* (ed. C. Bartholomew, C. Greene and K. Möller; SHS 1; Carlisle: Paternoster; Grand Rapids: Zondervan, 2000), 90–117

Wolterstorff, N., 'A Discussion of Oliver O'Donovan's *The Desire of the Nations*', *SJT* 54.1 (2001), 87–109

21

Response to Jonathan Chaplin

Oliver O'Donovan

It is a great satisfaction that the politics chair in Toronto's Institute for Christian Studies, founded by that fine teacher Bernard Zylstra, is now occupied by Jonathan Chaplin, who combines the neo-Calvinist theoretical richness with a critical finesse acquired, perhaps, in England – and Oxford can boast at least a contributory role in his development. I owe a great debt to his high-fidelity reading of my books, which has at several points helped me understand myself a little better, but especially for pointing out a contradiction which has hitherto gone unnoticed, by me at any rate, between *Resurrection and Moral Order* and *The Desire of the Nations*. In *Resurrection* I assumed that the subordination of power and tradition to justice was typical of all political authority; by the time of *Desire* I had reached the conclusion that it was a fruit of Christ's triumph.

Chaplin would like to draw me back to the view that I expressed in *Resurrection* and then forgot, by offering a more 'restorative' concept of God's action than shapes *Desire*. In other words, I must renounce the *felix culpa*.[1] It was always intended that justice should rule over tradition and Mary should be heaven's queen. Cain and Nimrod forgot it; but Jesus made it possible again. After the judges got it right, the equipoise was lost by Solomon, but then restored in David's true son and heir.

I find extraordinarily illuminating the way Chaplin connects this disagreement with my insistence on the 'Grotian negative'. In his famous definitions of 'right' in *De jure belli ac pacis* 1.1.1, Grotius first defines it as 'what is just – "just" being understood in a negative rather than a positive sense, to mean "what is not unjust"'. Injustice has epistemological priority over justice – which is to say, there are no 'principles' of justice before we render judgement on wrong. 'Wrong' in its turn is defined not in relation to any prior principles of justice, but in relation to created order.

This puts me into a deconstructive posture in relation to all abstract principles of justice from Aristotle to Rawls and, I would think, Chaplin. He himself

[1] For some further reflections on this theme see Chaplin's n. 150.

(n. 112) would like to distance himself from the opprobrious epithet 'abstract' by insisting on the relation of his principles of justice to created order, which is much to his credit. But there is a distinction to be made between justice as a 'special' virtue and the 'general justice' (or 'righteousness') that is simply the sum of all that is good to do. The law of creation is the reality that determines our ways. Justice, or right, is essentially *responsiveness* to the universal law, the successful determination of our ways under the authority of the law. Justice presupposes the possibility of injustice, as success presupposes the possibility of failure. Which is not to say that it presupposes the fall; it is founded on the alternative *posse vel peccare vel non peccare*, which belongs to the original createdness of humankind. Justice is the correspondence of our *self*-determination to our determination by the law; it is, in fact, obedience to the law. This is 'general justice' as Plato and Aristotle conceived it. Its ways are the ways of life. And at the level of general justice there are no 'principles of justice' other than the law of life itself, the order of things as they are.

Judgement, on the other hand, does presuppose the fall, for it is the response to actual wrong. Of judgement we can say that judgement is based on 'principles of justice', that is, of justice enacted as judgement, that are not simply repetitions of the law. For the ways of judgement are more limited than the ways of life, and its possibilities are more constrained than the possibilities of life. We are told, 'judge not, that you be not judged!', but never, 'refrain from justice!'. Judgement is a special activity that must be taken up and put down; there is a time for judgement and a time for abstaining from judgement, like the other activities in the preacher's list, though there is never a time for justice and a time for injustice. This special activity is governed by special principles, which are the principles of politics. It has its corresponding disciplines and virtues which we know as political virtues, and especially the virtue of 'special' justice. But these special principles and special virtues are not known directly from creation order; they are derived inductively, as heuristic descriptions, from the practice of judgement itself.

But judgement is the only practice of 'special justice' (or, in the unfortunate translation of Aristotle that gained pre-eminence in the West, 'particular' justice) that there is. There is no special virtue of justice, no special principles of justice, that are not *either* the law of the universe *or* the political principles by which judgement must be rendered. The virtue which Aristotle thought to identify and describe is an apparition on the borderline of political and non-political existence, formed out of the general obligation to obey particular judgements when they are made. If we single out some practice which we think of as 'just' in this special sense – say, paying bills in full and promptly – we may see that it is, on the one hand, generated by the special laws of our distinctive form of political existence. On the other hand, it is a function of our universal neighbourhood inseparable from the totality of what we owe one another as God's children. If we fail to pay a craftsman's bill, we are on the one hand failing to pay him due regard as a neighbour, in which case the 'injustice' of our failure is not interestingly different from any other species of malice to which he may fall victim, such as cruelty, greed or lust. If, on the other hand, we think we can recompense him by offering to give his daughter lessons in singing once a week, we are simply failing to understand or respect the contract-of-hire as a political form by which our relations are determined. The justice of paying bills arises from the meeting of the general justice to which we are universally bound and the special justice of a political device to which we are contingently bound. There is no middle-space between the two, independent of our moral obligation on the one hand, prior to our political obligation on the other; and the pursuit of such a middle-space is what I find 'abstract' in the idea of 'principles of justice'.

Chaplin invites me to acknowledge behind Leviticus 25 'a universal principle of justice requiring equitable distribution of essential material resources'. I do not need to acknowledge any such principle. It is enough to acknowledge the following features of created human society: a) the fundamentally common possession of material goods, and a secondary, administrative property in them; b) the multigenerational family as a productive economic unit in society and an object of proximate loyalty; c) territory as a defining material presupposition for the identity and effectiveness of social units. Given these three features, none of which are 'principles of justice', the destruction of family landholdings is a *prima facie* wrong, and the law protecting them is an act of judgement. If there is, nevertheless, a valid and useful principle of 'equitable distribution of resources', which there is, it will be serviceable only: a) in situations where distribution is necessary – which are actually rather specialized situations, and are certainly not envisaged in Leviticus 25; and b) in which the content of equity is moderately perspicuous. It will not as such help us decide whether the faculty of arts should get an equal share of the budget with the faculty of sciences, although the faculty of arts has twice as many students and a worse student-faculty ratio than the faculty of science, or whether adjustment should be made to enable the law faculty to pay salaries that can compete with the rewards of legal practice, or whether the medical school should count against the faculty of science, or be funded separately, and so on. The modest usefulness of the principle in calming the cruder form of budgetary warfare should not inspire us to promote it to the status of a universal principle of created order or to suggest that wherever justice is in question, this principle must be applied.

I agree that there is a proper distribution of functions within the work of government. In quarrelling with the notion of separation (not exclusively the US notion; I have Locke's view of the Williamite monarchy in my sights, too), I take issue on two points. 1) Accountability is not dependent upon the notion of separate powers; a court may be accountable to a higher court, an official to a higher official. Even where there is a highest figure, he can be accountable to a body with a different function without the two having to be constitutionally 'separated', as when a chairman is accountable to the very same board or committee which he ordinarily rules. 2) There must in any government be a point of closure, beyond which no further review of causes is possible; otherwise nothing could ever be settled. That is what is meant by 'sovereignty' in the older and less threatening sense, that is, *summa potestas*: some seat of authority settles arguments finally. A constitution must identify the seat of closure.

I don't 'advocate' unitary government, as Chaplin suggests, as though there were some other kind. I insist on it as a practical necessity of government. I am not even prepared to admit that I show a 'preference for a concentration rather than a dispersal of political power'. I simply dispute the theory of separate powers *as a theory*, challenging its ability to account plausibly for what really happens – in the United States or anywhere. It is a dangerous theory, not because it advocates a 'worse' form of government than unitary doctrines do, but simply because when taken literally (as political doctrines tend to be taken) it subverts government altogether. That is why I can appreciate, as Chaplin notes, the concrete steps taken in the sixteenth and seventeenth centuries to hold sovereigns accountable. Holding sovereigns accountable may be an excellent thing to do. My problem is with the doctrine that purports to explain *how* they are held accountable by positing three autonomous branches of government; but that was not the doctrine on which the sixteenth- and seventeenth-century constitutionalists, Calvinists among them, based themselves.

I add in passing, and by way of good humour, that I don't recognize the author of that famous epigram beginning 'all power corrupts' as any kind of representative of 'the Great Tradition', nor do I see it as a classically Christian idea that corruption is best spread as widely as possible!

Also in passing, I should acknowledge that what I wrote on the First Amendment in *Desire* may be historically wrong. I am prepared to listen sympathetically to the view that its original intention was to allow the states the prerogative of establishing religion and deny it only to the federal government. But the doctrine I wanted to identify was articulated elsewhere in the same period, and the point of the discussion was anyway not to answer the historical question of its source, but to examine a late-modern orthodoxy that nobody doubts prevailed eventually.

Chaplin offers as an alternative to my 'gentle support' for establishment a 'pluralist reading' of evangelical obedience, according to which 'the inner logic of the judicial task itself renders … privilege unacceptable in principle'. I insist on the 'public confession of Christian faith', while the pluralist holds that the state 'demonstrates its willingness to bow before the reign of Christ to the degree that … it relates to plural religious communities in an impartial way'. So far as I can see, our disagreement turns on this one proposition: that justice must include confessional silence, even in the face of error.[2] Which means that justice can be practised in community only when shorn of its fundamental reasons – reminiscent of Jacques Maritain and those 'private' reasons for teaching the democratic charter! The core of my anti-pluralism is the conviction that justice itself cannot survive such a scalping. Impartiality is not the essence of justice. Justice is a train of corrective reasoning about all the goods of human existence, from God to land allotments, and it can be nothing else. Cut it loose from such reasoning, and you have only an abstract formalism, a house swept and garnished waiting for seven worse devils, as the fate of recent Canadian jurisprudence has made shockingly evident. So we come back to the point of avoiding abstract principles of justice – that silence on my part about Rawls, which Chaplin kindly appreciated. But what of himself? Is he limping between two opinions, a neo-Calvinist YHWH-creator who made the world and all that is in it, and an English-speaking Baal of formal justice?

---

[2] Chaplin now responds to this characterization at his n. 106, but not so as to make me wish to withdraw it.

22

Revisiting Christendom: A Crisis of Legitimization

Colin J.D. Greene

Oliver O'Donovan's *The Desire of the Nations* has rightly been applauded as one of the most original, comprehensive and thoroughly biblically grounded works of political theology to appear in recent years. *DN* admirably demonstrates how imaginative biblical exegesis and interpretation, a profound grasp of the Christian tradition, and a trenchant refusal to engage in political theorizing in and for its own sake, can cast fresh light on both the political legacy of Christendom (that which O'Donovan refers to as early modern liberalism), and its dissolution in the social contract theories of modernity.

It is therefore potentially a contentious strategy, but nevertheless a necessary one, to claim that such a multifaceted and seminal work can in fact be better understood by highlighting its one central overarching thesis. While fully aware of the risks, I would like to suggest that what is so arresting and, for some theological commentators, so alarming, about *DN* is O'Donovan's rigorous and completely unapologetic attempt to retrieve the concept of authority as that which resides in every aspect of the biblical witness to God's revelatory covenant relationship with Israel, the Messiah, the church and the nations, and, so, correspondingly, as essential to the proper task of political theology today. In other words, the central and compelling thesis of *DN* is that 'theology, by developing its account of the reign of God, may recover the ground traditionally held by the notion of authority'.[1]

In what follows I would like to reinforce this perception and, to a certain extent, applaud its execution by tracing the role the concept of authority plays in the biblical foundation of O'Donovan's political theology. Secondly, I would like to take up a suggestion, only hinted at by O' Donovan himself, that there are other exegetical resources that one can marshal from the New Testament witness to the risen exalted Christ that show how this concept of authority inevitably collided with the political expectations of imperial

[1] *DN*, 19.

Rome. Thirdly, and most importantly from our point of view, I would like to argue that the fatal flaw in the impressive adventure of Christian mission we call Christendom was a fundamental conflict concerning how the triumph and authority of Christ should be realized among the nations. That conflict can be illustrated by reference to contradictory interpretations of one singularly important text, the Great Commission of Matthew 28:16–20,[2] which divided the political loyalties of East and West. In the course of this examination we will see that the system of dual authority (which O'Donovan, again, quite rightly derives from the biblical narrative), when applied to the realities of political power and rule in what has become known as the Christendom settlement, often rested on divergent and, many would contend, dubious, theological legitimization. This theological legitimization, it would appear to us at least, tended to confuse the notions of rule and society and so not surprisingly often skewed the practical realities of government both of church and empire in an absolutist direction. If, as it is often claimed, absolute power corrupts absolutely, or that bad theology inevitably leads to bad practice, then it was just such an insidious slide towards absolutism, with its corresponding proclivity for coercion, that sowed the seeds of destruction of the Christendom settlement. All of which is to claim that what O'Donovan refers to as the system of dual authority – that underlay the political aspirations of Christendom and manifested itself as a 'legal-constitutional conception'[3] – was in fact unsustainable. Nevertheless, it will also be our contention that it is precisely some such concept of dual authority, albeit in its original critically prophetic form, that we need to retrieve today to construct a viable political theology for our own time.

The Reign of God and the Concept of Authority

Critical interrogators of O'Donovan have sometimes protested that he spends an inordinate amount of time and exegetical energy investigating the Old Testament traditions concerning the rule and sovereignty of YHWH.[4] His primary reason for doing so, however, is to isolate the structure of authority that is inherent in the notion of divine rule. From this he extrapolates four

---

[2] This text in its present form is unique to Matthew and only hinted at in the reduced equivalents of Mk. 16:15–16 and Lk. 24:45–49.

[3] *DN*, 240.

[4] See, for instance, the rather carping criticism in this regard by Victor Paul Furnish, who accuses O' Donovan of privileging Israel's history 'as the medium through which God's rule is revealed' ('How Firm?', 19). To some extent, this theme is picked up by Walter Moberly's analysis of O'Donovan's use of the Old Testament in this volume.

complementary ways in which this rule or divine authority is expressed in Israel's history and community identity – salvation, judgement, possession and praise.

> YHWH's authority as king is established by the accomplishment of victorious deliverance, by the presence of judicial discrimination and by the continuity of a community-possession. To these three primary terms I add a fourth, which identifies the human response and acknowledgment of YHWH's reign: *t^e^hillāh* (praise).[5]

So God's authority translates into the realities of salvation or God's power over his creation, judgement and tradition. The appropriate human response to all of this is worship and obedience which refuses the pretensions of idolatry because 'the conjunction of power, judgment and tradition defines what political authority is'.[6] It is the primacy of such a notion of authority based on the idea of divine rule that O' Donovan vigorously defends as both ontologically prior and superior to other possible Old Testament political categories such as covenant, law and land.

The historical catastrophe and bitter experience of exile redefined Israel's understanding of political authority. From the fall of Jerusalem to the Babylonians and onwards, Israel had to learn to live with two authorities, two rules, indeed two conflicting political realities – Jerusalem and Babylon.

> Augustine did not misread the text in taking it as the model for his conception of two political entities coexistent in one time and space (*C. Faustum* XII.36; *City of God* 19.26). We need only enter the caveat that there are two ways of identifying the duality in this situation: on the one hand, there are two 'cities', the social entities of Israel and Babylon which live side by side; on the other, there are the two 'rules' under which Israel finds itself, that of Babylon and that of YHWH.[7]

According to O'Donovan, it is here that we locate the biblical conception of dual authority that now will persist for God's people until the eschaton.[8]

With the coming of the Messiah, however, this political configuration was destined to change. Indeed, it was decisively under threat because Jesus both proclaimed and embodied the primacy of YHWH's rule.

> Jesus' teaching-ministry, then, is taken by the evangelists to be something more than instruction. It is a disclosure of the reign of God, through which the authority of God asserts itself. Jesus' authority consists in his capacity to bring us directly into contact with God's authority.[9]

---

[5] *DN*, 36.
[6] *DN*, 233.
[7] *DN*, 83.
[8] This point is also drawn out by Wolterstorff in 'Discussion', 93.
[9] *DN*, 89.

O'Donovan's refusal to engage in the Enlightenment preference for a depoliticized Jesuology, in favour of a full-blown christological reformulation of the nature of political authority, eventuates in an interpretation of the Jesus story in terms of four central themes: advent, passion, resurrection and exaltation. Again, however, what is distinctive to all four movements within this overarching narrative is the mediation of God's authority. So advent, exemplified not primarily by the birth narratives found only in Luke and Matthew, but by the baptism of Jesus common to all the gospels, discloses that this 'event is focused upon the divine act of authorisation'.[10] Not surprisingly the passion constitutes the confrontation of divine authority, representatively expressed in the person of Jesus, with all other authorities and rulers who challenged his embodiment of the sovereignty of God's kingdom. In that sense, Jesus inevitably '... unsettled the Two Kingdoms conception, which had, in one way or another, shaped Israel's understanding of its political situation since the exile. He announced the coming of God's Kingdom to sweep away existing orders of government.'[11]

This, as O'Donovan claims quite rightly, is how the question of authority had to be settled. With this we would concur, because either Jesus' claim to represent the authority of God's rule is true, in which case it relativizes all other forms of authority or, as his persecutors thought, he was correctly indicted on the charge of blasphemy and public insurrection.[12]

The resurrection of Jesus is the restoration of God's created order, and as such represents the triumph of God's reign and authority over all that opposed it and the empowerment or authorization of the new humanity that Jesus' death and resurrection inaugurated. The exaltation or ascension of Jesus, which is deliberately described for us with coronation language (Ps. 2:1), is the vindication of Jesus as the Christ, the bearer of divine authority both in heaven and earth.

> This unspeakable event had political significance. It was not a private vindication but a public one; it was the fulfilment of the political promise which Jesus had come to bring, and his own authorisation as the representative of the Kingdom of God.[13]

These four interlocking motifs, taken together as a single story, constitute the historical and public manifestation of the authority of God's rule in the life history and destiny of Jesus of Nazareth. The coming of the Messiah, his death, resurrection and exaltation to the right hand of the Father, necessarily involves a christological regrounding of the nature of political power that

---

[10] *DN*, 134.
[11] *DN*, 137.
[12] *DN*, 138.
[13] *DN*, 145.

makes all other rules and authorities subordinate and subservient to his reign. 'He disarmed the rulers and authorities and made a public example of them, triumphing over them in it' (Col. 2:15).[14] 'That must be the primary eschatological assertion about the authorities, political and demonic, which govern the world: they have been made subject to God's sovereignty in the Exaltation of Christ.'[15]

In that sense, secular authority in the New Testament is simultaneously deauthorized and reauthorized. It is deauthorized in terms of the demonic and ultimately idolatrous ambitions of empire as graphically described for us in the apocalypse of John. It is reauthorized in terms of the limited authority now granted to state, nation or empire to provide a social space for the church's mission so that the Son of Man, who has been lifted up, can continue to draw all people to himself. This reauthorization of secular power is now limited to the judicial task. This is the surprising conclusion O'Donovan deduces from Paul's defence of secular authority in Romans 13:1–7, because this is how the wrath of God is realized in the affairs of government and empire.

> What has now changed is the privileging of this aspect of governmental authority, so that the whole rationale of government is seen to rest on its capacity to effect the judicial task. Here, it seems to me, is a novelty not anticipated either in classical or in Old Testament sources.[16]

This christological reauthorization of secular government allows not only a social space for the church's mission, but also a proper ecclesiological ordering of the church's authority as a political reality.

> Describing the church as a political society means to say that it is brought into being and held in being, not by a special function it has to fulfil, but by a government that it obeys in everything. It is ruled and authorised by the ascended Christ alone and supremely; it therefore has its own authority; and it is not answerable to any other authority that may attempt to subsume it.[17]

Consequently, Pentecost was the divine authorization of the church in its own unique mode of ecclesial existence. This existence recapitulates the narrative of Jesus' life so that his representative status as the new Adam is again discovered

---

[14] Colin Gunton notes, for instance, that 'There is a political Christ: not only the one depicted in the Gospels as coming to grief in the political-religious cauldron of first-century Judaea, but also the one crucified by "the rulers of this age" (1 Cor. 2:8), however those ambiguous entities be conceived' (*Yesterday and Today*, 199).

[15] *DN*, 146.

[16] *DN*, 148.

[17] *DN*, 159.

within the corporate life of the church. It is only when we perceive the church as rooted in the representative authority of the Christ-event that we can avoid the cardinal error of civil religion – a church answerable and subservient to other powers and thrones rather than that single power and authority by which alone it is legitimized. While the political authority of the church caught between the eschatological tension of the already and the not yet is by necessity therefore hidden and opaque, it is nevertheless capable of manifesting itself in historical form. It is at this juncture in his argument that O'Donovan introduces not his defence or exoneration of the Christendom ideal but, as he admits, an inevitably contested historical description and theological interpretation of how it came to embody what he refers to as the system of dual authorization.[18]

At this stage we need to say something about O'Donovan's methodological and interpretative framework as far as the biblical narrative is concerned. Clearly here is a moral and practical theologian who takes the Bible as Scripture, as sacred text, seriously. O'Donovan's riposte to those who complain that his story of Israel is a hermeneutical construct that we should not necessarily be too enamoured with would be, 'what story would you put in its place?' For surely a nineteenth-century history of religions story or an ideologically contaminated modern story is equally a hermeneutical construct. Like O'Donovan, I also wish to expostulate with those within the guild of biblical scholarship who continually privilege their own exegetical presuppositions by claiming that a narratival or a salvation history approach to Scripture is somehow an illegitimate conceptual construction that apparently ignores the plurality of contexts and sources within Scripture itself.[19] Similarly, to those who contend that this narrative leaves too little room for other stories about human identity and experience or indeed human possession and flourishing,[20] O'Donovan would reply that a biblical theologian receives and interprets all such alternatives through a given revelation. This revelation is the canonical narrative of a historically called and chastened Israel, whose vocation and identity comes to fruition and fulfilment in Jesus the Christ.[21] As Christian scholars we are, according to O'Donovan, involved in an exercise of deliberative reasoning that is at all times christologically grounded and conditioned. There is thus room for the paradigmatic status of Israel as witness to the rule of God among the nations, but this grounding also protects the necessary historical diastasis between the old and new covenants.

---

[18] See O'Donovan, 'Response', 104.

[19] In this regard see O'Donovan's critical engagement with Furnish over precisely this matter in 'Response', 95–97.

[20] See the criticism of O'Donovan in this regard by Wolterstorff, 'Discussion', and Schweiker, 'Freedom'.

[21] See O'Donovan's reply to both Wolterstorff and Schweiker in 'Deliberation'.

> 'Salvation-history', then, is not to be thought of as an ingenious 'method' brought to bear upon a long-suffering text. It proceeds simply from the canon and the *regula fidei*, that we allow room in reading Scripture both for the Jewish paradigm and for historical distance in relation to it.[22]

It should now be clear that O'Donovan's retrieval of the concept of authority as located in the biblical notion of God's rule pervades not just the exegetical heights he endeavours to scale, but also the subsequent political topography he intends to traverse. Modern people have repudiated all forms of authority, including that of Scripture, in favour of human autonomy. We, of course, have become used to hearing in the text the deafening roar of ideological or class interest. Therefore, not surprisingly, some have accused O'Donovan of simply shouting louder – but this time in the interests of 'a patrician defence of the hegemony of the ruling class'.[23] Others ask for a more pluralist approach to political theology that would reinstate other political concepts – for instance, that of shepherding or household governance[24] – apparently to blunt the rather hard-nosed realism of this premodern notion of authoritative government.

O'Donovan might have more readily convinced the doubters had he trawled more widely and brought some other significant christological exegetical material into the fray.[25] This would, if anything, have served to strengthen his case. We now turn to an investigation of one such exegetical resource – one which O'Donovan notes in passing before he moves on to concentrate on Jesus' role as the mediator of God's rule and as the representative individual.

> If political theology cannot perform its task by striking out on its own into Jesuology, it must learn how to perform it Christologically, making its way along that stream which flows from the apostles' proclamation of Christ as 'Lord' to the later, ontologically developed definitions of the ecumenical creeds.[26]

---

[22] O'Donovan, 'Deliberation', 141. Clearly, some of O'Donovan's interpreters wonder whether, in applying the maxim of historical distance, he does actually allow room for the discontinuities that this implies, or whether in the end deliberative reasoning privileges conceptual analysis over and against the inherent plasticity and superfluity of meaning found in the text. These issues, however, are mainly to do with the philosophy of language rather than being criticisms of the exegetical basis to O'Donovan's political theology.

[23] Gorringe, 'Authority', 25.

[24] So, e.g., Hauerwas and Fodor, 'Remaining', 47–48.

[25] This observation is turned into a complaint by Victor Paul Furnish when he asks of O'Donovan, 'Or again, why does he not look to *Jesus*' proclamation of God's reign, or to the earliest church's proclamation of Christ's lordship for his definitive political concepts?' ('How Firm?', 19). I would say that O'Donovan does pay sufficient attention to the former, but not to the latter.

[26] *DN*, 123.

Jesus: Lord of Lords

As long ago as 1977, James Dunn asked whether there is an underlying unity to the diverse christological confessions we find in the New Testament. In his seminal and important work *Unity and Diversity in the New Testament*, he attempted to demonstrate that there is a common core to the early Christian kerygma about Jesus, of which there are three components.

1. First of all, and most important for our purposes, is the proclamation of the present Lordship of Christ by virtue of his resurrection and exaltation.
2. Secondly, there is the call for a response of faith and commitment to Jesus as the risen Lord.
3. Thirdly, there is the promise of a continuing relationship between the one who believes and the exalted Christ – the experience of salvation.[27]

Dunn's search for a christological norm around which the New Testament witness to Jesus as the fulfilment of Israel's story might be grouped would be challenged nowadays by those who recognize and welcome the indisputable christological pluralism present in the New Testament writings themselves.[28] Indeed, Dunn's own subsequent work has moved in a similar direction.[29] Nevertheless, 'Jesus is Lord' is the principle confession of faith in the Pauline corpus. It occurs some 230 times in Paul's epistles alone.

> Jesus is Lord is the basic confession at conversion-initiation (Rom.10:9). Jesus is Lord is the distinguishing mark of inspiration by the Spirit of God (1 Cor. 12:3). Jesus is Lord is the climactic expression of the universe's worship in Phil. 2:11.[30]

The expression also appears many times in Luke-Acts. For instance, it is the basic content of the gospel Peter preached to his contemporaries in his Pentecost sermon: 'This Jesus whom you crucified, God has made both Lord and Christ' (Acts 2:36). While it is true that in the Gospels, where it occurs infrequently, the title may signify nothing more than an honorific address, after the resurrection this confession denotes a person who both possesses divinely given authority and shares God's divinity itself.

> Therefore God has highly exalted him and bestowed on him the name which is above every name, that at the name of Jesus every knee should bow, in heaven and earth and under the earth, and every tongue confess that Jesus Christ is Lord. (Phil. 2:9–11)

---

[27] Dunn, *Unity and Diversity*, 30.

[28] See Matera, *New Testament Christology*, also Powell and Bauer (eds.), *Who Do You Say that I Am?*.

[29] See, e.g., Dunn, *Christology*.

[30] Dunn, *Unity and Diversity*, 50.

Jesus himself acknowledged that his authority is a delegated one given to him by the Father: 'all authority in heaven and earth has been given to me' (Mt. 28:18). That authority is invested in him by virtue of his resurrection and exaltation. And it is an authority which he in turn can delegate to his disciples to baptize in the name, and therefore also in the power and authority, of the Father, Son and Holy Spirit.

There are, of course, different ways in which such a delegated authority can be understood. So, for instance, John Macquarrie, acknowledging his debt to Graham Stanton, asserts that, because the title *Kyrios* is one denoting rank or worth, it expresses Jesus' authority over the individual or the church. Consequently, he says, it is best understood as an existential Christology, pertaining only to the realm of personal relationships.[31]

Such a conclusion is only possible if we forget that, associated with the idea of authority, as O'Donovan has been at pains to point out, is the notion of kingship or reign, well expressed by the writer of the Apocalypse: 'the kingdom of the world has become the kingdom of our Lord and of his Christ and he shall reign for ever and ever' (Rev. 11:15). It is for this reason that Jesus can be hailed as 'Lord of lords and King of kings' in Revelation 17:14 – a text which, along with others, fuelled the millenarian hopes of the early church.[32] In 1 and 2 Thessalonians, for instance, the dignity and authority of Jesus the *Kyrios* are those of the returning eschatological judge, a conscious re-echoing of the Son of Man figure we find in Psalm 110:1 and Daniel 7:13.[33] In the present volume, Tom Wright, in discussion with other New Testament scholars, argues convincingly that the Pauline confession that Jesus is the *Kyrios*, the essential core of the gospel of salvation, was deliberately framed at least in Paul's letter to the Romans (with similar emphases in Philippians and Thessalonians) in such a way as to counteract the essentially idolatrous politico-religious aspirations of imperial Rome.[34] One makes such audacious claims from within the white heat of eschatological expectation and the imminent threat of martyrdom. Indeed, such millenarian hopes that Jesus the heavenly king would soon establish his kingdom here on earth carried on well into the second century, and it was such expectations that could not fail to be interpreted by the representatives of Caesar as a political threat.

---

[31] Macquarrie, *Jesus Christ*, 45–46; cf. also Stanton, 'Incarnational Christology', 155.

[32] In this regard, Rev. 20 was particularly important. Taking up the prophecy of Daniel (Dan. 7:17–27) concerning the four kingdoms, they interpreted the fourth as the Roman Empire.

[33] Cf. Marshall, *Origins*, 102–4.

[34] Wright, 'Paul and Caesar'.

The Early Church

In some respects, New Testament scholars are rediscovering what church historians have long recognized – namely, that in Roman society the religious cult of either a local deity or, later, of the emperor himself, guaranteed political and social stability and therefore was only to be interfered with on pain of death. To begin with, Christians were accused of being atheists. Justin acknowledged this charge, because they had forsaken belief in the traditional pagan gods. 'Thus, we are even called atheists. We do confess ourselves atheists before those whom you regard as gods, but not with respect to the Most True God.'[35] Their allegiance to Jesus as the *Kyrios*, however, inevitably relativized the absolute authority of the Roman emperor as well and brought down upon them a recurring cycle of indiscriminate persecution and social ostracism.

The account of the martyrdom of Polycarp of Smyrna stands as irrefutable evidence of such persecution. The proconsul demanded, 'swear by the genius of Caesar (in other words acknowledge Caesar as Lord and King) and I will release you: curse the Christ'. Polycarp replied, 'For 86 years I have been the servant of Jesus Christ and he never did me any injury. How then can I blaspheme my King who has saved me?'[36] Moreover, recent research has concluded that the imperial cult functioned as a kind of dominant ideological metanarrative, drawing all other religions and cultures under its sway and rewarding its devotees with Roman citizenship. Christians who refused to adjust their belief system accordingly risked economic and political isolation and alienation.[37]

Clearly the early Christians were not political revolutionaries engaged in a plot to overthrow the empire from below, and they protested their innocence in this regard on numerous occasions.[38] Similarly, the antimillenarians spiritualized the kingdom, claiming it was a kingdom not of this world, and they pointed to their custom of demonstrating loyalty to the empire through prayers for the safety of the empire and protection of the imperial house. But even they could pledge only loyalty and obedience, not worship – for that would be to accept the emperor as divine, indeed the *Kyrios*, a title reserved for Jesus alone.

Inevitably, therefore, the central Christian confession Jesus is *Kyrios* came into conflict with the imperial claims of Caesar for absolute sovereignty and rule. Christians could sanguinely acknowledge, if not fully participate in, the socio-economic benefits of the empire. But they could not bow the knee in

[35] Justin Martyr, *First Apology*, 6.38–39.

[36] Bettenson, *Documents*, 10.

[37] See Howard-Brook and Gwyther, *Unveiling Empire*.

[38] Tertullian, 'Christian Loyalty to the Emperor', *Apol.* xxix–xxxii; see Bettenson, *Documents*, 7.

political and religious homage to the emperor. The sovereignty of Rome had to give way to the absolute sovereignty of Jesus, Lord of lords and King of kings. The faith of the early first- and second-century Christians could not remain a private, individualized, personal religion. It inevitably became a public acknowledgement that the rule of Christ encompassed every domain of life. This explains, as Jaroslav Pelikan acknowledges, why it was some of the most morally and politically astute of the emperors, Marcus Aurelius and Diocletian, for instance, who persecuted Christians with a ferocity not previously experienced – simply because Christians could not afford to the emperor the absolute loyalty and allegiance he demanded in return for political stability and protection.[39] In this constellation of competing political ideologies there can only be one with ultimate authority. In that sense, the basic missionary proclamation Jesus is the *Kyrios*, when pitted against the claims of empire, could mean only one thing – all other powers and rules are subordinate and subservient to his reign. In a pagan environment where the emperor has assumed divinity to himself, this can only be a dangerous ideology as far as the gospel is concerned that must be exposed as such by recourse to a higher authority and name (Phil. 2:9–11; Rom. 14:11–12).

Romans 13

What, then, of Paul's acceptance, and indeed apparent legitimization, of the role and authority of both empire and emperor in the disputed passage of Romans 13? In this regard, a number of comments can be made. First of all, there is a fundamental difference between an explicit theological endorsement and a pragmatic Jewish acceptance of the role of governments, foreign or otherwise, in preventing a return to civil disorder and chaos. Both Deutero–Isaiah and the Wisdom of Solomon acknowledge that, even in the realm of international politics, the providential wisdom of God holds sway. In the light of Colossians 1:16 and 2:15, I suggest that Paul recognized that all things in heaven and earth can be both created and redeemed to serve the purposes of Christ – governments included. Would it be right to claim on the basis of these texts that here we have both a creational (Col. 1:16) and a christological (Col. 2:15) justification of the role of government respectively, or do these texts fall within that broader recognition of the providential role of civil authorities to which we have just eluded? Similarly, it seems that these texts do not necessarily imply a theological relegitimization that limits governments to being juridical instruments of the wrath of God. Indeed, Romans13:6–7 suggests that Paul recognized fiscal and civil responsibilities that are the lot of governments as agents of civil order as well.

[39] Pelikan, *Jesus*, 50.

Consequently, would not an explicit theological legitimization of the role of civil authority have to decide whether rulers, powers and governments belong to the created order, as Colossians 1:16 suggests, or to the realm of history, as O'Donovan claims, where politics always remains a matter of providential ordering which, according to Colossians 2:15, has now become diaphanous to the redeeming rule of Christ?[40] In Colossians, Paul appears to say both things without any apparent conflict of interest. And, in Romans 13, he may in fact be simply accepting the wisdom of Jewish tradition without attempting to construct a theological *tour de force* in respect to the role of the governing authorities *per se*.

In fact, the key to what is implied in Romans 13 could be found in the rest of his letter – namely, that the imperial ideology of Rome should be subversively undermined by doggedly proclaiming Jesus as the *Kyrios*, and by equally robustly preserving the unity of the church, which is the medium that legitimates the message. On the other hand, rulers and authorities that serve the providential interests of God by restraining the natural instincts and vice of humanity (Rom. 13:8–10), thereby allowing for the spread of the Christian gospel, belong to another, more restricted, level of theological adjudication. The gospel delegitimizes by refusing the office of divine authority to any other than the Christ who died and returned to life so that he could be Lord of all (Rom. 14:9). The same gospel, however, recognizes in a much more pragmatic sense the divinely ordained function of those persons and governments whose vocation it is to maintain the welfare of the city and all its inhabitants therein. We must now turn to the manner in which the same issues were pursued in a very different cultural and political context.

The Christendom Settlement

'When the Western world accepted Christianity, Caesar conquered; and the received text of Western theology was edited by his lawyers.'[41]

We now investigate the crisis of theological legitimization that ensued when the emperor accepted the faith his predecessors had tried unsuccessfully to eradicate. Again we will see that whether it was lawyers, bishops or theologians, the notion of dual authority, or church and state both under and sustainers of the rule and authority of the Word of God, became extraordinarily difficult to maintain.

In the annals of church history and Christian doctrine, nothing has provoked a more ambiguous reaction than the Emperor Constantine's

---

[40] O'Donovan, 'Deliberation', 137.

[41] Whitehead, *Process and Reality*, 520.

endorsement of the Christian faith with the Milan Protocol of 313. The decisive event in his career was his victory over Maxentius in 312 at the Milvian Bridge outside Rome. This gave him control over the whole of the west, including Rome, and he attributed his victory to the intervention of the deity who had chosen him to be an instrument of world government and so consolidate the famous *Pax Romana*. More specifically, according to Lactantius, a tutor in the emperor's household,[42] Constantine was supposedly directed in a dream before the battle to mark his soldiers' shields with a particular heavenly sign – the Greek letters *chi* and *rho* – later interpreted as the sign of the cross. The significance of Constantine's vision has been the subject of vigorous historical debate. Nevertheless, as T.D. Barnes observed:

> Since his accession, Constantine had given the Christian church political support; from the Battle of the Milvian Bridge onwards, he publicly proclaimed himself God's servant and the church's champion.[43]

Christians did not hesitate to interpret their change of fortunes as a sign of divine providence – an attitude that was later very evident in the triumphalist Christology of Eusebius of Caesarea.

Eusebius, friend of the emperor and court historian, worked out his imperial Christology in accord with the spirit of Origen.[44] The emperor is perceived as a copy, or image, of the divine Logos who rules in the heavenly spheres. As the Logos rules as vicegerent to the Father's kingdom, so the emperor rules and prepares his subjects for the rule of the Saviour. As the Logos fights against principalities and powers in the heavenly realm, so the emperor defeats the rulers of this present age in the power of the symbol of the conquering Saviour. The whole universe was in effect *logikos*, sustained by the Word and his image on earth, the emperor.

> The Word of God, the second person of the Trinity, mediates the kingship of God to facilitate the exercise of kingship by mankind, the 'kingly species'; so that the emperor, ruling first over himself and then over his empire, embodies at once God's kingship, as its 'image', and man's. He is at once law-governed (*ennomos*) and absolute (*autokratorike*). Again, since the unity is the presupposition of kingship, monotheism is the presupposition of its true exercise. Into this constellation of ideas Eusebius

---

[42] Lactantius, *Mort.*, 44; *Inst.*, 4.26–27; *Epit.*, 47, quoted in Pelikan, *Jesus*, notes for 48–58, 240.

[43] Barnes, *Constantine and Eusebius*, 43.

[44] Cf. von Balthasar, *Origenes*. Von Balthasar comments that if we remove the Origenistic shine from Eusebius, we are left with nothing but a second-rate, semi-Arian theologian. Quoted in Küng, *Great Christian Thinkers*, 44.

> draws Origen's conception of the providential role of the Roman Empire as a unifying force provided to facilitate the spread of the gospel.[45]

It is clear how Jesus' claim to divine authority in Matthew 28:18 is here being understood. God the Father, King of the universe, has conferred authority on Jesus, the representative of his kingship on earth. That authority has now been transferred to Jesus' vicegerent, the emperor. Here both divine rule and the rule of the emperor are conflated at the expense of adequately maintaining the distinction between church and empire. In effect, what emerges is a slide toward a Caesaro-papist conception of secular government. This was the system of political authority that evolved over three centuries in Byzantine Christendom, at least from the time of Constantine to Justinian the Great, and is well expressed in the Byzantine ceremony of coronation.[46] Here the intermingling of a religious and political settlement amounted to a theological reauthorization of secular government that could hardly concur with that limitation of secular political power which, according to O'Donovan, the resurrection and exaltation of Jesus demanded.

In fact, whether or not Constantine really accepted Christianity in a personal sense is in one way beside the point.[47] Clearly, as both O'Donovan and Barnes point out, a monarchical monotheism served the purposes of political monarchy represented by the absolutist emperor here on earth.[48] Christianity clearly fitted the bill in this regard, and the imperial Christology of Eusebius was a later theological construction that made precisely that point. Indeed, if Christ the King had elected to exercise his sovereignty over the world through the emperor, to whom he had appeared in visions and given victory in battle, then it was incumbent upon the emperor to call the first ecumenical council at Nicaea for the purpose of restoring doctrinal and political concord to both church and empire alike. According to Eusebius, the inclusion of the formula that Christ was of one being or substance with the Father was the result of a direct intervention by the emperor, which probably explains why a second-rate, semi-Arian theologian like Eusebius would have accepted the *homoousios* clause in the first place. What happened subsequently was, however, even more significant. Constantine then wrote to all of the churches in the provinces, explaining that 'whatever is determined in the holy assemblies of the bishops, is to be regarded as indicative of the divine will'. He then issued an edict against heretics, forbidding them to gather and confiscating all their church buildings.[49] Constantine remained much more implacably opposed to

---

[45] O'Donovan and O'Donovan, *Irenaeus*, 57.

[46] Pelikan, *Jesus*, 54.

[47] See the discussion on this matter by MacMullen, 'Christianity'.

[48] Barnes, *Constantine and Eusebius*, 43.

[49] Eusebius, *Constantine* 3.20, 64–65, quoted in Pelikan, *Jesus*, 240.

heretics than to pagans, because he recognized that unruly affairs of doctrine easily led to equally unruly affairs of state. Clearly, here is an emperor who does not see his role as solely limited to matters of juridical intent. Indeed, the christological cross-fertilization that resulted from this elevation of the emperor at least implied, if it did not always clearly articulate, precisely what Paul disallowed – namely, the divinization of imperial rule.

For instance, such a political use of Christology led to the emergence of imperial Christology. A transference took place in which titles originally given to the emperor were attributed to Christ, who became *Christus Imperator*, ruler or Lord of the world. Correspondingly, the emperor was given titles that originally referred to Christ, such as servant of God, shepherd and peace-maker.[50] The title 'Lord of Glory', which originally had an apocalyptic meaning, was also politicized. With the continuation of the Holy Roman Empire, Christ was viewed as the *Rex Gloriae*, the triumphant Lord, who continues to subdue the kingdoms of this world by the power of the emperor.

Quite apart from the issues of political expediency, it is clear, as is so often the case in christologies from above, that the *Christus Imperator* is one who has been surrounded by an ever-increasing weight of divinity, almost to the total exclusion of the real humanity of Christ. If more attention had been paid to the latter, then it would have been clear that the cross of Christ is the symbol of one who forsook political aggrandizement and refused to extend the Father's kingdom through the use of battalions and armies. Similarly, the *Rex Gloriae* is the one who, it was claimed, would, 'rule the nations with a rod of iron' (Rev. 2:27; 12:5; 19:15). Little or no account was taken, however, of the original references to Jeremiah 1:10; 23:29, where it is clearly the Word of God (the living personified word of God) which will rule in this manner. Nor was any real allowance made for the fact that the one who is worthy to occupy the throne of heaven is also the Lamb who was slain before the foundation of the world. These and other considerations show us, as Colin Gunton acknowledges, that:

> The imperial Christ was a product of dogmatic divinity abstracted from the gospel accounts of the human Jesus. When the divinity was separated from the humanity it became possible to adapt the doctrine of the divinity of Christ to the political needs of the day.[51]

Here, as is so often the case in the history of Christology, precisely what had been forbidden by Chalcedon – separation of Christ's divinity and humanity – had in fact taken place.

O'Donovan appears more sanguine about all of this, because he claims that Eusebius viewed Constantine as the royal man. The emperor was chosen by

---

[50] Cf. Studer, *Trinity*, 127–32.

[51] Gunton, *Yesterday and Today*, 198.

God to establish a viable political alternative to warring national factions, which were in turn the product of polytheism. The victory of Christ over the principalities and powers in the heavenlies was expressed on earth by a corresponding political settlement. The more insidious error with Eusebius' political Christology, according to O'Donovan, was the conflation of the imperial office with the notion of divine rule, with the consequent loss of the eschatological tension between this present age and the consummation of the divine rule that is yet to come.[52] But precisely that kind of illegitimate realized eschatology allowed the emperor to be perceived 'as a kind of Christ surrogate'[53] authorized by divine rule and participating in the divine being through the mediation of the divine Logos. In a neo-Platonic cosmology, imperial office receives its divine authorization through ontological participation in the reality of divine rule. For as Eusebius intones,

> This is he who holds a supreme dominion over this whole world, who is over and in all things and pervades all things visible and invisible, the Word of God. From whom and by whom our divinely favoured emperor, receiving as it were a transcript of the divine sovereignty, directs in imitation of God himself the administration of this world's affairs ...[54]

Similarly, in such a situation salvation was internalized and so inevitably the business of establishing the *imperium sacrum* was left to the emperors and the political processes over which they held sway.[55] So while in one sense it is correct to claim that the Christendom settlement in the East left the notion of two societies, church and state, more or less intact, it is difficult to see how this represents a system of dual authority. Constantine may have shown proper deference to the representatives of the church, but it is clear where the real power lay and how indeed an improper theological legitimization of this rule infringed upon the glory of the divinity of Christ, who alone holds sway over the kingdoms of the world.

The Christendom Settlement in the West

It is, however, possible to draw the lines of connection between the eternal kingship of Christ and the temporal kingship of earthly rulers in several different ways. In the East, the chain of command was understood to run from the

---

52 Cf. *DN*, 197–98.

53 *DN*, 197.

54 Eusebius, 'Speech', 60.

55 Moltmann, *Way*, 31.

Father to the Son, or Logos, and hence to the emperor, who was the Son's vicegerent on earth. As we have noted, this is one possible way of interpreting Jesus' words in the Great Commission. The model adopted by Constantine and Eusebius, however, was not the only alternative.

It was possible to interpret Jesus' words in a rather different sense, and this was the way things were understood in the Christian West. Christ's authority was given first of all to the apostles, an authority to make disciples and therefore ensure the spread and survival of the Christian church. To one of these, Peter, had already been given the authority to bind and loose sins and so, the theory went, this also included the authority to bind and loose political power. In this model, the line is drawn from God to Christ to Peter, the first pope, and from Peter to his successors and then to emperors and kings.[56]

The origins of this viewpoint can be seen in Ambrose of Milan's uncompromising attitude to successive Roman emperors. Indeed, in Ambrose's case we find a Christian bishop who

> ... could rally his church to a vision of church-world relations that has nothing in common with the Eusebian emperor-theology, and is heavy with echoes of the pre-Constantinian conflict, above all in the importance assigned to the memory of the martyrs. That church was coming to see its relation to the authorities in confrontational terms, as though nothing had changed.[57]

A classic example of such confrontational tactics was Ambrose's attitude to Theodosius the Great, who was hailed as the champion of Nicene orthodoxy at the Council of Constantinople in 381. Ambrose actually refused communion to Theodosius until he repented over his use of excessive force in the retaliatory measures taken in the case of a riot against the imperial garrison at Thessalonica. It is clear that Ambrose regarded the emperor, hailed as the saviour of the Catholic faith, as simply another lay Christian who must submit to episcopal discipline like everyone else. In Ambrose's opinion, the church needed to clear a space for herself in the affairs of the empire where she could protect her doctrinal heritage without interference from the emperor and express her witness to Christ in the preservation of civil liberties and in opposition to capital punishment and private wealth. As others have noted, here we have a credible *via media* between the political autocracy of Eusebius and the martyr church of Tertullian.[58]

---

[56] Cf. Pelikan, *Jesus*, 53–56.

[57] O'Donovan and O'Donovan, *Irenaeus*, 67.

[58] See O'Donovan and O'Donovan, *Irenaeus*, 23–25 (on Tertullian); 66–70 (on Ambrose).

> On the other hand, the emperor, refused the privilege of interfering in the church's affairs, was himself by no means immune from interference. 'In a case of faith', Ambrose reminded Valentinian, he was subject to the bishop's jurisdiction. The church expected the emperor to act like a Christian, and when he failed to do so it claimed the right to censure him. On several occasions Ambrose withdrew communion from emperors, sometimes for moral, sometimes for doctrinal causes.[59]

It is here that we really see the system of dual authority beginning to emerge. But first, as in Ambrose's case, its purpose is to rescue a political space for the church to both proclaim the gospel and exercise jurisdiction. With Ambrose there is but one rule – that of the risen exalted Lord – and there are two societies – church and empire, or 'religion' and 'judgement' – and it was the task of the former to continually confront the latter. As O'Donovan indicates, with Augustine there is a certain relaxation of this critical interface and tension by speaking of two loves and two cities that nevertheless coexist and intermingle. Nevertheless, 'Though mingled and confused, these were distinct social entities, each with its principle, "self love excluding God [made] the earthly city, love of God excluding self the heavenly", and each its political expression.'[60] Again, as O'Donovan accepts with Gelasius half a century after Augustine, the respective notions of rule and society are inverted. Now the world is ruled by princes and bishops within one universal society. While Gelasius could contend that only in Christ are the two rules combined so that both the sacral and the political must be separated, the two rules inevitably vied for supremacy. And once the move is made with the Carolingian age to say, 'Two there are by whom the *church* is ruled', then the tendency to absolutize either the king or the pope at the expense of the other is clearly a real temptation.[61] Once rule takes precedence over the distinction between church and society, then, as Ambrose clearly recognized, the sole rule of Christ is easily infringed by those lesser powers and authorities he has already led captive in his victory parade.

It is easy to see how such an attitude led to another expression of Christendom, that which O'Donovan refers to as 'the supremacy of spiritual authority',[62] where the imperial Christ sanctioned a particular doctrine of the church, this time most certainly modelled on the lines of imperial Rome. In the West, particularly during the mediaeval period, Christ was the King of kings, the church was a monarchy, the pope was a monarch, and it was by his authority that earthly monarchs exercised their own divinely derived authority and right to rule.

---

[59] *DN*, 200.

[60] *DN*, 203.

[61] *DN*, 203–4.

[62] *DN*, 205.

> The coronation of Charlemagne as emperor by Pope Leo III on Christmas Day in the year 800 at Saint Peter's in Rome became the model of how political sovereignty was believed in the West to have passed: from God to Christ, from Christ to the apostle Peter, from Peter to his successors on the 'throne of Peter', and from them to emperors and kings.[63]

Indeed, by the time of Gregory VII, another form of realized eschatology provided another form of ignoble theological legitimization by collapsing the distinction between church and kingdom to justify a supreme pontiff. Here the pope assumes the authority of both king and priest after the order of Melchizedek and he it is, like Abraham, to whom the kings of the earth must pay homage.[64] It is clear, therefore, that in the West as well as in the East, the theological legitimization of the Christendom experiment tended to move in an absolutist direction. Two there may have been whereby Christ the King exercised dual authority and jurisdiction over the kingdoms of this world, but the tendency was always to legitimize one at the expense of the other. My kingdom, Jesus had said in response to Pilate, does not belong to this world. His supporters and followers, in Western and in Eastern Christendom, seemingly begged to differ.

Revisiting Christendom

O'Donovan has now been credited with the dubious honour of having offered 'a defence of Christendom as a witness to the power of the Gospel'.[65] It would seem more appropriate to claim that he has defended the Christendom settlement as a viable, valid and courageous expression of Christian mission,[66] and in this regard Lesslie Newbigin clearly anticipated such an assessment.

> Much has been written about the harm done to the cause of the gospel when Constantine accepted baptism, and it is not difficult to expatiate on this theme. But could any other choice have been made? When the ancient classical world ... ran out of spiritual fuel and turned to the church as the one society that could hold a disintegrating world together, should the church have refused the appeal and washed its hands of responsibility for the political order? It is easy to see with hindsight how quickly the church fell into the temptation of worldly power. It is easy to point ... to the glaring contradiction between the Jesus of the Gospels and his followers occupying the seats of power and wealth. And yet we have to ask would God's purpose ... have been better served if the church had refused all political responsibility?[67]

---

[63] Pelikan, *Jesus*, 55.

[64] Cf. Pelikan, *Reformation*, 81–83.

[65] Hauerwas, cover endorsement of *DN*.

[66] This seems, at least, to be the tone of his remarks in 'Response', 102–5.

[67] Newbigin, *Foolishness*, 100f.

Not surprisingly the Christendom settlement has been the subject of much modern disputation and denunciation. Some of this is clearly justified because, as Newbigin implied, the church was not immune from the temptation to succumb to the acquisition of worldly power and wealth.[68] There is, however, a very modern tendency to read this important era of Christian mission and expansion through the eyes of liberal democracy or, indeed, through a decidedly Nietzschean assessment that Christendom represented nothing more than the naked will to power and domination. So, for instance, Stanley Hauerwas comes close to such a position when he conflates the Christendom idea with Constantinianism, which he regards quite starkly as the mistaken attempt to forward the influence and extent of the kingdom by the use of worldly power and violence.[69]

In dispute with Hauerwas, however, O'Donovan believes that this view is both historically inaccurate and theologically naïve. O'Donovan is surely correct when he asserts that Christians in those times were not prepared to return to the catacombs and indulge in a false quietism. Rather, they actively sought to realize in astute political form the triumph of Christ among the nations. O'Donovan is also correct in asserting that this is a very different motive than the desire of the oppressed to become the oppressor.

> It was the missionary imperative that compelled the church to take the conversion of the empire seriously and to seize the opportunities it offered. These were not merely opportunities for 'power'. They were opportunities for preaching the Gospel, baptising believers, curbing the violence and cruelty of empire and, perhaps most important of all, forgiving their former persecutors.[70]

Alan Kreider and Ramsey MacMullen, however, have recently entered this debate from a missiological and historical perspective, claiming that O'Donovan's view of Christendom overlooks two vital failings. First of all, there was a general accommodation of Christian teaching by the preachers and catechists of the post-Constantine era to the more favourable political circumstances that existed.

> A study of their preaching across the fourth century shows that they 'modulated their preaching' on wealth, to facilitate the conversion of the eminent and wealthy. A similar diachronic study of legislation shows that the Christian Empire had 'frequent resort to torture and executions in the name of justice'.[71]

---

[68] See Kreider, 'Changing Patterns of Conversion in the West', in *Origins*.

[69] Hauerwas, *After Christendom?*, 39.

[70] *DN*, 212.

[71] Kreider, *Change of Conversion*.

Secondly, the conversion of the masses was largely a 'carrot and stick' exercise. It was the stick in terms of 'swingeing penalties' for those who resisted the new legal and public status of the Christian faith, and the carrot for those who favoured the route of privilege and enrichment.[72] In that sense, the once persecuted Christian church became the persecutor of other sects and pagans. Consequently, dissent and heretical convictions were no longer tolerated.[73] Both Kreider and MacMullen provide significant historical evidence that might threaten the cogency of O'Donovan's argument that coercion was not endemic to the Christendom settlement.

Hauerwas' critique is more ecclesiological. He believes that the church simply failed to become in its own community life a radically subversive political reality, and so it accommodated itself to the advantageous political climate of the empire. Kreider and MacMullen see the same thing happening, but they interpret it as a failure of nerve and vision in terms of the practicalities of Christian mission and initiation. O'Donovan accepts that abuses and irregularities existed, and he indeed asks the fundamental question: must the Christendom settlement inevitably banish dissent and rely instead on coercion? Clearly he is right when he argues that this is not necessarily the case, particularly when the logic of the essential Christian story is recognized and upheld. 'The storytellers of Christendom do not celebrate coercion; they celebrate the power of God to humble the haughty ones of the earth and to harness them to the purposes of peace.'[74]

It is also true, however, that there have been many occasions in church history when the same storytellers mitigated the offence of the gospel to suit certain advantageous cultural and political conditions in an ill-informed endeavour to enhance the apparent credibility of their message. Carrot and stick evangelism has sullied the witness of the Christian church many times before, and no doubt it will continue to do so in the future.

It is probably this sort of conviction that lies behind Gorringe's claim that O'Donovan's account of the Christendom settlement is marred by idealism. 'Those who ruled in Christendom, O'Donovan tells us, intended to reflect Christ's coming reign… If one takes England, for example, I cannot think of a single ruler of whom this was true.'[75]

In all of this, of course, we are in the tricky terrain of historical judgement and interpretation and, as O'Donovan reminds us, there will always be different ways of reading this particular episode in the church's life and witness.

---

[72] Kreider, 'Changing Patterns of Conversion in the West', and MacMullen 'Christianity Shaped through its Mission', in Kreider (ed.), *Origins*.

[73] Cf. Butterfield, *Christianity*, 5.

[74] *DN*, 223.

[75] Gorringe, 'Authority', 27.

> The necessarily contested character of my reading of Christendom is like the necessarily contested character of my reading of modernity. There are, and always will be, other possible readings of Western social history than the reading of one as a history of Christian mission and of the other as apostasy.[76]

In some ways, Gorringe's complaint is more readily directed toward Aidan Nichols' uncompromising attempt to appropriate O'Donovan's analysis of the nature of political authority in terms of a reinvigoration of the Christendom ideal,[77] and unfortunately a reassertion of Roman Catholic hegemony.

Gorringe's complaint does, however, take us back to a central issue: O'Donovan's defence of authority as the objective correlate of freedom. In both *RMO* and *DN*, O'Donovan has trenchantly argued the case that authority derided and diminished is freedom lost and emaciated and, more recently, he makes the same point via Arendt's elegant refutation of the traditional liberal-conservative dichotomy.[78] Clearly some of O'Donovan's interlocutors, Gorringe and Shanks particularly, are not at home with the apparent hegemony of this concept of authority because, lurking in the background of their expositions, is the critique of modernity and of postmodernity – that such a rehabilitation of authority simply disguises the ideological or political self-interest of the ruling power.

Perhaps, however, it is not the nature of authority, as that which is located in the notion of divine sovereignty and rule, that is the real issue at stake in regard to the Christendom settlement. A lot depends on how one dates the ending of the Christendom experiment. O'Donovan opts for the duration between the Edict of Milan and the authorization of the First Amendment as part of the American Constitution in 1791. Like Richard John Neuhaus and others, however, I view the religious wars of the seventeenth century that followed in the wake of the Reformation as both the symbolic and historical end of Christendom.[79] Once again in the history of Christendom, the abuse of power reasserts itself and the unstable conflagration of political and religious interests proves unsustainable. The religious wars, brought to a merciful resolution by the Peace of Westphalia in 1648, not only undermined the theological and political conviction that it could only be the one, holy, catholic and apostolic church that guaranteed the political stability of Europe. These wars also exacerbated the mutually contradictory notions of devolved authority that separated Eastern Christendom from its Western equivalent. Here church, ruler, reformer and nation-state came into conflict with one another, and it was precisely the ferocity of the religious

---

[76] O'Donovan, 'Response', 104.

[77] Nichols, *Christendom*, 71–91.

[78] O'Donovan, 'Response', 99; see also Arendt, *Between Past and Future*, 100.

[79] See the chapter in this volume by Jonathan Chaplin, who suggests the French Revolution as another candidate for the symbolic end of Christendom.

conflict that 'virtually destroyed the political communities of Europe, impressing upon the minds of rulers and thoughtful citizens the necessity of confining religion and theological dispute to a spiritual sphere where they could not threaten public order'.[80] At least this was certainly Spinoza's view, and he wrote a theological and political treatise to prove his point.

Conclusion

It is a welcome sign that in recent years the Christendom settlement has quite rightly received more vigorous scholarly attention. In some ways this is hardly surprising, given the apparent bewilderment and impotence of the contemporary Christian church as it faces the missiological and political challenges of the twenty-first century. It is time now to try to adjudicate, recognizing, as O'Donovan reminds us, that every reading of the Christendom ideal, indeed, like every reading of Israel and the early Christian communities, will inevitably remain a contested exercise.

It has been our contention throughout that the system of dual authority upon which Christendom was predicated often relied on a flawed theological legitimization that reversed the epistemological and political significance of the categories of rule and society. There is but one rule and two societies, however, as soon as a triumphalist expression of human rule, be that of emperor, king or pope, subverts the one rule of the risen Christ. Then, at that point, inevitably, the important distinction between the sacred and the secular societies, and the relation of both to the larger reality of the kingdom of God, simply break down. At the same time there is an inevitable migration of power and authority in an absolutist direction that again infringes upon the sovereignty of the risen Christ. There is but one eternal verity – the kingdom of the Father whose rule is entrusted to the Son, making both dependent upon the realization of that authority in the history of humanity by the Spirit. The church is a prolepsis of the kingdom that should continually remind the state of its limited sphere of jurisdiction, in that way enabling secular power to manifest its role as a legal-constitutional settlement. If this observation is correct and perhaps deserves greater recognition, then it is not surprising that the Christendom settlement both in the East and the West was marred by insidious forms of coercion and compulsion which eroded the cogency of the Christian gospel. The rediscovery of personal religious freedom that epitomized the Reformation did not mark the end of Christendom, but replicated the weaknesses of both East and West in the Lutheran doctrine of the two kingdoms and the Calvinist attempts at mediated theocracy.

---

[80] Neuhaus, 'Commentary', 58.

The significance of the religious wars that followed in the wake of the Reformation in the seventeenth century can not be underestimated in the way O'Donovan apparently does. For this marks the end of the religious coercion that continually tarnished the Christendom ideal. While it is certainly true, as O'Donovan and others have pointed out, that both church and state continued to survive in the lengthening shadows of Christendom,[81] the religious wars unleashed both intellectual and political capital that continually bankrolled new humanist and secular ideals. Confessional pluralism raised the suspicion that the Christian faith was not based on divinely revealed and inspired truths and doctrines after all, but was in fact a mendacious conspiracy that blinded us to our true humanity and greatness.[82] The political and social revolutions of the eighteenth century founded that political capital on an alternative to catholic faith – namely, the myth of the social contract, based as it was on the equally spurious notion of universal human autonomy. It should not be surprising to those of us who have inherited this legacy that the legitimization of both depended upon the ideology and the coercion of the nation-state.[83]

Faced as we are with the reality of an acephalous society, we need once again to retrieve the notion of dual authority – but this time in its critically prophetic original form. In the early twenty-first century we stand with Israel in exile, with Paul writing to the Christian church in Rome, and with Ambrose in Milan. We desperately need to remind civil authority that its rule and authority are neither self-evident nor ubiquitous. Rather, liberal democracy requires a theological justification that would rob it of its pretensions toward absolute power and significance. Indeed, without this, democracy will find itself continually under threat from other usurpers who will undermine its political legitimacy – namely, global multinational capitalism and its counter-ego, militant Islam. For those whose task it is to reconfigure this prophetic critical engagement between church and state on the ground, so to speak, there will have to be a renewed commitment to vigorous political debate and at times, perhaps, a more confrontational stance. The future of liberal democracy could depend on a reinvigorated church that courageously sought to retrieve the Christian values and ideals out of which modernity was spawned.

---

[81] In this regard O'Donovan rightly draws attention to the work of J.C.D. Clark, *The Language of Liberty*, which demonstrates how confessional politics remained a factor up until the American Revolution and in England until 1828–32. My point would be to suggest that both church and state continued to draw on the legacy of Christendom without realizing how its spiritual capital had been devalued by what took place in Europe a century before.

[82] This, of course, was Nietzsche's view (in this regard see Ingraffia's fine study *Postmodern Theory and Biblical Theology*), but it was clearly anticipated in the rationalism of Leibniz and Locke, in the empiricism and scepticism of Hume, and in the secular humanism of Spinoza and Voltaire (see Byrne, *Glory, Jest and Riddle*).

[83] See the contribution to this volume by Joan Lockwood O'Donovan.

Bibliography

Arendt, H., *Between Past and Future* (London: Faber, 1961)

Balthasar, H.U. von, *Origenes: Geist und Feuer. Ein Aufbau aus seinen Schriften* (Salzburg, 1938)

Barnes, T.D., *Constantine and Eusebius* (Cambridge, MA: Harvard University Press, 1981)

Bettenson, H., *Documents of the Christian Church* (Oxford: OUP, 2nd edn, 1963)

Butterfield, H., *Christianity and History* (London: G. Bell & Sons, 1950)

Byrne, J., *Glory, Jest and Riddle: Religious Thought in the Enlightenment* (London: SCM Press, 1996)

Clark, J.C.D., *The Language of Liberty* (Cambridge: CUP, 1994)

Dunn, J., *Unity and Diversity in the New Testament: An Enquiry into the Character of Earliest Christianity* (London: SCM Press, 1977)

——, *Christology in the Making: An Inquiry into the Origins of the Doctrine of the Incarnation* (London: SCM Press, 1980)

Eusebius, 'From a Speech for the Thirtieth Anniversary of Constantine's Accession', in O'Donovan and O'Donovan, *From Irenaeus to Grotius: A Sourcebook in Christian Political Thought*, 60–65

Furnish, V.P., 'How Firm A Foundation? Some Questions about Scripture in *The Desire of the Nations*', *SCE* 11.2 (1998), 18–23

Gorringe, T., 'Authority, Plebs and Patricians', *SCE* 11.2 (1998), 24–29

Gunton, C., *Yesterday and Today: A Study of Continuities in Christology* (London: Darton, Longman & Todd, 1983)

Hauerwas, S., *After Christendom? How the Church Is to Behave if Freedom, Justice, and a Christian Nation are Bad Ideas* (Nashville: Abingdon Press, 1991)

——, and J. Fodor, 'Remaining in Babylon: Oliver O'Donovan's Defense of Christendom', *SCE* 11.2 (1998), 30–55

Howard-Brook, W., and A. Gwyther, *Unveiling Empire: Reading Revelation Then and Now* (Maryknoll, NY: Orbis Books, 1999)

Ingraffia, B., *Postmodern Theory and Biblical Theology: Vanquishing God's Shadow* (Cambridge: CUP, 1995)

Justin Martyr, *First Apology*, 6, in *Writings of Saint Justin Martyr* (trans. T.B. Falls; New York: Christian Heritage, 1948)

Kreider, A. (ed.), *The Origins of Christendom in the West* (Edinburgh: T. & T. Clark, 2001)

——, *The Change of Conversion and the Origin of Christendom: Christian Mission and Modern Culture* (Harrisburg, PA: Trinity Press International, 1999)

——, 'Response to Oliver O'Donovan's "Mission, coercion and Christendom"', in *The Gospel and Our Culture Network Newsletter*, 27 (Spring 2000), 5

Küng, H., *Great Christian Thinkers* (London: SCM Press, 1994)

MacMullen, R., 'Christianity Shaped through its Mission', in Kreider (ed.), *The Origins of Christendom in the West*, 97–117

Macquarrie, J., *Jesus Christ in Modern Thought* (London: SCM Press, 1990)

Marshall, I.H., *The Origins of New Testament Christology* (Leicester: IVP, 1990)

Matera, F.J., *New Testament Christology* (Louisville, KY: Westminster/John Knox Press, 1999)

Moltmann, J., *The Way of Jesus Christ: Christology in Messianic Dimensions* (London: SCM Press, 1990)

Newbigin, L., *Foolishness to the Greeks: The Gospel and Western Culture* (London: SPCK, 1986)

Neuhaus, R.J., 'Commentary on *The Desire of the Nations*', *SCE* 11.2 (1998), 56–61

Nichols, A., OP, *Christendom Awake: On Re-energising the Church in Culture* (Edinburgh: T. & T. Clark, 1999)

O'Donovan, O., *Resurrection and Moral Order: An Outline for Evangelical Ethics* (Leicester: IVP; Grand Rapids: Eerdmans, 2nd edn, 1994)

——, *The Desire of the Nations: Rediscovering the Roots of Political Theology* (Cambridge: CUP, 1996)

——, 'Response to Respondents: Behold the Lamb', *SCE* 11.2 (1998), 91–110

——, 'Deliberation, History and Reading: A Response to Schweiker and Wolterstorff', *SJT* 54.1 (2001), 127–44

——, and J.L. O'Donovan (eds.), *From Irenaeus to Grotius: A Sourcebook in Christian Political Thought 100–1625* (Grand Rapids: Eerdmans, 1999)

Pelikan, J., *Jesus Through the Centuries: His Place in the History of Culture* (New Haven: Yale University Press, 1985)

——, *Reformation of Church and Dogma (1300–1700)*, IV: *The Christian Tradition* (Chicago: University of Chicago Press, 1984)

Powell, M.A., and D.R. Bauer, *Who Do You Say that I Am? Essays on Christology* (Louisville, KY: Westminster/John Knox Press, 1999)

Schweiker, W., 'Freedom and Authority in Political Theology: A Response to Oliver O'Donovan's *The Desire of the Nations*', *SJT* 54.1 (2001), 110–26

Stanton, G., 'Incarnational Christology in the New Testament', in *Incarnation and Myth* (ed. M. Goulder; London: SCM Press, 1979)

Studer, B., *Trinity and Incarnation: The Faith of the Early Church* (ed. A. Louth; Edinburgh: T. & T. Clark, 1993)

Tertullian, 'Christian Loyalty to the Emperor', *Apol.* xxix–xxxii, in H. Bettenson, *Documents of the Christian Church*, 7

Whitehead, A.N., *Process and Reality: An Essay in Cosmology* (New York: Macmillan, 1929)

Wolterstorff, N., 'A Discussion of Oliver O'Donovan's *The Desire of the Nations*', *SJT* 54.1 (2001), 87–109

Wright, N.T., 'Paul and Caesar: A New Reading of Romans' (in the present volume)

23

Response to Colin Greene

Oliver O'Donovan

Colin Green is sympathetic to my theological contention that the authority of Christ is at the centre of the gospel, which is the important point for both of us. He is happy to reinforce my perception of the resurrection as a political event with further exegetical observations, while wishing to subvert my reading of Romans 13. He is more than prepared to be sympathetic to my 'defence' of Christendom – which, as I like to repeat, though often to deaf ears, is not so much a defence as some shrewd advice to Christendom's critics – at least to the point of agreeing that one key element to understanding it is to grasp its missiological concerns. His comparison of my project with that of Lesslie Newbigin is both apt and welcome. But he is not uninfluenced by the story told by some of Christendom's attackers – theologians, on the whole, rather than historians.

There is, for example, the story that Christendom ended with the Thirty Years' War, and that liberal indifference ruled from the Peace of Westphalia on. It has attracted major supporters (recently Pannenberg, who gets it from Dilthey), and there is certainly some relation between that traumatic experience and intellectual developments.[1] But, like the other popular story that the French Enlightenment was caused by the Lisbon earthquake (based on some scabrous remarks in Voltaire's *Candide*), it is oversimplified. In following Richard Neuhaus on this point, one should not ignore the personal importance for that vibrant Christian missionary of establishing that Lutheranism led to an *impasse* from the beginning. More importantly for our purposes, it does not account for the English-speaking world. The work of J.C.D. Clark on eighteenth-century England and America confirms how 'confessional' politics tended to be at least until the American Revolution, and in England until, as he would say, the crisis of 1828–32.[2] I am still persuaded in general

---

[1] W. Pannenberg, *Grundlagen der Ethik* (Göttingen: Vandenhoek & Ruprecht 1996), 9f.

[2] J.C.D. Clark, *The Language of Liberty 1660–1832* (Cambridge: CUP, 1994); *English Society 1660–1832* (Cambridge: CUP, 2nd edn, 2000).

terms that, if a threshold is wanted (and thresholds are only *conventional* historiographical devices), the American and French revolutions afford the obvious one.

Let us go back to Constantine, whose lawyers, in the memorable phrase Greene quotes from Whitehead, 'edited ... the received text of Western history'. It is impossible for anyone interested in the ideology of the Constantinian revolution not to take notice of Eusebius' two speeches and of his biographical sketch of the emperor; among the texts of that period they are exceptional for the thoroughgoing theological way in which they uphold the political settlement. But that poses a temptation to theologians who as moderns dislike Constantine, as Westerners dislike Eusebius' Origenism, and as free-churchmen dislike the Nicene Creed. What a fine story the Council of Nicaea offers, wrapping everything unlikeable about the fourth century into one package! Constantine promotes his political control, adopts Eusebius' theology and personally propounds a 'strictly monarchical' doctrine of the divinity of Christ. This event becomes an icon of Christendom itself. But the alliance of Constantine, Eusebius and monarchical theology was momentary; within eighteen months of the Council it was shattered. It took fifty years or so before an alliance between Nicene theology and the monarchs who were supposed to benefit from it could be patched up again – and on very different terms from anything Eusebius would have liked. It was not Constantine's lawyers who wrote the received text of history, but those bishops who challenged the authority of the imperial crown and won. Arguably the only solid achievement of imperial theological policy in the patristic period was the two-natures doctrine of Chalcedon.

Nor do other aspects of the story of the Constantinian fall fare much better. For the claim that post-Constantinian theologians 'modulated' their preaching on wealth I do not know the evidence; but I know that while second-century Clement of Alexandria and third-century Lactantius (before his employment by Constantine) both defended the principle of private property, fourth-century Ambrose and Chrysostom, preaching under the noses of emperors, denied it in the strongest terms. And while it is true that fourth-century government made free use of torture and the death penalty, it is also true that these quickly became defining issues in the relations between rulers and their Christian preachers. The story is an old one of how Ambrose, as an unbaptized governor, gave ostentatious orders for the interrogation of prisoners by torture in order to disqualify himself from baptism and ordination. More recently discovered is the story of Augustine's intercession with central government to stop a flourishing criminal racket that kidnapped inhabitants of lonely farms and sold them in the Eastern Mediterranean as slaves; but he warned the government that kidnappers must not be punished by scourging, for then the church would dissociate itself from the effort, and suspend its charitable practice of buying back the victims from the kidnappers.[3]

When we talk about Christendom, what 'it' thought and what 'it' intended, we need to remember who it is precisely that is thinking and intending in the texts that we read. Not the rulers, for rulers generally have little part in generating ideas. The ideas and ideals of Christendom were thought through by monks and bishops, counsellors and advisors. They proposed an ideal for the behaviour of government and the governed, and they gave reasons for it. Sometimes the ideal had effect in rulers' policies, sometimes in criticism of rulers' policies. Sometimes it was an inspiration to the ruler, sometimes an unwelcome drag. Christendom was not a guarantee of sanctity or single-mindedness among rulers; it simply constituted a set of reference points, which had to be included in any argument *pro* or *con* over any course of action. The story of Henry II and Becket is, in its way, archetypal, which is why it almost immediately achieved semi-mythical status. It was not that no Christian king could ever order the assassination of an awkward archbishop; but he could not do so without having to do public penance afterwards. And whether the penance was sincere or merely expedient, a strong negative judgement on arbitrary use of authority was shaping the conditions of the public realm one way or the other.

The record of historical Christendom, it is hardly necessary to repeat, was a very mixed one. I have never argued (*pace* Kreider) that a tendency to coercion was not 'endemic', merely that it was not logically implied by the concept of a Christian state. My interest in attending to it sympathetically, as Colin Greene appreciates, is to win some more satisfactory nourishment for our own political tasks than the thin gruel of late-modern political commonplace affords. The project of *Desire* is one of practical theology throughout. The reason we have to be grateful to our ancestors is that they wrestled with conceiving Christian politics in practical terms, where our contemporaries usually get no further than newspaper-editorializing. Those for whom a sharp and predictable denunciation is the last word in contemporary political responsibility will perhaps not appreciate why Joan and I have thought it worth our while to linger over those from the past who, with greater or lesser success, engaged in Christian deliberation for the welfare of their contemporaries.

---

[3] *Epistula* 10, in Augustine, *Epistolae ex duobus codicibus nuper in lucem prolatae* (ed. Johannes Divjak; Vindobonae: Hoelder-Pichler-Tempsky, 1981).

24

'Return to the Vomit of "Legitimation"'?[1] Scriptural Interpretation and the Authority of the Poor

Peter Scott

Authority of the Poor and the Poverty of Authority

In the opening chapter of *The Desire of the Nations*, in a discussion of the matter of authority, Oliver O'Donovan writes: 'But it is proper to say to theologians of the Southern school that, just as poverty was their issue first, but also ours, so authority is our issue first, but also theirs.'[2] What does O'Donovan intend by this comment, addressed to the 'Southern school' of political theology (including the liberation theology of Latin America)? The following may stand as an answer: As a matter of epistemological strategy, for the South the poor come first. However, in their desire to engage this matter theologically Southern theologians get lost in the dialectical manoeuvres of historicist idealism, and so in turn need to attend to the matter of authority. In their desire to avoid the charge of legitimation, the Southern theologians make a mistake: instead of attending to the notion of authority as the nerve of their position, they seek to avoid the charge of legitimation by drawing on the same critical theory from which the charge itself originates.

That the liberation theologians are working within a hermeneutic circle is obvious. Is the circle vicious, though? In considering this matter of authority, we should note that liberation theology is not without scriptural

---

1 O'Donovan, 'Political Theology', 241: 'Of course, no major movement of thought [sc. the theology of liberation] is unambiguous, especially not a movement of reaction. It is therefore quite possible to see this movement, as some influential liberal critics have seen it, as the dog's return to the vomit of "legitimation". In place of the statesman's advantage, it is said, there is the class advantage of the poor.'

2 *DN*, 16. The sentence is repeated verbatim in O'Donovan, 'Political Theology', 245.

commitments. The liberation theologians, as O'Donovan reports, have attended to *scriptural warrants* in their affirmation of 'the cause of the poor' (I shall say more on this phrase in a moment). The poor and the authority of Scripture imply each other, we might say, on account of God's affirmative action towards the poor reported in Scripture. As normative, Scripture authorizes the poor to be the primary locus of the reading of Scripture and discerning the eschatological signs of the times. Drawing from their own spiritual wells, the poor continue the mission authorized by Jesus Christ. Here is the core of the liberation strategy against the charge of legitimation in which the authority of the poor and scriptural authority are neither in balance nor in opposition.[3]

However, when addressing the theme of the roots of political theology in the North, O'Donovan heads straight for the notion of authority. The poor are of course an issue and a concern. But whereas the liberation theologians relate the poor and authority together, O'Donovan, articulating a Northern political theology, prefers to concentrate on authority alone. The response to the charge of legitimation must be rooted in a construal of Scripture as authoritative for a political theology so as to avoid 'the infinitely reflexive trajectory of modernity's self-critique'.[4] The focus is not, we may note, on authority *simpliciter.* O'Donovan contends that, 'Authority is the nuclear core, the all-present if unclarified source of rational energy that motivates the democratic bureaucratic organisations of the Northern hemisphere …'[5] Political authority is thereby an important political issue and problem for the North. However, scriptural authority is not paired, as in the Southern school, with a biblical-political notion; no Northern equivalent for the poor (such as 'the rich'?) is identified. Why is a biblical-political category, the poor, traded against a notion of the authority of Scripture? Given the original linking of authority and the poor, the significance of O'Donovan's de-coupling of the issue of the authority of the poor and scriptural authority in the consideration of a political theology for the North must be assessed. Has not the stress on the poor as a biblical-political concept been one of the central ways that liberation theology has overcome the divide between theology and the study of politics? And is not the overcoming of that divide what O'Donovan most admires in liberation theology?

In theological tradition, scriptural authority has been employed to answer the question, *where* should Christians turn for guidance in all matters, including politics?[6] O'Donovan follows this line, which is also affirmed by

---

[3] For Rowland and Corner, *Liberating Exegesis*, 46f., 'God sides with the poor' is the chief hermeneutical commitment of liberation theology.

[4] Schweiker, 'Freedom', 117; cf. 115: O'Donovan 'fold[s] his entire political theology within a specific reading of the biblical witness'.

[5] *DN*, 16.

[6] Fackre, *Doctrine*, 11.

liberation theology. Yet, liberation theologies also treat the poor, a political category and social agent, as a source of authority. Southern political theologies thereby privilege a particular group. Such specificity O'Donovan abjures. The approach taken by O'Donovan is, I think, linked to his account of the 'political act', which I confess I do not fully understand.[7] Nevertheless, my basic point is this: liberation theologians pair the authority of the poor and scriptural authority, whereas O'Donovan eschews the specificity of relating authority with any particular 'group', preferring to build his account of authority from the (biblical) ground up. Whereas O'Donovan calls for a fuller theological conceptuality in which to give an account of authority and the authorization of the political act, and argues (implicitly) that the liberation theologians draw from a set of too few concepts, his theological practice is to attend first and foremost to the theme of authority. A restriction is operative here. The liberation theologians wish to speak of scriptural authority and the poor in order to speak, in dependent fashion, of the authority of the poor: we drink from our own wells, as Gutiérrez remarks.[8] O'Donovan avoids such specificity.

That O'Donovan does not fully grasp the epistemological and hermeneutical significance of the liberation commitment to the authority of the poor may be gleaned from his characterization of liberation theology. 'The inspiration of the movement' has not, I fear, been 'to take up the cause of the poor';[9] the liberation church is not in service for the poor. Instead, the liberation church is theologically to be construed as the church *of* the poor in which the poor themselves, and not merely their cause, are granted standing and authority. This, in turn, throws some light on O'Donovan's resistance to aspects of liberation theology's use of social theory. He regards the use of dependency theory as authentically theological, whereas the use of class-conflict analysis is mistaken. Yet, for the liberation theologians, the poor is not simply a biblical-political category but also a social and economic one. Already, the divergence of scriptural authority and the authority of the poor is evident in O'Donovan's construal. The question that liberation theology poses is this: can the authority of the gospel be recognized without the authority of the poor? Is not the gospel itself of and for the poor? It is no wonder that the North struggles with the issue of scriptural authority, because in the failure to identify and acknowledge the *authority of the poor* the North discloses its own *poverty of authority*. Neither God's act in Jesus Christ

[7] See O'Donovan, 'Karl Barth', 23; and O'Donovan, 'Government', 37. In *DN*, 249, O'Donovan indicates that the full discussion of the political act is deferred until a later work on political ethics (cf. *DN*, 20–21).

[8] Gutiérrez, *We Drink*.

[9] *DN*, 11.

nor a political project worthy of Christian support may be explicated without reference to the poor.[10]

The Argument of this Paper

As the line of criticism I am developing, and the constructive position that lies behind it, are open to misunderstanding, I should at this point stress that I do not wish to trade off scriptural authority against some other form – the authority of solidarity, for example. In an over-hasty criticism of O'Donovan's position, for example, Andrew Shanks argues that '... the political theologian, one might say, has a primordial choice: either to prioritise the problematics of *authority* – or else to prioritise the problematics of *solidarity*'.[11] However, this is a false choice, as O'Donovan hints in his response to Shanks.[12] If there is a theological account of solidarity to be offered, it must be made in strict relation to the act of God in Christ. The question should be: what is the nature of the solidarity bestowed by God in Christ, and how might *that* solidarity function as a form of authority? Or, to put the matter dogmatically, the Holy Spirit is always the Spirit of Christ: the presentation of the theme of solidarity as the work of the Spirit cannot be made without reference to the 'career' of Jesus Christ.

Mention of Christ's career returns us to the theme of the poor as a biblical-political category. How so? Because the centrality of the poor to the political theologies of the liberation theologians is connected in some fashion to the solidarity of God with the poor in Jesus Christ. Yet the liberation theologians also insist that the poor is a political category. There are methodological difficulties in making the connection between the poor as biblical category and the poor as political category. Furthermore, liberation theology has been much criticized for the precise manner – that is, by reference to Marxian theory of class-conflict and neo-Marxist theories of dependency – in which the connection has been forged.[13] Nonetheless, although we do not have to treat the poor as liberation theology does, its basic insight is theological and sound: the poor are an important source of authority on account of God's solidarity with them. We should expect, then, that the spiritual wells of the poor will yield theological insight.

How shall we think of the poor for a political theology? In the following three ways, I suggest. First, the poor is a *soteriological* category. Of course, the poor is a soteriological category only contingently: God does not raise up the

---

[10] Míguez Bonino, 'Latin American Theology', 14.

[11] Shanks, 'Response', 86, first emphasis mine. In *God*, 92–95, Shanks revises this criticism.

[12] O'Donovan, 'Response', 100.

[13] Dorrien, *Reconstructing*, esp. ch. 6.

poor; material poverty is 'contrary to the will of God'.[14] Instead, God raises up a world, and then a community called Israel and, finally, raises one member of that people from the dead.[15] Nevertheless, the poor are, as Gustavo Gutiérrez argues, the primary witness to the universality of God's love for creation in Jesus Christ. That judgement, anyhow, is one way of interpreting Scripture as the drama of God's acts. 'The whole Bible', claims Gutiérrez, 'is marked by God's love and predilection for the weak and abused of human history',[16] culminating in the one who 'though he was rich, yet for your sakes he became poor' (2 Cor. 8:9) and so 'emptied himself, taking the form of a slave' (Phil. 2:7), and ending with God calling as church 'what is low and despised in the world' (1 Cor. 1:27). Of the option for the poor, Gutiérrez writes: 'It is a theocentric, prophetic option we make, one which strikes its roots deep in the gratuity of God's love and is demanded by that love.'[17] Theological attention must therefore be paid to the poor on account of *who God is*, and for no other reason. Are we to deduce from this claim that the poor are spiritually or morally superior? By no means: '...the poor are preferred not because they are necessarily better than others from a moral or religious standpoint', Gutiérrez argues, 'but because God is God'.[18] Of course, this position does not deny the ascription of a moral authority to the poor. However, such an authority is not innate but rather acquired: the moral authority of the poor is learned through its protest against material poverty. Such authority includes a call for repentance and conversion.[19] That is, the authority of the poor is also judgement on the poor.[20]

Second, the poor is an *anthropological* category. That is, the patterns of the production and distribution of power, wealth and goods as these place, engage and shape the poor – and are protested against by the poor – must also be analysed by a political theology. The situation of the contemporary poor, as O'Donovan rightly notes, must be *discerned*. Such discernment will require

---

[14] Gutiérrez, *Theology*, 291.

[15] At the consultation at which an earlier version of this paper was presented, Walter Moberly suggested that the poor is a theme in the New Testament rather than the Old. As will be clear from what follows, I read the exodus and the exile somewhat differently. Nor do I find Moberly's second suggestion that the Old Testament motif 'The fear of the Lord is the beginning of wisdom' (Ps. 111:10) is in opposition to the primacy being accorded here to the poor. After all, may not the rich use their position, wealth and possessions precisely as a guard against such fear?

[16] Gutiérrez, 'Option', 240.

[17] Gutiérrez, 'Option', 240.

[18] Gutiérrez, 'Option', 241. Cf. Gutiérrez, *Theology*, rev. edn, xxvii–xxviii.

[19] To all this, see Stephen J. Pope, 'Proper and Improper Impartiality', 242–71.

[20] I am indebted to Danny Carroll for this point.

some theory of society which aims not least to identify the agency of the poor. At the consultation at which this paper was first presented, Jonathan Chaplin proposed that a definition of the poor could be: 'those who are denied the goods of creation'. That is a very helpful suggestion. Nevertheless, a fuller account is also required of fundamental human needs *and the conditions for their fulfilment* if the anthropological construal of the poor is to be given developed content. Maria Mies offers the following list of nine needs:

> *subsistence* (health, food, shelter, clothing); *protection* (care, solidarity, work); *affection* (self-esteem, love, care, solidarity); *understanding* (study, learning, analysis); *participation* (responsibilities, sharing of rights and duties); *leisure/idleness* (curiosity, imagination, games, relaxation, fun); *creation* (intuition, imagination, work, curiosity); *identity* (sense of belonging, differentiation, self-esteem); *freedom* (autonomy, self-esteem, self-determination, equality).[21]

This account of fundamental human needs would need some reworking from a theological perspective. Nevertheless, from an amended list, the broadly political circumstance of the poor (as well as the rich) could be discerned. Not least, the difficulty that liberation theology has had – as Danny Carroll pointed out at the consultation – in acknowledging the 'rights' of native peoples can be identified by reference to the themes of identity and freedom. Such a list of basic needs indicates in addition that what contributes to human flourishing are not only economic matters but also a range of other resources, including the quality of one's habitat and social relations, access to good quality education, and a sense of identity and esteem.

Third, the poor is a *hermeneutical* category. As such, the poor under this third heading combines the imperatives of the first two senses: soteriological and anthropological tendencies converge to call into question dominant narratives and interpretations that obscure the poor and thereby obscure Jesus of Nazareth. As a hermeneutical category, the poor is *interruptive*: the 'wildness' and unseemliness of the interpretative principle of the poor is unavoidable. We should expect our soteriological and anthropological interpretations of the poor to be called into question as the authority of the poor functions as a *protest* against assimilationist construals of Christian Scripture. (And we should also expect that the hermeneutical category of the poor may also function in criticism of the poor. By such interruptive interpretation, the poor are also put in question.) In this connection, I do not think O'Donovan's suggestion – made in response to my paper – that the circumstance of the poor can be learned from 'looking around' is persuasive. I prefer his suggestion that 'experience cannot be our starting point, since experience is what is *problematised* in a deliberative

[21] Mies, 'Liberating', 255.

enquiry'.[22] And one way of seeking to make experience problematic will be to link central soteriological themes to anthropological issues: to join, to borrow two examples from *DN*, ecclesial joy with social suffering, and the vindication of created being with the scarcity (for some) of creation's goods.

So far, I have given an account of the status of the category of the poor in order to defend the claim of the authority of the poor. But what is this authority? What insights does it offer? My answer takes epistemological form. Beginning from O'Donovan's discussion of legitimation, I argue that the recovery of the possibilities of *true theological speech* under present political conditions is central. Theological counter-strategies to the charge of legitimation recover an account of Scripture as authoritative and thereby avoid the epistemological traps of legitimation. In turn, O'Donovan's reading of the Christ-event, its analogous 'rule' in society, and his construal of nature are criticized. (In putting the matter this way, I am moving in a different direction and employing different resources from those commonly used by liberation theologians. This paper, then, is not written 'from a liberation theology perspective'.) In a final coda, I express reservations on the use of Scripture in O'Donovan's political theology. In my view, Scripture functions in O'Donovan's work as the source and rationale for a deductive logic of revelation. In conclusion, I question the appropriateness and usefulness of such a view for a theologico-political hermeneutic.

Attending to Legitimation: True Speech and Ideology

Summarizing O'Donovan's position, Brent Waters has written:

> The most pressing task of political theology, then, is to give a theological account of Christ as the representative of God's triumphant Kingdom; i.e. to offer an explication of an unfolding political order in Christ's fulfilling of time.[23]

The issue, however, is less straightforward if we note, with Gustavo Gutiérrez, that the church, as the witness to this representative act, is part of a capitalist order.[24] To attend to an 'unfolding political order' is to do so from a position within the regnant, capitalist order, and to interpret the Christ-event from a perspective within that order. (This point is, arguably, of *greater* significance for the church in Europe and North America than for the church in Latin America.) From such a vantage point, the critical turn to praxis – in order to resituate the church at some epistemic distance from that hegemonic order – is

---

[22] O'Donovan, 'Deliberation', 128.

[23] Waters, 'Overview', 2.

[24] Gutiérrez, *Theology*, 175.

rendered intelligible, if not as yet persuasive. In order to give an account of the authority of the poor, a certain sort of historicizing is necessary. As I hope to show, such historicizing need not entail the scepticism of total suspicion.

In my view, true speech of the political cannot be secured without reference to a political order. Political discourse, in other words, is already shaped by the order that it seeks to name. As O'Donovan rightly notes, 'a tradition of explaining societies entirely by reference to efficient causes'[25] is unacceptable from a theological perspective. A political discourse that secures its status as legitimating through the affirmation of efficient causes alone, and thereby denies or obscures the transcendence of God, must be resisted by the theological critique of legitimation. In this narrow and restricted sense, the theologian may begin by exploring the operations of legitimation in order to demonstrate how notions of authority are deformed by political discourse. The theologian may concede, as John Milbank does, the historical relativity and contingency of our situation.[26] However, such a concession is not necessarily to cast oneself adrift on a sea of relativism; there may be normative aspects to the critique of legitimation. (Which, as we shall see, necessitates the critical turn to praxis and requires the theological development of standpoint epistemologies.)

O'Donovan takes a different view of the issue of legitimation. As suggested earlier, O'Donovan contrasts the recovery of authority and the critique of legitimation. In that the totalizing of suspicion is complete in our late-modern period, O'Donovan argues that politics is regarded as simply the advantage of a social interest: 'All of us have our political interests, especially class interests, so that all fine public sentiments may be unmasked, from whatever source.'[27]

O'Donovan acknowledges that liberation theology has attempted to break through this impasse but has done so by using counter-tendencies, especially idealist historicism, available in late-modern liberal culture. Nonetheless, whatever its successes may have been in overcoming the divide between theology and politics, liberation theology suffers from an important weakness: 'Building itself on an acephalous idea of society, dissolving government in deconstructive scepticism, lacking a point of view which can transcend given matrices of social engagement, liberation theology has lacked a concept of

[25] O'Donovan, 'Political Theology', 238.

[26] Milbank, *Theology*, 2.

[27] O'Donovan, 'Political Theology', 238. Of course, such criticism cannot be effectively totalizing otherwise the criticism of totalizing could not be made! If the perspective from a one-dimensional society is complete, then the affirmation of society as multi-dimensional is strictly impossible. A different way to attend to this problem would be to affirm that Christianity is exempt from the totalizing perspective; I do not think that O'Donovan is making a case for such an exemption. See *DN*, 272.

authority.'[28] Furthermore, O'Donovan argues that those Northern political theologies seeking to draw on liberation theology have encountered difficulties for precisely the same reason: they lack a notion of authority. Thus Northern political theologies too often are concerned with an account of society which downplays the issue of how we are politically governed; the critique of morality regards all positive accounts of the ends of human society as open to the charge of being merely to the 'statesman's advantage'; and knowledge gained in praxis is caught up in its situation rather than transcending the occasion of that knowledge's production. Indeed, we may conclude from O'Donovan's analysis that without an adequate construal of authority, Southern and Northern political theologies must oscillate between two debilitating positions: to affirm radical scepticism concerning all politico-moral claims; or, to the extent that such scepticism is in some fashion tempered, be charged with 'legitimation'.

Can a 'return to the vomit of "legitimation"' be avoided without lapsing into relativism? Only by way of a theological account of transcendence, I reply. But can a historicizing theology accept this 'interruption' by authority? Is not transcendence opposed to historicizing and is not the appeal to transcendence an attempt to sever the historical dialectic and bring history to a stop? How can such an arresting of history be described as anything other than legitimation? Defending the critique of legitimation as one part of the recovery of a socio-ethical account of transcendence, I shall argue that reference to transcendence is neither the halting of history nor pleading guilty to the charge of legitimation. Nor is there any good reason why the critique of legitimation may not serve as our point of departure: as O'Donovan himself notes, the *regula fidei* prescribes no single starting point for a political theology.[29] I hope to show, also, that despite beginning with the critique of legitimation, a political theology may proceed to reinterpret both the Christ-event and the political realm and thereby does not finish at the point where it began. (To remain at such a starting point is to accept that suspicion begets only more historicizing and thereby denies all claims to authority.)

So I turn now to the critique of legitimation. This critique, which emerges out of the encounter of historicist idealism with aspects of philosophical materialism, cannot be separated from a negative or critical conception of ideology. In western Marxism, the aim of such critical theory of ideology is to criticize ideas and discourses that obscure or misrepresent the true, emancipatory interests of social agents. If thought and social being do not coincide, as Karl Marx argued, ideas may serve the dominant order and legitimate and sustain relations of domination. On this view, note that legitimation is not the support of the

[28] O'Donovan, 'Political Theology', 245.
[29] O'Donovan, 'Political Theology', 241.

ideas of a statesman, or a class or group. If relations of domination are legitimated and sustained, these are the relations of a social *order*. Of course, certain individuals and/or groups may benefit from these social relations, but ideological ideas and discourses are not the 'invention' of the ruling few; a class-genetic view should be avoided.[30] The critique of legitimation thereby encompasses an epistemology for testing true and false knowledge and a critical theory of human freedom in society. What has this to do with political theology?

In theological discussion, the issue is old and new. '[T]he truth will make you free' (Jn. 8:32), a Jewish rabbi is reported as saying. What is the cognitive content of this truth and how is it emancipatory? As noted by O'Donovan, political theologies seek to break out of the corral that separates theology from the study of politics. But how is the cognitive content of the discourse of political theology to be interpreted? What is required, I consider, is the development of theological speech that specifies the social conditions of theology's emergence as discourse but is not reducible to these same conditions. Interpreted thus, the critique of legitimation may be understood as the political extension of the critique of idolatry: does the concept of God legitimate capitalist order and support relations of social domination? In any such ideological legitimation, the identity of the God of freedom is obscured and the liberating actions of God eclipsed.[31]

To put the matter differently, the critique of idolatry and true knowledge of political conditions are part of one epistemological act. Which means, in turn, that there can be no true knowledge of political conditions without reference to that which transcends those conditions: the actions and being of God. The criticism of legitimation, or the criticism of all forms of irrelation, is an important prolegomenon for the recovery of an account of the identity and presence of the triune God of relation. In a theologico-political hermeneutic, overcoming the eclipse of God is linked to emancipatory interventions in the political sphere. Or, as the liberation theologians are fond of putting the matter, to know God is to do justice.[32] For, as Nicholas Lash claims, 'The search for God is not the search for comfort or tranquillity, but for truth, for justice, faithfulness, integrity: these, as the prophets tirelessly reiterated, are the forms of God's appearance in the world.'[33]

What is this transcendence that has epistemological form? I have already indicated that the critique of legitimation is always ideology-critique. 'Ideology has to do with *legitimating* the power of a dominant social group or class',

---

[30] Eagleton, *Ideology*, 30.

[31] I have set out this position in detail in part I of my *Theology, Ideology and Liberation*.

[32] Gutiérrez, *Theology*, 194f. Cf. McDonagh, *Gracing*, 5, who reports a Catholic judgement to see 'the work of justice' as 'a constituent element of preaching the gospel'.

[33] Lash, *Beginning*, 179.

Terry Eagleton notes.[34] Ideology-critique is thereby an epistemological strategy which seeks to detect the relations of domination that ideology obscures. As John Thompson argues, 'to study ideology is to study the ways in which meaning serves to establish and sustain relations of domination'. For 'Ideological power ... is not just a matter of meaning, but of making a meaning *stick*.'[35] The concept of ideology with which I am working is therefore always negative, pejorative or critical.[36] Ideology is a lived practice and the criticism of ideology is thereby productive of enlightenment and emancipation. To put the matter differently, ideology-critique is part of the criticism of idolatry: in that our orientation on idols is a form of slavery, the criticism of ideology is the sustained attempt to free ourselves from false beliefs, attitudes and wants. As Raymond Geuss notes, 'Their ideology is what prevents the agents in the society from correctly perceiving their true interests; if they are to free themselves from social repression, the agents must rid themselves of ideological illusion.'[37] In a moment of socio-ethical transcendence, ideology-critique offers epistemological resources for the identification and criticism of idols.

To avoid the danger of biblical interpretation as a legitimating ideology, is the political theologian required immediately to invoke scriptural authority? Ideology-critique offers a different, yet complementary, route: the possibility of a construal of the authority of the poor. In other words, are the poor, as favoured by God, to be understood as occupying an especially favourable hermeneutical location for the interpretation of Scripture? This would mean that the nature and manner of the authorizing enacted by Scripture is linked epistemologically to the social location of the poor. Although such an approach may – but need not, as we shall see in the next section – fall into the trap of romanticizing and essentializing the suffering engendered by poverty, the location of the poor can in this fashion be understood as neither too close to, nor too distant from, social pressures. Located at a point whereby their interpretations are neither reactionary nor utopian, the poor names a liberative location of the criticism of ideology and a liberative place for the interpretation of Scripture.

Praxis and Knowledge

So far, I have argued that the criticism of strategies of legitimation in ideology-critique may be one way of construing the practice of socio-ethical

---

[34] Eagleton, *Ideology*, 5.

[35] Thompson, *Ideology*, 56 (italics removed); Thompson, *Studies*, 132.

[36] For more detail, see Scott, *Theology*, 36f.

[37] Geuss, *Idea*, 2–3.

transcendence, and as part of the critique of idolatry opens up the realm of politics and society to transcendent causes. If the poor are the preferential performers of such criticism, the authority of the poor may be invoked in the interpretation of Scripture. O'Donovan rejects such a construal of authority, which he calls the authority of 'knowledge won from action'.[38] On what grounds does O'Donovan reject such authority?

Again, it is to the notion of authority that O'Donovan turns: 'reflection upon praxis', he argues, is a flawed programme because any knowledge won from action does not require 'a moment of transcendent criticism, a moment of obedient attention to God's word'.[39] The two aspects of the process – namely, reflection and deliberation – are collapsed into one movement and thereby our 'practical engagements now seem to yield all the understanding that we need'. As there is no transcendent reference, O'Donovan concludes, there is no room for obedience. And if there is no epistemological space for obedience, then all such knowledge is generated through and through by the will. In short, such knowledge is inadequately *authorized*.

Is this a sound judgement, or can the authority of 'knowledge won from action', to use O'Donovan's unsatisfactory phrase, be recovered? For O'Donovan, transcendent reference may be secured at the point of 'reflection *upon* action that can situate our practical engagements within a vision of the world'.[40] Yet the position that I have sketched above does not rule out such a moment of transcendent criticism. Approached christologically, principles of judgement are embedded in the situation itself: in the praxis that seeks to act against ideology, and seeks to understand the restrictive force of ideology as Christians (and others) act against idolatry. 'Ideological suspicion is not something alien to the Gospel', writes James Alison, 'but is rather close to the heart of the project of the removing of idols which characterises Jesus' presence.'[41] Obedient attention to God's word may refer us to a praxis that seeks to be productive of enlightenment and emancipation, and resists blindness and slavery. That is, the discernment of true political interests may be assisted by 'learning' of the presence of God who engages people in the midst of life. (After all, according to theological tradition, Christ is never Lord without the Spirit.) And repentance of idolatry, and disobedience before idols, may be sourced to the praxis of ideology-critique: the attempt to transcend the idolatrous and self-deceiving forms of thought of a particular social and political order. There is no doubt that this position can, as O'Donovan rightly notes, lead in a technological direction. Yet technology is also an ideology, and so may be the subject of

---

38 *DN*, 12.

39 O'Donovan, 'Political Theology', 242.

40 O'Donovan, 'Political Theology', 242.

41 Alison, *Faith*, 50.

ideology-critique. There is no *necessary* reason, therefore, why the notion of knowledge formed in praxis must advance in a technological direction.[42]

We come now to the second part of O'Donovan's criticism. Does knowledge secured by praxis shape what is to be known? On the same grounds – namely that reference to transcendence is not required – O'Donovan also rejects this position. Any knowledge secured by praxis appears to have its source in 'a naked exercise of will' to which all transcendent reference is ruled out.[43] However, fuller consideration of the issue of 'standpoint epistemologies', as this issue has been named, leads to a different conclusion.

The issue of standpoint epistemologies emerges in debates in feminist theories of science. Yet, as Sandra Harding explains, its source is older: such standpoint theorizing 'originates in Hegel's thinking about the relationship between the master and slave and in the elaboration of this analysis in the writings of Marx, Engels, and the Hungarian Marxist theorist, G. Lukács'. How does standpoint epistemology operate? Harding again:

> Feminism and the women's movement provide the theory and motivation for inquiry and political struggle that can transform the perspective of women into a 'standpoint' – a morally and scientifically preferable grounding for our interpretations and explanations of nature and social life.[44]

The notion of a 'standpoint' is not restricted to feminism and the women's movement; Marxist-inspired socialist movements also lean on this epistemological development.

Such an epistemological privilege being granted to a group in a particular social location has been fiercely criticized within feminism. In 'A Cyborg Manifesto', Donna J. Haraway argues that such epistemologies require the presumption of a stable identity; this identity is however simply not available. We should, she maintains, be 'freed of the need to ground politics in "our" privileged position of the oppression that incorporates all other dominations, the innocence of the merely violated'. In the desire 'to construct a revolutionary subject from the perspective of a hierarchy of oppressions and/or a latent position of moral superiority, innocence, and greater closeness to nature', we may detect the Western self present through philosophical epistemologies. Indeed, we may also detect O'Donovan's concern with a kind of romanticized knowledge.[45] Appealing to a certain type of postmodernism, Haraway rejects the notions of identity and self which, in her judgement, such epistemologies require and entail.[46]

---

42 See Habermas, 'Technology', 81–122.

43 O'Donovan, 'Political Theology', 243.

44 Harding, *Science*, 26.

45 O'Donovan, 'Political Theology', 243.

46 Haraway, 'Cyborg', 176.

Yet, in later work,[47] Haraway – qualifying her social constructionism while still wishing to avoid the problems associated with claims to the impartiality of 'objective knowing' – moves closer to standpoint epistemologies.[48] Identifying the problem in epistemology as follows: 'how to have *simultaneously* an account of radical historical contingency for all knowledge claims and knowing subjects ... *and* a no-nonsense commitment to faithful accounts of a "real" world', she proposes

> ... politics and epistemologies of location, positioning, and situating, where partiality and not universality is the condition of being heard to make rational knowledge claims. These are claims on people's lives; the view from a body, always a complex, contradictory, structuring and structured body, versus the view from above, from nowhere, from simplicity.[49]

Given such commitments, standpoint epistemologies have a certain attractiveness in that these represent the views of agents from below. These Haraway calls 'subjugated knowledges'.

What is privileged is not 'the position of the poor', but rather the range of practices which identify – under present capitalist conditions – the location of the poor. Such an epistemology must be attentive to the *subjugated* or *disadvantaged* actions of the poor: its source lies not in some reified notion of the bodies of the poor, but in their position in a division of labour which, increasingly structured by micro-technology and founded on flows of information, makes of them an underclass. Such structuring remains classist and racist in that exclusion from technology and information is supported by social relations of exploitation shaped by post-Fordist de-industrialization. For example, 'piece work' undertaken by Asian women in Britain for miserly rates of pay is often located in areas that used to host 'heavy' industry such as steel making or shipbuilding.

All romanticism, as Haraway advises, must be rejected here: *social location* does not provide some automatic or innocent access to liberative knowledge; subjugated knowledges are not naturalized knowledge 'mysteriously' available if you inhabit the 'correct' body and position. If such knowledge is to be critical, it must be learned: 'To see from below is neither easily learned nor unproblematic', writes Haraway. '[*H*]*ow* to see from below is a problem requiring at least as much skill with bodies and language, with the mediations of vision, as the 'highest' techno-scientific visualizations'.[50] The crucial point here

---

[47] Haraway, 'Situated Knowledges', 199.

[48] This point is well made in a very helpful commentary on Haraway's work by Marsden, 'Virtual Sexes and Feminist Futures', 11.

[49] Haraway, 'Situated Knowledges', 187, 195.

[50] Haraway, 'Situated Knowledges', 191.

is not whether the poor are as easily identified – Mrs Gaskell fashion – as in the past, but whether or not the poor may identify *themselves*. Again, this is an issue of learning: a matter of political organization rather than social visibility.

Earlier, I employed the spatial metaphor of 'closeness and distance' to indicate the process of learning required, against the pressures of ideology, in order to validate such a standpoint epistemology.[51] For what is needed here is an account of the epistemological protocols which are operative to show how – under the deforming pressures of a patriarchal, capitalist hegemony – theological knowledge may be neither tied too closely to dominant practices nor utopian (in the bad sense).[52]

Whether or not Haraway's account of the contingency of all knowing can be combined with her desire to know the real world is not my concern here. It may be that her view requires a theological supplement to be persuasive, a comment that Haraway herself would vehemently reject. Still, if my argument is correct, in biblical interpretation, as in the production of knowledge more generally, social location is critical. It is not that location produces knowledge and thereby somehow produces also the objects of knowledge. It is rather that liberative knowledge is perspectival knowledge, and the attempt to operate a realist epistemology requires a standpoint. And, furthermore, such knowledge is always received rather than generated.

The two points made so far in this section converge on an affirmation of the authority of the poor. The relation between theory and praxis involves a transcendent reference: repentance and obedience are possible. And the reference to social location does not require the view that certain groups attempt the recreation of the world through epistemological acts of pure willing. The connection between praxis and standpoint epistemology links scriptural authority to the authority of the poor.

Christ and Political Order

Which means, in turn, that I cannot accept the account of 'an unfolding political order' presented by O'Donovan. The argument of *DN* moves through a graceful four-fold sequence of analogies (ending in each case with a disanalogy). I plan to attend, in reverse sequence, to two of these analogies as they relate to political order before turning, in the next section, to the consideration of Christology. The two series of analogies that I wish to discuss, in reverse order, are those of speech and the recovery of creation that begin from

[51] Cf. Scott, *Theology*, 33f.

[52] The historical reference is vital here; I intend no universal claim. Cf. Turner, *Marxism*, esp. part 2.

exaltation and restoration, respectively. These analogies, whose relations are presented through three chapters, have the following sequence: exaltation – prophecy and prayer – freedom of speech – distorted speech; and restoration – glad community – natural right/order[53] – arbitrary collective will.

To begin with the theme of Christ's exaltation: in the last section of the final chapter of *DN*, O'Donovan notes that political speech has lost its reference to the common good. Now serving competing wills, political discourse ends in a cacophony of claim and counter-claim. He concludes: 'The term "ideology" best expresses this meltdown of the democratic idea ... Self-posited speech destroys its own point and collapses into silence.'[54] Because ideological discourse on politics serves competing interests, O'Donovan claims, the achievement of some common good is always inhibited.

Problematic, in my view, is the way that such a rendering promotes an instrumentalist or functionalist reading of the notion of ideology. To an instrumentalist construal, reference to the common good may be an adequate response. But if, as suggested above, ideology-critique is a cognitive exercise, we must enquire both of the truth-telling quality of the discourses themselves and the social order that such discourses legitimate. We can be sure that our social order, which 'spontaneously' generates lived yet ideological relations, will yield no robust notion of the common good. Indeed, it may well be that the critique of legitimation requires us to conclude that the notion of common good can have no purchase under present political and economic arrangements. When O'Donovan somewhat loftily remarks that, 'The private or sectional good is of more interest to most people most of the time', he betrays his own liberalism: most people, it is implied, live behind some veil of ignorance from which they require emancipation. On such emancipation, these folk will, I presume, overcome their 'difficulty of achieving any public concern for the common good at all'.[55] However, the achievement of a common good may be a matter of social and political struggle rather than education. Indeed, I am unsure whether the notion of a common good is serviceable at all; and it may be the function of ideology – including an ideological theology – to convince us of the opposite.[56]

---

[53] Mostly, O'Donovan speaks of 'natural right', occasionally of 'natural order' (see *DN*, 250) – how this subtle change in terminology should be interpreted I cannot say.

[54] *DN*, 283.

[55] *DN*, 271.

[56] To speak of the common good is inherently difficult in a divided society; the dangers of 'false universalism' are always present (Hicks, *Inequality*, 172). Working from a standpoint epistemology, perhaps we may at most conclude that in a dialectically contradictory form, the poor both witness to, represent, and have the truest knowledge of the 'common good'. In anthropological perspective, the common good would thereby name a process of social conflict; in soteriological perspective, such language would be justified by reference to the eschatological judgement of all by Christ.

If such a criticism is sustainable, then O'Donovan's earlier discussion of prophecy and prayer, that in turn resources the openness to speech, and stands opposed to lapses into distorted speech, is rendered less persuasive. For prophecy as a form of social criticism is rendered exceedingly difficult. 'The church prophesies to the world', O'Donovan writes, 'discovering the situation of the world and passing judgment on it.'[57] Yet, as already suggested, discovering 'the situation of the world' is no easy task: we should ordinarily expect our language to be in the service of praise of idols. How does prophecy as social criticism counter, to borrow a phrase from Fredric Jameson, ideological strategies of containment? The adequacy of a response does not turn upon the vehemence of, say, the rejection of social atomism. For liberative speech not only exposes the discourse on atomism as false, but it also discloses the social order that requires such discourse. After all, the discourse of possessive individualism is a *social* phenomenon and thereby requires a *social* explanation that offers more than an (in fact, tautologous) account of the proclivities of individuals.

The second series of analogies on which I wish to comment, in reverse order again, is that which begins from Christ's restoration (restoration – glad community – natural right – arbitrary collective will). The attempt by society to save itself is linked by O'Donovan with the emasculation of the notion of natural right. These are, I consider, among the most interesting passages in *DN*: the treatment of the fate of equality under the conditions of modernity is both compelling and convincing.[58] Furthermore, I am sure that O'Donovan is right to argue that one strategy for overcoming the arbitrariness of our political orderings must be to move away from notions of society as 'self-posited' and to try to recover a sense of society as 'a gift to be received and appreciated' and thereby as enjoying the 'natural' marks of equality, affinity and reciprocity. This, in turn, means that we must pay theological attention to notions of nature and naturalness.

What conception of nature are we dealing with here? What is this nature in the perspective of the 'vindication of created being'?[59] O'Donovan is uncharacteristically reticent at this point, arguing only that the high tradition of political theology, within which he situates his own work, has not attended to the theme of 'the *creaturely cohabitation* of human and non-human species in a common world'.[60] As this tradition says little about ecological relations, O'Donovan thereby decides not to treat the issue. However, O'Donovan concludes that this high tradition is not called into question by

57 *DN*, 188.
58 *DN*, 278–81.
59 *DN*, 262.
60 *DN*, 262.

the ecological issue. Despite the fact that his theological enquiry is conducted by means of an analogical imagination, O'Donovan declines to attend to this important contemporary issue.

However, O'Donovan ventures more on the topic of the notion of nature than his comments reported above might indicate. In a discussion of 'the recovery of the creation order', linked to Christ's restoration, O'Donovan argues that, 'Activity [towards nature] is responsive; otherwise it becomes tyrannous and destructive.'[61] That is, human action towards nature encounters 'something *there*'. O'Donovan thereby offers an account of the goodness of creation as vindicated by the resurrection of Christ.

This is a welcome emphasis but does not, I fear, go far enough. For the vindication of creation must be seen, as O'Donovan would agree, as an eschatological act that, in turn, indicates that creation itself has a future in and for God.[62] There is, therefore, not only the 'raw givenness' of nature together with its 'possibilities for co-operation', but also the otherness of nature secured by its eschatological destiny in God. To speak of the fulfilment of nature is to narrate a destiny for nature that exceeds its usefulness to human beings. The ordering of nature is thereby an eschatological ordering; as eschatological, such an ordering is subject to alteration. In my view, nature, as oriented for its completion on God, provides a point of transcendent reference. We are presented not by 'the order God has made' in which we are invited to live joyfully, but rather by a natural ordering that God is making in which we are invited to live joyfully. Any political ordering is less static, more fluid, than is suggested by O'Donovan's presentation.

The focus through this section has been on the political ordering we may regard as authorized by the Christ-event. I have suggested that the connection between freedom of speech and distorted speech, as presented by O'Donovan, is too easily made. I doubt that free speech can correct distorted speech in the way that O'Donovan recommends. Additionally, I propose a more active construal of nature which may, in turn, suggest a rather more dynamic ordering of nature-society. By nature we are confronted with the authorizing 'otherness' of disorderliness. And to make the connection one more time with standpoint epistemologies, those who live 'closest' to nature, or who are the principal mediators of nature to society, or who are denied access to natural goods, may be those who are best able to speak of this dynamic order. Once more we are referred to the authority of the poor in a political theology.

---

[61] *DN*, 183.

[62] I have set out the case for this position in my 'Nature, Technology' and 'Future'.

In Jesus Christ, a Revolution

In many ways, I agree with the method by which O'Donovan constructs his political theology. As noted in the prologue to *DN*,

> The point is ... to push back the horizon of commonplace politics and open it up to the activity of God. .... [T]heology is political simply by responding to the dynamics of its own proper themes. Christ, salvation, the church, the Trinity: to speak about these has involved theologians in speaking of society, and has led them to formulate normative political ends.[63]

This is well and wonderfully said. Furthermore, I agree that theological attention should be directed to the Christ-event. But, in my view, the Christ-event makes true speech about society more difficult than it was before and invites us to think of nature in more dynamic ways. Theologically, true speech must therefore try to recover the conditions of speaking and acting that conform to the re-creation secured by the career of Jesus Christ. That must be so because Christ – the language of incarnation insists – is the transcendence of God. I have pressed the themes of ideology, praxis and political order to show that, immanently presented within our present social condition, there is transcendent reference. Such transcendent reference may be discerned not simply through attention to the word of Scripture, but by processes of discernment learned through the acquisition of 'sacramental vision' (Rowan Williams). Such vision, in its attention to otherness, permits both obedience and repentance.

In such fashion, the authority of the struggle to overcome the idolatry of ideology, the authority of knowledge gained in praxis, and the authority of engaging a dynamic order may be recovered. This I have glossed under the general heading, 'the authority of the poor'. My argument began, then, from a concern that O'Donovan drives apart the authority of Scripture and the authority of the poor. In response, I have tried to indicate how the notion of the authority of the poor may be recovered by and for political theology. I have also tried to show how my perspective raises questions regarding some of O'Donovan's findings. Any decent political theology, as already noted, will wish to avoid the 'modern' charge of legitimation. It can do so, my argument runs, without falling into a new legitimation. One way of securing this – as presented in my argument – is to attend to the authority of the poor.

---

[63] *DN*, 2, 3. Cf. McDonagh, *Gracing*, 2, 'Christian theology, in the doctrinal tradition, has been for too long removed from practical, social and political engagement – to the great impoverishment of theologians' understanding of God, Christ, salvation, church, grace.'

However, I am not seeking to oppose the authority of the poor to scriptural authority. In other words, I do not wish to end where the argument began. It is time to risk an interpretation of the political outworking of the Christ-event and to indicate any resulting implications for the construal of Scripture as authoritative. To these tasks, this section, and the next, are dedicated.

If we wish to reach for a slogan, we might say that in my view, the Gospel *socializes*, and thereby politicizes. The resurrection of Christ – named the restoration of Christ by O'Donovan – not only affirms the goodness of creation and freedom of speech but also instantiates a revolution in embodiment: in Jesus' body, and – by participation – in the body of Christ and the body politic of the poor.[64] The resurrection is a divine act whose closest analogy is, first, *creatio ex nihilo* and, second, the exodus. As Robert Jenson notes, 'God is whoever raised Jesus from the dead, having before raised Israel from Egypt.'[65] It is, further, this liberation from Egypt that, as Rowan Williams notes, provides the resources towards the development of the theme of creation out of nothing: 'the Exodus in turn comes to be seen as a sort of recapitulation of creation'.[66] Political theology is thereby tasked with the recovery of theologico-political speech that seeks to be true to the three levels – Christ, the church, and the poor – of this re-creative act of God. True theological speech invokes a political ordering that is oriented on this event, and the recovery of such theological discourse cannot be separated from a construal of this order; true speech is thereby always linked to practice. Any attempt to undo or minimize this linkage leads to the impoverishment of scriptural authority. The Christ-event is not the source of some grid of knowledge of political order, nor does the derived notion of the kingdom of God have to take all the weight for establishing criteria to develop our understanding of political order. Such a tendency to treat political and theological discourse as under our control is the final redoubt of bourgeois fantasy.

How is this christological construal the nerve of a 'sacramental vision'?[67] I have said that the principal analogue for the return of Jesus from the dead is creation out of nothing. Hence the association soon made by the early church between the free obedience of Jesus Christ and the creativity of God, who brings something to be out of nothing. Not only is creation vindicated, but the

---

64 For the detail of this position, see my *Theology*, part 3.

65 Jenson, *Triune God*, 63.

66 Williams, *Christian Theology*, 67. This is shorthand, of course: as Williams notes, the reconsideration of the exodus in relation to God's creating is given impetus and orientation by Israel's return from Babylonian exile.

67 Through this and the next paragraph, I am drawing on Williams, *Christian Theology*, esp. chs. 9, 14 and 15.

discontinuity of death is overcome: the gospel socializes by overcoming the final limit of sociality, which is death. Thus the early church understood itself to be charged with a mission: the gospel socializes by seeking to gather all into this covenant of the resurrected God-body, the promise of which endures through the caesura of death. The resurrection is thereby the nerve of a political theology, for it indicates the shape of the power and liberty which the church, as witnessing body, enacts. Rowan Williams puts the matter this way:

> In giving to the outcast, the powerless, the freedom to take their part in renewing the world and setting aside the existing tyranny of faceless powers and human betrayals, God brings life out of emptiness, reality out of nothing: Jesus Christ, as the bodily presence of that summons, the concrete medium for that gift to be given, is the presence in our world of the absolute creative resource of God, God's capacity to make the difference between something and nothing. God has chosen things low and contemptible, mere nothings to overthrow the existing order (I Cor. 1.28); Jesus, reaching out to those who are nothing, is the tangible form of God's creative choosing.[68]

What is rather hastily described in theological discourse as 'the incarnation' is thereby the gift of the liberty of God embedded in human life in all its aspects (including natural aspects). 'The "point" of the Incarnation', states Williams,

> is above all the establishing of human communion by showing what the ultimate foundation of common life is, and actively drawing us – with all the forms of common life we are already involved in and which define our existence – into the common life of God.[69]

The source and direction of human social life, the incarnation makes clear, is the life of God, a life of perfect community, to which death is no final interruption. The way of participating in such life is, of course, by the sacraments administered by the church: in the incarnation of the Son is the assumption of human nature; the assumption of such materiality is re-enacted in the non-identical acts of repetition[70] of the sacraments; the material elements indicate the assumption of the materiality of human nature.

All this is too condensed, but I hope what is intended by the phrase 'sacramental vision' is clearer. The invitation, represented by the sacraments, is for all to be drawn into the fellowship of the liberty and creativity of God, the medium of which is the God-body, Jesus Christ. The church undertakes its

---

68 Williams, *Christian Theology*, 'Incarnation and the Renewal of Community', 231.

69 Williams, *Christian Theology*, 'Incarnation', 226.

70 Pickstock, *After Writing*, 160.

mission and witness in the political realm to indicate the offer, and mode, of participation in that fellowship. The reality and offer of God's 'indiscriminate regard' in baptism and 'guarantee of hospitality' in the Eucharist, to borrow again from Rowan Williams, thereby have a critical edge. A sacramental vision indicates:

> the challenge of how there might be a social order in which the disadvantaged and even the criminal could *trust* that the common resources of a society would work for their good, and in which those who, at any given moment, enjoyed the advantage or power would be obliged to examine how their position could be aligned with the given fact of common or mutual need, how they would act so as to release others to become 'givers' to them.[71]

Perhaps the metaphor of vision, which in turn requires spatial imagery, is here unsatisfactory. A different way of making the point would be to speak of 'sacramental labour': the sacraments of baptism and Eucharist are indeed 'works', and the enactment of the sacramental vision is indeed a labour, including political labouring. Such sacramental labours are nerved by water, bread and wine as the way of participation in God's offer of hospitality and fellowship. And so the following question is immediately raised by such sacramental labouring: how do the present configurations of society deny people access to all kinds of materials? What must be drawn into the daylight are the ways in which the rich refuse to the poor access to material goods and the ways in which the rich refuse, or do not acknowledge, the gifts of the poor. Sacramental labour is thereby a 'way of struggle' (E.P. Thompson[72]) in which 'indiscriminate regard' and 'guarantee of hospitality' are employed as criteria of Christian judgement in the political realm.

The Christian stance is, we might say, that of militant impartiality: God's care, communicated through the resurrection of the God-body, is impartial in its regard and unbounded in its hospitality. However, such regard and hospitality put into question the actual configuration of a society in its distribution of material 'sacraments' and thereby require the militant, sacramental labour of the church's witness, both in its own life and outward testimony and practice. Through this militancy, the church asserts that societies are not best understood by attention only to efficient causes. Militant impartiality, a summary of sacramental labour, thereby includes a transcendent reference. And it is the poor, of course, who are likely to be more familiar with the interruptions in society's indiscriminate regard and failures in society's hospitality.[73]

---

[71] Williams, *Christian Theology*, 'Sacraments of the New Society', 220.

[72] Cited in Inglis, *Raymond Williams*, 171.

[73] Where the notion of sacramental vision is weak is in its construal of the political forms in society. I have learned this from reading O'Donovan's *The Desire of the*

Scriptural, Practical Reasoning?

Where have we got to? There is no single application of a method that rules the charge of a 'return to legitimation' out of court. However, perhaps the notion of scriptural authority may be recovered by reference to what is authorized by practical reasoning in the poor's social acts. This is neither the blessing of the class interest of the poor (ideology is anyway never class-ideology), nor a collapse into a praxiological immanentism (that lacks reference to the transcendent), nor a drift into sceptical relativism. Instead, it is to relocate a Christian account of authority in the relation between Scripture and the poor, and links the status of the poor to the 'reality' in word and sacrament (but not the 'actuality') of revelation.

Throughout, I have sought to maintain the connection between the authority of the poor and the authority of Scripture. These forms are not the same, nor are they on the same level. To argue for a connection is not to argue for equal standing; their relation is asymmetrical. Nevertheless, I have contended that overlooking the authority of the poor may be connected to the poverty of authority experienced in Northern attempts at political theology.

I have claimed already that Scripture functions in O'Donovan's work as the source and rationale for a deductive logic of revelation. In a comment on his four marks of the church, O'Donovan asks how the narrative coherence of these marks is to be grasped. His response is to press the matter of the 'inner logic of the sequence': 'The narrative we need to discern, however', he writes, 'is the inner logic of the sequence, the logic of the dawning Kingdom of God which the sequence itself makes plain.'[74] Amended somewhat, this

---

Nations, which is persuasive that too much political theology is dedicated to the theological treatment of society and insufficiently to the *polis*. In short, much political theology – including my own – falls into a trap set by sociology: to attend to the immanent workings of a society rather than the ways in which a society is politically governed. Too often the notion of politics, with which political theology deals, treats society as not politically formed. O'Donovan describes these as 'acephalous' accounts of society in which attention to the political head is missing. O'Donovan makes this point on a number of different occasions: see, *inter alia*, O'Donovan, 'Political Theology', 240, 245; and *DN*, 244–45, 246–47. But the question is: why does political theology deal so little with the political head? Is it because it is in fact concerned with social agency and ecclesial agency, which is very hard to imagine, at the end of socialism and the death of hope? On the matter of *agency*, O'Donovan is silent. Nor is the matter addressed in the essay, 'Government as Judgement', where attention is directed to the relation broadly construed between the legislature and the courts; the focus is resolutely on the functions of government.

[74] *DN*, 191.

expression can be offered as an account of the logic of revelation through *DN*: O'Donovan seeks to explicate the logic of the kingdom that has dawned, although not without preparation in and through Israel, in its eschatological mediator and representative, Jesus Christ. The career of this Christ – summarized in four moments – is, in two further deductive moves, the basis of the organization of the church and the redemption of society, whereas only one of the moments (judgement) relates to the *ruling* of society. From a scriptural rendering of this rule, all authorization flows, hence the importance of giving a full account of the content of this rule: the One who will gather, judge and vindicate in truth.

The identification of such a deductive logic raises anew the matter of the epistemic status of this notion of authority. Is *DN* an argument *from* scriptural authority for a political theology, or an argument *for* the scriptural authorizing of political theology? In other words, how should the critic respond to this text: is the most appropriate way to raise questions about the contours of the political theology, or to ask after the epistemological conditions from which these insights are derived? If the former, judgement is difficult; as O'Donovan notes of the contributions by modernity-critics, 'The interpretative decisions that are reached are unsusceptible of confirmation or rebuttal, and can only be, as it were, ventured.'[75] Does not the same apply to O'Donovan's position? Maybe, however, O'Donovan is proposing that his account of the authorizing of a political theology requires an account of *revelation* in order to answer the question: why that people, why this carpenter, why that community? But such an account of revelation requires a greater elaboration and defence than O'Donovan offers. Above all, as an account of revelation for a political theology, a fuller account of the politics of knowledge is required.

In dialogue with Oliver O'Donovan, to whose writing I am deeply indebted and from whom I have learned much, I have urged a slightly different view. Constitutive of scriptural, practical reasoning is the hermeneutic mediation of a philosophy of praxis. By such interaction, a relationship between the authority of the poor and the authority of Scripture is established. By such philosophical mediation, crucial issues for a theologico-political hermeneutic are raised: ideology, praxis, and the nature of political ordering. We might call these matters education by the Spirit.[76]

---

[75] *DN*, 272.

[76] I am unsure how to characterize my argument in the light of O'Donovan's typology of the various construals of the two cities approach, and their Thomist undermining (see O'Donovan, 'Political Thought', 66). For sure, my view does not require a commitment to 'the progressive transformation of the social order' (see O'Donovan, 'Augustine's *City*', 90). However, I am not convinced by O'Donovan's argument that to speak of 'the human good as social' only eschatologically entails a type of worldly

The praxis of closeness and distance is always a scriptural performance. The authority of the poor, as I have indicated, is a scriptural authorization. The praxis of closeness and distance is the attempt to speak the political truth in any situation in a fashion that is neither 'reformist' nor 'utopian'. The church speaks out of a sacramental vision and engages in the practice of sacramental labouring. And scriptural testimony is the source of this sacramental vision. More precisely, this vision is sourced to the revolution in embodiment in the resurrection of Jesus Christ, present today in the sacraments. The practice of that revolution today, I have called 'militant impartiality'.

'The church's identification with the poor', writes Oliver O'Donovan in his response to a draft of this paper, '...has to be the goal, not the presupposition, of social reflection in the North.' I would prefer to say that in attempting an authentic liturgical performance in word and sacrament, the church seeks rather to be in solidarity with the poor. What concerns me more, however, is the direction of O'Donovan's argument: that, to put the matter crudely, the church is something *before* its sought-after solidarity with the poor. But what, before its achieved solidarity with the poor, can the church be? Such a church misses its identity received and acquired in Christ. This church faces the face of Christ but is itself faceless. As identity-free, it is a church-from-nowhere whose scriptural interpretation will be exegesis-from-nowhere and whose preaching will be words-from-nowhere.

Of course, I accept that in its actual manifestation the Northern church is a bourgeois phenomenon. Perhaps that is what O'Donovan means to highlight. However, its constitution as a community by word and sacrament is always as a church of the poor. It sees truthfully only when it acts sacramentally and thereby seeks to relearn the identity that is already bestowed on it: as a body to a head (1 Cor. 12). Such sacramental practice governs its exegesis and its preaching. Through its core liturgical acts, the church receives its identity as a church of the poor and proclaims its solidarity with the poor. To argue differently is to fail to construe the identity of the church aright. That is why I find the language of 'social reflection' too anaemic. What is required theologically is not more 'reflection' on society. There is already too much of that! In other words, the church's persistent failure to construe its identity sacramentally ensures that its word is merely a 'social reflection', a mirror held up in gentle affirmation to contemporary society. When I suggested that what we have is a church-from-nowhere, exegesis-from-nowhere and preaching-from-nowhere, this description is not a full characterization. It is more accurate to say that such a

---

irrelevance ('Political Thought', 66); for eschatology is the way by which Christian theology acknowledges that 'all human life searches for a way forward, and thus seems wedded to the prospect of a good outcome from history' (Hardy, 'Eschatology', 153).

church, with its exegesis and preaching, occupies a position deep within the regnant social order. From such a position, in itself a failure to grasp the gift of sacramental identity, ecclesial solidarity with the poor is impossible. At issue here, then, is whether or not the church seeks to practice the identity given to it and extends that identity into society in its exegesis and preaching.

Nor is this difficulty eased by the correct suggestion that O'Donovan made at the consultation that 'the meaning of oppression is the denial of access to the empowering word'. Correctness is not yet truth, as Ernst Bloch once noted. If what is meant is that the word bypasses all materiality to reach us, I do not think that the phrase can be accepted. Such a 'truth' will not make free. The poor do not suddenly become 'spiritually poor' *despite* or *without reference to* their material circumstance. If, for example, the Eucharist is not accompanied by concrete acts of justice, then, as Gutiérrez notes, the ritual itself is an 'empty action'.[77]

If O'Donovan is arguing against a reduction to the material, his point is well taken. However, the word should not be used, in my view, to oppose spirit to matter, new life to context. For example, in a discussion of 'the natural' in Protestant theology, Dietrich Bonhoeffer writes: 'For some [the natural] was completely lost sight of in the darkness of general sinfulness, while for others, conversely, it was lighted up by the brilliance of absolute historicity.'[78] Thus Bonhoeffer notes a debilitating tendency in Protestant theology: the natural or material context is either obscured by sinfulness or occluded by reference to the 'historical' act of revelation. My stress on sacramental labouring is an attempt in the construal of the identity of the church to guard against such an opposition of the material and the spiritual.

An implication of this position must be noted. The oppressive situation of the poor is placed in a different theological context in their encounter with the word. The poor become 'poor' again, and thereby are re-established in their soteriological place as the primary interpreters of God's word. From which it follows that no-one is – in the soteriological sense – 'poor' until they have heard and responded to the word. Once more, we find that the interruptive power of the poor is in the convergence of soteriological and anthropological senses in the ecclesial life of the poor. Once again, we see that the church of Christ is already the poor church and is to be found wherever the poor gather to interpret and perform Scripture. This is the *concrete* church which the church as institution and as congregations seeks to discover through solidarity with the poor as a poor church.

So far, so good. However, an important question – vital to the project of the Scripture and Hermeneutics Seminar – still lurks: how should those of us who

---

[77] Gutiérrez, *Theology*, 265.
[78] Bonhoeffer, *Ethics*, 120.

are not poor read Scripture? Those of us who have extensive material interests in rendering the gospel abstractly, how is our practical reasoning authorized? O'Donovan's concern with framing the question this way is that the method to be followed will be some variant of that proposed by Elisabeth Schüssler Fiorenza in *Jesus: Miriam's Child, Sophia's Prophet.* In the opening chapters, a methodological *tour de force*, Schüssler Fiorenza insists that a 'critical feminist theology of liberation' must 'start with a hermeneutics of suspicion rather than with a hermeneutics of undiscriminating acceptance of Scripture and tradition'.[79] Such a hermeneutics of suspicion must critique current systems of domination (such an 'analytic' she terms 'kyriarchy'[80]), explore in a historicizing move the political pressures present in the formation of christological discourse, and secure an epistemological space, akin to the standpoint epistemologies discussed earlier, for women to assemble and develop counter-hegemonic politico-theological discourses (such a 'space' she dubs 'the ekklēsia of wo/men'). Later, she connects these commitments by arguing that feminist theology must be understood as grounded in the struggles of wo/men towards the transformation of 'kyriarchy'.

Given such an appeal to an authorizing ground, it should come as no surprise that, 'Scripture, tradition, theology, and Christology must therefore be critically analysed and tested for their ideological-political functions in legitimating or subverting kyriarchal structures and mind-sets of domination.'[81] Schüssler Fiorenza concludes that 'a feminist liberationist exploration of Christian Scriptures does not begin its work with the biblical text but with a critical articulation and analysis of the experiences of wo/men'. For the task of feminist theology at the present is not to discern the scriptural sources for Christology proper, but instead 'should test out the implications and elaborate the power of christological discourses either for legitimating or for changing kyriarchal relations of domination'.[82] In evaluating Schüssler Fiorenza's approach, much would depend, as O'Donovan rightly notes, whether or not her argument finishes where it began. However, I hope the argument of this paper is sufficiently developed to show that beginning where Schüssler Fiorenza begins does not preclude the construal of Scripture as authorizing.

Something like Schüssler Fiorenza's approach, once secured within a larger theological hermeneutic, is in my view fruitful in answering the question: how should those of us who are not poor read Scripture? We cannot answer without developing for theological purposes an analytic for discerning systems of

---

[79] Schüssler Fiorenza, *Jesus*, 12.

[80] 'Kyriarchy', Schüssler Fiorenza's preferred term to 'patriarchy', is defined as 'the rule of the emperor/master/lord/father/husband over his subordinates' (*Jesus*, 14).

[81] Schüssler Fiorenza, *Jesus*, 49.

[82] Schüssler Fiorenza, *Jesus*, 61.

domination, a radical affirmation of historical contingency and the development of standpoint epistemologies for testing the difference between truth and ideology. Militant impartiality may then stand also as the summary of the interpretative stance of those who read Christian Scripture, but are not poor. The *skandalon* of the creative liberty of the gospel can never be separated from the scandal of the restriction of justice, freedom, peace and truth[83] in any society.

The implications of militant impartiality for scriptural exegesis are profound and difficult. How *should* the rich interpret Scripture? Offering a 'political' reading of Scripture or concentrating on certain passages, such as Exodus or the parable of *Dives* and Lazarus or Jesus' proclamation of Jubilee (Lk. 4:16–21), is important yet insufficient. Any scriptural exegesis must not simply pronounce the normative 'political' contents of the gospel. It must also indicate how the Northern church in its very exegesis acknowledges how far it falls behind God's gathering of the church of the poor. To do otherwise would be to fall into sinful exegesis. Sin may be defined as 'what God does not want done'.[84] Sinful exegesis fails to give an account of our world in the perspective of God's act in Jesus Christ. For Christ is what God wants to do: 'He is the image of the invisible God, the firstborn of all creation' (Col. 1:15). True exegesis and true preaching in the North will therefore always follow a trajectory of confession and conversion. Not only to make strange and thereby attractive Christianity's basic story, but also to indicate the extent to which such a retelling is a confession of the failure of the poor church to accept its identity, and a renewal of the church's confession to face the God of the poor and not some idol. Without such confession and conversion, exegesis and preaching will be sinful. To be sure, the world may not use the term 'sinful'. Nevertheless, the world will recognize such a stance as unreal and without credibility: a church of the poor – of, that is, a very precise *somewhere* – presenting itself as a church-from-nowhere, with its exegesis-from-nowhere and preaching-from-nowhere in close attendance.

Acknowledgement: Thanks to M. Daniel Carroll, Andrew Lincoln, Oliver O'Donovan and Robert Song for insightful comments on a draft of this essay.

---

[83] This quaternity I have taken from McDonagh, *Gracing*, esp. 8–18, which I was prompted to read on account of a favourable notice in *DN*, 250.

[84] Jenson, *Works*, 133.

Bibliography

Alison, J., *Faith Beyond Resentment: Fragments Catholic and Gay* (London: Darton, Longman & Todd, 2001)

Bonhoeffer, D., *Ethics* (London: SCM Press, 1955/1978)

Dorrien, G., *Reconstructing the Common Good: Theology and the Social Order* (Maryknoll, NY: Orbis Books, 1990)

Eagleton, T., *Ideology: An Introduction* (London: Verso, 1991)

Fackre, G., *The Doctrine of Revelation: A Narrative Interpretation* (Edinburgh: Edinburgh University Press, 1997)

Geuss, R., *The Idea of a Critical Theory* (Cambridge: CUP, 1981)

Gutiérrez, G., *A Theology of Liberation* (London: SCM Press, 1974)

——, *We Drink from our Own Wells: The Spiritual Journey of a People* (London: SCM Press, 1984)

——, *A Theology of Liberation* (New York: Orbis Books, rev. edn, 1998)

——, 'Option for the Poor', in *Mysterium Liberationis: Fundamental Concepts of Liberation Theology* (ed. I. Ellacuría and J. Sobrino; Maryknoll, NY: Orbis Books, 1993), 235–50

Habermas, J., 'Technology and Science as "Ideology"', in Habermas, *Toward a Rational Society* (Cambridge: Polity Press, 1987), 81–122

Haraway, D.J., 'A Cyborg Manifesto: Science, Technology, and Socialist-Feminism in the Late Twentieth Century', in Haraway, *Simians, Cyborgs and Women: The Reinvention of Nature* (London: Free Association Books, 1991), 149–81

——, 'Situated Knowledges: The Science Question in Feminism and the Privilege of Partial Perspective', in Haraway, *Simians, Cyborgs and Women: The Reinvention of Nature* (London: Free Association Books, 1991), 183–201

Harding, S., *The Science Question in Feminism* (Ithaca, NY: Cornell University Press, 1986)

Hardy, D.W., 'Eschatology as a Challenge for Theology', in *The Future as God's Gift* (ed. D. Fergusson and M. Sarot; Edinburgh: T. & T. Clark, 2000), 151–58

Hicks, D.A., *Inequality and Christian Ethics* (Cambridge: CUP, 2000)

Inglis, F., *Raymond Williams* (London and New York: Routledge, 1995)

Jenson, R.W., *Systematic Theology* I, *The Triune God* (New York: OUP, 1997)

——, *Systematic Theology* II, *The Works of God* (New York: OUP, 1999)

Lash, N., *The Beginning and End of Religion* (Cambridge: CUP, 1996)

Marsden, J., 'Virtual Sexes and Feminist Futures: The Philosophy of "Cyberfeminism"', *Radical Philosophy* 78 (1996), 6–16

McDonagh, E., *The Gracing of Society* (Dublin: Gill and Macmillan, 1989)

Mies, M., 'Liberating the Consumer', in M. Mies and V. Shiva, *Ecofeminism* (London: Zed Books, 1993), 251–63

Míguez Bonino, J., 'Latin American Theology: Questions for Britain', in *Putting Theology to Work* (ed. Derek Winter; London: Conference for World Mission, 1980), 11–16

Milbank, J., *Theology and Social Theory: Beyond Secular Reason* (Oxford: Basil Blackwell, 1990)

O'Donovan, O., 'The Political Thought of the Book of Revelation', *TynBul* 37 (1986), 61–94

——, 'Augustine's *City of God* XIX and Western Political Thought', *Dionysius* XI (1987), 89–110

——, 'Karl Barth and Ramsey's "Uses of Power"', *JRE* 19.2 (1991), 1–30

——, *The Desire of the Nations: Rediscovering the Roots of Political Theology* (Cambridge: CUP, 1996)

——, 'Response to Respondents: Behold the Lamb!', *SCE* 11.2 (1998), 91–110

——, 'Political Theology, Tradition and Modernity', in *The Cambridge Companion to Liberation Theology* (ed. C. Rowland; Cambridge: CUP, 1999), 235–47

——, 'Government as Judgment', *First Things* 92 (1999), 36–44

——, 'Deliberation, Reading and History', *SJT* 54.1 (2001), 127–44

Pickstock, C., *After Writing: On the Liturgical Consummation of Philosophy* (Oxford: Basil Blackwell, 1998)

Pope, S.J., 'Proper and Improper Impartiality and the Preferential Option for the Poor', *TS* 54 (1993), 242–71

Rowland, C., and M. Corner, *Liberating Exegesis: The Challenge of Liberation Theology to Biblical Studies* (BFT; London: SPCK, 1990)

Schüssler Fiorenza, E., *Jesus: Miriam's Child, Sophia's Prophet* (London: SCM Press, 1994)

Schweiker, W., 'Freedom and Authority in Political Theology', *SJT* 54.1 (2001), 110–26

Scott, P., *Theology, Ideology and Liberation* (Cambridge: CUP, 1994)

——, 'The Future of Creation: Ecology and Eschatology', in *The Future as God's Gift* (ed. D. Fergusson and M. Sarot; Edinburgh: T. & T. Clark, 2000), 89–114

——, 'Nature, Technology and the Rule of God: Against the Disordering of Nature', in *Reordering Nature* (ed. C. Deane-Drummond; Edinburgh: T. & T. Clark, 2002)

Shanks, A., 'Response to *The Desire of the Nations*', *SCE* 11.2 (1998), 86–90

——, *God and Modernity: A New and Better Way to Do Theology* (London: Routledge, 1999)

Thompson, J.B., *Studies in the Theory of Ideology* (Cambridge: CUP, 1984)

——, *Ideology and Modern Culture* (Cambridge: Polity Press, 1990)

Turner, D., *Marxism and Christianity* (Oxford: Basil Blackwell, 1983)

Waters, B., '*The Desire of the Nations*: An Overview', *SCE* 11.2 (1998), 1–7

Williams, R., *On Christian Theology* (Oxford: Basil Blackwell, 2000)

25

Response to Peter Scott

Oliver O'Donovan

I came to the Southern School from a distance, finding its work intellectually unpalatable, abstractly dialectical and dogmatic by turns, and suspicious of its claims to a contextual truth. My eyes were opened by Gutiérrez's late work, *The Truth Shall Make You Free*, the fruit of the dialogue with the Vatican. My treatment in *Desire* was an attempt to make amends, especially on the point of contexuality, and to offer appreciation from a distance, taking a different path but with honour intact on both sides. Peter Scott may not object to the thought that his response to me is of the same genre. I am grateful for it, since appreciation from a distance can teach things that one cannot learn from nearer assessment. It is a condition of that kind of appreciation that one doesn't understand the other fully, and he and I need not reproach one another for that. He admits that he does not understand me on the political act – a pity, since it is my highest card as a revolutionary theologian! – and I admit that I do not understand his dialectical denial of the notion of the common good. I appreciate his willingness to appreciate; though I think he underestimates mine, interpreting me as more hostile to Liberation Theology than I feel myself to be on three points:

1. I do not challenge the claim that criticism of ideology is a necessary element in political theology, and that it has the character of resistance to idolatry. I only want to deny the totalizing of this move, and to insist that political theology has to get 'beyond suspicion' and take seriously the moment of transcendent authority. Scott gives an account of ideology-critique which, he says, 'does not rule out such a moment of transcendent criticism'. I agree, and can find no quarrel here between us.
2. I do not challenge the necessity of situated epistemologies, though I do not like everything he, or Harding, says about 'standpoints'. The impartiality of a universal view must wait for the kingdom of heaven. We must see from somewhere, and it matters where we see from. It matters in particular that we should try to see from some angle not immediately given to us – that is,

we should see with sympathy. But I object to the assumption that there are certain social standpoints from which everybody (at all times and in all places) ought to try to see – standpoints privileged universally and for all time. There is in fact only one such universal standpoint, and that is the entourage of an obscure Jewish rabbi in the first century. Historical change and cultural diversity do not permit given standpoints to remain unmodified from age to age and from place to place, and when we try to adopt one not of our time and place, we attribute transcendent significance to it, so that it becomes our faith. Either this is justified (as with the entourage of the Jewish rabbi), or it is not. When it is not, we have fallen victim to an idolatrous nostalgia, a self-falsification that vitiates practical engagement with the world.

3. I do not challenge the claim that the 'poor' is a biblical category, and therefore the poor have authority (in connection with, and not in opposition to, the authority of Scripture) that has to be responded to by any political theology. In the sentence that Peter Scott quotes at the beginning, I say as much. Nor do I challenge the claim that taking it up is a task for thought, not merely for service – that there is an epistemological, not only a moral, authority in it, though the sharpness with which Scott opposes these two slightly shocks me. The point of difference between North and South that I insist on is simply that for us this category cannot be a starting point, since where we live, the location of true poverty is hidden behind a veil of widespread wealth.

Scott says, 'there are methodological difficulties in making the connection between the poor as biblical category and the poor as political category', and that hits the nail on the head, except that the difficulties are more than 'methodological'. They have to do with discerning where in any society the 'poor' of whom the Scripture speaks are. 'The church ... is part of a capitalist order', he quotes Gutiérrez, though this is dialectically understood, in relation to 'the church of the poor'. A church of the poor thus situated in an alien order must clearly search for its identity-with-the-poor by 'seeing through' that order. Here I am in profound agreement with his quotation from Haraway: 'To see from below is neither easily learned nor unproblematic.'

Is Scott ready to 'see through' our Northern order? I am not sure. It depends on how he proposes to find out about it. Will he go to a political encyclopaedia (s.v. 'capitalism') or will he look around him? On page 18 of *Desire* I enumerated thirteen typical questions about our society, all obvious enough when one looks around, from checkouts in a supermarket to the nation-state; of these I said, rather cheekily, that 'political theology in its current [i.e. Southern-inspired] form sheds rather little light'. Scott, though he does not see himself as a representative of Liberation Theology, resembles it at least in taking no more notice of them! And when he speaks of classist,

> racist labour, I am afraid I sniff nostalgia. Of course, such perversions as classism and racism still arise among us; but if one has it in mind to denounce them, one will find oneself at the back of a long queue. The victims of such old-fashioned industrial violence are not the invisible oppressed of cyberspace society. Nor can his concern with the denial of 'access to all kinds of materials' be justified by Rowan Williams' conception of 'sacramental labouring'. A sacrament is constituted by a word as well as an element. Why should we not conclude from the same premise that the meaning of oppression is the denial of access to the empowering word? Certainly, when Williams speaks, with characteristic allusiveness, of 'what the ultimate foundation of common life is', I do not think he means simply material resources.

The church's identification with the poor, then, has to be the goal, not the presupposition, of social reflection in the North. Modern society has hidden the poor by distributing wealth and distributing power, and not distributing them together; so that even fairly poor people assume the attitudes that belong to power. When a clerical student, one of the materially poor of the earth, boasts that the internet has redefined our relation to space because we can buy things without going out, he commits the same error as an eighteenth-century slave-owner: he overlooks the fact that someone somewhere is running errands for him. To tyrannize over one's neighbour like a Roman emperor, one needs only the use of a computer and a phone-jack.

26

A Timely Conversation with *The Desire of the Nations* on Civil Society, Nation and State

Joan Lockwood O'Donovan

Throughout the twentieth century, the idea of the nation-state has pervaded the conceptualization of political order. The idea has been endorsed or attacked, and frequently both endorsed and attacked, but it has been ignored only with difficulty. For most of the century, it has played a strategic role in the formation of new political entities out of the old European and colonial empires: the Ottoman, Hapsburg and Tsarist empires in Europe and the Middle East, and the European colonial possessions throughout Africa, Asia and the Far East. In the course of imperial dismemberment, exacerbated by war, and of comprehensive decolonization, the idea of the nation-state has also been implicated in unprecedented state persecutions and territorial displacements of ethnic populations and the creation of 'stateless' peoples or official refugees. Thus, much ink has been spilt on the dramatic ambiguities of the concept for political morality. More recently, the idea has become a *locus* for a range of issues affecting liberal-democratic polities in the 'global' era of mass communications technology, mass immigration, multinational corporations, international finance and defence. The controlling question of these discussions concerns not so much the political morality as the political efficacy of the nation-state, whether it continues to be a viable and useful form of political organization in the contemporary world.

That the question of political morality continues to loom large in contemporary reflection on the nation-state is owing in part to the horrific events of 'ethnic cleansing' that have attracted universal attention over the last decade – in the former Yugoslav republics, in African countries such as Rwanda, Burundi, the Sudan and in Indonesia. To the extent that these assaults on civilian populations have been carried out by militias with various degrees of governmental backing, they are perceived to manifest not merely tribal lawlessness in an anarchic atmosphere, but perversions of the modern state, and so they stimulate us to reconsider the issues thrown up by the magnitude and global proliferation of such perversions in our century.

Should we want guidance in sifting through these issues, we are spoiled for resources, having at our disposal a massive array of investigations undertaken since the late 1930s into the origins, mechanisms, and effects of modern state domination. The more philosophically serious of these[1] have brought to light a pervasive political dynamic with two dialectical moments. One moment is the exclusive identification of the state with the perceived interests of a particular group – whether racial, ethnic, or social, such that the state becomes its instrument, to achieve its collective will. The other moment is the state's absolute self-elevation above the body politic: above its multiplicity of institutions, interests, authorities, communities, and moral sentiments, and above the inherited framework of customary and statutory law through which these are ordered. The state, it would seem, cannot be the slave of race, ethnicity, or social class without being unrestrained master of the commonwealth.

The challenge of overcoming this perverse political dynamic is that of reconstructing the government as a servant of the whole body politic in its authentic pluralism, willing and able to restrain the tyrannous aspirations of any single community. Needless to say, the obstacles to such a reconstruction in any society caught up in or emerging from this dynamic are formidable, even when the population is largely supportive of reforming measures – more so when the measures are, to some degree, being thrust upon a reluctant regime or population by international pressures. In such circumstances, the establishment of stable and effective government within a framework of law and public accountability, free and responsible social institutions, a climate of mutual tolerance, forbearance and respect among citizens, is nothing short of an awesome work of divine providence.

It is, however, a providential work that must be hoped and prayed for, and humanly abetted as much as possible, because the consequence of not overcoming nationalistic aggression and the tyrannical abuse of ethnic minorities is a continuous stream of wars of secession leading either to indefinitely protracted international protectorates of minority populations or to the birth of small, defensive and (most probably) intolerant new states. More than ever is it incumbent upon us in Western Europe and North America, who are playing and will play a vital role in the political future of many persecuted populations and secessionist movements throughout the world, to engage not only with the historical complexities behind present conflicts but also with the broadest

[1] Hannah Arendt's early work, *The Origins of Totalitarianism*, remains a masterpiece of historical interpretation and philosophical reflection which subsequent sociological and empirical investigations (e.g., by Carl Friedrich and Zbigniew Brzezinski) do not match.

theoretical issues that they raise. Since the 1930s, this engagement has moved within the conceptual framework of modern liberal-democratic pluralism, with its particular understandings of nation, state and civil society. While this framework has certain theoretical strengths, it is not without deficiencies serious enough (in my judgement) to contribute to the provocation and exacerbation of situations of political injustice and conflict.

Christian scholars who can lay hold of the resources of Scripture and the exegetical and theological traditions of the past are uniquely well-placed to perceive the shortcomings of the prevailing discussion and to reach for more theoretically adequate resolutions of these pressing issues. For in the revelation of God's historical dealings with Israel, fulfilled in the coming of Jesus Christ and the gathering of his kingdom, is given the reality of political authority and of political community – and therein the proper meaning of nation, state and civil polity in their interrelationship. And in the premodern and protomodern traditions of appropriating this meaning are developments that continue to have a crucial bearing on an adequate response to the political aberrations of our time. In my present attempt to address these aberrations out of the Christian resources, I am indebted to Oliver O'Donovan's *The Desire of the Nations* for its theological exposition of the elements and moments in the scriptural revelation of political authority and political community.

My argument has a critical and a constructive phase. In the first I explicate the interaction of romantic, civic and functional concepts of the nation in the thought of the last century, raising objections along the way. In the latter I indicate the biblical points of reference for a theological concept of the nation and their outworking in the formation of Western Christian nations.

The 'Romantic', the 'Civic' and the 'Functional' Nation

Intrinsic to contemporary usage of the term 'nation' is a conceptual ambiguity of decisive importance. On the one hand, the double-pronged noun 'nation-state' implies that the nation is a reality distinct not only from the mechanism of government (one meaning of 'state'), but also from the political community (another meaning of 'state'). On the other hand, 'nation' is frequently employed as a synonym for 'state' in its second meaning, most famously in the rubric of 'the United Nations'. The significance of this duality of meaning lies in the long-standing issues arising from it, concerning which referent has historical and moral priority so as to justify and determine the reality of the other.

The answer of *romantic nationalism* is that the nation as a unique communal totality, at once natural and historical, gives rise to and morally justifies the sovereign state. Constitutive of this prior totality, on the romantic view, are such features as a common language and ethnic inheritance, shared sentiments, mores, spiritual capacities and historical memories, and a continuous relation to a particular soil. When such an organic social-cultural reality becomes self-conscious, it seeks to express its subjectivity in the realms of power and law. In assuming statehood it becomes self-determining: it takes control of its historical destiny. This was the national idea that dominated Europe for a century after 1830, inspiring the partition of empires, projects of linguistic and cultural unification, and the formation of a host of new states in East and West. Its quintessential statement was Guiseppe Mazzini's call in 1857: 'Every nation a state' and 'only one state for the entire nation'.[2] The romantic principle, however, could give play to diverse political visions, as may be gauged by the distance between Mazzini's projected map of Europe consisting of 'a bare dozen states and federations' and the twenty-six European states produced by the peace treaties following World War I under the influence of Woodrow Wilson's version of the nationality idea. Whereas Mazzini's romantic nationalism was evidently adulterated by liberal-economic and progressivist notions inimical to the appearance of small states, President Wilson endorsed a purer strain of ethnic-linguistic nationhood sympathetic to the course of 'Balkanization'.

The constitution of all twenty-six new states as parliamentary democracies suggests the intimate relation between the romantic and the civic conceptions of the nation that existed in Europe from about 1870 onward. In contrast to the ethnic-linguistic nation, the *civic nation* was regarded not as a prior cause of the state but as coterminous with it and, to some extent, a consequence of it. The civic nation comprises the unifying moral and affective bonds of the citizenry in a free, democratic polity; it comprises the ongoing moral-political reality of the 'popular will' as a vital community of faith, sentiment and devotion. A rational communion, the civic nation is formed over time through the operation of political and legal institutions according to universal principles of justice. But it is also a deliberate project of public education and mobilization: of educating citizens in the principles of liberal democratic political culture and mobilizing them for political action.[3] Born in the crucible of late eighteenth-century revolutions, the civic nation has found its rational articulation in the equal rights of individual citizens: linguistic, cultural and religious, as well as civil and political rights. The civic nation requires that the state, understood as the permanent machinery and ongoing activity of government, be its subordinate agency, its instrument for defending and furthering the moral-juridical totality that it is.

---

[2] Hobsbawm, *Nations*, 101.

[3] Jacques Maritain, in his post-war writing *Man and the State*, presents the civic nation as both a spontaneous outgrowth of political activity and a conscious project of public education.

In the inter-war years, this *wedding of romantic and civic nations* proved catastrophic, a harbinger of the century's worsening political miseries. In the first place, the nation-states produced by the peace treaties in Eastern and Southern Europe were defective on both ethnic-linguistic and civic grounds, lacking homogenous populations, rootedness in the soil and a history of government. In the second place, the inevitable failure of the romantic-civic nation to produce justice for its 'minority peoples' was conceded from the start by the imposition of minority treaties, transferring the protection of minority rights to the international *League of Nations*. Precipitating the rising tide of refugees across Europe was the conviction of members of minority 'nations' that, without the 'popular sovereignty' provided by 'full national emancipation', they 'were deprived of human rights'.[4] With considerable penetration, some scholars have perceived Hitler's policies of invading neighbouring countries with German-speaking populations, repatriating Germans living on foreign soils, and depriving undesirable minorities of citizen-rights as following through the Wilsonian logic of national, democratic self-determination.[5] And not only Hitler's policies, we may add, but those of subsequent revolutionary and dictatorial regimes have also aggressively sought to recover or emancipate 'nationals' in foreign territories and/or have denationalized whole groups of citizens as beyond the pale of democratic rights.

It seems ironic, to say the least, that the post-World War II global political order defined by two decades of UN declarations should have as its twin planks the *equal and inalienable rights of individuals (including the 'right to a nationality')*[6] and *the equal and inalienable rights of 'peoples' to 'self-determination'*.[7] For the blend of civic and romantic nationalism has, arguably, been even less suited to the state-making of the decolonizing era. On the one hand, the liberal individualism of the United Nation's *Universal Declaration of Human Rights* (1948) has sat ill with the traditional social structures and political authorities of many decolonizing societies. On the other hand, the tantalizingly ambiguous promise of self-determination for 'peoples' has sat ill with the existing (colonial) boundaries of decolonized states. The combination of social disintegration under liberal ideological and economic pressures, mobilization of the political masses by 'democratic' dictators, and the absence of workable political institutions for incorporating traditional authorities and containing ethnic/tribal hostilities has contributed immeasurably to the unprecedented

4 Arendt, *Origins*, 272.

5 Arendt, *Origins*, 275; Hobsbawm, *Nations,* 133.

6 *Universal Declaration of Human Rights* (1948), Article 15 in Brownlie, *Basic Documents*, 24.

7 *Declaration on the Granting of Independence to Colonial Countries and Peoples* (1960), in Brownlie, *Basic Documents*, 29.

international problem of 'stateless' refugees. It is a most telling indictment of democratic nation-building that, by the 1980s, Africa could boast not only fifty new nation-states, but also a refugee population of over five million, 'an estimated one-half of the world's total'.[8] Moreover, even where traditional political and social arrangements have proved more stable, their deviation from international 'civic' norms has been a nagging source of public resentment, cynicism and polarization in these polities.

The relative persistence of colonial territorial boundaries in the post-colonial political order, despite the mooting of alternative visions of national emancipation, has reflected (among other factors) the continuing sway of *the 'functional' concept of the nation* – the nation conceived as meeting such 'functional' criteria as those of effective government, military capacity, constitutional order, unifying cultural traditions, social stability and economic development. The functional concept of the nation is bound to reinforce any relatively successful geopolitical status quo and to favour territorial units with more, rather than less, potential across the criteria. Its importance in the post-colonial context has been to counterbalance the impetus given by the principle of national self-determination to the emergence of 'paper states' ('juridical states'): functionally non-viable 'states' that are nonetheless 'guaranteed in their juridical sovereignty by the international community'.[9] Unfortunately, ideological resistance and imperial ambitions within the international community have not always allowed this concept to carry its proper weight.

Moreover, the theoretical achievement of the 'functional nation' has been marred by the long-standing liberal tendency to exaggerate the economic component. The tendency to understand and evaluate the nation chiefly as an economic organization, in terms of its benefits for industry, trade and finance, is as strong as ever in both the developed and the developing world – to the detriment of political discussion and deliberation. For instance, the seemingly interminable debate in Britain over the form of the European Community slogged on for many years without considerations beyond those of the 'national economy' surfacing in any coherent political manner. Only defence policy attracted comparable attention from time to time – as, indeed, it should. Not until recently have signs emerged of an appetite for a broader historical discussion of the distinctive political and legal traditions of European nations, and the consequences for them of the different avenues of European integration – whether federal, confederal or more loosely associative.

Post-colonial polities have shown themselves to be, if anything, even more susceptible to the excessive identification of 'national' with 'economic' objectives, on account of (among other factors) the weakness of indigenous political

---

[8] Mayall, *Nationalism*, 55.

[9] Mayall, *Nationalism*, 122.

traditions, widespread resentment over past economic exploitation, and the powerful models furnished by advanced industrial economies. Typically, rapid economic development has assumed disproportionate strategic and symbolic 'national' importance in these countries, with the deleterious economic, social and environmental consequences of which we are now all too aware. The 'debt mountain' of developing nations is one fairly predictable outcome of overly ambitious economic 'nation-making' undertaken in the highly disadvantageous conditions of international trade and finance.

Thus have the prevailing concepts of the nation over the last two centuries – the romantic, the civic and the functional – shown serious theoretical inadequacies in comprehending the *de facto* and *de jure* elements of concrete political order at the level of the nation-state. A Christian theological response to these failings has been made difficult by the apparent discontinuity between the modern ideas and projects of 'the nation' and the historical development of Christian nations. Even that minority of contemporary scholars who concede that 'the nation' came to light in the historical self-understanding of Christian polities, and that this self-understanding has theoretical and practical strengths lacking in modern successors, do not admit its relevance in the present.[10] At least they do not admit the full extent of its possible engagement with, and transformation of, contemporary political theory and practice – in the advanced West as well as in the recently liberated East and in the post-colonial world.

At the heart of the historical fatalism, or perhaps the 'historical impenitence' (to use Chesterton's pointed epithet) of contemporary scholarship, is acquiescence in the hegemony of the civic nation in the advanced West – in the seemingly irreversible ideological and institutional settlement of liberal-democratic pluralism. This settlement *prescribes* an *equality of individual right* to religious freedom that requires at best an *equal* representation of different religions in the public realm,[11] and at worst no religious representation at all. At the same time, it *proscribes* a unitary public confession of Christian belief and the establishment of one or more Christian churches. Running the gamut from deistic to agnostic to atheistic humanism, the advanced 'civic faith' has already determined the unifying culture of political society and does not welcome theological intrusions into its self-understanding. Reinforcing its anti-theological bias is a neurotic fear of theocratic nationalism (neurotic because counter-factual) fed by the emergence in Africa and Asia of anti-Western Islamic and Buddhist nations and national movements that are, in fact, less 'fundamentalist' (as they are

---

[10] Among such scholars I would include Hannah Arendt, E.J. Hobsbawm and Anthony D. Smith.

[11] The point here is that equality of religious representation is dogmatically required even where it may not be necessary for social peace and harmony.

commonly dubbed) than historically reactionary.[12] On their part, contemporary theologians have demonstrated too little appreciation of the theopolitical matrices of the formation of nations, especially the wide-ranging influence of the Old Testament. It is to these scriptural theological themes and their historical elaborations that I now turn.

The Nation as a Theological Construct

If we turn from the modern concepts of the nation to Oliver O'Donovan's exploration of God's historical self-revelation to Israel as her king in Chapter 2 of *DN*, we are immediately struck by his coherent theological exposition of all the ideas of the nation which we receive today in fragmentary and, dare I say, distorted, formulations. It becomes clear that Christian understandings of the nation have been, and must continue to be, shaped by the divine revelation of political authority and political community in the history of Israel. In the first place, God's royal rule is revealed in his acts of delivering his people from their enemies, of giving them his law and of judging them, through the human mediation of warrior-leaders, kings, priests and prophets. In the second place, the reality of God's kingdom is revealed in Israel's possession of the land as his gift, and in her possession of the law as the lasting record of God's royal judgements. In the third place, the Israelites are a people (*'am*) by virtue of their common ancestry, common language and common historical memories: by God's election of the twelve tribes as his covenanted people in their forefather Abraham and in successive generations of patriarchs with whom he confirmed his covenantal promises, by their common sufferings in Egypt and deliverance from them, by their wanderings in the desert and military conquest of Canaan for their promised homeland. In the fourth place, Israel perpetually receives her political identity through worshipping her divine saviour, judge, lawgiver and provider in public acts of thanksgiving, penitence and petition. Finally, her historical vocation as God's uniquely favoured people is to be a revelation of communal holiness to the gentile 'nations', who themselves have a divinely ordained political vocation which they forsake at their peril.

Inevitably, the model of Israel has played a leading role in the Christian formation of nations – not only in the emergence of modern Western nations from the fourteenth to the seventeenth centuries, but also in the emergence of their geopolitical predecessors – Ostrogothic and Burgundian kingdoms, Lombard Italy and Visigothic Spain, and the Western and Eastern Frankish

---

12 So-called Islamic fundamentalism is not an exegetical literalism in respect of the Koran, but reversion to a restrictive mediaeval codification of Islamic law and spirituality.

realms.[13] The reception of this model was invariably shaped by contemporary political traditions, whether indigenous Germanic or Roman imperial. Germanic Christian rulers and their European successors believed, with their subjects, that they held their thrones by divine appointment and by continuing divine favour. They cast themselves, and were cast, in the roles of Israelite rulers as they carried out their responsibilities of judging, legislating and waging war. David and Solomon provided the pervasive paradigm of royal rectitude by their knowledge of, and active obedience to, God's revealed law, and by their embodiment of divinely imparted wisdom. Christian rulers knew that their territorial kingdoms and their people's prosperity were not only given by God but removable by him in the event of their and/or their subjects' rebellion against his manifest will. They knew that because their nations were elect, they would incur greater judgement. They understood their realms to be bound together not only by historical, linguistic and cultural ties, but also preeminently by the ligaments of divine and human law. They saw their responsibility for public justice as extending to the public duty of rendering to God the worship of thankful, humble, obedient and contrite hearts owing to him. Later Christian commonwealths, in the sixteenth and seventeenth centuries, rested their political vocations on divine-human covenantal foundations, after the Israelite pattern.

In modelling their political self-understanding on Israel's, Christian polities always tread a perilous theological route. Their ever-present temptation was so to identify with God's *one elect nation* as to deny *the absolute historical uniqueness and universal representativeness of Israel's political vocation*. Whenever they succumbed to this temptation, with its destructive political baggage of holy war, theocratic legalism and messianism, so-called Christian nations refused to be Christian, refused to be subject to the kingship of Christ and the advent of his kingdom. They refused to follow Israel into exile, unfulfilled restoration and messianic expectancy, and they refused the fulfilment of Israel's vocation in the earthly ministry, death, resurrection and exaltation of Jesus Christ, continued in the earthly witness of Christ's faithful people to his coming kingdom. They refused the confrontation of Christ's rule of righteousness and love with *the nation as such*, the judgement of his justice and peace on the worldly polities' sinful and alienated strivings after justice and peace. They refused to acknowledge the new meaning of the nation created by the earthly presence of christological power, judgement, law and fellowship.

What is this new meaning? In the chapter of *DN* entitled 'The triumph of the Kingdom', Oliver O'Donovan conceives the meaning as taking shape in

---

[13] For the Christian formation of nations from the second to the seventeenth centuries, see O'Donovan and O'Donovan (eds.), *Sourcebook*, and for the formation of the English nation, see O'Donovan, *Theology of Law*.

the 'penumbra' of the church's eschatological witness in a sinful world. The nation is a concrete territorial order of political power, judgement and tradition that sustains a space within the sinful human condition for the gathering of Christ's faithful people through the work of the Holy Spirit. In a sense, the nation remains what Israel revealed it to be – its constitutive elements have not changed: a government that gives judgements, laws and protection from enemies; a population inhabiting a homeland, linked by historical, linguistic and cultural ties; and bound authoritatively by customs, laws and political judgements. But its theological significance has changed, its role in the divine economy *ad extra* has changed: it is no longer revealed to be the vehicle of salvation, but merely the guaranteed social space within which God's saving work proceeds. It is revealed to belong to the Father's sustaining governance of the world rather than his transforming governance through the Spirit of Christ. The nation is a reality of the old age which is passing away, but whose continuing sway serves the proclamatory mission of the renewed Israel.[14]

Only as the community of Pentecost – the Spirit-filled body of the exalted Christ – is grasped as the *telos* of earthly polity, do the *inherent* deficiencies and limitations of the nation come to light. These are the deficiencies, on the part of rulers, of coercive power, tragically inadequate judgement and weak vision; on the part of the ruled, of inequitable laws, incomplete consent and merely external and episodic obedience; on the part of the ethnic/cultural community, of narrow and exclusive self-definition.[15] The inevitability of these deficiencies becomes manifest only as they are judged by the church's fidelity to the worship and ministries appointed by Christ, for which she is empowered by the gifts of the Spirit. Conversely, evidence of grave and widespread unfaithfulness in the church provokes rulers and ruled alike to deny their inevitability. When church institutions have adopted non-christological modes of judgement, sought worldly power and riches, cultivated worldly virtues, turned away from the intellectual and moral stringency of the revealed word of Christ, civil rulers have frequently overstepped their vocations by engaging in defensive and offensive manoeuvres in spiritual control. The conception of the church as the 'nation at worship', which sprang up in the late Middle Ages in reaction to the exaggerated jurisdictional pretensions of the papal church, exemplifies such overstepping. For the nation can never coincide with the eschatological community of world-renunciation, suffering love, gospel proclamation and prophetic freedom that is the earthly 'bride' of the risen Christ.

---

[14] *DN*, 146–47.

[15] Of course, these deficiencies are always susceptible of becoming the more extreme political perversities of tyranny, persecution, anarchy, factionalism and national aggression.

While recognizing all the natural and historical elements of the nation, the reappraisal opened up by the Christ-event reinforces a certain primacy that is already revealed in the political identity of Israel: the primacy of authoritative judgement and communal law, that together constitute the tradition of legal justice. In the light of the advent of Christ's kingdom, we can discern the defining aspect of the earthly nation to be *the concrete rendering over time of legal justice, that is, the ongoing practice of judgement conducted through the medium of law.* It is this, rather than permanent territorial boundaries or ethnic/linguistic homogeneity or economic power, that gives political identity to a society. In the Christian political tradition, the defining primacy of legal justice has been elaborated in the twin theological themes of 1) the divine vicariate of the ruler and 2) the commonwealth as a body of law, both of which have been central pillars of the Christian formation of nations. The supersession of these themes in the modern concepts of the nation goes some way in accounting for the proliferating perversions of the nation-state in our time. Let us briefly indicate how their recovery in contemporary discussion may prove more efficacious in combating nationalist ideologies and averting their horrific consequences than any combination of the romantic and civic alternatives.

The divine vicariate of civil governors

To point out how inimical modern conceptions of the nation-state have been to the Christian idea that governors have a divine vicariate is to state the obvious. It is, however, instructive to indicate the misrepresentation of the Christian idea invariably involved in this hostility. We can detect this misrepresentation in Jacques Maritain's 1948 treatise entitled *Man and the State.* Here Maritain decries the exaltation of the totalitarian state above the body politic as the hypostasizing of the symbolic representation of political society into a transcendent substance, 'a metaphysical monad' or 'person', a separate and independent carrier of absolute political right.[16] He identifies this hypostasis with the modern doctrine of sovereignty as it developed from the sixteenth to the nineteenth centuries: behind Hegel's *totality of right* and Rousseau's *general will* lies Hobbes' *mortal God* and Bodin's *absolute power.* Maritain construes Bodin's *puissance absolue* as a theological-juridical construct involving the following logic: 'the people have absolutely deprived and divested themselves of their total power in order to transfer it to the Sovereign [prince]', thereby rendering him a superior subject of semi-divine power, conceived to be the 'image' or 'Vicar' of God, accountable to the divine Sovereign alone.[17]

[16] Maritain, *Man*, 13–14, 17.
[17] Maritain, *Man*, 30–36.

Against Bodin's legal-proprietary account of political institution in which a substantial possession (namely *power*, understood as the force by which persons are obliged to obey) is alienated from one owner to another, Maritain sets a 'moral' account in which the political community entrusts its natural and inalienable right to govern itself to a chosen representative, who exercises that right by participation, without possessing it. On the delegative or fiduciary theory of political authority, the government is the image not of God but of the people, subject and accountable to the people, the active 'instrument' of the will of the people.[18]

From a theological and historical point of view, Maritain's criticism of Bodin's theory of sovereignty is both penetrating and misleading. On the one hand, it pinpoints the problematic aspects of the idea of transferring political power from the community to the ruler. For ever since the mediaevals recovered the Roman law commentaries of early third-century jurists from which the idea arose,[19] civil lawyers had pondered the extent of this transference – whether it was total or partial – and its implications for the relative authority of different kinds of law: for example, imperial decree as compared with popular custom. Invariably, their discussions veered toward either monarchical absolutism, attributing all communal power to the ruler, or dualism of sovereignty, dividing power between ruler and community: in the first instance, substituting the head for the body and in the second, locking head and body in a struggle for power. Manifestly, the democratic understanding of political authority as delegated by and vicariously exercised for the people is one way of overcoming the inadequacies of the transference model. On the other hand, Maritain's criticism fails to recognize that the transference theory of political authority was never intrinsic to the *theology* of the ruler's divine vicariate, which for the better part of its history aimed at circumscribing political authority within the boundaries set by law, justice and the commonweal. Let me briefly dwell on the limiting and anti-despotic features of this theology.

---

[18] Maritain, *Man*, 126–32. Maritain explicitly aligns his fiduciary account of political authority with the neo-scholastic natural law thought of the Cardinals Cajetan and Bellarmine, and of Francisco de Suárez (133), all three of whom, it should be remarked, were bent on maximizing the distance between the divine vicariate of the pope and the natural vicariate of all temporal rulers, in response to the conciliarist and Protestant 'heresies' of the time. It is noteworthy, however, that Maritain is more liberal than any of these Thomists, and especially Suárez, whose thought is closer to Bodin's than to Maritain's.

[19] The *locus classicus* is the jurist Ulpian's observation in the *Digest* (1.4.1 pr., cf. *Inst.* 1.2.6) that what the prince pleases has the force of law because, by the royal law of the empire, the people have conferred on him all its political authority and power. ('*Quod principi placuit, legis habet vigorem utpote cum lege regia, quae de imperio ejus lata est, populus ei et in eum omne suum imperium et potestatem conferat.*')

The *locus classicus* for the divine vicariate of the ruler was biblical rather than Roman juristic: namely, St Paul's exhortation to obedience in Romans 13:1–7 which, it was commonly thought, acknowledged God's ordination of government as a social institution and his appointment of individual governors, for the purposes of rendering binding public judgement concerning matters of right and wrong, restraining evildoing by means of punishment and the fear of punishment and encouraging virtuous conduct by means of approval and other reward. From the New Testament's essentially juridical portrayal of government[20] developed the patristic systematization of rule as a postlapsarian divine ordinance that simultaneously manifested God's wrathful judgement on sinful humanity and his providential mercy toward it. In earthly government, the church fathers saw God acting to protect the fragile goods of human life from the assault of sinful human passions by providing a limited judgement and punishment of human wrongdoing, in lieu of the limitlessness of both divine judgement and the unrestrained human passion for vengeance.[21]

Contrary to contemporary theological instincts, most premodern theologians considered it imperative that the one who executes public judgement be the earthly representative, or even 'image', of the heavenly judge, in acknowledgement of two truths: first, of God's continuing sovereignty in judging his creatures, and second, of the radical equality of those created in his image, that forbade any of them coercively to judge his or her fellows. It was not enough for political authority to represent the whole community, the *universitas*, and express the common judgement of the people, as handed down in customary and statute law: for not even the whole community had the authority to take human life in punishment for crime, but God alone. Nevertheless, precisely as the human representative of a human community, the ruler received and exercised from God only delegated and participated power: 'Whatever the prince can do', said John of Salisbury in the twelfth century, 'is from God, so that power does not depart from God, but it is used as a substitute for His hand, making all things learn His justice and mercy.'[22]

And, moreover, it was *God's* justice and mercy, and not the prince's capricious and tyrannous whim, that the subject was to learn: delegated and

---

[20] Rom. 13:1–7 was heavily supported by 1 Pet. 2:13–15.

[21] The tendency among patristic and later Christian writers to locate the historical origin of political authority in Cain's building of a city suggests the link (probably intended by the Genesis redactor) between God's establishment of political authority and, on the one hand, the substitution of communal justice for private vengeance, and on the other, God's merciful deferring of divine judgement. Instead of striking down the murderer Cain or giving him over to his avengers, God places the protective 'mark' on him and allows him to take refuge in the city that he builds, away from God's presence (Gen. 4: 9–17).

[22] *Policraticus* 4. 1; Nederman, 28.

participated authority was formed and directed by God's revelation of his will in nature and Scripture. Even the most Byzantine conception of the ruler as a 'living law' (*lex animata, nomos empsychos*), transcending the exactions of the positive law, still cast him as interpreter of the divine Word in Christ and imitator of divine equity and virtue.[23] While not adequately expressing the fallibility and corruption of princely judgement, the Byzantine model did not remove it absolutely from prophetic counsel and admonition within the church. More consistently did the Western tradition of 'theocratic kingship' hold in theopolitical tension the public judgements of the ruler, judgements of the ruled formed and articulated independently of the ruler, and God's own judgements declared in his revealed Word by which both ruler and ruled are judged.

It is precisely this theopolitical tension that modern democratic liberalism has collapsed by casting the government *exclusively* as vicar of the people, thereby providing a necessary historical condition of modern political tyranny and totalitarianism, as thinkers as far apart as Pope Leo XIII and Hannah Arendt have perceived. Whether 'the people' that the government images is some fantastic racial essence, national folk spirit, avenging ethnic group, self-contained body of merely positive law, conflict of class interests and ideologies, or motor of economic development, it is a self-seeking, lawless and idolatrous community, and not a community of divine law and right. It cannot be, to use late mediaeval juristic language, a 'community of the realm' (*communitas regni*) or a 'mystical body of the commonweal' (*corpus reipublicae mysticum*) – not because there is lacking a monarch but because there is lacking the real moral bond of divine law between the governor and the governed that goes beyond the merely constitutional in the formal and procedural sense. Correspondingly, the modern totalitarian 'vicar of the people' is known by its emancipation from the divine commission to execute God's laws for the whole commonwealth, to give justice to *all* the persons within its territory.

Recognizing the divine vicariate of civil governors does not, of course, resolve the thorny problems of doing justice in the contemporary social setting. But it does dispel the dogma of popular sovereignty – that the popular will is the *source* of political authority and the *substance* of political judgement – which has infected all the aggressive nationalisms of our time. It cannot be the nation, understood as either a pre-political or a trans-governmental totality, that dispenses justice 'under God' through the vicarious instrumentality of its elected governors, but rather the governors (whether elected or holding some other legitimate title) that by their political judgements 'under God' constitute the nation as an ongoing reality. To grasp the dangerous theological error of the doctrine of self-government is to perceive its twin historical roots in late

---

[23] See the imperial panegyrics of Eusebius for Constantine I and of Agapetos in sixth-century Constantinople.

mediaeval corporatist voluntarism (closely associated with the northern Italian city-states) and the spiritualist tradition of communal perfectionism and Messianism (especially in the Reformation period), which, amalgamated, produced a mystical totality of absolute communal right constituted by the free consensus of individual wills. Manifestly, this hybrid conforms neither to the heavenly communion of saints, nor to the earthly church militant, nor to the civil polities through which fallen humanity is ordered.

Political society as a body of law in the 'penumbra' of the gospel

To focus the antipathy between the modern and the Christian concepts of political society, let us return to the blend of romantic and civic nationalism characteristic of the twentieth century, and notice the subtle shift in perspective from the inter-war to the post-war years. Whereas in Wilsonian thinking the ethnic-linguistic and the civic nations seemed to compose a symbiotic and harmonious fit, post-war thought lost confidence in this fit. The staggering task of raising civil societies out of the ashes of dictatorial and totalitarian regimes implied an arduous transformation of the ethnic-linguistic into the civic nation. Particularist society and its machinery of government had to be reconstructed on rational, universal principles of freedom, equality, participation and plurality, applied to individuals and groups. Only such a political therapy would place and maintain government in the role of instrument rather than master of the governed.

The United Nations *Universal Declaration of Human Rights* embodied the international consensus on the post-war programme of political renovation. This extensive catalogue of civil, political and social rights attributed chiefly to individuals expressed the form of the civic nation as a coherent communal project – 'a common standard of [communal] achievement'.[24] *In a comprehensive and universal moral-juridical code it articulated the unified communal will that was to constitute each and every society as a body politic or commonwealth, above and beyond its machinery of state and its whole fabric of statutory and customary laws.* The opening proclamation made clear that the civic nation as a body of programmatic rights was first and foremost a project of public education and citizen mobilization. Fifty years on, we cannot fail to be astonished by the systematic indoctrination envisaged and the religious fervour conveyed:[25]

---

[24] These rights not only included the venerable personal, political and religious rights: to individual life, liberty, security, property, freedoms of association, speech, religious belief and practice, and equality before the law. They also included the 'civic' right to equal political participation for all citizens, and the extensive catalogue of social rights that have become our public commonplaces: e.g., to humane employment, material security, medical care, suitable education and cultural involvement.

[25] Brownlie, *Basic Documents*, 22.

> The General Assembly proclaims *this universal declaration of human rights* as a common standard of achievement for all peoples and all nations to the end that every individual and every organ of society, keeping this Declaration constantly in mind, shall strive by teaching and education to promote respect for these rights and freedoms and by progressive measures, national and international, to secure their universal and effective recognition and observance ...

Thus was the civic nation and the civic community of nations to be constituted through the secular faith of the democratic creed. In the intervening years since the *Declaration*, the creedal unity of the civic nation has, if anything, intensified, especially with the welding of law and public ideology in constitutional bills of rights.[26] What has also become increasingly apparent is the debilitating effects on social moral agency of the abstract individualism and pluralism of the civil charter of rights – its frequent functioning in government legislation and judicial decision to undermine the legitimate representation of the moral and spiritual understandings within society.[27]

Against the ideological unification of the civil nation stands the witness of Scripture and the theopolitical tradition erected on it that the *political unity* of any society consists in its collective recognition of a political authority and consent to a body of laws – not in its subscription to a practical creed and plan of action. Through the judgements of its rulers accepted by the people, and in their obedience to laws – in other words, in the actual execution of public justice – its common good or common weal takes on definition. The fourteenth-century English jurist John Fortescue gave expression to this insight, widespread among his European contemporaries, when he referred to the legal constitution of the realm as 'the nerves and sinews of the body [politic]'.[28] In the feudal conception of the judge (whether king or lesser magistrate) as one who 'found' the law rather than 'made' it, and in the respect paid to the commonly 'found' customs of communities, the close relationship between the law and the moral judgement of both the one and the many was affirmed. And therein was also affirmed the close relation between laws and the broader sentiments, tastes, manners and affections of communal life.

---

[26] We should remark that the American Bill of Rights does not support the public moral programme of rights in its full social scope, in that it consists of constitutional amendments securing and extending the traditional liberties of British subjects for American citizens against the powers of government (especially the federal government) and an oppressive majority. For the role of the Bill of Rights within the American Constitution, see Goldwin, *Parchment*.

[27] Decisions of the Canadian judiciary in adjudicating cases under *The Charter of Rights and Freedoms* (1982) provide spectacular examples of such undermining of moral and spiritual community. See *UBCLR* 33 (2000).

[28] Fortescue, *Commendation*, 13.

Of course, beyond the ongoing achievement of public justice were the myriad articulations of the standards by which the achievement should be judged – by jurists, philosophers, theologians, bishops and the chief bishop – all appealing to the authoritative revelation of God's justice and God's law for human community in the scriptural witness to Christ. Beyond the realized political unity of society were the myriad authorities, goods, activities and institutions that composed it – all known to be equally ravaged by sin and equally objects of God's redemptive and sanctifying work. And, finally, all of redeemed society was known to be united within the body of Christ, the true *societas perfecta* of the universal church, one in Spirit and confession, the community of total and sufficient right, bound together in obedience to divine commandment and the realization of the absolute common good.

The theological naïvety which has gripped Christians and non-Christians in the last century – particularly in the latter half – is to think that two wholly unified and articulate common goods can coexist harmoniously and co-operatively: namely, the church of Christ and the civic nation united in the 'purely secular faith' of the 'democratic creed'. For the most part, Christians have not perceived the inflation of what belongs to Caesar in democratic civil religion, its capacity to tyrannize society like some 'Jacobin-at-large'. Both early critics of the totalitarian state, like Jacques Maritain, and later generations of critics, have failed to appreciate how the democratic creed itself functions as an ideology – a pseudo-religion justifying a false social totality. One early critic of totalitarianism, Hannah Arendt, always penetrating in her counter-suggestible historical and philosophical readings, approximated this insight in reflecting on the inability of modern states over the last two hundred years to protect the 'rights of man'.[29] Despite her penchant for regarding past beliefs as unworkable in the present because fatally anachronistic, she saw clearly that the advent of modern tyranny depended on the demise of a Christian political world where rulers were vicars of God rendering justice to *everyone within their territories*, and commonwealths were communities of obedience to divine and human law.[30] Arendt's resolution of the modern dilemma over the course of her distinguished career seems to have been to turn away from the unredeemable modern state to small communities of heightened political participation,[31]

[29] Arendt, *Origins*, 266–302.

[30] Indeed, the bitter irony of modern anti-Semitism for Arendt was that it depended on the abandonment of the model of Israel – the chosen people manifesting God's law before the nations – not only by Christian polities, but also by secular and assimilated Jews who, by thinking of themselves as a depoliticized 'chosen race', opened the floodgates of purely racial hatred on the part of European pan-national movements. Arendt, *Origins*, 72–74, 227–49.

[31] See esp. Arendt, *Revolution*, 215–81.

whereas the reaction of many of her contemporaries has been to promote the idea of transnational political and economic communities and governments. But neither resolution has tapped the full resources of the Christian political tradition for addressing the intimately related modern phenomena of unrestrained nationalism, dictatorial and totalitarian states, and the proliferation of ethnic polities.

Bibliography

Arendt, H., *The Origins of Totalitarianism* (London: André Deutsch, 1986)

——, *On Revolution* (Harmondsworth: Penguin Books, 1973)

Brownlie, I. (ed.), *Basic Documents on Human Rights* (Oxford: OUP, 2nd edn, 1981)

Fortescue, J., *A Treatise in Commendation of the Laws of England*, in *The Works of John Fortescue, Knight: His Life, Works, and Family History*, II (trans. F. Gregor; 2 vols.; London: 1869)

Goldwin, R.A., *From Parchment to Power: How James Madison Used the Bill of Rights to Save the Constitution* (Washington: AEI Press, 1997)

Greenfeld, L., *Nationalism: Five Roads to Modernity* (Cambridge, MA: Harvard University Press, 1992)

Hobsbawm, E.J., *Nations and Nationalism Since 1780: Programme, Myth, Reality* (Cambridge: CUP, 1990)

Maritain, J., *Man and the State* (Chicago: University of Chicago Press, 1951)

Mayall, J., *Nationalism and International Society* (Cambridge: CUP, 1990)

Nederman, C.J. (ed.), *Policraticus* (Cambridge: CUP, 1990)

O'Donovan, J., *Theology of Law and Authority in the English Reformation* (Atlanta: Scholars Press, 1991)

O'Donovan, O., *The Desire of the Nations: Rediscovering the Roots of Political Theology* (Cambridge: CUP, 1996)

——, and J. O'Donovan (eds.), *From Irenaeus to Grotius: A Sourcebook in Christian Political Thought 100–1625* (Grand Rapids: Eerdmans, 1999)

Smith, A.D., *Nations and Nationalism in a Global Era* (Cambridge: Polity Press, 1995)

University of British Columbia, *Law Review* 33 (2000) (*UBCLR*); Special Edition on *Religion, Morality and Law*

27

Response to Joan Lockwood O'Donovan

Oliver O'Donovan

Joan identifies three ways in which the nation is conceived: the *romantic nation*, in terms of a given cultural and historical homogeneity, the *civic nation*, in terms of a body of rights, and the *functional nation*, in terms of practical, especially economic, viability. The characteristic conceptions of modern nationalism are a blend of the first and the second; the third operates as a tool of anti-nationalist liberalism. But the blend of romantic and civic, based on the presumption of popular sovereignty, has proved to have horrible results. So, in reaction, the civic model has tended to gain predominance, and with it an attempt to purify nationalism by an ideological crusade which absorbs, and corrupts, all other practical endeavours we may have. In studying theology, for example, we justify ourselves by fashioning our theological investigations deliberately so as to heighten the awareness of individual rights. In place of all three she proposes a Christian conception of the nation as a 'concrete rendering over time of legal justice'. The bulk of the paper is critical, and with its critical edge I am in full agreement. The best comment I can make, then, is to elaborate what I suppose follows from the positive recommendations of the paper.

First a terminological point: we may free ourselves of the romantic overtones of the word 'nation' and the governmental overtones of the word 'state' by using the term 'people', in a concrete, not an abstract sense – that is, speaking of '*a* people', not of '*the* people', in place of 'nation-state'. To grasp ourselves as a people is a work of the moral imagination:

1. It is the largest corporate *agent* capable of uniting us to act together consistently and on an all-inclusive front. The 'people' is not included in any list of types of social organization: households, cities, provinces, nations, empires, and so on. It can take any of these forms, but is always the largest of them practically envisageable in current conditions. There is, then, a functional element in what counts as a people. A people can have no moral reality when for *practical* purposes its members turn to larger or smaller units. 'Scotland' may call itself a nation, and indeed retain a few remnants of that exclusive

co-operation which once made it a people, but its integration with the United Kingdom means that it is a people no longer – or, perhaps, not yet. The scholastics used the term 'perfect society' to describe this functional sufficiency, a term that has a certain usefulness, though Joan objects to some of the structural overtones it carries and, of course, it cannot be understood literally. If we use it, it should be taken to mean no more and no less than a society that is not too small to rally effectively against a threat, not too large and diverse to be interested in rallying against a threat.

2. As the largest body which effects our corporate agency, the people carries our corporate identity, and as such must be continuous with our common histories. The notion of identity is a chronological notion, a continuity between past, present and projected future. Peoples must have histories of some kind if they are to be peoples, for without a common past there can be no identity which can venture into agency. The notion of the 'founding act' of a nation is always a retrospective romanticism: the people comes into being in fact as existing histories converge and merge, so that certain kinds of common action become inevitable.
3. The idea of the people arises vis-à-vis the idea of the state. It does not pre-exist the idea of the state, as in the romantic-nation concept, where the nation comes first and then asserts a right to its own state. Neither is the idea of the people identical with the idea of a state, as in totalitarian conceptions from Hobbes to Marx, where the political organization 'is' the people. Political organization does not make a people; it finds it. The state-structure defends something other than the state-structure, a complex of social communications at many levels which have a real unity in themselves and subsist in relation to the structure which defends them. The people and the state are like the snail and its shell: the snail is not the shell, but the snail does not pre-exist the shell; the shell is the snail's shell, and the snail grows with its shell.

The recognition of the state, therefore, is a form of self-recognition: we see *ourselves* represented in the structure and leadership which defends *us* as a people. Precisely for that reason, the parallel and synchronous ideas of people-state or nation-state are always exposed to the temptation of idolatry, the worship of ourselves in an objectified symbol. There is no purely procedural or formal way of avoiding this sin. If we escape from the temptations of a popular unit based on the nation by joining multi-nation conglomerates or by breaking ourselves down into smaller popular units based on regions, we will find precisely the same temptation repeating itself at the new level. There are those who think that the morally problematic aspects of the nation-state Britain will be resolved if it dissolves into a United Europe in one direction and into the republics of Scotland, Wales, Northumbria, Devonia, and so on in the other. But the only defences against such moral problems are moral defences. They are: *a*) just and ordered relations with other peoples, which treat them as genuinely 'foreign' or 'external' – not as potential merger-partners or clients within our 'sphere of influence' – real foreign affairs, involving serious engagement with other peoples' practical problems, are a condition for any people's being able to cope with its own practical problems; *b*) a religious obedience to God that demands and enables constant self-criticism. To say that failures of religion undermine the existence of a people is not, of course, to promote 'civil religion', designed precisely for political purposes, which is already unbelief since it is fabricated and pretended. It is to say simply that the formation and sustaining of political identities is a cultural task, not a natural endowment; as a cultural task it depends strongly on virtues prior to those identities; and those virtues are not self-sown, but depend on a true relation between humankind and God.

This issue is a pressing one for Europeans. I judge myself to be politically a European and morally a *pro*-European, favouring attempts to highlight and promote co-operation among the peoples of Europe. But, within the current political options as usually described, I count as anti-European. Why this paradox? Because in the political vernacular 'Europe' has come to be used not as the name of a continental ensemble of peoples, but as the name of a *project*. But no political identity can be formed as a project. It can be formed only as we 'discover' the units within which we can and must practice justice, and as we develop traditions of judgement that serve those units. I am quite relaxed about the prospect that one day all the peoples of Europe may be a single people – though I think that development much more complex and improbable than the crystal-ball-gazers do. But if it is to be a happy development, it will have to happen because the communications of European governments have taken on that shape as they have striven to render justice within their spheres of responsibility. Otherwise, it will happen unhappily, which is to say that Europeans will feel themselves unfree, irrespective of any number of attempts to 'remedy the democratic deficit'. The approach of European governments to co-operation must be piecemeal: identifying at each moment the really urgent tasks of judgement which cannot be discharged without co-operation, and searching for ways and means of discharging them together. And then … just wait and see what happens!

28

Acting Politically in Biblical Obedience?

James W. Skillen

Introduction

The Center for Public Justice in the United States is a voluntary association of citizens. It was organized in 1977 to equip citizens, develop leaders, and shape policy. The Center is not a political party or lobbying organization, although it works to influence public officials in all branches of government by means of legal and public-policy arguments and proposals. Moreover, it exists as an explicit civic response to God's call to do justice in obedience to biblical revelation. Its mission to equip citizens and develop leaders aims to educate and motivate Christians to fulfill their civic responsibilities as part of their calling to be disciples of Christ in all of life. Consequently, the Center's purpose, philosophy, programs, daily actions, and very existence present a contemporary test case for this consultation.

The aim of this essay is threefold: first, to explain one of the Center's public-policy arguments which has had an impact on both officials and the law; second, to show how that argument has arisen from reading the Bible; and third, to enter into conversation with Oliver O'Donovan – particularly through his book, *The Desire of the Nations* – about differences in interpretation of, and action in response to, the Bible.

Welfare Policy and Religious Freedom

One consequence of a peculiarly American set of institutional arrangements and historical developments is that government-funded welfare programs were, by the 1960s, considered to be 'secular' in nature. 'Secular', in the American context, now means 'not religious'. That which is 'secular' is generally identified as nonsectarian and public, while 'religion' is identified as something sectarian and private. One implication of this is that major federal welfare programs, particularly those created in the 1960s and later, disallowed co-operation between government and religious ('sectarian') charities that serve the poor. Between 1994 and 1996, however, the federal and state governments engaged in a partial reform of welfare policies. The primary reason was the high cost and relative lack of success of many of the programs. Additionally, government was turning increasingly to non-government organizations for help. At this juncture, the Center for Public Justice helped to inject into federal welfare-reform legislation a provision that reflected its principled argument for two kinds of pluralism. The provision, which is now law, came to be called Charitable Choice.

The first principle of pluralism underlying Charitable Choice, for which the Center contended, is that government should recognize and deal justly with the diversity of non-government responsibilities that humans bear in God's creation. Humans bear different kinds of responsibility and exercise those responsibilities in a wide variety of relationships and institutions, including marriage, the family, education, business, the arts, the church and more. Thus, when government exercises its responsibility for the public's welfare, it should act in ways that fully respect and uphold the responsibilities that belong to other institutions and individuals in regard to that welfare. This has particular bearing on government's co-operation with non-government organizations in serving the poor. When government acts to address the needs of poor people, it does not do so *de novo*, as if poverty is simply a matter between government and poor individuals, unrelated to any other human relationship or responsibility. Rather, government addresses persons who also belong to, or are alienated from, families, schools, churches, places of employment, social service ministries and more. Thus, out of respect for the integrity of non-government organizations, government should not act as if such organizations are merely an extension of itself. When government co-operates with independent organizations in serving the poor, a real partnership should be created that establishes mutual respect for the integrity of each partner. The Charitable Choice provision entails precisely this kind of change in the definition of government's relation to non-government organizations. We can call this the principle of 'structural pluralism'.

The second principle of pluralism we refer to as 'confessional pluralism': government should act without discrimination toward the religions by which people live in public as well as in private life. The Charitable Choice provision of the 1996 welfare law declared that henceforth, when government co-operates with non-government organizations in providing welfare services to eligible recipients, it must no longer discriminate against religious service agencies by excluding them from partnership with government. Nor may government require that such organizations act in a 'secular' manner when they do co-operate with government. Government should neither favor nor disfavor an organization because of its 'secular' or 'religious' commitment as long as the organization demonstrates its ability to serve those in need.

When the new welfare law took effect in 1996, the Center for Public Justice became involved in explaining it to a wide public and advising both public officials and religious non-government organizations (now called 'faith-based' organizations) about the implications of Charitable Choice. This led to consultations between Stanley Carlson-Thies – the Center's lead figure in this area – and officials across the country, including the governor of Texas, George W. Bush, who became actively engaged in implementing Charitable Choice in Texas. When Bush became president, he established a new White House Office of Faith-Based and Community Initiatives with the aim of extending the reach of Charitable Choice principles to many more areas of policy. Dr Carlson-Thies was among the staff members President Bush hired to serve in the new office.

Action on Welfare Reform and Reading the Bible

How does the Center's argument for Charitable Choice and the two principles of pluralism reflect the organization's commitment to act in obedience to biblical revelation? Jesus Christ, according to the Bible, is King of kings and Lord of lords, the one who now claims all authority in heaven and on earth. Government, ordained by God, can thus have no authority except in subordination to Christ. Governments and citizens, whether conscious of it or not, bear God-given responsibility and are obligated to act in obedience to God. Part of that responsibility is for government to do justice – to give what is owed, to acknowledge and uphold – the responsibilities God has given directly to other human relationships and institutions. No human government holds omnicompetent authority. The principle of 'structural pluralism' is a direct response to this biblically illuminated reality.

It is also clear from the Bible that the fulfillment of Christ's judging and redeeming work lies in the future. God's rain and sunshine now fall on the just and unjust alike, and Christ's disciples have been given no authority to separate the wheat and the tares in the field of the divine kingdom. In fact, Christians have been called to honor government authorities and to try as far as is possible to live at peace with all people. Acting in obedience to these and other commandments is part of the way Christians bear witness to Christ's lordship. In other words, to act in civic obedience to Christ, who now exercises his all-embracing political authority with great patience and long-suffering, requires that we seek public laws and institutional arrangements that will give all citizens equal treatment under the law, including nondiscriminatory treatment of their religions, even false religions. Thus, 'confessional pluralism' is the right political response to Christ's call to follow and serve him.

The Center for Public Justice thus sees the Charitable Choice provision as flowing directly from the Center's purpose and as one example of the right exercise of government's authority in accord with Christ's patient and long-suffering kingship. In other words, the Center, as a free association of Christian citizens, represents a civic response of thankfulness to God for a political system in which its members are free to exercise civic responsibility. In exercising their civic responsibility, members of the Center seek to develop and articulate public-policy reforms that will bring government and the political community closer to the norm of justice. In the instance of Charitable Choice, the change of law from discrimination against explicitly religious groups to equal treatment of all social-service organizations, regardless of their faith commitments, is a change that the Center believes conforms to God's rule in Christ. The change is also one that advances government's exercise of respect for non-government organizations, which bear their own responsibilities. Thus, Charitable Choice represents a small step in the direction of advancing both structural and confessional pluralism.

The larger setting in which the Center's advocacy of Charitable Choice demonstrates its significance is in the contemporary public contention over the very nature and legitimacy of religion. Far too many Christians in the United States and elsewhere in the world act as if their Christian faith and practices are a private matter. They accept to some degree that politics is a secular, non-religious matter. On the other hand, quite in contrast, there are many Christians who believe that their religious allegiances should be expressed politically by trying to bring about some kind of Christian supremacy or hegemony in public life. Many Christians in the United States, for example, want to recover a 'Christian America'. The most consistent secularists, on the other hand, want to push all religious expression into private quarters.

In contrast to all of these views, the Center for Public Justice contends, as a consequence of its reading of the Bible, that religions, by their very nature, cannot be privatized, that all people will serve either the true God or false gods in their public lives as well as in their private lives. Thus Christians should, without embarrassment, act publicly, politically, as Christians. Yet in doing so, Christians should seek equal treatment for the public expression of all religious faiths, not just their own. And this means working to expose the deeply religious character of secularism and other self-styled 'non-religious' ways of life. The so-called culture wars in the United States represent a conflict *not* between religious conservatives and secular liberals, but rather between different religious ways of life (including secularism), each seeking dominance or monopoly over government's welfare and education policies, for example.

The Center for Public Justice engages publicly to try to demonstrate in political argument and public-policy proposals God's gracious rule in Christ, which makes possible government and civil rights themselves. Liberal secularists, neo-Marxists, free-market libertarians, American civil-religionists, and many others all contend politically from out of their deepest convictions and allegiance to their gods. The Center wants to manifest a humble, neighbor-serving, justice-seeking style of civic engagement, which it believes is a demonstration of Christian obedience required by God during the entire period between the first and second comings of Christ.

Reading O'Donovan

Let us now turn to the work of Oliver O'Donovan whose book *The Desire of the Nations*, in particular, bears directly on the purpose, philosophy and practices of the Center for Public Justice. In fact, much of what O'Donovan argues helps to make the case for, and ground the mission of, the Center.

In agreement with his earlier book, *Resurrection and Moral Order*, O'Donovan says in *DN* that it is a mistake to interpret the resurrection of Jesus Christ in a way that ignores its meaning as 'the restoration of creation'.[1] What God has done in Christ 'he has done for his creation and for his own sake as creator'. In death and in resurrection Christ was the representative of Israel, to be sure, but, as the apostle Paul explains, in that capacity he was also, by analogy, the representative of the human race. According to O'Donovan, 'The resurrection restores the life of all mankind, reversing the effects of sin' and reordering 'the disorder of which death is the emblem'. Christ thereby 'vindicates God's original act of creation'.[2] The kingdom of God 'has its origin in God's eternal purpose. It fulfils all that God intended in Creation. It is necessary, then, to say not simply that the Kingdom has appeared, but that it has been waiting to appear'.[3] 'When we say that the church is glad in the resurrection of Christ', O'Donovan writes, 'we point to the meaning of that event as the *recovery of creation order*. Gladness belongs essentially to the creature, as glory belongs to the creator.'[4] Among other things, I would say that O'Donovan's line of argument here lays the basis for government's responsibility to acknowledge and uphold all the non-government responsibilities God has given to human creatures.

O'Donovan speaks, however, of 'a puzzling feature about the interaction of politics and church in John of Patmos' vision [the book of Revelation]. Nowhere in the New Testament is such a broad array of political categories deployed to depict the eschatological triumph of the church. There is the true throne, of God and the Lamb; there is the true warfare which establishes it, and the true judgment.'[5] In fact, as it turns out, says O'Donovan, John's entire

[1] *DN*, 143.
[2] *DN*, 141–42.
[3] *DN*, 136.
[4] *DN*, 181.
[5] *DN*, 155.

vision encompasses a single political order – only one city – 'which is at once the Holy City trampled on by the Gentiles and the Great City where Christ was crucified. The community in which God and the Lamb have set their throne is one and the same with the community where Satan and the beast have set their throne.'[6] Believers, the followers of Christ, do not have a distinct social presence apart from the city, for they are there, in Christ, to 'claim back the Great City to become the Holy City'. O'Donovan solves this 'puzzle' in the following way:

> Just as there is only one true throne, so there is but one structured human community, and there can never be a second. Its name and aspect changes as the God who claims it wrests its government away from the pretender … The cry from heaven which John heard at the seventh trumpet, 'Sovereignty over the world has passed to our Lord and his Christ', was not only an announcement for the future; it was a commentary on the scene of the two martyrs, at the conclusion of which 'one tenth of the city collapsed … and the survivors, filled with fear, gave glory to the God of heaven' (11:13, 15). The outcome of the church's martyr-witness is to call forth the first hesitating and abashed confession of the rule of God, the beginning out of which the Holy City will come to be.[7]

From these comments, we may draw out the implication that Christ is lord and king of all creation right now and not only in the future, even though faithful service of Christ in this age may lead to martyrdom rather than to the exercise of political power. We may also conclude that God's purposes for creation, from the beginning, were to reveal the divine glory – including all of the political dimensions of that glory – in the city of God. Into this city all the achievements of the human generations – the faithful, earthly servant-rulers under the divine sovereign of the whole creation – would be gathered to the praise of God. Sin, which is human disobedience against God who created humans to rule the earth, threatens the Creator's purposes and has led to Satan's near triumph in gaining control over the emerging city. But Jesus Christ, the incarnate Son of God, through whom all things were created, was crucified for the sins of humankind and has been raised to new life by his Father. In the power of his resurrection, Christ recovers and restores obedient human authority over the whole creation for the glory of God and the fulfillment of humankind. He takes office as the King of kings and Lord of lords. The Holy City is not an afterthought of the Redeemer, but the intention of the Creator. In restoring creation, Christ leads humanity into the city of God.

This understanding of continuity from the beginning of creation to its fulfillment in the Holy City accords with O'Donovan's interpretation of the

---

6 *DN*, 156.

7 *DN*, 156.

creation's seven-day order in his earlier book, *RMO*. Interpreting Hebrews 4, where the author refers to God's promise of a final Sabbath rest still awaiting the people of God, O'Donovan says,

> For the author to the Hebrews, then, the completion of creation, so far from being put in doubt by the thought of a yet-to-be completed history, is the only ground on which we can take the latter seriously. Historical fulfilment means our entry into a completeness which is already present in the universe. Our sabbath rest is, as it were, a catching up with God's.[8]

The seven-day order of creation establishes the context and condition of human responsibility, according to O'Donovan. Christ's redemption of the world, which opens to the fulfillment of God's Sabbath,

> suggests the recovery of something given and lost. When we ask what it is that was given and lost, and must now be recovered, the answer is not just 'mankind', but mankind in his context as the ruler of the ordered creation that God has made; for the created order, too, cannot be itself while it lacks the authoritative and beneficent rule that man was to give it …
>
> The eschatological transformation of the world is neither the mere repetition of the created world nor its negation. It is its fulfilment, its *telos* or end. It is the historical *telos* of the origin, that which creation is intended *for*, and that which it points and strives *towards*.[9]

Given this reading of the Scripture by O'Donovan, it seems to me that all the *political* categories of throne, kingdom, king, judge, ruler, law and sovereignty of which the Bible speaks and which are in evidence in the revelation John received on Patmos, belong legitimately to the life of human creatures. Christ does not put on the garb of kingship uncomfortably, as if injecting something foreign into creation. The Scriptures reveal Christ as both the originator and the heir of David's throne. Jesus Christ takes up the throne intended for him from before David's time. The responsibility of human governance on earth reveals something true about God from the beginning, just as other dimensions of the image of God reveal something true about God. God, then, is political from the beginning to the end of creation, and human government, just as family life, friendship, agricultural and animal husbandry and much more, reveals or images the Creator. Creation fulfilled entails the realization of both God's kingship and human government under God. Christ's resurrection and ascension to the throne that is both human and divine restores creation and opens it to its fulfillment in the Holy City.

---

[8] *RMO*, 61–62.

[9] *RMO*, 54–55.

This sketch of the biblical story of creation (including human political responsibility) destined for fulfillment in God's Sabbath rest, represents the vision that grounds and inspires the work of the Center for Public Justice. However, the summary just presented does not capture the whole of what O'Donovan presents in *DN*. There are other elements and additional lines of argument that appear to me to be quite incompatible with, and even contradictory to, the interpretation just given.

Church, Society and Rulers

Let's begin with O'Donovan's understanding of the relation of the church to that which lies outside the church. O'Donovan speaks of the early church as addressing both society and rulers:

> The logic of this distinction is given in the very idea of God's rule in Christ. Society and rulers have different destinies: the former is to be transformed, shaped in conformity to God's purpose; the latter are to disappear, renouncing their sovereignty in the face of his. This distinction must, then, be reflected in our systematic thinking about the political content of the Gospel.[10]

But where does the church fit into this picture? Is not the church constituted by the very creatures whom God made in the first place for society and earthly governance? Why can only society be transformed, and not government?

O'Donovan does not answer this question in a general, structural way by referring to a calling for government or to a creation-order purpose for human politics. Instead, he speaks concretely about those who rule, and he sets rulers in the context of the doctrine of two ages. He says, the 'passing age of the principalities and powers has overlapped with the coming age of God's Kingdom'.[11] What is the relation of the two ages, as O'Donovan sees it? Are not both ages part of God's creation and subject to God's sovereignty? Are they not both ordered by the seven-day teleology of creation? Or does God's kingdom stand over against the principalities and powers of this passing age in a way that puts the creation at odds with itself? Where, in other words, does the passing age come from and who has authority over it? Furthermore, if both 'society' and 'rulers' belong to the passing age, do both pass away? Or is it only the rulers who disappear?

To deal with these questions, O'Donovan uses the word 'secular' (*saeculum*), which came into use in the patristic period of the church. He writes:

---

[10] *DN*, 193.

[11] *DN*, 211.

> Secular institutions have a role confined to this passing age (*saeculum*). They do not represent the arrival of the new age and the rule of God. They have to do with the perennial cycle of birth and death which makes tradition, not with the resurrection of the dead which supersedes all tradition. The corresponding term to 'secular' is not 'sacred', nor 'spiritual', but 'eternal'. Applied to political authorities, the term 'secular' should tell us that they are not agents of Christ, but are marked for displacement when the rule of God in Christ is finally disclosed. They are Christ's conquered enemies; yet they have an indirect testimony to give, bearing the marks of his sovereignty imposed upon them, negating their pretensions and evoking their acknowledgment.[12]

The picture O'Donovan presents here stands in considerable contrast, it seems to me, to the picture he paints elsewhere of a single creation fulfilled in Christ's kingly triumph. 'Secular institutions', as O'Donovan now puts it, do not represent the positive rule of God in Christ; they exist within the confines of the cycle of birth and death. Resurrection is something different, something beyond, something that transcends secular institutions. The latter are displaced by Christ's rule, not fulfilled by it. They bear testimony to Christ's authority not as revelatory parts of the creation striving to be fulfilled in God's kingdom, not as subordinate servants of divine sovereignty, but only as defeated enemies. Does O'Donovan really intend to say by this that every institution of this age will pass away and suffer defeat? Is the whole creation to be identified as merely secular? Did God then create the world only to triumph over and defeat it? If so, then what possible sense can there be of speaking of the Holy City of God as recovering and fulfilling creation? O'Donovan does not seem to want to reduce every part of creation to a merely secular existence, but that does seem to be his conclusion about government, for he says,

> Not only individuals, but families, tribes and nations may repent and believe the Gospel. Whether families, tribes and nations have an eternal destiny we may debate (though Israel has one – is that not enough?); but there is no difficulty in saying that they belong within the church. The ruler may belong within the church, too, but not *qua* ruler. The essential element in the conversion of the ruling power is the change in its self-understanding and its manner of government to suit the dawning age of Christ's own rule. The church has to instruct it in the ways of the humble state.[13]

Here the full ambiguity of O'Donovan's position comes through. The church apparently represents repentant sinners who have become believers in Christ and whose families, tribes and nations can enter the church. Society (at least part of it) can become part of the church, though O'Donovan remains

[12] *DN*, 211–12.
[13] *DN*, 219.

uncertain about whether such institutions, besides Israel, have an eternal destiny. Rulers, *qua* rulers, however, cannot belong within the church. They cannot be transformed. Their relation to Christ the King can only be that of defeated enemies. Nevertheless, despite all of this, O'Donovan says that rulers have a role to play in God's secular purposes. They cannot be 'agents of Christ', but the church can instruct them in the ways of 'the humble state'.[14] God has a role for rulers as servants of the church, though not as agents of Christ. And the church, which is Christ's agent, can instruct rulers to fulfill their humble role. What is this humble role? Are there criteria for humble political service? If there are such criteria, and if, at the same time, such humble servants are not 'agents of Christ', then it would appear that God's sovereignty over this secular age is exercised in two different ways. One way is through Christ; the other way is through secular agents that are not agents of Christ. What sense does it make, however, to speak of Christ triumphing over agents of God? Does this not put God in tension, if not in conflict, with Christ? And does it not limit Christ's authority over the creation?

The state, O'Donovan goes on to say, can serve God indirectly by facilitating the mission of the church even though it cannot belong to the church or pursue the mission of the church directly. It can facilitate the church's mission 'by performing its own business responsibly and with modest pretensions. In the Christian era there is no neutral performance on the part of rulers; either they accommodate to the energy of the divine mission, or they hurl themselves into defiance.'[15] But what does O'Donovan see as the state's 'own business', and how can that business be performed obediently or responsibly? If the state does what it should do and accommodates itself 'to the energy of the divine mission', then must it still be considered an enemy of Christ, able to show the signs of Christ's kingship only by the marks of its defeat?

It seems clear at this juncture in his argument that O'Donovan has nearly, if not entirely, lost from view the meaning of creation and creation redeemed. Or, perhaps more accurately, he has made clear that government and political institutions are not original with creation but came into existence only after the fall into sin to serve as secular institutions without an eternal destiny. The church, by contrast, is composed of redeemed sinners who do have an eternal destiny. Individuals, families and nations (though not rulers, *qua* rulers) can repent and 'belong to' the church. The implication is that certain creatures (including families) can be redeemed from sin. A person who once lived in defiance of God, with pretentious pride, can turn to God in Christ and become a renewed person. The same can be said for a family. Creation is, thus, redeemed in Christ. However, even if O'Donovan is not sure that families and

---

[14] *DN*, 211, 219.

[15] *DN*, 217.

nations have an eternal destiny, he nonetheless believes (contrary to one of his other statements) that the 'secular age' is not merely a cycle of birth and death, but is God's creation that can be redeemed. Death comes because of sin, but Christ has overcome death and thus is redeeming creation, not triumphing over it. Christ triumphs over and defeats sin, not creation. Prideful persons can become humble persons; pretentious families can become loving servants of the Lord. However, rulers, *qua* rulers, are not part of creation, cannot be redeemed, and have no eternal destiny.

Is this truly scriptural, however? The Scripture speaks repeatedly of God being like a father, a shepherd, a husband and a vineyard keeper. The creation reveals God through the image of God, through men and women who marry, and parent, and care for sheep, and tend vineyards. Yet it is also true that the Scriptures speak just as easily and as frequently of God being like a king, a judge, and a ruler, and the Bible treats human rulership as revelatory of God in the same way that human marriage and family and gardening reveal God. O'Donovan should not have been puzzled, therefore, when he noticed all the political categories in the book of Revelation. The most natural interpretation of that book follows from recognizing that God created humans for earthly government as one kind of humble service, which they owe to one another in obedience to the ultimate sovereign of the universe. To be sure, sinful disobedience can turn persons into killers and defilers of one another, and sin can turn rulers into pretentious, prideful predators who try to defy God. But the Scriptures tell the story of God's defeat of sinful governance and restoration of just and righteous human governance through Jesus Christ. Why, then, should we view rulers, *qua* rulers, as incapable of being Christ's servant-agents when we are able to see parents and shepherds and pastors as capable of being Christ's servants? Was King David not the very one whose throne Christ fulfilled forever? Did God not say of King Josiah that, in defending the cause of the poor and needy, he truly knew God (Jer. 22:16)? O'Donovan may be uncertain about whether families and nations have an eternal destiny, even though they are part of creation, yet he recognizes, in Revelation, that Christ's *kingship* is eternal. The Holy City, with its political throne, represents the recovered and transformed Great City of the earth. How is this possible if politics and government belong only to the secular age and have no creational origin, no agency under Christ, and no eternal destiny?

O'Donovan, it seems to me, in keeping with the church through much of its history, has simply not reconciled the biblical picture of 'creation redeemed' with the Graeco-Roman-Christian picture of an eternity that triumphs over or supersedes, rather than fulfills, the *saeculum*. The second picture dominates the first. In this regard, even his understanding of the church does not do justice to biblical revelation. Structurally speaking, the church in the New Testament is God's redeemed people, the disciples of Christ, the bride of Christ, the brothers and sisters of Christ, the body of Christ, the children of God, the household of faith, a kingdom of priests, the new Israel. None of these images allows for the church to be set off as one human institution among others, as a differentiated institution over against society and rulers. All of the biblical metaphors are rooted in creation and reveal something of who God is. Right within the epistles, for example, which are addressed to the church in Philippi or in Ephesus or in Rome, Paul addresses husbands and wives, citizens and rulers, parents and children, servants (or employees) and employers. The point is that *society* is not something outside God's redeemed people. The people of God represent and constitute society in repentance, the whole creation being redeemed. One may properly speak of Christian families addressing non-Christian families, or of Christian employers addressing non-Christian employers. But one may not speak of the church as an entity that stands over against families, businesses, and the rest of society. Of course, contemporary church institutions identified by reference to their separate legal status, or by their denominational names, or by their distinguishable organized authority-structures, can be distinguished from businesses, schools, states and labor unions. But that is not what the New Testament refers to with phrases like 'the body of Christ', or the 'bride of Christ', or 'the people of God'. Israel was an entire people, in contrast to other nations. Israel was not merely the Levitical priesthood set in contrast to the families, clans, businesses and political authorities within Israel. The new Israel, just as the old one, is a complex, full-bodied, multi-sided, multi-institutional community, encompassing all that is creationally possible for human beings to be.

Following this line of interpretation, there is nothing about the language of the New Testament, it seems to me, to suggest that rulers and governments exist only as enemies or defeated enemies of Christ rather than as agents of his authority. Yet most of *DN* is predicated on an institutional ontology that distinguishes the church from both society and the state in a way that requires government and politics to 'exist outside the perfection of Christ', as the Anabaptists of the Schleitheim Confession described it. In O'Donovan's view, it is 'the church which represents mankind under God's rule'.[16] His only question, then, is whether and to what extent 'secular authority' can be 'compatible with [the church's] mission and, so to speak, authorised by it?' Despite Jesus' words to his disciples after the resurrection that all authority in heaven and on earth had been given to him, O'Donovan sees only the church, not government rulers, as having authority under Christ. So his question about government's role and responsibility can only be one about how government serves the church's mission. Elsewhere he speaks of the state having its own business, but its authorization must somehow come from the church's mission.

[16] *DN*, 146.

Romans 13

The foregoing discussion establishes the framework for O'Donovan's interpretation of Romans 13. Christ's victory and authority, of which Paul is speaking, says O'Donovan, is 'the same victory that was promised to Israel over the nations, the victory of a God-filled and humanised social order over bestial and God-denying empires, a victory won for Israel on behalf of all mankind'.[17] The contrast here for O'Donovan is between Israel as a whole and 'the nations' as a whole. In light of the coming of Christ, O'Donovan then identifies the church with Israel (which is 'claimed for faith') and identifies rulers with the God-denying non-Israelite empires (who are 'claimed for obedience to Israel'). Consequently, O'Donovan reads what Paul says about the governing authorities in Romans, including the fact that God establishes them and that they are God's servants, through the lens that pre-colors them as defeated antagonists of Christ – the 'principalities and powers' that Christ has overcome by his death and resurrection.

The difficulty with this interpretation, however, is that Israel of old was not simply a cultic community, but it had a governance structure – rulers – in addition to the priests and the prophets. If the church is the new Israel, then why would one assume that all human rulers exist outside the people of God in Christ as antagonists of Christ? O'Donovan interprets Paul to say 'that it is by God's purpose that the structures of the old age "continue to exercise their sway" ... serving the church's mission'.[18] How do rulers 'exercise their sway' in service to the church? They may do so, says O'Donovan, only by exercising judgment. This is what O'Donovan draws from Romans 13:4, that government is 'an avenger to visit wrath on the wrongdoer'. He chooses to ignore the beginning of that verse, which says that government is 'God's servant to do you good'. However, according to O'Donovan, judgment 'in the ancient world always has in mind a decision between two parties (as in our civil rather than our criminal jurisdiction)', which means that a judgment against the evildoer also means 'praise' to 'the party who has acted rightly'.

Quite in contrast to this interpretation, it seems to me that Paul is telling the Roman Christians, who at the time did not hold positions of high governmental authority, to recognize the authorities as servants of God for their good. For that reason, they were to pay taxes, give honor, and not rebel. These authorities are first of all God's servants *for good*, and they are supposed to punish people only when they do wrong. O'Donovan, however, lays all the emphasis on judgment because of his previously established, elaborate argument (to which

---

[17] *DN*, 147.

[18] *DN*, 147.

we will turn below) that 'the whole rationale of government', after Christ's coming, 'is seen to rest on its capacity to effect the judicial task'.[19]

> Membership in Christ replaced all other political identities by which communities knew themselves. No respect can be paid to the role of government, then, as a focus of collective identity, either in Israel or in any other community. Judgment, on the other hand, must be respected, for it is the form in which God expresses his wrath; and that wrath cannot cease yet, for, as we will learn from Paul elsewhere, it is a restraining element in society which preserves the social order that furthers the spread of the Gospel.[20]

The casual reader of Romans 12 and 13 may find this reading of Paul quite idiosyncratic. Nevertheless, look closely at the last quotation. Even if we accept that government has only a restraining role to play, O'Donovan admits that this restraint helps preserve the social order. Yet if government is a preserver, it is doing good, is it not? It thus has a positive purpose, a constructive role to play in God's world. Why, then, does O'Donovan conclude that this constructive, preserving role arises only from the restraint of sin? Why does he not see that government performs a role that encourages and even constitutes legitimate public behavior? Moreover, what is behind O'Donovan's judgment that membership in Christ replaces all other political identities? Does membership in Christ also replace all other institutional identities? To the contrary, it seems to me (biblically speaking) that membership in Christ illuminates and restores our institutional responsibilities. Marriage relations are not replaced for Christians, but are shown to be revelatory of Christ's relation to the church. Families are not replaced by membership in Christ, but are shown to be revelatory of the higher meaning of being part of the family of God. In the same way, nothing in the New Testament suggests that membership in Christ replaces all other political identities. Rather, the New Testament, including this passage, suggests, if it does not teach, that political authority and political communities find their proper place under Christ's authority as revelatory of something larger and eschatologically fulfilling, namely the Holy City.

To read Paul in the way I am suggesting means reading him like one would read the Psalms, the Prophets, and the Law. God was the true and ultimate king of Israel and, when he gave Israel a king, he called on the people to recognize that such an office reflects and depends on God's superior kingship and anticipates the Messiah who will one day take that throne. Governmental authority was part of Israel's identity as much as prophetic authority, priestly authority, clan authority, and family authority were part of it. Israel represented redeemed humanity, including political governance. Of course, this reading presupposes

[19] *DN*, 148.

[20] *DN*, 148.

that political community is part of what God intended for humans in creation and that it points ahead in anticipation to the fulfillment of God's sovereignty in the city of God. This is precisely what O'Donovan seems to deny at many points in his book. So despite his puzzlement at the political language of Revelation, he reads the Scriptures in a way that identifies human government and political community as secular, outside the church, and as an agent of wrath that cannot be an agent of Christ.

This contrast is strengthened when O'Donovan says that, according to Romans 12–14, the life of the Christian community 'functions on an almost totally opposite principle to the judicial principle that serves the general needs of the world'.[21] Just before and just after Romans 13:1–7, according to O'Donovan, Paul tells the Roman church that 'there is to be no retaliation for evil received, no seeking of vengeance or vindication ... but only love for the enemy, which entrusts the whole of judgment to the decisive act of God'.[22] The implication, of course, is that the church's call to reconciling love is incompatible with punishment and vindication. Consequently, someone other than a Christian (or at least some office outside the institutional church) must act in these unloving, vengeance-taking ways. Again, this implies that if government is God's servant, it is a different kind of servant than Christ is and cannot be a direct agent of Christ's love. And yet, for O'Donovan, contradictory as it may sound, these agents 'outside the perfection of Christ' can be made to serve the church and somehow represent God. The 'structures of secular government', O'Donovan reads Paul as saying, 'are allowed to be an *anthrōpinē ktisis*, an institution that belongs to humankind as such, so that the common grace of God, rather than his saving purposes, forms the foundations of secular authority'.[23] For O'Donovan, God's restraining mercy exercised through a government that punishes evil stands in stark contrast to God's saving purposes in Christ. Lost from view, then, is O'Donovan's other argument about the integral creation, judged for its sinful disobedience and redeemed through Christ, who holds all authority in heaven and on earth and does not simply redeem a people out of this secular age.

From the more integral perspective of creation redeemed, however, one can read Romans 12–13 in a much less conflictual way, as follows. God has indeed called a people to himself in Christ, who is their King and Lord. In him, all of the good creation ordinances still hold: love your neighbors, even your enemies; don't do evil to them; don't take out personal vengeance against someone who harms you but trust God in Christ to ordain and carry out

---

[21] *DN*, 149.

[22] *DN*, 149.

[23] *DN*, 149.

retribution. That retribution, which is capable of discouraging evil and encouraging good, will be completed only in the final judgment. Nevertheless, even now, in order to displace human retaliation and spirals of vengeance, God appoints human authorities for the exact purpose of exercising *divine* punishment. These authorities are as much ordained by God, under Christ's authority, as are parents, and pastors and prophets. Heed them, as unto the Lord, and if you are ever called to such an office, as Joseph and Daniel and David once were, then exercise that authority as a member of the household of God in Christ, recognizing that this too should be done for the well-being of your neighbors, to protect the innocent, and to remind the evildoer through punishment that it is God who ultimately holds everyone accountable for his or her deeds. Outside that office of divine appointment a Christian should not, of course, act either as God or as a vengeance taker. Just as one ought to acknowledge Christ's authority in that office by fulfilling its functions, one should acknowledge Christ's authority outside that office by not trying to exercise its functions in a family, a church, a school, or a business enterprise. But this is saying no more than one would say about any authority ordained by God. Inside the parental office, act as a parent, as unto the Lord. Outside the office of parent, do not act as one. All human authority is given by God; all of it can be twisted by sinful disobedience; all of it is being judged and redeemed in Christ, our elder brother, husband of the church, and King of all kings on earth. In defeating sinful parenting, sinful spousal relations, and prideful governing, Christ also redeems those responsibilities through his sacrificial death and resurrection, bringing all human responsibilities to fulfillment in eschatological glory.

History and the State

Because O'Donovan sees earthly government, at least in part, as foreign to creation and not fully embraced by redemption in Christ, he develops an elaborate set of categories and theorems to explain how government came into existence in history and how it had to be modified historically by the coming of Christ. For example, instead of considering Israel, including its legal governance structure, to be the sign and example of redeemed humanity, O'Donovan arbitrarily abstracts three elements of that covenanted community and identifies them as the ones that constituted the unique, historical political order of Israel. The first element was Israel's *salvation* from Egypt, which represented God's victory. The second constituting factor was the responsibility to exercise *judgment* under God's law. The third was the promised land as Israel's *possession*. Later, when Israel was sent into exile, the law rather than the land became its possession.

When Christ came, according to O'Donovan, all of these elements were taken up into his kingship. Christ is now the *savior* from (*victor* over) the enemies of God's people. Christ fulfills the law in perfect *judgement* by both receiving God's judgment and being ordained the judge of all the earth. And Christ now becomes both the *possession* of his people and the one who possesses them. Historically, then, Christ takes hold of all governmental authority, requiring that his people have no other political identity or political community. Moreover, according to O'Donovan, after the coming of Christ, no government on earth has authority to constitute a people as a full political community – with salvation, judgment and a possession. 'No respect can be paid to the role of government, then, as a focus of collective identity, either in Israel or in any other community.'[24] Why? Because on the basis of Christ's victory over the powers, governments in the historical future are given only one task – and that is to make legal judgments.

As O'Donovan imagines it, God acts for the preservation of the secular world by giving earthly governments only one of the three functions taken up into Christ's authority, namely, the judicial functions that 'were once assigned to Israel's judges'.[25] No state or political authority can exist legitimately that claims more for itself than the right to make judgments. No political community may claim to *possess* the law or make law, but may only judge cases in the light of God's law. No government may claim to *save* or *give victory* to its citizens over its enemies. No political community may claim to possess the law or the promised land, because Christ alone possesses all of this.

In the latter part of *DN*, O'Donovan offers an interpretation of mediaeval and modern political history subsequent to Christ's victory over the powers. This is essentially a history of the church's influence, or lack of influence, on political traditions. For example, he tries to show how the historical influence of Israel and the church shaped the contours of modern constitutional government – the latter being one of the ways to define 'responsible government'. Responsible government exists when 'Rulers, overcome by Christ's victory, exist provisionally and on sufferance for specific purposes.'[26] O'Donovan's appeal to political principles is historically positivistic in the sense that he derives the principles from the historical experience of peoples and nations influenced by the impact of Christ's victory, mediated by the church. Thus, his argument that the state should be 'minimally coercive' and 'minimally representative' is 'not a restraint imposed by the nature of political authority as such' but 'is imposed by the limits conceded to secular authority by Christ's Kingdom'.[27] O'Donovan applauds all

[24] *DN*, 148.

[25] *DN*, 147.

[26] *DN*, 231.

[27] *DN*, 233.

the historical evidences that show governments accepting their limited judicial role, and he criticizes all indications of more expansive claims.

From this point of view, one might imagine that O'Donovan would approve of the American form of constitutional government which confines government to a rather narrow task, including the protection of religious freedom for all citizens. The First Amendment to the Constitution recognizes the freedom of churches and entails protection of the church by the government. This would appear to be an excellent example of state humility before Christ. However, O'Donovan criticizes the First Amendment because he sees it as 'the symbolic end of Christendom', a denial 'that the state should offer deliberate assistance to the church's mission'.[28] Apparently, for O'Donovan, God's restriction of government to the judicial role – nothing more than judging cases in the light of God's law – can be maintained only if the state also makes something of a public confession of faith. It is not enough for government simply to judge cases impartially in ways that allow the church to be the church; it should, in O'Donovan's view, actually privilege the church, even in its secular constitutional language, in order to demonstrate its submission to Christ's authority.

This is quite a different approach from the one taken by the Center for Public Justice with the Charitable Choice provision of welfare reform and with some of its other public policy proposals. The Center recognizes a positive role for government under Christ's authority. Yet, by virtue of its understanding of the normative differentiation of institutional responsibilities in God's creation, the Center contends that the state, as a differentiated political community, should not exhibit characteristics of a confessional community. The state shows its *direct* submission to Christ by establishing and upholding public justice, not by constitutionally professing its submission to the church. O'Donovan, by contrast, believes that God gives judicial authority to the state only in its capacity as a servant of the church. The Center believes that God holds political authorities *directly* responsible for their exercise of their governmental power. O'Donovan sees government existing outside, over against, and in service to the church. The Center sees government as existing under Christ's authority and thus as bearing responsibilities that Christians, *qua* Christian rulers, can bear in direct service to Christ.

In the end, it seems to me, O'Donovan's political theory is dominated not by a vision of creation regained, of Christ leading creation – including the fullness of humanity – into the Holy City, into which 'the kings of the earth will bring their splendor' (Rev. 21:24; cf. Isa. 60). Instead, O'Donovan's political theory is dominated by a structurally narrow understanding of the church as one institution among many in secular society, looking ahead to its eternal destiny while coexisting with governments that are destined to pass away.

---

[28] *DN*, 244.

'There is only one society which is incorporated into the Kingdom of God and which recapitulates the narrative of the Christ-event, and that is the church', says O'Donovan.[29] Society at large can be shaped by the church, but it is not the church. Thus, 'church and society are in a dialectical relation, distant from each other as well as identified'.[30] O'Donovan even submits 'divine law' to this dual framework of secular/eternal:

> The concept of divine law, as we have said, divides into two streams: secular government, on the one side, armed with the law of God under which it claims authority, encounters, on the other, the law of the Spirit of Christ, the law which has become prophecy, present wherever society has made a place for the church in its midst.[31]

In sum:

> The intelligibility of the secular authorities in the resurrection age depended on their being seen to carry forward what God had set himself to do. The secular function in society was to witness to divine judgment by, as it were, holding the stage for it; the church, on the other hand, must witness to divine judgment by no judgment, avoiding litigation and swallowing conflict in forgiveness. Society, respecting the judicial function as the core of political authority, must shape its conception of justice in the light of God's reconciling work.[32]

Conclusion

The many constructive things O'Donovan says about modern, limited governments and many of the insights he draws from Scripture and tradition must be attended to. His encompassing claim that government exists by the grace of God, who is active in history, not by the fiat of autonomous individuals, is potent today. Many Christians as well as secularized humanists see no connection between earthly government and God's purposes in history. O'Donovan is correct that, biblically speaking, no government exists except by God's grace in subservience to Jesus Christ. Nevertheless, O'Donovan's insights into creation regained are almost entirely overwhelmed, it seems to me, by a secular/eternal framework that is more Greek and Roman than it is biblical. In fact, I believe it is possible to demonstrate that the mediaeval synthesis of biblical and Graeco-Roman views of life is precisely what established the conditions for a secularizing modernity, which is the attempt to immanentize God's creative and redemptive power within human beings and their states. Consequently, O'Donovan's

---

[29] *DN*, 251.
[30] *DN*, 251.
[31] *DN*, 241.
[32] *DN*, 259.

critique of contemporary secular ideologies, including secular liberalism, lacks the punch that can come only by offering a full critique of the mediaeval synthesis that began to weaken the distinctively biblical understanding of God's creation, corrupted by human sin and judged and redeemed by Jesus Christ.

Despite O'Donovan's intent to develop a theological-political ethic, his framework is one that will, I fear, further encourage some Christian ethicists to disconnect church and state to such a degree that no basis will be left for a Christian understanding of the state. The Center for Public Justice cannot exist on that basis. Thus the challenge that O'Donovan's book poses for Christians is the need to gain a biblical understanding of creation, judgment, and redemption in Christ as the integral basis for properly formed political communities and properly exercised governmental authority.

Bibliography

Carlson-Thies, S., and J.W. Skillen, *Welfare in America: Christian Perspectives on a Policy in Crisis* (Grand Rapids: Eerdmans, 1996)

Chaplin, J., 'Christian Theories of Democracy', in *Contemporary Political Studies*, II (Political Studies Association of the United Kingdom, 1998), 988–1003

—— and P. Marshall (eds.), *Political Theory and Christian Vision: Essays in Memory of Bernard Zylstra* (Lanham, MD: University Press of America, 1994)

Dooyeweerd, H., *A New Critique of Theoretical Thought*, III (trans. D.H. Freeman and H. de Jongste; Philadelphia: Presbyterian and Reformed Publishing, 1957)

Goudzwaard, B., et al., *Globalization and the Kingdom of God* (Grand Rapids: Baker Book House, 2001)

O'Donovan, O., *Resurrection and Moral Order: An Outline for Evangelical Ethics* (Leicester: IVP; Grand Rapids: Eerdmans, 2nd edn, 1994)

——, *The Desire of the Nations: Rediscovering the Roots of Political Theology* (Cambridge: CUP, 1996)

——, and J.L. O'Donovan (eds.), *From Irenaeus to Grotius: A Sourcebook in Christian Political Thought 100–1625* (Grand Rapids: Eerdmans, 1999)

Skillen, J.W., *A Covenant to Keep: Meditations on the Biblical Theme of Justice* (Grand Rapids: CRC Publications, 2000)

——, 'E Pluribus Unum and Faith-Based Welfare Reform: A Kuyperian Moment for the Church in God's World', *PSB* XXII.3 (2001), 285–305

——, 'Politics in One World', *Philosophia Reformata* 66.1 (2001), 117–31

——, *Recharging the American Experiment: Principled Pluralism for Genuine Civic Community* (Grand Rapids: Baker Book House, 1994)

—— and R.M. McCarthy (eds.), *Political Order and the Plural Structure of Society* (Atlanta: Scholars Press, 1991)

29

Response to James W. Skillen

Oliver O'Donovan

It is especially welcome to have a contribution directly from the coalface of public Christian advocacy, and especially at a juncture when we can congratulate Jim Skillen's Center for Public Justice on its contribution to the reversal of a long-standing inequity in the US government's attitude to religious charitable bodies. I can only admire the achievement, though puzzled by some of the conceptual framework adduced to justify it, and not least by the role of that mantra-word 'choice'. And I cannot help wondering whether Hindus, Muslims and Jews in America feel that the government is really being non-discriminatory in referring to them as 'faith-based organizations' – 'faith' being, I suppose, a Christian word for a Christian thing – or in speaking of 'confessional pluralism' – 'confession' being a Christian word for a Christian activity. The jargon gives the whole project an atmosphere of 'anonymous Christianity'.

Without qualifying my enthusiasm for the achievement, I must identify three points at issue between myself and Skillen's argument:

1. *Pluralism*. There are, I think, two different principles being invoked under the term 'pluralism'. One is excellently stated: 'government [must] do justice ... to other human relationships and institutions'. The other is 'equal treatment for the public expression of all religious faiths'. The first is unexceptionable; the second is unexceptionable, too, but on one condition: that there really *exist* a plurality of equally positioned religious faiths, that a society actually has the plural form that pluralism attributes to it. But suppose there is only one 'religious faith' effectively operative in a society? Many Christians in Orthodox lands believe themselves to be in that situation and see 'pluralism' as the business of creating differences where they would not otherwise exist.

   I would like Skillen to say whether and how 'pluralism' can operate as a principle apart from the presupposition of plurality. If he thinks that a significant religious plurality always in fact exists, always has existed and always will exist, I can only say that this is an a priori judgement, not an empirical one. It indicates an interpretation of society that sets out to highlight differences. But how can such an a priori judgement be justified morally or theologically? By pointing to original sin, perhaps; but that can only be done in the context of God's will for human unity. How, in particular, is such an interpretation compatible with the Christian obligation to seek peace with all people, and especially with those who are of the household of faith? Is not pluralism hostile to ecumenism in principle, and ecumenism to pluralism?

When pluralists speak of 'different religious faiths', they tend to mean (among other things) Roman Catholics, Anglicans and Methodists. I don't regard these as different religious faiths at all, nor do I think there is any justification for regulating the relations among them on pluralist principles, rather than on the ecumenical principle of converging faith and practice: 'One Lord, one faith, one baptism, one God and Father of us all.' But the pluralist interpretation can hardly risk taking the ecumenical reality seriously. If it were prepared to count the Christian churches as one, that one would wholly outweigh, in terms of its claims on the right of tradition, all other religious traditions in the West. So the pluralist programme has to redescribe the Western church in such a way as to avoid any suggestion of Christian unity. I want to know whether Western Christians ought to put up with that, let alone encourage it. Furthermore, the programmatic character of Western pluralism can plausibly be charged with heightening religious intolerance and xenophobia in Eastern Europe, where established Orthodox churches see it as an assault on their position in society in the interests of fly-by-night US-based implants. The religious plurality is suppositious, plurality invented for the sake of pluralism.

And even in a genuinely plural society, where no group has a strongly dominant right of tradition, is it not hostile to civil peace to ignore convergences? There is, for example, a serious prospect that all religious bodies in this country would agree that the laws governing abortion are intolerably lax. 'Pluralism', not least by its counter-intuitive insistence that secularism is a religion just like any other, seems devoted to suppressing the public effect of any such convergence. It is a word that I think Christians should put their hands over their mouths before using.

2. *Confessionality.* 'Christians should, without embarrassment, act publicly, politically, as Christians' says Skillen, excellently. But he then says that the state 'should not exhibit characteristics of a confessional community'. How do these two pieces of advice work out for Christian office-holders: for presidents in the White House, for judges in the courts, and so on? Are Christian office-holders 'the state', which must not be confessional? Or are they 'Christians', who 'should, without embarrassment' be confessional?

What kind of freedom from embarrassment can they have if, as soon as they win office, they are silenced? What kind of non-confessionality can they represent if they are free to give their sincere religious reasons for every policy decision or court judgement with a plethora of scriptural quotations?

Behind this puzzle there lies the more formal question about who the political actors in a society really are. In defending a confessional political role for Christians, Jim Skillen seems to have voters in mind and, of course, policy organizations like his own, which appeal to voters. Without denying the importance of this emphasis, has his political conception nothing to say to the role of the Christian as an official, which would have been the chief emphasis of the political theology of Christendom? And if it has nothing to say to Christian confessionalism in that role, what is the relevance of Christian confessionalism among voters anyway? If as a Christian voter I must choose between voting for a non-Christian and a silenced Christian, why should I think the choice seriously engages my faith in any way?

3. *Eschatological supersession of government.* I am chided for my refusal to allow a final destiny to governments, 'like other institutions'. I fear that the term 'institution' has misled Jim Skillen here. It embraces created structures, providential orders, and, of course, voluntary organizations. The stock market, the symphony orchestra and the art gallery are 'human institutions', too, not only family and government. Just because we can say that they have a valuable role, we should not conclude that they are for eternity.

Jim Skillen lacks 'dispensationalism', as Jonathan Chaplin might say – a sense of the difference of the ages. Alternatively, he hasn't heard what Paul is saying to him. In fact, everything he finds puzzling about the role of government in my account has parallels in Paul's account of the law in Galatians and Romans. 'Is the law, then, sin?' 'No, the law is holy, just and good.' But in the new age we are delivered from it, all the same.

The concrete functions of government-as-judgement, it would seem to me, absolutely require a notion of eschatological supersession. Governments condemn – but 'there is now no condemnation'; governments exercise terror – but 'perfect love casts out fear'; governments say 'Know the Lord!', or perhaps, in the US, 'Know the God of your choice!' – but 'they shall no longer say "Know the Lord", for they shall all know me.' Jesus taught that marriage is superseded in heaven. That, surely, would be enough to put the question of supersession of government on the table, even if there were nothing in the New Testament to suggest that the crowned heads of this world would cast their crowns before the throne of God and the Lamb.

University of Gloucestershire, Theology and Religious Studies

In October 2001, Cheltenham and Gloucester College of Higher Education received University title and became the University of Gloucestershire. Since then several areas of research in the University, including Theology and Religious Studies, have been assessed in the national Research Assessment Exercise as having attained a level of excellence.

The University is pleased that the partnership with the Bible Society in the Scripture and Hermeneutics Seminar is continuing, and we are delighted that the third volume, *A Royal Priesthood? The Use of the Bible Ethically and Politically*, is now published. We thank the contributors and editors for their work on this volume and trust that readers will find it informative and challenging in their use of the Bible.

To promote further research activity in biblical interpretation, an International Centre for Biblical Interpretation was launched in Cheltenham in 2001. Tom Wright's chapter in this volume, 'Paul and Caesar: A New Reading of Romans', is a revised version of the leture he gave at the launch of ICBI.

Relating the Bible to ethics and politics is sometimes seen as highly controversial. Nevertheless, attention to issues such as government, law, power and social care is important if the church is to avoid a serious failure of engagement with contemporary life. In exploring these issues we have been considerably helped by Professor Oliver O'Donovan, Regius Professor of Moral and Pastoral Theology and Canon of Christ Church at the University of Oxford. His willingness to speak to us and dialogue with us has been much appreciated. The importance of these issues has been emphasized by the events of 11 September 2001.

The first two volumes in this series have been well received, and the Seminar is increasingly recognized as a unique means of debate for leading scholars. We remain committed to making their work available to the wider academic and church communities.

To extend the work of the Seminar in North America, we are delighted to have been able to form a link with Baylor University, Texas, and look forward to working together in the future.

In May 2002, the Scripture and Hermeneutics Seminar held a fifth consultation in Boston, USA. The theme was *History and Biblical Interpretation*, and papers from that consultation are being prepared for volume 4, to be published in November 2003.

Dr Fred Hughes
Head of Theology and Religious Studies
University of Gloucestershire
Francis Close Hall
Swindon Road, Cheltenham, Gloucestershire GL50 4AZ
< www.glos.ac.uk/humanities/contents.asp?rid=14 >

The British and Foreign Bible Society

The Scripture and Hermeneutics Seminar is now five years old. The preliminary consultation in 1989, on the relevance of speech-act theory to the discipline of biblical scholarship, launched a ten-year research programme. Some of the fruits of that initial consultation crystallized in volume 2 of the series, *After Pentecost: Language and Biblical Interpretation*.

Those of us who have enjoyed the immense privilege of being part of this exciting venture from the moment of its inception to the present stage in its development know that both the level of scholarship and the strenuous engagement with important hermeneutical and exegetical issues have exceeded our expectations. This is due in no small measure to two particular factors.

First, and probably most importantly, the interdisciplinary nature of our conversations has been crucial. It has become clear to us that biblical studies is not a discreet discipline, but does in fact draw from literary, philosophical, historical and socio-political sources in a way rarely acknowledged by the fraternity of biblical scholars. If this issue was ever in doubt, then this present volume in the series should reinforce such an observation. The consultation from which this volume emanated unearthed a rich vein of scholarship that owes a debt to the manner in which Oliver O'Donovan combines biblical, historical and political investigations to construct a viable political theology for our generation. Part of the wide-ranging interest that O'Donovan's work generates stems from his astute ability to be both firmly biblical and cross-disciplinary at the same time. And why should this surprise us? Archbishop Desmond Tutu, interviewed recently on radio in Britain, remarked, 'If I was to give one piece of advice to anyone trying to run an oppressive regime it would be, ban the Bible, because once people begin to read that book the liberation cat is out of the bag.' Quite so, and it is towards the liberation of biblical studies for the good of all that the Scripture and Hermeneutics Seminar directs most of its energy and commitment.

In order to achieve that aim, however, this expanding network of scholars and practitioners must be prepared to take the long route round and deal with the most elemental hermeneutical issues with patience and rigour. This has been the other characteristic feature of our annual consultations and the preparation and editing of the papers that make up each volume. There are no quick fix solutions to the issues that continually infiltrate biblical interpretation, and it is always our hope that the volumes that continue to come from the Seminar will stimulate further debate and discussion.

The British and Foreign Bible Society has recently endorsed a new change of direction, one that seeks to make the Bible heard in the public life of society. In order to achieve that we require the help and assistance of the best in the world of biblical scholarship. Similarly, recent tumultuous events in the world of international politics make it even more imperative both for the church and the academy that the ethical and political implications of the biblical story are clearly heard and understood within the multicultural and global realities of our world today. We warmly commend this present volume, *A Royal Priesthood? The Use of the Bible Ethically and Politically* as an important contribution toward that end.

Revd Dr Colin J.D. Greene
Head of Theology and Public Policy
British and Foreign Bible Society

Baylor University

Baylor University is honored to be able to identify with the University of Gloucestershire and the British and Foreign Bible Society in supporting the Scripture and Hermeneutics Seminar as North American partner. As a university community with 157 years of commitment to Christian higher education and the largest Baptist University in the world, we are deeply interested in the kinds of issues the Seminar pursues. In particular we are grateful to the larger community of scholars whose purpose it is to situate the study of Scripture firmly in relationship to the intellectual life of a wide range of academic disciplines.

Interdisciplinary scholarship is an increasingly necessary and highly productive feature of academic life. Nowhere, perhaps, is it more necessary or productive than when the goal of biblical scholars is to make the full potential of biblical scholarship available to the life of the Church.

We congratulate the editors and contributors to the present volume on the vigor and quality of their exchange of views. We look forward to working with the Seminar in the years ahead and to hosting a future Consultation here on the campus at Baylor University.

David Lyle Jeffrey
Distinguished Professor of Literature and Humanities
Senior Vice Provost
Baylor University
PO Box 97404
Waco
Texas 76798-7404
USA

Scripture Index

Old Testament

New Testament

Name Index

Subject Index

The delegates at the 2001 Consultation

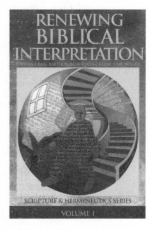

IS THERE A MEANING IN THIS TEXT?

The Bible, the Reader, and the Morality of Literary Knowledge

KEVIN J. VANHOOZER

Is there a meaning in the Bible, or is meaning rather a matter of who is reading or of how one reads? Does Christian doctrine have anything to contribute to debates about interpretation, literary theory, and postmodernity? These are questions of crucial importance for contemporary biblical studies and theology alike.

Is There a Meaning in This Text? guides the student toward greater confidence in the authority, clarity, and relevance of Scripture, and a well-reasoned expectation to understand accurately the message of the Bible.

Is There a Meaning in This Text? is a comprehensive and creative analysis of current debates over biblical hermeneutics that draws on interdisciplinary resources, all coordinated by Christian theology. It makes a significant contribution to biblical interpretation that will be of interest to readers in a number of fields. The intention of the book is to revitalize and enlarge the concept of author-oriented interpretation and to restore confidence that readers of the Bible can reach understanding. The result is a major challenge to the central assumptions of postmodern biblical scholarship and a constructive alternative proposal—an Augustinian hermeneutic—that reinvigorates the notion of biblical authority and finds a new exegetical practice that recognizes the importance of both the reader's situation and the literal sense.

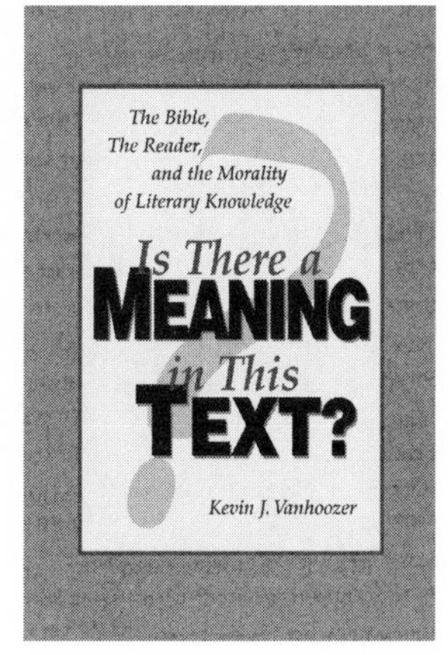

Hardcover: ISBN 0-310-21156-5

ZONDERVAN™

GRAND RAPIDS, MICHIGAN 49530 USA

WWW.ZONDERVAN.COM